Blackstone's Statutes on
Environmental Law

Blackstone's Statutes on
Environmental Law

....

Fourth Edition

Edited by

R. M. C. Duxbury

LLB, Barrister

Principal Lecturer in Law, Nottingham Law School, Nottingham Trent University

S. G. C. Morton

LLB, Solicitor

Senior Lecturer in Law, Nottingham Law School, Nottingham Trent University

OXFORD

UNIVERSITY PRESS

Great Clarendon Street, Oxford OX2 6DP

Oxford University Press is a department of the University of Oxford.
It furthers the University's objective of excellence in research, scholarship,
and education by publishing worldwide in

Oxford New York

Auckland Bangkok Buenos Aires Cape Town Chennai
Dar es Salaam Delhi Hong Kong Istanbul Karachi Kolkata
Kuala Lumpur Madrid Melbourne Mexico City Mumbai Nairobi
São Paulo Shanghai Taipei Tokyo Toronto

Oxford is a registered trade mark of Oxford University Press
in the UK and in certain other countries

Published in the United States
by Oxford University Press Inc., New York

First published by Blackstone Press

First published 1994
Second edition 1995
Third edition 2000
Fourth edition 2002

British Library Cataloguing in Publication Data
Data available

Crown Copyright material is reproduced with permission of
the Controller of HMSO and the Queen's Printer for Scotland

ISBN 0–19–925528–8

1 3 5 7 9 10 8 6 4 2

Typeset in ITC Stone Serif and ITC Stone Sans
by RefineCatch Limited, Bungay, Suffolk
Printed in Great Britain by
Antony Rowe Limited, Chippenham and Reading

CONTENTS

EDITORS' PREFACE TO THE FOURTH EDITION

The previous edition of this book was published two years ago but Environmental Law has moved on since then and we have therefore included a substantial amount of new law in this edition.

To the collection of primary legislation we have added extracts from the Freedom of Information Act 2000. The Act enables the implementation of the Aarhus Convention insofar as it relates to the provision of access to environmental information.

We have included a number of statutory instruments, which either amend existing legislation or introduce new law. Possibly the most significant of these is the Landfill (England and Wales) Regulations 2002 which set out a pollution control regime for the purpose of implementing the Landfill Directive. There have also been some changes to the Pollution Prevention and Control Regulations (as they appeared in the previous edition of this book), and amendments have been made to the regulations on Waste Management Licensing and Special Waste.

Obligations have been imposed on those having custody or control of oil under the Control of Pollution (Oil Storage) (England) Regulations 2001; and the Environmental Impact Assessment (EIA) (Amendment) Regulations 2000 supplement the 1999 regulations so as to ensure compliance with European law by bringing old mining permissions within the scope of EIA requirements

We have found space for the Air Quality Limit Values Regulations 2001 but editorial constraints preclude inclusion of the Drinking Water (Undertakings) (England and Wales) Regulations and Climate Change Levy (Registration and Miscellaneous Provisions) Regulations of 2000 and 2001 respectively.

We would like to thank our publishers for their support in the preparation of this new edition. May we once again express the hope that those involved in Environmental Law will find the book of some use.

Robert Duxbury
Sandra Morton
Nottingham Law School
June 2002

EDITORS' PREFACE TO THE FIRST EDITION

Although laws relating to the environment have been studied for many years in one form or another, the appearance of a subject called 'environmental law' is a relatively new phenomenon. It no doubt reflects a fashionable concern with the so-called 'green' agenda but it also owes much to the introduction, at the beginning of the decade, of comprehensive legislation dealing with pollution and waste management with its 'integrated' approach to the environment. A further factor has been the gradual coalescing of the well-established planning system with wider environmental considerations, prompted in large measure by the impetus of European environmental law and policy.

In 1991 the editors of this book introduced an Environmental Law course on the LLB degree at Nottingham Law School. The need for a readily accessible collection of statutes and statutory instruments — for teaching, private study and examining — was obvious. Having decided to put together our own selection, as it were, 'in-house', we approached Blackstone Press to see if commercial publication was a possibility. They responded with characteristic enthusiasm.

We realise, however, that we have set ourselves a daunting task. Unlike courses on, say, contract law, environmental law programmes differ greatly from institution to institution in coverage, emphasis and approach. Our aim has been to bring together what we feel to be the most important and widely referred-to sections of statutes and statutory instruments in the field of environmental law. Given the inevitable limitations of space set by our publishers we have had to make some difficult decisions as to what to include and what to leave out. In particular, and with regret, we felt that there would be no room for reference to many other EC directives, UK statutory instruments or to government circulars and policy guidance. Provisions relating to Scotland or Northern Ireland have also been omitted. Readers will need to look elsewhere for these.

The extracts are set out in chronological order. Subsequent amendments to statutes are denoted by square brackets ([]) with no reference to the amending statute. Thus the extensive changes to the Town and Country Planning Act 1990 made by the Planning and Compensation Act 1991 are indicated in this way. In those very few cases where we have not cited a section in full, the omitted material is denoted by three dots (. . .) and sub-sections which have been repealed are indicated thus, ([. . .]). With the exception of the footnotes, the recently issued Waste Management Licensing Regulations have been reproduced in full because of their impact on the implementation of Part II of the Environmental Protection Act and the requirements relating to 'Directive waste'.

We would like to thank those colleagues at other institutions who, when approached by the publishers as to the potential coverage of this book, gave most helpful advice. A debt of gratitude is also owed to our publishers for their support and encouragement. We sincerely hope that those concerned with environmental law will find the book of some use.

Robert Duxbury
Sandra Morton

PART I

EC Treaty

Consolidated Version of the Treaty Establishing the European Community

PART ONE   PRINCIPLES

Article 1   (ex Article 1)

By this Treaty, the High Contracting Parties establish among themselves a European Community.

Article 2   (ex Article 2)

The Community shall have as its task, by establishing a common market and an economic and monetary union and by implementing common policies or activities referred to in Articles 3 and 4, to promote throughout the Community a harmonious, balanced and sustainable development of economic activities, a high level of employment and of social protection, equality between men and women, sustainable and non-inflationary growth, a high degree of competitiveness and convergence of economic performance, a high level of protection and improvement of the quality of the environment, the raising of the standard of living and quality of life, and economic and social cohesion and solidarity among Member States.

Article 3   (ex Article 3)

1. For the purposes set out in Article 2, the activities of the Community shall include, as provided in this Treaty and in accordance with the timetable set out therein:

    (a) the prohibition, as between Member States, of customs duties and quantitative restrictions on the import and export of goods, and of all other measures having equivalent effect;

    (b) a common commercial policy;

    (c) an internal market characterised by the abolition, as between Member States, of obstacles to the free movement of goods, persons, services and capital;

    (d) measures concerning the entry and movement of persons as provided for in Title IV;

    (e) a common policy in the sphere of agriculture and fisheries;

    (f) a common policy in the sphere of transport;

    (g) a system ensuring that competition in the internal market is not distorted;

    (h) the approximation of the laws of Member States to the extent required for the functioning of the common market;

    (i) the promotion of coordination between employment policies of the Member States with a view to enhancing their effectiveness by developing a coordinated strategy for employment;

    (j) a policy in the social sphere comprising a European Social Fund;

    (k) the strengthening of economic and social cohesion;

    (l) a policy in the sphere of the environment;

    (m) the strengthening of the competitiveness of Community industry;

    (n) the promotion of research and technological development;

    (o) encouragement for the establishment and development of trans-European networks;

    (p) a contribution to the attainment of a high level of health protection;

    (q) a contribution to education and training of quality and to the flowering of the cultures of the Member States;

    (r) a policy in the sphere of development cooperation;

    (s) the association of the overseas countries and territories in order to increase trade and promote jointly economic and social development;

    (t) a contribution to the strengthening of consumer protection;

    (u) measures in the spheres of energy, civil protection and tourism.

2. In all the activities referred to in this Article, the Community shall aim to eliminate inequalities, and to promote equality, between men and women.

Article 4   (ex Article 3a)

1. For the purposes set out in Article 2, the activities of the Member States and the Community shall include, as provided in this Treaty and in accordance with the timetable set out therein, the adoption of an economic policy which is based on the close coordination of Member States' economic policies, on the internal market and on the definition of common objectives, and conducted in accordance with the principle of an open market economy with free competition.

2. Concurrently with the foregoing, and as provided in this Treaty and in accordance with the timetable and the procedures set out therein, these activities shall include the irrevocable fixing of exchange rates leading to the introduction of a single currency, the ECU, and the definition and conduct of a single monetary policy and exchange rate policy the primary objective of both of which shall be to maintain price stability and, without prejudice to this objective, to support the general economic policies in the Community, in accordance with the principle of an open market economy with free competition.

3. These activities of the Member States and the Community shall entail compliance with the following guiding principles: stable prices, sound public finances and monetary conditions and a sustainable balance of payments.

Article 5   (ex Article 3b)

The Community shall act within the limits of the powers conferred upon it by this Treaty and of the objectives assigned to it therein.

In areas which do not fall within its exclusive competence, the Community shall take action, in accordance with the principle of subsidiarity, only if and insofar as the objectives of the proposed action cannot be sufficiently achieved by the Member States and can therefore, by reason of the scale or effects of the proposed action, be better achieved by the Community.

Any action by the Community shall not go beyond what is necessary to achieve the objectives of this Treaty.

Article 6   (ex Article 3c)

Environmental protection requirements must be integrated into the definition and implementation of the Community policies and activities referred to in Article 3, in particular with a view to promoting sustainable development.

Article 10   (ex Article 5)

Member States shall take all appropriate measures, whether general or particular, to ensure fulfilment of the obligations arising out of this Treaty or resulting from action taken by the institutions of the Community. They shall facilitate the achievement of the Community's tasks.

They shall abstain from any measure which could jeopardise the attainment of the objectives of this Treaty.

PART THREE   COMMUNITY POLICIES

TITLE I   FREE MOVEMENT OF GOODS

CHAPTER 2   PROHIBITION OF QUANTITATIVE RESTRICTIONS BETWEEN MEMBER STATES

Article 28   (ex Article 30)
Quantitative restrictions on imports and all measures having equivalent effect shall be prohibited between Member States.

Article 30   (ex Article 36)
The provisions of Articles 28 and 29 shall not preclude prohibitions or restrictions on imports, exports or goods in transit justified on grounds of public morality, public policy or public security; the protection of health and life of humans, animals or plants; the protection of national treasures possessing artistic, historic or archaeological value; or the protection of industrial and commercial property. Such prohibitions or restrictions shall not, however, constitute a means of arbitrary discrimination or a disguised restriction on trade between Member States.

TITLE VI (ex Title V)   COMMON RULES ON COMPETITION, TAXATION AND APPROXIMATION OF LAWS

CHAPTER 3   APPROXIMATION OF LAWS

Article 94   (ex Article 100)
The Council shall, acting unanimously on a proposal from the Commission and after consulting the European Parliament and the Economic and Social Committee, issue directives for the approximation of such laws, regulations or administrative provisions of the Member States as directly affect the establishment or functioning of the common market.

Article 95   (ex Article 100a)
1. By way of derogation from Article 94 and save where otherwise provided in this Treaty, the following provisions shall apply for the achievement of the objectives set out in Article 14. The Council shall, acting in accordance with the procedure referred to in Article 251 and after consulting the Economic and Social Committee, adopt the measures for the approximation of the provisions laid down by law, regulation or administrative action in Member States which have as their object the establishment and functioning of the internal market.

2. Paragraph 1 shall not apply to fiscal provisions, to those relating to the free movement of persons nor to those relating to the rights and interests of employed persons.

3. The Commission, in its proposals envisaged in paragraph 1 concerning health, safety, environmental protection and consumer protection, will take as a base a high level of protection, taking account in particular of any new development based on scientific facts. Within their respective powers, the European Parliament and the Council will also seek to achieve this objective.

4. If, after the adoption by the Council or by the Commission of a harmonisation measure, a Member State deems it necessary to maintain national provisions on grounds of major needs referred to in Article 30, or relating to the protection of the environment or the working environment, it shall notify the Commission of these provisions as well as the grounds for maintaining them.

5. Moreover, without prejudice to paragraph 4, if, after the adoption by the Council or by the Commission of a harmonisation measure, a Member State deems it necessary to introduce national provisions based on new scientific evidence relating to the protection of the environment or the working environment on grounds of a problem specific to that Member State arising after the adoption of the harmonisation measure, it shall notify the Commission of the envisaged provisions as well as the grounds for introducing them.

6.   The Commission shall, within six months of the notifications as referred to in paragraphs 4 and 5, approve or reject the national provisions involved after having verified whether or not they are a means of arbitrary discrimination or a disguised restriction on trade between Member States and whether or not they shall constitute an obstacle to the functioning of the internal market.

In the absence of a decision by the Commission within this period the national provisions referred to in paragraphs 4 and 5 shall be deemed to have been approved.

When justified by the complexity of the matter and in the absence of danger for human health, the Commission may notify the Member State concerned that the period referred to in this paragraph may be extended for a further period of up to six months.

7.   When, pursuant to paragraph 6, a Member State is authorised to maintain or introduce national provisions derogating from a harmonisation measure, the Commission shall immediately examine whether to propose an adaptation to that measure.

8.   When a Member State raises a specific problem on public health in a field which has been the subject of prior harmonisation measures, it shall bring it to the attention of the Commission which shall immediately examine whether to propose appropriate measures to the Council.

9.   By way of derogation from the procedure laid down in Articles 226 and 227, the Commission and any Member State may bring the matter directly before the Court of Justice if it considers that another Member State is making improper use of the powers provided for in this Article.

10.   The harmonisation measures referred to above shall, in appropriate cases, include a safeguard clause authorising the Member States to take, for one or more of the non-economic reasons referred to in Article 30, provisional measures subject to a Community control procedure.

TITLE XIX (ex Title XVI)   ENVIRONMENT

Article 174   (ex Article 130r)

1. Community policy on the environment shall contribute to pursuit of the following objectives:

— preserving, protecting and improving the quality of the environment;
— protecting human health;
— prudent and rational utilisation of natural resources;
— promoting measures at international level to deal with regional or worldwide environmental problems.

2. Community policy on the environment shall aim at a high level of protection taking into account the diversity of situations in the various regions of the Community. It shall be based on the precautionary principle and on the principles that preventive action should be taken, that environmental damage should as a priority be rectified at source and that the polluter should pay.

In this context, harmonisation measures answering environmental protection requirements shall include, where appropriate, a safeguard clause allowing Member States to take provisional measures, for non-economic environmental reasons, subject to a Community inspection procedure.

3. In preparing its policy on the environment, the Community shall take account of:
— available scientific and technical data;
— environmental conditions in the various regions of the Community;
— the potential benefits and costs of action or lack of action;
— the economic and social development of the Community as a whole and the balanced development of its regions.

4. Within their respective spheres of competence, the Community and the Member States shall cooperate with third countries and with the competent international organisations. The arrangements for Community cooperation may be the subject of agreements between the Community and the third parties concerned, which shall be negotiated and concluded in accordance with Article 300.

The previous subparagraph shall be without prejudice to Member States' competence to negotiate in international bodies and to conclude international agreements.

Article 175   (ex Article 130s)

1. The Council, acting in accordance with the procedure referred to in Article 251 and after consulting the Economic and Social Committee and the Committee of the Regions, shall decide what action is to be taken by the Community in order to achieve the objectives referred to in Article 174.

2. By way of derogation from the decision-making procedure provided for in paragraph 1 and without prejudice to Article 95, the Council, acting unanimously on a proposal from the Commission and after consulting the European Parliament, the Economic and Social Committee and the Committee of the Regions, shall adopt:
— provisions primarily of a fiscal nature;
— measures concerning town and country planning, land use with the exception of waste management and measures of a general nature, and management of water resources;
— measures significantly affecting a Member State's choice between different energy sources and the general structure of its energy supply.

The Council may, under the conditions laid down in the preceding subparagraph, define those matters referred to in this paragraph on which decisions are to be taken by a qualified majority.

3. In other areas, general action programmes setting out priority objectives to be attained shall be adopted by the Council, acting in accordance with the procedure referred to in Article 251 and after consulting the Economic and Social Committee and the Committee of the Regions.

The Council, acting under the terms of paragraph 1 or paragraph 2 according to the case, shall adopt the measures necessary for the implementation of these programmes.

4. Without prejudice to certain measures of a Community nature, the Member States shall finance and implement the environment policy.

5. Without prejudice to the principle that the polluter should pay, if a measure based on the provisions of paragraph 1 involves costs deemed disproportionate for the public authorities of a Member State, the Council shall, in the act adopting that measure, lay down appropriate provisions in the form of:
— temporary derogations, and/or
— financial support from the Cohesion Fund set up pursuant to Article 161.

Article 176   (ex Article 130t)

The protective measures adopted pursuant to Article 175 shall not prevent any Member State from maintaining or introducing more stringent protective measures. Such measures must be compatible with this Treaty. They shall be notified to the Commission.

PART FIVE   INSTITUTIONS OF THE COMMUNITY

TITLE I   PROVISIONS GOVERNING THE INSTITUTIONS

CHAPTER 1   THE INSTITUTIONS

SECTION 2   THE COUNCIL

Article 205   (ex Article 148)

1. Save as otherwise provided in this Treaty, the Council shall act by a majority of its members.

2. Where the Council is required to act by a qualified majority, the votes of its members shall be weighted as follows:

Belgium	5
Denmark	3
Germany	10
Greece	5
Spain	8
France	10
Ireland	3
Italy	10
Luxembourg	2
Netherlands	5
Austria	4
Portugal	5
Finland	3
Sweden	4
United Kingdom	10

For their adoption, acts of the Council shall require at least:
— 62 votes in favour where this Treaty requires them to be adopted on a proposal from the Commission,
— 62 votes in favour, cast by at least 10 members, in other cases.

3. Abstentions by members present in person or represented shall not prevent the adoption by the Council of acts which require unanimity.

SECTION 3   COMMISSION

Article 211   (ex Article 155)

In order to ensure time proper functioning and development of the common market, the Commission shall:
— ensure that the provisions of this Treaty and the measures taken by the institutions pursuant thereto are applied;
— formulate recommendations or deliver opinions on matters dealt with in this Treaty, if it expressly so provides or if the Commission considers it necessary;
— have its own power of decision and participate in the shaping of measures taken by the Council and by the European Parliament in the manner provided for in this Treaty;
— exercise time powers conferred on it by the Council for the implementation of the rules laid down by the latter.

SECTION 4   THE COURT OF JUSTICE

Article 226   (ex Article 169)

If the Commission considers that a Member State has failed to fulfil an obligation under this Treaty, it shall deliver a reasoned opinion on the matter after giving the State concerned the opportunity to submit its observations.

If the State concerned does not comply with the opinion within the period laid down by the Commission, the latter may bring the matter before the Court of Justice.

Article 227   (ex Article 170)

A Member State which considers that another Member State has failed to fulfil an obligation under this Treaty may bring the matter before the Court of Justice.

Before a Member State brings an action against another Member State for an alleged infringement of an obligation under this Treaty, it shall bring the matter before the Commission.

The Commission shall deliver a reasoned opinion after each of the States concerned has been given the opportunity to submit its own case and its observations on the other party's case both orally and in writing.

If the Commission has not delivered an opinion within three months of the date on which the matter was brought before it, the absence of such opinion shall not prevent the matter from being brought before the Court of Justice.

Article 228   (ex Article 171)

1. If the Court of Justice finds that a Member State has failed to fulfil an obligation under this Treaty, the State shall be required to take the necessary measures to comply with the judgment of the Court of Justice.

2. If the Commission considers that the Member State concerned has not taken such measures it shall, after giving that State the opportunity to submit its observations, issue a reasoned opinion specifying the points on which the Member State concerned has not complied with the judgment of the Court of Justice.

If the Member State concerned fails to take the necessary measures to comply with the Court's judgment within the time-limit laid down by the Commission, the latter may bring the case before the Court of Justice. In so doing it shall specify the amount of the lump sum or penalty payment to be paid by the Member State concerned which it considers appropriate in the circumstances.

If the Court of Justice finds that the Member State concerned has not complied with its judgment it may impose a lump sum or penalty payment on it.

This procedure shall be without prejudice to Article 227.

Article 230   (ex Article 173)

The Court of Justice shall review the legality of acts adopted jointly by the European Parliament and the Council, of acts of the Council, of the Commission and of the ECB, other than recommendations and opinions, and of acts of the European Parliament intended to produce legal effects vis-à-vis third parties.

It shall for this purpose have jurisdiction in actions brought by a Member State, the Council or the Commission on grounds of lack of competence, infringement of an essential procedural requirement, infringement of this Treaty or of any rule of law relating to its application, or misuse of powers.

The Court of Justice shall have jurisdiction under the same conditions in actions brought by the European Parliament, by the Court of Auditors and by the ECB for the purpose of protecting their prerogatives.

Any natural or legal person may, under the same conditions, institute proceedings against a decision addressed to that person or against a decision which, although in the form of a regulation or a decision addressed to another person, is of direct and individual concern to the former.

The proceedings provided for in this Article shall be instituted within two months of the publication of the measure, or of its notification to the plaintiff, or, in the absence thereof, of the day on which it came to the knowledge of the latter, as the case may be.

Article 234   (ex Article 177)

The Court of Justice shall have jurisdiction to give preliminary rulings concerning:

    (a) the interpretation of this Treaty;

    (b) the validity and interpretation of acts of the institutions of the Community and of the ECB;

    (c) the interpretation of the statutes of bodies established by an act of the Council, where those statutes so provide.

Where such a question is raised before any court or tribunal of a Member State, that court or tribunal may, if it considers that a decision on the question is necessary to enable it to give judgment, request the Court of Justice to give a ruling thereon.

Where any such question is raised in a case pending before a court or tribunal of a Member State against whose decisions there is no judicial remedy under national law, that court or tribunal shall bring the matter before the Court of Justice.

CHAPTER 2   PROVISIONS COMMON TO SEVERAL INSTITUTIONS

Article 249   (ex Article 189)

In order to carry out their task and in accordance with the provisions of this Treaty, the European Parliament acting jointly with time Council, the Council and the Commission shall make regulations and issue directives, take decisions, make recommendations or deliver opinions.

A regulation shall have general application. It shall be binding in its entirety and directly applicable in all Member States.

A directive shall be binding, as to the result to be achieved, upon each Member State to which it is addressed, but shall leave to the national authorities the choice of form and methods.

A decision shall be binding in its entirety upon those to whom it is addressed. Recommendations and opinions shall have no binding force.

Article 250   (ex Article 189a)

1. Where, in pursuance of this Treaty, the Council acts on a proposal front time Commission, unanimity shall be required for an act constituting an amendment to that proposal, subject to Article 251(4) and (5).

2. As long as the Council has not acted, the Commission may alter its proposal at any time during the procedures leading to the adoption of a Community act.

Article 251   (ex Article 189b)

1. Where reference is made in this Treaty to this Article for the adoption of an act, the following procedure shall apply.

2. The Commission shall submit a proposal to the European Parliament and the Council.

The Council, acting by a qualified majority after obtaining the opinion of the European Parliament,

    — if it approves all the amendments contained in the European Parliament's opinion, may adopt the proposed act thus amended;

— if the European Parliament does not propose any amendments, may adopt the proposed act;

— shall otherwise adopt a common position and communicate it to the European Parliament. The Council shall inform the European Parliament fully of the reasons which led it to adopt its common position. The Commission shall inform the European Parliament fully of its position.

If, within three months of such communication, the European Parliament:

(a) approves the common position or has not taken a decision, the act in question shall be deemed to have been adopted in accordance with that common position;

(b) rejects, by an absolute majority of its component members, the common position, the proposed act shall be deemed not to have been adopted;

(c) proposes amendments to the common position by an absolute majority of its component members, the amended text shall be forwarded to the Council and to the Commission, which shall deliver an opinion on those amendments.

3. If, within three months of the matter being referred to it, the Council, acting by a qualified majority, approves all the amendments of the European Parliament, the act in question shall be deemed to have been adopted in the form of the common position thus amended; however, the Council shall act unanimously on the amendments on which the Commission has delivered a negative opinion. If the Council does not approve all the amendments, the President of the Council, in agreement with the President of the European Parliament, shall within six weeks convene a meeting of the Conciliation Committee.

4. The Conciliation Committee, which shall be composed of the members of the Council or their representatives and an equal number of representatives of the European Parliament, shall have the task of reaching agreement on a joint text, by a qualified majority of the members of the Council or their representatives and by a majority of the representatives of the European Parliament. The Commission shall take part in the Conciliation Committee's proceedings and shall take all the necessary initiatives with a view to reconciling the positions of the European Parliament and the Council. In fulfilling this task, time Conciliation Committee shall address the common position on the basis of the amendments proposed by the European Parliament.

5. If, within six weeks of its being convened, the Conciliation Committee approves a joint text, the European Parliament, acting by an absolute majority of the votes cast, and the Council, acting by a qualified majority, shall each have a period of six weeks from that approval in which to adopt the act in question in accordance with the joint text. If either of the two institutions fails to approve the proposed act within that period, it shall be deemed not to have been adopted.

6. Where the Conciliation Committee does not approve a joint text, the proposed act shall be deemed not to have been adopted.

7. The periods of three months and six weeks referred to in this Article shall be extended by a maximum of one month and two weeks respectively at the initiative of the European Parliament or the Council.

Article 252   (ex Article 189c)

Where reference is made in this Treaty to this Article for the adoption of an act, the following procedure shall apply:

(a) The Council, acting by a qualified majority on a proposal from the Commission and after obtaining the opinion of the European Parliament, shall adopt a common position.

(b) The Council's common position shall be communicated to the European Parliament. The Council and the Commission shall inform the European Parliament fully of the reasons which led the Council to adopt its common position and also of the Commission's position.

If, within three months of such communication, the European Parliament approves this common position or has not taken a decision within that period, the Council shall definitively adopt the act in question in accordance with the common position.

(c) The European Parliament may, within the period of three months referred to in point (b), by an absolute majority of its component Members, propose amendments to the Council's common position. The European Parliament may also, by the same majority, reject the Council's common position. The result of the proceedings shall be transmitted to the Council and the Commission.

If the European Parliament has rejected the Council's common position, unanimity shall be required for the Council to act on a second reading.

(d) The Commission shall, within a period of one month, re-examine the proposal on the basis of which the Council adopted its common position, by taking into account the amendments proposed by the European Parliament.

The Commission shall forward to the Council, at the same time as its re-examined proposal, the amendments of the European Parliament which it has not accepted, and shall express its opinion on them. The Council may adopt these amendments unanimously.

(e) The Council, acting by a qualified majority, shall adopt the proposal as re-examined by the Commission.

Unanimity shall be required for the Council to amend the proposal as re-examined by the Commission.

(f) In the cases referred to in points (c), (d) and (e), the Council shall be required to act within a period of three months. If no decision is taken within this period, the Commission proposal shall be deemed not to have been adopted.

(g) The periods referred to in points (b) and (f) may be extended by a maximum of one month by common accord between the Council and the European Parliament.

PART II

UK Legislation

European Communities Act 1972
(1972, c. 68)

2.—(1) All such rights, powers, liabilities, obligations and restrictions from time to time created or arising by or under the Treaties, and all such remedies and procedures from time to time provided for by or under the Treaties, as in accordance with the Treaties are without further enactment to be given legal effect or used in the United Kingdom shall be recognised and available in law, and be enforced, allowed and followed accordingly; and the expression 'enforceable Community right' and similar expressions shall be read as referring to one to which this subsection applies.

(2) Subject to Schedule 2 to this Act, at any time after its passing Her Majesty may by Order in Council, and any designated Minister or department may by regulations, make provision—

    (a) for the purpose of implementing any Community obligation of the United Kingdom, or enabling any such obligation to be implemented, or of enabling any rights enjoyed or to be enjoyed by the United Kingdom under or by virtue of the Treaties to be exercised; or

    (b) for the purpose of dealing with matters arising out of or related to any such obligation or rights or the coming into force, or the operation from time to time, of subsection (1) above;

and in the exercise of any statutory power or duty, including any power to give directions or to legislate by means of orders, rules, regulations or other subordinate instrument, the person entrusted with the power or duty may have regard to the objects of the Communities and to any such obligation or rights as aforesaid.

In this subsection 'designated Minister or department' means such Minister of the Crown or government department as may from time to time be designated by Order in Council in relation to any matter or for any purpose, but subject to such restrictions or conditions (if any) as may be specified by the Order in Council.

(3) . . .

(4) The provision that may be made under subsection (2) above includes, subject to Schedule 2 to this Act, any such provision (of any such extent) as might be made by Act of Parliament, and any enactment passed or to be passed, other than one contained in this part of this Act, shall be construed and have effect subject to the foregoing provisions of this sections; but, except as may be provided by any Act passed after this Act, Schedule 2 shall have effect in connection with the powers conferred by this and the following sections of this Act to make Orders in Council and regulations.

(5) . . .

(6) . . .

3.—(1) For the purposes of all legal proceedings any question as to the meaning or effect of any of the Treaties, or as to the validity, meaning or effect of any Community instrument, shall be treated as a question of law (and, if not referred to the European Court, be for determination as such in accordance with the principles laid down by and any relevant [decision of the European Court or any court attached thereto)].

(2) Judicial notice shall be taken of the Treaties, of the Official Journal of the Communities and of any decision of, or expression of opinion by, the European Court [or any court attached thereto] on any such question as aforesaid; and the Official Journal shall be admissible as evidence of any instrument or other act thereby communicated of any of the Communities or of any Community institution.

SCHEDULE 2   PROVISIONS AS TO SUBORDINATE LEGISLATION

2.—(1) . . . where a provision contained in any section of this Act confers power to make regulations (otherwise than by modification or extension of an existing power), the power shall be exercisable by statutory instrument.

(2) Any statutory instrument containing an Order in Council or regulations made in the exercise of a power so conferred, if made without a draft having been approved by resolution of each House of Parliament, shall be subject to annulment in pursuance of a resolution of either House.

3. . . .

Salmon and Freshwater Fisheries Act 1975
(1975, c. 51)

PART I   PROHIBITION OF CERTAIN MODES OF TAKING OR DESTROYING FISH, ETC.

4   Poisonous matter and polluting effluent

(1) Subject to subsection (2) below, any person who causes or knowingly permits to flow, or puts or knowingly permits to be put, into any waters containing fish or into any tributaries of waters containing fish, any liquid or solid matter to such an extent as to cause the waters to be poisonous or injurious to fish or the spawning grounds, spawn or food of fish, shall be guilty of an offence.

(2) A person shall not be guilty of an offence under subsection (1) above for any act done in the exercise of any right to which he is by law entitled or in continuance of a method in use in connection with the same premises before 18th July 1923, if he proves to the satisfaction of the court that he has used the best practicable means, within a reasonable cost, to prevent such matter from doing injury to fish or to the spawning grounds, spawn or food of fish.

(3) Proceedings under this section shall not be instituted except by [the Agency] or by a person who has first obtained a certificate from the Minister that he has a material interest in the waters alleged to be affected.

Control of Pollution (Amendment) Act 1989
(1989, c. 14)

1   Offence of transporting controlled waste without registering

(1) Subject to the following provisions of this section, it shall be an offence for any person who is not a registered carrier of controlled waste, in the course of any business of his or otherwise with a view to profit, to transport any controlled waste to or from any place in Great Britain.

(2) A person shall not be guilty of an offence under this section in respect of—

    (a) the transport of controlled waste within the same premises between different places in those premises;

    (b) the transport to a place in Great Britain of controlled waste which has been brought from a country or territory outside Great Britain and is not landed in Great Britain until it arrives at that place;

    (c) the transport by air or sea of controlled waste from a place in Great Britain to a place outside Great Britain.

(3) The Secretary of State may by regulations provide that a person shall not be required for the purposes of this section to be a registered carrier of controlled waste if—

    (a) he is a prescribed person or a person of such a description as may be prescribed; or

    (b) without prejudice to paragraph (a) above, he is a person in relation to whom the prescribed requirements under the law of any other member State are satisfied.

(4) In proceedings against any person for an offence under this section in respect of the transport of any controlled waste it shall be a defence for that person to show—

    (a) that the waste was transported in an emergency of which notice was given, as soon as practicable after it occurred, to the [regulation] authority in whose area the emergency occurred;

    (b) that he neither knew nor had reasonable grounds for suspecting that what was being transported was controlled waste and took all such steps as it was reasonable to take for ascertaining whether it was such waste; or

    (c) that he acted under instructions from his employer.

(5) A person guilty of an offence under this section shall be liable on summary conviction to a fine not exceeding level 5 on the standard scale.

(6) In this section 'emergency', in relation to the transport of any controlled waste, means any circumstances in which, in order to avoid, remove or reduce any serious danger to the public or serious risk of damage to the environment, it is necessary for the waste to be transported from one place to another without the use of a registered carrier of such waste.

2 Registration of carriers

(1) Subject to section 3 below, the Secretary of State may by regulations make provision for the registration of persons with [regulation] authorities as carriers of controlled waste and, for that purpose, for the establishment and maintenance by such authorities, in accordance with the regulations, of such registers as may be prescribed.

(2) Regulations under this section may—

    (a) make provision with respect to applications for registration;

    (b) impose requirements with respect to the manner in which [regulation] authorities maintain registers of carriers of controlled waste;

    (c) provide for the issue of a certificate of registration free of charge to a registered carrier of controlled waste both on his registration and on the making of any alteration of any entry relating to him in a register of such carriers;

    (d) provide for such a certificate to be in such form and to contain such information as may be prescribed;

    (e) provide that the provision by a [regulation] authority to a registered carrier of such copies of a certificate of registration as are provided in addition to the certificate provided free of charge in pursuance of provision made by virtue of paragraph (c) above is to be made subject to the payment of a charge imposed under the regulations.

(3) Provision contained in any regulations under this section by virtue of subsection (2)(a) above may, in particular, include provision which—

    (a) prescribes the manner of determining the [regulation] authority to which an application is to be made;

(b) prescribes the form on which and other manner in which an application is to be made;

(c) prescribes the period within which an application for the renewal of any registration which is due to expire is to be made;

(d) imposes requirements with respect to the information which is to be provided by an applicant to the authority to which his application is made;

(e) [. . .]

[(3A) Without prejudice to the generality of paragraphs (b) and (d) of subsection (3) above—

(a) the power to prescribe a form under paragraph (b) of that subsection includes power to require an application to be made on any form of any description supplied for the purpose by the regulation authority to which the application is to be made; and

(b) The power to impose requirements with respect to information under paragraph (d) of that subsection includes power to make provision requiring an application to be accompanied by such information as may reasonably be required by the regulation authority to which it is to be made.]

(4) Provision contained in any regulations under this section by virtue of subsection (2)(b) above may, in particular, include provision—

(a) specifying or describing the information to be incorporated in any register maintained by a [regulation] authority in pursuance of any such regulations;

(b) requiring a registered carrier of controlled waste to notify a [regulation] authority which maintains such a register of any change of circumstances affecting information contained in the entry relating to that carrier in that register;

(c) requiring a [regulation] authority, to such extent and in such manner as may be prescribed, to make the contents of any such register available for public inspection free of charge; and

(d) requiring such an authority, on payment of such charges as may be imposed under the regulations, to provide such copies of the contents of any such register to any person applying for a copy as may be prescribed.

(5) Subsections (2) to (4) above are without prejudice to the generality of subsection (1) above.

3   Restrictions on power under section 2

(1) Nothing in any regulations under section 2 above shall authorise a [regulation] authority to refuse an application for registration except where—

(a) there has, in relation to that application, been a contravention of the requirements of any regulations made by virtue of subsection (2)(a) of that section; or

(b) the applicant or another relevant person has been convicted of a prescribed offence and, in the opinion of the authority, it is undesirable for the applicant to be authorised to transport controlled waste.

(2) Nothing in any regulations under section 2 above shall authorise any [regulation] authority to revoke any person's registration as a carrier of controlled waste except where—

(a) that person or another relevant person has been convicted of a prescribed offence; and

(b) in the opinion of the authority, it is undesirable for the registered carrier to continue to be authorised to transport controlled waste; but registration in accordance with any regulations under that section shall cease to have effect after such period as may be prescribed or if the registered carrier gives written notice requiring the removal of his name from the register.

(3) Regulations under section 2 above may require every registration in respect of a business which is or is to be carried on by a partnership to be a registration of all the partners

and to cease to have effect if any of the partners ceases to be registered or if any person who is not registered becomes a partner.

(4) Nothing in any regulations under section 2 above shall have the effect of bringing the revocation of any person's registration as a carrier of controlled waste into force except—

(a) after the end of such period as may be prescribed for appealing against the revocation under section 4 below; or

(b) where that person has indicated, within that period, that he does not intend to make or continue with an appeal.

(5) In relation to any applicant for registration or registered carrier, another relevant person shall be treated for the purposes of any provision made by virtue of subsection (1) or (2) above as having been convicted of a prescribed offence if—

(a) any person has been convicted of a prescribed offence committed by him in the course of his employment by the applicant or registered carrier or in the course of the carrying on of any business by a partnership one of the members of which was the applicant or registered carrier;

(b) a body corporate has been convicted of a prescribed offence committed at a time when the applicant or registered carrier was a director, manager, secretary or other similar officer of that body corporate; or

(c) where the applicant or registered carrier is a body corporate, a person who is a director, manager, secretary or other similar officer of that body corporate—

(i) has been convicted of a prescribed offence; or

(ii) was a director, manager, secretary or other similar officer of another body corporate at a time when a prescribed offence for which that other body corporate has been convicted was committed.

(6) In determining for the purposes of any provision made by virtue of subsection (1) or (2) above whether it is desirable for any individual to be or to continue to be authorised to transport controlled waste, a [regulation] authority shall have regard, in a case in which a person other than the individual has been convicted of a prescribed offence, to whether that individual has been a party to the carrying on of a business in a manner involving the commission of prescribed offences.

4   Appeals against refusal of registration etc

(1) Where a person has applied to a [regulation] authority to be registered in accordance with any regulations under section 2 above, he may appeal to the Secretary of State if—

(a) his application is refused; or

(b) the relevant period from the making of the application has expired without his having been registered;

and for the purposes of this subsection the relevant period is two months or, except in the case of an application for the renewal of his registration by a person who is already registered, such longer period as may be agreed between the applicant and the [regulation] authority in question.

(2) A person whose registration as a carrier of controlled waste has been revoked may appeal against the revocation to the Secretary of State.

(3) On an appeal under this section the Secretary of State may, as he thinks fit, either dismiss the appeal or give the [regulation] authority in question a direction to register the appellant or, as the case may be, to cancel the revocation.

(4) Where on an appeal made by virtue of subsection (1)(b) above the Secretary of State dismisses an appeal, he shall direct the [regulation] authority in question not to register the appellant.

(5) It shall be the duty of a [regulation] authority to comply with any direction under this section.

(6) The Secretary of State may by regulations make provision as to the manner in which

and time within which an appeal under this section is to be made and as to the procedure to be followed on any such appeal.

(7) Where an appeal under this section is made in accordance with regulations under this section—

(a) by a person whose appeal is in respect of such an application for the renewal of his registration as was made, in accordance with regulations under section 2 above, at a time when he was already registered; or

(b) by a person whose registration has been revoked, that registration shall continue in force, notwithstanding the expiry of the prescribed period or the revocation, until the appeal is disposed of.

(8) For the purposes of subsection (7) above an appeal is disposed of when any of the following occurs, that is to say—

(a) the appeal is withdrawn;

(b) the appellant is notified by the Secretary of State or the [regulation] authority in question that his appeal has been dismissed; or

(c) the [regulation] authority comply with any direction of the Secretary of State to renew the appellant's registration or to cancel the revocation.

[(9) This section is subject to section 114 of the Environment Act 1995 (delegation or reference of appeals etc).]

5   Duty to produce authority to transport controlled waste

(1) If it reasonably appears to any duly authorised officer of a [regulation] authority or to a constable that any controlled waste is being or has been transported in contravention of section 1(1) above, he may—

(a) stop any person appearing to him to be or to have been engaged in transporting that waste and require that person to produce his authority or, as the case may be, his employer's authority for transporting that waste; and

(b) search any vehicle that appears to him to be a vehicle which is being or has been used for transporting that waste, carry out tests on anything found in any such vehicle and take away for testing samples of anything so found.

(2) Nothing in subsection (1) above shall authorise any person other than a constable in uniform to stop a vehicle on any road.

(3) Subject to the following provisions of this section, a person who is required by virtue of this section to produce an authority for transporting controlled waste shall do so by producing it forthwith to the person making the requirement, by producing it at the prescribed place and within the prescribed period or by sending it to that place within that period.

(4) A person shall be guilty of an offence under this section if he—

(a) intentionally obstructs any authorised officer of a [regulation] authority or constable in the exercise of the power conferred by subsection (1) above; or

(b) subject to subsection (5) below, fails without reasonable excuse to comply with a requirement imposed in exercise of that power;

and in paragraph (b) above the words 'without reasonable excuse' shall be construed in their application to . . . England and Wales, as making it a defence for a person against whom proceedings for the failure are brought to show that there was a reasonable excuse for the failure, rather than as requiring the person bringing the proceedings to show that there was no such excuse.

(5) A person shall not be guilty of an offence by virtue of subsection (4)(b) above unless it is shown—

(a) that the waste in question was controlled waste; and

(b) that that person did transport it to or from a place in Great Britain.

(6) For the purposes of this section a person's authority for transporting controlled waste is—

(a) his certificate of registration as a carrier of controlled waste or such a copy of that certificate as satisfies prescribed requirements; or

(b) such evidence as may be prescribed that he is not required to be registered as a carrier of controlled waste.

(7) A person guilty of an offence under this section shall be liable on summary conviction to a fine not exceeding level 5 on the standard scale.

6   Seizure and disposal of vehicles used for illegal waste disposal

(1) A justice of the peace . . . may issue a warrant to a [regulation] authority for the seizure of any vehicle if he is satisfied, on sworn information in writing—

(a) that there are reasonable grounds for believing—

(i) that an offence under section 3 of the Control of Pollution Act 1974 [or section 33 of the Environmental Protection Act 1990] (prohibition on unlicensed [deposit, treatment or] disposal of waste) has been committed; and

(ii) that that vehicle was used in the commission of the offence;

(b) that proceedings for that offence have not yet been brought against any person; and

(c) that the authority have failed, after taking the prescribed steps, to ascertain the name and address of any person who is able to provide them with the prescribed information about who was using the vehicle at the time when the offence was committed.

(2) Subject to subsections (3) and (4) below, where a warrant under this section has been issued to a [regulation] authority in respect of any vehicle, any duly authorised officer of the disposal authority or any constable may stop the vehicle and, on behalf of the authority, seize the vehicle and its contents.

(3) Nothing in this section shall authorise any person other than a constable in uniform to stop a vehicle on any road; and a duly authorised officer of a [regulation] authority shall not be entitled to seize any property under this section unless he is accompanied by a constable.

(4) A warrant under this section shall continue in force until its purpose is fulfilled; and any person seizing any property under this section shall, if required to do so, produce both the warrant and any authority in pursuance of which he is acting under the warrant.

(5) Where any property has been seized under this section on behalf of a [regulation] authority, the authority may, in accordance with regulations made by the Secretary of State, remove it to such place as the authority consider appropriate and may retain custody of it until either—

(a) it is returned, in accordance with the regulations, to a person who establishes that he is entitled to it; or

(b) it is disposed of by the authority in exercise of a power conferred by the regulations to sell or destroy the property or to deposit it at any place.

[(6) Regulations under this section shall not authorise a regulation authority to sell or destroy any property or to deposit any property at any place unless—

(a) the following conditions are satisfied, that is to say—

(i) the authority have published such notice, and taken such other steps (if any), as may be prescribed for informing persons who may be entitled to the property that it has been seized and is available to be claimed; and

(ii) the prescribed period has expired without any obligation arising under the regulations for the regulation authority to return the property to any person; or

(b) the condition of the property requires it to be disposed of without delay.]

(7) Regulations under this section may—

(a) impose obligations on a [regulation] authority to return any property which has been seized under this section to a person who claims to be entitled to it and satisfies such requirements for establishing his entitlement, and such other requirements, as may be prescribed;

(b) provide for the manner in which the person entitled to any such property is to be determined where there is more than one claim to it;

(c) provide for the proceeds of sale of any property sold by a [regulation] authority under the regulations to be applied towards meeting expenses incurred by the authority in exercising their functions by virtue of this section and, in so far as they are not so applied, to be applied in such other manner as may be prescribed;

(d) make provision which treats a person who establishes that he is entitled to a vehicle as having established for the purposes of regulations under this section that he is also entitled to its contents.

(8) Subject to their powers by virtue of any regulations under this section to sell or destroy any property or to dispose of it by depositing it at any place, it shall be the duty of a [regulation] authority, while any property is in their custody by virtue of a warrant under this section, to take such steps as are reasonably necessary for the safe custody of that property.

(9) Any person who intentionally obstructs any authorised officer of a [regulation] authority or constable in the exercise of any power conferred by virtue of a warrant under this section shall be guilty of an offence and liable, on summary conviction, to a fine not exceeding level 5 on the standard scale.

7 Further enforcement provisions

(1) Subject to subsection (2) below, the provisions of [section 71] of the [Environmental Protection Act 1990 (powers of entry, of dealing with imminent pollution or to obtain information)] shall have effect as if the provisions of this Act were provisions of that Act and as if, in those sections, references to a relevant authority were references to a [regulation] authority.

(2) [. . .]

(3) A person shall be guilty of an offence under this subsection if he—

(a) fails, without reasonable excuse, to comply with any requirement in pursuance of regulations under this Act to provide information to the Secretary of State or a [regulation] authority; or

(b) in complying with any such requirement, provides information which he knows to be false [or misleading] in a material particular or recklessly provides information which is false [or misleading] in a material particular;

and in paragraph (a) above the words 'without reasonable excuse' shall be construed in their application to . . . England and Wales, as making it a defence for a person against whom proceedings for the failure are brought to show that there was a reasonable excuse for the failure, rather than as requiring the person bringing the proceedings to show that there was no such excuse.

(4) A person guilty of an offence under subsection (3) above shall be liable on summary conviction to a fine not exceeding level 5 on the standard scale.

(5) Where the commission by any person of an offence under this Act is due to the act or default of some other person, that other person shall also be guilty of the offence; and a person may be charged with and convicted of an offence by virtue of this subsection whether or not proceedings for the offence are taken against any other person.

(6) Where a body corporate is guilty of an offence under this Act (including where it is so guilty by virtue of subsection (5) above) in respect of any act or omission which is shown to have been committed with the consent or connivance of, or to be attributable to any neglect on the part of, any director, manager, secretary or other similar officer of the body corporate or any person who was purporting to act in any such capacity, he, as well as the body corporate, shall be guilty of that offence and shall be liable to be proceeded against and punished accordingly.

(7) Where the affairs of a body corporate are managed by its members, subsection (6)

above shall apply in relation to the acts and defaults of a member in connection with his functions of management as if he were a director of the body corporate.

(8) [. . .]

8 Regulations

(1) The powers of the Secretary of State under this Act to make regulations shall be exercisable by statutory instrument subject to annulment in pursuance of a resolution of either House of Parliament.

(2) Regulations made in exercise of any such power may—

(a) contain such supplemental, consequential and transitional provision as the Secretary of State considers appropriate; and

(b) make different provision for different cases (including different provision for different persons, circumstances or localities).

9 Interpretation

(1) In this Act—

'controlled waste' has, [at any time], the same meaning as [for the purposes of Part II of the Environmental Protection Act 1990];

[. . .]

'prescribed' means prescribed by regulations made by the Secretary of State;

['regulation authority' means—

(a) in relation to England and Wales, the Environment Agency; and

(b) . . .

and any reference to the area of a regulation authority shall accordingly be construed as a reference to any area in England and Wales . . .]

'road' has the same meaning as in the Road Traffic Act 1988;

'transport', in relation to any controlled waste, includes the transport of that waste by road or rail or by air, sea or inland waterway but does not include moving that waste from one place to another by means of any pipe or other apparatus that joins those two places.

'vehicle' means any motor vehicle or trailer within the meaning of the Road Traffic Regulation Act 1984.

(2) [. . .]

Town and Country Planning Act 1990
(1990, c. 8)

PART I   PLANNING AUTHORITIES

1   Local planning authorities: general

(1) In a non-metropolitan county—

(a) the council of a county is the county planning authority for the county, and

(b) the council of a district is the district planning authority for the district, and references in the planning Acts to a local planning authority in relation to a non-metropolitan county shall be construed, subject to any express provision to the contrary, as references to both the county planning authority and the district planning authorities.

[(1A) Subsection (1) does not apply in relation to Wales.]

[(1B) In Wales—

(a) the local planning authority for a county is the county council; and

(b) the local planning authority for a county borough is the county borough council.]

(2) The council of a metropolitan district is the local planning authority for the district and the council of a London borough is the local planning authority for the borough.

(3) In England (exclusive of the metropolitan counties, Greater London and the Isles of Scilly) [. . .] all functions conferred on local planning authorities by or under the planning Acts shall be exercisable both by county planning authorities and district planning authorities.

(4) In this Act 'mineral planning authority' means—

    (a) in respect of a site in a non-metropolitan county, the county planning authority; and

    (b) in respect of a site in a metropolitan district or London borough, the local planning authority.

[(4A) Subsection (4) does not apply in relation to Wales.]

[(4B) As to any site in Wales, the local planning authority is also the mineral planning authority.]

(5) This section has effect subject to any express provision to the contrary in the planning Acts and, in particular—

    (a) [this section has] effect subject to [sections 4A to] [8A] of this Act [and] [. . .]

    (b) subsections (1) to (2) have effect subject to sections 2 and 9; and

    (c) subsection (3) has effect subject to [. . .] Schedule 1 (which contains provisions as to the exercise of certain functions under this Act by particular authorities and liaison between them).

[(6) The exercise, in relation to Wales, of functions conferred on local planning authorities is subject to [. . .] Schedule 1A.]

[4A National Parks with National Park authorities

(1) Where a National Park authority has been established for any area, this section, [. . .] shall apply, as from such time as may be specified for the purposes of this section in the order establishing that authority, in relation to the Park for which it is the authority.

(2) Subject to subsections (4) and (5) below, the National Park authority for the Park shall be the sole local planning authority for the area of the Park and, accordingly—

    (a) functions conferred by or under the planning Acts on a planning authority of any description (including the functions of a mineral planning authority under those Acts and under the Planning and Compensation Act 1991) shall, in relation to the Park, be functions of the National Park authority, and not of any other authority; and

    (b) so much of the area of any other authority as is included in the Park shall be treated as excluded from any area for which that other authority is a planning authority of any description.

(3) For the purposes of subsection (2) above functions under the planning Acts which (apart from this section) are conferred—

    (a) in relation to some areas on the county or district planning authorities for those areas, and

    (b) in relation to other areas on the councils for those areas, shall be treated, in relation to those other areas, as conferred on each of those councils as the local planning authority for their area.

(4) The functions of a local planning authority by virtue of sections 198 to 201, 206 to 209 and 211 to 215, so far as they are functions of a National Park authority by virtue of this section, shall be exercisable as respects any area which is or is included in an area for which there is a district council, concurrently with the National Park authority, by that council.

(5) For the purposes of any enactment relating to the functions of a district planning authority, the functions of a district council by virtue of subsection (4) above shall be deemed

to be conferred on them as a district planning authority and as if the district were the area for which they are such an authority.]

6   Enterprise zones

(1) An order under paragraph 5 of Schedule 32 to the Local Government, Planning and Land Act 1980 (designation of enterprise zone) may provide that the enterprise zone authority shall be the local planning authority for the zone for such purposes of the planning Acts and in relation to such kinds of development as may be specified in the order.

(2) Without prejudice to the generality of paragraph 15(1) of that Schedule (modification of orders by the Secretary of State), an order under that paragraph may provide that the enterprise zone authority shall be the local planning authority for the zone for different purposes of the planning Acts or in relation to different kinds of development.

(3) Where such provision as is mentioned in subsection (1) or (2) is made by an order designating an enterprise zone or, as the case may be, an order modifying such an order, while the zone subsists the enterprise zone authority shall be, to the extent mentioned in the order (as it has effect subject to any such modifications) and to the extent that it is not already, the local planning authority for the zone in place of any authority who would otherwise be the local planning authority for the zone.

(4) The Secretary of State may by regulations make transitional and supplementary provision in relation to a provision of an order under paragraph 5 of that Schedule made by virtue of subsection (1).

(5) Such regulations may modify any provision of the planning Acts or any instrument made under any of them or may apply any such enactment or instrument (with or without modification) in making such transitional or supplementary provision.

PART II   DEVELOPMENT PLANS

11   Survey of planning areas

(1) The local planning authority—
  (a) shall keep under review the matters which may be expected to affect the development of their area or the planning of its development; and
  (b) may, if they think fit, institute a survey or surveys of their area or any part of their area for examining those matters.

(2) Without prejudice to the generality of subsection (1), the matters to be kept under review or examined under that subsection shall include—
  (a) the principal physical and economic characteristics of the area of the authority (including the principal purposes for which land is used) and, so far as they may be expected to affect that area, of any neighbouring areas;
  (b) the size, composition and distribution of the population of that area (whether resident or otherwise);
  (c) without prejudice to paragraph (a), the communications, transport system and traffic of that area and, so far as they may be expected to affect that area, of any neighbouring areas;
  (d) any considerations not mentioned in paragraphs (a), (b) and (c) which may be expected to affect any matters mentioned in them;
  (e) such other matters as may be prescribed or as the Secretary of State may in a particular case direct;
  (f) any changes already projected in any of the matters mentioned in any of paragraphs (a) to (e) and the effect which those changes are likely to have on the development of that area or the planning of such development.

(3) A local planning authority shall, for the purpose of discharging their functions under this section of keeping under review and examining any matters relating to the area of another such authority, consult with that other authority about those matters.

12   Preparation of unitary development plan

(1) The local planning authority shall, within such period (if any) as the Secretary of State may direct, prepare for their area a plan to be known as a unitary development plan.

(2) A unitary development plan shall comprise two parts.

(3) Part I of a unitary development plan shall consist of a written statement formulating the authority's general policies in respect of the development and other [use of land in their area.]

[(3A) The policies shall, subject to subsection (3B), include policies in respect of—

   (a) the conservation of the natural beauty and amenity of the land;
   (b) the improvement of the physical environment; and
   (c) the management of traffic.]

[(3B) Regulations under this section may prescribe the aspects of such development and use with which the general policies in Part I of a unitary development plan are to be concerned, in which case the policies shall be concerned with those aspects and no others.]

[(3C) In the case of a London borough, Part I of the unitary development plan shall be in general conformity with the spatial development strategy for the time being in force.]

(4) Part II of a unitary development plan shall consist of—

   (a) a written statement formulating in such detail as the authority think appropriate (and so as to be readily distinguishable from the other contents of the plan) their proposals for the development and use of land in their area;
   (b) a map showing those proposals on a geographical basis;
   (c) a reasoned justification of the general policies in Part I of the plan and of the proposals in Part II of it; and
   (d) such diagrams, illustrations or other descriptive or explanatory matter in respect of the general policies in Part I of the plan or the proposals in Part II of it as the authority think appropriate or as may be prescribed.

(5) A unitary development plan shall also contain such other matters as may be prescribed or as the Secretary of State may in any particular case direct.

[(6) In formulating the general policies in Part I of a unitary development plan the authority shall have regard to—

   (a) any regional or strategic planning guidance given by the Secretary of State to assist them in the preparation of the plan;
   (b) current national policies;
   (c) the resources likely to be available; and
   (d) such other matters as the Secretary of State may prescribe or, in a particular case, direct.]

(7) The proposals in Part II of a unitary development plan shall be in general conformity with Part I [and, in the case of a London Borough Council, with the spatial development strategy.]

[(7A) In formulating their proposals in Part II of a unitary development plan, the authority shall have regard to such information and other considerations as the Secretary of State may prescribe or, in a particular case, direct.]

(8) Part II of a unitary development plan may designate any part of the authority's area as an action area, that is to say, an area which they have selected for the commencement during a prescribed period of comprehensive treatment by development, redevelopment or improvement (or partly by one and partly by another method) and if an area is so designated that Part of the plan shall contain a description of the treatment proposed by the authority.

(9) In preparing a unitary development plan the authority shall take into account the provisions of any scheme under paragraph 3 of Schedule 32 to the Local Government, Planning and Land Act 1980 relating to land in their area which has been designated under that Schedule as an enterprise zone.

[(10) Regulations under this section may make different provision for different cases and shall be subject to any direction given, in a particular case, by the Secretary of State.]

[(11) Any provision made by regulations under this section in its application by virtue of section 10 may differ from that made under this section in its application by virtue of section 10A.]

27 Meaning of 'development plan' in Greater London and metropolitan counties

For the purposes of this Act and any other enactment relating to town and country planning, the Land Compensation Act 1961 and the Highways Act 1980, the development plan for any district in Greater London or a metropolitan county (whether the whole or part of the area of a local planning authority) shall be taken as consisting of—

(a) the provisions of the unitary development plan for the time being in force for that area or the relevant part of it, together with a copy of the local planning authority's resolution of adoption or the Secretary of State's notice of approval or, where part of the plan has been adopted and the remainder approved, copies of the resolution and the notice; and

(b) any alteration to that plan, together with a copy of the authority's resolution of adoption, or the Secretary of State's notice of approval, of the alteration or, where part of the alteration has been adopted and the remainder approved, copies of the resolution and the notice.

31 Structure plans: continuity, form and content

(1) Each structure plan approved by the Secretary of State under the 1971 Act with respect to the area of a local planning authority which is in operation immediately before the commencement of this Act shall continue in force after its commencement (subject to any alterations then in operation and to the following provisions of this Part).

[(2) A structure plan shall contain a written statement formulating the authority's general policies in respect of the development and use of land in their area.]

[(3) The policies shall, subject to subsection (4), include policies in respect of—

(a) the conservation of the natural beauty and amenity of the land;

(b) the improvement of the physical environment; and

(c) the management of traffic.]

[(4) Regulations under this section may prescribe the aspects of such development and use with which the general policies in a structure plan are to be concerned, in which case the policies shall be concerned with those aspects and no others.]

[(5) A structure plan shall also contain—

(a) such diagrams, illustrations or other descriptive or explanatory matter in respect of the general policies as may be prescribed; and

(b) such other matters as the Secretary of State may, in any particular case, direct.]

[(6) In formulating their general policies the authority shall have regard to—

(a) any regional or strategic planning guidance given by the Secretary of State to assist them in the preparation of the plan;

(b) current national policies;

(c) the resources likely to be available; and

(d) such other matters as the Secretary of State may prescribe or, in a particular case, direct.]

[(7) Where there is in operation, by virtue of section 7(7) of the 1971 Act, a structure plan relating to part of the area of a local planning authority, the authority shall, within such period (if any) as the Secretary of State may direct, prepare proposals for replacing the structure plans for the time being in operation with a single structure plan relating to the whole of their area.]

[(8) The following provisions of this Chapter apply to such replacement as they apply to replacement in exercise of the power in section 32(1)(b).]

[(9) Regulations under this section may make different provision for different cases and shall be subject to any direction given, in a particular case, by the Secretary of State.]

[(10) For the purposes of this section, except subsection (6)(b), 'policies' includes proposals.]

32 [Alteration and replacement of structure plans

(1) A local planning authority may at any time prepare proposals—

    (a) for alterations to the structure plan for their area; or

    (b) for its replacement.

(2) If the Secretary of State directs them to do so, the authority shall prepare, within such time as he may direct, proposals for—

    (a) such alterations to the structure plan as he directs; or

    (b) its replacement.

(3) An authority shall not, without the consent of the Secretary of State, prepare proposals in respect of a structure plan if the plan or any part of it has been approved by the Secretary of State under section 35A.

(4) Proposals for the alteration of a structure plan may relate to the whole or part of the area to which the plan relates.

(5) Proposals prepared under this section shall be accompanied by an explanatory memorandum.

(6) The explanatory memorandum shall state—

    (a) the reasons which in the opinion of the authority justify each of their proposals;

    (b) any information on which the proposals are based;

    (c) the relationship of the proposals to general policies for the development and use of land in neighbouring areas which may be expected to affect the area to which the proposals relate,

and may contain such illustrative material as the authority think appropriate.

(7) Proposals for the alteration or replacement of a structure plan shall not become operative unless they are—

    (a) adopted by the authority (under section 35); or

    (b) approved by the Secretary of State (under section 35A).]

33 [Public participation

(1) When preparing proposals for the alteration or replacement of a structure plan for their area and before finally determining their contents the local planning authority shall—

    (a) comply with—

        (i) any requirements imposed by regulations made under section 53; and

        (ii) any particular direction given to them by the Secretary of State with respect to a matter falling within any of paragraphs (a) to (c) or (e) of subsection (2) of that section; and

    (b) consider any representations made in accordance with those regulations.

(2) Where the authority have prepared proposals for the alteration or replacement of a structure plan they shall—

    (a) make copies of the proposals and the explanatory memorandum available for inspection at such places as may be prescribed by those regulations;

    (b) send a copy of the proposals and the explanatory memorandum to the Secretary of State; and

    (c) comply with any requirements imposed by those regulations.

(3) Each copy made available for inspection or sent under subsection (2) shall be accompanied by a statement of the prescribed period within which objections may be made to the authority.

(4) In this section 'the prescribed period' means such period as may be prescribed by or determined in accordance with regulations made under section 53 and in this Chapter 'objections made in accordance with the regulations' means objections made—

    (a) in accordance with regulations made under that section; and

    (b) within the prescribed period.

(5) The persons who may make objections in accordance with the regulations include, in particular, the Secretary of State.

(6) The proposals shall not be adopted by the authority under section 35 until—

    (a) after they have considered any objections made in accordance with the regulations; or

    (b) if no such objections are made, after the expiry of the prescribed period.]

34   [Withdrawal of proposals for alteration and replacement of structure plans

(1) Proposals for the alteration or replacement of a structure plan may be withdrawn by the local planning authority at any time before they have adopted them or the Secretary of State has approved them.

(2) On the withdrawal of such proposals, the authority shall—

    (a) withdraw the copies made available for inspection in accordance with section 33(2); and

    (b) give notice that the proposals have been withdrawn to every person who has made an objection to them.]

35   [Adoption of proposals

(1) Subject to subsection (3) and sections 35A and 35B, the local planning authority may by resolution adopt proposals for the alteration or replacement of a structure plan, either as originally prepared or as modified so as to take account of—

    (a) any objections to the proposals; or

    (b) any other considerations which appear to them to be material.

(2) If it appears to the Secretary of State that the proposals are unsatisfactory he may, at any time before the local planning authority have adopted the proposals, direct the authority to modify the proposals in such respects as are indicated in the direction.

(3) An authority to whom such a direction is given shall not adopt the proposals unless—

    (a) they satisfy the Secretary of State that they have made the modifications necessary to conform with the direction; or

    (b) the direction is withdrawn.

(4) Subject to the following provisions of this Chapter and to section 287, proposals for the alteration or replacement of a structure plan shall become operative on the date on which they are adopted.]

35A   [Calling in of proposals for approval by Secretary of State

(1) The Secretary of State may, at any time before the local planning authority have adopted proposals for the alteration or replacement of a structure plan, direct that all or any part of the proposals shall be submitted to him for his approval.

(2) If he gives such a direction—

    (a) the local planning authority shall not take any further steps for the adoption of any of the proposals until the Secretary of State has given his decision on the proposals or the relevant part of the proposals; and

    (b) the proposals or the relevant part of the proposals shall not have effect unless approved by him and shall not require adoption by the authority under section 35.

(3) Subsection (2)(a) applies in particular to holding or proceeding with an examination in public under section 35B(1).

(4) The Secretary of State may, after considering proposals submitted to him in compliance with a direction under subsection (1)—

    (a) approve them, in whole or in part and with or without modifications or reservations; or

    (b) reject them.

(5) In considering proposals so submitted to him the Secretary of State—

    (a) shall take into account any objections made in accordance with the regulations; and

    (b) may take into account any matters which he thinks relevant, whether or not they were taken into account in preparing the proposals.

(6) For the purpose of taking into account any objection or matter, the Secretary of State may, but need not, consult with any local planning authority or other person.

(7) The Secretary of State shall give the authority such statement as he considers appropriate of the reasons governing his decision on any proposals submitted to him.

(8) Subject to section 287, proposals approved by the Secretary of State under this section shall become operative on such day as he may appoint.]

35B [Examination in public

(1) Before adopting proposals for the alteration or replacement of a structure plan, the local planning authority shall, unless the Secretary of State otherwise directs, cause an examination in public to be held of such matters affecting the consideration of the proposals as—

    (a) they consider ought to be so examined; or

    (b) the Secretary of State directs.

(2) Where proposals are submitted to the Secretary of State in compliance with a direction under section 35A(1), he may cause an examination in public to be held of any matter specified by him.

(3) An examination in public shall be conducted by a person or persons appointed by the Secretary of State for the purpose.

(4) No person shall have a right to be heard at an examination in public.

(5) The following may take part in an examination in public—

    (a) in the case of an examination held under subsection (1), the local planning authority; and

    (b) in any case, any person invited to do so by the person or persons holding the examination or the person causing the examination to be held.

(6) The Secretary of State may, after consultation with the Lord Chancellor, make regulations with respect to the procedure to be followed at any examination in public.

(7) An examination in public shall constitute a statutory inquiry for the purposes of section 1(1)(c) of the Tribunals and Inquiries Act [1992] but shall not constitute such an inquiry for any other purpose of that Act.]

35C [Duties to notify authorities responsible for local plans

(1) An authority responsible for a structure plan shall, where any proposals of theirs for the alteration or replacement of a structure plan are adopted or approved—

    (a) notify any authority responsible for a local plan in their area that the proposals have been adopted or approved; and

    (b) supply that authority with a statement that the local plan is or, as the case may be, is not in general conformity with the altered or new structure plan.

(2) A statement that a local plan is not in general conformity with a structure plan shall specify the respects in which it is not in such conformity.

(3) An authority responsible for a structure plan shall, where any proposals of theirs for the alteration or replacement of a structure plan are withdrawn, notify any authority responsible for a local plan in their area that the proposals have been withdrawn.

(4) Nothing in this section requires an authority to notify or supply a statement to themselves.

(5) For the purposes of this section an authority shall be regarded as responsible—

    (a) for a structure plan, if they are entitled to prepare proposals for its alteration or replacement; and

    (b) for a local plan, if they are under a duty to prepare a local plan or are entitled to prepare proposals for its alteration or replacement.]

36 [Local plans

(1) The local planning authority shall, within such period (if any) as the Secretary of State may direct, prepare for their area a plan to be known as a local plan.

(2) A local plan shall contain a written statement formulating the authority's detailed policies for the development and use of land in their area.

(3) The policies shall include policies in respect of—

    (a) the conservation of the natural beauty and amenity of the land;

    (b) the improvement of the physical environment; and

    (c) the management of traffic.

(4) A local plan shall be in general conformity with the structure plan.

(5) A local plan shall not contain—

    (a) any policies in respect of the winning and working of minerals or the depositing of mineral waste, unless it is a plan for a National Park;

    (b) any policies in respect of the depositing of refuse or waste materials other than mineral waste, unless it is a plan for a National Park or for an area where such depositing is not a county matter for the purposes of Schedule 1.

(6) A local plan shall also contain—

    (a) a map illustrating each of the detailed policies; and

    (b) such diagrams, illustrations or other descriptive or explanatory matter in respect of the policies as may be prescribed,

and may contain such descriptive or explanatory matter as the authority think appropriate.

(7) A local plan may designate any part of the authority's area as an action area, that is to say, an area which they have selected for the commencement during a prescribed period of comprehensive treatment by development, redevelopment or improvement (or partly by one and partly by another method).

(8) If an area is so designated the plan shall contain a description of the treatment proposed by the authority.

(9) In formulating their detailed policies, the authority shall have regard to—

    (a) such information and other considerations as the Secretary of State may prescribe or, in a particular case, direct; and

    (b) the provisions of any scheme under paragraph 3 of Schedule 32 to the Local Government, Planning and Land Act 1980 relating to land in their area which has been designated under that Schedule as an enterprise zone.

(10) Subject to the following provisions of this Chapter and section 287, a local plan shall become operative on the date on which it is adopted.

(11) For the purposes of this section 'policies' includes proposals.]

37 [Minerals local plans

(1) A mineral planning authority for an area other than a National Park shall, within such period (if any) as the Secretary of State may direct, prepare for their area a plan to be known as a minerals local plan.

(2) A minerals local plan shall contain a written statement formulating the authority's detailed policies for their area in respect of development consisting of the winning and working of minerals or involving the depositing of mineral waste.

(3) The local planning authority for a National Park shall, within such period (if any) as the Secretary of State may direct—

    (a) prepare for their area a plan to be known as a minerals local plan; or

    (b) include in their local plan their detailed policies in respect of development consisting of the winning and working of minerals or involving the depositing of mineral waste.

(4) In formulating the policies in a minerals local plan, the authority shall have regard to such information and other considerations as the Secretary of State may prescribe or, in a particular case, direct.

(5) Subsections (4), (6), (10) and (11) of section 36 apply with respect to minerals local plans as they apply with respect to local plans.

(6) The following provisions of this Chapter apply with respect to minerals local plans as they apply with respect to local plans, but as if references to a local planning authority were, in relation to an area other than a National Park, references to a mineral planning authority.]

38   [Waste policies

(1) In this section—

'waste policies' means detailed policies in respect of development which involves the depositing of refuse or waste materials other than mineral waste; and

'waste local plan' means a plan containing waste policies.

(2) A local planning authority other than an excluded authority shall, within such period (if any) as the Secretary of State may direct—

    (a) prepare a waste local plan for their area; or

    (b) include their waste policies in their minerals local plan.

(3) A local planning authority are an excluded authority for the purposes of subsection (2) if they are an authority—

    (a) for a National Park;

    (b) for an area where waste policies are not a county matter for the purposes of Schedule 1.

(4) A local planning authority for a National Park shall within such period (if any) as the Secretary of State may direct—

    (a) prepare a waste local plan for their area; or

    (b) include their waste policies in—

        (i) their minerals local plan; or

        (ii) their local plan.

(5) In formulating their waste policies, the authority shall have regard to such information and other considerations as the Secretary of State may prescribe or, in a particular case, direct.

(6) Subsections (4), (6), (10) and (11) of section 36 apply with respect to waste local plans as they apply with respect to local plans.

(7) The following provisions of this Chapter apply with respect to waste local plans as they apply with respect to local plans, but as if references to a local planning authority were references to the authority who are entitled to prepare a waste local plan.]

39   [Alteration and replacement of local plans

(1) A local planning authority may at any time prepare proposals—

    (a) for alterations to the local plan for their area; or

    (b) for its replacement.

(2) A local planning authority shall—

    (a) consider whether they need to prepare such proposals, if they have been supplied with a statement under section 35C that the local plan is not in general conformity with the structure plan; and

    (b) prepare such proposals, if they are directed to do so by the Secretary of State, within such period (if any) as he may direct.

(3) An authority shall not, without the consent of the Secretary of State, prepare such proposals if the plan or any part of it has been approved by the Secretary of State.

(4) Proposals for the alteration of a local plan may relate to the whole or part of the area to which the plan relates.

(5) Subject to the following provisions of this Chapter and section 287, proposals for the alteration or replacement of a local plan shall become operative on the date on which they are adopted.]

40   [Public participation

(1) When preparing a local plan for their area or proposals for its alteration or replacement and before finally determining the contents of the plan or the proposals the local planning authority shall—

   (a) comply with—
      (i) any requirements imposed by regulations made under section 53; and
      (ii) any particular direction given to them by the Secretary of State with respect to a matter falling within any of paragraphs (a) to (c) or (e) of subsection (2) of that section; and
   (b) consider any representations made in accordance with those regulations.

(2) Subject to section 46(1), where the authority have prepared a local plan or proposals for its alteration or replacement they shall—

   (a) make copies of the relevant documents available for inspection at such places as may be prescribed by those regulations.
   (b) send a copy of the relevant documents to the Secretary of State; and
   (c) comply with any requirements imposed by those regulations.

(3) In subsection (2) 'the relevant documents' means—

   (a) the plan or the proposals; and
   (b) any statement supplied under section 46(2).

(4) Each copy made available for inspection or sent under subsection (2) shall be accompanied by a statement of the prescribed period within which objections may be made to the authority.

(5) In this section 'the prescribed period' means such period as may be prescribed by or determined in accordance with regulations made under section 53 and in this Chapter 'objections made in accordance with the regulations' means objections made—

   (a) in accordance with regulations made under that section; and
   (b) within the prescribed period.

(6) The persons who may make objections in accordance with the regulations include, in particular, the Secretary of State.

(7) A local plan or proposals for its alteration or replacement shall not be adopted by the authority under section 43 until—

   (a) after they have considered any objections made in accordance with the regulations; or
   (b) if no such objections are made, after the expiry of the prescribed period.]

42   [Objections: local inquiry or other hearing]

[(1) Where any objections have been made, in accordance with the regulations, to proposals for a local plan or for its alteration or replacement copies of which have been made available for inspection under section 40(2), the local planning authority shall cause a local inquiry or other hearing to be held for the purpose of considering the objections.]

[(2) The local planning authority may cause a local inquiry or other hearing to be held for the purpose of considering any other objections to the proposals.]

[(2A) No local inquiry or other hearing need be held under this section if all persons who have made objections have indicated in writing that they do not wish to appear.]

(3) A local inquiry or other hearing shall be held by a person appointed by the Secretary of State or, in such cases as may be prescribed, by the authority themselves.

(4) Regulations may—

    (a) make provision with respect to the appointment, and qualifications for appointment, of persons to hold a local inquiry or other hearing;

    (b) include provision enabling the Secretary of State to direct a local planning authority to appoint a particular person, or one of a specified list or class of persons;

    (c) make provision with respect to the remuneration and allowances of the person appointed.

(5) Subsections (2) and (3) of section 250 of the Local Government Act 1972 (power to summon and examine witnesses) apply to an inquiry held under this section.

(6) The Tribunals and Inquiries Act [1992] shall apply to a local inquiry or other hearing held under this section as it applies to a statutory inquiry held by the Secretary of State, but as if in [section 10(1)] of that Act (statement of reasons for decisions) the reference to any decision taken by the Secretary of State were a reference to a decision taken by a local authority.

43   Adoption of proposals

[(1) Subject to the following provisions of this section and section 44, the local planning authority may by resolution adopt proposals for a local plan or for its alteration or replacement, either as originally prepared or as modified so as to take account of—

    (a) any objections to the plan; or

    (b) any other considerations which appear to them to be material.]

(2) [. . .]

(3) The authority shall not adopt any proposals which do not conform generally to the structure plan.

(4) After copies of the proposals have been sent to the Secretary of State and before they have been adopted by the local planning authority, the Secretary of State may, if it appears to him that the proposals are unsatisfactory, direct the authority to [modify] the proposals in such respects as are indicated in the direction.

(5) An authority to whom a direction is given shall not adopt the proposals unless they satisfy the Secretary of State that they have made the modifications necessary to conform with the direction or the direction is withdrawn.

(6) [. . .]

44   Calling in of proposals for approval by Secretary of State

(1) After copies of proposals have been sent to the Secretary of State and before they have been adopted by the local planning authority, the Secretary of State may direct that the proposals [or any part of them] shall be submitted to him for his approval.

[(2) If he gives such a direction—

    (a) the authority shall not take any further steps for the adoption of any of the proposals until the Secretary of State has given his decision on the proposals or the relevant part of the proposals; and

    (b) the proposals or the relevant part of the proposals shall not have effect unless approved by him and shall not require adoption by the authority under section 43.]

(3) [. . .]

45   Approval of proposals by Secretary of State

(1) The Secretary of State may after considering proposals submitted to him under section 44 either approve them (in whole or in part and with or without modifications or reservations) or reject them.

(2) In considering the proposals he may take into account any matters he thinks are relevant, whether or not they were taken into account in the proposals as submitted.

(3) Where on taking the proposals into consideration the Secretary of State does not determine then to reject them, he shall before determining whether or not to approve them—

(a) consider any objections to them made in accordance with [the] regulations,

(b) give any person who made such an objection which has not been withdrawn an opportunity of appearing before and being heard by a person appointed by him for the purpose, and

(c) if a local inquiry or other hearing is held, also give such an opportunity to the authority and such other persons as he thinks fit,

except so far as the objections have already been considered, or a local inquiry or other hearing into the objections has already been held, by the authority.

(4) In considering the proposals the Secretary of State may consult with or consider the views of any local planning authority or any other person; but he need not do so, or give an opportunity for the making of representations or objections, or cause a local inquiry or other hearing to be held, except as provided by subsection (3).

[(5) Subject to section 287, proposals approved by the Secretary of State under this section shall become operative on such day as he may appoint.]

46 [Conformity between plans

(1) An authority responsible for a local plan shall not make copies available as mentioned in section 40(2) unless—

(a) they have served on the authority responsible for the structure plan in their area a copy of the plan or the proposals; and

(b) such period as may be prescribed has elapsed since they served the copy of the plan or proposals.

(2) Where a local planning authority have been served with a copy as mentioned in subsection (1) they shall, before the end of any period prescribed for the purposes of that subsection, supply the authority responsible for the local plan with—

(a) a statement that the plan or the proposals are in general conformity with the structure plan; or

(b) a statement that the plan or the proposals are not in such conformity.

(3) A statement that a plan or proposals are not in such conformity shall specify the respects in which the plan or proposals are not in such conformity.

(4) Any such statement shall be treated for the purposes of this Chapter as an objection made in accordance with the regulations.

(5) Nothing in this section requires an authority to serve a copy on or supply a statement to themselves.

(6) Where—

(a) a local planning authority propose to make, alter or replace a local plan;

(b) copies of proposals for the alteration or replacement of the structure plan for their area have been made available for inspection under section 33(2); and

(c) the authority mentioned in paragraph (a) include in any relevant copy of the plan or proposals a statement that they are making the permitted assumption,

the permitted assumption shall, subject to subsection (9), be made for all purposes (including in particular any question as to conformity between plans).

(7) In this section 'the permitted assumption' means the assumption that—

(a) the proposals mentioned in subsection (6)(b); or

(b) if any proposed modifications to those proposals are published in accordance with regulations made under section 53, the proposals as so modified,

have been adopted.

(8) For the purposes of subsection (6)(c) a copy is a relevant copy of a plan or proposals if it is—

(a) served under subsection (1)(a); or

(b) made available or sent under section 40(2).

(9) The permitted assumption shall not be made at any time after the authority mentioned in subsection (6)(a) know that the proposals mentioned in subsection (6)(b) have been withdrawn.

(10) The provisions of a local plan prevail for all purposes over any conflicting provisions in the relevant structure plan unless the local plan is one—

(a) stated under section 35C not to be in general conformity with the structure plan; and

(b) neither altered nor replaced after the statement was supplied.

(11) The Secretary of State may make regulations with respect to cases where—

(a) provisions in a structure plan or a local plan conflict with provisions in—

(i) a minerals local plan; or

(ii) a waste local plan;

(b) a structure plan and a local plan are made by the same authority and the provisions of the two plans conflict.

(12) Subsection (5) of section 35C applies for the purposes of this section as it applies for the purposes of that.]

54   Meaning of 'development plan' outside Greater London and the metropolitan counties

(1) Subject to subsection (4), for the purposes of this Act and any other enactment relating to town and country planning, the Land Compensation Act 1961 and the Highways Act 1980, the development plan for any district outside Greater London and the metropolitan counties (whether the whole or part of the area of a local planning authority) shall be taken as consisting of—

[(a) the provisions of the structure plan for the time being in operation in the area;

(b) any alterations to that structure plan;

(c) the provisions of the local plan and any minerals local plan or waste local plan for the time being in operation in the area;

(d) any alterations to that local plan or minerals local plan or waste local plan, together with the resolutions of the authority who made or altered the plan or, as the case may be the Secretary of State's notice of approval.]

(2) References in subsection (1) to the provisions of any plan, notices of approval, alterations and resolutions of adoption shall, in relation to a district forming part of the area to which they are applicable, be respectively construed as references to so much of those provisions, notices, alterations and resolutions as is applicable to the district.

(3) References in subsection (1) to notices of approval shall, in relation to any plan or alteration made by the Secretary of State under section 51, be construed as references to notices of the making of the plan or alteration.

(4) This section has effect subject to Part III of Schedule 2 (old development plans) [and Part III of Schedule 4 to the Planning and Compensation Act 1991].

(5) Any reference in the Land Compensation Act 1961 to an area defined in the current development plan as an area of comprehensive development shall be construed as a reference to an action area for which a local plan is in force.

54A   [Status of development plans

Where, in making any determination under the planning Acts, regard is to be had to the development plan, the determination shall be made in accordance with the plan unless material considerations indicate otherwise.]

PART III   CONTROL OVER DEVELOPMENT

55   Meaning of 'development' and 'new development'

(1) Subject to the following provisions of this section, in this Act, except where the context otherwise requires, 'development,' means the carrying out of building, engineering, mining or other operations in, on, over or under land, or the making of any material change in the use of any buildings or other land.

[(1A) For the purposes of this Act 'building operations' includes—

(a) demolition of buildings;

(b) rebuilding;

(c) structural alterations of or additions to buildings; and

(d) other operations normally undertaken by a person carrying on business as a builder.]

(2) The following operations or uses of land shall not be taken for the purposes of this Act to involve development of the land—

(a) the carrying out for the maintenance, improvement or other alteration of any building of works which—

(i) affect only the interior of the building, or

(ii) do not materially affect the external appearance of the building, and are not works for making good war damage or works begun after 5th December 1968 for the alteration of a building by providing additional space in it underground;

(b) the carrying out on land within the boundaries of a road by a local highway authority of any works required for the maintenance or improvement of the road; [but, in the case of any such works which are not exclusively for the maintenance of the road, not including any works which may have significant adverse effects on the environment.]

(c) the carrying out by a local authority or statutory undertakers of any works for the purpose of inspecting, repairing or renewing any sewers, mains, pipes, cables or other apparatus, including the breaking open of any street or other land for that purpose;

(d) the use of any buildings or other land within the curtilage of a dwellinghouse for any purpose incidental to the enjoyment of the dwellinghouse as such;

(e) the use of any land for the purposes of agriculture or forestry (including afforestation) and the use for any of those purposes of any building occupied together with land so used;

(f) in the case of buildings or other land which are used for a purpose of any class specified in an order made by the Secretary of State under this section, the use of the buildings or other land or, subject to the provisions of the order, of any part of the buildings or the other land, for any other purpose of the same class.

[(g) the demolition of any description of building specified in a direction given by the Secretary of State to local planning authorities generally or to a particular local planning authority.]

(3) For the avoidance of doubt it is hereby declared that for the purpose of this section—

(a) the use as two or more separate dwellinghouses of any building previously used as a single dwellinghouse involves a material change in the use of the building and of each part of it which is so used;

(b) the deposit of refuse or waste materials on land involves a material change in its use, notwithstanding that the land is comprised in a site already used for that purpose, if—

(i) the superficial area of the deposit is extended, or

(ii) the height of the deposit is extended and exceeds the level of the land adjoining the site.

(4) For the purposes of this Act mining operations include—

(a) the removal of material of any description—

(i) from a mineral-working deposit;

(ii) from a deposit of pulverised fuel ash or other furnace ash or clinker; or

(iii) from a deposit of iron, steel or other metallic slags; and

(b) the extraction of minerals from a disused railway embankment.

[(4A) Where the placing or assembly of any tank in any part of any inland waters for the purpose of fish farming there would not, apart from this subsection, involve development of the land below, this Act shall have effect as if the tank resulted from carrying out engineering operations over that land; and in this subsection—

'fish farming' means the breeding, rearing or keeping of fish or shellfish (which includes any kind of crustacean and mollusc);

'inland waters' means waters which do not form part of the sea or of any creek, bay or estuary or of any river as far as the tide flows; and

'tank' includes any cage and any other structure for use in fish farming.]

(5) Without prejudice to any regulations made under the provisions of this Act relating to the control of advertisements, the use for the display of advertisements of any external part of a building which is not normally used for that purpose shall be treated for the purposes of this section as involving a material change in the use of that part of the building.

56 Time when development begun

(1) Subject to the following provisions of this section, for the purposes of this Act development of land shall be taken to be initiated—

(a) if the development consists of the carrying out of operations, at the time when those operations are begun;

(b) if the development consists of a change in use, at the time when the new use is instituted;

(c) if the development consists both of the carrying out of operations and of a change in use, at the earlier of the times mentioned in paragraphs (a) and (b).

(2) For the purposes of the provisions of this Part mentioned in subsection (3) development shall be taken to be begun on the earliest date on which any material operation comprised in the development begins to be carried out.

(3) The provisions referred to in subsection (2) are sections 85(2), 86(6), 87(4), [89,] 91, 92 and 94.

(4) In subsection (2) 'material operation' means—

(a) any work of construction in the course of the erection of a building;

[(aa) any work of demolition of a building;]

(b) the digging of a trench which is to contain the foundations, or part of the foundations, of a building;

(c) the laying of any underground main or pipe to the foundations, or part of the foundations, of a building or to any such trench as is mentioned in paragraph (b);

(d) any operation in the course of laying out or constructing a road or part of a road;

(e) any change in the use of any land which constitutes material development.

(5) In subsection (4)(e) 'material development' means any development other than—

(a) development for which planning permission is granted by a general development order for the time being in force and which is carried out so as to comply with any condition or limitation subject to which planning permission is so granted;

[(b) development of a class specified in paragraph 1 or 2 of Schedule 3;]

(c) development of any class prescribed for the purposes of this subsection.

(6) In subsection (5) 'general development order' means a development order (within the meaning of section 59) made as a general order applicable (subject to such exceptions as may be specified in it) to all land in England and Wales.

57   Planning permission required for development

(1) Subject to the following provisions of this section, planning permission is required for the carrying out of any development of land.

(2) Where planning permission to develop land has been granted for a limited period, planning permission is not required for the resumption, at the end of that period, of its use for the purpose for which it was normally used before the permission was granted.

(3) Where by a development order planning permission to develop land has been granted subject to limitations, planning permission is not required for the use of that land which (apart from its use in accordance with that permission) is its normal use.

(4) Where an enforcement notice has been issued in respect of any development of land, planning permission is not required for its use for the purpose for which (in accordance with the provisions of this Part of this Act) it could lawfully have been used if that development had not been carried out.

(5) In determining for the purposes of subsections (2) and (3) what is or was the normal use of land, no account shall be taken of any use begun in contravention of this Part or of previous planning control.

(6) For the purposes of this section a use of land shall be taken to have been begun in contravention of previous planning control if it was begun in contravention of Part III of the 1947 Act, Part III of the 1962 Act or Part III of the 1971 Act.

(7) Subsection (1) has effect subject to Schedule 4 (which makes special provision about use of land on 1st July 1948).

58   Granting of planning permission: general

(1) Planning permission may be granted—
  (a) by a development order;
  (b) by the local planning authority (or, in the cases provided in this Part, by the Secretary of State) on application to the authority in accordance with a development order;
  (c) on the adoption or approval of a simplified planning zone scheme or alterations to such a scheme in accordance with section 82 or, as the case may be, section 86; or
  (d) on the designation of an enterprise zone or the approval of a modified scheme under Schedule 32 to the Local Government, Planning and Land Act 1980 in accordance with section 88 of this Act.

(2) Planning permission may also be deemed to be granted under section 90 (development with government authorisation).

(3) This section is without prejudice to any other provisions of this Act providing for the granting of permission.

70   Determination of applications: general considerations

(1) Where an application is made to a local planning authority for planning permission—
  (a) subject to sections 91 and 92, they may grant planning permission, either unconditionally or subject to such conditions as they think fit; or
  (b) they may refuse planning permission.

(2) In dealing with such an application the authority shall have regard to the provisions of the development plan, so far as material to the application, and to any other material considerations.

(3) Subsection (1) has effect subject to [section 65] and to the following provisions of this Act, to sections 66, 67, 72 and 73 of the Planning (Listed Buildings and Conservation Areas) Act 1990 and to section 15 of the Health Services Act 1976.

70A   [Power of local planning authority to decline to determine applications

(1) A local planning authority may decline to determine an application for planning permission for the development of any land if—

(a) within the period of two years ending with the date on which the application is received, the Secretary of State has refused a similar application referred to him under section 77 or has dismissed an appeal against the refusal of a similar application; and

(b) in the opinion of the authority there has been no significant change since the refusal or, as the case may be, dismissal mentioned in paragraph (a) in the development plan, so far as material to the application, or in any other material considerations.

(2) For the purposes of this section an application for planning permission for the development of any land shall only be taken to be similar to a later application if the development and the land to which the applications relate are in the opinion of the local planning authority the same or substantially the same.

(3) The reference in subsection (1)(a) to an appeal against the refusal of an application includes an appeal under section 78(2) in respect of an application.]

72   Conditional grant of planning permission

(1) Without prejudice to the generality of section 70(1), conditions may be imposed on the grant of planning permission under that section—

(a) for regulating the development or use of any land under the control of the applicant (whether or not it is land in respect of which the application was made) or requiring the carrying out of works on any such land, so far as appears to the local planning authority to be expedient for the purposes of or in connection with the development authorised by the permission;

(b) for requiring the removal of any buildings or works authorised by the permission, or the discontinuance of any use of land so authorised, at the end of a specified period, and the carrying out of any works required for the reinstatement of land at the end of that period.

(2) A planning permission granted subject to such a condition as is mentioned in subsection (1)(b) is in this Act referred to as 'planning permission granted for a limited period'.

. . .

73   Determination of applications to develop land without compliance with conditions previously attached

(1) This section applies, subject to subsection (4), to applications for planning permission for the development of land without complying with conditions subject to which a previous planning permission was granted.

(2) On such an application the local planning authority shall consider only the question of the conditions subject to which planning permission should be granted, and—

(a) if they decide that planning permission should be granted subject to conditions differing from those subject to which the previous permission was granted, or that it should be granted unconditionally, they shall grant planning permission accordingly, and

(b) if they decide that planning permission should be granted subject to the same conditions as those subject to which the previous permission was granted, they shall refuse the application.

(3) Special provision may be made with respect to such applications—

(a) by regulations under section 62 as regards the form and content of the application, and

(b) by a development order as regards the procedure to be followed in connection with the application.

(4) This section does not apply if the previous planning permission was granted subject to a condition as to the time within which the development to which it related was to be begun and that time has expired without the development having been begun.

75 Effect of planning permission

(1) Without prejudice to the provisions of this Part as to the duration, revocation or modification of planning permission, any grant of planning permission to develop land shall (except in so far as the permission otherwise provides) enure for the benefit of the land and of all persons for the time being interested in it.

(2) Where planning permission is granted for the erection of a building, the grant of permission may specify the purposes for which the building may be used.

(3) If no purpose is so specified, the permission shall be construed as including permission to use the building for the purpose for which it is designed.

77 Reference of applications to Secretary of State

(1) The Secretary of State may give directions requiring applications for planning permission, or for the approval of any local planning authority required under a development order, to be referred to him instead of being dealt with by local planning authorities.

(2) A direction under this section—
  (a) may be given either to a particular local planning authority or to local planning authorities generally; and
  (b) may relate either to a particular application or to applications of a class specified in the direction.

(3) Any application in respect of which a direction under this section has effect shall be referred to the Secretary of State accordingly.

(4) Subject to subsection (5), where an application for planning permission is referred to the Secretary of State under this section, sections [70, 72(1) and (5), 73 and 73A] shall apply, with any necessary modifications, as they apply to such an application which falls to be determined by the local planning authority [and a development order may apply, with or without modifications, to an application so referred any requirements imposed by such an order by virtue of section 65 or 71.]

(5) Before determining an application referred to him under this section, the Secretary of State shall, if either the applicant or the local planning authority wish, give each of them an opportunity of appearing before, and being heard by, a person appointed by the Secretary of State for the purpose.

(6) Subsection (5) does not apply to an application for planning permission referred to a Planning Inquiry Commission under section 101.

(7) The decision of the Secretary of State on any application referred to him under this section shall be final.

78 Right to appeal against planning decisions and failure to take such decisions

(1) Where a local planning authority—
  (a) refuse an application for planning permission or grant it subject to conditions;
  (b) refuse an application for any consent, agreement or approval of that authority required by a condition imposed on a grant of planning permission or grant it subject to conditions; or
  (c) refuse an application for any approval of that authority required under a development order or grant it subject to conditions,
the applicant may by notice appeal to the Secretary of State.

(2) A person who has made such an application may also appeal to the Secretary of State if the local planning authority have [done none of the following]

(a) given notice to the applicant of their decision on the application;

[(aa) given notice to the applicant that they have exercised their power under section 70A to decline to determine the application;]

(b) given notice to him that the application has been referred to the Secretary of State in accordance with directions given under section 77,

within such period as may be prescribed by the development order or within such extended period as may at any time be agreed upon in writing between the applicant and the authority.

. . .

79 Determination of appeals

(1) On an appeal under section 78 the Secretary of State may—

(a) allow or dismiss the appeal, or

(b) reverse or vary any part of the decision of the local planning authority (whether the appeal relates to that part of it or not),

and may deal with the application as if it had been made to him in the first instance.

(2) Before determining an appeal under section 78 the Secretary of State shall, if either the appellant or the local planning authority so wish, give each of them an opportunity of appearing before and being heard by a person appointed by the Secretary of State for the purpose.

(3) Subsection (2) does not apply to an appeal referred to a Planning Inquiry Commission under section 101.

(4) Subject to subsection (2), the provisions of sections [70, 72(1) and (5), 73 and 73A] and Part I of Schedule 5 shall apply, with any necessary modifications, in relation to an appeal to the Secretary of State under section 78 as they apply in relation to an application for planning permission which falls to be determined by the local planning authority [and a development order may apply, with or without modifications, to such an appeal any requirements imposed by a development order by virtue of section 65 or 71]

(5) The decision of the Secretary of State on such an appeal shall be final.

(6) If, before or during the determination of such an appeal in respect of an application for planning permission to develop land, the Secretary of State forms the opinion that, having regard to the provisions of sections 70 and 72(1), the development order and any directions given under that order, planning permission for that development—

(a) could not have been granted by the local planning authority; or

(b) could not have been granted otherwise than subject to the conditions imposed,

he may decline to determine the appeal or to proceed with the determination.

[(6A) If at any time before or during the determination of such an appeal it appears to the Secretary of State that the appellant is responsible for undue delay in the progress of the appeal, he may—

(a) give the appellant notice that the appeal will be dismissed unless the appellant takes, within the period specified in the notice, such steps as are specified in the notice for the expedition of the appeal; and

(b) if the appellant fails to take those steps within that period, dismiss the appeal accordingly.]

. . .

82 Simplified planning zones

(1) A simplified planning zone is an area in respect of which a simplified planning zone scheme is in force.

(2) The adoption or approval of a simplified planning zone scheme has effect to grant in relation to the zone, or any part of it specified in the scheme, planning permission—

(a) for development specified in the scheme, or

(b) for development of any class so specified.

(3) Planning permission under a simplified planning zone scheme may be unconditional or subject to such conditions, limitations or exceptions as may be specified in the scheme.

83   Making of simplified planning zone schemes

(1) Every local planning authority shall consider, as soon as practicable after 2nd November 1987, the question for which part or parts of their area a simplified planning zone scheme is desirable, and then shall keep that question under review.

(2) If as a result of their original consideration or of any such review a local planning authority decide that it is desirable to prepare a scheme for any part of their area they shall do so; and a local planning authority may at any time decide—

(a) to make a simplified planning zone scheme, or

(b) to alter a scheme adopted by them, or

(c) with the consent of the Secretary of State, to alter a scheme approved by him.

(3) Schedule 7 has effect with respect to the making and alteration of simplified planning zone schemes and other related matters.

88   Planning permission for development in enterprise zones

(1) An order designating an enterprise zone under Schedule 32 to the Local Government, Planning and Land Act 1980 shall (without more) have effect on the date on which the order designating the zone takes effect to grant planning permission for development specified in the scheme or for development of any class so specified.

(2) The approval of a modified scheme under paragraph 11 of that Schedule shall (without more) have effect on the date on which the modifications take effect to grant planning permission for development specified in the modified scheme or for development of any class so specified.

(3) Planning permission so granted shall be subject to such conditions or limitations as may be specified in the scheme or modified scheme or, if none is specified, shall be unconditional.

(4) Subject to subsection (5), where planning permission is so granted for any development or class of development the enterprise zone authority may direct that the permission shall not apply in relation—

(a) to a specified development; or

(b) to a specified class of development; or

(c) to a specified class of development in a specified area within the enterprise zone.

(5) An enterprise zone authority shall not give a direction under subsection (4) unless—

(a) they have submitted it to the Secretary of State, and

(b) he has notified them that he approves of their giving it.

(6) If the scheme or the modified scheme specifies, in relation to any development it permits, matters which will require approval by the enterprise zone authority, the permission shall have effect accordingly.

(7) The Secretary of State may by regulations make provision as to—

(a) the procedure for giving a direction under subsection (4); and

(b) the method and procedure relating to the approval of matters specified in a scheme or modified scheme as mentioned in subsection (6).

(8) Such regulations may modify any provision of the planning Acts or any instrument made under them or may apply any such provision or instrument (with or without modification) in making any such provision as is mentioned in subsection (7).

(9) Nothing in this section prevents planning permission being granted in relation to land in an enterprise zone otherwise than by virtue of this section (whether the permission is granted in pursuance of an application made under this Part or by a development order).

(10) Nothing in this section prejudices the right of any person to carry out development apart from this section.

91   General condition limiting duration of planning permission

(1) Subject to the provisions of this section, every planning permission granted or deemed to be granted shall be granted or, as the case may be, be deemed to be granted, subject to the condition that the development to which it relates must be begun not later than the expiration of—

(a) five years beginning with the date on which the permission is granted or, as the case may be, deemed to be granted; or

(b) such other period (whether longer or shorter) beginning with that date as the authority concerned with the terms of planning permission may direct.

(2) The period mentioned in subsection (1)(b) shall be a period which the authority consider appropriate having regard to the provisions of the development plan and to any other material considerations.

(3) If planning permission is granted without the condition required by subsection (1), it shall be deemed to have been granted subject to the condition that the development to which it relates must be begun not later than the expiration of five years beginning with the date of the grant.

(4) Nothing in this section applies—

(a) to any planning permission granted by a development order;

(b) to any planning permission granted [for development carried out before the grant of that permission.]

(c) to any planning permission granted for a limited period;

[(d) to any planning permission for development consisting of the winning and working of minerals or involving the depositing of mineral waste which is granted (or deemed to be granted) subject to a condition that the development to which it relates must be begun before the expiration of a specified period after—

(i) the completion of other development consisting of the winning and working of minerals already being carried out by the applicant for the planning permission; or

(ii) the cessation of depositing of mineral waste already being carried out by the applicant for the planning permission;]

(e) to any planning permission granted by an enterprise zone scheme;

(f) to any planning permission granted by a simplified planning zone scheme; or

(g) to any outline planning permission, as defined by section 92.

92   Outline planning permission

(1) In this section and section 91 'outline planning permission' means planning permission granted, in accordance with the provisions of a development order, with the reservation for subsequent approval by the local planning authority or the Secretary of State of matters not particularised in the application ('reserved matters').

(2) Subject to the following provisions of this section, where outline planning permission is granted for development consisting in or including the carrying out of building or other operations, it shall be granted subject to conditions to the effect—

(a) that, in the case of any reserved matter, application for approval must be made not later than the expiration of three years beginning with the date of the grant of outline planning permission; and

(b) that the development to which the permission relates must be begun not later than—

(i) the expiration of five years from the date of the grant of outline planning permission; or

(ii) if later, the expiration of two years from the final approval of the reserved matters or, in the case of approval on different dates, the final approval of the last such matter to be approved.

(3) If outline planning permission is granted without the conditions required by subsection (2), it shall be deemed to have been granted subject to those conditions.

(4) The authority concerned with the terms of an outline planning permission may, in applying subsection (2), substitute, or direct that there be substituted, for the periods of three years, five years or two years referred to in that subsection such other periods respectively (whether longer or shorter) as they consider appropriate.

(5) They may also specify, or direct that there be specified, separate periods under paragraph (a) of subsection (2) in relation to separate parts of the development to which the planning permission relates; and, if they do so, the condition required by paragraph (b) of that subsection shall then be framed correspondingly by reference to those parts, instead of by reference to the development as a whole.

(6) In considering whether to exercise their powers under subsections (4) and (5), the authority shall have regard to the provisions of the development plan and to any other material considerations.

106   [Planning obligations

(1) Any person interested in land in the area of local planning authority may, by agreement or otherwise, enter into an obligation (referred to in this section and sections 106A and 106B as 'a planning obligation'), enforceable to the extent mentioned in subsection (3)—

    (a) restricting the development or use of the land in any specified way;

    (b) requiring specified operations or activities to be carried out in, on, under or over the land;

    (c) requiring the land to be used in any specified way; or

    (d) requiring a sum or sums to be paid to the authority on a specified date or dates or periodically.

(2) A planning obligation may—

    (a) be unconditional or subject to conditions;

    (b) impose any restriction or requirement mentioned in subsection (1)(a) to (c) either indefinitely or for such period or periods as may be specified; and

    (c) if it requires a sum or sums to be paid, require the payment of a specified amount or an amount determined in accordance with the instrument by which the obligation is entered into and, if it requires the payment of periodical sums, require them to be paid indefinitely or for a specified period.

(3) Subject to subsection (4) a planning obligation is enforceable by the authority identified in accordance with subsection (9)(d)—

    (a) against the person entering into the obligation; and

    (b) against any person deriving title from that person.

(4) The instrument by which a planning obligation is entered into may provide that a person shall not be bound by the obligation in respect of any period during which he no longer has an interest in the land.

(5) A restriction or requirement imposed under a planning obligation is enforceable by injunction.

(6) Without prejudice to subsection (5), if there is a breach of a requirement in a planning obligation to carry out any operations in, on, under or over the land to which the obligation relates, the authority by whom the obligation is enforceable may—

    (a) enter the land and carry out the operations; and

    (b) recover from the person or persons against whom the obligation is enforceable any expenses reasonably incurred by them in doing so.

(7) Before an authority exercise their power under subsection (6)(a) they shall give not less than twenty-one days' notice of their intention to do so to any person against whom the planning obligation is enforceable.

(8) Any person who wilfully obstructs a person acting in the exercise of a power under subsection (6)(a) shall be guilty of an offence and liable on summary conviction to a fine not exceeding level 3 on the standard scale.

(9) A planning obligation may not be entered into except by an instrument executed as a deed which—

(a) states that the obligation is a planning obligation for the purposes of this section;

(b) identifies the land in which the person entering into the obligation is interested;

(c) identifies the person entering into the obligation and states what his interest in the land is; and

(d) identifies the local planning authority by whom the obligation is enforceable.

(10) A copy of any such instrument shall be given to the authority so identified.

(11) A planning obligation shall be a local land charge and for the purposes of the Local Land Charges Act 1975 the authority by whom the obligation is enforceable shall be treated as the originating authority as respects such a charge.

(12) Regulations may provide for the charging on the land of—

(a) any sum or sums required to be paid under a planning obligation; and

(b) any expenses recoverable by a local planning authority under subsection (6)(b),

and this section and sections 106A and 106B shall have effect subject to any such regulations.

(13) In this section 'specified' means specified in the instrument by which the planning obligation is entered into and in this section and section 106A 'land' has the same meaning as in the Local Land Charges Act 1975.]

106A   [Modification and discharge of planning obligations.

(1) A planning obligation may not be modified or discharged except—

(a) by agreement between the authority by whom the obligation is enforceable and the person or persons against whom the obligation is enforceable; or

(b) in accordance with this section and section 106B.

(2) An agreement falling within subsection (1)(a) shall not be entered into except by an instrument executed as a deed.

(3) A person against whom a planning obligation is enforceable may, at any time after the expiry of the relevant period, apply to the local planning authority by whom the obligation is enforceable for the obligation—

(a) to have effect subject to such modifications as may be specified in the application; or

(b) to be discharged.

(4) In subsection (3) 'the relevant period' means—

(a) such period as may be prescribed; or

(b) if no period is prescribed, the period of five years beginning with the date on which the obligation is entered into.

(5) An application under subsection (3) for the modification of a planning obligation may not specify a modification imposing an obligation on any other person against whom the obligation is enforceable.

(6) Where an application is made to an authority under subsection (3), the authority may determine—

(a) that the planning obligation shall continue to have effect without modification;

(b) if the obligation no longer serves a useful purpose, that it shall be discharged; or

(c) if the obligation continues to serve a useful purpose, but would serve that purpose equally well if it had effect subject to the modifications specified in the application, that it shall have effect subject to those modifications.

(7) The authority shall give notice of their determination to the applicant within such period as may be prescribed.

(8) Where an authority determine that a planning obligation shall have effect subject to

modifications specified in the application, the obligation as modified shall be enforceable as if it had been entered into on the date on which notice of the determination was given to the applicant.

(9) Regulations may make provision with respect to—

(a) the form and content of applications under subsection (3);

(b) the publication of notices of such applications;

(c) the procedures for considering any representations made with respect to such applications; and

(d) the notices to be given to applicants of determinations under subsection (6).

(10) Section 84 of the Law of Property Act 1925 (power to discharge or modify restrictive covenants affecting land) does not apply to a planning obligation.]

106B [Appeals

(1) Where a local planning authority—

(a) fail to give notice as mentioned in section 106A(7); or

(b) determine that a planning obligation shall continue to have effect without modification,

the applicant may appeal to the Secretary of State.

(2) For the purposes of an appeal under subsection (1)(a), it shall be assumed that the authority have determined that the planning obligation shall continue to have effect without modification.

(3) An appeal under this section shall be made by notice served within such period and in such manner as may be prescribed.

(4) Subsections (6) to (9) of section 106A apply in relation to appeals to the Secretary of State under this section as they apply in relation to applications to authorities under that section.

(5) Before determining the appeal the Secretary of State shall, if either the applicant or the authority so wish, give each of them an opportunity of appearing before and being heard by a person appointed by the Secretary of State for the purpose.

(6) The determination of an appeal by the Secretary of State under this section shall be final.

(7) Schedule 6 applies to appeals under this section.]

PART VII   ENFORCEMENT

[Introductory]

171A [Expressions used in connection with enforcement

(1) For the purposes of this Act—

(a) carrying out development without the required planning permission; or

(b) failing to comply with any condition or limitation subject to which planning permission has been granted,

constitutes a breach of planning control.

(2) For the purposes of this Act—

(a) the issue of an enforcement notice (defined in section 172); or

(b) the service of a breach of condition notice (defined in section 187A),

constitutes taking enforcement action.

(3) In this Part 'planning permission' includes permission under Part III of the 1947 Act, of the 1962 Act or of the 1971 Act.]

171B [Time limits

(1) Where there has been a breach of planning control consisting in the carrying out without planning permission of building, engineering, mining or other operations in,

on, over or under land, no enforcement action may be taken after the end of the period of four years beginning with the date on which the operations were substantially completed.

(2) Where there has been a breach of planning control consisting in the change of use of any building to use as a single dwellinghouse, no enforcement action may be taken after the end of the period of four years beginning with the date of the breach.

(3) In the case of any other breach of planning control, no enforcement action may be taken after the end of the period of ten years beginning with the date of the breach.

(4) The preceding subsections do not prevent—

    (a) the service of a breach of condition notice in respect of any breach of planning control if an enforcement notice in respect of the breach is in effect; or

    (b) taking further enforcement action in respect of any breach of planning control if, during the period of four years ending with that action being taken, the local planning authority have taken or purported to take enforcement action in respect of that breach.]

171C   [Power to require information about activities on land

(1) Where it appears to the local planning authority that there may have been a breach of planning control in respect of any land, they may serve notice to that effect (referred to in this Act as a 'planning contravention notice') on any person who—

    (a) is the owner or occupier of the land or has any other interest in it; or

    (b) is carrying out operations on the land or is using it for any purpose.

(2) A planning contravention notice may require the person on whom it is served to give such information as to—

    (a) any operations being carried out on the land, any use of the land and any other activities being carried out on the land; and

    (b) any matter relating to the conditions or limitations subject to which any planning permission in respect of the land has been granted,

as may be specified in the notice.

(3) Without prejudice to the generality of subsection (2), the notice may require the person on whom it is served, so far as he is able—

    (a) to state whether or not the land is being used for any purpose specified in the notice or any operations or activities specified in the notice are being or have been carried out on the land;

    (b) to state when any use, operations or activities began;

    (c) to give the name and address of any person known to him to use or have used the land for any purpose or to be carrying out, or have carried out, any operations or activities on the land;

    (d) to give any information he holds as to any planning permission for any use or operations or any reason for planning permission not being required for any use or operations;

    (e) to state the nature of his interest (if any) in the land and the name and address of any other person known to him to have an interest in the land.

(4) A planning contravention notice may give notice of a time and place at which—

    (a) any offer which the person on whom the notice is served may wish to make to apply for planning permission, to refrain from carrying out any operations or activities or to undertake remedial works; and

    (b) any representations which he may wish to make about the notice, will be considered by the authority, and the authority shall give him an opportunity to make in person any such offer or representations at that time and place.

(5) A planning contravention notice must inform the person on whom it is served—

(a) of the likely consequences of his failing to respond to the notice and, in particular, that enforcement action may be taken; and

(b) of the effect of section 186(5)(b).

(6) Any requirement of a planning contravention notice shall be complied with by giving information in writing to the local planning authority.

(7) The service of a planning contravention notice does not affect any other power exercisable in respect of any breach of planning control.

(8) In this section references to operations or activities on land include operations or activities in, under or over the land.]

171D   [Penalties for non-compliance with planning contravention notice

(1) If, at any time after the end of the period of twenty-one days beginning with the day on which a planning contravention notice has been served on any person, he has not complied with any requirement of the notice, he shall be guilty of an offence.

(2) An offence under subsection (1) may be charged by reference to any day or longer period of time and a person may be convicted of a second or subsequent offence under that subsection by reference to any period of time following the preceding conviction for such an offence.

(3) It shall be a defence for a person charged with an offence under subsection (1) to prove that he had a reasonable excuse for failing to comply with the requirement.

(4) A person guilty of an offence under subsection (1) shall be liable on summary conviction to a fine not exceeding level 3 on the standard scale.

(5) If any person—

(a) makes any statement purporting to comply with a requirement of a planning contravention notice which he knows to be false or misleading in a material particular; or

(b) recklessly makes such a statement which is false or misleading in a material particular,

he shall be guilty of an offence.

(6) A person guilty of an offence under subsection (5) shall be liable on summary conviction to a fine not exceeding level 5 on the standard scale.]

172   [Issue of enforcement notice

[(1) The local planning authority may issue a notice (in this Act referred to as an 'enforcement notice') where it appears to them—

(a) that there has been a breach of planning control; and

(b) that it is expedient to issue the notice, having regard to the provisions of the development plan and to any other material considerations.

(2) A copy of an enforcement notice shall be served—

(a) on the owner and on the occupier of the land to which it relates; and

(b) on any other person having an interest in the land, being an interest which, in the opinion of the authority, is materially affected by the notice.

(3) The service of the notice shall take place—

(a) not more than twenty-eight days after its date of issue; and

(b) not less than twenty-eight days before the date specified in it as the date on which it is to take effect.]

173   [Contents and effect of notice

(1) An enforcement notice shall state—

(a) the matters which appear to the local planning authority to constitute the breach of planning control; and

(b) the paragraph of section 171A(1) within which, in the opinion of the authority, the breach falls.

(2) A notice complies with subsection (1)(a) if it enables any person on whom a copy of it is served to know what those matters are.

(3) An enforcement notice shall specify the steps which the authority require to be taken, or the activities which the authority require to cease, in order to achieve, wholly or partly, any of the following purposes.

(4) Those purposes are—

    (a) remedying the breach by making any development comply with the terms (including conditions and limitations) of any planning permission which has been granted in respect of the land, by discontinuing any use of the land or by restoring the land to its condition before the breach took place; or

    (b) remedying any injury to amenity which has been caused by the breach.

(5) An enforcement notice may, for example, require—

    (a) the alteration or removal of any buildings or works;

    (b) the carrying out of any building or other operations;

    (c) any activity on the land not to be carried on except to the extent specified in the notice; or

    (d) the contour of a deposit of refuse or waste materials on land to be modified by altering the gradient or gradients of its sides.

(6) Where an enforcement notice is issued in respect of a breach of planning control consisting of demolition of a building, the notice may require the construction of a building (in this section referred to as a 'replacement building') which, subject to subsection (7), is as similar as possible to the demolished building.

(7) A replacement building—

    (a) must comply with any requirement imposed by any enactment applicable to the construction of buildings;

    (b) may differ from the demolished building in any respect which, if the demolished building had been altered in that respect, would not have constituted a breach of planning control;

    (c) must comply with any regulations made for the purposes of this subsection (including regulations modifying paragraphs (a) and (b)).

(8) An enforcement notice shall specify the date on which it is to take effect and, subject to sections 175(4) and 289(4A), shall take effect on that date.

(9) An enforcement notice shall specify the period at the end of which any steps are required to have been taken or any activities are required to have ceased and may specify different periods for different steps or activities; and, where different periods apply to different steps or activities, references in this Part to the period for compliance with an enforcement notice, in relation to any step or activity, are to the period at the end of which the step is required to have been taken or the activity is required to have ceased.

(10) An enforcement notice shall specify such additional matters as may be prescribed, and regulations may require every copy of an enforcement notice served under section 172 to be accompanied by an explanatory note giving prescribed information as to the right of appeal under section 174.

(11) Where—

    (a) an enforcement notice in respect of any breach of planning control could have required any buildings or works to be removed or any activity to cease, but does not do so; and

    (b) all the requirements of the notice have been complied with, then, so far as the notice did not so require, planning permission shall be treated as having been granted by virtue of section 73A in respect of development consisting of the construction of the buildings or works or, as the case may be, the carrying out of the activities.

(12) Where—

(a) an enforcement notice requires the construction of a replacement building;

(b) all the requirements of the notice with respect to that construction have been complied with,

planning permission shall be treated as having been granted by virtue of section 73A in respect of development consisting of that construction.]

173A   **[Variation and withdrawal of enforcement notices**

(1) The local planning authority may—

(a) withdraw an enforcement notice issued by them; or

(b) waive or relax any requirement of such a notice and, in particular, may extend any period specified in accordance with section 173(9).

(2) The powers conferred by subsection (1) may be exercised whether or not the notice has taken effect.

(3) The local planning authority shall, immediately after exercising the powers conferred by subsection (1), give notice of the exercise to every person who has been served with a copy of the enforcement notice or would, if the notice were re-issued, be served with a copy of it.

(4) The withdrawal of an enforcement notice does not affect the power of the local planning authority to issue a further enforcement notice.]

174   **Appeal against enforcement notice**

(1) A person having an interest in the land to which an enforcement notice relates or a relevant occupier may appeal to the Secretary of State against the notice, whether or not a copy of it has been served on him.

[(2) An appeal may be brought on any of the following grounds—

(a) that, in respect of any breach of planning control which may be constituted by the matters stated in the notice, planning permission ought to be granted or, as the case may be, the condition or limitation concerned ought to be discharged;

(b) that those matters have not occurred;

(c) that those matters (if they occurred) do not constitute a breach of planning control;

(d) that, at the date when the notice was issued, no enforcement action could be taken in respect of any breach of planning control which may be constituted by those matters;

(e) that copies of the enforcement notice were not served as required by section 172;

(f) that the steps required by the notice to be taken, or the activities required by the notice to cease, exceed what is necessary to remedy any breach of planning control which may be constituted by those matters or, as the case may be, to remedy any injury to amenity which has been caused by any such breach;

(g) that any period specified in the notice in accordance with section 173(9) falls short of what should reasonably be allowed.

(3) An appeal under this section shall be made either—

(a) by giving written notice of the appeal to the Secretary of State before the date specified in the enforcement notice as the date on which it is to take effect; or

(b) by sending such notice to him in a properly addressed and pre-paid letter posted to him at such time that, in the ordinary course of post, it would be delivered to him before that date.]

(4) A person who gives notice under subsection (3) shall submit to the Secretary of State, either when giving the notice or within the prescribed time, a statement in writing—

(a) specifying the grounds on which he is appealing against the enforcement notice; and

(b) giving such further information as may be prescribed.

(5) If, where more than one ground is specified in that statement, the appellant does not give information required under subsection (4)(b) in relation to each of those grounds within the prescribed time, the Secretary of State may determine the appeal without considering any ground as to which the appellant has failed to give such information within that time.

(6) In this section 'relevant occupier' means a person who—

(a) on the date on which the enforcement notice is issued occupies the land to which the notice relates by virtue of a licence; and

(b) continues so to occupy the land when the appeal is brought.

176   [General provisions relating to determination of appeals

(1) On an appeal under section 174 the Secretary of State may—

(a) correct any defect, error or misdescription in the enforcement notice; or

(b) vary the terms of the enforcement notice, if he is satisfied that the correction or variation will not cause injustice to the appellant or the local planning authority.]

[(2) Where the Secretary of State determines to allow the appeal, he may quash the notice.]

[(2A) The Secretary of State shall give any directions necessary to give effect to his determination on the appeal.]

(3) The Secretary of State—

(a) may dismiss an appeal if the appellant fails to comply with section 174(4) within the prescribed time; and

(b) may allow an appeal and quash the enforcement notice if the local planning authority fail to comply with any requirement of regulations made by virtue of paragraph (a), (b), or (d) of section 175(1) within the prescribed period.

(4) If the Secretary of State proposes to dismiss an appeal under paragraph (a) of subsection (3) or to allow an appeal and quash the enforcement notice under paragraph (b) of that subsection, he need not comply with section 175(3).

(5) Where it would otherwise be a ground for determining an appeal under section 174 in favour of the appellant that a person required to be served with a copy of the enforcement notice was not served, the Secretary of State may disregard that fact if neither the appellant nor that person has been substantially prejudiced by the failure to serve him.

179   [Offence where enforcement notice not complied with

(1) Where, at any time after the end of the period for compliance with an enforcement notice, any step required by the notice to be taken has not been taken or any activity required by the notice to cease is being carried on, the person who is then the owner of the land is in breach of the notice.

(2) Where the owner of the land is in breach of an enforcement notice he shall be guilty of an offence.

(3) In proceedings against any person for an offence under subsection (2), it shall be a defence for him to show that he did everything he could be expected to do to secure compliance with the notice.

(4) A person who has control of or an interest in the land to which an enforcement notice relates (other than the owner) must not carry on any activity which is required by the notice to cease or cause or permit such an activity to be carried on.

(5) A person who, at any time after the end of the period for compliance with the notice, contravenes subsection (4) shall be guilty of an offence.

(6) An offence under subsection (2) or (5) may be charged by reference to any day or longer period of time and a person may be convicted of a second or subsequent offence under the subsection in question by reference to any period of time following the preceding conviction for such an offence.

(7) Where—

(a) a person charged with an offence under this section has not been served with a copy of the enforcement notice; and

(b) the notice is not contained in the appropriate register kept under section

it shall be a defence for him to show that he was not aware of the existence of the notice.

(8) A person guilty of an offence under this section shall be liable—

(a) on summary conviction, to a fine not exceeding £20,000; and

(b) on conviction on indictment, to a fine.

(9) In determining the amount of any fine to be imposed on a person convicted of an offence under this section, the court shall in particular have regard to any financial benefit which has accrued or appears likely to accrue to him in consequence of the offence.]

183   Stop notices

[(1) Where the local planning authority consider it expedient that any relevant activity should cease before the expiry of the period for compliance with an enforcement notice, they may, when they serve the copy of the enforcement notice or afterwards, serve a notice (in this Act referred to as a 'stop notice') prohibiting the carrying out of that activity on the land to which the enforcement notice relates, or any part of that land specified in the stop notice.]

[(2) In this section and sections 184 and 186 'relevant activity' means any activity specified in the enforcement notice as an activity which the local planning authority require to cease and any activity carried out as part of that activity or associated with that activity.]

[(3) A stop notice may not be served where the enforcement notice has taken effect.]

[(4) A stop notice shall not prohibit the use of any building as a dwellinghouse.]

[(5) A stop notice shall not prohibit the carrying out of any activity if the activity has been carried out (whether continuously or not) for a period of more than four years ending with the service of the notice; and for the purposes of this subsection no account is to be taken of any period during which the activity was authorised by planning permission.]

[(5A) Subsection (5) does not prevent a stop notice prohibiting any activity consisting of, or incidental to, building, engineering, mining or other operations or the deposit of refuse or waste materials.]

(6) A stop notice may be served by the local planning authority on any person who appears to them to have an interest in the land or to be engaged in any activity prohibited by the notice.

(7) The local planning authority may at any time withdraw a stop notice (without prejudice to their power to serve another) by serving notice to that effect on persons served with the stop notice.

184   Stop notices: supplementary provisions

(1) A stop notice must refer to the enforcement notice to which it relates and have a copy of that notice annexed to it.

(2) A stop notice must specify the date on which it will take effect (and it cannot be contravened until that date).

[(3) That date—

(a) must not be earlier than three days after the date when the notice is served, unless the local planning authority consider that there are special reasons for specifying an earlier date and a statement of those reasons is served with the stop notice; and

(b) must not be later than twenty-eight days from the date when the notice is first served on any person.]

(4) A stop notice shall cease to have effect when—

(a) the enforcement notice to which it relates is withdrawn or quashed; or

(b) the [period for compliance with the enforcement notice] expires; or

(c) notice of the withdrawal of the stop notice is first served under section 183(7).

(5) A stop notice shall also cease to have effect if or to the extent that the activities prohibited by it cease, on a variation of the enforcement notice, to be included [relevant activities].

(6) Where a stop notice has been served in respect of any land, the local planning authority may display there a notice (in this section and section 187 referred to as a 'site notice')—

(a) stating that a stop notice has been served and that any person contravening it may be prosecuted for an offence under section 187,

(b) giving the date when the stop notice takes effect, and

(c) indicating its requirements.

(7) If under section 183(7) the local planning authority withdraw a stop notice in respect of which a site notice was displayed, they must display a notice of the withdrawal in place of the site notice.

(8) A stop notice shall not be invalid by reason that a copy of the enforcement notice to which it relates was not served as required by section [172] if it is shown that the local planning authority took all such steps as were reasonably practicable to effect proper service.

186 Compensation for loss due to stop notice

(1) Where a stop notice is served under section 183 compensation may be payable under this section in respect of a prohibition contained in the notice only if—

(a) the enforcement notice is quashed on grounds other than those mentioned in paragraph (a) of section 174(2);

(b) the enforcement notice is varied (otherwise than on the grounds mentioned in that paragraph) so that [any activity the carrying out of which is prohibited by the stop notice ceases to be a relevant activity];

(c) the enforcement notice is withdrawn by the local planning authority otherwise than in consequence of the grant by them of planning permission for the development to which the notice relates; or

(d) the stop notice is withdrawn.

(2) A person who, when the stop notice is first served, has an interest in or occupies the land to which the notice relates shall be entitled to be compensated by the local planning authority in respect of any loss or damage directly attributable to the prohibition contained in the notice or, in a case within subsection (1)(b), [the prohibition of such of the activities prohibited by the stop notice as cease to be relevant activities].

(3) A claim for compensation under this section shall be made to the local planning authority within the prescribed time and in the prescribed manner.

(4) The loss or damage in respect of which compensation is payable under this section in respect of a prohibition shall include any sum payable in respect of a breach of contract caused by the taking of action necessary to comply with the prohibition.

[(5) No compensation is payable under this section—

(a) in respect of the prohibition in a stop notice of any activity which, at any time when the notice is in force, constitutes or contributes to a breach of planning control; or

(b) in the case of a claimant who was required to provide information under section 171C or 330 or section 16 of the Local Government (Miscellaneous Provisions) Act 1976, in respect of any loss or damage suffered by him which could have been avoided if he had provided the information or had otherwise co-operated with the local planning authority when responding to the notice.]

(6) Except in so far as may be otherwise provided by any regulations made under this Act, any question of disputed compensation under this Part shall be referred to and determined by the Lands Tribunal.

(7) In relation to the determination of any such question, the provisions of sections 2 and 4 of the Land Compensation Act 1961 shall apply subject to any necessary modifications and to the provisions of any regulations made under this Act.

187   Penalties for contravention of stop notice

[(1) If any person contravenes a stop notice after a site notice has been displayed or the stop notice has been served on him he shall be guilty of an offence.]

[(1A) An offence under this section may be charged by reference to any day or longer period of time and a person may be convicted of a second or subsequent offence under this section by reference to any period of time following the preceding conviction for such an offence.]

[(1B) References in this section to contravening a stop notice include causing or permitting its contravention.]

[(2) A person guilty of an offence under this section shall be liable—

(a) on summary conviction, to a fine not exceeding £20,000; and

(b) on conviction on indictment, to a fine.]

[(2A) In determining the amount of any fine to be imposed on a person convicted of an offence under this section, the court shall in particular have regard to any financial benefit which has accrued or appears likely to accrue to him in consequence of the offence.]

(3) In proceedings for an offence under this section it shall be a defence for the accused to prove—

(a) that the stop notice was not served on him, and

(b) that he did not know, and could not reasonably have been expected to know, of its existence.

187A   [Enforcement of conditions

(1) This section applies where planning permission for carrying out any development of land has been granted subject to conditions.

(2) The local planning authority may, if any of the conditions is not complied with, serve a notice (in this Act referred to as a 'breach of condition notice') on—

(a) any person who is carrying out or has carried out the development; or

(b) any person having control of the land,

requiring him to secure compliance with such of the conditions as are specified in the notice.

(3) References in this section to the person responsible are to the person on whom the breach of condition notice has been served.

(4) The conditions which may be specified in a notice served by virtue of subsection (2)(b) are any of the conditions regulating the use of the land.

(5) A breach of condition notice shall specify the steps which the authority consider ought to be taken, or the activities which the authority consider ought to cease, to secure compliance with the conditions specified in the notice.

(6) The authority may by notice served on the person responsible withdraw the breach of condition notice, but its withdrawal shall not affect the power to serve on him a further breach of condition notice in respect of the conditions specified in the earlier notice or any other conditions.

(7) The period allowed for compliance with the notice is—

(a) such period of not less than twenty-eight days beginning with the date of service of the notice as may be specified in the notice; or

(b) that period as extended by a further notice served by the local planning authority on the person responsible.

(8) If, at any time after the end of the period allowed for compliance with the notice—

(a) any of the conditions specified in the notice is not complied with; and

(b) the steps specified in the notice have not been taken or, as the case may be, the activities specified in the notice have not ceased,

the person responsible is in breach of the notice.

(9) If the person responsible is in breach of the notice he shall be guilty of an offence.

(10) An offence under subsection (9) may be charged by reference to any day or longer period of time and a person may be convicted of a second or subsequent offence under that subsection by reference to any period of time following the preceding conviction for such an offence.

(11) It shall be a defence for a person charged with an offence under subsection (9) to prove—

(a) that he took all reasonable measures to secure compliance with the conditions specified in the notice; or

(b) where the notice was served on him by virtue of subsection (2)(b), that he no longer had control of the land.

(12) A person who is guilty of an offence under subsection (9) shall be liable on summary conviction to a fine not exceeding level 3 on the standard scale.

(13) In this section—

(a) 'conditions' includes limitations; and

(b) references to carrying out any development include causing or permitting another to do so.]

187B   [Injunctions restraining breaches of planning control

(1) Where a local planning authority consider it necessary or expedient for any actual or apprehended breach of planning control to be restrained by injunction, they may apply to the court for an injunction, whether or not they have exercised or are proposing to exercise any of their other powers under this Part.

(2) On an application under subsection (1) the court may grant such an injunction as the court thinks appropriate for the purpose of restraining the breach.

(3) Rules of court may provide for such an injunction to be issued against a person whose identity is unknown.

(4) In this section 'the court' means the High Court or the county court.]

191   [Certificate of lawfulness of existing use or development

(1) If any person wishes to ascertain whether—

(a) any existing use of buildings or other land is lawful;

(b) any operations which have been carried out in, on, over or under land are lawful; or

(c) any other matter constituting a failure to comply with any condition or limitation subject to which planning permission has been granted is lawful,

he may make an application for the purpose to the local planning authority specifying the land and describing the use, operations or other matter.

(2) For the purposes of this Act uses and operations are lawful at any time if—

(a) no enforcement action may then be taken in respect of them (whether because they did not involve development or require planning permission or because the time for enforcement action has expired or for any other reason); and

(b) they do not constitute a contravention of any of the requirements of any enforcement notice then in force.

(3) For the purposes of this Act any matter constituting a failure to comply with any condition or limitation subject to which planning permission has been granted is lawful at any time if—

(a) the time for taking enforcement action in respect of the failure has then expired; and

(b) it does not constitute a contravention of any of the requirements of any enforcement notice or breach of condition notice then in force.

(4) If, on an application under this section, the local planning authority are provided with information satisfying them of the lawfulness at the time of the application of the use, operations or other matter described in the application, or that description as modified by the

local planning authority or a description substituted by them, they shall issue a certificate to that effect; and in any other case they shall refuse the application.

(5) A certificate under this section shall—

(a) specify the land to which it relates;

(b) describe the use, operations or other matter in question (in the case of any use falling within one of the classes specified in an order under section 55(2)(f), identifying it by reference to that class);

(c) give the reasons for determining the use, operations or other matter to be lawful; and

(d) specify the date of the application for the certificate.

(6) The lawfulness of any use, operations or other matter for which a certificate is in force under this section shall be conclusively presumed.

(7) A certificate under this section in respect of any use shall also have effect, for the purposes of the following enactments, as if it were a grant of planning permission—

(a) section 3(3) of the Caravan Sites and Control of Development Act 1960;

(b) section 5(2) of the Control of Pollution Act 1974; and

(c) section 36(2)(a) of the Environmental Protection Act 1990.]

192   [Certificate of lawfulness of proposed use or development

(1) If any person wishes to ascertain whether—

(a) any proposed use of buildings or other land; or

(b) any operations proposed to be carried out in, on, over or under land, would be lawful, he may make an application for the purpose to the local planning authority specifying the land and describing the use or operations in question.

(2) If, on an application under this section, the local planning authority are provided with information satisfying them that the use or operations described in the application would be lawful if instituted or begun at the time of the application, they shall issue a certificate to that effect; and in any other case they shall refuse the application.

(3) A certificate under this section shall—

(a) specify the land to which it relates;

(b) describe the use or operations in question (in the case of any use falling within one of the classes specified in an order under section 55(2)(f), identifying it by reference to that class);

(c) give the reasons for determining the use or operations to be lawful; and

(d) specify the date of the application for the certificate.

(4) The lawfulness of any use or operations for which a certificate is in force under this section shall be conclusively presumed unless there is a material change, before the use is instituted or the operations are begun, in any of the matters relevant to determining such lawfulness.]

193   [Certificates under sections 191 and 192: supplementary provisions

(1) An application for a certificate under section 191 or 192 shall be made in such manner as may be prescribed by a development order and shall include such particulars, and be verified by such evidence, as may be required by such an order or by any directions given under such an order or by the local planning authority.

(2) Provision may be made by a development order for regulating the manner in which applications for certificates under those sections are to be dealt with by local planning authorities.

(3) In particular, such an order may provide for requiring the authority—

(a) to give to any applicant within such time as may be prescribed by the order such notice as may be so prescribed as to the manner in which his application has been dealt with; and

(b) to give to the Secretary of State and to such other persons as may be prescribed by or under the order, such information as may be so prescribed with respect to such applications made to the authority, including information as to the manner in which any application has been dealt with.

(4) A certificate under either of those sections may be issued—

(a) for the whole or part of the land specified in the application; and

(b) where the application specifies two or more uses, operations or other matters, for all of them or some one or more of them;

and shall be in such form as may be prescribed by a development order.

(5) A certificate under section 191 or 192 shall not affect any matter constituting a failure to comply with any condition or limitation subject to which planning permission has been granted unless that matter is described in the certificate.

(6) In section 69 references to applications for planning permission shall include references to applications for certificates under section 191 or 192.

(7) A local planning authority may revoke a certificate under either of those sections if, on the application for the certificate—

(a) a statement was made or document used which was false in a material particular; or

(b) any material information was withheld.

(8) Provision may be made by a development order for regulating the manner in which certificates may be revoked and the notice to be given of such revocation.]

194   [Offences

(1) If any person, for the purpose of procuring a particular decision on an application (whether by himself or another) for the issue of a certificate under section 191 or 192—

(a) knowingly or recklessly makes a statement which is false or misleading in a material particular;

(b) with intent to deceive, uses any document which is false or misleading in a material particular; or

(c) with intent to deceive, withholds any material information, he shall be guilty of an offence.

(2) A person guilty of an offence under subsection (1) shall be liable—

(a) on summary conviction, to a fine not exceeding the statutory maximum; or

(b) on conviction on indictment, to imprisonment for a term not exceeding two years, or a fine, or both.

(3) Notwithstanding section 127 of the Magistrates' Courts Act 1980, a magistrates' court may try an information in respect of an offence under subsection (1) whenever laid.]

PART VIII   TREES

197   Planning permission to include appropriate provision for preservation and planting of trees

It shall be the duty of the local planning authority—

(a) to ensure, whenever it is appropriate, that in granting planning permission for any development adequate provision is made, by the imposition of conditions, for the preservation or planting of trees; and

(b) to make such orders under section 198 as appear to the authority to be necessary in connection with the grant of such permission, whether for giving effect to such conditions or otherwise.

198   Power to make tree preservation orders

(1) If it appears to a local planning authority that it is expedient in the interests of amenity to make provision for the preservation of trees or woodlands in their area, they may

for that purpose make an order with respect to such trees, groups of trees or woodlands as may be specified in the order.

(2) An order under subsection (1) is in this Act referred to as a 'tree preservation order'.

(3) A tree preservation order may, in particular, make provision—

   (a) for prohibiting (subject to any exemptions for which provision may be made by the order) the cutting down, topping, lopping, uprooting, wilful damage or wilful destruction of trees except with the consent of the local planning authority, and for enabling that authority to give their consent subject to conditions;

   (b) for securing the replanting, in such manner as may be prescribed by or under the order, of any part of a woodland area which is felled in the course of forestry operations permitted by or under the order;

   (c) for applying, in relation to any consent under the order, and to applications for such consent, any of the provisions of this Act mentioned in subsection (4), subject to such adaptations and modifications as may be specified in the order.

(4) The provisions referred to in subsection (3)(c) are—

   (a) the provisions of Part III relating to planning permission and to applications for planning permission, except sections 56, 62, 65, 69(3) and (4), 71, 91 to 96, 100 and 101 and Schedule 8; and

   (b) sections 137 to 141, 143 and 144 (except so far as they relate to purchase notices served in consequence of such orders as are mentioned in section 137(1)(b) or (c));

   (c) section 316.

(5) A tree preservation order may be made so as to apply, in relation to trees to be planted pursuant to any such conditions as are mentioned in section 197(a), as from the time when those trees are planted.

(6) Without prejudice to any other exemptions for which provision may be made by a tree preservation order, no such order shall apply—

   (a) to the cutting down, uprooting, topping or lopping of trees which are dying or dead or have become dangerous, or

   (b) to the cutting down, uprooting, topping or lopping of any trees in compliance with any obligations imposed by or under an Act of Parliament or so far as may be necessary for the prevention or abatement of a nuisance.

(7) This section shall have effect subject to—

   (a) section 39(2) of the Housing and Planning Act 1986 (saving for effect of section 2(4) of the Opencast Coal Act 1958 on land affected by a tree preservation order despite its repeal); and

   (b) section 15 of the Forestry Act 1967 (licences under that Act to fell trees comprised in a tree preservation order).

Land adversely affecting amenity of neighbourhood

215 Power to require proper maintenance of land

(1) If it appears to the local planning authority that the amenity of a part of their area, or of an adjoining area, is adversely affected by the condition of land in their area, they may serve on the owner and occupier of the land a notice under this section.

(2) The notice shall require such steps for remedying the condition of the land as may be specified in the notice to be taken within such period as may be so specified.

(3) Subject to the following provisions of this Chapter, the notice shall take effect at the end of such period as may be specified in the notice.

(4) That period shall not be less than 28 days after the service of the notice.

Advertisements

220 Regulations controlling display of advertisements

(1) Regulations under this Act shall make provision for restricting or regulating the display of advertisements so far as appears to the Secretary of State to be expedient in the interests of amenity or public safety.

(2) Without prejudice to the generality of subsection (1), any such regulations may provide—

(a) for regulating the dimensions, appearance and position of advertisements which may be displayed, the sites on which advertisements may be displayed and the manner in which they are to be affixed to the land;

(b) for requiring the consent of the local planning authority to be obtained for the display of advertisements, or of advertisements of any class specified in the regulations;

(c) for applying, in relation to any such consent and to applications for such consent, any of the provisions mentioned in subsection (3), subject to such adaptations and modifications as may be specified in the regulations;

(d) for the constitution, for the purposes of the regulations, of such advisory committees as may be prescribed by the regulations, and for determining the manner in which the expenses of any such committee are to be defrayed.

(3) The provisions referred to in subsection (2)(c) are—

(a) the provisions of Part III relating to planning permission and to applications for planning permission, except sections 56, 62, 65, 69(3) and (4), 71, 91 to 96, 100 and 101 and Schedule 8;

(b) sections 137 to 141, 143 and 144 (except so far as they relate to purchase notices served in consequence of such orders as are mentioned in section 137(1)(b) or (c));

(c) section 316.

. . .

PART XII

288 Proceedings for questioning the validity of other orders, decisions and directions

(1) If any person—

(a) is aggrieved by any order to which this section applies and wishes to question the validity of that order on the grounds—

(i) that the order is not within the powers of this Act, or

(ii) that any of the relevant requirements have not been complied with in relation to that order; or

(b) is aggrieved by any action on the part of the Secretary of State to which this section applies and wishes to question the validity of that action on the grounds—

(i) that the action is not within the powers of this Act, or

(ii) that any of the relevant requirements have not been complied with in relation to that action,

he may make an application to the High Court under this section.

(2) Without prejudice to subsection (1), if the authority directly concerned with any order to which this section applies, or with any action on the part of the Secretary of State to which this section applies, wish to question the validity of that order or action on any of the grounds mentioned in subsection (1), the authority may make an application to the High Court under this section.

(3) An application under this section must be made within six weeks from the date on which the order is confirmed (or, in the case of an order under section 97 which takes effect

under section 99 without confirmation, the date on which it takes effect) or, as the case may be, the date on which the action is taken.

(4) This section applies to any such order as is mentioned in subsection (2) of section 284 and to any such action on the part of the Secretary of State as is mentioned in subsection (3) of that section.

(5) On any application under this section the High Court—

    (a) may, subject to subsection (6), by interim order suspend the operation of the order or action, the validity of which is questioned by the application, until the final determination of the proceedings;

    (b) if satisfied that the order or action in question is not within the powers of this Act, or that the interests of the applicant have been substantially prejudiced by a failure to comply with any of the relevant requirements in relation to it, may quash that order or action.

(6) Paragraph (a) of subsection (5) shall not apply to applications questioning the validity of tree preservation orders.

(7) In relation to a tree preservation order, or to an order made in pursuance of section 221(5), the powers conferred on the High Court by subsection (5) shall be exercisable by way of quashing or (where applicable) suspending the operation of the order either in whole or in part, as the court may determine.

(8) References in this section to the confirmation of an order include the confirmation of an order subject to modifications as well as the confirmation of an order in the form in which it was made.

(9) In this section 'the relevant requirements', in relation to any order or action to which this section applies, means any requirements of this Act or of the Tribunals and Inquiries Act [1992], or of any order, regulations or rules made under this Act or under that Act which are applicable to that order or action.

(10) Any reference in this section to the authority directly concerned with any order or action to which this section applies—

    (a) in relation to any such decision as is mentioned in section 284(3)(f), is a reference to the council on whom the notice in question was served and, in a case where the Secretary of State has modified such a notice, wholly or in part, by substituting another local authority or statutory undertakers for that council, includes a reference to that local authority or those statutory undertakers;

    (b) in any other case, is a reference to the authority who made the order in question or made the decision or served the notice to which the proceedings in question relate, or who referred the matter to the Secretary of State, or, where the order or notice in question was made or served by him, the authority named in the order or notice.

PART XV

336 Interpretation

(1) In this Act, except in so far as the context otherwise requires and subject to the following provisions of this section and to any transitional provision made by the Planning (Consequential Provisions) Act 1990—

. . .

'advertisement' means any word, letter, model, sign, placard, board, notice, [awning, blind], device or representation, whether illuminated or not, in the nature of, and employed wholly or partly for the purposes of, advertisement, announcement or direction, and (without prejudice to the previous provisions of this definition), includes any hoarding or similar structure used, [or designed] or adapted for use [and anything else principally used, or designed or adapted principally for use], for the display of advertisements, and references to the display of advertisements shall be construed accordingly;

. . .

'agriculture' includes horticulture, fruit growing, seed growing, dairy farming, the breeding and keeping of livestock (including any creature kept for the production of food, wool, skins or fur, or for the purpose of its use in the farming of land), the use of land as grazing land, meadow land, osier land, market gardens and nursery grounds, and the use of land for woodlands where that use is ancillary to the farming of land for other agricultural purposes, and 'agricultural' shall be construed accordingly;

. . .

'building' includes any structure or erection, and any part of a building, as so defined, but does not include plant or machinery comprised in a building;

. . .

['building operations' has the meaning given by section 55]

. . .

'engineering operations' includes the formation or laying out of means of access to highways;

. . .

'means of access' includes any means of access, whether private or public, for vehicles or for foot passengers, and includes a street;

. . .

'minerals' includes all minerals and substances in or under land of a kind ordinarily worked for removal by underground or surface working, except that it does not include peat cut for purposes other than sale;

. . .

'open space' means any land laid out as a public garden, or used for the purposes of public recreation, or land which is a disused burial ground;

. . .

'owner', in relation to any land, means a person, other than a mortgagee not in possession, who, whether in his own right or as trustee for any other person, is entitled to receive the rack rent of the land or, where the land is not let at a rack rent, would be so entitled if it were so let;

. . .

'the planning Acts' means this Act, the Planning (Listed Buildings and Conservation Areas) Act 1990, the Planning (Hazardous Substances) Act 1990 and the Planning (Consequential Provisions) Act 1990;

. . .

'use', in relation to land, does not include the use of land for the carrying out of any building or other operations on it;

. . .

Planning (Listed Buildings and Conservation Areas) Act 1990

(1990, c. 9)

PART I   LISTED BUILDINGS

1   Listing of buildings of special architectural or historic interest

(1) For the purposes of this Act and with a view to the guidance of local planning authorities in the performance of their functions under this Act and the principal Act in relation to

buildings of special architectural or historic interest, the Secretary of State shall compile lists of such buildings, or approve, with or without modifications, such lists compiled by the Historic Buildings and Monuments Commission for England (in this Act referred to as 'the Commission') or by other persons or bodies of persons, and may amend any list so compiled or approved.

(2) The Secretary of State shall not approve any list compiled by the Commission if the list contains any building situated outside England.

(3) In considering whether to include a building in a list compiled or approved under this section, the Secretary of State may take into account not only the building itself but also—

(a) any respect in which its exterior contributes to the architectural or historic interest of any group of buildings of which it forms part; and

(b) the desirability of preserving, on the ground of its architectural or historic interest, any feature of the building consisting of a man-made object or structure fixed to the building or forming part of the land and comprised within the curtilage of the building.

(4) Before compiling, approving (with or without modifications) or amending any list under this section the Secretary of State shall consult—

(a) in relation to buildings which are situated in England, with the Commission; and

(b) with such other persons or bodies of persons as appear to him appropriate as having special knowledge of, or interest in, buildings of architectural or historic interest.

(5) In this Act 'listed building' means a building which is for the time being included in a list compiled or approved by the Secretary of State under this section; and for the purposes of this Act—

(a) any object or structure fixed to the building;

(b) any object or structure within the curtilage of the building which, although not fixed to the building, forms part of the land and has done so since before 1st July 1948,

shall be treated as part of the building.

(6) Schedule I shall have effect for the purpose of making provision as to the treatment as listed buildings of certain buildings formerly subject to building preservation orders.

3 Temporary listing: building preservation notices

(1) If it appears to a local planning authority [in Wales, or to a local planning authority in England who are not] a county planning authority, that a building in their area which is not a listed building—

(a) is of special architectural or historic interest; and

(b) is in danger of demolition or of alteration in such a way as to affect its character as a building of such interest,

they may serve on the owner and occupier of the building a notice (in this Act referred to as a 'building preservation notice').

(2) A building preservation notice served by a local planning authority shall—

(a) state that the building appears to them to be of special architectural or historic interest and that they have requested the Secretary of State to consider including it in a list compiled or approved under section 1; and

(b) explain the effect of subsections (3) to (5) and Schedule 2.

(3) A building preservation notice—

(a) shall come into force as soon as it has been served on both the owner and occupier of the building to which it relates; and

(b) subject to subsection (4), shall remain in force for six months from the date when it is served or, as the case may be, last served.

(4) A building preservation notice shall cease to be in force if the Secretary of State—

(a) includes the building in a list compiled or approved under section 1, or

(b) notifies the local planning authority in writing that he does not intend to do so

(5) While a building preservation notice is in force with respect to a building, the provisions of this Act (other than section 59) and the principal Act shall have effect in relation to the building as if it were a listed building.

(6) If, following the service of a building preservation notice, the Secretary of State notifies the local planning authority that he does not propose to include the building in a list compiled or approved under section 1, the authority shall immediately give notice of that decision to the owner and occupier of the building.

(7) Following such a notification by the Secretary of State no further building preservation notice in respect of the building shall be served by the local planning authority within the period of 12 months beginning with the date of the notification.

(8) The Commission shall, as respects any London borough, have concurrently with the council of that borough the functions of a local planning authority under this section; and references to the local planning authority shall be construed accordingly.

4 Temporary listing in urgent cases

(1) If it appears to the local planning authority to be urgent that a building preservation notice should come into force, they may, instead of serving the notice on the owner and occupier of the building, affix the notice conspicuously to some object on the building.

(2) The affixing of a notice under subsection (1) shall be treated for all the purposes of section 3, this section, sections 5 and 10 to 26 and Schedule 2 as service of the notice.

(3) A notice which is so affixed must explain that by virtue of being so affixed it is treated as being served for those purposes.

(4) The Commission shall, as respects any London borough, have concurrently with the council of that borough the functions of a local planning authority under this section; and references to the local planning authority shall be construed accordingly.

6 Issue of certificate that building not intended to be listed

(1) Where—

(a) application has been made for planning permission for any development involving the alteration, extension or demolition of a building; or

(b) any such planning permission has been granted; the Secretary of State may, on the application of any person, issue a certificate stating that he does not intend to list the building.

(2) The issue of such a certificate in respect of a building shall—

(a) preclude the Secretary of State for a period of 5 years from the date of issue from exercising in relation to that building any of the powers conferred on him by section 1; and

(b) preclude the local planning authority for that period from serving a building preservation notice in relation to it.

(3) Notice of an application under subsection (1) shall be given to the local planning authority within whose area the building is situated at the same time as the application is submitted to the Secretary of State.

(4) In this section 'local planning authority', in relation to a building in Greater London, includes the Commission.

7 Restriction on works affecting listed buildings

Subject to the following provisions of this Act, no person shall execute or cause to be executed any works for the demolition of a listed building or for its alteration or extension in any manner which would affect its character as a building of special architectural or historic interest, unless the works are authorised.

9 Offences

(1) If a person contravenes section 7 he shall be guilty of an offence.

(2) Without prejudice to subsection (1), if a person executing or causing to be executed any works in relation to a listed building under a listed building consent fails to comply with any condition attached to the consent, he shall be guilty of an offence.

(3) In proceedings for an offence under this section it shall be a defence to prove the following matters—

(a) that works to the building were urgently necessary in the interests of safety or health or for the preservation of the building;

(b) that it was not practicable to secure safety or health or, as the case may be, the preservation of the building by works of repair or works for affording temporary support or shelter;

(c) that the works carried out were limited to the minimum measures immediately necessary; and

(d) that notice in writing justifying in detail the carrying out of the works was given to the local planning authority as soon as reasonably practicable.

[(4) A person who is guilty of an offence under this section shall be liable—

(a) on summary conviction, to imprisonment for a term not exceeding six months or a fine not exceeding £20,000, or both; or

(b) on conviction on indictment, to imprisonment for a term not exceeding two years or a fine, or both.]

(5) In determining the amount of any fine to be imposed on a person convicted of an offence under this section, the court shall in particular have regard to any financial benefit which has accrued or appears likely to accrue to him in consequence of the offence.

29 Compensation for loss or damage caused by service of building preservation notice

(1) This section applies where a building preservation notice ceases to have effect without the building having been included in a list compiled or approved by the Secretary of State under section 1.

(2) Any person who at the time when the notice was served had an interest in the building shall, on making a claim to the authority within the prescribed time and in the prescribed manner, be entitled to be paid compensation by the local planning authority in respect of any loss or damage directly attributable to the effect of the notice.

(3) The loss or damage in respect of which compensation is payable under subsection (2) shall include a sum payable in respect of any breach of contract caused by the necessity of discontinuing or countermanding any works to the building on account of the building preservation notice being in force with respect to it.

38 Power to issue listed building enforcement notice

(1) Where it appears to the local planning authority—

(a) that any works have been or are being executed to a listed building in their area; and

(b) that the works are such as to involve a contravention of section 9(1) or (2), they may, if they consider it expedient to do so having regard to the effect of the works on the character of the building as one of special architectural or historic interest, issue a notice under this section (in this Act referred to as a 'listed building enforcement notice').

(2) A listed building enforcement notice shall specify the alleged contravention and require such steps as may be specified in the notice to be taken—

(a) for restoring the building to its former state; or

(b) if the authority consider that such restoration would not be reasonably practicable or would be undesirable, for executing such further works specified in the notice as they consider necessary to alleviate the effect of the works which were carried out without listed building consent; or

(c) for bringing the building to the state in which it would have been if the terms and conditions of any listed building consent which has been granted for the works had been complied with.

[(3) A listed building enforcement notice—

(a) shall specify the date on which it is to take effect and, subject to sections 39(3) and 65(3A), shall take effect on that date, and

(b) shall specify the period within which any steps are required to be taken and may specify different periods for different steps,

and, where different periods apply to different steps, references in this Part to the period for compliance with a listed building enforcement notice, in relation to any step, are to the period within which the step is required to be taken.]

(4) A copy of a listed building enforcement notice shall be served, not later than 28 days after the date of its issue and not later than 28 days before the [date specified in it as the date on which it is to take effect]—

(a) on the owner and on the occupier of the building to which it relates; and

(b) on any other person having an interest in that building which in the opinion of the authority is materially affected by the notice.

[(5) The local planning authority may—

(a) withdraw a listed building enforcement notice (without prejudice to their power to issue another); or

(b) waive or relax any requirement of such a notice and, in particular, may extend the period specified in accordance with section 38(3),

and the powers conferred by this subsection may be exercised whether or not the notice has taken effect.

(6) The local planning authority shall, immediately after exercising the powers conferred by subsection (5), give notice of the exercise to every person who has been served with a copy of the listed building enforcement notice or would, if the notice were re-issued, be served with a copy of it.]

(7) Where a listed building enforcement notice imposes any such requirement as is mentioned in subsection (2)(b), listed building consent shall be deemed to be granted for any works of demolition, alteration or extension of the building executed as a result of compliance with the notice.

39 Appeal against listed building enforcement notice

(1) A person having an interest in the building to which a listed building enforcement notice relates or a relevant occupier may appeal to the Secretary of State against the notice on any of the following grounds—

(a) that the building is not of special architectural or historic interest;

[(b) that the matters alleged to constitute a contravention of section 9(1) or (2) have not occurred;

(c) that those matters (if they occurred) do not constitute such a contravention];

(d) that works to the building were urgently necessary in the interests of safety or health or for the preservation of the building, that it was not practicable to secure safety or health or, as the case may be, the preservation of the building by works of repair or works for affording temporary support or shelter, and that the works carried out were limited to the minimum measures immediately necessary;

(e) that listed building consent ought to be granted for the works, or that any relevant condition of such consent which has been granted ought to be discharged, or different conditions substituted;

(f) that copies of the notice were not served as required by section 38(4);

(g) except in relation to such a requirement as is mentioned in section 38(2)(b) or (c), that the requirements of the notice exceed what is necessary for restoring the building to its condition before the works were carried out;

(h) that the period specified in the notice as the period within which any step required by the notice is to be taken falls short of what should reasonably be allowed;

(i) that the steps required by the notice for the purpose of restoring the character of the building to its former state would not serve that purpose;

(j) that steps required to be taken by virtue of section 38(2)(b) exceed what is necessary to alleviate the effect of the works executed to the building;

(k) that steps required to be taken by virtue of section 38(2)(c) exceed what is necessary to bring the building to the state in which it would have been if the terms and conditions of the listed building consent had been complied with.

[(2) An appeal under this section shall be made either—

(a) by giving written notice of the appeal to the Secretary of State before the date specified in the listed building enforcement notice as the date on which it is to take effect; or

(b) by sending such notice to him in a properly addressed and prepaid letter posted to him at such time that, in the ordinary course of post, it would be delivered to him before that date.]

(3) Where such an appeal is brought the listed building enforcement notice shall [subject to any order under section 65(3A)] be of no effect pending the final determination or the withdrawal of the appeal.

(4) A person who gives notice of appeal under this section shall submit to the Secretary of State, either when giving the notice or within such time as may be prescribed, a statement in writing—

(a) specifying the grounds on which he is appealing against the listed building enforcement notice; and

(b) giving such further information as may be prescribed.

(5) If, where more than one ground is specified in the statement, the appellant does not give information required under subsection (4)(b) in relation to each of those grounds within the prescribed time, the Secretary of State may determine the appeal without considering any ground as to which the appellant has failed to give such information within that time.

(6) Where any person has appealed to the Secretary of State under this section against a notice, no person shall be entitled, in any other proceedings instituted after the making of the appeal, to claim that the notice was not duly served on the person who appealed.

(7) In this section 'relevant occupier' means a person who—

(a) on the date on which the listed building enforcement notice is issued occupies the building to which the notice relates by virtue of a licence; and

(b) continues so to occupy the building when the appeal is brought.

43 **[Offence where listed building enforcement notice not complied with**

(1) Where, at any time after the end of the period for compliance with the notice, any step required by a listed building enforcement notice to be taken has not been taken, the person who is then owner of the land is in breach of the notice.

(2) If at any time the owner of the land is in breach of a listed building enforcement notice he shall be guilty of an offence.

(3) An offence under this section may be charged by reference to any day or longer period of time and a person may be convicted of a second or subsequent offence under this section by reference to any period of time following the preceding conviction for such an offence.

(4) In proceedings against any person for an offence under this section, it shall be a defence for him to show—

    (a) that he did everything he could be expected to do to secure that all the steps required by the notice were taken; or

    (b) that he was not served with a copy of the listed building enforcement notice and was not aware of its existence.

(5) A person guilty of an offence under this section shall be liable—

    (a) on summary conviction, to a fine not exceeding £20,000; and

    (b) on conviction on indictment, to a fine.

(6) In determining the amount of any fine to be imposed on a person convicted of an offence under this section, the court shall in particular have regard to any financial benefit which has accrued or appears likely to accrue to him in consequence of the offence.]

44A   [Injunctions

(1) Where a local planning authority consider it necessary or expedient for any actual or apprehended contravention of section 9(1) or (2) to be restrained by injunction, they may apply to the court for an injunction, whether or not they have exercised or are proposing to exercise any of their other powers under this Part.

(2) In an application under subsection (1) the court may grant such an injunction as the court thinks appropriate for the purpose of restraining the contravention.

(3) Rules of court may, in particular, provide for such an injunction to be issued against a person whose identity is unknown.

(4) The references in subsection (1) to a local planning authority include, as respects England, the Commission.

(5) In this section 'the court' means the High Court or the county court.]

47   Compulsory acquisition of listed building in need of repair

(1) If it appears to the Secretary of State that reasonable steps are not being taken for properly preserving a listed building he—

    (a) may authorise the appropriate authority to acquire compulsorily under this section the building and any relevant land; or

    (b) may himself compulsorily acquire them under this section.

(2) The Acquisition of Land Act 1981 shall apply to compulsory acquisition under this section.

(3) The Secretary of State shall not make or confirm a compulsory purchase order for the acquisition of any building by virtue of this section unless—

    (a) in the case of the acquisition of a building situated in England otherwise than by the Commission, he has consulted with the Commission; and

    (b) in any case, he is satisfied that it is expedient to make provision for the preservation of the building and to authorise its compulsory acquisition for that purpose.

(4) Any person having an interest in a building which it is proposed to acquire compulsorily under this section may, within 28 days after the service of the notice required by section 12 of that Act of 1981 or, as the case may be, paragraph 3(1) of Schedule 1 to that Act, apply to a magistrates' court acting for the petty sessions area within which the building is situated for an order staying further proceedings on the compulsory purchase order.

(5) If on an application under subsection (4) the court is satisfied that reasonable steps have been taken for properly preserving the building, the court shall make an order accordingly.

(6) Any person aggrieved by the decision of a magistrates' court on an application under subsection (4) may appeal against the decision to the Crown Court.

(7) In this section—

'the appropriate authority' means—

(a) the council of the county, [county borough] or district in which the building is situated, or

(b) in the case of a building situated in Greater London, the Commission or the council of the London borough in which the building is situated, or

(c) in the case of a building situated outside Greater London, the joint planning board for the area in which the building is situated; or

(d) in the case of a building situated within the Broads, the Broads Authority;

'relevant land', in relation to any building, means the land comprising or contiguous or adjacent to it which appears to the Secretary of State to be required for preserving the building or its amenities, or for affording access to it, or for its proper control or management.

48 Repairs notice as preliminary to acquisition under s. 47

(1) The compulsory purchase of a building under section 47 shall not be started by the appropriate authority or by the Secretary of State unless at least two months previously the authority or, as the case may be, the Secretary of State has served on the owner of the building a notice under this section (in this section referred to as a 'repairs notice')—

(a) specifying the works which the appropriate authority or, as the case may be, the Secretary of State considers reasonably necessary for the proper preservation of the building; and

(b) explaining the effect of sections 47 to 50,

and the repairs notice has not been withdrawn.

(2) Where—

(a) a building is demolished after a repairs notice has been served in respect of it by an appropriate authority or the Secretary of State, but

(b) the Secretary of State is satisfied that he would have confirmed or, as the case may be, would have made a compulsory purchase order in respect of the building had it not been demolished,

the demolition of the building shall not prevent the authority or the Secretary of State from being authorised under section 47 to acquire compulsorily the site of the building.

(3) An appropriate authority or the Secretary of State may at any time withdraw a repairs notice served by them on any person; and if they do so, they shall immediately give him notice of the withdrawal.

(4) The Secretary of State shall consult with the Commission before he serves or withdraws a repairs notice in relation to a building situated in England.

(5) Where a repairs notice has been served on a person in respect of a building, he shall not be entitled to serve a listed building purchase notice in respect of it—

(a) until the expiration of three months beginning with the date of the service of the repairs notice; or

(b) if during that period the compulsory acquisition of the building is begun under section 47, unless and until the compulsory acquisition is discontinued.

(6) For the purposes of this section a compulsory acquisition—

(a) is started when the notice required by section 12 of the Acquisition of Land Act 1981 or, as the case may be, paragraph 3(1) of Schedule 1 to that Act is served; and

(b) is discontinued—

(i) in the case of acquisition by the Secretary of State, when he decides not to make the compulsory purchase order; and

(ii) in any other case, when the order is withdrawn or the Secretary of State decides not to confirm it.

(7) In this section 'appropriate authority' has the same meaning as in section 47.

49 Compensation on compulsory acquisition of listed building

Subject to section 50, for the purpose of assessing compensation in respect of any compulsory acquisition of land including a building which immediately before the date of the compulsory purchase order was listed, it shall be assumed that listed building consent would be granted for any works—

(a) for the alteration or extension of the building; or

(b) for the demolition of the building for the purpose of development of any class specified in Schedule 3 to the principal Act (development not constituting new development).

50   Minimum compensation in case of listed building deliberately left derelict

(1) Where the appropriate authority within the meaning of section 47—

(a) propose to acquire a building compulsorily under that section; and

(b) are satisfied that the building has been deliberately allowed to fall into disrepair for the purpose of justifying its demolition and the development or redevelopment of the site or any adjoining site,

they may include in the compulsory purchase order as submitted to the Secretary of State for confirmation a direction for minimum compensation.

(2) Subject to the provisions of this section, where the Secretary of State acquires a building compulsorily under section 47, he may, if he is satisfied as mentioned in subsection (1)(b), include a direction for minimum compensation in the compulsory purchase order.

(3) Without prejudice to so much of section 12 of the Acquisition of Land Act 1981 or, as the case may be, paragraph 3(1) of Schedule 1 to that Act (notices stating effect of compulsory purchase order or, as the case may be, draft order) as requires the notice to state the effect of the order, the notice required to be served in accordance with that provision shall—

(a) include a statement that a direction for minimum compensation has been included in the order or, as the case may be, in the draft order prepared by the Secretary of State in accordance with Schedule 1 to that Act; and

(b) explain the meaning of the expression 'direction for minimum compensation'.

(4) A direction for minimum compensation, in relation to a building compulsorily acquired, is a direction that for the purpose of assessing compensation it is to be assumed, notwithstanding anything to the contrary in the Land Compensation Act 1961, the principal Act, or this Act—

(a) that planning permission would not be granted for any development or re-development of the site of the building; and

(b) that listed building consent would not be granted for any works for the demolition, alteration or extension of the building other than development or works necessary for restoring it to and maintaining it in a proper state of repair.

(5) If a compulsory purchase order is confirmed or made with the inclusion of a direction for minimum compensation, the compensation in respect of the compulsory acquisition shall be assessed in accordance with the direction.

(6) Where such a direction is included in a compulsory purchase order or, as the case may be, in a draft order prepared by the Secretary of State, any person having an interest in the building may, within 28 days after the service of the notice mentioned in subsection (3), apply to a magistrates' court acting for the petty sessions area in which the building is situated for an order that no such direction be included in the compulsory purchase order as confirmed or made by the Secretary of State.

(7) If the court to which an application is made under subsection (6) is satisfied that the building in respect of which the application is made has not been deliberately allowed to fall into disrepair for the purpose mentioned in subsection (1)(b) the court shall make the order applied for.

(8) A person aggrieved by the decision of a magistrates' court on an application under subsection (6) may appeal against the decision to the Crown Court.

(9) The rights conferred by subsections (6) and (8) shall not prejudice those conferred by section 47(4) and (6).

54   Urgent works to preserve unoccupied listed buildings

(1) A local authority may execute any works which appear to them to be urgently necessary for the preservation of a listed building in their area.

(2) If it appears to the Secretary of State that any works are urgently necessary for the preservation of a listed building—

- (a) if the building is in England, he shall authorise the Commission to execute any works specified in the authorisation which appear to him to be urgently necessary for its preservation; or
- (b) if the building is in Wales, he may himself execute any works which appear to him to be urgently necessary for its preservation.

(3) The works which may be executed under this section may consist of or include works for affording temporary support or shelter for the building.

(4) If the building is occupied works may be carried out only to those parts which are not in use.

(5) The owner of the building must be given not less than seven days' notice in writing of the intention to carry out the works and, in the case of works authorised under subsection (2)(a), the Commission shall give that notice.

(6) A notice under subsection (5) shall describe the works proposed to be carried out.

(7) As respects buildings in Greater London, the functions of a local authority under this section are exercisable concurrently by the Commission and the relevant London borough council.

55   Recovery of expenses of works under s. 54

(1) This section has effect for enabling the expenses of works executed under section 54 to be recovered by the authority who carried out the works, that is to say the local authority, the Commission or the Secretary of State or, in the case of works carried out by the Commission on behalf of the Secretary of State, the Secretary of State.

(2) That authority may give notice to the owner of the building requiring him to pay the expenses of the works.

(3) Where the works consist of or include works for affording temporary support or shelter for the building—

- (a) the expenses which may be recovered include any continuing expenses involved in making available the apparatus or materials used; and
- (b) notices under subsection (2) in respect of any such continuing expenses may be given from time to time.

(4) The owner may within 28 days of the service of the notice represent to the Secretary of State—

- (a) that some or all of the works were unnecessary for the preservation of the building; or
- (b) in the case of works for affording temporary support or shelter, that the temporary arrangements have continued for an unreasonable length of time; or
- (c) that the amount specified in the notice is unreasonable; or
- (d) that the recovery of that amount would cause him hardship, and the Secretary of State shall determine to what extent the representations are justified.

(5) The Secretary of State shall give notice of his determination, the reasons for it and the amount recoverable—

- (a) to the owner of the building; and
- (b) if the authority who gave notice under subsection (2) is a local authority or the Commission, to them.

66   General duty as respects listed buildings in exercise of planning functions

(1) In considering whether to grant planning permission for development which affects a listed building or its setting, the local planning authority or, as the case may be, the Secretary of State shall have special regard to the desirability of preserving the building or its setting or any features of special architectural or historic interest which it possesses.

(2) Without prejudice to section 72, in the exercise of the powers of appropriation, disposal and development (including redevelopment) conferred by the provisions of sections 232, 233 and 235(1) of the principal Act, a local authority shall have regard to the desirability of preserving features of special architectural or historic interest, and in particular, listed buildings.

(3) The reference in subsection (2) to a local authority includes a reference to a joint planning board [. . .]

67   Publicity for applications affecting setting of listed buildings

(1) This section applies where an application for planning permission for any development of land is made to a local planning authority and the development would, in the opinion of the authority, affect the setting of a listed building.

(2) The local planning authority shall—

  (a) publish in a local newspaper circulating in the locality in which the land is situated; and

  (b) for not less than seven days display on or near the land, a notice indicating the nature of the development in question and naming a place within the locality where a copy of the application, and of all plans and other documents submitted with it, will be open to inspection by the public at all reasonable hours during the period of 21 days beginning with the date of publication of the notice under paragraph (a).

(3) In a case where the land is situated in England, the local planning authority shall send a copy of the notice to the Commission.

(4) Where the Secretary of State, after consulting with the Commission, notifies a local planning authority in writing that subsection (3) shall not affect the authority as regards any notice relating to any kind of application specified in the notification, then that subsection shall not affect the authority as regards any such notice.

(5) The Secretary of State shall send the Commission a copy of any notification made under subsection (4).

(6) The application shall not be determined by the local planning authority before—

  (a) the expiry of the period of 21 days referred to in subsection (2); or

  (b) if later, the expiry of the period of 21 days beginning with the date on which the notice required by that subsection to be displayed was first displayed.

(7) In determining any application for planning permission to which this section applies, the local planning authority shall take into account any representations relating to the application which are received by them before the periods mentioned in subsection (6) have elapsed.

[(8) In this section references to planning permission do not include references to planning permissions falling within section 73A of the principal Act.]

PART II

69   Designation of conservation areas

(1) Every local planning authority—

  (a) shall from time to time determine which parts of their area are areas of special architectural or historic interest the character or appearance of which it is desirable to preserve or enhance, and

  (b) shall designate those areas as conservation areas.

(2) It shall be the duty of a local planning authority from time to time to review the past exercise of functions under this section and to determine whether any parts or any further parts of their area should be designated as conservation areas; and, if they so determine, they shall designate those parts accordingly.

(3) The Secretary of State may from time to time determine that any part of a local planning authority's area which is not for the time being designated as a conservation area is an area of special architectural or historic interest the character or appearance of which it is desirable to preserve or enhance; and, if he so determines, he may designate that part as a conservation area.

(4) The designation of any area as a conservation area shall be a local land charge.

71 Formulation and publication of proposals for preservation and enhancement of conservation areas

(1) It shall be the duty of a local planning authority from time to time to formulate and publish proposals for the preservation and enhancement of any parts of their area which are conservation areas.

(2) Proposals under this section shall be submitted for consideration to a public meeting in the area to which they relate.

(3) The local planning authority shall have regard to any views concerning the proposals expressed by persons attending the meeting.

72 General duty as respects conservation areas in exercise of planning functions

(1) In the exercise, with respect to any buildings or other land in a conservation area, of any [functions under or by virtue of] any of the provisions mentioned in subsection (2), special attention shall be paid to the desirability of preserving or enhancing the character or appearance of that area.

(2) The provisions referred to in subsection (1) are the planning Acts and Part I of the Historic Buildings and Ancient Monuments Act 1953 [and sections 70 and 73 of the Leasehold Reform, Housing and Urban Development Act 1993].

73 Publicity for applications affecting conservation areas

(1) Where an application for planning permission for any development of land is made to a local planning authority and the development would, in the opinion of the authority, affect the character or appearance of a conservation area, subsections (2) to (7) of section 67 shall apply as they apply in the circumstances mentioned in subsection (1) of that section.

[(2) In this section references to planning permission do not include references to planning permissions falling within section 73A of the principal Act.]

74 Control of demolition in conservation areas

(1) A building in a conservation area shall not be demolished without the consent of the appropriate authority (in this Act referred to as 'conservation area consent').

(2) The appropriate authority for the purposes of this section is—

    (a) in relation to applications for consent made by local planning authorities, the Secretary of State; and

    (b) in relation to other applications for consent, the local planning authority or the Secretary of State.

(3) Sections 7 to 26, 28, 32 to 46, 56, 62 to 65, 66(1), 82(2) to (4), 83(1)(b), (3) and (4) and 90(2) to (4) have effect in relation to buildings in conservation areas as they have effect in relation to listed buildings subject to such exceptions and modifications as may be prescribed by regulations.

(4) Any such regulations may make different provision—

    (a) in relation to applications made by local planning authorities, and

    (b) in relation to other applications.

75 Cases in which s. 74 does not apply

(1) Section 74 does not apply to—

    (a) listed buildings;

    (b) ecclesiastical buildings which are for the time being used for ecclesiastical purposes;

    (c) buildings for the time being included in the schedule of monuments compiled and maintained under section 1 of the Ancient Monuments and Archaeological Areas Act 1979; or

    (d) buildings in relation to which a direction under subsection (2) is for the time being in force.

(2) The Secretary of State may direct that section 74 shall not apply to any description of buildings specified in the direction.

(3) A direction under subsection (2) may be given either to an individual local planning authority exercising functions under that section or to local planning authorities generally.

(4) The Secretary of State may vary or revoke a direction under subsection (2) by a further direction under that subsection.

(5) For the purposes of subsection (1)(b), a building used or available for use by a minister of religion wholly or mainly as a residence from which to perform the duties of his office shall be treated as not being an ecclesiastical building.

(6) For the purposes of sections 7 to 9 as they apply by virtue of section 74(3) a building shall be taken to be used for the time being for ecclesiastical purposes if it would be so used but for the works in question.

(7) The Secretary of State may by order provide for restricting or excluding the operation of subsection (1)(b) in such cases as may be specified in the order.

(8) An order under subsection (7) may—

    (a) make provision for buildings generally, for descriptions of building or for particular buildings;

    (b) make different provision for buildings in different areas, for buildings of different religious faiths or denominations or according to the use made of the building;

    (c) make such provision in relation to a part of a building (including, in particular, an object or structure falling to be treated as part of the building by virtue of section 1(5)) as may be made in relation to a building and make different provision for different parts of the same building;

    (d) make different provision with respect to works of different descriptions or according to the extent of the works;

    (e) make such consequential adaptations or modifications of the operation of any other provision of this Act or the principal Act, or of any instrument made under either of those Acts, as appear to the Secretary of State to be appropriate.

(9) Regulations under this Act may provide that subsections (5) to (8) shall have effect subject to such exceptions and modifications as may be prescribed, and any such regulations may make different provision—

    (a) in relation to applications made by local planning authorities, and

    (b) in relation to other applications.

(10) Any proceedings on or arising out of an application for conservation area consent made while section 74 applies to a building shall lapse if it ceases to apply to it, and any such consent granted with respect to the building shall also lapse.

(11) The fact that that section has ceased to apply to a building shall not affect the liability of any person to be prosecuted and punished for an offence under section 9 or 43 committed with respect to the building while that section did apply to it.

Environmental Protection Act 1990
(1990, c. 43)

PART I   INTEGRATED POLLUTION CONTROL AND AIR
POLLUTION CONTROL BY LOCAL AUTHORITIES

1   Preliminary

(1) The following provisions have effect for the interpretation of this Part.

(2) The 'environment' consists of all, or any, of the following media, namely, the air, water and land; and the medium of air includes the air within buildings and the air within other natural or man-made structures above or below ground.

(3) 'Pollution of the environment' means pollution of the environment due to the release (into any environmental medium) from any process of substances which are capable of causing harm to man or any other living organisms supported by the environment.

(4) 'Harm' means harm to the health of living organisms or other interference with the ecological systems of which they form part and, in the case of man, includes offence caused to any of his senses or harm to his property; and 'harmless' has a corresponding meaning.

(5) 'Process' means any activities carried on in Great Britain, whether on premises or by means of mobile plant, which are capable of causing pollution of the environment and 'prescribed process' means a process prescribed under section 2(1) below.

(6) For the purposes of subsection (5) above—

'activities' means industrial or commercial activities or activities of any other nature whatsoever (including, with or without other activities, the keeping of a substance);

'Great Britain' includes so much of the adjacent territorial sea as is, or is treated as, relevant territorial waters for the purposes of [Part III of the Water Act 1991] . . .

'mobile plant' means plant which is designed to move or to be moved whether on roads or otherwise.

(7) The 'enforcing authority', in relation to England and Wales, is [the Environment Agency or the local authority by which], under section 4 below, the functions conferred or imposed by this Part otherwise than on the Secretary of State are for the time being exercisable in relation respectively to releases of substances into the environment or into the air; and 'local enforcing authority' means any such local authority.

(8) . . .

(9) 'Authorisation' means an authorisation for a process (whether on premises or by means of mobile plant) granted under section 6 below; and a reference to the conditions of an authorisation is a reference to the conditions subject to which at any time the authorisation has effect.

(10) A substance is 'released' into any environmental medium whenever it is released directly into that medium whether it is released into it within or outside Great Britain and 'release' includes—

(a)   in relation to air, any emission of the substance into the air;

(b)   in relation to water, any entry (including any discharge) of the substance into water;

(c)   in relation to land, any deposit, keeping or disposal of the substance in or on land;

and for this purpose 'water' and 'land' shall be construed in accordance with subsections (11) and (12) below.

(11) For the purpose of determining into what medium a substance is released—

(a)   any release into—

(i)   the sea or the surface of the seabed,

(ii)   any river, watercourse, lake, loch or pond (whether natural or artificial or above or below ground) or reservoir or the surface of the riverbed or of other land supporting such waters, or

(iii) ground waters,

is a release into water;

(b) any release into—

(i) land covered by water falling outside paragraph (a) above or the water covering such land; or

(ii) the land beneath the surface of the seabed or of other land supporting waters falling within paragraph (a)(ii) above,

is a release into land; and

(c) any release into a sewer (within the meaning of the [Water Industry Act 1991] . . .) shall be treated as a release into water;

but a sewer and its contents shall be disregarded in determining whether there is pollution of the environment at any time.

(12) In subsection (11) above 'ground waters' means any waters contained in underground strata, or in—

(a) a well, borehole or similar work sunk into underground strata, including any adit or passage constructed in connection with the well, borehole or work for facilitating the collection of water in the well, borehole or work; or

(b) any excavation into underground strata where the level of water in the excavation depends wholly or mainly on water entering it from the strata.

(13) 'Substance' shall be treated as including electricity or heat and 'prescribed substance' has the meaning given by section 2(7) below.

[(14) In this Part 'the appropriate Agency' means—

(a) in relation to England and Wales, the Environment Agency; and

(b) . . .]

2   Prescribed processes and prescribed substances

(1) The Secretary of State may, by regulations, prescribe any description of process as a process for the carrying on of which after a prescribed date an authorisation is required under section 6 below.

(2) Regulations under subsection (1) above may frame the description of a process by reference to any characteristics of the process or the area or other circumstances in which the process is carried on or the description of person carrying it on.

(3) Regulations under subsection (1) above may prescribe or provide for the determination under the regulations of different dates for different descriptions of persons and may include such transitional provisions as the Secretary of State considers necessary or expedient as respects the making of applications for authorisations and suspending the application of section 6(1) below until the determination of applications made within the period allowed by the regulations.

(4) Regulations under subsection (1) above shall, as respects each description of process, designate it as one for central control or one for local control.

(5) The Secretary of State may, by regulations, prescribe any description of substance as a substance the release of which into the environment is subject to control under sections 6 and 7 below.

(6) Regulations under subsection (5) above may—

(a) prescribe separately, for each environmental medium, the substances the release of which into that medium is to be subject to control; and

(b) provide that a description of substance is only prescribed, for any environmental medium, so far as it is released into that medium in such amounts over such periods, in such concentrations or in such other circumstances as may be specified in the regulations; and in relation to a substance of a description which is prescribed for releases into the air, the regulations may designate the substance as one for central control or one for local control.

(7) In this Part 'prescribed substance' means any substance of a description prescribed in regulations under subsection (5) above or, in the case of a substance of a description prescribed only for releases in circumstances specified under subsection (6)(b) above, means any substance of that description which is released in those circumstances.

3   Emission etc. limits and quality objectives

(1) The Secretary of State may make regulations under subsection (2) or (4) below establishing standards, objectives or requirements in relation to particular prescribed processes or particular substances.

(2) Regulations under this subsection may—

- (a) in relation to releases of any substance from prescribed processes into any environmental medium, prescribe standard limits for—
  - (i) the concentration, the amount or the amount in any period of that substance which may be so released; and
  - (ii) any other characteristic of that substance in any circumstances in which it may be so released;
- (b) prescribe standard requirements for the measurement or analysis of, or of releases of, substances for which limits have been set under paragraph (a) above; and
- (c) in relation to any prescribed process, prescribe standards or requirements as to any aspect of the process.

(3) Regulations under subsection (2) above may make different provision in relation to different cases, including different provision in relation to different processes, descriptions of person, localities or other circumstances.

(4) Regulations under this subsection may establish for any environmental medium (in all areas or in specified areas) quality objectives or quality standards in relation to any substances which may be released into that or any other medium from any process.

(5) The Secretary of State may make plans for—

- (a) establishing limits for the total amount, or the total amount in any period, of any substance which may be released into the environment in, or in any area within, the United Kingdom;
- (b) allocating quotas as respects the release of substances to persons carrying on processes in respect of which any such limit is established;
- (c) establishing limits of the descriptions specified in subsection (2)(a) above so as progressively to reduce pollution of the environment;
- (d) the progressive improvement in the quality objectives and quality standards established by regulations under subsection (4) above;

and the Secretary of State may, from time to time, revise any plan so made.

(6) Regulations or plans under this section may be made for any purposes of this Part or for other purposes.

(7) The Secretary of State shall give notice in the London Gazette . . . of the making and the revision of any plan under subsection (5) above and shall make the documents containing the plan, or the plan as so revised, available for inspection by members of the public at the places specified in the notice.

(8) . . .

4   Discharge and scope of functions

(1) This section determines the authority by whom the functions conferred or imposed by this Part otherwise than on the Secretary of State are exercisable and the purposes for which they are exercisable.

(2) Those functions, in their application to prescribed processes designated for central control, shall be functions of [the appropriate Agency] and shall be exercisable for the purpose

of preventing or minimising pollution of the environment due to the release of substances into any environmental medium.

(3) Subject to subsection (4) below, those functions, in their application to prescribed processes designated for local control, shall be functions of—

[(a) in the case of a prescribed process carried on (or to be carried on) by means of a mobile plant, where the person carrying on the process has his principal place of business—

(i) in England and Wales, the local authority in whose area that place of business is;

(ii) . . .

(b) in any other cases, where the prescribed processes are (or are to be) carried on—

(i) in England and Wales, the local authority in whose area they are (or are to be) carried on;

(ii) . . .]

and the functions applicable to such processes shall be exercisable for the purpose of preventing or minimising pollution of the environment due to the release of substances into the air (but not into any other environmental medium).

(4) The Secretary of State may, as respects the functions under this Part being exercised by a local authority specified in the direction, direct that those functions shall be exercised instead by [the Environmental Agency] while the direction remains in force or during a period specified in the direction.

[(4A) In England and Wales, a local authority, in exercising the functions conferred or imposed on it under this Part by virtue of subsection (3) above, shall have regard to the strategy for the time being published pursuant to section 80 of the Environment Act 1995.]

(5) A transfer of functions under subsection (4) above to [the Environment Agency] does not make them exercisable by [that Agency] for the purpose of preventing or minimising pollution of the environment due to releases of substances into any other environmental medium than the air.

(6) A direction under subsection (4) above may transfer those functions as exercisable in relation to all or any description of prescribed processes carried on by all or any description of persons (a 'general direction') or in relation to a prescribed process carried on by a specified person (a 'specific direction').

(7) A direction under subsection (4) above may include such saving and transitional provisions as the Secretary of State considers necessary or expedient.

(8) The Secretary of State, on giving or withdrawing a direction under subsection (4) above, shall—

(a) in the case of a general direction—

(i) forthwith serve notice of it on [the Environment Agency] and on the local enforcing authorities affected by the direction; and

(ii) cause notice of it to be published as soon as practicable in the London Gazette [. . .] and in at least one newspaper circulating in the area of each authority affected by the direction;

(b) in the case of a specific direction—

(i) forthwith serve notice of it on [the Environment Agency], the local enforcing authority and the person carrying on or appearing to the Secretary of State to be carrying on the process affected, and

(ii) cause notice of it to be published as soon as practicable in the London Gazette [. . .] and in at least one newspaper circulating in the authority's area;

and any such notice shall specify the date at which the direction is to take (or took) effect and (where appropriate) its duration.

[(8A) The requirements of sub-paragraph (ii) of paragraph (a) or, as the case may be, of paragraph (b) of subsection (8) above shall not apply in any case where, in the opinion of the

Secretary of State, the publication of notice in accordance with that sub-paragraph would be contrary to the interests of national security.

(8B) ...]

[(9) It shall be the duty of local authorities to follow such developments in technology and techniques for preventing or reducing pollution of the environment due to releases of substances from prescribed processes as concern releases into the air of substances from prescribed processes designated for local control.]

(10) It shall be the duty of [the Environment Agency] ... and the local enforcing authorities to give effect to any directions given to them under any provision of this Part.

(11) In this Part 'local authority' means, subject to subsection (12) below—

(a) in Greater London, a London borough council, the Common Council of the City of London, the Sub-Treasurer of the Inner Temple and the Under Treasurer of the Middle Temple;

(b) [in England and Wales,] outside Greater London, a district council and the Council of the Isles of Scilly; and

(12) Where, by an order under section 2 of the Public Health (Control of Disease) Act 1984, a port health authority has been constituted for any port health district, the port health authority shall have by virtue of this subsection, as respects its district, the functions conferred or imposed by this Part and no such order shall be made assigning those functions; and 'local authority' and 'area' shall be construed accordingly.

Authorisations

6   Authorisations: general provisions

(1) No person shall carry on a prescribed process after the date prescribed or determined for that description of process by or under regulations under section 2(1) above (but subject to any transitional provision made by the regulations) except under an authorisation granted by the enforcing authority and in accordance with the conditions to which it is subject.

(2) An application for an authorisation shall be made to the enforcing authority in accordance with Part I of Schedule 1 to this Act and shall be accompanied by

[(a) in a case where, by virtue of section 41 of the Environment Act 1995, a charge prescribed by a charging scheme under that section is required to be paid to the appropriate Agency in respect of the application, the charge so prescribed; or

(b) in any other case,]

the fee prescribed under section 8(2)(a) below.

(3) Where an application is duly made to the enforcing authority, the authority shall either grant the authorisation subject to the conditions required or authorised to be imposed by section 7 below or refuse the application.

(4) An application shall not be granted unless the enforcing authority considers that the applicant will be able to carry on the process so as to comply with the conditions which would be included in the authorisation.

(5) The Secretary of State may, if he thinks fit in relation to any application for an authorisation, give to the enforcing authority directions as to whether or not the authority should grant the authorisation.

[(6) Subject to subsection (6A) below,] the enforcing authority shall, as respects each authorisation in respect of which it has functions under this Part, from time to time but not less frequently than once in every period of four years, carry out a review of the conditions of the authorisation.

[(6A) Subsection (6) above shall not require a review of the conditions of an authorisation to be carried out if—

(a) the prescribed process covered by the authorisation is carried on in a new Part A installation or by means of a new Part A mobile plant;

(b) the prescribed process covered by the authorisation is carried on in an existing Part A installation or by means of an existing Part A mobile plant and the review would be carried out within the period of two years ending at the beginning of the relevant period for that installation or mobile plant; or

(c) the prescribed process covered by the authorisation is carried on in an existing Part B installation or by means of an existing Part B mobile plant and the review would be carried out within the period of two years ending on the relevant date for that installation or mobile plant.

(6B) In subsection (6A) above, 'new Part A installation', 'existing Part A installation', 'new Part A mobile plant', 'existing Part A mobile plant', 'relevant period', 'existing Part B installation', 'existing Part B mobile plant' and 'relevant date' have the meaning given in Schedule 3 to the Pollution Prevention and Control (England and Wales) Regulations 2000.]

(7) The Secretary of State may, by regulations, substitute for the period for the time being specified in subsection (6) above such other period as he thinks fit.

(8) Schedule 1 to this Act (supplementary provisions) shall have effect in relation to authorisations.

7   Conditions of authorisations

(1) There shall be included in an authorisation—

(a) subject to paragraph (b) below, such specific conditions as the enforcing authority considers appropriate, when taken with the general condition implied by subsection (4) below, for achieving the objectives specified in subsection (2) below;

(b) such conditions as are specified in directions given by the Secretary of State under subsection (3) below; and

(c) such other conditions (if any) as appear to the enforcing authority to be appropriate;

but no conditions shall be imposed for the purpose only of securing the health of persons at work (within the meaning of Part I of the Health and Safety at Work etc. Act 1974).

(2) Those objectives are—

(a) ensuring that, in carrying on a prescribed process, the best available techniques not entailing excessive cost will be used—

(i) for preventing the release of substances prescribed for any environmental medium into that medium or, where that is not practicable by such means, for reducing the release of such substances to a minimum and for rendering harmless any such substances which are so released; and

(ii) for rendering harmless any other substances which might cause harm if released into any environmental medium;

(b) compliance with any directions by the Secretary of State given for the implementation of any obligations of the United Kingdom under the Community Treaties or international law relating to environmental protection;

(c) compliance with any limits or requirements and achievement of any quality standards or quality objectives prescribed by the Secretary of State under any of the relevant enactments;

(d) compliance with any requirements applicable to the grant of authorisations specified by or under a plan made by the Secretary of State under section 3(5) above.

(3) Except as respects the general condition implied by subsection (4) below, the Secretary of State may give directions to the enforcing authorities as to the conditions which are, or are not, to be included in all authorisations, in authorisations of any specified description or in any particular authorisation.

(4) Subject to subsections (5) and (6) below, there is implied in every authorisation a

general condition that, in carrying on the process to which the authorisation applies, the person carrying it on must use the best available techniques not entailing excessive cost—

>   (a) for preventing the release of substances prescribed for any environmental medium into that medium or, where that is not practicable by such means, for reducing the release of such substances to a minimum and for rendering harmless any such substances which are so released; and

>   (b) for rendering harmless any other substances which might cause harm if released into any environmental medium.

(5) In the application of subsections (1) to (4) above to authorisations granted by a local enforcing authority references to the release of substances into any environmental medium are to be read as references to the release of substances into the air.

(6) The obligation implied by virtue of subsection (4) above shall not apply in relation to any aspect of the process in question which is regulated by a condition imposed under subsection (1) above.

(7) The objectives referred to in subsection (2) above shall, where the process—

>   (a) is one designated for central control; and

>   (b) is likely to involve the release of substances into more than one environmental medium;

include the objective of ensuring that the best available techniques not entailing excessive cost will be used for minimising the pollution which may be caused to the environment taken as a whole by the releases having regard to the best practicable environmental option available as respects the substances which may be released.

(8) An authorisation for carrying on a prescribed process may, without prejudice to the generality of subsection (1) above, include conditions—

>   (a) imposing limits on the amount or composition of any substance produced by or utilised in the process in any period; and

>   (b) requiring advance notification of any proposed change in the manner of carrying on the process.

(9) This section has effect subject to section 28 below [. . .]

(10) References to the best available techniques not entailing excessive cost, in relation to a process, include (in addition to references to any technical means and technology) references to the number, qualifications, training and supervision of persons employed in the process and the design, construction, lay-out and maintenance of the buildings in which it is carried on.

(11) It shall be the duty of enforcing authorities to have regard to any guidance issued to them by the Secretary of State for the purposes of the application of subsections (2) and (7) above as to the techniques and environmental options that are appropriate for any description of prescribed process.

(12) In subsection (2) above 'the relevant enactments' are any enactments or instruments contained in or made for the time being under—

>   (a) section 2 of the Clean Air Act 1968;

>   (b) section 2 of the European Communities Act 1972;

>   (c) Part I of the Health and Safety at Work etc. Act 1974;

>   (d) Parts II, III or IV of the Control of Pollution Act 1974;

>   (e) [the Water Resources Act 1991]; and

>   (f) section 3 of this Act [and

>   (g) section 87 of the Environment Act 1995.]

8 Fees and charges for authorisations

(1) There shall be charged by and paid to the [local enforcing authority] such fees and charges as may be prescribed from time to time by a scheme under subsection (2) below (whether by being specified in or made calculable under the scheme).

(2) The Secretary of State may, with the approval of the Treasury, make, and from time to time revise, a scheme prescribing—

(a) fees payable in respect of applications for authorisations;

(b) fees payable by persons holding authorisations in respect of, or of applications for, the variation of authorisations; and

(c) charges payable by such persons in respect of the subsistence of their authorisations.

(3) The Secretary of State shall, on making or revising a scheme under subsection (2) above, lay a copy of the scheme or of the alterations made in the scheme or, if he considers it more appropriate, the scheme as revised, before each House of Parliament.

(4) [. . .]

(5) A scheme under subsection (2) above may, in particular—

(a) make different provision for different cases, including different provision in relation to different persons, circumstances or localities;

(b) allow for reduced fees or charges to be payable in respect of authorisations for a number of prescribed processes carried on by the same person;

(c) provide for the times at which and the manner in which the payments required by the scheme are to be made; and

(d) make such incidental, supplementary and transitional provision as appears to the Secretary of State to be appropriate.

(6) The Secretary of State, in framing a scheme under subsection (2) above, shall, so far as practicable, secure that the fees and charges payable under the scheme are sufficient, taking one financial year with another, to cover the relevant expenditure attributable to authorisations.

(7) The 'relevant expenditure attributable to authorisations' is the expenditure incurred by the [local enforcing authorities] in exercising their functions under this Part in relation to authorisations [. . .][together with the expenditure incurred by the Environment Agency in exercising, in relation to authorisations granted by local enforcing authorities or the prescribed processes to which such authorisations relate, such of its functions as are specified in the scheme.]

(8) If it appears to the [local enforcing authority] that the holder of an authorisation has failed to pay a charge due in consideration of the subsistence of the authorisation, it may, by notice in writing served on the holder, revoke the authorisation.

(9) [. . .]

(10) . . .

(11) [. . .]

9   Transfer of authorisations

(1) An authorisation for the carrying on of any prescribed process may be transferred by the holder to a person who proposes to carry on the process in the holder's place.

(2) Where an authorisation is transferred under this section, the person to whom it is transferred shall notify the enforcing authority in writing of that fact not later than the end of the period of twenty-one days beginning with the date of the transfer.

(3) An authorisation which is transferred under this section shall have effect on and after the date of the transfer as if it had been granted to that person under section 6 above, subject to the same conditions as were attached to it immediately before that date.

10   Variation of authorisations by enforcing authority

(1) The enforcing authority may at any time, subject to the requirements of section 7 above, and, in cases to which they apply, the requirements of Part II of Schedule 1 to this Act, vary an authorisation and shall do so if it appears to the authority at that time that that section requires conditions to be included which are different from the subsisting conditions.

(2) Where the enforcing authority has decided to vary an authorisation under subsection

(1) above the authority shall notify the holder of the authorisation and serve a variation notice on him.

(3) In this Part a 'variation notice' is a notice served by the enforcing authority on the holder of an authorisation—

(a) specifying variations of the authorisation which the enforcing authority has decided to make; and

(b) specifying the date or dates on which the variations are to take effect;

and, unless the notice is withdrawn [or is varied under subsection (3A) below], the variations specified in a variation notice shall take effect on the date or dates so specified.

[(3A) An enforcing authority which has served a variation notice may vary that notice by serving on the holder of the authorisation in question a further notice—

(a) specifying the variations which the enforcing authority has decided to make to the variation notice; and

(b) specifying the date or dates on which the variations specified in the variation notice, as varied by the further notice, are to take effect;

and any reference in this Part to a variation notice, or to a variation notice served under subsection (2) above, includes a reference to such a notice as varied by a further notice served under this subsection.]

(4) A variation notice served under subsection (2) above shall also—

(a) require the holder of the authorisation, within such period as may be specified in the notice, to notify the authority what action (if any) he proposes to take to ensure that the process is carried on in accordance with the authorisation as varied by the notice; and

[(b) require the holder to pay, within such period as may be specified in the notice,—

(i) in a case where the enforcing authority is the Environment Agency . . ., the charge (if any) prescribed for the purpose by a charging scheme under section 41 of the Environment Act 1995; or

(ii) in any other case, the fee (if any) prescribed by a scheme under section 8 above.]

(5) Where in the opinion of the enforcing authority any action to be taken by the holder of an authorisation in consequence of a variation notice served under subsection (2) above will involve a substantial change in the manner in which the process is being carried on, the enforcing authority shall notify the holder of its opinion.

(6) The Secretary of State may, if he thinks fit in relation to authorisations of any description or particular authorisations, direct the enforcing authorities—

(a) to exercise their powers under this section, or to do so in such circumstances as may be specified in the directions, in such manner as may be so specified; or

(b) not to exercise those powers, or not to do so in such circumstances or such manner as may be so specified;

and the Secretary of State shall have the corresponding power of direction in respect of the powers of the enforcing authorities to vary authorisations under section 11 below.

(7) In this section and section 11 below a 'substantial change', in relation to a prescribed process being carried on under an authorisation means a substantial change in the substances released from the process or in the amount or any other characteristic of any substance so released; and the Secretary of State may give directions to the enforcing authorities as to what does or does not constitute a substantial change in relation to processes generally, any description of process or any particular process.

(8) In this section and section 11 below—

'prescribed' means prescribed in regulations made by the Secretary of State;

'vary',

[(a)] in relation to the subsisting conditions or other provisions of an authorisation, means adding to them or varying or rescinding any of them; [and

(b) in relation to a variation notice, means adding to, or varying or rescinding the notice or any of its contents;]

and 'variation' shall be construed accordingly.

11   Variation of conditions etc: applications by holders of authorisations

(1) A person carrying on a prescribed process under an authorisation who wishes to make a relevant change in the process may at any time—

(a) notify the enforcing authority in the prescribed form of that fact, and

(b) request the enforcing authority to make a determination, in relation to the proposed change, of the matters mentioned in subsection (2) below;

and a person making a request under paragraph (b) above shall furnish the enforcing authority with such information as may be prescribed or as the authority may by notice require.

(2) On receiving a request under subsection (1) above the enforcing authority shall determine—

(a) whether the proposed change would involve a breach of any condition of the authorisation;

(b) if it would not involve such a breach, whether the authority would be likely to vary the conditions of the authorisation as a result of the change;

(c) if it would involve such a breach, whether the authority would consider varying the conditions of the authorisation so that the change may be made; and

(d) whether the change would involve a substantial change in the manner in which the process is being carried on;

and the enforcing authority shall notify the holder of the authorisation of its determination of those matters.

(3) Where the enforcing authority has determined that the proposed change would not involve a substantial change, but has also determined under paragraph (b) or (c) of subsection (2) above that the change would lead to or require the variation of the conditions of the authorisation then—

(a) the enforcing authority shall (either on notifying its determination under that subsection or on a subsequent occasion) notify the holder of the authorisation of the variations which the authority is likely to consider making; and

(b) the holder may apply in the prescribed form to the enforcing authority for the variation of the conditions of the authorisation so that he may make the proposed change.

(4) Where the enforcing authority has determined that a proposed change would involve a substantial change that would lead to or require the variation of the conditions of the authorisation, then—

(a) the authority shall (either on notifying its determination under subsection (2) above or on a subsequent occasion) notify the holder of the authorisation of the variations which the authority is likely to consider making; and

(b) the holder of the authorisation shall, if he wishes to proceed with the change, apply in the prescribed form to the enforcing authority for the variation of the conditions of the authorisation.

(5) The holder of an authorisation may at any time, unless he is carrying on a prescribed process under the authorisation and wishes to make a relevant change in the process, apply to the enforcing authority in the prescribed form for the variation of the conditions of the authorisation.

(6) A person carrying on a process under an authorisation who wishes to make a relevant change in the process may, where it appears to him that the change will require the variation of the conditions of the authorisation, apply to the enforcing authority in the prescribed form for the variation of the conditions of the authorisation specified in the application.

(7) person who makes an application for the variation of the conditions of an authorisation shall furnish the authority with such information as may be prescribed or as the authority may by notice require.

(8) On an application for variation of the conditions of an authorisation under any provision of this section—

(a) the enforcing authority may, having fulfilled the requirements of Part II of Schedule 1 to this Act in cases to which they apply, as it thinks fit either refuse the application or, subject to the requirements of section 7 above, vary the conditions or, in the case of an application under subsection (6) above, treat the application as a request for a determination under subsection (2) above; and

(b) if the enforcing authority decides to vary the conditions, it shall serve a variation notice on the holder of the authorisation.

[(9) Any application to the enforcing authority under this section shall be accompanied—

(a) in a case where the enforcing authority is the Environment Agency . . ., by the charge (if any) prescribed for the purpose by a charging scheme under section 41 of the Environment Act 1995; or

(b) in any other case, by the fee (if any) prescribed by a scheme under section 8 above.]

(10) This section applies to any provision other than a condition which is contained in an authorisation as it applies to a condition with the modification that any reference to the breach of a condition shall be read as a reference to acting outside the scope of the authorisation.

(11) For the purposes of this section a relevant change in a prescribed process is a change in the manner of carrying on the process which is capable of altering the substances released from the process or of affecting the amount or any other characteristic of any substance so released.

12 Revocation of authorisation

(1) The enforcing authority may at any time revoke an authorisation by notice in writing to the person holding the authorisation.

(2) Without prejudice to the generality of subsection (1) above, the enforcing authority may revoke an authorisation where it has reason to believe that a prescribed process for which the authorisation is in force has not been carried on or not for a period of twelve months.

(3) The revocation of an authorisation under this section shall have effect from the date specified in the notice; and the period between the date on which the notice is served and the date so specified shall not be less than twenty-eight days.

(4) The enforcing authority may, before the date on which the revocation of an authorisation takes effect, withdraw the notice or vary the date specified in it.

(5) The Secretary of State may, if he thinks fit in relation to an authorisation, give to the enforcing authority directions as to whether the authority should revoke the authorisation under this section.

13 Enforcement notices

(1) If the enforcing authority is of the opinion that the person carrying on a prescribed process under an authorisation is contravening any condition of the authorisation, or is likely to contravene any such condition, the authority may serve on him a notice ('an enforcement notice').

(2) An enforcement notice shall—

(a) state that the authority is of the said opinion;

(b) specify the matters constituting the contravention or the matters making it likely that the contravention will arise, as the case may be;

(c) specify the steps that must be taken to remedy the contravention or to remedy the matters making it likely that the contravention will arise, as the case may be; and

(d) specify the period within which those steps must be taken.

(3) The Secretary of State may, if he thinks fit in relation to the carrying on by any person of a prescribed process, give to the enforcing authority directions as to whether the authority should exercise its powers under this section and as to the steps which are to be required to be taken under this section.

[(4) The enforcing authority may, as respects any enforcement notice it has issued to any person, by notice in writing served on that person, withdraw the notice.]

14 Prohibition notices

(1) If the enforcing authority is of the opinion, as respects the carrying on of a prescribed process under an authorisation, that the continuing to carry it on, or the continuing to carry it on in a particular manner, involves an imminent risk of serious pollution of the environment the authority shall serve a notice (a 'prohibition notice') on the person carrying on the process.

(2) A prohibition notice may be served whether or not the manner of carrying on the process in question contravenes a condition of the authorisation and may relate to any aspects of the process, whether regulated by the conditions of the authorisation or not.

(3) A prohibition notice shall—

(a) state the authority's opinion;

(b) specify the risk involved in the process;

(c) specify the steps that must be taken to remove it and the period within which they must be taken; and

(d) direct that the authorisation shall, until the notice is withdrawn, wholly or to the extent specified in the notice cease to have effect to authorise the carrying on of the process;

and where the direction applies to part only of the process it may impose conditions to be observed in carrying on the part which is authorised to be carried on.

(4) The Secretary of State may, if he thinks fit in relation to the carrying on by any person of a prescribed process, give to the enforcing authority directions as to—

(a) whether the authority should perform its duties under this section; and

(b) the matters to be specified in any prohibition notice in pursuance of subsection (3) above which the authority is directed to issue.

(5) The enforcing authority shall, as respects any prohibition notice it has issued to any person, by notice in writing served on that person, withdraw the notice when it is satisfied that the steps required by the notice have been taken.

15 Appeals as respects authorisations and against variation, enforcement and prohibition notices

(1) The following persons, namely—

(a) a person who has been refused the grant of an authorisation under section 6 above;

(b) a person who is aggrieved by the conditions attached, under any provision of this Part, to his authorisation;

(c) a person who has been refused a variation of an authorisation on an application under section 11 above;

(d) a person whose authorisation has been revoked under section 12 above; may appeal against the decision of the enforcing authority to the Secretary of State (except where the decision implements a direction of his).

(2) A person on whom a variation notice, an enforcement notice or a prohibition notice is served may appeal against the notice to the Secretary of State [except where the notice implements a direction of his.]

[(3) This section is subject to section 114 of the Environment Act 1995 (delegation or reference of appeals etc).]

(4) An appeal under this section shall, if and to the extent required by regulations under subsection (10) below, be advertised in such manner as may be prescribed by regulations under that subsection.

[(5) Before determining an appeal under this section, the Secretary of State may, if he thinks fit—

(a)   cause the appeal to take or continue in the form of a hearing (which may, if the person hearing the appeal so decides, be held, or held to any extent, in private); or

(b)   cause a local inquiry to be held; and the Secretary of State shall act as mentioned in paragraph (a) or (b) above if a request is made by either party to the appeal to be heard with respect to the appeal.]

(6) On determining an appeal against a decision of an enforcing authority under subsection (1) above, the Secretary of State—

(a)   may affirm the decision;

(b)   where the decision was a refusal to grant an authorisation or a variation of an authorisation, may direct the enforcing authority to grant the authorisation or to vary the authorisation, as the case may be;

(c)   where the decision was as to the conditions attached to an authorisation, may quash all or any of the conditions of the authorisation;

(d)   where the decision was to revoke an authorisation, may quash the decision; and where he exercises any of the powers in paragraphs (b), (c) or (d) above, he may give directions as to the conditions to be attached to the authorisation.

(7) On the determination of an appeal under subsection (2) above the Secretary of State may either quash or affirm the notice and, if he affirms it, may do so either in its original form or with such modifications as he may in the circumstances think fit.

(8) Where an appeal is brought under subsection (1) above against the revocation of an authorisation, the revocation shall not take effect pending the final determination or the withdrawal of the appeal.

(9) Where an appeal is brought under subsection (2) above against a notice, the bringing of the appeal shall not have the effect of suspending the operation of the notice.

(10) Provision may be made by the Secretary of State by regulations with respect to appeals under this section and in particular—

(a)   as to the period within which and the manner in which appeals are to be brought; and

(b)   as to the manner in which appeals are to be considered

[and any such regulations may make different provision for different cases or different circumstances.]

19   Obtaining of information from persons and authorities

(1) For the purposes of the discharge of his functions under this Part, the Secretary of State may, by notice in writing served on an enforcing authority, require the authority to furnish such information about the discharge of its functions as an enforcing authority under this Part as he may require.

(2) For the purposes of the discharge of their respective functions under this Part, the following authorities, that is to say—

(a)   the Secretary of State,

(b)   a local enforcing authority,

(c)   [the Environment Agency, and]

(d)   . . .

may, by notice in writing served on any person, require that person to furnish to the authority such information which the authority reasonably considers that it needs as is specified in the notice, in such form and within such period following service of the notice [, or at such time,] as is so specified.

(3) For the purposes of this section the discharge by the Secretary of State of an obligation of the United Kingdom under the Community Treaties or any international agreement relating to environmental protection shall be treated as a function of his under this Part.

20   Public registers of information

(1) It shall be the duty of each enforcing authority, as respects prescribed processes for which it is the enforcing authority, to maintain, in accordance with regulations made by the Secretary of State, a register containing prescribed particulars of or relating to—

(a) applications for authorisations made to that authority;

(b) the authorisations which have been granted by that authority or in respect of which the authority has functions under this Part;

(c) variation notices, enforcement notices and prohibition notices issued by that authority;

(d) revocations of authorisations effected by that authority;

(e) appeals under section 15 above;

(f) convictions for such offences under section 23(1) below as may be prescribed;

(g) information obtained or furnished in pursuance of the conditions of authorisations or under any provision of this Part;

(h) directions given to the authority under any provision of this Part by the Secretary of State; and

(i) such other matters relating to the carrying on of prescribed processes or any pollution of the environment caused thereby as may be prescribed;

but that duty is subject to sections 21 and 22 below.

(2) Subject to subsection (4) below, the register maintained by a local enforcing authority [in England and Wales] shall also contain prescribed particulars of such information contained in any register maintained by [the Environment Agency] as relates to the carrying on in the area of the authority of prescribed processes in relation to which [the Environment Agency] has functions under this Part; and [the Environment Agency] shall furnish each authority with the particulars which are necessary to enable it to discharge its duty under this subsection.

(3) [. . .]

(4) Subsection (2) above does not apply to port health authorities but each local enforcing authority [in England and Wales] whose area adjoins that of a port health authority shall include corresponding information in the register maintained by it; and [the Environment Agency] shall furnish each such local enforcing authority with the particulars which are necessary to enable it to discharge its duty under this subsection.

(5) Where information of any description is excluded from any register by virtue of section 22 below, a statement shall be entered in the register indicating the existence of information of that description.

(6) The Secretary of State may give to enforcing authorities directions requiring the removal from any register of theirs of any specified information not prescribed for inclusion under subsection (1) or (2) above or which, by virtue of section 21 or 22 below, ought to have been excluded from the register.

(7) It shall be the duty of each enforcing authority—

(a) to secure that the registers maintained by them under this section are available, at all reasonable times, for inspection by the public free of charge; and

(b) to afford to members of the public facilities for obtaining copies of entries, on payment of reasonable charges

[and, for the purposes of this subsection, places may be prescribed by the Secretary of State at which any such registers or facilities as are mentioned in paragraph (a) or (b) above are to be available or afforded to the public in pursuance of the paragraph in question.]

(8) Registers under this section may be kept in any form.

(9) [. . .]

(10) In this section 'prescribed' means prescribed in regulations under this section.

21   Exclusion from registers of information affecting national security

(1) No information shall be included in a register maintained under section 20 above if and so long as, in the opinion of the Secretary of State, the inclusion in the register of that information, or information of that description, would be contrary to the interests of national security.

(2) The Secretary of State may, for the purpose of securing the exclusion from registers of information to which subsection (1) above applies, give to enforcing authorities directions—

(a) specifying information, or descriptions of information, to be excluded from their registers; or

(b) specifying descriptions of information to be referred to the Secretary of State for his determination;

and no information referred to the Secretary of State in pursuance of paragraph (b) above shall be included in any such register until the Secretary of State determines that it should be so included.

(3) The enforcing authority shall notify the Secretary of State of any information it excludes from the register in pursuance of directions under subsection (2) above.

(4) A person may, as respects any information which appears to him to be information to which subsection (1) above may apply, give a notice to the Secretary of State specifying the information and indicating its apparent nature; and, if he does so—

(a) he shall notify the enforcing authority that he has done so; and

(b) no information so notified to the Secretary of State shall be included in any such register until the Secretary of State has determined that it should be so included.

22   Exclusion from registers of certain confidential information

(1) No information relating to the affairs of any individual or business shall be included in a register maintained under section 20 above, without the consent of that individual or the person for the time being carrying on that business, if and so long as the information—

(a) is, in relation to him, commercially confidential; and

(b) is not required to be included in the register in pursuance of directions under subsection (7) below;

but information is not commercially confidential for the purposes of this section unless it is determined under this section to be so by the enforcing authority or, on appeal, by the Secretary of State.

(2) Where information is furnished to an enforcing authority for the purpose of—

(a) an application for an authorisation or for the variation of an authorisation;

(b) complying with any condition of an authorisation; or

(c) complying with a notice under section 19(2) above; then, if the person furnishing it applies to the authority to have the information excluded from the register on the ground that it is commercially confidential (as regards himself or another person), the authority shall determine whether the information is or is not commercially confidential.

(3) A determination under subsection (2) above must be made within the period of fourteen days beginning with the date of the application and if the enforcing authority fails to make a determination within that period it shall be treated as having determined that the information is commercially confidential.

(4) Where it appears to an enforcing authority that any information (other than information furnished in circumstances within subsection (2) above) which has been obtained

by the authority under or by virtue of any provision of this Part might be commercially confidential, the authority shall—

  (a) give to the person to whom or whose business it relates notice that that information is required to be included in the register unless excluded under this section; and

  (b) give him a reasonable opportunity—

   (i) of objecting to the inclusion of the information on the ground that it is commercially confidential; and

   (ii) of making representations to the authority for the purpose of justifying any such objection;

and, if any representations are made, the enforcing authority shall, having taken the representations into account, determine whether the information is or is not commercially confidential.

   (5) Where, under subsection (2) or (4) above, an authority determines that information is not commercially confidential—

  (a) the information shall not be entered [in the register] until the end of the period of twenty-one days beginning with the date on which the determination is notified to the person concerned;

  (b) that person may appeal to the Secretary of State against the decision; and, where an appeal is brought in respect of any information, the information shall not be entered [in the register until the end of the period of seven days following the day on which the appeal is finally determined or withdrawn.]

   [(6) Subsections (5) and (10) of section 15 above shall apply in relation to an appeal under subsection (5) above as they apply in relation to an appeal under that section, but—

  (a) subsection (5) of that section shall have effect for the purposes of this subsection with the substitution for the words from '(which may' onwards of the words '(which must be held in private)'; and

  (b) subsection (5) above is subject to section 114 of the Environment Act 1995 (delegation or reference of appeals etc).]

   (7) The Secretary of State may give to the enforcing authorities directions as to specified information, or descriptions of information, which the public interest requires to be included in registers maintained under section 20 above notwithstanding that the information may be commercially confidential.

   (8) Information excluded from a register shall be treated as ceasing to be commercially confidential for the purposes of this section at the expiry of the period of four years beginning with the date of the determination by virtue of which it was excluded; but the person who furnished it may apply to the authority for the information to remain excluded from the register on the ground that it is still commercially confidential and the authority shall determine whether or not that is the case.

   (9) Subsections (5) and (6) above shall apply in relation to a determination under subsection (8) above as they apply in relation to a determination under subsection (2) or (4) above.

   (10) The Secretary of State may, by order, substitute for the period for the time being specified in subsection (3) above such other period as he considers appropriate.

   (11) Information is, for the purposes of any determination under this section, commercially confidential, in relation to any individual or person, if its being contained in the register would prejudice to an unreasonable degree the commercial interests of that individual or person.

23 Offences

   (1) It is an offence for a person—

  (a) to contravene section 6(1) above;

  (b) to fail to give the notice required by section 9(2) above;

(c) to fail to comply with or contravene any requirement or prohibition imposed by an enforcement notice or a prohibition notice;

(d) [. . .]

(e) [. . .]

(f) [. . .]

(g) to fail, without reasonable excuse, to comply with any requirement imposed by a notice under section 19(2) above;

(h) to make a statement which he knows to be false or misleading in a material particular, or recklessly to make a statement which is false or misleading in a material particular, where the statement is made—

    (i) in purported compliance with a requirement to furnish any information imposed by or under any provision of this Part; or

    (ii) for the purpose of obtaining the grant of an authorisation to himself or any other person or the variation of an authorisation;

(i) intentionally to make a false entry in any record required to be kept under section 7 above;

(j) with intent to deceive, to forge or use a document issued or authorised to be issued under section 7 above or required for any purpose thereunder or to make or have in his possession a document so closely resembling any such document as to be likely to deceive;

(k) [. . .]

(l) to fail to comply with an order made by a court under section 26 below.

(2) A person guilty of an offence under paragraph (a), (c) or (l) of subsection (1) above shall be liable:

(a) on summary conviction, to a fine not exceeding £20,000 [or to imprisonment for a term not exceeding three months, or to both.]

(b) on conviction on indictment, to a fine or to imprisonment for a term not exceeding two years, or to both.

(3) A person guilty of an offence under paragraph (b), (g), (h), (i) or (j) of subsection (1) above shall be liable—

(a) on summary conviction, to a fine not exceeding the statutory maximum;

(b) on conviction on indictment, to a fine or to imprisonment for a term not exceeding two years, or to both.

(4) [. . .]

(5) [. . .]

24 Enforcement by High Court

If the enforcing authority is of the opinion that proceedings for an offence under section 23(1)(c) above would afford an ineffectual remedy against a person who has failed to comply with the requirements of an enforcement notice or a prohibition notice, the authority may take proceedings in the High Court . . . for the purpose of securing compliance with the notice.

25 Onus of proof as regards techniques and evidence

(1) In any proceedings for an offence under section 23(1)(a) above consisting in a failure to comply with the general condition implied in every authorisation by section 7(4) above, it shall be for the accused to prove that there was no better available technique not entailing excessive cost than was in fact used to satisfy the condition.

(2) Where—

(a) an entry is required under section 7 above to be made in any record as to the observance of any condition of an authorisation; and

(b) the entry has not been made; that fact shall be admissible as evidence that that condition has not been observed.

[(3) Subsection (2) above shall not have effect in relation to any entry required to be made in any record by virtue of a condition of a relevant licence, within the meaning of section 111 of the Environment Act 1995 (which makes corresponding provision in relation to such licences).]

26 Power of court to order cause of offence to be remedied

(1) Where a person is convicted of an offence under section 23(1)(a) or (c) above in respect of any matters which appear to the court to be matters which it is in his power to remedy, the court may, in addition to or instead of imposing any punishment, order him, within such time as may be fixed by the order, to take such steps as may be specified in the order for remedying those matters.

(2) The time fixed by an order under subsection (1) above may be extended or further extended by order of the court on an application made before the end of the time as originally fixed or as extended under this subsection, as the case may be.

(3) Where a person is ordered under subsection (1) above to remedy any matters, that person shall not be liable under section 23 above in respect of those matters in so far as they continue during the time fixed by the order or any further time allowed under subsection (2) above.

27 Power of chief inspector to remedy harm

(1) Where the commission of an offence under section 23(1)(a) or (c) above causes any harm which it is possible to remedy, [the appropriate Agency] may, subject to subsection (2) below—

(a) arrange for any reasonable steps to be taken towards remedying the harm; and

(b) recover the cost of taking those steps from any person convicted of that offence.

(2) [The Environment Agency . . . shall not exercise its] powers under this section except with the approval in writing of the Secretary of State and, where any of the steps are to be taken on or will affect land in the occupation of any person other than the person on whose land the prescribed process is being carried on, with the permission of that person.

28 Authorisations and other statutory controls

(1) No condition shall at any time be attached to an authorisation so as to regulate the final disposal by deposit in or on land of controlled waste (within the meaning of Part II), nor shall any condition apply to such a disposal; [. . .]

(2) Where any of the activities comprising a prescribed process are regulated both by an authorisation granted by the enforcing authority under this Part and by a registration or authorisation under the Radioactive Substances Act 1960, then, if different obligations are imposed as respects the same matter by a condition attached to the authorisation under this Part and a condition attached to the registration or authorisation under that Act, the condition imposed by the authorisation under this Part shall be treated as not binding the person carrying on the process.

(3) [. . .]

(4) [. . .]

PART II   WASTE ON LAND

29 Preliminary

(1) The following provisions have effect for the interpretation of this Part.

(2) The 'environment' consists of all, or any, of the following media, namely land, water and the air.

(3) 'Pollution of the environment' means pollution of the environment due to the release or escape (into any environmental medium) from—

(a) the land on which controlled waste is treated,

(b) the land on which controlled waste is kept,

(c) the land in or on which controlled waste is deposited,

(d) fixed plant by means of which controlled waste is treated, kept or disposed of,

of substances or articles constituting or resulting from the waste and capable (by reason of the quantity or concentrations involved) of causing harm to man or any other living organisms supported by the environment.

(4) Subsection (3) above applies in relation to mobile plant by means of which controlled waste is treated or disposed of as it applies to plant on land by means of which controlled waste is treated or disposed of.

(5) For the purposes of subsections (3) and (4) above 'harm' means harm to the health of living organisms or other interference with the ecological systems of which they form part and in the case of man includes offence to any of his senses or harm to his property; and 'harmless' has a corresponding meaning.

(6) The 'disposal' of waste includes its disposal by way of deposit in or on land and, subject to subsection (7) below, waste is 'treated' when it is subjected to any process, including making it re-usable or reclaiming substances from it and 'recycle' (and cognate expressions) shall be construed accordingly.

(7) Regulations made by the Secretary of State may prescribe activities as activities which constitute the treatment of waste for the purposes of this Part or any provision of this Part prescribed in the regulations.

(8) 'Land' includes land covered by waters where the land is above the low water mark of ordinary spring tides and references to land on which controlled waste is treated, kept or deposited are references to the surface of the land (including any structure set into the surface).

(9) 'Mobile plant' means, subject to subsection (10) below, plant which is designed to move or be moved whether on roads or other land.

(10) Regulations made by the Secretary of State may prescribe descriptions of plant which are to be treated as being, or as not being, mobile plant for the purposes of this Part.

(11) 'Substance' means any natural or artificial substance, whether in solid or liquid form or in the form of a gas or vapour.

30   Authorities for purposes of this Part

[(1) Any reference in this Part to a waste regulation authority—

(a) in relation to England and Wales, is a reference to the Environment Agency; and

(b) . . .

and any reference in this Part to the area of a waste regulation authority shall accordingly be taken as a reference to the area over which the Environment Agency . . . exercises its functions or, in the case of any particular function, the function in question.]

(2) For the purposes of this Part the following authorities are waste disposal authorities, namely—

(a) for any non-metropolitan county in England, the county council;

(b) in Greater London, the following—

(i) for the area of a London waste disposal authority, the authority constituted as the waste disposal authority for that area;

(ii) for the City of London, the Common Council;

(iii) for any other London borough, the council of the borough;

(c) in the metropolitan county of Greater Manchester, the following—

(i) for the metropolitan district of Wigan, the district council;

(ii) for all other areas in the county, the authority constituted as the Greater Manchester Waste Disposal Authority;

(d) for the metropolitan county of Merseyside, the authority constituted as the Merseyside Waste Disposal Authority;

(e) for any district in any other metropolitan county in England, the council of the district;

(f) for any district in Wales, the council of the district;

(g) ...

(3) For the purposes of this Part the following authorities are waste collection authorities—

(a) for any district in England and Wales not within Greater London, the council of the district;

(b) in Greater London, the following—

(i) for any London borough, the council of the borough;

(ii) for the City of London, the Common Council;

(iii) for the Temples, the Sub-Treasurer of the Inner Temple and the Under Treasurer of the Middle Temple respectively;

(c) ...

(4) In this section references to particular authorities having been constituted as waste disposal [. . .] or regulation authorities are references to their having been so constituted by the Waste Regulation and Disposal (Authorities) Order 1985 made by the Secretary of State under section 10 of the Local Government Act 1985 and the reference to London waste disposal authorities is a reference to the authorities named in Parts I, II, III, IV and V of Schedule 1 to that Order and this section has effect subject to any order made under the said section 10 [. . .].

(5) In this Part 'waste disposal contractor' means a person who in the course of a business collects, keeps, treats or disposes of waste, being either—

(a) a company formed for all or any of those purposes by a waste disposal authority whether in pursuance of section 32 below or otherwise; or

(b) either a company formed for all or any of those purposes by other persons or a partnership or an individual;

and 'company' has the same meaning as in the Companies Act 1985 and 'formed', in relation to a company formed by other persons, includes the alteration of the objects of the company.

(6) [. . .]

(7) [. . .]

(8) [. . .]

32 Transition to waste disposal companies etc

(1) In this section 'existing disposal authority' means any authority (including any joint authority) constituted as a waste disposal authority for any area before the day appointed for this section to come into force.

(2) The Secretary of State shall, subject to subsection (3) below, give directions to existing disposal authorities or, in the case of joint authorities, to the constituent authorities requiring them, before specified dates, to—

(a) form or participate in forming waste disposal companies; and

(b) transfer to the companies so formed, by and in accordance with a scheme made in accordance with Schedule 2 to this Act, the relevant part of their undertakings;

and a waste disposal authority shall accordingly have power to form, and hold securities in, any company so established.

(3) Subject to subsection (4) below, the Secretary of State shall not give any direction under subsection (2) above to an existing disposal authority, or to the constituent authorities of an existing disposal authority, as respects which or each of which he is satisfied that the authority—

(a) has formed or participated in forming a waste disposal company and transferred to it the relevant part of its undertaking;

(b) has, in pursuance of arrangements made with other persons, ceased to carry on itself the relevant part of its undertaking;

(c) has made arrangements with other persons to cease to carry on itself the relevant part of its undertaking; or

(d) has, in pursuance of arrangements made with other persons, ceased to provide places at which and plant and equipment by means of which controlled waste can be disposed of or deposited for the purposes of disposal.

(4) Subsection (3) above does not apply in a case falling within paragraph (a) unless it appears to the Secretary of State that—

(a) the form of the company and the undertaking transferred are satisfactory; and

(b) the requirements of subsections (8) and (9) below are fulfilled; and 'satisfactory' means satisfactory by reference to the corresponding arrangements to which he would give his approval for the purposes of a transfer scheme under Schedule 2 to this Act.

(5) Where the Secretary of State is precluded from giving a direction under subsection (2) above to any authority by reason of his being satisfied as to the arrangements mentioned in subsection (3)(c) above, then, if those arrangements are not implemented within what appears to him to be a reasonable time, he may exercise his power to give directions under subsection (2) above as respects that authority.

(6) Part I of Schedule 2 to this Act has effect for the purposes of this section and Part II for regulating the functions of waste disposal authorities and the activities of waste disposal contractors.

(7) Subject to subsection (8) below, the activities of a company which a waste disposal authority has formed or participated in forming (whether in pursuance of subsection (2)(a) above or otherwise) may include activities which are beyond the powers of the authority to carry on itself, but, in the case of a company formed otherwise than in pursuance of subsection (2)(a) above, only if the Secretary of State has determined under subsection (4)(a) above that the form of the company and the undertaking transferred to it are satisfactory.

(8) A waste disposal authority shall, for so long as it controls a company which it has formed or participated in forming (whether in pursuance of subsection (2)(a) above or otherwise), so exercise its control as to secure that the company does not engage in activities other than the following activities or any activities incidental or conducive to, or calculated to facilitate, them, that is to say, the disposal, keeping or treatment of waste and the collection of waste.

(9) Subject to subsection (10) below, a waste disposal authority shall, for so long as it controls a company which it has formed or participated in forming (whether in pursuance of subsection (2)(a) above or otherwise), so exercise its control as to secure that, for the purposes of Part V of the Local Government and Housing Act 1989, the company is an arm's length company.

(10) Subsection (9) above shall not apply in the case of a company which a waste disposal authority has formed or participated in forming in pursuance of subsection (2)(a) above until after the vesting date for that company.

(11) In this section and Schedule 2 to this Act—

'control' (and cognate expressions) is to be construed in accordance with section 68 or, as the case requires, section 73 of the Local Government and Housing Act 1989;

'the relevant part' of the undertaking of an existing disposal authority is that part which relates to the disposal, keeping or treatment or the collection of waste;

and in this section 'securities' and 'vesting date' have the same meaning as in Schedule 2.

(12) . . .

33   Prohibition on unauthorised or harmful deposit, treatment or disposal etc. of waste

(1) Subject to subsection (2) and (3) below . . . a person shall not—

  (a) deposit controlled waste, or knowingly cause or knowingly permit controlled waste to be deposited in or on any land unless a waste management licence authorising the deposit is in force and the deposit is in accordance with the licence;

  (b) treat, keep or dispose of controlled waste, or knowingly cause or knowingly permit controlled waste to be treated, kept or disposed of—

  (i) in or on any land, or

  (ii) by means of any mobile plant, except under and in accordance with a waste management licence;

  (c) treat, keep or dispose of controlled waste in a manner likely to cause pollution of the environment or harm to human health.

(2) Subsection (1) above does not apply in relation to household waste from a domestic property which is treated, kept or disposed of within the curtilage of the dwelling by or with the permission of the occupier of the dwelling.

(3) Subsection (1)(a), (b) or (c) above do not apply in cases prescribed in regulations made by the Secretary of State and the regulations may make different exceptions for different areas.

(4) The Secretary of State, in exercising his power under subsection (3) above, shall have regard in particular to the expediency of excluding from the controls imposed by waste management licences—

  (a) any deposits which are small enough or of such a temporary nature that they may be so excluded;

  (b) any means of treatment or disposal which are innocuous enough to be so excluded;

  (c) cases for which adequate controls are provided by another enactment than this section.

(5) Where controlled waste is carried in and deposited from a motor vehicle, the person who controls or is in a position to control the use of the vehicle shall, for the purposes of subsection (1)(a) above, be treated as knowingly causing the waste to be deposited whether or not he gave any instructions for this to be done.

(6) A person who contravenes subsection (1) above or any condition of a waste management licence commits an offence.

(7) It shall be a defence for a person charged with an offence under this section to prove—

  (a) that he took all reasonable precautions and exercised all due diligence to avoid the commission of the offence; or

  (b) that he acted under instructions from his employer and neither knew nor had reason to suppose that the acts done by him constituted a contravention of subsection (1) above; or

  [(c) that the acts alleged to constitute the contravention were done in an emergency in order to avoid danger to human health in a case where—

  (i) he took all such steps as were reasonably practicable in the circumstances for minimising pollution of the environment and harm to human health; and

  (ii) particulars of the acts were furnished to the waste regulation authority as soon as reasonably practicable after they were done.]

(8) Except in a case falling within subsection (9) below, a person who commits an offence under this section shall be liable—

  (a) on summary conviction, to imprisonment for a term not exceeding six months or a fine not exceeding £20,000 or both; and

(b) on conviction on indictment, to imprisonment for a term not exceeding two years or a fine or both.

(9) A person who commits an offence under this section in relation to special waste shall be liable—

(a) on summary conviction, to imprisonment for a term not exceeding six months or a fine not exceeding £20,000 or both;

(b) on conviction on indictment, to imprisonment for a term not exceeding five years or a fine or both.

34 Duty of care etc. as respects waste

(1) Subject to subsection (2) below, it shall be the duty of any person who imports, produces, carries, keeps, treats or disposes of controlled waste or, as a broker, has control of such waste, to take all such measures applicable to him in that capacity as are reasonable in the circumstances—

(a) to prevent any contravention by any other person of section 33 above;

[(aa) to prevent any contravention by any other person of regulation 9 of the Pollution Prevention and Control (England and Wales) Regulations 2000 or of a condition of a permit granted under regulation 10 of those Regulations;]

(b) to prevent the escape of the waste from his control or that of any other person; and

(c) on the transfer of the waste, to secure—

(i) that the transfer is only to an authorised person or to a person for authorised transport purposes; and

(ii) that there is transferred such a written description of the waste as will enable other persons to avoid a contravention of that section [or any condition of a permit granted under regulation 10 of those Regulations] and to comply with the duty under this subsection as respects the escape of waste.

(2) The duty imposed by subsection (1) above does not apply to an occupier of domestic property as respects the household waste produced on the property.

(3) The following are authorised persons for the purpose of subsection (1)(c) above—

(a) any authority which is a waste collection authority for the purposes of this Part;

(b) any person who is the holder of a waste management licence under section 35 below [. . .]

(c) any person to whom section 33(1) above does not apply by virtue of regulations under subsection (3) of that section;

(d) any person registered as a carrier of controlled waste under section 2 of the Control of Pollution (Amendment) Act 1989;

(e) any person who is not required to be so registered by virtue of regulations under section 1(3) of that Act; and

(f) . . .

[(3A) The Secretary of State may by regulations amend subsection (3) above so as to add, whether generally or in such circumstances as may be prescribed in the regulations, any person specified in the regulations, or any description of person so specified, to the persons who are authorised persons for the purposes of subsection (1)(c) above.]

(4) The following are authorised transport purposes for the purposes of subsection (1)(c) above—

(a) the transport of controlled waste within the same premises between different places in those premises;

(b) the transport to a place in Great Britain of controlled waste which has been brought from a country or territory outside Great Britain not having been landed in Great Britain until it arrives at that place; and

(c) the transport by air or sea of controlled waste from a place in Great Britain to a place outside Great Britain;

and 'transport' has the same meaning in this subsection as in the Control of Pollution (Amendment) Act 1989.

[(4A) For the purposes of subsection (1)(c)(ii) above—

(a) a transfer of waste in stages shall be treated as taking place when the first stage of the transfer takes place, and

(b) a series of transfers between the same parties of waste of the same description shall be treated as a single transfer taking place when the first of the transfers in the series takes place.]

(5) The Secretary of State may, by regulations, make provision imposing requirements on any person who is subject to the duty imposed by subsection (1) above as respects the making and retention of documents and the furnishing of documents or copies of documents.

(6) Any person who fails to comply with the duty imposed by subsection (1) above or with any requirement imposed under subsection (5) above shall be liable—

(a) on summary conviction, to a fine not exceeding the statutory maximum; and

(b) on conviction on indictment, to a fine.

(7) The Secretary of State shall, after consultation with such persons or bodies as appear to him representative of the interests concerned, prepare and issue a code of practice for the purpose of providing to persons practical guidance on how to discharge the duty imposed on them by subsection (1) above.

(8) The Secretary of State may from time to time revise a code of practice issued under subsection (7) above by revoking, amending or adding to the provisions of the code.

(9) The code of practice prepared in pursuance of subsection (7) above shall be laid before both Houses of Parliament.

(10) A code of practice issued under subsection (7) above shall be admissible in evidence and if any provision of such a code appears to the court to be relevant to any question arising in the proceedings it shall be taken into account in determining that question.

(11) Different codes of practice may be prepared and issued under subsection (7) above for different areas.

35   Waste management licences: general

(1) A waste management licence is a licence granted by a waste regulation authority authorising the treatment, keeping or disposal of any specified description of controlled waste in or on specified land or the treatment or disposal of any specified description of controlled waste by means of specified mobile plant.

(2) A licence shall be granted to the following person, that is to say—

(a) in the case of a licence relating to the treatment, keeping or disposal of waste in or on land, to the person who is in occupation of the land; and

(b) in the case of a licence relating to the treatment or disposal of waste by means of mobile plant, to the person who operates the plant.

(3) A licence shall be granted on such terms and subject to such conditions as appear to the waste regulation authority to be appropriate and the conditions may relate—

(a) to the activities which the licence authorises, and

(b) to the precautions to be taken and works to be carried out in connection with or in consequence of those activities:

and accordingly requirements may be imposed in the licence which are to be complied with before the activities which the licence authorises have begun or after the activities which the licence authorises have ceased.

(4) Conditions may require the holder of a licence to carry out works or do other things notwithstanding that he is not entitled to carry out the works or do the thing and any person

whose consent would be required shall grant, or join in granting, the holder of the licence such rights in relation to the land as will enable the holder of the licence to comply with any requirements imposed on him by the licence.

(5) Conditions may relate, where waste other than controlled waste is to be treated, kept or disposed of, to the treatment, keeping or disposal of that other waste.

(6) The Secretary of State may, by regulations, make provision as to the conditions which are, or are not, to be included in a licence; and regulations under this subsection may make different provision for different circumstances.

(7) The Secretary of State may, as respects any licence for which an application is made to a waste regulation authority, give to the authority directions as to the terms and conditions which are, or are not, to be included in the licence; and it shall be the duty of the authority to give effect to the directions.

[(7A) In any case where—

    (a) an entry is required under this section to be made in any record as to the observance of any condition of a licence, and

    (b) the entry has not been made, that fact shall be admissible as evidence that that condition has not been observed.

(7B) Any person who—

    (a) intentionally makes a false entry in any record required to be kept under any condition of a licence, or

    (b) with intent to deceive, forges or uses a licence or makes or has in his possession a document so closely resembling a licence as to be likely to deceive, shall be guilty of an offence.

(7C) A person guilty of an offence under subsection (7B) above shall be liable— (a) on summary conviction, to a fine not exceeding the statutory maximum;

    (b) on conviction on indictment, to a fine or to imprisonment for a term not exceeding two years, or to both.]

(8) It shall be the duty of waste regulation authorities to have regard to any guidance issued to them by the Secretary of State with respect to the discharge of their functions in relation to licences.

(9) A licence may not be surrendered by the holder except in accordance with section 39 below.

(10) A licence is not transferable by the holder but the waste regulation authority may transfer it to another person under section 40 below.

(11) A licence shall continue in force until [it ceases to have effect under subsection (11A) below,] it is revoked entirely by the waste regulation authority under section 38 below or it is surrendered or its surrender is accepted under section 39 below.

[(11A) A licence shall cease to have effect if and to the extent that the treatment, keeping or disposal of waste authorised by the licence is authorised by a permit granted under regulations under section 2 of the Pollution Prevention and Control Act 1999.]

(12) In this Part 'licence' means a waste management licence and 'site licence' and 'mobile plant licence' mean, respectively, a licence authorising the treatment, keeping or disposal of waste in or on land and a licence authorising the treatment or disposal of waste by means of mobile plant.

[35A   Compensation where rights granted pursuant to section 35(4) or 38(9A)

(1) This section applies in any case where—

    (a) the holder of a licence is required—

        (i) by the conditions of the licence; or

        (ii) by a requirement imposed under section 38(9) below, to carry out any works or do any other thing which he is not entitled to carry out or do;

    (b) a person whose consent would be required has, pursuant to the requirements of section 35(4) above or 38(9A) below, granted, or joined in granting, to the holder of the licence any rights in relation to any land; and

(c) those rights, or those rights together with other rights, are such as will enable the holder of the licence to comply with any requirements imposed on him by the licence or, as the case may be, under section 38(9) below.

(2) In a case where this section applies, any person who has granted, or joined in granting, the rights in question shall be entitled to be paid compensation under this section by the holder of the licence.

(3) The Secretary of State shall by regulations provide for the discriptions of loss and damage for which compensation is payable under this section.

(4) The Secretary of State may by regulations—

(a) provide for the basis on which any amount to be paid by way of compensation under this section is to be assessed;

(b) without prejudice to the generality of subsection (3) and paragraph (a) above provide for compensation under this section to be payable in respect of—
    (i) any effect of any rights being granted, or
    (ii) any consequence of the exercise of any rights which have been granted;

(c) provide for the times at which any entitlement to compensation under this secton is to arise or at which any such compensation is to become payable;

(d) provide for the persons or bodies by whom, and the manner in which, any dispute—
    (i) as to whether any, and (if so) how much and when, compensation under this section is payable; or
    (ii) as to the person to or by whom it shall be paid, is to be determined;

(e) provide for when or how applications may be made for compensation under this section;

(f) without prejudice to the generality of pargraph (d) above, provide for when or how applications may be made for the determination of any such disputes as are mentioned in that paragraph;

(g) without prejudice to the generality of paragraphs (e) and (f) above, prescribe the form in which any such applications as are mentioned in those paragraphs are to be made;

(h) make provision similar to any provision made by paragraph 8 or Schedule 19 to the Water Resources Act 1991;

(j) make different provision for different cases, including different provision in relation to different persons or circumstances;

(k) include such incidental, supplemental, consequential or transitional provision as the Secretary of State considers appropriate.]

36 Grant of licences

(1) An application for a licence shall be made—

(a) in the case of an application for a site licence, to the waste regulation authority in whose area the land is situated; and

(b) in the case of an application for a mobile plant licence, to the waste regulation authority in whose area the operator of the plant has his principal place of business; [and shall be made on a form provided for the purpose by the waste regulation authority and accompanied by such information as that authority reasonably requires and the charge prescribed for the purpose by a charging scheme under section 41 of the Environment Act 1995.

(1A) Where an applicant for a licence fails to provide the waste regulation authority with any information required under subsection (1) above, the authority may refuse to proceed with the application, or refuse to proceed with it until the information is provided.]

(2) A licence shall not be issued for a use of land for which planning permission is required in pursuance of the Town and Country Planning Act 1990 . . . unless—

(a) such planning permission is in force in relation to that use of the land, or
(b) an established use certificate is in force under section 192 of the said Act of 1990 . . . in relation to that use of the land.

(3) Subject to subsection (2) above and subsection (4) below, a waste regulation authority to which an application for a licence has been duly made shall not reject the application if it is satisfied that the applicant is a fit and proper person unless it is satisfied that its rejection is necessary for the purpose of preventing—

(a) pollution of the environment;
(b) harm to human health; or
(c) serious detriment to the amenities of the locality; but paragraph (c) above is inapplicable where planning permission is in force in relation to the use to which the land will be put under the licence.

(4) Where the waste regulation authority proposes to issue a licence, the authority must, before it does so—

(a) refer the proposal to [the appropriate planning authority] and the Health and Safety Executive; and
(b) consider any representations about the proposal which the [authority] or the Executive makes to it during the allowed period.

(5) [. . .]
(6) [. . .]
(7) Where any part of the land to be used is land which has been notified under section 28(1) of the Wildlife and Countryside Act 1981 (protection for certain areas) and the waste regulation authority proposes to issue a licence, the authority must, before it does so—

(a) refer the proposal to the appropriate nature conservation body; and
(b) consider any representations about the proposal which the body makes to it during the allowed period;

and in this section any reference to the appropriate nature conservation body is a reference to the Nature Conservancy Council for England . . . or the Countryside Council for Wales, according as the land is situated in England . . . or Wales.

(8) [. . .]
(9) If within the period of four months beginning with the date on which a waste regulation authority received an application for the grant of a licence, or within such longer period as the authority and the applicant may at any time agree in writing, the authority has neither granted the licence in consequence of the application nor given notice to the applicant that the authority has rejected the application, the authority shall be deemed to have rejected the application.

[(9A) Subsection (9) above—

(a) shall not have effect in any case where, by virtue of subsection (1A) above, the waste regulation authority refuses to proceed with the application in question, and
(b) shall have effect in any case where, by virtue of subsection (1A) above, the waste regulation authority refuses to proceed with it until the required information is provided, with the substitution for the period of four months there mentioned of the period of four months beginning with the date on which the authority received the information.

(10) The period allowed to the appropriate planning authority, the Health and Safety Executive or the appropriate nature conservancy body for the making of representations under subsection (4) or (7) above about a proposal is the period of twenty-eight days beginning with the day on which the proposal is received by the waste regulation authority or

such longer period as the waste regulation authority, the appropriate planning authority, the Executive or the body, as the case may be, agree in writing.

(11) In this section—

'the appropriate planning authority' means—

    (a) where the relevant land is situated in the area of a London borough council, that London borough council;

    (b) where the relevant land is situated in the City of London, the Common Council of the City of London;

    (c) where the relevant land is situated in a non-metropolitan county in England, the council of that county;

    (d) where the relevant land is situated in a National Park or the Broads, the National Park authority for that National Park or, as the case may be, the Broads Authority;

    (e) where the relevant land is situated elsewhere in England or Wales, the council of the district or, in Wales, the county or county borough, in which the land is situated;

    (f) . . .

'the Broads' has the same meaning as in the Norfolk and Suffolk Broads Act 1988;

'National Park authority', [. . .] means a National Park authority established under section 63 of the Environment Act 1995 which has become the local planning authority for the National Park in question;

'the relevant land' means—

    (a) in relation to a site licence, the land to which the licence relates; and

    (b) in relation to a mobile plant licence, the principal place of business of the operator of the plant to which the licence relates.

(12) [. . .]

(13) The Secretary of State may by regulations amend the definition of 'appropriate planning authority" in subsection (11) above.

(14) This section shall have effect subject to section 36A below.]

[36A   Consultation before the grant of certain licences

(1) This section applies where an application for a licence has been duly made to a waste regulation authority, and the authority proposes to issue a licence subject (by virtue of section 35(4) above) to any condition which might require the holder of the licence to—

    (a) carry out any works, or

    (b) do any other thing, which he might not be entitled to carry out or do.

(2) Before issuing the licence, the waste regulation authority shall serve on every person appearing to the authority to be a person failing within subsection (3) below a notice which complies with the requirements set out in subsection (4) below.

(3) A person falls within this subsection if—

    (a) he is the owner, lessee or occupier of any land; and

    (b) that land is land in relation to which it is likely that, as a consequence of the licence being issued subject to the condition in question, rights will have to be granted by virtue of section 35(4) above to the holder of the licence.

(4) A notice served under subsection (2) above shall—

    (a) set out the condition in question;

    (b) indicate the nature of the works or other things which that condition might require the holder of the licence to carry out or do; and

    (c) specify the date by which, and the manner in which, any representations relating to the condition or its possible effects are to be made to the waste regulation authority by the person on whom the notice is served.

(5) The date which, pursuant to subsection (4)(c) above, is specified in a notice shall be a date not earlier than the date on which expires the period—

    (a) beginning with the date on which the notice is served, and

    (b) of such length as may be prescribed in regulations made by the Secretary of State.

(6) Before the waste regulation authority issues the licence it must, subject to subsection (7) below, consider any representations made in relation to the condition in question, or its possible effects, by any person on whom a notice has been served under subsection (2) above.

(7) Subsection (6) above does not require the waste regulation authority to consider any representations made by a person after the date specified in the notice served on him under subsection (2) above as the date by which his representations in relation to the condition or its possible effects are to be made.

(8) In subsection (3) above

'owner', in relation to any land in England and Wales, means the person who—

    (a) is for the time being receiving the rack-rent of the land, whether on his own account or as agent or trustee for another person; or

    (b) would receive the rack-rent if the land were let at a rack-rent, but does not include a mortgagee not in possession; and

  . . .]

37 Variation of licences

(1) While a licence issued by a waste regulation authority is in force, the authority may, subject to regulations under section 35(6) above and to subsection (3) below,—

    (a) on its own initiative, modify the conditions of the licence to any extent which, in the opinion of the authority, is desirable and is unlikely to require unreasonable expense on the part of the holder; and

    (b) on the application of the licence holder accompanied by [the charge prescribed for the purpose by a charging scheme under section 41 of the Environment Act 1995,] modify the conditions of his licence to the extent requested in the application.

(2) While a licence issued by a waste regulation authority is in force, the authority shall, except where it revokes the licence entirely under section 38 below, modify the conditions of the licence—

    (a) to the extent which in the opinion of the authority is required for the purpose of ensuring that the activities authorised by the licence do not cause pollution of the environment or harm to human health or become seriously detrimental to the amenities of the locality affected by the activities; and

    (b) to the extent required by any regulations in force under section 35(6) above.

(3) The Secretary of State may, as respects any licence issued by a waste regulation authority, give to the authority directions as to the modifications which are to be made in the conditions of the licence under subsection (1)(a) or (2)(a) above; and it shall be the duty of the authority to give effect to the directions.

(4) Any modification of a licence under this section shall be effected by notice served on the holder of the licence and the notice shall state the time at which the modification is to take effect.

(5) Section 36(4), [. . .] (7), [. . .] and (10) above shall with the necessary modifications apply to a proposal by a waste regulation authority to modify a licence under subsection (1) or (2)(a) above as they apply to a proposal to issue a licence, except that—

    (a) the authority may postpone the reference so far as the authority considers that by reason of an emergency it is appropriate to do so; and

    (b) the authority need not consider any representations as respects a modification which, in the opinion of the waste regulation authority, will not affect any authority mentioned in the subsections so applied.

(6) If within the period of two months beginning with the date on which a waste regulation authority received an application by the holder of a licence for a modification of it, or within such longer period as the authority and the applicant may at any time agree in writing, the authority has neither granted a modification of the licence in consequence of the application nor given notice to the applicant that the authority has rejected the application, the authority shall be deemed to have rejected the application.

[(7) This section shall have effect subject to section 37A below.]

[37A   Consultation before certain variations

(1) This section applies where—

(a) a waste regulation authority proposes to modify a licence under section 37(1) or (2)(a) above; and

(b) the licence, if modified as proposed, would be subject to a relevant new condition.

(2) For the purposes of this section, a 'relevant new condition' is any condition by virtue of which the holder of the licence might be required to carry out any works or do any other thing—

(a) which he might not be entitled to carry out or do, and

(b) which he could not be required to carry out or do by virtue of the conditions to which, prior to the modification, the licence is subject.

(3) Before modifying the licence, the waste regulation authority shall serve on every person appearing to the authority to be a person failing within subsection (4) below a notice which complies with the requirements set out in subsection (5) below.

(4) A person falls within this subsection if—

(a) he is the owner, lessee or occupier of any land; and

(b) that land is land in relation to which it is likely that, as a consequence of the licence being modified so as to be subject to the relevant new condition in question, rights will have to be granted by virtue of section 35(4) above to the holder of the licence.

(5) A notice served under subsection (3) above shall—

(a) set out the relevant new condition in question;

(b) indicate the nature of the works or other things which that condition might require the holder of the licence to carry out or do but which he could not be required to carry out or do by virtue of the conditions (if any) to which, prior to the modification, the licence is subject; and

(c) specify the date by which, and the manner in which, any representations relating to the condition or its possible effects are to be made to the waste regulation authority by the person on whom the notice is served.

(6) The date which, pursuant to subsection (5)(c) above, is specified in a notice shall be a date not earlier than the date on which expires the period—

(a) beginning with the date on which the notice is served, and

(b) of such length as may be prescribed in regulations made by the Secretary of State.

(7) Before the waste regulation authority issues the licence it must, subject to subsection (8) below, consider any representations made in relation to the condition in question, or its possible effects, by any person on whom a notice has been served under subsection (3) above.

(8) Subsection (7) above does not require the waste regulation authority to consider any representations made by a person after the date specified in the notice served on him under subsection (3) above as the date by which his representations in relation to the condition or its possible effects are to be made.

(9) A waste regulation authority may postpone the service of any notice or the consideration of any representations required under the foregoing provisions of this section so far as the authority considers that by reason of an emergency it is appropriate to do so.

(10) In subsection (3) above, 'owner' has the same meaning as it has in subsection (3) of section 36A above by virtue of subsection (8) of that section.]

38 **Revocation and suspension of licences**

(1) Where a licence granted by a waste regulation authority is in force and it appears to the authority—

(a) that the holder of the licence has ceased to be a fit and proper person by reason of his having been convicted of a relevant offence; or

(b) that the continuation of the activities authorised by the licence would cause pollution of the environment or harm to human health or would be seriously detrimental to the amenities of the locality affected; and

(c) that the pollution, harm or detriment cannot be avoided by modifying the conditions of the licence;

the authority may exercise, as it thinks fit, either of the powers conferred by subsections (3) and (4) below.

(2) Where a licence granted by a waste regulation authority is in force and it appears to the authority that the holder of the licence has ceased to be a fit and proper person by reason of the management of the activities authorised by the licence having ceased to be in the hands of a technically competent person, the authority may exercise the power conferred by subsection (3) below.

(3) The authority may, under this subsection, revoke the licence so far as it authorises the carrying on of the activities specified in the licence or such of them as the authority specifies in revoking the licence.

(4) The authority may, under this subsection, revoke the licence entirely.

(5) A licence revoked under subsection (3) above shall cease to have effect to authorise the carrying on of the activities specified in the licence or, as the case may be, the activities specified by the authority in revoking the licence but shall not affect the requirements imposed by the licence which the authority, in revoking the licence, specify as requirements which are to continue to bind the licence holder.

(6) Where a licence granted by a waste regulation authority is in force and it appears to the authority—

(a) that the holder of the licence has ceased to be a fit and proper person by reason of the management of the activities authorised by the licence having ceased to be in the hands of a technically competent person; or

(b) that serious pollution of the environment or serious harm to human health has resulted from, or is about to be caused by, the activities to which the licence relates or the happening or threatened happening of an event affecting those activities; and

(c) that the continuing to carry on those activities, or any of those activities, in the circumstances will continue or, as the case may be, cause serious pollution of the environment or serious harm to human health;

the authority may suspend the licence so far as it authorises the carrying on of the activities specified in the licence or such of them as the authority specifies in suspending the licence.

(7) The Secretary of State may, if he thinks fit in relation to a licence granted by a waste regulation authority, give to the authority directions as to whether and in what manner the authority should exercise its powers under this section; and it shall be the duty of the authority to give effect to the directions.

(8) A licence suspended under subsection (6) above shall, while the suspension has effect, be of no effect to authorise the carrying on of the activities specified in the licence or, as the case may be, the activities specified by the authority in suspending the licence.

(9) Where a licence is suspended under subsection (6) above, the authority, in suspending

it or at any time while it is suspended, may require the holder of the licence to take such measures to deal with or avert the pollution or harm as the authority considers necessary.

[(9A) A requirement imposed under subsection (9) above may require the holder of a licence to carry out works or do other things notwithstanding that he is not entitled to carry out the works or do the thing and any person whose consent would be required shall grant, or join in granting, the holder of the licence such rights in relation to the land as will enable the holder of the licence to comply with any requirements imposed on him under that subsection.

(9B) Subsections (2) to (8) of section 36A above shall, with the necessary modifications, apply where the authority proposes to impose a requirement under subsection (9) above which may require the holder of a licence to carry out any such works or do any such thing as is mentioned in subsection (9A) above as they apply where the authority proposes to issue a licence subject to any such condition as is mentioned in subsection (1) of that section, but as if—

(a) the reference in subsection (3) of that section to section 35(4) above were a reference to subsection (9A) above; and

(b) any reference in those subsections—

(i) to the condition, or the condition in question, were a reference to the requirement; and

(ii) to issuing a licence were a reference to serving a notice, under subsection (12) below, effecting the requirement.

(9C) The authority may postpone the service of any notice or the consideration of any representations required under section 36A above, as applied by subsection (9B) above, so far as the authority considers that by reason of an emergency it is appropriate to do so.]

(10) A person who, without reasonable excuse, fails to comply with any requirement imposed under subsection (9) above otherwise than in relation to special waste shall be liable—

(a) on summary conviction, to a fine of an amount not exceeding the statutory maximum; and

(b) on conviction on indictment, to imprisonment for a term not exceeding two years or a fine or both.

(11) A person who, without reasonable excuse, fails to comply with any requirement imposed under subsection (9) above in relation to special waste shall be liable—

(a) on summary conviction, to imprisonment for a term not exceeding six months or a fine not exceeding the statutory maximum or both; and

(b) on conviction on indictment, to imprisonment for a term not exceeding five years or a fine or both.

(12) Any revocation or suspension ora licence or requirement imposed during the suspension of a licence under this section shall be effected by notice served on the holder of the licence and the notice shall state the time at which the revocation or suspension or the requirement is to take effect and, in the case of suspension, the period at the end of which, or the event on the occurrence of which, the suspension is to cease.

[(13) If a waste regulation authority is of the opinion that proceedings for an offence under subsection (10) or (11) above would afford an ineffectual remedy against a person who has failed to comply with any requirement imposed under subsection (9) above, the authority may take proceedings in the High Court . . .]

39   Surrender of licences

(1) A licence may be surrendered by its holder to the authority which granted it but, in the case of a site licence, only if the authority accepts the surrender.

(2) The following provisions apply to the surrender and acceptance of the surrender of a site licence.

(3) The holder of a site licence who desires to surrender it shall make an application for that purpose to the authority [on a form provided by the authority for the purpose, giving such information and accompanied by such evidence as the authority reasonably requires and accompanied by the charge prescribed for the purpose by a charging scheme under section 41 of the Environment Act 1995.]

(4) An authority which receives an application for the surrender of a site licence—

(a) shall inspect the land to which the licence relates, and

(b) may require the holder of the licence to furnish to it further information or further evidence.

(5) The authority shall determine whether it is likely or unlikely that the condition of the land, so far as that condition is the result of the use of the land for the treatment, keeping or disposal of waste (whether or not in pursuance of the licence), will cause pollution of the environment or harm to human health.

(6) If the authority is satisfied that the condition of the land is unlikely to cause the pollution or harm mentioned in subsection (5) above, the authority shall, subject to subsection (7) below, accept the surrender of the licence; but otherwise the authority shall refuse to accept it.

(7) Where the authority proposes to accept the surrender of a site licence, the authority must, before it does so,—

(a) refer the proposal to [the appropriate planning authority]; and

(b) consider any representations about the proposal which [the appropriate planning authority] makes to it during the allowed period;

[. . .]

(8) [. . .]

(9) Where the surrender of a licence is accepted under this section the authority shall issue to the applicant, with the notice of its determination, a certificate (a 'certificate of completion') stating that it is satisfied as mentioned in subsection (6) above and, on the issue of that certificate, the licence shall cease to have effect.

(10) If within the period of three months beginning with the date on which an authority receives an application to surrender a licence, or within such longer period as the authority and the applicant may at any time agree in writing, the authority has neither issued a certificate of completion nor given notice to the applicant that the authority has rejected the application, the authority shall be deemed to have rejected the application.

(11) Section 36(10) above applies for the interpretation of the 'allowed period' in [subsection (7) above].

[(12) In this section—

'the appropriate planning authority' means—

(a) where the relevant land is situated in the area of a London borough council, that London borough council;

(b) where the relevant land is situated in the City of London, the Common Council of the City of London;

(c) where the relevant land is situated in a non-metropolitan county in England, the council of that county;

(d) where the relevant land is situated in a National Park or the Broads, the National Park authority for that National Park or, as the case may be, the Broads Authority;

(e) where the relevant land is situated elsewhere in England or Wales, the council of the district or, in Wales, the county or county borough, in which the land is situated;

(f) . . .

'the Broads' has the same meaning as in the Norfolk and Suffolk Broads Act 1988;

'National Park authority', subject to subsection (13) below, means a National Park authority established under section 63 of the Environment Act 1995 which has become the local planning authority for the National Park in question;

'the relevant land', in the case of any site licence, means the land to which the licence relates.

(13) As respects any period before a National Park authority established under section 63 of the Environment Act 1995 in relation to a National Park becomes the local planning authority for that National Park, any reference in this section to a National Park authority shall be taken as a reference to the National Park Committee or joint or special planning board for that National Park.

(14) The Secretary of State may by regulations amend the definition of 'appropriate planning authority' in subsection (12) above.]

40   Transfer of licences

(1) A licence may be transferred to another person in accordance with subsections (2) to (6) below and may be so transferred whether or not the licence is partly revoked or suspended under any provision of this Part.

(2) Where the holder of a licence desires that the licence be transferred to another person ('the proposed transferee') the licence holder and the proposed transferee shall jointly make an application to the waste regulation authority which granted the licence for a transfer of it.

(3) An application under subsection (2) above for the transfer of a licence shall be made [on a form provided by the authority for the purpose, accompanied by such information as the authority may reasonably require, the charge prescribed for the purpose by a charging scheme under section 41 of the Environment Act 1995] and the licence.

(4) If, on such an application, the authority is satisfied that the proposed transferee is a fit and proper person the authority shall effect a transfer of the licence to the proposed transferee.

(5) The authority shall effect a transfer of a licence under the foregoing provisions of this section by causing the licence to be endorsed with the name and other particulars of the proposed transferee as the holder of the licence from such date specified in the endorsement as may be agreed with the applicants.

(6) If within the period of two months beginning with the date on which the authority receives an application for the transfer of a licence, or within such longer period as the authority and the applicants may at any time agree in writing, the authority has neither effected a transfer of the licence nor given notice to the applicants that the authority has rejected the application, the authority shall be deemed to have rejected the application.

42   Supervision of licensed activities

(1) While a licence is in force it shall be the duty of the waste regulation authority which granted the licence to take the steps needed—

    (a) for the purpose of ensuring that the activities authorised by the licence do not cause pollution of the environment or harm to human health or become seriously detrimental to the amenities of the locality affected by the activities; and

    (b) for the purpose of ensuring that the conditions of the licence are complied with.

(2) [. . .]

(3) For the purpose of performing the duty imposed on it by subsection (1) above, any officer of the authority authorised in writing for the purpose by the authority may, if it appears to him that by reason of an emergency it is necessary to do so, carry out work on the land or in relation to plant or equipment on the land to which the licence relates or, as the case may be, in relation to the mobile plant to which the licence relates.

(4) Where a waste regulation authority incurs any expenditure by virtue of subsection (3) above, the authority may recover the amount of the expenditure from [the holder, or (as the case may be) the former holder, of the licence] except where the holder or former holder of

the licence shows that there was no emergency requiring any work or except such of the expenditure as he shows was unnecessary.

(5) Where it appears to a waste regulation authority that a condition of a licence granted by it is not being complied with, [or is likely not to be complied with,] then, without prejudice to any proceedings under section 33(6) above, the authority may—

[(a) serve on the holder of the licence a notice—

    (i) stating that the authority is of the opinion that a condition of the licence is not being complied with or, as the case may be, is likely not to be complied with;

    (ii) specifying the matters which constitute the non-compliance or, as the case may be, which make the anticipated non-compliance likely;

    (iii) specifying the steps which must be taken to remedy the non-compliance or, as the case may be, to prevent the anticipated non-compliance from occurring; and

    (iv) specifying the period within which those steps must be taken; and]

(b) if in the opinion of the authority the licence holder [has not taken the steps specified in the notice within the period so specified,] exercise any of the powers specified in subsection (6) below.

(6) The powers which become exercisable in the event mentioned in subsection (5)(b) above are the following—

(a) to revoke the licence so far as it authorises the carrying on of the activities specified in the licence or such of them as the authority specifies in revoking the licence;

(b) to revoke the licence entirely; and

(c) to suspend the licence so far as it authorises the carrying on of the activities specified in the licence or, as the case may be, the activities specified by the authority in suspending the licence.

[(6A) If a waste regulation authority is of the opinion that revocation or suspension of the licence, whether entirely or to any extent, under subsection (6) above would afford an ineffectual remedy against a person who has failed to comply with any requirement imposed under subsection (5)(a) above, the authority may take proceedings in the High Court . . . for the purpose of securing compliance with the requirement.]

(7) Where a licence is revoked or suspended under subsection (6) above, [subsections (5) and (12) or, as the case may be, subsections (8) to (12) of section 38] above shall apply with the necessary modifications as they respectively apply to revocations or suspensions of licences under that section; [. . .]

(8) The Secretary of State may, if he thinks fit in relation to a licence granted by a waste regulation authority, give to the authority directions as to whether and in what manner the authority should exercise its powers under this section; and it shall be the duty of the authority to give effect to the directions.

43 Appeals to Secretary of State from decisions with respect to licences

(1) Where, except in pursuance of a direction given by the Secretary of State,—

(a) an application for a licence or a modification of the conditions of a licence is rejected;

(b) a licence is granted subject to conditions;

(c) the conditions of a licence are modified;

(d) a licence is suspended;

(e) a licence is revoked under section 38 or 42 above;

(f) an application to surrender a licence is rejected; or

(g) an application for the transfer of a licence is rejected;

then, except in the case of an application for a transfer, the applicant for the licence or, as the case may be, the holder or former holder of it may appeal from the decision to the Secretary of State and, in the case of an application for a transfer, the proposed transferee may do so.

(2) Where an appeal is made to the Secretary of State—

[. . .]

    (a) [. . .]

    (b) [. . .]

    (c) if a party to the appeal so requests, or the Secretary of State so decides, the appeal shall be or continue in the form of a hearing (which may, if the person hearing the appeal so decides, be held or held to any extent in private).

[(2A) This section is subject to section 114 of the Environment Act 1995 (delegation or reference of appeals etc).]

(3) Where, on such an appeal, the Secretary of State or other person determining the appeal determines that the decision of the authority shall be altered it shall be the duty of the authority to give effect to the determination.

(4) While an appeal is pending in a case falling within subsection (1)(c) or (e) above, the decision in question shall, subject to subsection (6) below, be ineffective; and if the appeal is dismissed or withdrawn the decision shall become effective from the end of the day on which the appeal is dismissed or withdrawn.

(5) Where an appeal is made in a case falling within subsection (1)(d) above, the bringing of the appeal shall have no effect on the decision in question.

(6) Subsection (4) above shall not apply to a decision modifying the conditions of a licence under section 37 above or revoking a licence under section 38 or 42 above in the case of which the notice effecting the modification or revocation includes a statement that in the opinion of the authority it is necessary for the purpose of preventing or, where that is not practicable, minimising pollution of the environment or harm to human health that that subsection should not apply.

(7) Where the decision under appeal is one falling within subsection (6) above or is a decision to suspend a licence, if, on the application of the holder or former holder of the licence, the Secretary of State or other person determining the appeal determines that the authority acted unreasonably in excluding the application of subsection (4) above or, as the case may be, in suspending the licence, then—

    (a) if the appeal is still pending at the end of the day on which the determination is made, subsection (4) above shall apply to the decision from the end of that day; and

    (b) the holder or former holder of the licence shall be entitled to recover compensation from the authority in respect of any loss suffered by him in consequence of the exclusion of the application of that subsection or the suspension of the licence;

and any dispute as to a person's entitlement to such compensation or as to the amount of it shall be determined by arbitration or in Scotland by a single arbiter appointed, in default of agreement between the parties concerned, by the Secretary of State on the application of any of the parties.

(8) Provision may be made by the Secretary of State by regulations with respect to appeals under this section and in particular—

    (a) as to the period within which and the manner in which appeals are to be brought; and

    (b) as to the manner in which appeals are to be considered.

[44 Offences of making false or misleading statements or false entries

(1) A person who—

    (a) in purported compliance with a requirement to furnish any information imposed by or under any provision of this Part, or

(b) for the purpose of obtaining for himself or another any grant of a licence, any modification of the conditions of a licence, any acceptance of the surrender of a licence or any transfer of a licence,

makes a statement which he knows to be false or misleading in a material particular, or recklessly makes any statement which is false or misleading in a material particular, commits an offence.

(2) A person who intentionally makes a false entry in any record required to be kept by virtue of a licence commits an offence.

(3) A person who commits an offence under this section shall be liable—

(a) on summary conviction, to a fine not exceeding the statutory maximum;

(b) on conviction on indictment, to a fine or to imprisonment for a term not exceeding two years, or to both.]

[44A National waste strategy: England and Wales

(1) The Secretary of State shall as soon as possible prepare a statement ('the strategy') containing his policies in relation to the recovery and disposal of waste in England and Wales.

(2) The strategy shall consist of or include—

(a) a statement which relates to the whole of England and Wales; or

(b) two or more statements which between them relate to the whole of England and Wales.

(3) The Secretary of State may from time to time modify the strategy.

(4) Without prejudice to the generality of what may be included in the strategy, the strategy must include—

(a) a statement of the Secretary of State's policies for attaining the objectives specified in Schedule 2A to this Act;

(b) provisions relating to each of the following, that is to say—

(i) the type, quantity and origin of waste to be recovered or disposed of;

(ii) general technical requirements; and

(iii) any special requirements for particular wastes.

(5) In preparing the strategy or any modification of it, the Secretary of State—

(a) shall consult the Environment Agency,

(b) shall consult—

(i) such bodies or persons appearing to him to be representative of the interests of local government, and

(ii) such bodies or persons appearing to him to be representative of the interests of industry,

as he may consider appropriate, and

(c) may consult such other bodies or persons as he considers appropriate,

(6) Without prejudice to any power to give directions conferred by section 38 of the Environment Act 1995, the Secretary of State may give directions to the Environment Agency requiring it—

(a) to advise him on the policies which are to be included in the strategy;

(b) to carry out a survey of or investigation into—

(i) the kinds or quantities of waste which it appears to that Agency is likely to be situated in England and Wales,

(ii) the facilities which are or appear to that Agency likely to be available or needed in England and Wales for recovering or disposing of any such waste,

(iii) any other matter upon which the Secretary of State wishes to be informed in connection with his preparation of the strategy or any modification of it,

and to report its findings to him.

(7) A direction under subsection (6)(b) above—

    (a) shall specify or describe the matters or the areas which are to be the subject of the survey or investigation; and

    (b) may make provision in relation to the manner in which—

        (i) the survey or investigation is to be carried out, or

        (ii) the findings are to be reported or made available to other persons.

    (8) Where a direction is given under subsection (6)(b), the Environment Agency shall, in accordance with any requirement of the direction,—

    (a) before carrying out the survey or investigation, consult—

        (i) such bodies or persons appearing to it to be representative of local planning authorities, and

        (ii) such bodies or persons appearing to it to be representative of the interests of industry,

as it may consider appropriate; and

    (b) make its findings available to those authorities.

    (9) In this section—

'local planning authority' has the same meaning as in the Town and Country Planning Act 1990;

'strategy' includes the strategy as modified from time to time and 'statement' shall be construed accordingly.

    (10) This section makes provision for the purpose of implementing Article 7 of the directive of the Council of the European Communities, dated 15th July 1975, on waste, as amended by—

    (a) the directive of that Council, dated 18th March 1991, amending directive 75/442/EEC on waste; and

    (b) the directive of that Council, dated 23rd December 1991, standardising and rationalising reports on the implementation of certain Directives relating to the environment.

44B . . .]

45 **Collection of controlled waste**

    (1) It shall be the duty of each waste collection authority—

    (a) to arrange for the collection of household waste in its area except waste—

        (i) which is situated at a place which in the opinion of the authority is so isolated or inaccessible that the cost of collecting it would be unreasonably high, and

        (ii) as to which the authority is satisfied that adequate arrangements for its disposal have been or can reasonably be expected to be made by a person who controls the waste; and

    (b) if requested by the occupier of premises in its area to collect any commercial waste from the premises, to arrange for the collection of the waste.

    (2) Each waste collection authority may, if requested by the occupier of premises in its area to collect any industrial waste from the premises, arrange for the collection of the waste; but a collection authority in England and Wales shall not exercise the power except with the consent of the waste disposal authority whose area includes the area of the waste collection authority.

    (3) No charge shall be made for the collection of household waste except in cases prescribed in regulations made by the Secretary of State; and in any of those cases—

    (a) the duty to arrange for the collection of the waste shall not arise until a person who controls the waste requests the authority to collect it; and

    (b) the authority may recover a reasonable charge for the collection of the waste from the person who made the request.

    (4) A person at whose request waste other than household waste is collected under this section shall be liable to pay a reasonable charge for the collection and disposal of the waste to

the authority which arranged for its collection; and it shall be the duty of that authority to recover the charge unless in the case of a charge in respect of commercial waste the authority considers it inappropriate to do so.

(5) It shall be the duty of each waste collection authority—

(a) to make such arrangements for the emptying, without charge, of privies serving one or more private dwellings in its area as the authority considers appropriate;

(b) if requested by the person who controls a cesspool serving only one or more private dwellings in its area to empty the cesspool, to remove such of the contents of the cesspool as the authority considers appropriate on payment, if the authority so requires, of a reasonable charge.

(6) A waste collection authority may, if requested by the person who controls any other privy or cesspool in its area to empty the privy or cesspool, empty the privy or, as the case may be, remove from the cesspool such of its contents as the authority consider appropriate on payment, if the authority so requires, of a reasonable charge.

(7) A waste collection authority may—

(a) construct, lay and maintain, within or outside its area, pipes and associated works for the purpose of collecting waste;

(b) contribute towards the cost incurred by another person in providing or maintaining pipes or associated works connecting with pipes provided by the authority under paragraph (a) above.

(8) A waste collection authority may contribute towards the cost incurred by another person in providing or maintaining plant or equipment intended to deal with commercial or industrial waste before it is collected under arrangements made by the authority under subsection (1)(b) or (2) above.

(9) Subject to section 48(1) below, anything collected under arrangements made by a waste collection authority under this section shall belong to the authority and may be dealt with accordingly.

(10) ...

(11) ...

(12) In this section 'privy' means a latrine which has a moveable receptacle and 'cesspool' includes a settlement tank or other tank for the reception or disposal of foul matter from buildings.

46 Receptacles for household waste

(1) Where a waste collection authority has a duty by virtue of section 45(1)(a) above to arrange for the collection of household waste from any premises, the authority may, by notice served on him, require the occupier to place the waste for collection in receptacles of a kind and number specified.

(2) The kind and number of the receptacles required under subsection (1) above to be used shall be such only as are reasonable but, subject to that, separate receptacles or compartments of receptacles may be required to be used for waste which is to be recycled and waste which is not.

(3) In making requirements under subsection (1) above the authority may, as respects the provision of the receptacles—

(a) determine that they be provided by the authority free of charge;

(b) propose that they be provided, if the occupier agrees, by the authority on payment by him of such a single payment or such periodical payments as he agrees with the authority;

(c) require the occupier to provide them if he does not enter into an agreement under paragraph (b) above within a specified period; or

(d) require the occupier to provide them.

(4) In making requirements as respects receptacles under subsection (1) above, the authority may, by the notice under that subsection, make provision with respect to—

    (a) the size, construction and maintenance of the receptacles;

    (b) the placing of the receptacles for the purpose of facilitating the emptying of them, and access to the receptacles for that purpose;

    (c) the placing of the receptacles for that purpose on highways . . .

    (d) the substances or articles which may or may not be put into the receptacles or compartments of receptacles of any description and the precautions to be taken where particular substances or articles are put into them; and

    (e) the steps to be taken by occupiers of premises to facilitate the collection of waste from the receptacles.

(5) No requirement shall be made under subsection (1) above for receptacles to be placed on a highway or, as the case may be, road, unless—

    (a) the relevant highway authority or roads authority have given their consent to their being so placed; and

    (b) arrangements have been made as to the liability for any damage arising out of their being so placed.

(6) person who fails, without reasonable excuse, to comply with any requirements imposed under subsection (1), (3)(c) or (d) or (4) above shall be liable on summary conviction to a fine not exceeding level 3 on the standard scale.

(7) Where an occupier is required under subsection (1) above to provide any receptacles he may, within the period allowed by subsection (8) below, appeal to a magistrates' court . . . against any requirement imposed under subsection (1), subsection (3)(c) or (d) or (4) above on the ground that—

    (a) the requirement is unreasonable; or

    (b) the receptacles in which household waste is placed for collection from the premises are adequate.

(8) The period allowed to the occupier of premises for appealing against such a requirement is the period of twenty-one days beginning—

    (a) in a case where a period was specified under subsection (3)(c) above, with the end of that period; and

    (b) where no period was specified, with the day on which the notice making the requirement was served on him.

(9) Where an appeal against a requirement is brought under subsection (7) above—

    (a) the requirement shall be of no effect pending the determination of the appeal;

    (b) the court shall either quash or modify the requirement or dismiss the appeal; and

    (c) no question as to whether the requirement is, in any respect, unreasonable shall be entertained in any proceedings for an offence under subsection (6) above.

(10) In this section—

'receptacle' includes a holder for receptacles; and

'specified' means specified in a notice under subsection (1) above.

47 Receptacles for commercial or industrial waste

(1) A waste collection authority may, at the request of any person, supply him with receptacles for commercial or industrial waste which he has requested the authority to arrange to collect and shall make a reasonable charge for any receptacle supplied unless in the case of a receptacle for commercial waste the authority considers it appropriate not to make a charge.

(2) If it appears to a waste collection authority that there is likely to be situated, on any premises in its area, commercial waste or industrial waste of a kind which, if the waste is not stored in receptacles of a particular kind, is likely to cause a nuisance or to be detrimental to the amenities of the locality, the authority may, by notice served on him, require the occupier

of the premises to provide at the premises receptacles for the storage of such waste of a kind and number specified.

(3) The kind and number of the receptacles required under subsection (2) above to be used shall be such only as are reasonable.

(4) In making requirements as respects receptacles under subsection (2) above, the authority may, by the notice under that subsection, make provision with respect to—

(a) the size, construction and maintenance of the receptacles;

(b) the placing of the receptacles for the purpose of facilitating the emptying of them, and access to the receptacles for that purpose;

(c) the placing of the receptacles for that purpose on highways . . .

(d) the substances or articles which may or may not be put into the receptacles and the precautions to be taken where particular substances or articles are put into them; and

(e) the steps to be taken by occupiers of premises to facilitate the collection of waste from the receptacles.

(5) No requirement shall be made under subsection (2) above for receptacles to be placed on a highway . . . unless—

(a) the relevant highway authority . . . have given their consent to their being so placed; and

(b) arrangements have been made as to the liability for any damage arising out of their being so placed.

(6) A person who fails, without reasonable excuse, to comply with any requirements imposed under subsection (2) or (4) above shall be liable on summary conviction to a fine not exceeding level 3 on the standard scale.

(7) Where an occupier is required under subsection (2) above to provide any receptacles he may, within the period allowed by subsection (8) below, appeal to a magistrates' court . . . against any requirement imposed under subsection (2) or (4) above on the ground that—

(a) the requirement is unreasonable; or

(b) the waste is not likely to cause a nuisance or be detrimental to the amenities of the locality.

(8) The period allowed to the occupier of premises for appealing against such a requirement is the period of twenty-one days beginning with the day on which the notice making the requirement was served on him.

(9) Where an appeal against a requirement is brought under subsection (7) above—

(a) the requirement shall be of no effect pending the determination of the appeal; and

(b) the court shall either quash or modify the requirement or dismiss the appeal; and

(c) no question as to whether the requirement is, in any respect, unreasonable shall be entertained in any proceedings for an offence under subsection (6) above.

(10) In this section—

'receptacle' includes a holder for receptacles; and

'specified' means specified in a notice under subsection (2) above.

48   Duties of waste collection authorities as respects disposal of waste collected

(1) Subject to subsections (2) and (6) below, it shall be the duty of each waste collection authority to deliver for disposal all waste which is collected by the authority under section 45 above to such places as the waste disposal authority for its area directs.

(2) The duty imposed on a waste collection authority by subsection (1) above does not, except in cases falling within subsection (4) below, apply as respects household waste or commercial waste for which the authority decides to make arrangements for recycling the waste; and the authority shall have regard, in deciding what recycling arrangements to make, to its waste recycling plan under section 49 below.

(3) A waste collection authority which decides to make arrangements under subsection (2) above for recycling waste collected by it shall, as soon as reasonably practicable, by notice in writing, inform the waste disposal authority for the area which includes its area of the arrangements which it proposes to make.

(4) Where a waste disposal authority has made with a waste disposal contractor arrangements, as respects household waste or commercial waste in its area or any part of its area, for the contractor to recycle the waste, or any of it, the waste disposal authority may, by notice served on the waste collection authority, object to the waste collection authority having the waste recycled; and the objection may be made as respects all the waste, part only of the waste or specified descriptions of the waste.

(5) Where an objection is made under subsection (4) above, subsection (2) above shall not be available to the waste collection authority to the extent objected to.

(6) A waste collection authority may, subject to subsection (7) below, provide plant and equipment for the sorting and baling of waste retained by the authority under subsection (2) above.

(7) Subsection (6) above does not apply to an authority which is also a waste disposal authority; but, in such a case, the authority may make arrangements with a waste disposal contractor for the contractor to deal with the waste as mentioned in that subsection.

(8) A waste collection authority may permit another person to use facilities provided by the authority under subsection (6) above and may provide for the use of another person any such facilities as the authority has power to provide under that subsection; and—

(a) subject to paragraph (b) below, it shall be the duty of the authority to make a reasonable charge in respect of the use by another person of the facilities, unless the authority considers it appropriate not to make a charge;

(b) no charge shall be made under this subsection in respect of household waste; and

(c) anything delivered to the authority by another person in the course of using the facilities shall belong to the authority and may be dealt with accordingly.

(9) . . .

49   Waste recycling plans by collection authorities

(1) It shall be the duty of each waste collection authority, as respects household and commercial waste arising in its area—

(a) to carry out an investigation with a view to deciding what arrangements are appropriate for dealing with the waste by separating, baling or otherwise packaging it for the purpose of recycling it;

(b) to decide what arrangements are in the opinion of the authority needed for that purpose;

(c) to prepare a statement ('the plan') of the arrangements made and proposed to be made by the authority and other persons for dealing with waste in those ways;

(d) to carry out from time to time further investigations with a view to deciding what changes in the plan are needed; and

(e) to make any modification of the plan which the authority thinks appropriate in consequence of any such further investigation.

(2) In considering any arrangements or modification for the purposes of subsection (1)(c) or (e) above it shall be the duty of the authority to have regard to the effect which the arrangements or modification would be likely to have on the amenities of any locality and the likely cost or saving to the authority attributable to the arrangements or modification.

(3) It shall be the duty of a waste collection authority to include in the plan information as to—

(a) the kinds and quantities of controlled waste which the authority expects to collect during the period specified in the plan;

(b) the kinds and quantities of controlled waste which the authority expects to purchase during that period;

(c) the kinds and quantities of controlled waste which the authority expects to deal with in the ways specified in subsection (1)(a) above during that period;

(d) the arrangements which the authority expects to make during that period with waste disposal contractors or, in Scotland, waste disposal authorities and waste disposal contractors for them to deal with waste in those ways;

(e) the plant and equipment which the authority expects to provide under section 48(6) above or 53 below; and

(f) the estimated costs or savings attributable to the methods of dealing with the waste in the ways provided for in the plan.

(4) It shall be the duty of a waste collection authority, before finally determining the content of the plan or a modification, to send a copy of it in draft to the Secretary of State for the purpose of enabling him to determine whether subsection (3) above has been complied with; and, if the Secretary of State gives any directions to the authority for securing compliance with that subsection, it shall be the duty of the authority to comply with the direction.

(5) When a waste collection authority has determined the content of the plan or a modification it shall be the duty of the authority—

(a) to take such steps as in the opinion of the authority will give adequate publicity in its area to the plan or modification; and

(b) to send to the waste disposal authority and waste regulation authority for the area which includes its area a copy of the plan or, as the case may be, particulars of the modification.

(6) It shall be the duty of each waste collection authority to keep a copy of the plan and particulars of any modifications to it available at all reasonable times at its principal offices for inspection by members of the public free of charge and to supply a copy of the plan and of the particulars of any modifications to it to any person who requests one, on payment by that person of such reasonable charge as the authority requires.

(7) The Secretary of State may give to any waste collection authority directions as to the time by which the authority is to perform any duty imposed by this section specified in the direction; and it shall be the duty of the authority to comply with the direction.

51 Functions of waste disposal authorities

(1) It shall be the duty of each waste disposal authority to arrange—

(a) for the disposal of the controlled waste collected in its area by the waste collection authorities; and

(b) for places to be provided at which persons resident in its area may deposit their household waste and for the disposal of waste so deposited;

in either case by means of arrangements made (in accordance with Part II of Schedule 2 to this Act) with waste disposal contractors, but by no other means.

(2) The arrangements made by a waste disposal authority under subsection (1)(b) above shall be such as to secure that—

(a) each place is situated either within the area of the authority or so as to be reasonably accessible to persons resident in its area;

(b) each place is available for the deposit of waste at all reasonable times (including at least one period on the Saturday or following day of each week except a week in which the Saturday is 25th December or 1st January);

(c) each place is available for the deposit of waste free of charge by persons resident in the area;

but the arrangements may restrict the availability of specified places to specified descriptions of waste.

(3) A waste disposal authority may include in arrangements made under subsection (1)(b) above arrangements for the places provided for its area for the deposit of household waste free of charge by residents in its area to be available for the deposit of household or other controlled waste by other persons on such terms as to payment (if any) as the authority determines.

(4) For the purpose of discharging its duty under subsection (1)(a) above as respects controlled waste collected as mentioned in that paragraph a waste disposal authority—

(a) shall give directions to the waste collection authorities within its area as to the persons to whom and places at which such waste is to be delivered;

(b) may arrange for the provision, within or outside its area, by waste disposal contractors of places at which such waste may be treated or kept prior to its removal for treatment or disposal;

(c) may make available to waste disposal contractors (and accordingly own) plant and equipment for the purpose of enabling them to keep such waste prior to its removal for disposal or to treat such waste in connection with so keeping it or for the purpose of facilitating its transportation;

(d) may make available to waste disposal contractors (and accordingly hold) land for the purpose of enabling them to treat, keep or dispose of such waste in or on the land;

(e) may contribute towards the cost incurred by persons who produce commercial or industrial waste in providing and maintaining plant or equipment intended to deal with such waste before it is collected; and

(f) may contribute towards the cost incurred by persons who produce commercial or industrial waste in providing or maintaining pipes or associated works connecting with pipes provided by a waste collection authority within the area of the waste disposal authority.

(5) For the purpose of discharging its duties under subsection (1)(b) above as respects household waste deposited as mentioned in that paragraph a waste disposal authority—

(a) may arrange for the provision, within or outside its area, by waste disposal contractors of places at which such waste may be treated or kept prior to its removal for treatment or disposal;

(b) may make available to waste disposal contractors (and accordingly own) plant and equipment for the purpose of enabling them to keep such waste prior to its removal for disposal or to treat such waste in connection with so keeping it or for the purpose of facilitating its transportation; and

(c) may make available to waste disposal contractors (and accordingly hold) land for the purpose of enabling them to treat, keep or dispose of such waste in or on the land.

(6) Where the arrangements made under subsection (1)(b) include such arrangements as are authorised by subsection (3) above, subsection (5) above applies as respects household or other controlled waste as it applies as respects household waste.

(7) Subsection (1) above is subject to section 77.

(8) . . .

52 Payments for recycling and disposal etc. of waste

(1) Where, under section 48(2) above, a waste collection authority retains for recycling waste collected by it under section 45 above, the waste disposal authority for the area which includes the area of the waste collection authority shall make to that authority payments, in respect of the waste so retained, of such amounts representing its net saving of expenditure on the disposal of the waste as the authority determines.

(2) Where, by reason of the discharge by a waste disposal authority of its functions, waste arising in its area does not fall to be collected by a waste collection authority under section 45

above, the waste collection authority shall make to the waste disposal authority payments, in respect of the waste not falling to be so collected, of such amounts representing its net saving of expenditure on the collection of the waste as the authority determines.

(3) Where a person other than a waste collection authority, for the purpose of recycling it, collects waste arising in the area of a waste disposal authority which would fall to be collected under section 45 above, the waste disposal authority may make to that person payments, in respect of the waste so collected, of such amounts representing its net saving of expenditure on the disposal of the waste as the authority determines.

(4) Where a person other than a waste collection authority, for the purpose of recycling it, collects waste which would fall to be collected under section 45 above, the waste collection authority may make to that person payments, in respect of the waste so collected, of such amounts representing its net saving of expenditure on the collection of the waste as the authority determines.

(5) The Secretary of State may, by regulations, impose on waste disposal authorities a duty to make payments corresponding to the payments which are authorised by subsection (3) above to such persons in such circumstances and in respect of such descriptions or quantities of waste as are specified in the regulations.

(6) For the purposes of subsections (1), (3) and (5) above the net saving of expenditure of a waste disposal authority on the disposal of any waste retained or collected for recycling is the amount of the expenditure which the authority would, but for the retention or collection, have incurred in having it disposed of less any amount payable by the authority to any person in consequence of the retention or collection for recycling (instead of the disposal) of the waste.

(7) For the purposes of subsections (2) and (4) above the net saving of expenditure of a waste collection authority on the collection of any waste not falling to be collected by it is the amount of the expenditure which the authority would, if it had had to collect the waste, have incurred in collecting it.

(8) The Secretary of State shall, by regulations, make provision for the determination of the net saving of expenditure for the purposes of subsections (1), (2), (3), (4) and (5) above.

(9) A waste disposal authority shall be entitled to receive from a waste collection authority such sums as are needed to reimburse the waste disposal authority the reasonable cost of making arrangements under section 51(1) above for the disposal of commercial and industrial waste collected in the area of the waste disposal authority.

(10) A waste disposal authority shall pay to a waste collection authority a reasonable contribution towards expenditure reasonably incurred by the waste collection authority in delivering waste, in pursuance of a direction under section 51(4)(a) above, to a place which is unreasonably far from the waste collection authority's area.

(11) Any question arising under subsection (9) or (10) above shall, in default of agreement between the two authorities in question, be determined by arbitration.

55 Powers for recycling waste

(1) This section has effect for conferring on waste disposal authorities and waste collection authorities powers for the purposes of recycling waste.

(2) A waste disposal authority may—

    (a) make arrangements with waste disposal contractors for them to recycle waste as respects which the authority has duties under section 51(1) above or agrees with another person for its disposal or treatment;

    (b) make arrangements with waste disposal contractors for them to use waste for the purpose of producing from it heat or electricity or both;

    (c) buy or otherwise acquire waste with a view to its being recycled;

    (d) use, sell or otherwise dispose of waste as respects which the authority has duties under section 51(1) above or anything produced from such waste.

(3) A waste collection authority may—
  (a) buy or otherwise acquire waste with a view to recycling it;
  (b) use, or dispose of by way of sale or otherwise to another person, waste belonging to the authority or anything produced from such waste.

(4) . . .

57 Power of Secretary of State to require waste to be accepted, treated, disposed of or delivered

(1) The Secretary of State may, by notice in writing, direct the holder of any waste management licence to accept and keep, or accept and treat or dispose of, controlled waste at specified places on specified terms.

(2) The Secretary of State may, by notice in writing, direct any person who is keeping controlled waste on any land to deliver the waste to a specified person on specified terms with a view to its being treated or disposed of by that other person.

(3) A direction under this section may impose a requirement as respects waste of any specified kind or as respects any specified consignment of waste.

(4) A direction under subsection (2) above may require the person who is directed to deliver the waste to pay to the specified person his reasonable costs of treating or disposing of the waste.

(5) A person who fails, without reasonable excuse, to comply with a direction under this section shall be liable on summary conviction to a fine not exceeding level 5 on the standard scale.

(6) A person shall not be guilty of an offence under any other enactment prescribed by the Secretary of State by regulations made for the purposes of this subsection by reason only of anything necessarily done or omitted in order to comply with a direction under this section.

(7) The Secretary of State may, where the costs of the treatment or disposal of waste are not paid or not fully paid in pursuance of subsection (4) above to the person treating or disposing of the waste, pay the costs or the unpaid costs, as the case may be, to that person.

(8) In this section 'specified' means specified in a direction under this section.

59 Powers to require removal of waste unlawfully deposited

(1) If any controlled waste is deposited in or on any land in the area of a waste regulation authority or waste collection authority in contravention of section 33(1) above, the authority may, by notice served on him, require the occupier to do either or both of the following, that is—
  (a) to remove the waste from the land within a specified period not less than a period of twenty-one days beginning with the service of the notice;
  (b) to take within such a period specified steps with a view to eliminating or reducing the consequences of the deposit of the waste.

(2) A person on whom any requirements are imposed under subsection (1) above may, within the period of twenty-one days mentioned in that subsection, appeal against the requirement to a magistrates' court . . .

(3) On any appeal under subsection (2) above the court shall quash the requirement if it is satisfied that—
  (a) the appellant neither deposited nor knowingly caused nor knowingly permitted the deposit of the waste; or
  (b) there is a material defect in the notice; and in any other case shall either modify the requirement or dismiss the appeal.

(4) Where a person appeals against any requirement imposed under subsection (1) above, the requirement shall be of no effect pending the determination of the appeal; and where the court modifies the requirement or dismisses the appeal it may extend the period specified in the notice.

(5) If a person on whom a requirement imposed under subsection (1) above fails, without reasonable excuse, to comply with the requirement he shall be liable, on summary conviction, to a fine not exceeding level 5 on the standard scale and to a further fine of an amount equal to one-tenth of level 5 on the standard scale for each day on which the failure continues after conviction of the offence and before the authority has begun to exercise its powers under subsection (6) below.

(6) Where a person on whom a requirement has been imposed under subsection (1) above by an authority fails to comply with the requirement the authority may do what that person was required to do and may recover from him any expenses reasonably incurred by the authority in doing it.

(7) If it appears to a waste regulation authority or waste collection authority that waste has been deposited in or on any land in contravention of section 33(1) above and that—

(a) in order to remove or prevent pollution of land, water or air or harm to human health it is necessary that the waste be forthwith removed or other steps taken to eliminate or reduce the consequences of the deposit or both; or

(b) there is no occupier of the land; or

(c) the occupier neither made nor knowingly permitted the deposit of the waste; the authority may remove the waste from the land or take other steps to eliminate or reduce the consequences of the deposit or, as the case may require, to remove the waste and take those steps.

(8) Where an authority exercises any of the powers conferred on it by subsection (7) above it shall be entitled to recover the cost incurred by it in removing the waste or taking the steps or both and in disposing of the waste—

(a) in a case falling within subsection (7)(a) above, from the occupier of the land unless he proves that he neither made nor knowingly caused nor knowingly permitted the deposit of the waste;

(b) in any case, from any person who deposited or knowingly caused or knowingly permitted the deposit of any of the waste;

except such of the cost as the occupier or that person shows was incurred unnecessarily.

(9) Any waste removed by an authority under subsection (7) above shall belong to that authority and may be dealt with accordingly.

60   Interference with waste sites and receptacles for waste

(1) No person shall sort over or disturb—

(a) anything deposited at a place for the deposit of waste provided by a waste collection authority, by a waste disposal contractor under arrangements made with a waste disposal authority or by any other local authority or person . . .

(b) anything deposited in a receptacle for waste, whether for public or private use, provided by a waste collection authority, by a waste disposal contractor under arrangements made with a waste disposal authority, by a parish or community council or by a holder of a waste management licence or . . .

(c) the contents of any receptacle for waste which, in accordance with a requirement under section 46 or 47 above, is placed on any highway . . . or in any other place with a view to its being emptied;

unless he has the relevant consent or right to do so specified in subsection (2) below.

(2) The consent or right that is relevant for the purposes of subsection (1)(a), (b) or (c) above is—

(a) in the case of paragraph (a), the consent of the authority, contractor or other person who provides the place for the deposit of the waste;

(b) in the case of paragraph (b), the consent of the authority, contractor or other person who provides the receptacle for the deposit of the waste;

(c) in the case of paragraph (c), the right to the custody of the receptacle, the consent of the person having the right to the custody of the receptacle or the right conferred by the function by or under this Part of emptying such receptacles.

(3) A person who contravenes subsection (1) above shall be liable on summary conviction to a fine of an amount not exceeding level 3 on the standard scale.

62 Special provision with respect to certain dangerous or intractable waste

(1) If the Secretary of State considers that controlled waste of any kind is or may be so dangerous or difficult to treat, keep or dispose of that special provision is required for dealing with it he shall make provision by regulations for the treatment, keeping or disposal of waste of that kind ('special waste').

(2) Without prejudice to the generality of subsection (1) above, the regulations may include provision—

(a) for the giving of directions by waste regulation authorities with respect to matters connected with the treatment, keeping or disposal of special waste;

(b) for securing that special waste is not, while awaiting treatment or disposal in pursuance of the regulations, kept at any one place in quantities greater than those which are prescribed and in circumstances which differ from those which are prescribed;

(c) in connection with requirements imposed on consignors or consignees of special waste, imposing, in the event of non-compliance, requirements on any person carrying the consignment to re-deliver it as directed;

(d) for requiring the occupier of premises on which special waste is situated to give notice of that fact and other prescribed information to a prescribed authority;

(e) for the keeping of records by waste regulation authorities and by persons who import, export, produce, keep, treat or dispose of special waste or deliver it to another person for treatment or disposal, for the inspection of the records and for the furnishing by such persons to waste regulation authorities of copies of or information derived from the records;

(f) for the keeping in the register under section 64(1) below of copies of such of those records, or such information derived from those records, as may be prescribed;

(g) providing that a contravention of the regulations shall be an offence and pre-scribing the maximum penalty for the offence, which shall not exceed, on summary conviction, a fine at level 5 on the standard scale and, on conviction on indictment, imprisonment for a term of two years or a fine or both.

(3) Without prejudice to the generality of subsection (1) above, the regulations may include provision—

[(a) for the supervision by waste regulation authorities—

(i) of activities authorised by virtue of the regulations or of activities by virtue of carrying on which persons are subject to provisions of the regulations, or

(ii) of persons who carry on activities authorised by virtue of the regulations or who are subject to provisions of the regulations,

and for the recovery from persons falling within sub-paragraph (ii) above of the costs incurred by waste regulation authorities in performing functions conferred upon those authorities by the regulations;]

(b) as to the recovery of expenses or other charges for the treatment, keeping or disposal or the re-delivery of special waste in pursuance of the regulations;

(c) as to appeals to the Secretary of State from decisions of waste regulation author-ities under the regulations.

[(3A) This section is subject to section 114 of the Environment Act 1995 (delegation or reference of appeals etc).]

(4) . . .

63 Waste other than controlled waste

(1) The Secretary of State may, after consultation with such bodies as he considers appropriate, make regulations providing that prescribed provisions of this Part shall have effect in a prescribed area—

(a) as if references in those provisions to controlled waste or controlled waste of a kind specified in the regulations included references to such waste as is mentioned in section 75(7)(c) below which is of a kind so specified; and

(b) with such modifications as may be prescribed; and the regulations may make such modifications of other enactments as the Secretary of State considers appropriate.

[(2) A person who deposits, or knowingly causes or knowingly permits the deposit of, any waste—

(a) which is not controlled waste, but

(b) which, if it were controlled waste, would be special waste,

in a case where he would be guilty of an offence under section 33 above if the waste were special waste and any waste management licence were not in force, shall, subject to subsection (3) below, be guilty of that offence and punishable as if the waste were special waste.]

(3) No offence is committed by virtue of subsection (2) above if the act charged was done under and in accordance with any consent, licence, approval or authority granted under any enactment (excluding any planning permission under the enactments relating to town and country planning).

(4) Section 45(2) and section 47(1) above shall apply to waste other than controlled waste as they apply to controlled waste.

64 Public registers

(1) Subject to sections 65 and 66 below, it shall be the duty of each waste regulation authority to maintain a register containing prescribed particulars of or relating to—

(a) current or recently current licences ('licences') granted by the authority;

(b) current or recently current applications to the authority for licences;

(c) applications made to the authority under section 37 above for the modifi-cation of licences;

(d) notices issued by the authority under section 37 above effecting the modifi-cation of licences;

(e) notices issued by the authority under section 38 above effecting the revocation or suspension of licences or imposing requirements on the holders of licences;

(f) appeals under section 43 above relating to decisions of the authority;

(g) certificates of completion issued by the authority under section 39(9) above;

(h) notices issued by the authority imposing requirements on the holders of licences under section 42(5) above;

(i) convictions of the holders of licences granted by the authority for any offence under this Part (whether in relation to a licence so granted or not);

(j) the occasions on which the authority has discharged any function under section 42 or 61 above;

(k) directions given to the authority under any provision of this Part by the Secretary of State;

(l) [...]

(m) such matters relating to the treatment, keeping or disposal of waste in the area of the authority or any pollution of the environment caused thereby as may be prescribed;

and any other document or information required to be kept in the register under any provision of this Act.

(2) Where information of any description is excluded from any register by virtue of section 66 below, a statement shall be entered in the register indicating the existence of information of that description.

[(2A) The Secretary of State may give to a waste regulation authority directions requiring the removal from any register of its of any specified information not prescribed for inclusion under subsection (1) above or which, by virtue of section 65 or 66 below, ought to be excluded from the register.]

(3) For the purposes of subsection (1) above licences are 'recently' current for the period of twelve months after they cease to be in force and applications for licences are 'recently' current if they relate to a licence which is current or recently current or, in the case of an application which is rejected, for the period of twelve months beginning with the date on which the waste regulation authority gives notice of rejection or, as the case may be, on which the application is deemed by section 36(9) above to have been rejected.

(4) It shall be the duty of each waste collection authority in England [or Wales] [. . .] to maintain a register containing prescribed particulars of such information contained in any register maintained under subsection (1) above as relates to the treatment, keeping or disposal of controlled waste in the area of the authority.

[(5) The waste regulation authority in relation to England and Wales shall furnish any waste collection authorities in its area with the particulars necessary to enable them to discharge their duty under subsection (4) above.]

(6) Each waste regulation authority and waste collection authority

[(a)] shall secure that any register maintained under this section is open to inspection [. . .] by members of the public free of charge at all reasonable hours; and

[(b)] shall afford to members of the public reasonable facilities for obtaining, on payment of reasonable charges, copies of entries in the register

[and, for the purposes of this subsection, places may be prescribed by the Secretary of State at which any such registers or facilities as are mentioned in paragraph (a) or (b) above are to be available or afforded to the public in pursuance of the paragraph in question.]

(7) Registers under this section may be kept in any form.

(8) In this section 'prescribed' means prescribed in regulations by the Secretary of State.

65 Exclusion from registers of information affecting national security

(1) No information shall be included in a register maintained under section 64 above (a 'register') if and so long as, in the opinion of the Secretary of State, the inclusion in the register of that information, or information of that description, would be contrary to the interests of national security.

(2) The Secretary of State may, for the purpose of securing the exclusion from registers of information to which subsection (1) above applies, give to the authorities maintaining registers directions—

(a) specifying information, or descriptions of information, to be excluded from their registers; or

(b) specifying descriptions of information to be referred to the Secretary of State for his determination;

and no information referred to the Secretary of State in pursuance of paragraph (b) above shall be included in any such register until the Secretary of State determines that it should be so included.

(3) An authority maintaining a register shall notify the Secretary of State of any information it excludes from the register in pursuance of directions under subsection (2) above.

(4) A person may, as respects any information which appears to him to be information to which subsection (1) above may apply, give a notice to the Secretary of State specifying the information and indicating its apparent nature; and, if he does so—

    (a) he shall notify the authority concerned that he has done so; and

    (b) no information so notified to the Secretary of State shall be included in the register kept by that authority until the Secretary of State has determined that it should be so included.

66 Exclusion from registers of certain confidential information

(1) No information relating to the affairs of any individual or business shall be included in a register maintained under section 64 above (a 'register'), without the consent of that individual or the person for the time being carrying on that business, if and so long as the information—

    (a) is, in relation to him, commercially confidential; and

    (b) is not required to be included in the register in pursuance of directions under subsection (7) below;

but information is not commercially confidential for the purposes of this section unless it is determined under this section to be so by the authority maintaining the register or, on appeal, by the Secretary of State.

(2) Where information is furnished to an authority maintaining a register for the purpose of—

    (a) an application for, or for the modification of, a licence;

    (b) complying with any condition of a licence; or

    (c) complying with a notice under section 71(2) below;

then, if the person furnishing it applies to the authority to have the information excluded from the register on the ground that it is commercially confidential (as regards himself or another person), the authority shall determine whether the information is or is not commercially confidential.

(3) A determination under subsection (2) above must be made within the period of fourteen days beginning with the date of the application and if the authority fails to make a determination within that period it shall be treated as having determined that the information is commercially confidential.

(4) Where it appears to an authority maintaining a register that any information (other than information furnished in circumstances within subsection (2) above) which has been obtained by the authority under or by virtue of any provision of this Part might be commercially confidential, the authority shall—

    (a) give to the person to whom or whose business it relates notice that that information is required to be included in the register unless excluded under this section; and

    (b) give him a reasonable opportunity—

        (i) of objecting to the inclusion of the information on the grounds that it is commercially confidential; and

       (ii) of making representations to the authority for the purpose of justifying any such objection;

and, if any representations are made, the authority shall, having taken the representations into account, determine whether the information is or is not commercially confidential.

(5) Where, under subsection (2) or (4) above, an authority determines that information is not commercially confidential—

    (a) the information shall not be entered in the register until the end of the period of twenty-one days beginning with the date on which the determination is notified to the person concerned;

    (b) that person may appeal to the Secretary of State against the decision; and, where an appeal is brought in respect of any information, the information shall not be entered in the register [until the end of the period of seven days following the day on which the appeal is finally determined or withdrawn].

[(6) Subsections (2) and (8) of section 43 above shall apply in relation to appeals under subsection (5) above as they apply in relation to appeals under that section; but

(a) subsection (2)(c) of that section shall have effect for the purposes of this subsection with the substitution for the words from '(which may' onwards of the words '(which must be held in private)'; and

(b) subsection (5) above is subject to section 114 of the Environment Act 1995 (delegation or reference of appeals etc).]

(7) The Secretary of State may give to the authorities maintaining registers directions as to specified information, or descriptions of information, which the public interest requires to be included in the registers notwithstanding that the information may be commercially confidential.

(8) Information excluded from a register shall be treated as ceasing to be commercially confidential for the purposes of this section at the expiry of the period of four years beginning with the date of the determination by virtue of which it was excluded; but the person who furnished it may apply to the authority for the information to remain excluded from the register on the ground that it is still commercially confidential and the authority shall determine whether or not that is the case.

(9) Subsections (5) and (6) above shall apply in relation to a determination under subsection (8) above as they apply in relation to a determination under subsection (2) or (4) above.

(10) The Secretary of State may, by order, substitute for the period for the time being specified in subsection (3) above such other period as he considers appropriate.

(11) Information is, for the purposes of any determination under this section, commercially confidential, in relation to any individual or person, if its being contained in the register would prejudice to an unreasonable degree the commercial interests of that individual or person.

71   Obtaining of information from persons and authorities

(1) [. . .]

(2) For the purpose of the discharge of their respective functions under this Part—

(a) the Secretary of State, and

(b) a waste regulation authority,

may, by notice in writing served on him, require any person to furnish such information specified in the notice as the Secretary of State or the authority, as the case may be, reasonably considers he or it needs, in such form and within such period following service of the notice [or at such time,] as is so specified.

(3) A person who—

(a) fails, without reasonable excuse, to comply with a requirement imposed under subsection (2) above; [. . .]

(b) [. . .]

shall be liable—

(i) on summary conviction, to a fine not exceeding the statutory maximum;

(ii) on conviction on indictment, to a fine or to imprisonment for a term not exceeding two years, or to both.

73   Appeals and other provisions relating to legal proceedings and civil liability

(1) An appeal against any decision of a magistrates' court under this Part (other than a decision made in criminal proceedings) shall lie to the Crown Court at the instance of any party to the proceedings in which the decision was given if such an appeal does not lie to the Crown Court by virtue of any other enactment.

(2) . . .

(3) Where a person appeals to the Crown Court . . . against a decision of a magistrates'

court ... dismissing an appeal against any requirement imposed under this Part which was suspended pending determination of that appeal, the requirement shall again be suspended pending the determination of the appeal to the Crown Court ...

(4) Where an appeal against a decision of any authority lies to a magistrates' court ... by virtue of any provision of this Part, it shall be the duty of the authority to include in any document by which it notifies the decision to the person concerned a statement indicating that such an appeal lies and specifying the time within which it must be brought.

(5) Where on an appeal to any court against or arising out of a decision of any authority under this Part the court varies or reverses the decision it shall be the duty of the authority to act in accordance with the court's decision.

(6) Where any damage is caused by waste which has been deposited in or on land, any person who deposited it, or knowingly caused or knowingly permitted it to be deposited, in either case so as to commit an offence under section 33(1) or 63(2) above, is liable for the damage except where the damage—

(a) was due wholly to the fault of the person who suffered it; or

(b) was suffered by a person who voluntarily accepted the risk of the damage being caused;

but without prejudice to any liability arising otherwise than under this subsection.

(7) The matters which may be proved by way of defence under section 33(7) above may be proved also by way of defence to an action brought under subsection (6) above.

(8) In subsection (6) above—

'damage' includes the death of, or injury to, any person (including any disease and any impairment of physical or mental condition); and

'fault' has the same meaning as in the Law Reform (Contributory Negligence) Act 1945.

(9) For the purposes of the following enactments—

(a) the Fatal Accidents Act 1976;

(b) the Law Reform (Contributory Negligence) Act 1945; and

(c) the Limitation Act 1980;

... any damage for which a person is liable under subsection (6) shall be treated as due to his fault.

74 Meaning of 'fit and proper person'

(1) The following provisions apply for the purposes of the discharge by a waste regulation authority of any function under this Part which requires the authority to determine whether a person is or is not a fit and proper person to hold a waste management licence.

(2) Whether a person is or is not a fit and proper person to hold a licence is to be determined by reference to the carrying on by him of the activities which are or are to be authorised by the licence and the fulfilment of the requirements of the licence.

(3) Subject to subsection (4) below, a person shall be treated as not being a fit and proper person if it appears to the authority—

(a) that he or another relevant person has been convicted of a relevant offence;

(b) that the management of the activities which are or are to be authorised by the licence are not or will not be in the hands of a technically competent person; or

(c) that the person who holds or is to hold the licence has not made and either has no intention of making or is in no position to make financial provision adequate to discharge the obligations arising from the licence.

(4) The authority may, if it considers it proper to do so in any particular case, treat a person as a fit and proper person notwithstanding that subsection (3)(a) above applies in his case.

(5) It shall be the duty of waste regulation authorities to have regard to any guidance

issued to them by the Secretary of State with respect to the discharge of their functions of making the determinations to which this section applies.

(6) The Secretary of State may, by regulations, prescribe the offences that are relevant for the purposes of subsection (3)(a) above and the qualifications and experience required of a person for the purposes of subsection (3)(b) above.

(7) For the purposes of subsection (3)(a) above, another relevant person shall be treated, in relation to the licence holder or proposed licence holder, as the case may be, as having been convicted of a relevant offence if—

(a) any person has been convicted of a relevant offence committed by him in the course of his employment by the holder or, as the case may be, the proposed holder of the licence or in the course of the carrying on of any business by a partnership one of the members of which was the holder or, as the case may be, the proposed holder of the licence;

(b) a body corporate has been convicted of a relevant offence committed when the holder or, as the case may be, the proposed holder of the licence was a director, manager, secretary or other similar officer of that body corporate; or

(c) where the holder or, as the case may be, the proposed holder of the licence is a body corporate, a person who is a director, manager, secretary or other similar officer of that body corporate—

  (i) has been convicted of a relevant offence; or

  (ii) was a director, manager, secretary or other similar officer of another body corporate at a time when a relevant offence for which that other body corporate has been convicted was committed.

75 Meaning of 'waste' and household, commercial and industrial waste and special waste

(1) The following provisions apply for the interpretation of this Part.

[(2) 'Waste' means any substance or object in the categories set out in Schedule 2B to this Act which the holder discards or intends or is required to discard; and for the purposes of this definition—

'holder' means the producer of the waste or the person who is in possession of it; and

'producer' means any person whose activities produce waste or any person who carries out pre-processing, mixing or other operations resulting in a change in the nature or composition of this waste.]

(3) [. . .]

(4) 'Controlled waste' means household, industrial and commercial waste or any such waste.

(5) Subject to subsection (8) below, 'household waste' means waste from—

(a) domestic property, that is to say, a building or self-contained part of a building which is used wholly for the purposes of living accommodation;

(b) a caravan (as defined in section 29(1) of the Caravan Sites and Control of Development Act 1960) which usually and for the time being is situated on a caravan site (within the meaning of that Act);

(c) a residential home;

(d) premises forming part of a university or school or other educational establishment;

(e) premises forming part of a hospital or nursing home.

(6) Subject to subsection (8) below, 'industrial waste' means waste from any of the following premises—

(a) any factory (within the meaning of the Factories Act 1961);

(b) any premises used for the purposes of, or in connection with, the provision to the public of transport services by land, water or air;

(c) any premises used for the purposes of, or in connection with, the supply to the public of gas, water or electricity or the provision of sewerage services; or

(d) any premises used for the purposes of, or in connection with, the provision to the public of postal or telecommunications services.

(7) Subject to subsection (8) below, 'commercial waste' means waste from premises used wholly or mainly for the purposes of a trade or business or the purposes of sport, recreation or entertainment excluding—

(a) household waste;

(b) industrial waste;

(c) waste from any mine or quarry and waste from premises used for agriculture within the meaning of the Agriculture Act 1947 . . . and

(d) waste of any other description prescribed by regulations made by the Secretary of State for the purposes of this paragraph.

(8) Regulations made by the Secretary of State may provide that waste of a description prescribed in the regulations shall be treated for the purposes of provisions of this Part prescribed in the regulations as being or not being household waste or industrial waste or commercial waste; but no regulations shall be made in respect of such waste as is mentioned in subsection (7)(c) above and references to waste in subsection (7) above and this subsection do not include sewage (including matter in or from a privy) except so far as the regulations provide otherwise.

(9) 'Special waste' means controlled waste as respects which regulations are in force under section 62 above.

[(10) Schedule 2B to this Act (which reproduces Annex I to the Waste Directive) shall have effect.

(11) Subsection (2) above is substituted, and Schedule 2B to this Act is inserted, for the purpose of assigning to 'waste' in this Part the meaning which it has in the Waste Directive by virtue of paragraphs (a) to (c) of Article 1 of, and Annex I to, that Directive, and those provisions shall be construed accordingly.

(12) In this section 'the Waste Directive' means the directive of the Council of the European Communities, dated 15th July 1975, on waste, as amended by—

(a) the directive of that Council, dated 18th March 1991, amending directive 75/442/EEC on waste; and

(b) the directive of that Council, dated 23rd December 1991, standardising and rationalising reports on the implementation of certain Directives relating to the environment.]

77 Transition from Control of Pollution Act 1974 to this Part

(1) This section has effect for the purposes of the transition from the provisions of Part I of the Control of Pollution Act 1974 ('the 1974 Act') to the corresponding provisions of this Part of this Act and in this section—

'existing disposal authority' has the same meaning as in section 32 above;

'existing disposal licence' means a disposal licence under section 5 of the 1974 Act subsisting on the day appointed under section 164(3) below for the repeal of sections 3 to 10 of the 1974 Act and 'relevant appointed day for licences' shall be construed accordingly;

'existing disposal plan' means a plan under section 2 of the 1974 Act subsisting on the day appointed under section 164(3) below for the repeal of that section and 'relevant appointed day for plans' shall be construed accordingly;

'relevant part of its undertaking', in relation to an existing disposal authority, has the same meaning as in section 32 above; and

'the vesting date', in relation to an existing disposal authority and its waste disposal contractors, means the vesting date under Schedule 2 to this Act.

(2) [Subject to section 4 of the Pollution Prevention and Control Act 1999,] an existing disposal licence shall, on and after the relevant appointed day for licences, be treated as a site licence until it expires or otherwise ceases to have effect; and accordingly it shall be variable and subject to revocation or suspension under this Part of this Act and may not be surrendered or transferred except under this Part of this Act.

(3) The restriction imposed by section 33(1) above shall not apply in relation to land occupied by an existing disposal authority for which a resolution of the authority subsists under section 11 of the 1974 Act on the relevant appointed day for licences until the following date, that is to say—

(a) in the case of an authority which transfers the relevant part of its undertaking in accordance with a scheme under Schedule 2 to this Act, the date which is the vesting date for that authority; and

(b) in any other case, the date on which the authority transfers, or ceases itself to carry on, the relevant part of its undertaking or ceases to provide places at which and plant and equipment by means of which controlled waste can be disposed of or deposited for the purposes of disposal.

(4) Any existing disposal plan of an existing disposal authority shall, on and after the relevant appointed day for plans, be treated as the plan of that authority under section 50 above and that section shall accordingly have effect as if references in it to 'the plan' included the existing disposal plan of that authority.

(5) . . .

(6) Subject to subsection (7) below, as respects any existing disposal authority—

(a) the restriction imposed by section 51(1) of this Act on the means whereby the authority arranges for the disposal of controlled waste shall not apply to the authority—

(i) in the case of an authority which transfers the relevant part of its undertaking in accordance with a scheme under Schedule 2 to this Act, until the date which is the vesting date for that authority; and

(ii) in any other case, until the date on which the authority transfers, or ceases itself to carry on, the relevant part of its undertaking or ceases to provide places at which and plant and equipment by means of which controlled waste can be disposed of or deposited for the purposes of disposal; and

(b) on and after that date, section 14(4) of the 1974 Act shall not authorise the authority to arrange for the disposal of controlled waste except by means of arrangements made (in accordance with Part II of Schedule 2 to this Act) with waste disposal contractors.

(7) The Secretary of State may, as respects any existing disposal authority, direct that the restriction imposed by section 51(1) above shall not apply in the case of that authority until such date as he specifies in the direction and where he does so paragraph (a) of subsection (6) above shall not apply and paragraph (b) shall be read as referring to the date so specified.

(8) In section 14(4) of the 1974 Act, after the words 'this subsection', there shall be inserted the words 'but subject to subsection (6) of section 77 of the Environmental Protection Act 1990 as respects any time after the date applicable to the authority under paragraph (a) or (b) of that subsection'.

(9) As respects any existing disposal authority, until the date which is, under subsection (6)(a) above, the date until which the restriction imposed by section 51(1) of this Act is disapplied,—

(a) the powers conferred on a waste disposal authority by section 55(2)(a) and (b) of this Act as respects the recycling of waste and the use of waste to produce heat or electricity shall be treated as powers which the authority may exercise itself; and

(b) the power conferred on a waste disposal authority by section 48(4) of this Act to object to a waste collection authority having waste recycled where the disposal authority has made arrangements with a waste disposal contractor for the contractor to recycle the waste shall be available to the waste disposal authority where it itself has the waste recycled.

78   This Part and radioactive substances

Except as provided by regulations made by the Secretary of State under this section, nothing in this Part applies to radioactive waste within the meaning of the Radioactive Substances Act 1960; but regulations may—

(a) provide for prescribed provisions of this Part to have effect with such modifications as the Secretary of State considers appropriate for the purposes of dealing with such radioactive waste;

(b) make such modifications of the Radioactive Substances Act 1960 and any other Act as the Secretary of State considers appropriate.

[PART IIA   CONTAMINATED LAND

78A   Preliminary

(1) The following provisions have effect for the interpretation of this Part.

(2) 'Contaminated land' is any land which appears to the local authority in whose area it is situated to be in such a condition, by reason of substances in, on or under the land, that—

(a) significant harm is being caused or there is a significant possibility of such harm being caused; or

(b) pollution of controlled waters is being, or is likely to be, caused; and, in determining whether any land appears to be such land, a local authority shall, subject to subsection (5) below, act in accordance with guidance issued by the Secretary of State in accordance with section 78YA below with respect to the manner in which that determination is to be made.

(3) A 'special site' is any contaminated land—

(a) which has been designated as such a site by virtue of section 78C(7) or 78D(6) below; and

(b) whose designation as such has not been terminated by the appropriate Agency under section 78Q(4) below.

(4) 'Harm' means harm to the health of living organisms or other interference with the ecological systems of which they form part and, in the case of man, includes harm to his property.

(5) The questions—

(a) what harm is to be regarded as 'significant',

(b) whether the possibility of significant harm being caused is 'significant',

(c) whether pollution of controlled waters is being, or is likely to be caused,

shall be determined in accordance with guidance issued for the purpose by the Secretary of State in accordance with section 78YA below.

(6) Without prejudice to the guidance that may be issued under subsection (5) above, guidance under paragraph (a) of that subsection may make provision for different degrees of importance to be assigned to, or for the disregard of,—

(a) different descriptions of living organisms or ecological systems;

(b) different descriptions of places; or

(c) different descriptions of harm to health or property, or other interference;

and guidance under paragraph (b) of that subsection may make provision for different degrees of possibility to be regarded as 'significant' (or as not being 'significant') in relation to different descriptions of significant harm.

(7) 'Remediation' means—

(a) the doing of anything for the purpose of assessing the condition of—

   (i)   the contaminated land in question;

   (ii) any controlled waters affected by that land; or

   (iii) any land adjoining or adjacent to that land;

(b) the doing of any works, the carrying out of any operations or the taking of any steps in relation to any such land or waters for the purpose—

   (i)   of preventing or minimising, or remedying or mitigating the effects of, any significant harm, or any pollution of controlled waters, by reason of which the contaminated land is such land; or

   (ii) of restoring the land or waters to their former state; or

(c) the making of subsequent inspections from time to time for the purpose of keeping under review the condition of the land or waters;

and cognate expressions shall be construed accordingly.

(8) Controlled waters are 'affected by' contaminated land if (and only if) it appears to the enforcing authority that the contaminated land in question is, for the purposes of subsection (2) above, in such a condition, by reason of substances in, on or under the land, that pollution of those waters is being, or is likely to be caused.

(9) The following expressions have the meaning respectively assigned to them—

'the appropriate Agency' means—

(a) in relation to England and Wales, the Environment Agency;

(b) . . .

'appropriate person' means any person who is an appropriate person, determined in accordance with section 78F below, to bear responsibility for any thing which is to be done by way of remediation in any particular case;

'charging notice' has the meaning given by section 78P(3)(b) below;

'controlled waters'—

(a) in relation to England and Wales, has the same meaning as in Part III of the Water Resources Act 1991; and

(b) . . .

. . .

'enforcing authority' means—

(a) in relation to a special site, the appropriate Agency;

(b) in relation to contaminated land other than a special site, the local authority in whose area the land is situated;

. . .

'local authority' in relation to England and Wales means—

(a) any unitary authority;

(b) any district council, so far as it is not a unitary authority;

(c) the Common Council of the City of London and, as respects the Temples, the Sub-Treasurer of the Inner Temple and the Under-Treasurer of the Middle Temple respectively;

. . .

'notice' means notice in writing;

'notification' means notification in writing;

'owner', in relation to any land in England and Wales, means a person (other than a mortgagee not in possession) who, whether in his own right or as trustee for any other person, is entitled to receive the rack rent of the land, or, where the land is not let at a rack rent, would be so entitled if it were so let;

. . .

'pollution of controlled waters' means the entry into controlled waters of any poisonous, noxious or polluting matter or any solid waste matter;

'prescribed' means prescribed by regulations;

'regulations' means regulations made by the Secretary of State;

'remediation declaration' has the meaning given by section 78H(6) below;

'remediation notice" has the meaning given by section 78E(1) below;

'remediation statement' has the meaning given by section 78H(7) below;

'required to be designated as a special site' shall be construed in accordance with section 78C(8) below;

'substance' means any natural or artificial substance, whether in solid or liquid form or in the form of a gas or vapour;

'unitary authority' means—

    (a) the council of a county, so far as it is the council of an area for which there are no district councils;

    (b) the council of any district comprised in an area for which there is no county council;

    (c) the council of a London borough;

    (d) the council of a county borough in Wales.

78B   Identification of contaminated land

(1) Every local authority shall cause its area to be inspected from time to time for the purpose—

    (a) of identifying contaminated land; and

    (b) of enabling the authority to decide whether any such land is land which is required to be designated as a special site.

(2) In performing its functions under subsection (1) above a local authority shall act in accordance with any guidance issued for the purpose by the Secretary of State in accordance with section 78R below.

(3) If a local authority identifies any contaminated land in its area, it shall give notice of that fact to—

    (a) the appropriate Agency;

    (b) the owner of the land;

    (c) any person who appears to the authority to be in occupation of the whole or any part of the land; and

    (d) each person who appears to the authority to be an appropriate person; and any notice given under this subsection shall state by virtue of which of paragraphs (a) to (d) above it is given.

(4) If, at any time after a local authority has given any person a notice pursuant to subsection (3)(d) above in respect of any land, it appears to the enforcing authority that another person is an appropriate person, the enforcing authority shall give notice to that other person—

    (a) of the fact that the local authority has identified the land in question as contaminated land; and

    (b) that he appears to the enforcing authority to be an appropriate person.

78C   Identification and designation of special sites

(1) If at any time it appears to a local authority that any contaminated land in its area might be land which is required to be designated as a special site, the authority—

    (a) shall decide whether or not the land is land which is required to be so designated; and

    (b) if the authority decides that the land is land which is required to be so designated, shall give notice of that decision to the relevant persons.

(2) For the purposes of this section 'the relevant persons' at any time in the case of any land are the persons who at that time fall within paragraphs (a) to (d) below that is to say—

    (a) the appropriate Agency;

    (b) the owner of the land;

    (c) any person who appears to the local authority concerned to be in occupation of the whole or any part of the land; and

    (d) each person who appears to that authority to be an appropriate person.

(3) Before making a decision under paragraph (a) of subsection (1) above in any particular case, a local authority shall request the advice of the appropriate Agency, and in making its decision shall have regard to any advice given by that Agency in response to the request.

(4) If at any time the appropriate Agency considers that any contaminated land is land which is required to be designated as a special site, that Agency may give notice of that fact to the local authority in whose area the land is situated.

(5) Where notice under subsection (4) above is given to a local authority, the authority shall decide whether the land in question—

    (a) is land which is required to be designated as a special site, or

    (b) is not land which is required to be so designated, and shall give notice of that decision to the relevant persons.

(6) Where a local authority makes a decision falling within subsection (1)(b) or 5(a) above, the decision shall, subject to section 78D below, take effect on the day after whichever of the following events first occurs, that is to say—

    (a) the expiration of the period of twenty-one days beginning with the day on which the notice required by virtue of subsection (1)(b) or, as the case may be, (5)(a) above is given to the appropriate Agency; or

    (b) if the appropriate Agency gives notification to the local authority in question that it agrees with the decision, the giving of that notification;

and where a decision takes effect by virtue of this subsection, the local authority shall give notice of that fact to the relevant persons.

(7) Where a decision that any land is land which is required to be designated as a special site takes effect in accordance with subsection (6) above, the notice given under subsection (1)(b) or, as the case may be, (5)(a) above shall have effect, as from the time when the decision takes effect, as the designation of that land as such a site.

(8) For the purposes of this Part, land is required to be designated as a special site if, and only if, it is land of a description prescribed for the purposes of this subsection.

(9) Regulations under subsection (8) above may make different provision for different cases or circumstances or different areas or localities and may, in particular, describe land by reference to the area or locality in which it is situated.

(10) Without prejudice to the generality of his power to prescribe any description of land for the purposes of subsection (8) above, the Secretary of State, in deciding whether to prescribe a particlar description of contaminated land for those purposes, may, in particular, have regard to—

    (a) whether land of the description in question appears to him to be land which is likely to be in such a condition, by reason of substances in, on or under the land that—

        (i) serious harm would or might be caused, or

        (ii) serious pollution of controlled waters would be, or would be likely to be, caused; or

    (b) whether the appropriate Agency is likely to have expertise in dealing with the kind of significant harm, or pollution of controlled waters, by reason of which land of the description in question is contaminated land.

78D   Referral of special site decisions to the Secretary of State

    (1) In any case where—

(a) a local authority gives notice of a decision to the appropriate Agency pursuant to subsection (1)(b) or (5)(b) of section 78C above, but

(b) before the expiration of the period of twenty-one days beginning with the day on which that notice is so given,

that Agency gives the local authority notice that it disagrees with the decision, together with a statement of its reasons for disagreeing, the authority shall refer the decision to the Secretary of State and shall send to him a statement of its reasons for reaching the decision.

(2) Where the appropriate Agency gives notice to a local authority under paragraph (b) of subsection (1) above, it shall also send to the Secretary of State a copy of the notice and of the statement given under that paragraph.

(3) Where a local authority refers a decision to the Secretary of State under subsection (1) above, it shall give notice of that fact to the relevant persons.

(4) Where a decision of a local authority is referred to the Secretary of State under subsection (1) above, he—

(a) may confirm or reverse the decision with respect to the whole or any part of the land to which it relates; and

(b) shall give notice of this decision on the referral—

(i) to the relevant persons; and

(ii) to the local authority.

(5) Where a decision of a local authority is referred to the Secretary of State under subsection (1) above, the decision shall not take effect until the day after that on which the Secretary of State gives the notice required by subsection (4) above to the persons there mentioned and shall then take effect as confirmed or reversed by him.

(6) Where a decision which takes effect in accordance with subsection (5) above is to the effect that at least some land is land which is required to be designated as a special site, the notice given under subsection (4)(b) above shall have effect, as from the time when the decision takes effect, as the designation of that land as such a site.

(7) In this section 'the relevant persons' has the same meaning as in section 78C above.

78E Duty of enforcing authority to require remediation of contaminated land etc.

(1) In any case where—

(a) any land has been designated as a special site by virtue of section 78C(7) or 78D(6) above, or

(b) a local authority has identified any contaminated land (other than a special site) in its area,

the enforcing authority shall, in accordance with such procedure as may be prescribed and subject to the following provisions of this Part, serve on each person who is an appropriate person a notice (in this Part referred to as a 'remediation notice') specifying what that person is to do by way of remediation and the periods within which he is required to do each of the things so specified.

(2) Different remediation notices requiring the doing of different things by way of remediation may be served on different persons in consequence of the presence of different substances in, on or under any land or waters.

(3) Where two or more persons are appropriate persons in relation to any particular thing which is to be done by way of remediation, the remediation notice served on each of them shall state the proportion, determined under section 78F(7) below, of the cost of doing that thing which each of them respectively is liable to bear.

(4) The only things by way of remediation which the enforcing authority may do, or require to be done, under or by virtue of this Part are things which it considers reasonable, having regard to—

(a) the cost which is likely to be involved; and

(b) the seriousness of the harm, or pollution of controlled waters, in question.

(5) In determining for any purpose of this Part—

(a) what is to be done (whether by an appropriate person, the enforcing authority or any other person) by way of remediation in any particular case,

(b) the standard to which any land is, or waters are, to be remediated pursuant to the notice, or

(c) what is, or is not, to be regarded as reasonable for the purposes of subsection (4) above,

the enforcing authority shall have regard to any guidance issued for the purpose by the Secretary of State.

(6) Regulations may make provision for or in connection with—

(a) the form or content of remediation notices; or

(b) any steps of a procedural nature which are to be taken in connection with, or in consequence of, the service of a remediation notice.

78F Determination of the appropriate person to bear responsibility for remediation

(1) This section has effect for the purpose of determining who is the appropriate person to bear responsibility for any particular thing which the enforcing authority determines is to be done by way of remediation in any particular case.

(2) Subject to the following provisions of this section, any person, or any of the persons, who caused or knowingly permitted the substances, or any of the substances, by reason of which the contaminated land in question is such land to be in, on or under that land is an appropriate person.

(3) A person shall only be an appropriate person by virtue of subsection (2) above in relation to things which are to be done by way of remediation which are to any extent referable to substances which he caused or knowingly permitted to be present in, on or under the contaminated land in question.

(4) If no person has, after reasonable inquiry, been found who is by virtue of subsection (2) above an appropriate person to bear responsibility for the things which are to be done by way of remediation, the owner or occupier for the time being of the contaminated land in question is an appropriate person.

(5) If, in consequence of subsection (3) above, there are things which are to be done by way of remediation in relation to which no person has, after reasonable inquiry, been found who is an appropriate person by virtue of subsection (2) above, the owner or occupier for the time being of the contaminated land in question is an appropriate person in relation to those things.

(6) Where two or more persons would, apart from this subsection, be appropriate persons in relation to any particular thing which is to be done by way of remediation, the enforcing authority shall determine in accordance with guidance issued for the purpose by the Secretary of State whether any, and if so which, of them is to be treated as not being an appropriate person in relation to that thing.

(7) Where two or more persons are appropriate persons in relation to any particular thing which is to be done by way of remediation, they shall be liable to bear the cost of doing that thing in proportions determined by the enforcing authority in accordance with guidance issued for the purpose by the Secretary of State.

(8) Any guidance issued for the purposes of subsection (6) or (7) above shall be issued in accordance with section 78YA below.

(9) A person who has caused or knowingly permitted any substance ('substance A') to be in, or under any land shall also be taken for the purposes of this section to have caused or knowingly permitted there to be in, on or under that land any substance

which is there as a result of a chemical reaction or biological process affecting substance A.

(10) A thing which is to be done by way of remediation may be regarded for the purposes of this Part as referable to the presence of any substance notwithstanding that the thing in question would not have to be done—

(a) in consequence only of the presence of that substance in any quantity; or

(b) in consequence only of the quantity of that substance which any particular person caused or knowingly permitted to be present.

78G   Grant of, and compensation for, rights of entry etc.

(1) A remediation notice may require an appropriate person to do things by way of remediation, notwithstanding that he is not entitled to do those things.

(2) Any person whose consent is required before any thing required by a remediation notice may be done shall grant, or join in granting, such rights in relation to any of the relevant land or waters as will enable the appropriate person to comply with any requirements imposed by the remediation notice.

(3) Before serving a remediation notice, the enforcing authority shall reasonably endeavour to consult every person who appears to the authority—

(a) to be the owner or occupier of any of the relevant land or waters, and

(b) to be a person who might be required by subsection (2) above to grant, or join in granting, any rights,

concerning the rights which that person may be so required to grant.

(4) Subsection (3) above shall not preclude the service of a remediation notice in any case where it appears to the enforcing authority that the contaminated land in question is in such a condition, by reason of substances in, on or under the land, that there is imminent danger of serious harm or serious pollution of controlled waters, being caused.

(5) A person who grants, or joins in granting, any rights pursuant to subsection (2) above shall be entitled, on making an application within such period as may be prescribed and in such manner as may be prescribed to such person as may be prescribed, to be paid by the appropriate person compensation of such amount as may be determined in such manner as may be prescribed.

(6) Without prejudice to the generality of the regulations that may be made by virtue of subsection (5) above regulations by virtue of that subsection may make such provision in relation to compensation under this section as may be made by regulations by virtue of subsection (4) of section 35A above in relation to compensation under that section.

(7) In this section, 'relevant land or waters' means—

(a) the contaminated land in question;

(b) any controlled waters affected by that land; or

(c) any land adjoining or adjacent to that land or those waters.

78H   Restrictions and prohibitions on serving remediation notices

(1) Before serving a remediation notice, the enforcing authority shall reasonably endeavour to consult—

(a) the person on whom the notice is to be served,

(b) the owner of any land to which the notice relates,

(c) any person who appears to that authority to be in occupation of the whole or any part of the land, and

(d) any person of such other description as may be prescribed, concerning what is to be done by way of remediation.

(2) Regulations may make provision for, or in connection with, steps to be taken for the purposes of subsection (1) above.

(3) No remediation notice shall be served on any person by reference to any contaminated land during any of the following periods, that is to say—

(a) the period—
  (i) beginning with the identification of the contaminated land in question pursuant to section 78B(1) above, and
  (ii) ending with the expiration of the period of three months beginning with the day on which the notice required by subsection (3)(d) or, as the case may be, (4) of section 78B above is given that person in respect of that land;

(b) if a decision falling within paragraph (b) of section 78C(1) above is made in relation to the contaminated land in question, the period beginning with the making of the decision and ending with the expiration of the perod of three months beginning with—
  (i) in a case where the decision is not referred to the Secretary of State under section 78D above, the day on which the notice required by section 78C(6) above is given, or
  (ii) in a case where the decision is referred to the Secretary of State under section 78D above, the day on which he gives the notice required by subsection (4)(b) of that section;

(c) if the appropriate Agency gives a notice under subsection (4) of section 78C above to a local authority in relation to the contaminated land in question, the period beginning with the day on which that notice is given and endng with the expiration of the period of three months beginning with—
  (i) in a case where notice is given under subsection (6) of that section, the day on which that notice is given;
  (ii) in a case where the authority makes a decision falling within subsection (5)(b) of that section and the appropriate Agency fails to give notice under paragraph (b) of section 78D(1) above, the day following the expiration of the period of twenty-one days mentioned in that paragraph; or
  (iii) in a case where the authority makes a decision falling within section 78C(5)(b) above which is referred to the Secretary of State under section 78D above, the day on which the Secretary of State gives the notice required by subsection (4)(b) of that section.

(4) Neither subsection (1) nor subsection (3) above shall preclude the service of a remediation notice in any case where it appears to the enforcing authority that th land in question is in such a condition, by reason of substances in, on or under the land, that there is imminent danger of serious harm, or serious pollution of controlled waters, being caused.

(5) The enforcing authority shall not serve a remediation notice on a person if and so long as any one or more of the following conditions is for the time being satisfied in the particular case, that is to say—
  (a) the authority is satisfied, in consequence of section 78E(4) and (5) above, that there is nothing by way of remediation which could be specified in a remediation notice served on that person;
  (b) the authority is satisfied that appropriate things are being, or will be, done by way of remediation without the service of a remediation notice on that person;
  (c) it appears to the authority that the person on whom the notice would be served is the authority itself; or
  (d) the authority is satisfied that the powers conferred on it by section 78N below to do what is appropriate by way of remediation are exercisable.

(6) Where the enforcing authority is precluded by virtue of section 78E(4) or (5) above from specifying in a remediation notice any particular thing by way of remediation which it would othewise have specified in such a notice, the authority shall prepare and publish a document (in this Part referred to as a 'remediation declaration') which shall record—

(a) the reasons why the authority would have specified that thing; and

(b) the grounds on which the authority is satisfied that it is precluded from specifying that thing in such a notice.

(7) In any case where the enforcing authority is precluded, by virtue of paragraph (b), (c) or (d) of subsection (5) above, from serving a remediation notice, the responsible person shall prepare and publish a document (in this Part referred to as a 'remediation statement') which shall record—

(a) the things which are being, have been, or are expected to be, done by way of remediation in the particular case;

(b) the name and address of the person who is doing, has done, or is expected to do, each of those things; and

(c) the periods within which each of those things is being, or is expected to be, done.

(8) For the purposes of subsection (7) above, the 'responsible person' is—

(a) in a case where the condition in paragraph (b) of subsection (5) above is satisfied, the person who is doing or has done, or who the enforcing authority is satisfied will do, the things there mentioned; or

(b) in a case where the condition in paragrah (c) or (d) of that subsection is satisfied, the enforcing authority.

(9) If a person who is required by virtue of subsection (8)(a) above to pepare and publish a remediation statement fails to do so within a reasonable time after the date on which a remediation notice specifying the things there mentioned could, apart from subsection (5) above, have been served, the enforcing authority may itself prepare and publish the statement and may recover its reasonable costs of doing so from that person.

(10) Where the enforcing authority has been precluded by virtue only of subsection (5) above from serving a remediation notice on an appropriate person but—

(a) none of the conditions in that subsection is for the time being satisified in the particular case, and

(b) the authority is not precluded by any other provison of this Part from serving a remediation notice on that appropriate person,

the authority shall serve a remediation notice on that person; and any such notice may be so served without any further endeavours by the authority to consult persons pursuant to subsection (1) above, if and to the extent that that person has been consulted pursuant to that subsection concerning the things which will be specified in the notice.

78J   Restrictions on liability relating to the pollution of controlled waters

(1) This section applies where any land is contaminated land by virtue of paragraph (b) of subsection (2) of section 78A above (whether or not the land is also contaminated land by virtue of paragraph (a) of that subsection).

(2) Where this section applies, no remediation notice given in consequence of the land in question being contaminated land shall require a person who is an appropriate person by virtue of section 78F(4) or (5) above to do anything by way of remediation to that or any other land, or any waters, which he could not have been required to do by such a notice had paragraph (b) of section 78A(2) above (and all other references to pollution of controlled waters) been omitted from this Part.

(3) If, in a case where this section applies, a person permits, has permitted, or might permit, water from an abandoned mine or part of a mine—

(a) to enter any controlled waters, or

(b) to reach a place from which it is or, as the case may be, was likely, in the opinion of the enforcing authority, to enter such waters,

no remediation notice shall require him in consequence to do anything by way of remediation (whether to the contaminated land in question or to any other land or waters) which he could not have been required to do by such a notice had paragraph (b) of section

78A(2) above (and all other references to pollution of controlled waters) been omitted from this Part.

(4) Subsection (3) above shall not apply to the owner or former operator of any mine or part of a mine if the mine or part in question became abandoned after 31st December 1999.

(5) In determining for the purposes of subsection (4) above whether a mine or part of a mine became abandoned before, on or after 31st December 1999 in a case where the mine or part has become abandoned on two or more occasions, of which—

(a) at least one falls on or before that date, and

(b) at least one falls after that date,

the mine or part shall be regarded as becoming abandoned after that date (but without prejudice to the operation of subsection (3) above in relation to that mine or part at, or in relation to, any time before the first of those occasions which fall after that date).

(6) Where, immediately before a part of a mine becomes abandoned, that part is the only part of the mine not falling to be regarded as abandoned for the time being, the abandonment of that part shall not be regarded for the purposes of subsection (4) or (5) above as constituting the abandonment of the mine, but only of that part of it.

(7) Nothing in subsection (2) or (3) above prevents the enforcing authority from doing anything by way of remediation under section 78N below which it could have done apart from that subsection, but the authority shall not be entitled under section 78P below to recover from any person any part of the cost incurred by the authority in doing by way of remediation anything which it is precluded by subsection (2) or (3) above from requiring that person to do.

(8) In this section 'mine' has the same meaning as in the Mines and Quarries Act 1954.

78K Liability in respect of contaminating substances which escape to other land

(1) A person who has caused or knowingly permitted any substances to be in, on or under any land shall also be taken for the purposes of this Part to have caused or, as the case may be, knowingly permitted those substances to be in, on or under any other land to which they appear to have escaped.

(2) Subsections (3) and(4) below apply in any case where it appears that any substances are or have been in, on or under any land (in this section referred to as 'land A') as a result of their escape, whether directly or indirectly from other land in, on or under which a person caused or knowingly permitted them to be.

(3) Where this subsection applies, no remediation notice shall require a person—

(a) who is the owner or occupier of land A, and

(b) who has not caused or knowingly permitted the substances in question to be in, on or under that land,

to do anything by way of remediation to any land or waters (other than land or waters of which he is the owner or occupier) in consequence of land A appearing to be in such a condition, by reason of the presence of those substances in, on or under it, that significant harm is being caused, or there is a significant possibility of such harm being caused, or that pollution of controlled waters is being, or is likely to be caused.

(4) Where this subsection applies, no remediation notice shall require a person—

(a) who is the owner or occupier of land A, and

(b) who has not caused or knowingly permitted the substances in question to be in, on or under that land,

to do anything by way of remediation in consequence of any further land in, on or under which those substances or any of them appear to be or to have been present as a result of their escape from land A ('land B') appearing to be in such a condition, by reason of the presence of those substances in, on or under it, that significant harm is being caused, or there is a significant possibility of such harm being caused, or that pollution of controlled waters is being, or is likely to be caused, unless he is also the owner or occupier of land B.

(5) In any case where—

    (a) a person ('person A') has caused or knowingly permitted any substances to be in, on, or under any land,

    (b) another person ('person B') who has not caused or knowingly permitted those substances to be in, or under that land becomes the owner or occupier of that land, and

    (c) the substances, or any of the substances, mentioned in paragraph (a) above appear to have escaped to other land,

no remediation notice shall require person B to do anything by way of remediation to that other land in consequence of the apparent acts or omissions of person A, except to the extent that person B caused or knowingly permitted the escape.

(6) Nothing in subsection (3), (4) or (5) above prevents the enforcing authority from doing anything by way of remediation under section 78N below which it could have done apart from that subsection, but the authority shall not be entitled under section 78P below to recover from any person any part of the cost incurred by the authority in doing by way of remediation anything which it is precluded by subsection (3), (4) or (5) above from requiring that person to do.

(7) In this section, 'appear' means appear to the enforcing authority, and cognate expressions shall be construed accordingly.

78L   Appeals against remediation notices

(1) A person on whom a remediation notice is served may, within the period of twenty-one days beginning with the day on which the notice is served, appeal against the notice—

    (a) if it was served by a local authority, to a magistrates' court or, . . . or

    (b) if it was served by the appropriate Agency, to the Secretary of State;

and in the following provisions of this section 'the appellate authority' means the magistrates' court, the sheriff or the Secretary of State, as the case may be.

(2) On any appeal under subsection (1) above the appellate authority—

    (a) shall quash the notice, if it is satisfied that there is a material defect in the notice; but

    (b) subject to that, may confirm the remediation notice, with or without modification, or quash it.

(3) Where an appellate authority confirms a remediation notice, with or without modification, it may extend the period specified in the notice for doing what the notice requires to be done.

(4) Regulations may make provision with respect to—

    (a) the grounds on which appeals under subsection (1) above may be made;

    (b) the cases in which, grounds on which, court or tribunal to which, or person at whose instance, an appeal against a decision of a magistrates' court or sheriff court in pursuance of an appeal under subsection (1) above shall lie; or

    (c) the procedure on an appeal under subsection (1) above or on an appeal by virtue of paragraph (b) above.

(5) Regulations under subsection (4) above may (among other things)—

    (a) include provisions comparable to those in section 290 of the Public Healh Act 1936 (appeals againt notices requiring the execution of works);

    (b) prescribe the cases in which a remediation notice is, or is not, to be suspended until the appeal is decided, or until some other stage in proceedings;

    (c) prescribe the cases in which the decision on an appeal may in some respects be less favourable to the appellant than the remediation notice against which he is appealing;

(d) prescribe the cases in which the appellant may claim that a remediation notice should have been served on some other person and prescribe the procedure to be followed in those cases;

(e) make provision as respects—

    (i) the particulars to be included in the notice of appeal;

    (ii) the persons on whom notice of appeal is to be served and the particulars, if any, which are to accompany the notice; and

    (iii) the abandonment of an appeal;

(f) make different provision for different cases or classes of case.

(6) This section, so far as relating to appeals to the Secretary of State, is subject to section 114 of the Environment Act 1995 (delegation or reference of appeals etc).

78M Offences of not complying with a remediation notice

(1) If a person on whom an enforcing authority serves a remediation notice fails, without reasonable excuse, to comply with any of the requirements of the notice, he shall be guilty of an offence.

(2) Where the remediation notice in question is one which was required by section 78E(3) above to state, in relation to the requirement which has not been complied with, the proportion of the cost involved which the person charged with the offence is liable to bear, it shall be a defence for that person to prove that the only reason why he has not complied with the requirement is that one or more of the other persons who are liable to bear a proportion of that cost refused, or was not able, to comply with the requirement.

(3) Except in a case falling within subsection (4) below, a person who commits an offence under subsection (1) above shall be liable, on summary conviction, to a fine not exceeding level 5 on the standard scale and to a further fine of an amount equal to one-tenth of level 5 on the standard scale for each day on which the failure continues after conviction of the offence and before the enforcing authority has begun to exercise its powers by virtue of section 78N(3)(c) below.

(4) A person who commits an offence under subsection (1) above in a case where the contaminated land to which the remediation notice relates is industrial, trade or business premises shall be liable on summary conviction to a fine not exceeding £20,000 or such greater sum as the Secretary of State may from time to time by order substitute and to a further fine of an amount equal to one-tenth of that sum for each day on which the failure continues after conviction of the offence and before the enforcing authority has begun to exercise its powers by virtue of section 78N(3)(c) below.

(5) If the enforcing authority is of the opinion that proceedings for an offence under this section would afford an ineffectual remedy against a person who has failed to comply with any of the requirements of a remediation notice which that authority has served on him, that authority may take proceedings in the High Court . . . for the purpose of securing compliance with the remediation notice.

(6) In this section 'industrial, trade or business premises' means premises used for any industrial, trade or business purposes or premises not so used on which matter is burnt in connection with any industrial, trade or business process, and premises are used for industrial purposes where they are used for the purposes of any treatment or process as well as where they are used for the purpose of manufacturing.

(7) No order shall be made under subsection (4) above unless a draft of the order has been laid before, and approved by a resolution of, each House of Parliament.

78N Powers of the enforcing authority to carry out remediation

(1) Where this section applies, the enforcing authority shall itself have power, in a case falling within paragraph (a) or (b) of section 78E(1) above, to do what is appropriate by way of remediation to the relevant land or waters.

(2) Subsection (1) above shall not confer power on the enforcing authority to do anything by way of remediation if the authority would, in the particular case, be precluded by section 78YB below from serving a remediation notice requiring that thing to be done.

(3) This section applies in each of the following cases, that is to say—

(a) where the enforcing authority considers it necessary to do anything itself by way of remediation for the purpose of preventing the occurrence of any serious harm, or serious pollution of controlled waters, of which there is imminent danger;

(b) where an appropriate person has entered into a written agreement with the enforcing authority for that authority to do, at the cost of that person, that which he would otherwise be required to do under this Part by way of remediation;

(c) where a person on whom the enforcing authority serves a remediation notice fails to comply with any of the requirements of the notice;

(d) where the enforcing authority is precluded by section 78J or 78K above from including something by way of remediation in a remediation notice;

(e) where the enforcing authority considers that, were it to do some particular thing by way of remediation, it would decide, by virtue of subsection (2) of section 78P below or any guidance issued under that subsection,—

(i) not to seek to recover under subsection (1) of that section any of the reasonable cost incurred by it in doing that thing; or

(ii) to seek so to recover only a portion of that cost;

(f) where no person has, after reasonable inquiry, been found who is an appropriate person in relation to any particular thing.

(4) Subject to section 78E(4) and (5) above, for the purposes of this section, the things which it is appropriate for the enforcing authority to do by way of remediation are—

(a) in a case falling within paragraph (a) of subsection (3) above, anything by way of remediation which the enforcing authority considers necessary for the purpose mentioned in that paragraph;

(b) in a case falling within paragraph (b) of that subsection, anything specified in, or determined under, the agreement mentioned in that paragraph;

(c) in a case falling within paragraph (c) of that subsection, anything which the person mentioned in that paragraph was required to do by virtue of the remediation notice;

(d) in a case falling within paragraph (d) of that subsection, anything by way of remediation which the enforcing authority is precluded by section 78J or 78K above from including in a remediation notice;

(e) in a case falling within paragraph (e) or (f) of that subsection, the particular thing mentioned in the paragraph in question.

(5) In this section 'the relevant land or waters' means—

(a) the contaminated land in question;

(b) any controlled waters affected by that land; or

(c) any land adjoining or adjacent to that land or those waters.

78P   Recovery of, and security for, the cost of remediation by the enforcing authority

(1) Where, by virtue of section 78N(3)(a), (c), (e) or (f) above, the enforcing authority does any particular thing by way of remediation, it shall be entitled, subject to section 78J(7) and 78K(6) above, to recover the reasonable cost incurred in doing it from the appropriate person or, if there are two or more appropriate persons in proportions determined pursuant to section 78F(7) above.

(2) In deciding whether to recover the cost, and, if so, how much of the cost, which it is entitled to recover under subsection (1) above, the enforcing authority shall have regard—

(a) to any hardship which the recovery may cause to the person from whom the cost is recoverable; and

(b) to any guidance issued by the Secretary of State for the purposes of this subsection.

(3) Subsection (4) below shall apply in any case where—

(a) any cost is recoverable under subsection (1) above from a person—

(i) who is the owner of any premises which consist of or include the contaminated land in question; and

(ii) who caused or knowingly permitted the substances, or any of the substances, by reason of which the land is contaminated land to be in, on or under the land; and

(b) the enforcing authority serves a notice under this subsection (in this Part referred to as a 'charging notice') on that person.

(4) Where this subsection applies—

(a) the cost shall carry interest, at such reasonable rate as the enforcing authority may determine, from the date of service of the notice until the whole amount is paid; and

(b) subject to the following provisions of this section, the cost and accrued interest shall be a charge on the premises mentioned in subsection (3)(a)(i) above.

(5) A charging notice shall—

(a) specify the amount of the cost which the enforcing authority claims is irrecoverable;

(b) state the effect of subsection (4) above and the rate of interest determined by the authority under that subsection; and

(c) state the effect of subsections (7) and (8) below.

(6) On the date on which an enforcing authority serves a charging notice on a person, the authority shall also serve a copy of the notice on every other person who, to the knowledge of the authority, has an interest in the premises capable of being affected by the charge.

(7) Subject to any order under subsection (9)(b) or (c) below, the amount of any cost specified in a charging notice and the accrued interest shall be a charge on the premises—

(a) as from the end of the period of twenty-one days beginning with the service of the charging notice, or

(b) where an appeal is brought under subsection (8) below, as from the final determination or (as the case may be) the withdrawal, of the appeal,

until the cost and interest are recovered.

(8) A person served with a charging notice or a copy of a charging notice may appeal against the notice to a county court within the period of twenty-one days beginning with the date of service.

(9) On an appeal under subsection (8) above, the court may—

(a) confirm the notice without modification;

(b) order that the notice is to have effect with the substitution of a different amount for the amount originally specified in it; or

(c) order that the notice is to be of no effect.

(10) Regulations may make provision with respect to—

(a) the grounds on which appeals under this section may be made; or

(b) the procedure on any such appeal.

(11) An enforcing authority shall, for the purpose of enforcing a charge under this section, have all the same powers and remedies under the Law of Property Act 1925, and otherwise, as if it were a mortgagee by deed having powers of sale and lease, of accepting surrenders of leases and of appointing a receiver.

(12) Where any cost is a charge on premises under this section, the enforcing authority may by order declare the cost to be payable with interest by instalments within the specified period until the whole amount is paid.

(13) In subsection (12) above—

'interest' means interest at the rate determined by the enforcing authority under subsection (4) above; and

'the specified period' means such period of thirty years or less from the date of service of the charging notice as is specified in the order.

(14) ...

78Q   Special sites

(1) If, in a case where a local authority has served a remediation notice, the contaminated land in question becomes a special site, the appropriate Agency may adopt the remediation notice and, if it does so,—

    (a) it shall give notice of its decision to adopt the remediation notice to the appropriate person and to the local authority;

    (b) the remediation notice shall have effect, as from the time at which the appropriate Agency decides to adopt it, as a remediation notice given by that Agency; and

    (c) the validity of the remediation notice shall not be affected by—

        (i) the contaminated land having become a special site;

        (ii) the adoption of the remediation notice by the appropriate Agency; or

        (iii) anything in paragraph (b) above.

(2) Where a local authority has, by virtue of section 78N above, begun to do anything, or any series of things, by way of remediation—

    (a) the authority may continue doing that thing, or that series of things, by virtue of that section, notwithstanding that the contaminated land in question becomes a special site; and

    (b) section 78P above shall apply in relation to the reasonable cost incurred by the authority in doing that thing or those things as if that authority were the enforcing authority.

(3) If and so long as any land is a special site, the appropriate Agency may from time to time inspect that land for the purpose of keeping its condition under review.

(4) If it appears to the appropriate Agency that a special site is no longer land which is required to be designated as such a site, the appropriate Agency may give notice—

    (a) to the Secretary of State, and

    (b) to the local authority in whose area the site is situated,

terminating the designation of the land in question as a special site as from such date as may be specified in the notice.

(5) A notice under subsection (4) above shall not prevent the land, or any of the land, to which the notice relates beng designated as a special site on a subsequent occasion.

(6) In exercising its functions under subsection (3) or (4) above, the appropriate Agency shall act in accordance with any guidance given for the purpose by the Secretary of State.

78R   Registers

(1) Every enforcing authority shall maintain a register containing prescribed particulars of or relating to—

    (a) remediation notices served by that authority;

    (b) appeals against any such remediation notices;

    (c) remediation statements or remediation declarations prepared and published under section 78H above;

    (d) in relation to an enforcing authority in England and Wales, appeals against charging notices served by that authority;

    (e) notices under subsection (1)(b) or (5)(a) of section 78C above which have effect by virtue of subsection (7) of that section as the designation of any land as a special site;

   (f) notices under subsection (4)(b) of section 78D above which have effect by virtue of subsection (6) of that section as the designation of any land as a special site;

   (g) notices given by or to the enforcing authority under section 78Q(4) above terminating the designation of any land as a special site;

   (h) notifications given to that authority by persons—
      (i) on whom a remediation notice has been served, or
      (ii) who are or were required by virtue of section 78H(8)(a) above to prepare and publish a remediation statement,
    of what they claim has been done by them by way of remediation;

   (j) notifications given to that authority by owners or occupiers of land—
      (i) in respect of which a remediation notice has been served, or
      (ii) in respect of which a remediation statement has been prepared and published,
    of what they claim has been done on the land in question by way of remediation;

   (k) convictions for such offences under section 78M above as may be prescribed;

   (l) such other matters relating to contaminated land as may be prescribed; but that duty is subject to sections 78S and 78T below.

(2) The form of, and the descriptions of information to be contained in, notifications for the purposes of subsection (1)(h) or (j) above may be prescribed by the Secretary of State.

(3) No entry made in a register by virtue of subsection (1)(h) or (j) above constitutes a repesentation by the body maintaining the register or, in a case where the entry is made by virtue of subsection (6) below, the authority which sent the copy of the particulars in question pursuant to subsection (4) or (5) below—

   (a) that what is stated in the entry to have been done has in fact been done; or

   (b) as to the manner in which it has been done.

(4) Where any particulars are entered on a register maintained under this section by the appropriate Agency, the appropriate Agency shall send a copy of those particulars to the local authority in whose area is situated the land to which the particulars relate.

(5) In any case where—

   (a) any land is treated by virtue of section 78X(2) below as situated in the area of a local authority other than the local authority in whose area it is in fact situated, and

   (b) any particulars relating to that land are entered on the register maintained under this section by the local authority in whose area the land is so treated as situated, that authority shall send a copy of those particulars to the local authority in whose area the land is in fact situated.

(6) Where a local authority receives a copy of any particulars sent to it pursuant to sub-section (4) or (5) above, it shall enter those particulars on the register maintained by it under this section.

(7) Where information of any description is excluded by virtue of section 78T below from any register maintained under this section, a statement shall be entered in the register indicating the existence of information of that description.

(8) It shall be the duty of each enforcing authority—

   (a) to secure that the registers maintained by it under this section are available, at all reasonable times, for inspection by the public free of charge; and

   (b) to afford to members of the public facilities for obtaining copies of entries, on payment of reasonable charges;

and, for the purposes of this subsection, places may be prescribed by the Secretary of State at which any such registers or facilities as are mentioned in paragraph (a) or (b) above are to be available or afforded to the public in pursuance of the paragraph in question.

(9) Registers under this section may be kept in any form.

78S   Exclusion from registers of information affecting national security

(1) No information shall be included in a register maintained under section 78R above if and so long as, in the opinion of the Secretary of State, the inclusion in the register of that information, or information of that description, would be contrary to the interests of national security.

(2) The Secretary of State may, for the purpose of securing the exclusion from registers of information to which subsection (1) above applies, give to enforcing authorities directions—

(a) specifying information, or descriptions of information, to be excluded from their registers; or

(b) specifying descriptions of information to be referred to the Secretary of State for his determination;

and no information referred to the Secretary of State in pursuance of paragraph (b) above shall be in any such register until the Secretary of State determines that it should be so included.

(3) The enforcing authority shall notify the Secretary of State of any information which it excludes from the register in pursuance of directions under subsection (2) above.

(4) A person may, as respects any information which appears to him to be information to which subsection (1) above may apply, give a notice to the Secretary of State specifying the information and indicating its apparent nature; and, if he does so—

(a) he shall notify the enforcing authority that he has done so; and

(b) no information so notified to the Secretary of State shall be included in any such register until the Secretary of State has determined that it should be so included.

78T   Exclusion from registers of certain confidential information

(1) No information relating to the affairs of any individual or business shall be included in a register maintained under section 78R above, without the consent of that individual or the person for the time being carrying on that business, if and so long as the information—

(a) is, in relation to him, commercially confidential; and

(b) is not required to be included in the register in pursuance of directions under subsection (7) below;

but information is not commercially confidential for the purposes of this section unless it is determined under this section to be so by the enforcing authority or, on appeal, by the Secretary of State.

(2) Where it appears to an enforcing authority that any information which has been obtained by the authority under or by virtue of any provision of this Part might be commercially confidential, the authority shall—

(a) give to the person to whom or whose business it relates notice that that information is required to be included in the register unless excluded under this section; and

(b) give him a reasonable opportunity—

(i) of objecting to the inclusion of the information on the ground that it is commercially confidential; and

(ii) of making representations to the authority for the purpose of justifying any such objection;

and, if any representations are made, the enforcing authority shall, having taken the representations into account, determine whether the information is or is not commercially confidential.

(3) Where, under subsection (2) above, an authority determines that information is not commercially confidential—

(a) the information shall not be entered in the register until the end of the period of twenty-one days beginning with the date on which the determination is notified to the person concerned;

(b) that person may appeal to the Secretary of State against the decision;

and, where an appeal is brought in respect of any information, the information shall not be entered in the register until the end of the period of seven days following the day on which the appeal is finally determined or withdrawn.

(4) An appeal under subsection (3) above shall, if either party to the appeal so requests or the Secretary of State so decides, take or continue in the form of a hearing (which must be held in private).

(5) Subsection (10) of section 15 above shall apply in relation to an appeal under subsection (3) above as it applies in relation to an appeal under that section.

(6) Subsection (3) above is subject to section 114 of the Environment Act 1995 (delegation or reference of appeals etc).

(7) The Secretary of State may give to the enforcing authorities directions as to specified information, or descriptions of information, which the public interest requires to be included in registers maintained under section 78R above notwithstanding that the information may be commercially confidential.

(8) Information excluded from a register shall be treated as ceasing to be commercially confidential for the purposes of this section at the expiry of the period of four years beginning with the date of the determination by virtue of which it was excluded; but the person who furnished it may apply to the authority for the information to remain excluded from the register on the ground that it is still commercially confidential and the authority shall determine whether or not that is the case.

(9) Subsections (3) to (6) above shall apply in relation to a determination under subsection (8) above as they apply in relation to a determination under subsection (2) above.

(10) Information is, for the purposes of any determination under this section, commercially confidential, in relation to any individual or person, if its being contained in the register would prejudice to an unreasonable degree the commercial interests of that individual or person.

(11) For the purposes of subsection (10) above, there shall be disregarded any prejudice to the commercial interests of any individual or person so far as relating only to the value of the contaminated land in question or otherwise to the ownership or occupation of that land.

78U   Reports by the appropriate Agency on the state of contaminated land

(1) The appropriate Agency shall—

    (a) from time to time, or

    (b) if the Secretary of State at any time so requests,

prepare and publish a report on the state of contaminated land in England and Wales . . . as the case may be.

(2) A local authority shall, at the written request of the appropriate Agency, furnish the appropriate Agency with such information to which this subsection applies as the appropriate Agency may require for the purpose of enabling it to perform its functions under subsection (1) above.

(3) The information to which subsection (2) above applies is such information as the local authority may have, or may reasonably be expected to obtain, with respect to the condition of contaminated land in its area, being information which the authority has acquired or may acquire in the exercise of its functions under this Part.

78V   Site-specific guidance by the appropriate Agency concerning contaminated land

(1) The appropriate Agency may issue guidance to any local authority with respect to the exercise or performance of the authority's powers or duties under this Part in relation to any particular contaminated land; and in exercising or performing those powers or duties in relation to that land the authority shall have regard to any such guidance so issued.

(2) If and to the extent that any guidance issued under subsection (1) above to a local authority is inconsistent with any guidance issued under this Part by the Secretary of State, the local authority shall disregard the guidance under that subsection.

(3) A local authority shall, at the written request of the appropriate Agency, furnish the appropriate Agency with such information to which this subsection applies as the appropriate Agency may require for the purpose of enabling it to issue guidance for the purposes of subsection (1) above.

(4) The information to which subsection (3) above applies is such information as the local authority may have, or may reasonably be expected to obtain, with respect to any contaminated land in its area, being information which the authority has acquired, or may acquire, in the exercise of its functions under this Part.

78W   The appropriate Agency to have regard to guidance given by the Secretary of State

(1) The Secretary of State may issue guidance to the appropriate Agency with respect to the exercise or performance of that Agency's powers or duties under this Part; and in exercising or performing those powers or duties the appropriate Agency shall have regard to any such guidance so issued.

(2) The duty imposed on the appropriate Agency by subsection (1) above is without prejudice to any duty imposed by any other provision of this Part on that Agency to act in accordance with guidance issued by the Secretary of State.

78X   Supplementary provisions

(1) Where it appears to a local authority that two or more different sites, when considered together, are in such a condition, by reason of substances in, on or under the land, that—

(a) significant harm is being caused or there is a significant possibility of such harm being caused, or

(b) pollution of controlled waters is being, or is likely to be, caused,

this Part shall apply in relation to each of those sites, whether or not the condition of the land at any of them, when considered alone, appears to the authority to be such that significant harm is being caused, or there is a significant possibility of such harm being caused, or that pollution of controlled waters is being or is likely to be caused.

(2) Where it appears to a local authority that any land outside, but adjoining or adjacent to, its area is in such a condition, by reason of substances in, on or under the land, that significant harm is being caused, or there is a significant possibility of such harm being caused, or that pollution of controlled waters is being, or is likely to be, caused within its area—

(a) the authority may, in exercising its functions under this Part, treat that land as if it were land situated within its area; and

(b) except in this subsection, any reference—

(i) to land within the area of a local authority, or

(ii) to the local authority in whose area any land is situated,

shall be construed accordingly;

but this subsection is without prejudice to the functions of the local authority in whose area the land is in fact situated.

(3) A person acting in a relevant capacity—

(a) shall not thereby be personally liable, under this Part, to bear the whole or any part of the cost of doing any thing by way of remediation, unless that thing is to any extent referable to substances whose presence in, on or under the contaminated land in question is a result of any act done or omission made by him which it was unreasonable for a person acting in that capacity to do or make; and

(b) shall not thereby be guilty of an offence under or by virtue of section 78M above unless the requirement which has not been complied with is a requirement to do some particular thing for which he is personally liable to bear the whole or any part of the cost.

(4) In subsection (3) above, 'person acting in a relevant capacity' means—

    (a) a person acting as an insolvency practitioner, within the meaning of section 388 of the Insolvency Act 1986 (includng that section as it applies in relation to an insolvent partnership by virtue of any order made under section 421 of that Act);

    (b) the official receiver acting in a capacity in which he would be regarded as acting as an insolvency practitioner within the meaning of section 388 of the Insolvency Act 1986 if subsection (5) of that section were disregarded;

    (c) the official receiver acting as receiver or manager;

    (d) a person acting as a special manager under section 177 or 370 of the Insolvency Act 1986;

    (e) . . .

    (f) a person acting as a receiver or receiver and manager—

        (i) under or by virtue of any enactment; or

        (ii) by virtue of his appointment as such by an order of a court or by any other instrument.

(5) Regulations may make different provision for different cases or circumstances.

78Y . . .

78YA Supplementary provisions with respect to guidance by the Secretary of State

(1) Any power of the Secretary of State to issue guidance under this Part shall only be exercisable after consultation with the appropriate Agency and such other bodies or persons as he may consider it appropriate to consult in relation to the guidance in question.

(2) A draft of any guidance proposed to be issued under section 78A(2) or (5), 78B(2) or 78F(6) or (7) above shall be laid before each House of Parliament and the guidance shall not be issued until after the period of 40 days beginning with the day on which the draft was so laid or, if the draft is laid on different days, the later of the two days.

(3) If, within the period mentioned in subsection (2) above, either House resolves that the guidance, the draft of which was laid before it, should not be issued, the Secretary of State shall not issue that guidance.

(4) In reckoning any period of 40 days for the purposes of subsection (2) or (3) above, no account shall be taken of any time during which Parliament is dissolved or prorogued or during which both Houses are adjourned for more than four days.

(5) The Secretary of State shall arrange for any guidance issued by him under this Part to be published in such manner as he considers appropriate.

78YB Interaction of this Part with other enactments

(1) A remediation notice shall not be served if and to the extent that it appears to the enforcing authority that the powers of the appropriate Agency under section 27 above may be exercised in relation to—

    (a) the significant harm (if any), and

    (b) the pollution of controlled waters (if any), by reason of which the contaminated land in question is such land.

(2) Nothing in this Part shall apply in relation to any land in respect of which there is for the time being in force a site licence under Part II above, except to the extent that any significant harm, or pollution of controlled waters, by reason of which that land would otherwise fall to be regarded as contaminated land is attributable to causes other than—

    (a) breach of the conditions of the licence; or

    (b) the carrying on, in accordance with the conditions of the licence, of any activity authorised by the licence.

[(2A) This Part shall not apply if and to the extent that—

(a) any significant harm, or pollution of controlled waters, by reason of which the land would otherwise fall to be regarded as contaminated, is attributable to the final disposal by deposit in or on land of controlled waste, and

(b) enforcement action may be taken in relation to that disposal.

(2B) A remediation notice shall not be served in respect of contaminated land if and to the extent that—

(a) the significant harm, or pollution of controlled waters, by reason of which the contaminated land is such land is attributable to an activity other than the final disposal by deposit in or on land of controlled waste, and

(b) enforcement action may be taken in relation to that activity.

(2C) In subsections (2A) and (2B) above—

'controlled waste' has the meaning given in section 75(4) of this Act; and

'enforcement action' means action under regulation 24 (enforcement notices) or regulation 26(2) (power of regulator to remedy pollution) of the Pollution Prevention and Control (England and Wales) Regulations 2000.]

(3) If, in a case falling within subsection (1) or (7) of section 59 above, the land in question is contaminated land, or becomes such land by reason of the deposit of the controlled waste in question, a remediation notice shall not be served in respect of that land by reason of that waste or any consequences of its deposit, if and to the extent that it appears to the enforcing authority that the powers of a waste regulation authority or waste collection authority under that section may be exercised in relation to that waste or the consequences of its deposit.

(4) No remediation notice shall require a person to do anything the effect of which would be to impede or prevent the making of a discharge in pursuance of a consent given under Chapter II of Part III of the Water Resources Act 1991 (pollution offences). . . .

78YC This Part and radioactivity

Except as provided by regulations, nothing in this Part applies in relation to harm, or pollution of controlled waters, so far as attributable to any radioactivity possessed by any substance; but regulations may—

(a) provide for prescribed provisions of this Part to have effect with such modifications as the Secretary of State considers appropriate for the purpose of dealing with harm, or pollution of controlled waters, so far as attributable to any radioactivity possessed by any substances; or

(b) make such modifications of the Radioactive Substances Act 1993 or any other Act as the Secretary of State considers appropriate.]

PART III   STATUTORY NUISANCES AND CLEAN AIR

79 Statutory nuisances and inspections therefor

(1) [Subject to subsections (1A) to (6A)] below, the following matters constitute 'statutory nuisances' for the purposes of this Part, that is to say—

(a) any premises in such a state as to be prejudicial to health or a nuisance;

(b) smoke emitted from premises so as to be prejudicial to health or a nuisance;

(c) fumes or gases emitted from premises so as to be prejudicial to health or a nuisance;

(d) any dust, steam, smell or other effluvia arising on industrial, trade or business premises and being prejudicial to health or a nuisance;

(e) any accumulation or deposit which is prejudicial to health or a nuisance;

(f) any animal kept in such a place or manner as to be prejudicial to health or a nuisance;

(g) noise emitted from premises so as to be prejudicial to health or a nuisance;

[(ga) noise that is prejudicial to health or a nuisance and is emitted from or caused by a vehicle, machinery or equipment in a street . . .]

(h) any other matter declared by any enactment to be a statutory nuisance;

and it shall be the duty of every local authority to cause its area to be inspected from time to time to detect any statutory nuisances which ought to be dealt with under sections 80 [and 80A] below and, where a complaint of a statutory nuisance is made to it by a person living within its area, to take such steps as are reasonably practicable to investigate the complaint.

[(1A) No matter shall constitute a statutory nuisance to the extent that it consists of, or is caused by, any land being in a contaminated state.

(1B) Land is in a 'contaminated state' for the purposes of subsection (1A) above if, and only if, it is in such a condition, by reason of substances in, on or under the land, that—

(a) harm is being caused or there is a possibility of harm being caused; or

(b) pollution of controlled waters is being, or is likely to be, caused;

and in this subsection 'harm', 'pollution of controlled waters' and 'substance' have the same meaning as in Part IIA of this Act.]

(2) Subsection (1)(b) and (g) above do not apply in relation to premises—

(a) occupied on behalf of the Crown for naval, military or air force purposes or for the purposes of the department of the Secretary of State having responsibility for defence, or

(b) occupied by or for the purposes of a visiting force;

and 'visiting force' means any such body, contingent or detachment of the forces of any country as is a visiting force for the purposes of any of the provisions of the Visiting Forces Act 1952.

(3) Subsection (1)(b) above does not apply to—

(i) smoke emitted from a chimney of a private dwelling within a smoke control area,

(ii) dark smoke emitted from a chimney of a building or a chimney serving the furnace of a boiler or industrial plant attached to a building or for the time being fixed to or installed on any land,

(iii) smoke emitted from a railway locomotive steam engine, or

(iv) dark smoke emitted otherwise than as mentioned above from industrial or trade premises.

(4) Subsection (1)(c) above does not apply in relation to premises other than private dwellings.

(5) Subsection (1)(d) above does not apply to steam emitted from a railway locomotive engine.

(6) Subsection (1)(g) above does not apply to noise caused by aircraft other than model aircraft.

[(6A) Subsection (1)(ga) above does not apply to noise made—

(a) by traffic,

(b) by any naval, military or air force of the Crown or by a visiting force (as defined in subsection (2) above), or

(c) by a political demonstration or a demonstration supporting or opposing a cause or campaign.]

(7) In this Part—

'chimney' includes structures and openings of any kind from or through which smoke may be emitted;

'dust' does not include dust emitted from a chimney as an ingredient of smoke;

['equipment' includes a musical instrument;]

'fumes' means any airborne solid matter smaller than dust;

'gas' includes vapour and moisture precipitated from vapour;

'industrial, trade or business premises' means premises used for any industrial, trade or business purposes or premises not so used on which matter is burnt in connection with any industrial, trade or business process, and premises are used for industrial purposes where they are used for the purposes of any treatment or process as well as where they are used for the purposes of manufacturing;

'local authority' means, subject to subsection (8) below,—

    (a) in Greater London, a London borough council, the Common Council of the City of London and, as respects the Temples, the Sub-Treasurer of the Inner Temple and the Under-Treasurer of the Middle Temple respectively;

    (b) [in England and Wales] outside Greater London, a district council; [. . .]

    (c) the Council of the Isles of Scilly;

    (d) . . .

'noise' includes vibration;

['person responsible'—

    (a) in relation to a statutory nuisance, means the person to whose act, default or sufferance the nuisance is attributable;

    (b) in relation to a vehicle, includes the person in whose name the vehicle is for the time being registered under the Vehicles (Excise) Act 1971 and any other person who is for the time being the driver of the vehicle;

    (c) in relation to machinery or equipment, includes any person who is for the time being the operator of the machinery or equipment;]

'prejudicial to health' means injurious, or likely to cause injury, to health;

'premises' includes land and, subject to subsection (12) [and [in relation to England and Wales] section 81A(9)] below, any vessel;

'private dwelling' means any building, or part of a building, used or intended to be used, as a dwelling;

['road' has the same meaning as in Part IV of the New Roads and Street Works Act 1991:]

'smoke' includes soot, ash, grit and gritty particles emitted in smoke;

['street' means a highway and any other road, footway, square or court that is for the time being open to the public;]

and any expressions used in this section and in [the Clean Air Act 1993] have the same meaning in this section as in that Act and [section 3 of the Clean Air Act 1993] shall apply for the interpretation of the expression 'dark smoke' and the operation of this Part in relation to it.

(8) Where, by an order under section 2 of the Public Health (Control of Disease) Act 1984, a port health authority . . . has been constituted for any port health district, the port health authority . . . shall have by virtue of this subsection, as respects its district, the functions conferred or imposed by this Part in relation to statutory nuisances other than a nuisance falling within paragraph (g) [or (ga)] of subsection (1) above and no such order shall be made assigning those functions; and 'local authority' and 'area' shall be construed accordingly.

(9) In this Part 'best practicable means' is to be interpreted by reference to the following provisions—

    (a) 'practicable' means reasonably practicable having regard among other things to local conditions and circumstances, to the current state of technical knowledge and to the financial implications;

    (b) the means to be employed include the design, installation, maintenance and manner and periods of operation of plant and machinery, and the design. construction and maintenance of buildings and structures;

    (c) the test is to apply only so far as compatible with any duty imposed by law;

(d) the test is to apply only so far as compatible with safety and safe working conditions, and with the exigencies of any emergency or unforeseeable circumstances;

and, in circumstances where a code of practice under section 71 of the Control of Pollution Act 1974 (noise minimisation) is applicable, regard shall also be had to guidance given in it.

(10) A local authority shall not without the consent of the Secretary of State institute summary proceedings under this Part in respect of a nuisance falling within paragraph (b), (d) [(e) or (g)] . . . of subsection (1) above if proceedings in respect thereof might be instituted under Part I [or under regulations under section 2 of the Pollution Prevention and Control Act 1999.]

(11) The area of a local authority which includes part of the seashore shall also include for the purposes of this Part the territorial sea lying seawards from that part of the shore; and subject to subsection (12) [in relation to England and Wales,] [and section 81A(9)] below, this Part shall have effect, in relation to any area included in the area of a local authority by virtue of this subsection—

(a) as if references to premises and the occupier of premises included respectively a vessel and the master of a vessel; and

(b) with such other modifications, if any, as are prescribed in regulations made by the Secretary of State.

(12) A vessel powered by steam reciprocating machinery is not a vessel to which this Part of this Act applies.

80 Summary proceedings for statutory nuisances

(1) Where a local authority is satisfied that a statutory nuisance exists, or is likely to occur or recur, in the area of the authority, the local authority shall serve a notice ('an abatement notice') imposing all or any of the following requirements—

(a) requiring the abatement of the nuisance or prohibiting or restricting its occurrence or recurrence;

(b) requiring the execution of such works, and the taking of such other steps, as may be necessary for any of those purposes,

and the notice shall specify the time or times within which the requirements of the notice are to be complied with.

(2) [Subject to section 80A(1) below,] the abatement notice shall be served—

(a) except in a case falling within paragraph (b) or (c) below, on the person responsible for the nuisance;

(b) where the nuisance arises from any defect of a structural character, on the owner of the premises;

(c) where the person responsible for the nuisance cannot be found or the nuisance has not yet occurred, on the owner or occupier of the premises.

[(3) A person served with an abatement notice] may appeal against the notice to a magistrates' court . . . within the period of twenty-one days beginning with the date on which he was served with the notice.

(4) If a person on whom an abatement notice is served, without reasonable excuse, contravenes or fails to comply with any requirement or prohibition imposed by the notice, he shall be guilty of an offence.

(5) Except in a case falling within subsection (6) below, a person who commits an offence under subsection (4) above shall be liable on summary conviction to a fine not exceeding level 5 on the standard scale together with a further fine of an amount equal to one-tenth of that level for each day on which the offence continues after the conviction.

(6) A person who commits an offence under subsection (4) above on industrial, trade or business premises shall be liable on summary conviction to a fine not exceeding £20,000.

(7) Subject to subsection (8) below, in any proceedings for an offence under subsection (4) above in respect of a statutory nuisance it shall be a defence to prove that the best practicable means were used to prevent, or to counteract the effects of, the nuisance.

(8) The defence under subsection (7) above is not available—

    (a) in the case of a nuisance falling within paragraph (a), (d), (e), (f) or (g) of section 79(1) above except where the nuisance arises on industrial, trade or business premises;

    [(aa) in the case of a nuisance falling within paragraph (ga) of section 79(1) above except where the noise is emitted from or caused by a vehicle, machinery or equipment being used for industrial, trade or business purposes;]

    (b) in the case of a nuisance falling within paragraph (b) of section 79(1) above except where the smoke is emitted from a chimney; and

    (c) in the case of a nuisance falling within paragraph (c) or (h) of section 79(1) above.

(9) In proceedings for an offence under subsection (4) above in respect of a statutory nuisance falling within paragraph (g) [or (ga)] of section 79(1) above where the offence consists in contravening requirements imposed by virtue of subsection (1)(a) above it shall be a defence to prove—

    (a) that the alleged offence was covered by a notice served under section 60 or a consent given under section 61 or 65 of the Control of Pollution Act 1974 (construction sites, etc); or

    (b) where the alleged offence was committed at a time when the premises were subject to a notice under section 66 of that Act (noise reduction notice), that the level of noise emitted from the premises at that time was not such as to a constitute a contravention of the notice under that section; or

    (c) where the alleged offence was committed at a time when the premises were not subject to a notice under section 66 of that Act, and when a level fixed under section 67 of that Act (new buildings liable to abatement order) applied to the premises, that the level of noise emitted from the premises at that time did not exceed that level.

(10) Paragraphs (b) and (c) of subsection (9) above apply whether or not the relevant notice was subject to appeal at the time when the offence was alleged to have been committed.

80A   [Abatement notice in respect of noise in street

    (1) In the case of a statutory nuisance within section 79(1)(ga) above that—

    (a) has not yet occurred, or

    (b) arises from noise emitted from or caused by an unattended vehicle or unattended machinery or equipment,

the abatement notice shall be served in accordance with subsection (2) below.

    (2) The notice shall be served—

    (a) where the person responsible for the vehicle, machinery or equipment can be found, on that person;

    (b) where that person cannot be found or where the local authority determines that this paragraph should apply, by fixing the notice to the vehicle, machinery or equipment.

    (3) Where—

    (a) an abatement notice is served in accordance with subsection (2)(b) above by virtue of a determination of the local authority, and

    (b) the person responsible for the vehicle, machinery or equipment can be found and served with a copy of the notice within an hour of the notice being fixed to the vehicle, machinery or equipment,

a copy of the notice shall be served on that person accordingly.

(4) Where an abatement notice is served in accordance with subsection (2)(b) above by virtue of a determination of the local authority, the notice shall state that, if a copy of the notice is subsequently served under subsection (3) above, the time specified in the notice as the time within which its requirements are to be complied with is extended by such further period as is specified in the notice.

(5) Where an abatement notice is served in accordance with subsection (2)(b) above, the person responsible for the vehicle, machinery or equipment may appeal against the notice under section 80(3) above as if he had been served with the notice on the date on which it was fixed to the vehicle, machinery or equipment.

(6) Section 80(4) above shall apply in relation to a person on whom a copy of an abatement notice is served under subsection (3) above as if the copy were the notice itself.

(7) A person who removes or interferes with a notice fixed to a vehicle, machinery or equipment in accordance with subsection (2)(b) above shall be guilty of an offence, unless he is the person responsible for the vehicle, machinery or equipment or he does so with the authority of that person.

(8) A person who commits an offence under subsection (7) above shall be liable on summary conviction to a fine not exceeding level 3 on the standard scale.]

81 Supplementary provisions

(1) [Subject to subsection (1A) below, where] more than one person is responsible for a statutory nuisance section 80 above shall apply to each of those persons whether or not what any one of them is responsible for would by itself amount to a nuisance.

[(1A) In relation to a statutory nuisance within section 79(1)(ga) above for which more than one person is responsible (whether or not what any one of those persons is responsible for would by itself amount to such a nuisance), section 80(2)(a) above shall apply with the substitution of 'any one of the persons' for 'the person'.

(1B) In relation to a statutory nuisance within section 79(1)(ga) above caused by noise emitted from or caused by an unattended vehicle or unattended machinery or equipment for which more than one person is responsible, section 80A above shall apply with the substitution—

    (a) in subsection (2)(a), of 'any of the persons' for 'the person' and of 'one such person' for 'that person',
    (b) in subsection (2)(b), of 'such a person' for 'that person',
    (c) in subsection (3), of 'any of the persons' for 'the person' and of 'one such person' for 'that person',
    (d) in subsection (5), of 'any person' for 'the person', and
    (e) in subsection (7), of 'a person' for 'the person' and of 'such a person' for 'that person'.]

(2) Where a statutory nuisance which exists or has occurred within the area of a local authority, or which has affected any part of that area, appears to the local authority to be wholly or partly caused by some act or default committed or taking place outside the area, the local authority may act under section 80 above as if the act or default were wholly within that area, except that any appeal shall be heard by a magistrates' court ... having jurisdiction where the act or default is alleged to have taken place.

(3) Where an abatement notice has not been complied with the local authority may, whether or not they take proceedings for an offence ... under section 80(4) above, abate the nuisance and do whatever may be necessary in execution of the notice.

(4) Any expenses reasonably incurred by a local authority in abating, or preventing the recurrence of, a statutory nuisance under subsection (3) above may be recovered by them from the person by whose act or default the nuisance was caused and, if that person is the owner of the premises, from any person who is for the time being the owner thereof; and the court ...

may apportion the expenses between persons by whose acts or defaults the nuisance is caused in such manner as the court consider . . . fair and reasonable.

(5) If a local authority is of opinion that proceedings for an offence under section 80(4) above would afford an inadequate remedy in the case of any statutory nuisance, they may, subject to subsection (6) below, take proceedings in the High Court . . . for the purpose of securing the abatement, prohibition or restriction of the nuisance, and the proceedings shall be maintainable notwithstanding the local authority have suffered no damage from the nuisance.

(6) In any proceedings under subsection (5) above in respect of a nuisance falling within paragraph (g) [or (ga)] of section 79(1) above, it shall be a defence to prove that the noise was authorised by a notice under section 60 or a consent under section 61 (construction sites) of the Control of Pollution Act 1974.

(7) The further supplementary provisions in Schedule 3 to this Act shall have effect.

81A [Expenses recoverable from owner to be a charge on premises

(1) Where any expenses are recoverable under section 81(4) above from a person who is the owner of the premises there mentioned and the local authority serves a notice on him under this section—

   (a) the expenses shall carry interest, at such reasonable rate as the local authority may determine, from the date of service of the notice until the whole amount is paid, and

   (b) subject to the following provisions of this section, the expenses and accrued interest shall be a charge on the premises.

(2) A notice served under this section shall—

   (a) specify the amount of the expenses that the local authority claims is recoverable,

   (b) state the effect of subsection (1) above and the rate of interest determined by the local authority under that subsection, and

   (c) state the effect of subsections (4) to (6) below.

(3) On the date on which a local authority serves a notice on a person under this section the authority shall also serve a copy of the notice on every other person who, to the knowledge of the authority, has an interest in the premises capable of being affected by the charge.

(4) Subject to any order under subsection (7)(b) or (c) below, the amount of any expenses specified in a notice under this section and the accrued interest shall be a charge on the premises—

   (a) as from the end of the period of twenty-one days beginning with the date of service of the notice, or

   (b) where an appeal is brought under subsection (6) below, as from the final determination of the appeal,

until the expenses and interest are recovered.

(5) For the purposes of subsection (4) above, the withdrawal of an appeal has the same effect as a final determination of the appeal.

(6) A person served with a notice or copy of a notice under this section may appeal against the notice to the county court within the period of twenty-one days beginning with the date of service.

(7) On such an appeal the court may—

   (a) confirm the notice without modification,

   (b) order that the notice is to have effect with the substitution of a different amount for the amount originally specified in it, or

   (c) order that the notice is to be of no effect.

(8) A local authority shall, for the purpose of enforcing a charge under this section, have all the same powers and remedies under the Law of Property Act 1925, and otherwise, as if it

were a mortgagee by deed having powers of sale and lease, of accepting surrenders of leases and of appointing a receiver.

(9) In this section—

'owner', in relation to any premises, means a person (other than a mortgagee not in possession) who, whether in his own right or as trustee for any other person, is entitled to receive the rack rent of the premises or, where the premises are not let at a rack rent, would be so entitled if they were so let, and

'premises' does not include a vessel.

(10) . . .

81B   Payment of expenses by instalments

(1) Where any expenses are a charge on premises under section 81A above, the local authority may by order declare the expenses to be payable with interest by instalments within the specified period, until the whole amount is paid.

(2) In subsection (1) above—

'interest' means interest at the rate determined by the authority under section 81A (1) above, and

'the specified period' means such period of thirty years or less from the date of service of the notice under section 81A above as is specified in the order.

(3) Subject to subsection (5) below, the instalments and interest, or any part of them, may be recovered from the owner or occupier for the time being of the premises.

(4) Any sums recovered from an occupier may be deducted by him from the rent of the premises.

(5) An occupier shall not be required to pay at any one time any sum greater than the aggregate of—

(a) the amount that was due from him on account of rent at the date on which he was served with a demand from the local authority together with a notice requiring him not to pay rent to his landlord without deducting the sum demanded, and

(b) the amount that has become due from him on account of rent since that date.]

(6) . . .

82   Summary proceedings by persons aggrieved by statutory nuisances

(1) A magistrates' court may act under this section on a complaint . . . made by any person on the ground that he is aggrieved by the existence of a statutory nuisance.

(2) If the magistrates' court . . . is satisfied that the alleged nuisance exists, or that although abated it is likely to recur on the same premises [or, in the case of a nuisance within section 79(1)(ga) above, in the same street . . .], thecourt . . . shall make an order for either or both of the following purposes—

(a) requiring the defendant . . . to abate the nuisance, within a time specified in the order, and to execute any works necessary for that purpose;

(b) prohibiting a recurrence of the nuisance, and requiring the defendant . . . within a time specified in the order, to execute any works necessary to prevent the recurrence;

and may also impose on the defendant a fine not exceeding level 5 on the standard scale.

(3) If the magistrates' court . . . is satisfied that the alleged nuisance exists and is such as, in the opinion of the court . . . torender premises unfit for human habitation, an order under subsection (2) above may prohibit the use of the premises for human habitation until the premises are, to the satisfaction of the court . . ., rendered fit for that purpose.

(4) Proceedings for an order under subsection (2) above shall be brought—

(a) except in a case falling within [paragraph (b), (c) or (d) below], against the person responsible for the nuisance;

(b) where the nuisance arises from any defect of a structural character, against the owner of the premises;

(c) where the person responsible for the nuisance cannot be found, against the owner or occupier of the premises.

[(d) in the case of a statutory nuisance within section 79(1)(ga) above caused by noise emitted from or caused by an unattended vehicle or unattended machinery or equipment, against the person responsible for the vehicle, machinery or equipment.]

[(5) Subject to subsection (5A) below, where] more than one person is responsible for a statutory nuisance, subsections (1) to (4) above shall apply to each of those persons whether or not what any one of them is responsible for would by itself amount to a nuisance.

[(5A) In relation to a statutory nuisance within section 79(1)(ga) above for which more than one person is responsible (whether or not what any one of those persons is responsible for would by itself amount to such a nuisance), subsection (4)(a) above shall apply with the substitution of 'each person responsible for the nuisance who can be found' for 'the person responsible for the nuisance'.

(5B) In relation to a statutory nuisance within section 79(1)(ga) above caused by noise emitted from or caused by an unattended vehicle or unattended machinery or equipment for which more than one person is responsible, subsection (4)(d) above shall apply with the substitution of 'any person' for 'the person'.]

(6) Before instituting proceedings for an order under subsection (2) above against any person, the person aggrieved by the nuisance shall give to that person such notice in writing of his intention to bring the proceedings as is applicable to proceedings in respect of a nuisance of that description and the notice shall specify the matter complained of.

(7) The notice of the bringing of proceedings in respect of a statutory nuisance required by subsection (6) above which is applicable is—

(a) in the case of a nuisance falling within paragraph (g) [or (ga)] of section 79(1) above, not less than three days' notice; and

(b) in the case of a nuisance of any other description, not less than twenty-one days' notice;

but the Secretary of State may, by order, provide that this subsection shall have effect as if such period as is specified in the order were the minimum period of notice applicable to any description of statutory nuisance specified in the order.

(8) A person who, without reasonable excuse, contravenes any requirement or prohibition imposed by an order under subsection (2) above shall be guilty of an offence and liable on summary conviction to a fine not exceeding level 5 on the standard scale together with a further fine of an amount equal to one-tenth of that level for each day on which the offence continues after the conviction.

(9) Subject to subsection (10) below, in any proceedings for an offence under subsection (8) above in respect of a statutory nuisance it shall be a defence to prove that the best practicable means were used to prevent, or to counteract the effects of, the nuisance.

(10) The defence under subsection (9) above is not available—

(a) in the case of a nuisance falling within paragraph (a), (d), (e), (f) or (g) of section 79(1) above except where the nuisance arises on industrial, trade or business premises;

[(aa) in the case of a nuisance falling within paragraph (ga) of section 79(1) above except where the noise is emitted from or caused by a vehicle, machinery or equipment being used for industrial, trade or business purposes;]

(b) in the case of a nuisance falling within paragraph (b) of section 79(1) above except where the smoke is emitted from a chimney;

(c) in the case of a nuisance falling within paragraph (c) or (h) of section 79(1) above; and

(d) in the case of a nuisance which is such as to render the premises unfit for human habitation.

(11) If a person is convicted of an offence under subsection (8) above, a magistrates' court . . . may, after giving the local authority in whose area the nuisance has occurred an opportunity of being heard, direct the authority to do anything which the person convicted was required to do by the order to which the conviction relates.

(12) Where on the hearing of proceedings for an order under subsection (2) above it is proved that the alleged nuisance existed at the date of the making of the complaint . . ., then, whether or not at the date of the hearing it still exists or is likely to recur, the court . . . shall order the defendant . . . (or defendants . . . in such proportions as appears fair and reasonable) to pay to the person bringing the proceedings such amount as the court . . . considers reasonably sufficient to compensate him for any expenses properly incurred by him in the proceedings.

(13) If it appears to the magistrates' court . . . that neither the person responsible for the nuisance nor the owner or occupier of the premises [or (as the case may be) the person responsible for the vehicle, machinery or equipment] can be found the court . . . may, after giving the local authority in whose area the nuisance has occurred an opportunity of being heard, direct the authority to do anything which the court . . . would have ordered that person to do.

PART VII   NATURE CONSERVATION IN GREAT BRITAIN AND COUNTRYSIDE MATTERS IN WALES

128   Creation and constitution of new Councils

(1) There shall be three councils, to be called the Nature Conservancy Council for England, the Nature Conservancy Council for Scotland, and the Countryside Council for Wales (in this Part referred to as 'the Councils').

(2) The Councils shall have the following membership, that is to say—

    (a) the Nature Conservancy Council for England shall have not less than 10 nor more than 14 members;

    (b) the Nature Conservancy Council for Scotland shall have not less than 8 nor more than 12 members; and

    (c) the Countryside Council for Wales shall have not less than 8 nor more than 12 members;

and those members shall be appointed by the Secretary of State.

(3) The Secretary of State may by order amend paragraph (a), (b) or (c) of subsection (2) above so as to substitute for the number for the time being specified as the maximum membership of a Council such other number as he thinks appropriate.

(4) The Councils shall establish a committee to be called the Joint Nature Conservation Committee (in this Part referred to as 'the joint committee').

(5) Schedules 6 and 7 to this Act shall have effect with respect to the constitution and proceedings of the Councils and of the joint committee and related matters.

130   Countryside functions of Welsh Council

(1) The Countryside Council for Wales shall, in place of the Commission established under section 1 of the National Parks and Access to the Countryside Act 1949 (so far as concerns Wales), have such of the functions under the Acts amended by Schedule 8 to this Act (which relates to countryside matters) as are assigned to them in accordance with the amendments effected by that Schedule.

(2) The Countryside Council for Wales shall discharge those functions—

    (a) for the conservation and enhancement of natural beauty in Wales and of the natural beauty and amenity of the countryside in Wales, both in the areas designated under the National Parks and Access to the Countryside Act 1949 as National Parks or as areas of outstanding natural beauty and elsewhere;

(b) for encouraging the provision or improvement, for persons resorting to the countryside in Wales, of facilities for the enjoyment thereof and for the enjoyment of the opportunities for open-air recreation and the study of nature afforded thereby; and shall have regard to the social and economic interests of rural areas in Wales.

(3) The reference in subsection (2) above to the conservation of the natural beauty of the countryside includes the conservation of its flora, fauna and geological and physiographical features.

(4) The Countryside Council for Wales and the Countryside Commission shall discharge their respective functions under those Acts (as amended by Schedule 8) on and after a day to be appointed by an order made by the Secretary of State.

131   Nature conservation functions: preliminary

(1) For the purposes of nature conservation, and fostering the understanding thereof, the Councils shall, in place of the Nature Conservancy Council established under the Nature Conservancy Council Act 1973, have the functions conferred on them by sections 132 to 134 below (which are in this Part referred to as 'nature conservation functions').

(2) It shall be the duty of the Councils in discharging their nature conservation functions to take appropriate account of actual or possible ecological changes.

(3) The Councils shall discharge their nature conservation functions on and after a day to be appointed by an order made by the Secretary of State.

(4) The Secretary of State may give the Councils, or any of them, directions of a general or specific character with regard to the discharge of any of their nature conservation functions other than those conferred on them by section 132(1)(a) below.

(5) Any reference in this section to the Councils includes a reference to the joint committee and, accordingly, directions under subsection (4) above may be given to the joint committee as respects any of the functions dischargeable by them (other than under section 133(2)(a)).

(6) In this Part 'nature conservation' means the conservation of flora, fauna or geological or physiographical features.

132   General functions of the Councils

(1) The Councils shall each have the following functions, namely—

(a) such of the functions previously discharged by the Nature Conservancy Council under the Acts amended by Schedule 9 to this Act as are assigned to them in accordance with the amendments effected by that Schedule;

(b) the establishment, maintenance and management of nature reserves (within the meaning of section 15 of the National Parks and Access to the Countryside Act 1949) in their area;

(c) the provision of advice for the Secretary of State or any other Minister on the development and implementation of policies for or affecting nature conservation in their area;

(d) the provision of advice and the dissemination of knowledge to any persons about nature conservation in their area or about matters arising from the discharge of their functions under this section or section 134 below;

(e) the commissioning or support (whether by financial means or otherwise) of research which in their opinion is relevant to any of their functions under this section or section 134 below;

and the Councils shall, in discharging their functions under this section, have regard to any advice given to them by the joint committee under section 133(3) below.

(2) The Councils shall each have power—

(a) to accept any gift or contribution made to them for the purposes of any of the functions conferred on them by subsection (1) above or section 134 below and, subject to the terms of the gift or contribution, to apply it to those purposes;

(b) to initiate and carry out such research directly related to those functions as it is appropriate that they should carry out instead of commissioning or supporting other persons under paragraph (e) of that subsection;

and they may do all such other things as are incidental or conducive to those functions including (without prejudice to the generality of this provision) making charges and holding land or any interest in or right over land.

(3) Nothing in this section shall be taken as preventing any of the Councils—

(a) if consulted by another of the Councils about a matter relating to the functions of that other Council, from giving that other Council any advice or information which they are able to give; or

(b) from giving advice or information to the joint committee about any matter relating to any of the functions conferred by section 133(2) and (3) below.

133   Special functions of Councils

(1) The Councils shall jointly have the following functions which may, however, be discharged only through the joint committee; and in this section the functions so dischargeable are referred to as 'special functions'.

(2) The special functions of the Councils are—

(a) such of the functions previously discharged by the Nature Conservancy Council under the Wildlife and Countryside Act 1981 as are assigned to the Councils jointly as special functions in accordance with the amendments to that Act effected by Schedule 9 to this Act;

(b) the provision of advice for the Secretary of State or any other Minister on the development and implementation of policies for or affecting nature conservation for Great Britain as a whole or nature conservation outside Great Britain;

(c) the provision of advice and the dissemination of knowledge to any persons about nature conservation for Great Britain as a whole or nature conservation outside Great Britain;

(d) the establishment of common standards throughout Great Britain for the monitoring of nature conservation and for research into nature conservation and the analysis of the resulting information;

(e) the commissioning or support (whether by financial means or otherwise) of research which in the opinion of the joint committee is relevant to any matter mentioned in paragraphs (a) to (d) above;

and section 132(2) above shall apply to the special functions as it applies to the functions conferred by subsection (1) of that section.

(3) The joint committee may give advice or information to any of the Councils on any matter arising in connection with the functions of that Council under section 132 above which, in the opinion of the committee, concerns nature conservation for Great Britain as a whole or nature conservation outside Great Britain.

(4) For the purposes of this section, references to nature conservation for Great Britain as a whole are references to—

(a) any nature conservation matter of national or international importance or which otherwise affects the interests of Great Britain as a whole; or

(b) any nature conservation matter which arises throughout Great Britain and raises issues common to England, Scotland and Wales,

and it is immaterial for the purposes of paragraph (a) above that a matter arises only in relation to England, to Scotland or to Wales.

(5) The Secretary of State may, as respects any matter arising in connection with—

(a) any special function of the Councils, or

(b) the function of the joint committee under subsection (3) above,

give directions to any of the Councils requiring that Council (instead of the joint committee) to discharge that function in relation to that matter.

PART VIII   MISCELLANEOUS

140   Power to prohibit or restrict the importation, use, supply or storage of injurious substances or articles

(1) The Secretary of State may by regulations prohibit or restrict—

(a) the importation into and the landing and unloading in the United Kingdom,

(b) the use for any purpose,

(c) the supply for any purpose, and

(d) the storage,

of any specified substance or article if he considers it appropriate to do so for the purpose of preventing the substance or article from causing pollution of the environment or harm to human health or to the health of animals or plants.

(2) Any such prohibition or restriction may apply—

(a) in all, or only in specified, areas;

(b) in all, or only in specified, circumstances or if conditions imposed by the regulations are not complied with; and

(c) to all, or only to specified descriptions of, persons.

(3) Regulations under this section may—

(a) confer on the Secretary of State power to direct that any substance or article whose use, supply or storage is prohibited or restricted is to be treated as waste or controlled waste of any description and in relation to any such substance or article—

(i) to apply, with or without modification, specified provisions of Part II; or

(ii) to direct that it be disposed of or treated in accordance with the direction;

(b) confer on the Secretary of State power, where a substance or article has been imported, landed or unloaded in contravention of a prohibition or restriction imposed under subsection (1)(a) above, to require that the substance or article be disposed of or treated in or removed from the United Kingdom;

(c) confer powers corresponding to those conferred by section 17 above on persons authorised for any purpose of the regulations by the Secretary of State or any local or other authority; and

(d) include such other incidental and supplemental, and such transitional provisions, as the Secretary of State considers appropriate.

(4) The Secretary of State may, by regulations under this section, direct that, for the purposes of any power conferred on him under subsection (3)(b) above, any prohibition or restriction on the importation into or the landing and unloading in the United Kingdom imposed—

(a) by or under any Community instrument, or

(b) by or under any enactment,

shall be treated as imposed under subsection (1)(a) above and any power conferred on him under subsection (3)(b) above shall be exercisable accordingly.

(5) The Secretary of State may by order establish a committee to give him advice in relation to the exercise of the power to make regulations under this section and Schedule 12 to this Act shall have effect in relation to it.

(6) Subject to subsection (7) below, it shall be the duty of the Secretary of State before he makes any regulations under this section other than regulations under subsection (4) above—

(a) to consult the committee constituted under subsection (5) above about the proposed regulations;

(b) having consulted the committee, to publish in the London Gazette . . . and in any other publication which he considers appropriate, a notice indicating the effect of the proposed regulations and specifying—

(i)   the date on which it is proposed that the regulations will come into force;

(ii) a place where a draft of the proposed regulations may be inspected free of charge by members of the public during office hours; and

(iii) a period of not less than fourteen days, beginning with the date on which the notice is first published, during which representations in writing may be made to the Secretary of State about the proposed regulations; and

(c) to consider any representations which are made to him in accordance with the notice.

(7) The Secretary of State may make regulations under this section in relation to any substance or article without observing the requirements of subsection (6) above where it appears to him that there is an imminent risk, if those requirements are observed, that serious pollution of the environment will be caused.

(8) The Secretary of State may, after performing the duty imposed on him by subsection (6) above with respect to any proposed regulations, make the regulations either—

(a) in the form of the draft mentioned in subsection (6)(b) above, or

(b) in that form with such modifications as he considers appropriate;

but the Secretary of State shall not make any regulations incorporating modifications unless he is of opinion that it is appropriate for the requirements of subsection (6) above to be disregarded.

(9) Regulations under this section may provide that a person who contravenes or fails to comply with a specified provision of the regulations or causes or permits another person to contravene or fail to comply with a specified provision of the regulations commits an offence and may prescribe the maximum penalty for the offence.

(10) No offence under the regulations shall be made punishable with imprisonment for more than two years or punishable on summary conviction with a fine exceeding level 5 on the standard scale (if not calculated on a daily basis) or, in the case of a continuing offence, exceeding one-tenth of the level on the standard scale specified as the maximum penalty for the original offence.

(11) In this section—

'the environment' means the air, water and land, or any of those media, and the medium of air includes the air within buildings and the air within other natural or man-made structures above or below ground;

'specified' means specified in the regulations; and

'substance' means any natural or artificial substance, whether in solid or liquid form or in the form of a gas or vapour and it includes mixtures of substances.

141   Power to prohibit or restrict the importation or exportation of waste

(1) The Secretary of State may, for the purpose of preventing any risk of pollution of the environment or of harm to human health arising from waste being imported or exported or of conserving the facilities or resources for dealing with waste, make regulations prohibiting or restricting, or providing for the prohibition or restriction of—

(a) the importation into and the landing and unloading in the United Kingdom, or

(b) the exportation, or the loading for exportation, from the United Kingdom, of waste of any description.

(2) Regulations under this section may make different provision for different descriptions of waste or waste of any description in different circumstances.

(3) Regulations under this section may, as respects any description of waste, confer or impose on waste regulation authorities or any of them such functions in relation to the importation of waste as appear to be appropriate to the Secretary of State, subject to such limitations and conditions as are specified in the regulations.

(4) Regulations under this section may confer or impose on waste regulation authorities or any of them functions of enforcing any of the regulations on behalf of the Secretary of State whether or not the functions fall within subsection (3) above.

(5) Regulations under this section may—

    (a) as respects functions conferred or imposed on waste regulation authorities—

        (i) make them exercisable in relation to individual consignments or consignments in a series by the same person but not in relation to consignments or descriptions of consignments generally; [. . .]

        (ii) [. . .]

    (b) impose or provide for the imposition of prohibitions either absolutely or only if conditions or procedures prescribed in or under the regulations are not complied with;

    (c) impose duties to be complied with before, on or after any importation or exportation of waste by persons who are, or are to be, consignors, consignees, carriers or holders of the waste or any waste derived from it;

    (d) confer powers corresponding to those conferred by section 69(3) above;

    (e) provide for appeals to the Secretary of State from determinations made by authorities under the regulations;

    (f) provide for the keeping by the Secretary of State, waste regulation authorities and waste collection authorities of public registers of information relating to the importation and exportation of waste and for the transmission of such information between any of those persons;

    (g) create offences, subject to the limitation that no offence shall be punishable with imprisonment for more than two years or punishable on summary conviction with imprisonment for more than six months or a fine exceeding level 5 on the standard scale (if not calculated on a daily basis) or, in the case of a continuing offence, exceeding one-tenth of the level on the standard scale specified as the maximum penalty for the original offence.

(6) In this section—

'the environment' means land, water and air or any of them;

'harm' includes offence to any of man's senses;

'waste', 'waste collection authority', and 'waste regulation authority' have the same meaning as in Part II; and

'the United Kingdom' includes its territorial sea.

(7) . . .

142 Powers to obtain information about potentially hazardous substances

(1) The Secretary of State may, for the purpose of assessing their potential for causing pollution of the environment or harm to human health, by regulations make provision for and in connection with the obtaining of relevant information relating to substances which may be specified by him by order for the purposes of this section.

(2) The Secretary of State shall not make an order under subsection (1) above specifying any substance—

    (a) which was first supplied in any member State on or after 18th September 1981; or

    (b) in so far as it is a regulated substance for the purposes of any relevant enactment.

(3) The Secretary of State shall not make an order under subsection (1) above specifying any substance without consulting the committee established under section 140(5) except

where it appears to him that information about the substance needs to be obtained urgently under this section.

(4) Regulations under this section may—

(a) prescribe the descriptions of relevant information which are to be furnished under this section in relation to specified substances;

(b) impose requirements on manufacturers, importers or suppliers generally to furnish information prescribed under paragraph (a) above;

(c) provide for the imposition of requirements on manufacturers, importers or suppliers generally to furnish relevant information relating to products or articles containing specified substances in relation to which information has been furnished in pursuance of paragraph (b) above;

(d) provide for the imposition of requirements on particular manufacturers, importers or suppliers to furnish further information relating to specified substances in relation to which information has been furnished in pursuance of paragraph (b) above;

(e) provide for the imposition of requirements on particular manufacturers or importers to carry out tests of specified substances and to furnish information of the results of the tests;

(f) authorise persons to comply with requirements to furnish information imposed on them by or under the regulations by means of representative persons or bodies;

(g) impose restrictions on the disclosure of information obtained under this section and provide for determining what information is, and what information is not, to be treated as furnished in confidence;

(h) create offences, subject to the limitation that no offence shall be punishable with imprisonment or punishable on summary conviction with a fine exceeding level 5 on the standard scale;

(i) make any public authority designated by the regulations responsible for the enforcement of the regulations to such extent as may be specified in the regulations;

(j) include such other incidental and supplemental, and such transitional, provisions as the Secretary of State considers appropriate.

(5) The Secretary of State shall have regard, in imposing or providing for the imposition of any requirement under subsection (4)(b), (c), (d) or (e) above, to the cost likely to be involved in complying with the requirement.

(6) In this section—

'the environment' means the air, water and land or any of them;

'relevant information', in relation to substances, products or articles, means information relating to their properties, production, distribution, importation or use or intended use and, in relation to products or articles, to their disposal as waste;

'substance' means any natural or artificial substance, whether in solid or liquid form or in the form of a gas or vapour and it includes mixtures of substances.

(7) The enactments which are relevant for the purposes of subsection (2)(b) above are the following—

the Explosive Substances Act 1875;

the Radioactive Substances Act 1960;

Parts II, III and VIII of the Medicines Act 1968;

Part IV of the Agriculture Act 1970;

the Misuse of Drugs Act 1971;

Part III of the Food and Environment Protection Act 1985; and

the Food Safety Act 1990;

and a substance is a regulated substance for the purposes of any such enactment in so far as any prohibition, restriction or requirement is imposed in relation to it by or under the enactment for the purposes of that enactment.

PART IX　GENERAL

156　Power to give effect to Community and other international obligations etc.

(1) The Secretary of State may by regulations provide that the provisions to which this section applies shall have effect with such modifications as may be prescribed for the purpose of enabling Her Majesty's Government in the United Kingdom—

    (a)　to give effect to any Community obligation or exercise any related right; or

    (b)　to give effect to any obligation or exercise any related right under any international agreement to which the United Kingdom is for the time being a party.

(2) This section applies to the following provisions of this Act—

    (a)　Part I;

    (b)　Part II;

    (c)　Part VI; and

    (d)　in Part VIII, sections 140, 141 or 142;

and the provisions of the Radioactive Substances Act 1960.

(3) In this section—

'modifications' includes additions, alterations and omissions;

'prescribed' means prescribed in regulations under this section; and

'related right', in relation to an obligation, includes any derogation or other right to make more onerous provisions available in respect of that obligation.

(4) ...

157　Offences by bodies corporate

(1) Where an offence under any provision of this Act committed by a body corporate is proved to have been committed with the consent or connivance of, or to have been attributable to any neglect on the part of, any director, manager, secretary or other similar officer of the body corporate or a person who was purporting to act in any such capacity, he as well as the body corporate shall be guilty of that offence and shall be liable to be proceeded against and punished accordingly.

(2) Where the affairs of a body corporate are managed by its members, subsection (1) above shall apply in relation to the acts or defaults of a member in connection with his functions of management as if he were a director of the body corporate.

158　Offences under Parts I, II, IV, VI, etc. due to fault of others

Where the commission by any person of an offence under Part I, II, IV, or VI, or section 140, 141 or 142 above is due to the act or default of some other person, that other person may be charged with and convicted of the offence by virtue of this section whether or not proceedings for the offence are taken against the first-mentioned person.

159　Application to Crown

(1) Subject to the provisions of this section, the provisions of this Act and of regulations and orders made under it shall bind the Crown.

(2) No contravention by the Crown of any provision of this Act or of any regulations or order made under it shall make the Crown criminally liable; but the High Court ... may, on the application of any public or local authority charged with enforcing that provision, declare unlawful any act or omission of the Crown which constitutes such a contravention.

(3) Notwithstanding anything in subsection (2) above, the provisions of this Act and of regulations and orders made under it shall apply to persons in the public service of the Crown as they apply to other persons.

(4) If the Secretary of State certifies that it appears to him, as respects any Crown premises and any powers of entry exercisable in relation to them specified in the certificate that it is

requisite or expedient that, in the interests of national security, the powers should not be exercisable in relation to the premises, those powers shall not be exercisable in relation to those premises; and in this subsection 'Crown premises' means premises held or used by or on behalf of the Crown.

(5) Nothing in this section shall be taken as in any way affecting Her Majesty in her private capacity; and this subsection shall be construed as if section 38(3) of the Crown Proceedings Act 1947 (interpretation of references in that Act to Her Majesty in her private capacity) were contained in this Act.

(6) References in this section to regulations or orders are references to regulations or orders made by statutory instrument.

(7) For the purposes of this section in its application to Part II and Part IV the authority charged with enforcing the provisions of those Parts in its area is—

(a) in the case of Part II, any waste regulation authority, and

(b) in the case of Part IV, any principal litter authority.

[Sections 44A and 44B   SCHEDULE 2A

OBJECTIVES FOR THE PURPOSES OF THE NATIONAL WASTE STRATEGY

1. Ensuring that waste is recovered or disposed of without endangering human health and without using processes or methods which could harm the environment and, in particular, without—

(a) risk to water, air, soil, plants or animals;

(b) causing nuisance through noise or odours; or

(c) adversely affecting the countryside or places of special interest.

2. Establishing an integrated and adequate network of waste disposal installations, taking account of the best available technology not involving excessive costs.

3. Ensuring that the network referred to in paragraph 2 above enables—

(a) the European Community as a whole to become self-sufficient in waste disposal, and the Member States individually to move towards that aim, taking into account geographical circumstances or the need for specialised installations for certain types of waste; and

(b) waste to be disposed of in one of the nearest appropriate installations, by means of the most appropriate methods and technologies in order to ensure a high level of protection for the environment and public health.

4. Encouraging the prevention or reduction of waste production and its harmfulness, in particular by—

(a) the development of clean technologies more sparing in their use of natural resources;

(b) the technical development and marketing of products designed so as to make no contribution or to make the smallest possible contribution, by the nature of their manufacture, use or final disposal, to increasing the amount or harmfulness of waste and pollution hazards; and

(c) the development of appropriate techniques for the final disposal of dangerous substances contained in waste destined for recovery.

5. Encouraging—

(a) the recovery of waste by means of recycling, re-use or reclamation or any other process with a view to extracting secondary raw materials; and

(b) the use of waste as a source of energy.]

[SCHEDULE 2B   CATEGORIES OF WASTE

1. Production or consumption residues not otherwise specified below.
2. Off-specification products.
3. Products whose date for appropriate use has expired.
4. Materials spilled, lost or having undergone other mishap, including any materials, equipment, etc, contaminated as a result of the mishap.
5. Materials contaminated or soiled as a result of planned actions (e.g. residues from cleaning operations, packing materials, containers, etc.).
6. Unusable parts (e.g. reject batteries, exhausted catalysts, etc.).
7. Substances which no longer perform satisfactorily (e.g. contaminated acids, contaminated solvents, exhausted tempering salts, etc.).
8. Residues of industrial processes (e.g. slags, still bottoms, etc.).
9. Residues from pollution abatement processes (e.g. scrubber sludges, baghouse dusts, spent filters, etc.).
10. Machining or finishing residues (e.g. lathe turnings, mill scales, etc.).
11. Residues from raw materials extraction and processing (e.g. mining residues, oil field slops, etc.).
12. Adulterated materials (e.g. oils contaminated with PCBs, etc.).
13. Any materials, substances or products whose use has been banned by law.
14. Products for which the holder has no further use (e.g. agricultural, household, office, commercial and shop discards, etc.).
15. Contaminated materials, substances or products resulting from remedial action with respect to land.
16. Any materials, substances or products which are not contained in the above categories.]

Section 81   SCHEDULE 3

STATUTORY NUISANCES: SUPPLEMENTARY PROVISIONS

Appeals to magistrates' court

1.—(1) This paragraph applies in relation to appeals under section 80(3) against an abatement notice to a magistrates' court.

(2) An appeal to which this paragraph applies shall be by way of complaint for an order and the Magistrates' Courts Act 1980 shall apply to the proceedings.

(3) An appeal against any decision of a magistrates' court in pursuance of an appeal to which this paragraph applies shall lie to the Crown Court at the instance of any party to the proceedings in which the decision was given.

(4) The Secretary of State may make regulations as to appeals to which this paragraph applies and the regulations may in particular—

(a) include provisions comparable to those in section 290 of the Public Health Act 1936 (appeals against notices requiring the execution of works);
(b) prescribe the cases in which an abatement notice is, or is not, to be suspended until the appeal is decided, or until some other stage in the proceedings;
(c) prescribe the cases in which the decision on appeal may in some respects be less favourable to the appellant than the decision from which he is appealing;
(d) prescribe the cases in which the appellant may claim that an abatement notice should have been served on some other person and prescribe the procedure to be followed in those cases.

1A . . .

Powers of entry etc.

2.—(1) Subject to sub-paragraph (2) below, any person authorised by a local authority may, on production (if so required) of his authority, enter any premises at any reasonable time—

    (a) for the purpose of ascertaining whether or not a statutory nuisance exists; or

    (b) for the purpose of taking any action, or executing any work, authorised or required by Part III.

(2) Admission by virtue of sub-paragraph (1) above to any premises used wholly or mainly for residential purposes shall not except in an emergency be demanded as of right unless twenty-four hours notice of the intended entry has been given to the occupier.

(3) If it is shown to the satisfaction of a justice of the peace on sworn information in writing—

    (a) that admission to any premises has been refused, or that refusal is apprehended, or that the premises are unoccupied or the occupier is temporarily absent, or that the case is one of emergency, or that an application for admission would defeat the object of the entry; and

    (b) that there is reasonable ground for entry into the premises for the purpose for which entry is required,

the justice may by warrant under his hand authorise the local authority by any authorised person to enter the premises, if need be by force.

(4) An authorised person entering any premises by virtue of sub-paragraph (1) or a warrant under sub-paragraph (3) above may—

    (a) take with him such other persons and such equipment as may be necessary;

    (b) carry out such inspections, measurements and tests as he considers necessary for the discharge of any of the local authority's functions under Part III; and

    (c) take away such samples or articles as he considers necessary for that purpose.

(5) On leaving any unoccupied premises which he has entered by virtue of sub-paragraph (1) above or a warrant under sub-paragraph (3) above the authorised person shall leave them as effectually secured against trespassers as he found them.

(6) A warrant issued in pursuance of sub-paragraph (3) above shall continue in force until the purpose for which the entry is required has been satisfied.

(7) Any reference in this paragraph to an emergency is a reference to a case where the person requiring entry has reasonable cause to believe that circumstances exist which are likely to endanger life or health and that immediate entry is necessary to verify the existence of those circumstances or to ascertain their cause and to effect a remedy.

[2A.—(1) Any person authorised by a local authority may on production (if so required) of his authority—

    (a) enter or open a vehicle, machinery or equipment, if necessary by force, or

    (b) remove a vehicle, machinery or equipment from a street to a secure place,

for the purpose of taking any action, or executing any work, authorised by or required under Part III in relation to a statutory nuisance within section 79(1)(ga) above caused by noise emitted from or caused by the vehicle, machinery or equipment.

(2) On leaving any unattended vehicle, machinery or equipment that he has entered or opened under sub-paragraph (1) above, the authorised person shall (subject to sub-paragraph (3) below) leave it secured against interference or theft in such manner and as effectually as he found it.

(3) If the authorised person is unable to comply with sub-paragraph (2) above, he shall for the purpose of securing the unattended vehicle, machinery or equipment either—

    (a) immobilise it by such means as he considers expedient, or

    (b) remove it from the street to a secure place.

(4) In carrying out any function under sub-paragraph (1), (2) or (3) above, the authorised person shall not cause more damage than is necessary.

(5) Before a vehicle, machinery or equipment is entered, opened or removed under sub-paragraph (1) above, the local authority shall notify the police of the intention to take action under that sub-paragraph.

(6) After a vehicle, machinery or equipment has been removed under sub-paragraph (1) or (3) above, the local authority shall notify the police of its removal and current location.

(7) Notification under sub-paragraph (5) or (6) above may be given to the police at any police station in the local authority's area or, in the case of the Temples, at any police station of the City of London Police.

(8) For the purposes of section 81(4) above, any expenses reasonably incurred by a local authority under sub-paragraph (2) or (3) above shall be treated as incurred by the authority under section 81(3) above in abating or preventing the recurrence of the statutory nuisance in question.]

Offences relating to entry

3.—(1) A person who wilfully obstructs any person acting in the exercise of any powers conferred by paragraph 2 [or 2A] above shall be liable, on summary conviction, to a fine not exceeding level 3 on the standard scale.

(2) If a person discloses any information relating to any trade secret obtained in the exercise of any powers conferred by paragraph 2 above he shall, unless the disclosure was made in the performance of his duty or with the consent of the person having the right to disclose the information, be liable, on summary conviction, to a fine not exceeding level 5 on the standard scale.

Default powers

4.—(1) This paragraph applies to the following function of a local authority, that is to say its duty under section 79 to cause its area to be inspected to detect any statutory nuisance which ought to be dealt with under [sections 80 and 80A] and its powers under paragraph 2 [or 2A] above.

(2) If the Secretary of State is satisfied that any local authority has failed, in any respect, to discharge the function to which this paragraph applies which it ought to have discharged, he may make an order declaring the authority to be in default.

(3) An order made under sub-paragraph (2) above which declares an authority to be in default may, for the purpose of remedying the default, direct the authority ('the defaulting authority') to perform the function specified in the order and may specify the manner in which and the time or times within which the function is to be performed by the authority.

(4) If the defaulting authority fails to comply with any direction contained in such an order the Secretary of State may, instead of enforcing the order by mandamus, make an order transferring to himself the function of the authority specified in the order.

(5) Where the function of a defaulting authority is transferred under subparagraph (4) above, the amount of any expenses which the Secretary of State certifies were incurred by him in performing the function shall on demand be paid to him by the defaulting authority.

(6) Any expenses required to be paid by a defaulting authority under subpara-graph (5) above shall be defrayed by the authority in like manner, and shall be debited to the like account, as if the function had not been transferred and the expenses had been incurred by the authority in performing them.

(7) The Secretary of State may by order vary or revoke any order previously made by him under this paragraph.

(8) Any order under this paragraph may include such incidental, supplemental and transitional provisions as the Secretary of State considers appropriate.

Protection from personal liability

5.   Nothing done by, or by a member of, a local authority or by any officer of or other person authorised by a local authority shall, if done in good faith for the purpose of executing Part III, subject them or any of them personally to any action, liability, claim or demand whatsoever (other than any liability under section 19 or 20 of the Local Government Finance Act 1982 (powers of district auditor and court)).

Statement of right of appeal in notices

6.   Where an appeal against a notice served by a local authority lies to a magistrates' court by virtue of section 80, it shall be the duty of the authority to include in such a notice a statement indicating that such an appeal lies as aforesaid and specifying the time within which it must be brought.

Water Industry Act 1991
(1991, c. 56)

PART II

CHAPTER II   ENFORCEMENT AND INSOLVENCY

18   Orders for securing compliance with certain provisions

(1) Subject to subsection (2) and sections 19 and 20 below, where in the case of any company holding an appointment under Chapter I of this Part the Secretary of State or the Director is satisfied—

- (a) that that company is contravening—
  - (i) any condition of the company's appointment in relation to which he is the enforcement authority; or
  - (ii) any statutory or other requirement which is enforceable under this section and in relation to which he is the enforcement authority;

    or
- (b) that that company has contravened any such condition or requirement and is likely to do so again,

he shall by a final enforcement order make such provision as is requisite for the purpose of securing compliance with that condition or requirement.

(2) Subject to section 19 below, where in the case of any company holding an appointment under Chapter I of this Part—

- (a) it appears to the Secretary of State or the Director as mentioned in paragraph (a) or (b) of subsection (1) above; and
- (b) it appears to him that it is requisite that a provisional enforcement order be made,

he may (instead of taking steps towards the making of a final order) by a provisional enforcement order make such provision as appears to him requisite for the purpose of securing compliance with the condition or requirement in question.

(3) In determining for the purposes of subsection (2)(b) above whether it is requisite that a provisional enforcement order be made, the Secretary of State or, as the case may be, the Director shall have regard, in particular, to the extent to which any person is likely to sustain loss or damage in consequence of anything which, in contravention of any condition or of any statutory or other requirement enforceable under this section, is likely to be done, or omitted to be done, before a final enforcement order may be made.

(4) Subject to sections 19 and 20 below, where the Secretary of State or the Director has

made a provisional enforcement order, he shall confirm it, with or without modifications, if—

- (a) he is satisfied that the company to which the order relates—
    - (i) is contravening any condition or statutory or other requirement in relation to which he is the enforcement authority; or
    - (ii) has contravened any such condition or requirement and is likely to do so again;

    and
- (b) the provision made by the order (with any modifications) is requisite for the purpose of securing compliance with that condition or requirement.

(5) An enforcement order—

- (a) shall require the company to which it relates (according to the circumstances of the case) to do, or not to do, such things as are specified in the order or are of a description so specified;
- (b) shall take effect at such time, being the earliest practicable time, as is determined by or under the order; and
- (c) may be revoked at any time by the enforcement authority who made it.

(6) For the purposes of this section and the following provisions of this Act—

- (a) the statutory and other requirements which shall be enforceable under this section in relation to a company holding an appointment under Chapter I of this Part shall be such of the requirements of any enactment or of any subordinate legislation as—
    - (i) are imposed in consequence of that appointment; and
    - (ii) are made so enforceable by that enactment or subordinate legislation;
- (b) the Director shall be the enforcement authority in relation to the conditions of an appointment under Chapter I of this Part; and
- (c) the enforcement authority in relation to each of the statutory and other requirements enforceable under this section shall be the Secretary of State, the Director or either of them, according to whatever provision is made by the enactment or subordinate legislation by which the requirement is made so enforceable.

(7) In this section and the following provisions of this Chapter—

'enforcement order' means a final enforcement order or a provisional enforcement order;

'final enforcement order' means an order under this section other than a provisional enforcement order;

'provisional enforcement order' means an order under this section which, if not previously confirmed in accordance with subsection (4) above, will cease to have effect at the end of such period (not exceeding three months) as is determined by or under the order.

(8) Where any act or omission constitutes a contravention of a condition of an appointment under Chapter I of this Part or of a statutory or other requirement enforceable under this section, the only remedies for that contravention, apart from those available by virtue of this section, shall be those for which express provision is made by or under any enactment and those that are available in respect of that act or omission otherwise than by virtue of its constituting such a contravention.

[PART IIIA   PROMOTION OF THE EFFICIENT USE OF WATER

93A   Duty to promote the efficient use of water

(1) It shall be the duty of every water undertaker to promote the efficient use of water by its customers.

(2) The duty of a water undertaker under this section shall be enforceable under section 18 above—

(a) by the Secretary of State; or

(b) with the consent of or in accordance with a general authorisation given by the Secretary of State, by the Director.

(3) Nothing in this Part shall have effect to authorise or require a water undertaker to impose any requirement on any of its customers or potential customers.

93B   Power of Director to impose requirements on water undertakers

(1) The Director may require a water undertaker, in its performance of its duty under section 93A above, to—

(a) take any such action; or

(b) achieve any such overall standards of performance,

as he may specify in the document imposing the requirement.

(2) Where the Director, in the document imposing a requirement on a water undertaker under subsection (1) above, stipulates that any contravention of the requirement by the undertaker will be a breach of its duty under section 93A above, any contravention of that requirement by the undertaker shall be a breach of that duty.

(3) Without prejudice to the generality of subsection (1) above, a requirement under that subsection may—

(a) require a water undertaker to make available to its customers or potential customers such facilities as may be specified in the document imposing the requirement;

(b) require a water undertaker to provide or make available to its customers or potential customers such information as may be specified in the document imposing the requirement, and may specify the form in which, the times at which or the frequency with which any such information is to be provided or made available.

(4) In exercising his powers under this section in relation to any water undertaker the Director shall have regard to the extent to which water resources are available to that undertaker.

(5) Before imposing any requirement on a water undertaker under subsection (1) above the Director shall consult that undertaker.

(6) Nothing in this section authorises the Director to impose any requirement on a water undertaker which has or may have the effect of authorising or requiring that undertaker to impose any requirement on any of its customers or potential customers.

93C   Publicity of requirements imposed under section 93B

(1) Where, under section 93B(1) above, the Director imposes any requirement on a water undertaker, the Director may arrange for that requirement to be publicised in any such manner as he may consider appropriate for the purpose of bringing it to the attention of that undertaker's customers.

(2) Without prejudice to the generality of subsection (1) above, the Director may arrange for such publicising of the requirement as is mentioned in that subsection by—

(a) himself publicising the requirement or causing it to be publicised; or

(b) directing the undertaker to inform or arrange to inform its customers of the requirement.

93D   Information as to compliance with requirements under section 93B

(1) Where a water undertaker is subject to any requirement imposed under section 93B(1) above, the Director may arrange for there to be given to the customers of that undertaker at any such times or with such frequency, and in any such manner, as he may consider appropriate, such information about the level of performance achieved by the undertaker in relation to that requirement as appears to the Director to be expedient to be given to those customers.

(2) Without prejudice to the generality of subsection (1) above, the Director may arrange for such giving of information as is mentioned in that subsection by—

(a) himself disseminating the information or causing it to be disseminated; or

(b) directing the undertaker to give or arrange to give the information to its customers.

(3) At such times and in such form or manner as the Director may direct, a water undertaker shall provide the Director with such information as may be specified in the direction in connection with the undertaker's performance in relation to any requirement imposed upon the undertaker under section 93B(1) above.

(4) A water undertaker who fails without reasonable excuse to do anything required of him by virtue of subsection (3) above shall be guilty of an offence and liable on summary conviction to a fine not exceeding level 5 on the standard scale.]

PART IV   SEWERAGE SERVICES

CHAPTER I   GENERAL FUNCTIONS OF SEWERAGE UNDERTAKERS

94   General duty to provide sewerage system

(1) It shall be the duty of every sewerage undertaker—

(a) to provide, improve and extend such a system of public sewers (whether inside its area or elsewhere) and so to cleanse and maintain those sewers as to ensure that that area is and continues to be effectually drained; and

(b) to make provision for the emptying of those sewers and such further provision (whether inside its area or elsewhere) as is necessary from time to time for effectually dealing, by means of sewage disposal works or otherwise, with the contents of those sewers.

(2) It shall be the duty of a sewerage undertaker in performing its duty under subsection (1) above to have regard—

(a) to its existing and likely future obligations to allow for the discharge of trade effluent into its public sewers; and

(b) to the need to provide for the disposal of trade effluent which is so discharged.

(3) The duty of a sewerage undertaker under subsection (1) above shall be enforceable under section 18 above—

(a) by the Secretary of State; or

(b) with the consent of or in accordance with a general authorisation given by the Secretary of State, by the Director.

(4) The obligations imposed on a sewerage undertaker by the following Chapters of this Part, and the remedies available in respect of contraventions of those obligations, shall be in addition to any duty imposed or remedy available by virtue of any provision of this section or section 95 below and shall not be in any way qualified by any such provision.

(5) In this section 'trade effluent' has the same meaning as in Chapter III of this Part.

95   Standards of performance in connection with provision of sewerage services

(1) For the purpose—

(a) of facilitating the determination of the extent to which breaches of the obligations imposed by virtue of the following provisions of this Part are to amount to breaches of the duty imposed by section 94 above; or

(b) of supplementing that duty by establishing overall standards of performance in relation to the provision of sewerage services by any sewerage undertaker,

the Secretary of State may, in accordance with section 96 below, by regulations provide for contraventions of such requirements as may be prescribed to be treated for the purposes of this Act as breaches of that duty.

(2) The Secretary of State may, in accordance with section 96 below, by regulations prescribe such standards of performance in connection with the provision of sewerage services as, in his opinion, ought to be achieved in individual cases.

(3) Regulations under subsection (2) above may provide that, if a sewerage undertaker fails to meet a prescribed standard, it shall pay such amount as may be prescribed to any person who is affected by the failure and is of a prescribed description.

(4) Without prejudice to the generality of the power conferred by subsection (2) above, regulations under that subsection may—

> (a) include in a standard of performance a requirement for a sewerage under-taker, in prescribed circumstances, to inform a person of his rights by virtue of any such regulations;
>
> (b) provide for any dispute under the regulations to be referred by either party to the dispute to the Director;
>
> (c) make provision for the procedure to be followed in connection with any such reference and for the Director's determination on such a reference to be enforceable in such manner as may be prescribed;
>
> (d) prescribe circumstances in which a sewerage undertaker is to be exempted from requirements of the regulations.

(5) Where the Director determines any dispute in accordance with regulations under this section he shall, in such manner as may be specified in the regulations, give his reasons for reaching his decision with respect to the dispute.]

CHAPTER II   PROVISION OF SEWERAGE SERVICES

Provision of public sewers otherwise than by requisition

101A   Further duty to provide sewers

(1) Without prejudice to section 98 . . ., it shall be the duty of a sewerage undertaker to provide a public sewer to be used for the drainage for domestic sewerage purposes of premises in a particular locality in its area if the conditions specified in subsection (2) below are satisfied.

(2) The conditions mentioned in subsection (1) above are—

> (a) that the premises in question, or any of those premises, are premises on which there are buildings each of which, with the exception of any shed, glasshouse or other outbuilding appurtenant to a dwelling and not designed or occupied as living accommodation, is a building erected before, or whose erection was substantially completed by, 20th June 1995;
>
> (b) that the drains or sewers used for the drainage for domestic sewerage purposes of the premises in question do not, either directly or through an intermediate drain or sewer, connect with a public sewer; and
>
> (c) that the drainage of any of the premises in question in respect of which the condition specified in paragraph (a) above is satisfied is giving, or is likely to give, rise to such adverse effects to the environment or amenity that it is appropriate, having regard to any guidance issued under this section by the Secretary of State and all other relevant considerations, to provide a public sewer for the drainage for domestic sewerage purposes of the premises in question.

(3) Without prejudice to the generality of subsection (2)(c) above, regard shall be had to the following considerations, so far as relevant, in determining whether it is appropriate for any sewer to be provided by virtue of this section—

> (a) the geology of the locality in question or of any other locality;
>
> (b) the number of premises, being premises on which there are buildings, which might reasonably be expected to be drained by means of that sewer;
>
> (c) the costs of providing that sewer;

(d) the nature and extent of any adverse effects to the environment or amenity arising, or likely to arise, as a result of the premises or, as the case may be, the locality in question not being drained by means of a public sewer; and

(e) the extent to which it is practicable for those effects to be overcome otherwise than by the provision (whether by virtue of this section or otherwise) of public sewers, and the costs of so overcoming those effects.

(4) Guidance issued by the Secretary of State under this section may—

(a) relate to how regard is to be had to the considerations mentioned in paragraphs (a) to (e) of subsection (3) above;

(b) relate to any other matter which the Secretary of State considers may be a relevant consideration in any case and to how regard is to be had to any such matter;

(c) set out considerations, other than those mentioned in paragraphs (a) to (e) of subsection (3) above, to which (so far as relevant) regard shall be had in determining whether it is appropriate for any sewer to be provided by virtue of this section;

(d) relate to how regard is to be had to any such consideration as is mentioned in paragraph (c) above;

(e) without prejudice to paragraphs (a) to (d) above, relate to how a sewerage undertaker is to discharge its functions under this section.

(5) Before issuing guidance under this section the Secretary of State shall consult—

(a) the Environment Agency;

(b) the Director; and

(c) such other bodies or persons as he considers appropriate;

and the Secretary of State shall arrange for any guidance issued by him under this section to be published in such manner as he considers appropriate.

(6) Subject to the following provisions of this section, the duty of a sewerage undertaker by virtue of subsection (1) above shall be enforceable under section 18 above—

(a) by the Secretary of State; or

(b) with the consent of or in accordance with a general authorisation given by the Secretary of State, by the Director.

(7) Any dispute between a sewerage undertaker and an owner or occupier of any premises in its area as to—

(a) whether the undertaker is under a duty by virtue of subsection (1) above to provide a public sewer to be used for any such drainage of those premises as is mentioned in that subsection;

(b) the domestic sewerage purposes for which any such sewer should be provided; or

(c) the time by which any such duty of the undertaker should be performed,

shall be determined by the Environment Agency, and may be referred to the Environment Agency for determination by either of the parties to the dispute.

(8) The Environment Agency—

(a) shall notify the parties of the reasons for its decision on any dispute referred to it under subsection (7) above; and

(b) may make any such recommendations, or give any such guidance, relating to or in connection with the drainage of the premises or locality in question as it considers appropriate.

(9) The decision of the Environment Agency on any dispute referred to it under subsection (7) above shall be final.

(10) A sewerage undertaker shall only be taken to be in breach of its duty under subsection (1) above where, and to the extent that, it has accepted, or the Environment Agency has determined under this section, that it is under such a duty and where any time accepted by it, or determined by the Environment Agency under this section, as the time by which the duty is to that extent to be performed has passed.]

106   Right to communicate with public sewers

(1) Subject to the provisions of this section—

    (a) the owner or occupier of any premises [. . .]; or

    (b) the owner of any private sewer draining premises [. . .],

shall be entitled to have his drains or sewer communicate with the public sewers of that undertaker and thereby to discharge foul water and surface water from those premises or that private sewer.

(2) Subject to the provisions of Chapter III of this Part, nothing in subsection (1) above shall entitle any person—

    (a) to discharge directly or indirectly into any public sewer—

        (i) any liquid from a factory, other than domestic sewage or surface or storm water, or any liquid from a manufacturing process; or

        (ii) any liquid or other matter the discharge of which into public sewers is prohibited by or under any enactment; or

    (b) where separate public sewers are provided for foul water and for surface water, to discharge directly or indirectly—

        (i) foul water into a sewer provided for surface water; or

        (ii) except with the approval of the undertaker, surface water into a sewer provided for foul water; or

    (c) to have his drains or sewer made to communicate directly with a storm-water overflow sewer.

(3) A person desirous of availing himself of his entitlement under this section shall give notice of his proposals to the sewerage undertaker in question.

(4) At any time within twenty-one days after a sewerage undertaker receives a notice under subsection (3) above, the undertaker may by notice to the person who gave the notice refuse to permit the communication to be made, if it appears to the undertaker that the mode of construction or condition of the drain or sewer is such that the making of the communication would be prejudicial to the undertaker's sewerage system

(5) For the purpose of examining the mode of construction and condition of a drain or sewer to which a notice under subsection (3) above relates a sewerage undertaker may, if necessary, require it to be laid open for inspection.

(6) Any question arising under subsections (3) to (5) above between a sewerage undertaker and a person proposing to make a communication as to—

    (a) the reasonableness of the undertaker's refusal to permit a communication to be made; or

    (b) as to the reasonableness of any requirement under subsection (5) above,

may, on the application of that person, be determined by [the Director under section 30A above].

(7) [. . .]

(8) Where a person proposes under this section to make a communication between a drain or sewer and such a public sewer in Greater London as is used for the general reception of sewage from other public sewers and is not substantially used for the reception of sewage from private sewers and drains—

    (a) the grounds on which a sewerage undertaker may refuse to permit the communication shall be such grounds as the undertaker thinks fit; and

    (b) no application to [the Director] may be made under subsection (6) above in respect of any refusal under this subsection.

(9) In this section 'factory' has the same meaning as in the Factories Act 1961.

111   Restrictions on use of public sewers

(1) Subject to the provisions of Chapter III of this Part, no person shall throw, empty or

turn, or suffer or permit to be thrown or emptied or to pass, into any public sewer, or into any drain or sewer communicating with a public sewer—

    (a) any matter likely to injure the sewer or drain, to interfere with the free flow of its contents or to affect prejudicially the treatment and disposal of its contents; or

    (b) any such chemical refuse or waste steam, or any such liquid of a temperature higher than one hundred and ten degrees Fahrenheit, as by virtue of subsection (2) below is a prohibited substance; or

    (c) any petroleum spirit or carbide of calcium.

(2) For the purposes of subsection (1) above, chemical refuse, waste steam or a liquid of a temperature higher than that mentioned in that subsection is a prohibited substance if (either alone or in combination with the contents of the sewer or drain in question) it is or, in the case of the liquid, is when so heated—

    (a) dangerous;

    (b) the cause of a nuisance; or

    (c) injurious, or likely to cause injury, to health.

(3) A person who contravenes any of the provisions of this section shall be guilty of an offence and liable—

    (a) on summary conviction, to a fine not exceeding the statutory maximum and to a further fine not exceeding £50 for each day on which the offence continues after conviction;

    (b) on conviction on indictment, to imprisonment for a term not exceeding two years or to a fine or to both.

(4) For the purposes of so much of subsection (3) above as makes provision for the imposition of a daily penalty—

    (a) the court by which a person is convicted of the original offence may fix a reasonable date from the date of conviction for compliance by the defendant with any directions given by the court; and

    (b) where a court has fixed such a period, the daily penalty shall not be imposed in respect of any day before the end of that period.

(5) In this section the expression 'petroleum spirit' means any such—

    (a) crude petroleum;

    (b) oil made from petroleum or from coal, shale, peat or other bituminous substances; or

    (c) product of petroleum or mixture containing petroleum,

as, when tested in the manner prescribed by or under the Petroleum (Consolidation) Act 1928, gives off an inflammable vapour at a temperature of less than seventy-three degrees Fahrenheit.

CHAPTER III   TRADE EFFLUENT

118   Consent required for discharge of trade effluent into public sewer

(1) Subject to the following provisions of this Chapter, the occupier of any trade premises in the area of a sewerage undertaker may discharge any trade effluent proceeding from those premises into the undertaker's public sewers if he does so with the undertaker's consent.

(2) Nothing in this Chapter shall authorise the discharge of any effluent into a public sewer otherwise than by means of a drain or sewer.

(3) The following, that is to say—

    (a) the restrictions imposed by paragraphs (a) and (b) of section 106(2) above; and

    (b) section 111 above so far as it relates to anything falling within paragraph (a) or (b) of subsection (1) of that section, shall not apply to any discharge of trade effluent which is lawfully made by virtue of this Chapter.

(4) Accordingly, subsections (3) to (8) of section 106 above and sections 108 and 109 above shall have effect in relation to communication with a sewer for the purpose of making any discharge which is lawfully made by virtue of this Chapter as they have effect in relation to communication with a sewer for the purpose of making discharges which are authorised by subsection (1) of section 106 above.

(5) If, in the case of any trade premises, any trade effluent is discharged without such consent or other authorisation as is necessary for the purposes of this Chapter, the occupier of the premises shall be guilty of an offence and liable—

(a) on summary conviction, to a fine not exceeding the statutory maximum; and

(b) on conviction on indictment, to a fine.

119 Application for consent

(1) An application to a sewerage undertaker for a consent to discharge trade effluent from any trade premises into a public sewer of that undertaker shall be by notice served on the undertaker by the owner or occupier of the premises.

(2) An application under this section with respect to a proposed discharge of any such effluent shall state—

(a) the nature or composition of the trade effluent;

(b) the maximum quantity of the trade effluent which it is proposed to discharge on any one day; and

(c) the highest rate at which it is proposed to discharge the trade effluent.

120 Applications for the discharge of special category effluent

(1) Subject to subsection (3) below, where a notice containing an application under section 119 above is served on a sewerage undertaker with respect to discharges of any special category effluent, it shall be the duty of the undertaker to refer to [the Environment Agency] the questions—

(a) whether the discharges to which the notice relates should be prohibited; and

(b) whether, if they are not prohibited, any requirements should be imposed as to the conditions on which they are made.

(2) Subject to subsection (3) below, a reference which is required to be made by a sewerage undertaker by virtue of subsection (1) above shall be made before the end of the period of two months beginning with the day after the notice containing the application is served on the undertaker.

(3) There shall be no obligation on a sewerage undertaker to make a reference under this section in respect of any application if, before the end of the period mentioned in subsection (2) above, there is a refusal by the undertaker to give any consent on the application.

(4) It shall be the duty of a sewerage undertaker where it has made a reference under this section not to give any consent, or enter into any agreement, with respect to the discharges to which the reference relates at any time before [the Environment Agency] serves notice on the undertaker of his determination on the reference.

(5) Every reference under this section shall be made in writing and shall be accompanied by a copy of the notice containing the application in respect of which it is made.

(6) It shall be the duty of a sewerage undertaker, on making a reference under this section, to serve a copy of the reference on the owner or the occupier of the trade premises in question, according to whether the discharges to which the reference relates are to be by the owner or by the occupier.

(7) [. . .]

(8) [. . .]

[(9) If a sewerage undertaker fails, within the period provided by subsection (2) above, to refer to the Environment Agency any question which he is required by subsection (1) above to refer to the Agency, the undertaker shall be guilty of an offence and liable—

(a) on summary conviction, to a fine not exceeding the statutory maximum;

(b) on conviction on indictment, to a fine.

(10) If the Environment Agency becomes aware of any such failure as is mentioned in subsection (9) above, the Agency may—

(a) if a consent under this Chapter to make discharges of any special category effluent has been granted on the application in question, exercise its powers of review under section 127 or 131 below, notwithstanding anything in subsection (2) of the section in question; or

(b) in any other case, proceed as if the reference required by this section had been made.]

121 Conditions of consent

(1) The power of a sewerage undertaker, on an application under section 119 above, to give a consent with respect to the discharge of any trade effluent shall be a power to give a consent either unconditionally or subject to such conditions as the sewerage undertaker thinks fit to impose with respect to—

(a) the sewer or sewers into which the trade effluent may be discharged;

(b) the nature or composition of the trade effluent which may be discharged;

(c) the maximum quantity of trade effluent which may be discharged on any one day, either generally or into a particular sewer; and

(d) the highest rate at which trade effluent may be discharged, either generally or into a particular sewer.

(2) Conditions with respect to all or any of the following matters may also be attached under this section to a consent to the discharge of trade effluent from any trade premises—

(a) the period or periods of the day during which the trade effluent may be discharged from the trade premises into the sewer;

(b) the exclusion from the trade effluent of all condensing water;

(c) the elimination or diminution, in cases falling within subsection (3) below, of any specified constituent of the trade effluent, before it enters the sewer;

(d) the temperature of the trade effluent at the time when it is discharged into the sewer, and its acidity or alkalinity at that time;

(e) the payment by the occupier of the trade premises to the undertaker of charges for the reception of the trade effluent into the sewer and for the disposal of the effluent;

(f) the provision and maintenance of such an inspection chamber or manhole as will enable a person readily to take samples, at any time, of what is passing into the sewer from the trade premises;

(g) the provision, testing and maintenance of such meters as may be required to measure the volume and rate of discharge of any trade effluent being discharged from the trade premises into the sewer;

(h) the provision, testing and maintenance of apparatus for determining the nature and composition of any trade effluent being discharged from the premises into the sewer;

(i) the keeping of records of the volume, rate of discharge, nature and composition of any trade effluent being discharged and, in particular, the keeping of records of readings of meters and other recording apparatus provided in compliance with any other condition attached to the consent; and

(j) the making of returns and giving of other information to the sewerage undertaker concerning the volume, rate of discharge, nature and composition of any trade effluent discharged from the trade premises into the sewer.

(3) A case falls within this subsection where the sewerage undertaker is satisfied that the

constituent in question, either alone or in combination with any matter with which it is likely to come into contact while passing through any sewers—

    (a) would injure or obstruct those sewers, or make the treatment or disposal of the sewage from those sewers specially difficult or expensive; or

    (b) in the case of trade effluent which is to be or is discharged—

        (i) into a sewer having an outfall in any harbour or tidal water; or

        (ii) into a sewer which connects directly or indirectly with a sewer or sewage disposal works having such an outfall,

would cause or tend to cause injury or obstruction to the navigation on, or the use of, the harbour or tidal water.

(4) In the exercise of the power conferred by virtue of subsection (2)(e) above, regard shall be had—

    (a) to the nature and composition and to the volume and rate of discharge of the trade effluent discharged;

    (b) to any additional expense incurred or likely to be incurred by a sewerage undertaker in connection with the reception or disposal of the trade effluent; and

    (c) to any revenue likely to be derived by the undertaker from the trade effluent.

(5) If, in the case of any trade premises, a condition imposed under this section is contravened, the occupier of the premises shall be guilty of an offence and liable—

    (a) on summary conviction, to a fine not exceeding the statutory maximum; and

    (b) on conviction on indictment, to a fine.

(6) In this section 'harbour' and 'tidal water' have the same meanings as in the Merchant Shipping Act 1894.

(7) This section has effect subject to the provisions of sections 133 and 135(3) below.

122   Appeals to the Director with respect to decisions on applications etc.

(1) Any person aggrieved by—

    (a) the refusal of a sewerage undertaker to give a consent for which application has been duly made to the undertaker under section 119 above;

    (b) the failure of a sewerage undertaker to give such a consent within the period of two months beginning with the day after service of the notice containing the application; or

    (c) any condition attached by a sewerage undertaker to such a consent, may appeal to the Director.

(2) On an appeal under this section in respect of a refusal or failure to give a consent, the Director may give the necessary consent, either unconditionally or subject to such conditions as he thinks fit to impose for determining any of the matters as respects which the undertaker has power to impose conditions under section 121 above.

(3) On an appeal under this section in respect of a condition attached to a consent, the Director may take into review all the conditions attached to the consent, whether appealed against or not, and may—

    (a) substitute for them any other set of conditions, whether more or less favourable to the appellant; or

    (b) annul any of the conditions.

(4) The Director may, under subsection (3) above, include provision as to the charges to be made in pursuance of any condition attached to a consent for any period before the determination of the appeal.

(5) On any appeal under this section, the Director may give a direction that the trade effluent in question shall not be discharged until a specified date.

(6) Any consent given or conditions imposed by the Director under this section in respect of discharges of trade effluent shall have effect for the purposes of this Chapter as if given or imposed by the sewerage undertaker in question.

(7) The powers of the Director under this section shall be subject to the provisions of sections 123, 128, 133, 135 and 137 below.

123   Appeals with respect to the discharge of special category effluent

(1) Where a reference is made to [the Environment Agency] under section 120 above, the period mentioned in paragraph (b) of subsection (1) of section 122 above shall not begin to run for the purposes of that subsection, in relation to the application to which the reference relates, until the beginning of the day after [the Environment Agency] serves notice on the sewerage undertaker in question of his determination on the reference.

(2) If, on an appeal under section 122 above, it appears to the Director—

    (a) that the case is one in which the sewerage undertaker in question is required to make a reference under section 120 above before giving a consent; and

    (b) that the undertaker has not made such a reference, whether because the case falls within subsection (3) of that section or otherwise,

the Director shall not be entitled to determine the appeal, otherwise than by upholding a refusal, except where the conditions set out in subsection (3) below are satisfied.

(3) The conditions mentioned in subsection (2) above are satisfied if the Director—

    (a) has himself referred the questions mentioned in section 120(1) above to [the Environment Agency]; and

    (b) has been sent a copy of the notice of [the Environment Agency's] determination on the reference.

(4) Every reference under this section shall be made in writing and shall be accompanied by a copy of the notice containing the application in respect of which the appeal and reference is made.

(5) It shall be the duty of the Director, on making a reference under this section, to serve a copy of the reference—

    (a) on the owner or the occupier of the trade premises in question, according to whether the discharges to which the reference relates are to be by the owner or by the occupier; and

    (b) on the sewerage undertaker in question.

124   Variation of consents

(1) Subject to sections 128, 133 and 135(3) below, a sewerage undertaker may from time to time give a direction varying the conditions which have been attached to any of its consents under this Chapter to the discharge of trade effluent into a public sewer.

(2) Subject to subsections (3) and (4) and section 125 below, no direction shall be given under this section with respect to a consent under this Chapter—

    (a) within two years from the date of the consent; or

    (b) where a previous direction has been given under this section with respect to that consent, within two years from the date on which notice was given of that direction.

(3) Subsection (2) above shall not prevent a direction being given before the time specified in that subsection if it is given with the consent of the owner and occupier of the trade premises in question.

(4) A direction given with the consent mentioned in subsection (3) above shall not affect the time at which any subsequent direction may be given.

(5) The sewerage undertaker shall give to the owner and occupier of the trade premises to which a consent under this Chapter relates notice of any direction under this section with respect to that consent.

(6) A notice under subsection (5) above shall—

    (a) include information as to the right of appeal conferred by subsection (1) of section 126 below; and

(b) state the date, being a date not less than two months after the giving of the notice, on which (subject to subsection (2) of that section) the direction is to take effect.

(7) For the purposes of this section references to the variation of conditions include references to the addition or annulment of a condition and to the attachment of a condition to a consent to which no condition was previously attached.

125   Variations within time limit

(1) A sewerage undertaker may give a direction under section 124 above before the time specified in subsection (2) of that section and without the consent required by subsection (3) of that section if it considers it necessary to do so in order to provide proper protection for persons likely to be affected by the discharges which could lawfully be made apart from the direction.

(2) Subject to section 134(3) below, where a sewerage undertaker gives a direction by virtue of subsection (1) above, the undertaker shall be liable to pay compensation to the owner and occupier of the trade premises to which the direction relates, unless the undertaker is of the opinion that the direction is required—

(a) in consequence of a change of circumstances which—
   (i)   has occurred since the beginning of the period of two years in question; and
   (ii) could not reasonably have been foreseen at the beginning of that period; and
(b) otherwise than in consequence of consents for discharges given after the beginning of that period.

(3) Where a sewerage undertaker gives a direction by virtue of subsection (1) above and is of the opinion mentioned in subsection (2) above, it shall be the duty of the undertaker to give notice of the reasons for its opinion to the owner and occupier of the premises in question.

(4) For the purposes of this section the circumstances referred to in subsection (2)(a) above may include the information available as to the discharges to which the consent in question relates or as to the interaction of those discharges with other discharges or matter.

(5) The Secretary of State may by regulations make provision as to the manner of determining the amount of any compensation payable under this section, including the factors to be taken into account in determining that amount.

126   Appeals with respect to variations of consent

(1) The owner or occupier of any trade premises may—

(a) within two months of the giving to him under subsection (5) of section 124 above of a notice of a direction under that section; or
(b) with the written permission of the Director, at any later time,

appeal to the Director against the direction.

(2) Subject to subsection (3) below, if an appeal against a direction is brought under subsection (1) above before the date specified under section 124(6)(b) above in the notice of the direction, the direction shall not take effect until the appeal is withdrawn or finally disposed of.

(3) In so far as the direction which is the subject of an appeal relates to the making of charges payable by the occupier of any trade premises, it may take effect on any date after the giving of the notice.

(4) On an appeal under subsection (1) above with respect to a direction, the Director shall have power—

(a) to annul the direction given by the sewerage undertaker; and
(b) to substitute for it any other direction, whether more or less favourable to the appellant;

and any direction given by the Director may include provision as to the charges to be made for any period between the giving of the notice by the sewerage undertaker and the determination of the appeal.

(5) A person to whom notice is given in pursuance of section 125(3) above may, in accordance with regulations made by the Secretary of State, appeal to the Director against the notice on the ground that compensation should be paid in consequence of the direction to which the notice relates.

(6) On an appeal under subsection (5) above the Director may direct that section 125 above shall have effect as if the sewerage undertaker in question were not of the opinion to which the notice relates.

(7) Any consent given or conditions imposed by the Director under this section in respect of discharges of trade effluent shall have effect for the purposes of this Chapter as if given or imposed by the sewerage undertaker in question.

(8) The powers of the Director under this section shall be subject to the provisions of sections 133, 135 and 137 below.

127 Review by [the Environment Agency] of consents relating to special category effluent

(1) Where any person, as the owner or occupier of any trade premises, is (whether or not in accordance with a notice under section 132 below) for the time being authorised by virtue of a consent under this Chapter to make discharges of any special category effluent from those premises into a sewerage undertaker's public sewer, [the Environment Agency] may review the questions—

    (a) whether the discharges authorised by the consent should be prohibited; and

    (b) whether, if they are not prohibited, any requirements should be imposed as to the conditions on which they are made.

(2) Subject to subsection (3) below, [the Environment Agency] shall not review any question under this section unless—

    (a) the consent or variation by virtue of which the discharges in question are made has not previously been the subject-matter of a review and was given or made—

        (i) before 1st September 1989; or

        (ii) in contravention of section 133 below;

    (b) a period of more than two years has elapsed since the time, or last time, when notice of [the Environment Agency's] determination on any reference or review relating to that consent or the consent to which that variation relates was served under section 132 below on the owner or occupier of the trade premises in question; or

    (c) there has, since the time, or last time, when such a notice was so served, been a contravention of any provision which was included in compliance with a requirement of a notice under section 132 below in the consent or variation by virtue of which the discharges in question are made.

(3) Subsection (2) above shall not apply if the review is carried out—

    (a) for the purpose of enabling Her Majesty's Government in the United Kingdom to give effect to any Community obligation or to any international agreement to which the United Kingdom is for the time being a party; or

    (b) for the protection of public health or of flora and fauna dependent on an aquatic environment.

128 Application for variation of time for discharge

(1) If, after a direction has been given under any of the preceding provisions of this Chapter requiring that trade effluent shall not be discharged until a specified date, it appears to the sewerage undertaker in question that in consequence—

    (a) of a failure to complete any works required in connection with the reception and
        disposal of the trade effluent; or

    (b) of any other exceptional circumstances, a later date ought to be substituted for the
        date so specified in the direction, the undertaker may apply to the Director for
        such a substitution.

(2) The Director shall have power, on an application under subsection (1) above, to vary
the direction so as to extend the period during which the trade effluent may not be discharged
until the date specified in the application or, if he thinks fit, any earlier date.

(3) Not less than one month before making an application under subsection (1) above a
sewerage undertaker shall give notice of its intention to the owner and occupier of the trade
premises from which the trade effluent is to be discharged.

(4) The Director, before varying a direction on an application under subsection (1) above,
shall take into account any representations made to him by the owner or occupier of the trade
premises in question.

129 Agreements with respect to the disposal etc of trade effluent

(1) Subject to sections 130 and 133 below, a sewerage undertaker may enter into and carry
into effect—

    (a) an agreement with the owner or occupier of any trade premises within its area for
        the reception and disposal by the undertaker of any trade effluent produced on
        those premises;

    (b) an agreement with the owner or occupier of any such premises under which it
        undertakes, on such terms as may be specified in the agreement, to remove and
        dispose of substances produced in the course of treating any trade effluent on or in
        connection with those premises.

(2) Without prejudice to the generality of subsection (1) above, an agreement such as is
mentioned in paragraph (a) of that subsection may, in particular, provide—

    (a) for the construction or extension by the sewerage undertaker of such works as may
        be required for the reception or disposal of the trade effluent; and

    (b) for the repayment by the owner or occupier, as the case may be, of the whole or
        part of the expenses incurred by the undertaker in carrying out its obligations
        under the agreement.

(3) It is hereby declared that the power of a sewerage undertaker to enter into an agreement under this section includes a power, by that agreement, to authorise such a discharge as
apart from the agreement would require a consent under this Chapter.

**130 Reference to [the Environment Agency] of agreements relating to special
category effluent**

(1) Where a sewerage undertaker and the owner or occupier of any trade premises are
proposing to enter into an agreement under section 129 above with respect to, or to any
matter connected with, the reception or disposal of any special category effluent, it shall be
the duty of the undertaker to refer to [the Environment Agency] the questions—

    (a) whether the operations which would, for the purposes of or in connection with
        the reception or disposal of that effluent, be carried out in pursuance of the
        proposed agreement should be prohibited; and

    (b) whether, if they are not prohibited, any requirements should be imposed as to the
        conditions on which they are carried out.

(2) It shall be the duty of a sewerage undertaker where it has made a reference under this
section not to give any consent or enter into any agreement with respect to any such operations as are mentioned in subsection (1)(a) above at any time before [the Environment
Agency] serves notice on the undertaker of his determination on the reference.

(3) Every reference under this section shall be made in writing and shall be accompanied
by a copy of the proposed agreement.

(4) It shall be the duty of a sewerage undertaker, on making a reference under this section, to serve a copy of the reference on the owner or the occupier of the trade premises in question, according to whether it is the owner or occupier who is proposing to be a party to the agreement.

(5) [. . .]

(6) [. . .]

[(7) If a sewerage undertaker fails, before giving any consent or entering into any agreement with respect to any such operations as are mentioned in paragraph (a) of subsection (1) above, to refer to the Environment Agency any question which he is required by that subsection to refer to the Agency, the undertaker shall be guilty of an offence and liable—

(a) on summary conviction, to a fine not exceeding the statutory maximum;

(b) on conviction on indictment, to a fine.

(8) If the Environment Agency becomes aware—

(a) that a sewerage undertaker and the owner or occupier of any trade premises are proposing to enter into any such agreement as is mentioned in subsection (1) above, and

(b) that the sewerage undertaker has not referred to the Agency any question which it is required to refer to the Agency by that subsection,

the Agency may proceed as if the reference required by that subsection had been made.

(9) If the Environment Agency becomes aware that any consent has been given or agreement entered into with respect to any such operations as are mentioned in paragraph (a) of subsection (1) above without the sewerage undertaker in question having referred to the Environment Agency any question which he is required by that subsection to refer to the Agency, the Agency may exercise its powers of review under section 127 above or, as the case may be, section 131 below, notwithstanding anything in subsection (2) of the section in question.]

131 Review by [the Environment Agency] of agreements relating to special category effluent

(1) Where any person, as the owner or occupier of any trade premises, is (whether or not in accordance with a notice under section 132 below) for the time being a party to any agreement under section 129 above with respect to, or to any matter connected with, the reception or disposal of special category effluent, [the Environment Agency] may review the questions—

(a) whether the operations which, for the purposes of or in connection with the reception or disposal of that effluent, are carried out in pursuance of the agreement should be prohibited; and

(b) whether, if they are not prohibited, any requirements should be imposed as to the conditions on which they are carried out.

(2) Subject to subsection (3) below, [the Environment Agency] shall not review any question under this section unless—

(a) the agreement by virtue of which the operations in question are carried out has not previously been the subject-matter of a review and was entered into—
   (i) before 1st September 1989; or
   (ii) in contravention of section 133 below;

(b) a period of more than two years has elapsed since the time, or last time, when notice of [the Environment Agency's] determination on any reference or review relating to that agreement was served under section 132 below on the owner or occupier of the trade premises in question; or

(c) there has, since the time, or last time, when such a notice was so served, been a contravention of any provision which was included in compliance with a requirement of a notice under section 132 below in the agreement by virtue of which the operations in question are carried out.

(3) Subsection (2) above shall not apply if the review is carried out—

(a) for the purpose of enabling Her Majesty's Government in the United Kingdom to give effect to any Community obligation or to any international agreement to which the United Kingdom is for the time being a party; or

(b) for the protection of public health or of flora and fauna dependent on an aquatic environment.

(4) References in this section to an agreement include references to an agreement as varied from time to time by a notice under section 132 below.

132   Powers and procedure on references and reviews

(1) This section applies to—

(a) any reference to [the Environment Agency] under section 120, 123 or 130 above; and

(b) any review by [the Environment Agency] under section 127 or 131 above.

(2) On a reference or review to which this section applies, it shall be the duty of [the Environment Agency], before determining the questions which are the subject-matter of the reference or review—

(a) to give an opportunity of making representations or objections to [the Environment Agency]—

(i) to the sewerage undertaker in question; and

(ii) to the following person, that is to say, the owner or the occupier of the trade premises in question, according to whether it is the owner or the occupier of those premises who is proposing to be, or is, the person making the discharges or, as the case may be, a party to the agreement;

and

(b) to consider any representations or objections which are duly made to [the Agency] with respect to those questions by a person to whom [the Agency] is required to give such an opportunity and which are not withdrawn.

(3) On determining any question on a reference or review to which this section applies, [the Environment Agency] shall serve notice on the sewerage undertaker in question and on the person specified in subsection (2)(a)(ii) above.

(4) A notice under this section shall state, according to what has been determined—

(a) that the discharges or operations to which, or to the proposals for which, the reference or review relates, or such of them as are specified in the notice, are to be prohibited; or

(b) that those discharges or operations, or such of them as are so specified, are to be prohibited except in so far as they are made or carried out in accordance with conditions which consist in or include conditions so specified; or

(c) that [the Environment Agency] has no objection to those discharges or operations and does not intend to impose any requirements as to the conditions on which they are made or carried out.

(5) Without prejudice to section 133 below, a notice under this section, in addition to containing such provision as is specified in sub-paragraph (4) above, may do one or both of the following, that is to say—

(a) vary or revoke the provisions of a previous notice with respect to the discharges or operations in question; and

(b) for the purpose of giving effect to any prohibition or other requirement contained in the notice, vary or revoke any consent under this Chapter or any agreement under section 129 above.

(6) Nothing in subsection (1) or (2) of section 121 above shall be construed as restricting the power of [the Environment Agency], by virtue of subsection (4)(b) above, to specify such conditions as [the Agency] considers appropriate in a notice under this section.

(7) [. . .]

(8) The Secretary of State shall send a copy of every notice served under this section to the Director.

133   Effect of determination on reference or review

(1) Where a notice under section 132 above has been served on a sewerage undertaker, it shall be the duty—

(a) of the undertaker; and

(b) in relation to that undertaker, of the Director,

so to exercise the powers to which this section applies as to secure compliance with the provisions of the notice.

(2) This paragraph applies to the following powers, that is to say—

(a) in relation to a sewerage undertaker, its power to give a consent under this Chapter, any of its powers under section 121 or 124 above and any power to enter into or vary an agreement under section 129 above; and

(b) in relation to the Director, any of his powers under this Chapter.

(3) Nothing in subsection (1) or (2) of section 121 above shall be construed as restricting the power of a sewerage undertaker, for the purpose of complying with this section, to impose any condition specified in a notice under section 132 above.

(4) [. . .]

[(5) A sewerage undertaker which fails to perform its duty under subsection (1) above shall be guilty of an offence and liable—

(a) on summary conviction, to a fine not exceeding the statutory maximum;

(b) on conviction on indictment, to a fine.

(6) The Environment Agency may, for the purpose of securing compliance with the provisions of a notice under section 132 above, by serving notice on the sewerage undertaker in question and on the person specified in section 132(2)(a)(ii) above, vary or revoke—

(a) any consent given under this Chapter to make discharges of any special category effluent, or

(b) any agreement under section 129 above.]

134   Compensation in respect of determinations made for the protection of public health etc

(1) Subject to subsection (2) below, [the Environment Agency] shall be liable to pay compensation to the relevant person in respect of any loss or damage sustained by that person as a result of any notice under section 132 above containing [the Environment Agency's] determination on a review which—

(a) has been carried out for the protection of public health or of flora and fauna dependent on an aquatic environment; and

(b) but for being so carried out would have been prohibited by virtue of section 127(2) or 131(2) above.

(2) [The Environment Agency] shall not be required to pay any compensation under this section if the determination in question is shown to have been given in consequence of—

(a) a change of circumstances which could not reasonably have been foreseen at the time when the period of two years mentioned in section 127(2) or, as the case may be, section 131(2) above began to run; or

(b) consideration by [the Environment Agency] of material information which was not reasonably available to [the Agency] at that time.

(3) No person shall be entitled to any compensation under section 125 above in respect of anything done in pursuance of section 133 above.

(4) In this section 'the relevant person', in relation to a review, means the owner or the occupier of the trade premises in question, according to whether it is the owner or the

occupier who makes the discharges to which the review relates or, as the case may be, is a party to the agreement to which it relates.

135   Restrictions on power to fix charges under Chapter III

(1) On any appeal under section 122 or 126(1) above conditions providing for the payment of charges to the sewerage undertaker in question shall not be determined by the Director except in so far as no provision is in force by virtue of a charges scheme under section 143 below in respect of any such receptions, discharges, removals or disposals of effluent or substances as are of the same description as the reception, discharge, removal or disposal which is the subject-matter of the appeal.

(2) In so far as any such conditions as are mentioned in subsection (1) above do fall to be determined by the Director, they shall be determined having regard to the desirability of that undertaker's—

    (a) recovering the expenses of complying with its obligations in consequence of the consent or agreement to which the conditions relate; and

    (b) securing a reasonable return on its capital.

(3) To the extent that subsection (1) above excludes any charges from a determination on an appeal those charges shall be fixed from time to time by a charges scheme under section 143 below but not otherwise.

[135A   Power of the Environment Agency to acquire information for the purpose of its functions in relation to special category effluent

(1) For the purpose of the discharge of its functions under this Chapter, the Environment Agency may, by notice in writing served on any person, require that person to furnish such information specified in the notice as that Agency reasonably considers it needs, in such form and within such period following service of the notice, or at such time, as is so specified.

(2) A person who—

    (a) fails, without reasonable excuse, to comply with a requirement imposed under subsection (1) above, or

    (b) in furnishing any information in compliance with such a requirement, makes any statement which he knows to be false or misleading in a material particular, or recklessly makes a statement which is false or misleading in a material particular,

shall be guilty of an offence.

(3) A person guilty of an offence under subsection (2) above shall be liable—

    (a) on summary conviction, to a fine not exceeding the statutory maximum;

    (b) on conviction on indictment, to a fine or to imprisonment for a term not exceeding two years, or to both.]

136   Evidence from meters etc.

Any meter or apparatus provided in pursuance of this Chapter in any trade premises for the purpose of measuring, recording or determining the volume, rate of discharge, nature or composition of any trade effluent discharged from those premises shall be presumed in any proceedings to register accurately, unless the contrary is shown.

137   Statement of case on appeal

(1) At any stage of the proceedings on an appeal under section 122 or 126(1) above, the Director may, and if so directed by the High Court shall, state in the form of a special case for the decision of the High Court any question of law arising in those proceedings.

(2) The decision of the High Court on a special case under this section shall be deemed to be a judgment of the Court within the meaning of section 16 of the Supreme Court Act 1981 (which relates to the jurisdiction of the Court of Appeal); but no appeal to the Court of Appeal shall be brought by virtue of this subsection except with the leave of the High Court or of the Court of Appeal.

138 Meaning of 'special category effluent'

(1) Subject to [subsections (1A) and] (2) below, trade effluent shall be special category effluent for the purposes of this Chapter if—

    (a) such substances as may be prescribed under this Act are present in the effluent or are present in the effluent in prescribed concentrations; or

    (b) the effluent derives from any such process as may be so prescribed or from a process involving the use of prescribed substances or the use of such substances in quantities which exceed the prescribed amounts.

[(1A) If trade effluent is produced, or to be produced, by operating any installation or plant or otherwise carrying on any activity, the operation or carrying on of which requires a permit, that effluent shall not be special category effluent for the purposes of this Chapter as from the determination date relating to the installation, plant or activity in question.

(1B) In subsection (1A)—

    (a) 'determination date', in relation to an installation, plant or activity, means—

        (i) in the case of an installation, plant or activity in relation to which a permit is granted, the date on which it is granted, whether in pursuance of the application, or on an appeal, of a direction to grant it;

        (ii) in the case of an installation, plant or activity in relation to which the grant of a permit is refused, the date of refusal or, on appeal, of the affirmation of the refusal, and in this paragraph the references to an appeal are references to an appeal under regulations under section 2 of the Pollution Prevention and Control Act 1999;

    (b) 'permit' means a permit granted, under regulations under that section, by an authority exercising functions under the regulations that are exercisable for the purpose of preventing or reducing emissions into the air, water and land.]

(2) Trade effluent shall not be special category effluent for the purposes of this Chapter if it is produced, or to be produced, in any process which is a prescribed process designated for central control as from the date which is the determination date for that process.

(3) In subsection (2) above 'determination date', in relation to a prescribed process, means—

    (a) in the case of a process for which authorisation is granted, the date on which the enforcing authority grants it, whether in pursuance of the application or, on an appeal, of a direction to grant it;

    (b) in the case of a process for which authorisation is refused, the date of refusal or, on appeal, of the affirmation of the refusal.

(4) [In subsection (2) and (3) above]—

    (a) 'authorisation', 'enforcing authority' and 'prescribed process' have the meanings given by section 1 of the Environmental Protection Act 1990; and

    (b) the references to designation for central control and to an appeal are references, respectively, to designation under section 4 of that Act and to an appeal under section 15 of that Act.

(5) Without prejudice to the power in subsection (3) of section 139 below, nothing in this Chapter shall enable regulations under this section to prescribe as special category effluent any liquid or matter which is not trade effluent but falls to be treated as such for the purposes of this Chapter by virtue of an order under that section.

139 Power to apply Chapter III to other effluents

(1) The Secretary of State may by order provide that, subject to section 138(5) above, this Chapter shall apply in relation to liquid or other matter of any description specified in the order which is discharged into public sewers as it applies in relation to trade effluent.

(2) An order applying the provisions of this Chapter in relation to liquid or other matter of any description may provide for it to so apply subject to such modifications (if any) as

may be specified in the order and, in particular, subject to any such modification of the meaning for the purposes of this Chapter of the expression 'trade premises' as may be so specified.

(3) The Secretary of State may include in an order under this section such provisions as appear to him expedient for modifying any enactment relating to sewage as that enactment applies in relation to the discharge into sewers of any liquid or other matter to which any provisions of this Chapter are applied by an order under this section.

(4) The Secretary of State may include in an order under this section such other supplemental, incidental and transitional provision as appears to him to be expedient.

(5) The power to make an order under this section shall be exercisable by statutory instrument; and no order shall be made under this section unless a draft of it has been laid before, and approved by a resolution of, each House of Parliament.

140   Pre-1989 Act authority for trade effluent discharges etc.

Schedule 8 to this Act shall have effect (without prejudice to the provisions of the Water Consolidation (Consequential Provisions) Act 1991 or to sections 16 and 17 of the Interpretation Act 1978) for the purpose of making provision in respect of certain cases where trade effluent was discharged in accordance with provision made before the coming into force of the Water Act 1989.

141   Interpretation of Chapter III

(1) In this Chapter, except in so far as the context otherwise requires—

'special category effluent' has the meaning given by section 138 above;

'trade effluent'—

    (a) ameans any liquid, either with or without particles of matter in suspension in the liquid, which is wholly or partly produced in the course of any trade or industry carried on at trade premises; and

    (b) in relation to any trade premises, means any such liquid which is so produced in the course of any trade or industry carried on at those premises, but does not include domestic sewage;

'trade premises' means, subject to subsection (2) below, any premises used or intended to be used for carrying on any trade or industry.

(2) For the purposes of this Chapter any land or premises used or intended for use (in whole or in part and whether or not for profit)—

    (a) for agricultural or horticultural purposes or for the purposes of fish farming; or

    (b) for scientific research or experiment,

shall be deemed to be premises used for carrying on a trade or industry; and the references to a trade or industry in the definition of 'trade effluent' in subsection (1) above shall include references to agriculture, horticulture, fish farming and scientific research or experiment.

(3) Every application or consent made or given under this Chapter shall be made or given in writing.

(4) Nothing in this Chapter shall affect any right with respect to water in a river stream or watercourse, or authorise any infringement of such a right, except in so far as any such right would dispense with the requirements of this Chapter so far as they have effect by virtue of any regulations under section 138 above.

PART V   FINANCIAL PROVISIONS

CHAPTER I   CHARGES

143   Charges schemes

(1) A relevant undertaker may make a scheme ('a charges scheme') which does any one or more of the following, that is to say—

    (a) fixes the charges to be paid for any services provided by the undertaker in the course of carrying out its functions;

(b) in the case of a sewerage undertaker, requires such charges as may be fixed by the scheme to be paid to the undertaker where, in the circumstances set out in the scheme—

    (i) a notice containing an application for a consent is served on the undertaker under section 119 above;

    (ii) such a consent as is necessary for the purposes of Chapter III of Part IV of this Act is given by the undertaker; or

    (iii) a discharge is made in pursuance of such a consent; and

(c) makes provision with respect to the times and methods of payment of the charges fixed by the scheme.

(2) The persons who may be required by a charges scheme to pay any charge fixed by virtue of subsection (1)(b) above shall be the person who serves the notice, the person to whom the consent is given or, as the case may be, any person who makes a discharge in pursuance of the consent at any time during the period to which, in accordance with the scheme, the charge relates.

(3) A charges scheme which requires the payment of charges where a discharge has been made in pursuance of such a consent as is mentioned in subsection (1)(b) above may impose—

(a) a single charge in respect of the whole period for which the consent is in force;

(b) separate charges in respect of different parts of that period; or

(c) both such a single charge and such separate charges.

[(3A) A sewerage undertaker is under a duty to ensure that any charges scheme made by the undertaker, so far as having effect to recover the undertaker's costs of providing a sewer by virtue of its duty under section 101A(1) above, causes those costs to be borne by the undertaker's customers generally; and a sewerage undertaker's duty under this subsection shall be enforceable under section 18 above—

(a) by the Secretary of State; or

(b) with the consent of or in accordance with a general authorisation given by the Secretary of State, by the Director.]

(4) A charges scheme may—

(a) make different provision for different cases, including different provision in relation to different circumstances or localities; and

(b) contain supplemental, consequential and transitional provision for the purposes of the scheme;

and such a scheme may revoke or amend a previous charges scheme.

(5) Nothing in any charges scheme shall affect—

(a) any power of a relevant undertaker to enter into such an agreement with any person in any particular case as determines the charges to be made for the services provided to that person by the undertaker; or

(b) the power of a sewerage undertaker to enter into any agreement under section 129 above on terms that provide for the making of payments to the undertaker.

PART VII   INFORMATION PROVISIONS

196 Trade effluent registers

(1) It shall be the duty of every sewerage undertaker to secure that copies of—

(a) every consent given or having effect as if given by the undertaker under Chapter III of Part IV of this Act;

(b) every direction given or having effect as if given by the undertaker under that Chapter;

(c) every agreement entered into or having effect as if entered into by the undertaker under section 129 above; and

(d) every notice served on the undertaker under section 132 above, are kept available, at all reasonable times, for inspection by the public free of charge at the offices of the undertaker.

(2) It shall be the duty of every sewerage undertaker, on the payment of such sum as may be reasonable, to furnish a person who requests it with a copy of, or of an extract from, anything kept available for inspection under this section.

(3) The duties of a sewerage undertaker under this section shall be enforceable under section 18 above by the Director.

204   Provision of information to sewerage undertakers with respect to trade effluent discharges

(1) The owner or occupier of any land on or under which is situated any sewer, drain, pipe, channel or outlet used or intended to be used for discharging any trade effluent into a sewer of a sewerage undertaker shall, when requested to do so by the undertaker—

(a) produce to the undertaker all such plans of the sewer, drain, pipe, channel or outlet as the owner or, as the case may be, occupier possesses or is able without expense to obtain;

(b) allow copies of the plans so produced by him to be made by, or under the directions of, the undertaker; and

(c) furnish to the undertaker all such information as the owner or, as the case may be, occupier can reasonably be expected to supply with respect to the sewer, drain, pipe, channel or outlet.

(2) A request by a sewerage undertaker for the purposes of this section shall be made in writing.

(3) Every person who fails to comply with this section shall be guilty of an offence and liable, on summary conviction to a fine not exceeding level 3 on the standard scale.

(4) Expressions used in this section and in Chapter III of Part IV of this Act have the same meanings in this section as in that Chapter; and, accordingly, section 139 above shall have effect for the purposes of this section as it has effect for the purposes of that Chapter.

PART VIII   MISCELLANEOUS AND SUPPLEMENTAL

120   Offences by bodies corporate

(1) Where a body corporate is guilty of an offence under this Act and that offence is proved to have been committed with the consent or connivance of, or to be attributable to any neglect on the part of, any director, manager, secretary or other similar officer of the body corporate or any person who was purporting to act in any such capacity, then he, as well as the body corporate, shall be guilty of that offence and shall be liable to be proceeded against and punished accordingly.

(2) Where the affairs of a body corporate are managed by its members, subsection (1) above shall apply in relation to the acts and defaults of a member in connection with his functions of management as if he were a director of the body corporate.

211   Limitation on right to prosecute in respect of sewerage offences

Proceedings in respect of an offence created by or under any of the relevant sewerage provisions shall not, without the written consent of the Attorney-General, be taken by any person other than—

(a) a party aggrieved;

(b) a sewerage undertaker; or

(c) a body whose function it is to enforce the provisions in question.

219 General interpretation

(1) In this Act, except in so far as the context otherwise requires—

. . .

'drain' means (subject to subsection (2) below) a drain used for the drainage of one building or of any buildings or yards appurtenant to buildings within the same curtilage;

'effluent' means any liquid, including particles of matter and other substances in suspension in the liquid;

. . .

'owner', in relation to any premises, means the person who—

(a) is for the time being receiving the rack-rent of the premises, whether on his own account or as agent or trustee for another person; or

(b) would receive the rack-rent if the premises were let at a rack-rent, and cognate expressions shall be construed accordingly;

. . .

'public sewer' means a sewer for the time being vested in a sewerage undertaker in its capacity as such, whether vested in that undertaker by virtue of a scheme under Schedule 2 to the Water Act 1989 or Schedule 2 to this Act or under section 179 above or otherwise, and 'private sewer' shall be construed accordingly;

. . .

'sewer' includes (without prejudice to subsection (2) below) all sewers and drains (not being drains within the meaning given by this subsection) which are used for the drainage of buildings and yards appurtenant to buildings;

. . .

(2) In this Act—

(a) references to a pipe, including references to a main, a drain or a sewer, shall include references to a tunnel or conduit which serves or is to serve as the pipe in question and to any accessories for the pipe; and

(b) references to any sewage disposal works shall include references to the machinery and equipment of those works and any necessary pumping stations and outfall pipes;

and, accordingly, references to the laying of a pipe shall include references to the construction of such a tunnel or conduit, to the construction or installation of any such accessories and to the making of a connection between one pipe and another.

. . .

[221 Crown application

(1) Subject to the provisions of this section, this Act shall bind the Crown.

(2) No contravention by the Crown of any provision made by or under this Act shall make the Crown criminally liable; but the High Court may, on the application of the Environment Agency, a water undertaker or a sewerage undertaker, declare unlawful any act or omission of the Crown which constitutes such a contravention.

(3) Notwithstanding anything in subsection (2) above, any provision made by or under this Act shall apply to persons in the public service of the Crown as it applies to other persons.

(4) If the Secretary of State certifies that it appears to him, as respects any Crown premises and any powers of entry exercisable in relation to them specified in the certificate, that it is requisite or expedient that, in the interests of national security, the powers should not be exercisable in relation to those premises, those powers shall not be exercisable in relation to those premises.

(5) Nothing in this section shall be taken as in any way affecting Her Majesty in her private capacity; and this subsection shall be construed as if section 38(3) of the Crown Proceedings Act 1947 (interpretation of references to Her Majesty in her private capacity) were contained in this Act.

(6) . . .

(7) In this section—

'the appropriate authority' has the same meaning as it has in Part XIII of the Town and Country Planning Act 1990 by virtue of section 293(2) of that Act;

'Crown or Duchy interest' means an interest which belongs to Her Majesty in right of the Crown or of the Duchy of Lancaster, or to the Duchy of Cornwall, or belonging to a government department or held in trust for Her Majesty for the purposes of a government department;

'Crown premises' means premises held by or on behalf of the Crown.

(8) The provisions of subsection (3) of section 293 of the Town and Country Planning Act 1990 (questions relating to Crown application) as to the determination of questions shall apply for the purposes of this section.]

Section 140   SCHEDULE 8

PRE-1989 ACT TRANSITIONAL AUTHORITY FOR TRADE EFFLUENT DISCHARGES ETC.

1.—Nothing in Chapter III of Part IV of this Act (except so far as it relates to special category effluent) or in the repeals made by the Water Consolidation (Consequential Provisions) Act 1991 shall affect—

    (a) any agreement with respect to any trade effluent to which a sewerage undertaker is a party by virtue of its having been duly made before 1st July 1937 between a predecessor of the undertaker and the owner or occupier of any trade premises; or

    (b) any agreement saved by section 63(8) of the Public Health Act 1961 (pre-1961 Act agreements with respect to discharges from premises used for farming or for scientific research or experiment).

2.—(1) Where, by virtue of section 43(2) of the Control of Pollution Act 1974 there is, immediately before the commencement of this Act, a deemed consent for the purposes of the Public Health (Drainage of Trade Premises) Act 1937 which has effect under the Water Act 1989 in relation to any sewerage undertaker, that deemed consent shall have effect as a deemed consent for the purposes of Chapter III of Part IV of this Act subject to the following provisions of this paragraph.

    (2) The sewerage undertaker—

        (a) may at any time; and

        (b) shall if requested to do so by any person entitled to make a discharge in pursuance of the deemed consent,

by notice served on the owner and any occupier of the premises in question cancel the deemed consent and, subject to sub-paragraph (3) below, give its actual consent for such discharges as were authorised by the deemed consent.

    (3) An actual consent given under sub-paragraph (2) above shall be so given either conditionally or subject to any conditions which may be attached to consents by virtue of section 121 of this Act.

    (4) It is hereby declared that the provisions of Chapter III of Part IV of this Act with respect to the variation of conditions of a consent apply in relation to an actual consent under sub-paragraph (2) above as they apply in relation to any other actual consent under Chapter III of Part IV of this Act.

    (5) A notice signifying an actual consent under sub-paragraph (2) above shall indicate that a right of appeal is conferred under the following paragraph in respect of the notice.

Appeals in respect of consents under paragraph 2

3.—(1) A person on whom notice is served in pursuance of paragraph 2(2) above may, in accordance with regulations made by the Secretary of State, appeal to the Director.

(2) Section 137 of this Act shall apply, with the necessary modifications, in relation to appeals under this paragraph as it applies in relation to appeals under section 122 of this Act.

(3) On an appeal under this paragraph the Director may give the sewerage undertaker in question any such direction as he thinks fit with respect to the notice and it shall be the duty of the undertaker to comply with the direction.

Determinations of disputes as to transitional matters

4.—(1) Any dispute in so far as it—

    (a) arises after the commencement of this Act and relates to a deemed consent in respect of discharges previously authorised under section 4 of the Public Health (Drainage of Trade Premises) Act 1937; and

    (b) is a dispute as to the nature or composition of any trade effluent discharged from any trade premises into a sewer during any period, as to the quantity of trade effluent so discharged on any one day during any period or as to the rate of trade effluent so discharged during any period,

shall, unless the parties otherwise agree, be referred to the Director for determination.

(2) On a reference under this paragraph the Director may make such order in the matter as he thinks just.

(3) An order on a reference under this paragraph shall be final; but section 137 of this Act shall apply, with the necessary modifications, in relation to references under this paragraph as it applies in relation to appeals under section 122 of this Act.

Regulations as to residue of agreements

5.—The Secretary of State may by regulations make provisions in relation to the provisions of any agreement to which subsection (1) of section 43 of the Control of Pollution Act 1974 applied and which apart from that section would be in force after the commencement of this Act—

    (a) for determining, by arbitration or otherwise, whether any such agreement continues to have effect as relating to a matter other than the discharge of trade effluent into a sewerage undertaker's sewer;

    (b) for determining, by arbitration or otherwise, what modifications (if any) are appropriate in consequence of any prescribed provision of section 43 of that Act or any provision of this Schedule re-enacting any such provision; and

    (c) in a case in which the conditions on which any discharges authorised by such an agreement included, immediately before the coming into force of section 43 of that Act, a condition as to charges in respect of the discharges and other matters—

        (i) for determining, by arbitration or otherwise, the proportion of the charges attributable to the discharges; and

        (ii) for limiting accordingly the conditions which are to be treated by virtue of section 43 of that Act as included in the deemed consent which has effect by virtue of this Schedule.

Water Resources Act 1991
(1991, c. 57)

PART III   CONTROL OF POLLUTION OF WATER RESOURCES

CHAPTER I   QUALITY OBJECTIVES

82   Classification of quality of waters

(1) The Secretary of State may, in relation to any description of controlled waters (being a description applying to some or all of the waters of a particular class or of two or more different classes), by regulations prescribe a system of classifying the quality of those waters according to criteria specified in the regulations.

(2) The criteria specified in regulations under this section in relation to any classification shall consist of one or more of the following, that is to say—

(a) general requirements as to the purposes for which the waters to which the classification is applied are to be suitable;

(b) specific requirements as to the substances that are to be present in or absent from the water and as to the concentrations of substances which are or are required to be present in the water;

(c) specific requirements as to other characteristics of those waters;

and for the purposes of any such classification regulations under this section may provide that the question whether prescribed requirements are satisfied may be determined by reference to such samples as may be prescribed.

83   Water quality objectives

(1) For the purpose of maintaining and improving the quality of controlled waters the Secretary of State may, by serving a notice on the [Agency] specifying—

(a) one or more of the classifications for the time being prescribed under section 82 above; and

(b) in relation to each specified classification, a date,

establish the water quality objectives for any waters which are, or are included in, waters of a description prescribed for the purposes of that section.

(2) The water quality objectives for any waters to which a notice under this section relates shall be the satisfaction by those waters, on and at all times after each date specified in the notice, of the requirements which at the time of the notice were the requirements for the classification in relation to which that date is so specified.

(3) Where the Secretary of State has established water quality objectives under this section for any waters he may review objectives for those waters if—

(a) five years or more have elapsed since the service of the last notice under subsection (1) or (6) of this section to be served in respect of those waters; or

(b) the [Agency], after consultation with such water undertakers and other persons as it considers appropriate, requests a review;

and the Secretary of State shall not exercise his power to establish objectives for any waters by varying the existing objectives for those waters except in consequence of such a review.

(4) Where the Secretary of State proposes to exercise his power under this section to establish or vary the objectives for any waters he shall—

(a) give notice setting out his proposal and specifying the period (not being less than three months from the date of publication of the notice) within which representations or objections with respect to the proposal may be made; and

(b) consider any representations or objections which are duly made and not withdrawn;

and, if he decides, after considering any such representations or objections, to exercise his power to establish or vary those objectives, he may do so either in accordance with the proposal contained in the notice or in accordance with that proposal as modified in such manner as he considers appropriate.

(5) A notice under subsection (4) above shall be given—

    (a) by publishing the notice in such manner as the Secretary of State considers appropriate for bringing it to the attention of persons likely to be affected by it; and

    (b) by serving a copy of the notice on the [Agency].

(6) If, on a review under this section or in consequence of any representations or objections made following such a review for the purposes of subsection (4) above, the Secretary of State decides that the water quality objectives for any waters should remain unchanged, he shall serve notice of that decision on the [Agency].

84 General duties to achieve and maintain objectives etc.

(1) It shall be the duty of the Secretary of State and of the [Agency] to exercise the powers conferred on him or it by or under the water pollution provisions of this Act (other than the preceding provisions of this Chapter and sections 104 and 192 below) in such manner as ensures, so far as it is practicable by the exercise of those powers to do so, that the water quality objectives specified for any waters in—

    (a) a notice under section 83 above; or

    (b) . . .

are achieved at all times.

(2) It shall be the duty of the [Agency], for the purposes of the carrying out of its functions under the water pollution provisions of this Act—

    (a) to monitor the extent of pollution in controlled waters; and

    (b) to consult, in such cases as it may consider appropriate, with river purification authorities in Scotland.

CHAPTER II   POLLUTION OFFENCES

85 Offences of polluting controlled waters

(1) A person contravenes this section if he causes or knowingly permits any poisonous, noxious or polluting matter or any solid waste matter to enter any controlled waters.

(2) A person contravenes this section if he causes or knowingly permits any matter, other than trade effluent or sewage effluent, to enter controlled waters by being discharged from a drain or sewer in contravention of a prohibition imposed under section 86 below.

(3) A person contravenes this section if he causes or knowingly permits any trade effluent or sewage effluent to be discharged—

    (a) into any controlled waters; or

    (b) from land in England and Wales, through a pipe, into the sea outside the seaward limits of controlled waters.

(4) A person contravenes this section if he causes or knowingly permits any trade effluent or sewage effluent to be discharged, in contravention of any prohibition imposed under section 86 below, from a building or from any fixed plant—

    (a) on to or into any land; or

    (b) into any waters of a lake or pond which are not inland freshwaters.

(5) A person contravenes this section if he causes or knowingly permits any matter whatever to enter any inland freshwaters so as to tend (either directly or in combination with other matter which he or another person causes or permits to enter those waters) to impede the proper flow of the waters in a manner leading, or likely to lead, to a substantial aggravation of—

(a) pollution due to other causes; or

(b) the consequences of such pollution.

(6) Subject to the following provisions of this Chapter, a person who contravenes this section or the conditions of any consent given under this Chapter for the purposes of this section shall be guilty of an offence and liable—

(a) on summary conviction, to imprisonment for a term not exceeding three months or to a fine not exceeding £20,000 or to both;

(b) on conviction on indictment, to imprisonment for a term not exceeding two years or to a fine or to both.

86   Prohibition of certain discharges by notice or regulations

(1) For the purposes of section 85 above a discharge of any effluent or other matter is, in relation to any person, in contravention of a prohibition imposed under this section if, subject to the following provisions of this section—

(a) the [Agency] has given that person notice prohibiting him from making or, as the case may be, continuing the discharge; or

(b) the [Agency] has given that person notice prohibiting him from making or, as the case may be, continuing the discharge unless specified conditions are observed, and those conditions are not observed.

(2) For the purposes of section 85 above a discharge of any effluent or other matter is also in contravention of a prohibition imposed under this section if the effluent or matter discharged—

(a) contains a prescribed substance or a prescribed concentration of such a substance; or

(b) derives from a prescribed process or from a process involving the use of prescribed substances or the use of such substances in quantities which exceed the prescribed amounts.

(3) Nothing in subsection (1) above shall authorise the giving of a notice for the purposes of that subsection in respect of discharges from a vessel; and nothing in any regulations made by virtue of subsection (2) above shall require any discharge from a vessel to be treated as a discharge in contravention of a prohibition imposed under this section.

(4) A notice given for the purposes of subsection (1) above shall expire at such time as may be specified in the notice.

(5) The time specified for the purposes of subsection (4) above shall not be before the end of the period of three months beginning with the day on which the notice is given, except in a case where the [Agency] is satisfied that there is an emergency which requires the prohibition in question to come into force at such time before the end of that period as may be so specified.

(6) Where, in the case of such a notice for the purposes of subsection (1) above as (but for this subsection) would expire at a time at or after the end of the said period of three months, an application is made before that time for a consent under this Chapter in respect of the discharge to which the notice relates, that notice shall be deemed not to expire until the result of the application becomes final—

(a) on the grant or withdrawal of the application;

(b) on the expiration, without the bringing of an appeal with respect to the decision on the application, of any period prescribed as the period within which any such appeal must be brought; or

(c) on the withdrawal or determination of any such appeal.

87   Discharges into and from public sewers etc.

[(1) This section applies for the purpose of determining liability where sewage effluent is discharged as mentioned in subsection (3) or (4) of section 85 above from any sewer or works ('the discharging sewer') vested in a sewerage undertaker ('the discharging undertaker').

(1A) If the discharging undertaker did not cause, or knowingly permit, the discharge it shall nevertheless be deemed to have caused the discharge if—

(a) matter included in the discharge was received by it into the discharging sewer or any other sewer or works vested in it;

(b) it was bound (either unconditionally or subject to conditions which were observed) to receive that matter into that sewer or works; and

(c) subsection (1B) below does not apply.

(1B) This subsection applies where the sewage effluent was, before being discharged from the discharging sewer, discharged through a main connection into that sewer or into any other sewer or works vested in the discharging undertaker by another sewerage undertaker ('the sending undertaker') under an agreement having effect between the discharging undertaker and the sending undertaker under section 110A of the Water Industry Act 1991.

(1C) Where subsection (1B) above applies, the sending undertaker shall be deemed to have caused the discharge if, although it did not cause, or knowingly permit, the sewage effluent to be discharged into the discharging sewer, or into any other sewer or works of the discharging undertaker—

(a) matter included in the discharge was received by it into a sewer or works vested in it; and

(b) it was bound (either unconditionally or subject to conditions which were observed) to receive that matter into that sewer or works.]

(2) A sewerage undertaker shall not be guilty of an offence under section 85 above by reason only of the fact that a discharge from a sewer or works vested in the undertaker contravenes conditions of a consent relating to the discharge if—

(a) the contravention is attributable to a discharge which another person caused or permitted to be made into the sewer or works;

(b) the undertaker either was not bound to receive the discharge into the sewer or works or was bound to receive it there subject to conditions which were not observed; and

(c) the undertaker could not reasonably have been expected to prevent the discharge into the sewer or works.

(3) A person shall not be guilty of an offence under section 85 above in respect of a discharge which he caused or permitted to be made into a sewer or works vested in a sewerage undertaker if the undertaker was bound to receive the discharge there either unconditionally or subject to conditions which were observed.

[(4) In this section 'main connection' has the same meaning as in section 110A of the Water Industry Act 1991.]

88   Defence to principal offences in respect of authorised discharges

(1) Subject to the following provisions of this section, a person shall not be guilty of an offence under section 85 above in respect of the entry of any matter into any waters or any discharge if the entry occurs or the discharge is made under and in accordance with, or as a result of any act or omission under and in accordance with—

(a) a consent given under this Chapter . . .;

[(aa) a permit granted, under regulations under section 2 of the Pollution Prevention and Control Act 1999, by an authority exercising functions under the regulations that are exercisable for the purpose of preventing or reducing emissions into the air, water and land;]

(b) an authorisation for a prescribed process designated for central control granted under Part I of the Environmental Protection Act 1990;

(c) a waste management or disposal licence;

(d) a licence granted under Part II of the Food and Environment Protection Act 1985;

(e) section 163 below or section 165 of the Water Industry Act 1991 (discharges for works purposes);

(f) any local statutory provision or statutory order which expressly confers power to discharge effluent into water; or

(g) any prescribed enactment.

(2) Schedule 10 to this Act shall have effect, subject to section 91 below, with respect to the making of applications for consents under this Chapter for the purposes of subsection (1)(a) above and with respect to the giving, revocation and modification of such consents.

(3) Nothing in any disposal licence shall be treated for the purposes of subsection (1) above as authorising—

(a) any such entry or discharge as is mentioned in subsections (2) to (4) of section 85 above; or

(b) any act or omission so far as it results in any such entry or discharge.

(4) In this section—

'disposal licence' means a licence issued in pursuance of section 5 of the Control of Pollution Act 1974;

'statutory order' means—

(a) any order under section 168 below or section 167 of the Water Industry Act 1991 (compulsory works orders); or

(b) any order, byelaw, scheme or award made under any other enactment, including an order or scheme confirmed by Parliament or brought into operation in accordance with special parliamentary procedure;

and

'waste management licence' means such a licence granted under Part II of the Environmental Protection Act 1990.

89   Other defences to principal offences

(1) A person shall not be guilty of an offence under section 85 above in respect of the entry of any matter into any waters or any discharge if—

(a) the entry is caused or permitted, or the discharge is made, in an emergency in order to avoid danger to life or health;

(b) that person takes all such steps as are reasonably practicable in the circumstances for minimising the extent of the entry or discharge and of its polluting effects; and

(c) particulars of the entry or discharge are furnished to the [Agency] as soon as reasonably practicable after the entry occurs.

(2) A person shall not be guilty of an offence under section 85 above by reason of his causing or permitting any discharge of trade or sewage effluent from a vessel.

(3) A person shall not be guilty of an offence under section 85 above by reason only of his permitting water from an abandoned mine [or an abandoned part of a mine] to enter controlled waters.

[(3A) Subsection (3) above shall not apply to the owner or former operator of any mine or part of a mine if the mine or part in question became abandoned after 31st December 1999.

(3B) In determining for the purposes of subsection (3A) above whether a mine or part of a mine became abandoned before, on or after 31st December 1999 in a case where the mine or part has become abandoned on two or more occasions, of which—

(a) at least one falls on or before that date, and

(b) at least one falls after that date,

the mine or part shall be regarded as becoming abandoned after that date (but without prejudice to the operation of subsection (3) above in relation to that mine or part at, or in relation to, any time before the first of those occasions which falls after that date).

(3C) Where, immediately before a part of a mine becomes abandoned, that part is the only part of the mine not falling to be regarded as abandoned for the time being, the abandonment of that part shall not be regarded for the purposes of subsection (3A) or (3B) above as constituting the abandonment of the mine, but only of that part of it.]

(4) A person shall not, otherwise than in respect of the entry of any poisonous, noxious or polluting matter into any controlled waters, be guilty of an offence under section 85 above by reason of his depositing the solid refuse of a mine or quarry on any land so that it falls or is carried into inland freshwaters if—

(a) the deposits the refuse on the land with the consent of the [Agency];

(b) no other site for the deposit is reasonably practicable; and

(c) he takes all reasonably practicable steps to prevent the refuse from entering those inland freshwaters.

(5) A highway authority or other person entitled to keep open a drain by virtue of section 100 of the Highways Act 1980 shall not be guilty of an offence under section 85 above by reason of his causing or permitting any discharge to be made from a drain kept open by virtue of that section unless the discharge is made in contravention of a prohibition imposed under section 86 above.

(6) In this section 'mine' and 'quarry' have the same meanings as in the Mines and Quarries Act 1954.

90   Offences in connection with deposits and vegetation in rivers

(1) A person shall be guilty of an offence under this section if, without the consent of the [Agency], he—

(a) removes from any part of the bottom, channel or bed of any inland freshwaters a deposit accumulated by reason of any dam, weir or sluice holding back the waters; and

(b) does so by causing the deposit to be carried away in suspension in the waters.

(2) A person shall be guilty of an offence under this section if, without the consent of the [Agency], he—

(a) causes or permits a substantial amount of vegetation to be cut or uprooted in any inland freshwaters, or to be cut or uprooted so near to any such waters that it falls into them; and

(b) fails to take all reasonable steps to remove the vegetation from those waters.

(3) A person guilty of an offence under this section shall be liable, on summary conviction, to a fine not exceeding level 4 on the standard scale.

(4) Nothing in subsection (1) above applies to anything done in the exercise of any power conferred by or under any enactment relating to land drainage, flood prevention or navigation.

(5) In giving a consent for the purposes of this section the [Agency] may make the consent subject to such conditions as it considers appropriate.

(6) The Secretary of State may by regulations provide that any reference to inland freshwaters in subsection (1) or (2) above shall be construed as including a reference to such coastal waters as may be prescribed.

[Consents for the purposes of sections 88 to 90

90A   Applications for consent under section 89 or 90

(1) Any application for a consent for the purposes of section 89(4)(a) or 90(1) or (2) above—

(a) must be made on a form provided for the purpose by the Agency, and

(b) must be advertised in such manner as may be required by regulations made by the Secretary of State,

except that paragraph (b) above shall not have effect in the case of an application of any class or description specified in the regulations as being exempt from the requirements of that paragraph.

(2) The applicant for such a consent must, at the time when he makes his application, provide the Agency—

(a) with all such information as it reasonably requires; and

(b) with all such information as may be prescribed for the purpose by the Secretary of State.

(3) The information required by subsection (2) above must be provided either on, or together with, the form mentioned in subsection (1) above.

(4) The Agency may give the applicant notice requiring him to provide it with all such further information of any description specified in the notice as it may require for the purpose of determining the application.

(5) If the applicant fails to provide the Agency with any information required under subsection (4) above, the Agency may refuse to proceed with the application or refuse to proceed with it until the information is provided.

90B   Enforcement notices

(1) If the Agency is of the opinion that the holder of a relevant consent is contravening any condition of the consent, or is likely to contravene any such condition, the Agency may serve on him a notice (an 'enforcement notice').

(2) An enforcement notice shall—

(a) state that the Agency is of the said opinion;

(b) specify the matters constituting the contravention or the matters making it likely that the contravention will arise;

(c) specify the steps that must be taken to remedy the contravention or, as the case may be, to remedy the matters making it likely that the contravention will arise; and

(d) specify the period within which those steps must be taken.

(3) Any person who fails to comply with any requirement imposed by an enforcement notice shall be guilty of an offence and liable—

(a) on summary conviction, to imprisonment for a term not exceeding three months or to a fine not exceeding £20,000 or to both;

(b) on conviction on indictment, to imprisonment for a term not exceeding two years or to a fine or to both.

(4) If the Agency is of the opinion that proceedings for an offence under subsection (3) above would afford an ineffectual remedy against a person who has failed to comply with the requirements of an enforcement notice, the Agency may take proceedings in the High Court for the purpose of securing compliance with the notice.

(5) The Secretary of State may, if he thinks fit in relation to any person, give to the Agency directions as to whether the Agency should exercise its powers under this section and as to the steps which must be taken.

(6) In this section—

'relevant consent' means—

(a) a consent for the purposes of section 89(4)(a) or 90(1) or (2) above; or

(b) a discharge consent, within the meaning of section 91 below; and

'the holder', in relation to a relevant consent, is the person who has the consent in question.]

91   Appeals in respect of consents under Chapter II

(1) This section applies where the [Agency], otherwise than in pursuance of a direction of the Secretary of State—

(a) on an application for a consent under this Chapter for the purposes of section 88(1)(a) above, has refused a consent for any discharges;

(b) in giving a discharge consent, has made that consent subject to conditions;

(c) has revoked a discharge consent, modified the conditions of any such consent or provided that any such consent which was unconditional shall be subject to conditions;

(d) has, for the purposes of paragraph [8(1)] or (2) of Schedule 10 to this Act, specified a period in relation to a discharge consent without the agreement of the person who proposes to make, or makes, discharges in pursuance of that consent;

(e) has refused a consent for the purposes of section 89(4)(a) above for any deposit;

(f) has refused a consent for the purposes of section 90 above for the doing of anything by any person or, in giving any such consent, made that consent subject to conditions.

(2) The person, if any, who applied for the consent [or variation] in question, or any person whose deposits, discharges or other conduct is or would be authorised by the consent [or the person on whom the enforcement notice was served,] may appeal against the decision to the Secretary of State.

[(2A) This section is subject to section 114 of the 1995 Act (delegation or reference of appeals etc).

(2B) An appeal under this section shall, if and to the extent required by regulations under subsection (2K) below, be advertised in such manner as may be prescribed by regulations under that subsection.

(2C) If either party to the appeal so requests or the Secretary of State so decides, an appeal shall be or continue in the form of a hearing (which may, if the person hearing the appeal so decides, be held, or held to any extent, in private).

(2D) On determining an appeal brought by virtue of any of paragraphs (a) to (g) of subsection (1) above against a decision of the Agency, the Secretary of State—

(a) may affirm the decision;

(b) where the decision was a refusal to grant a consent or a variation of a consent, may direct the Agency to grant the consent or to vary the consent, as the case may be;

(c) where the decision was as to the conditions of a consent, may quash all or any of those conditions;

(d) where the decision was to revoke a consent, may quash the decision;

(e) where the decision relates to a period specified for the purposes of paragraph 8(1) or (2) of Schedule 10 to this Act, may modify any provisions specifying that period;

and where he exercises any of the powers in paragraphs (b), (c) or (d) above, he may give directions as to the conditions to which the consent is to be subject.

(2E) On the determination of an appeal brought by virtue of paragraph (h) of subsection (1) above, the Secretary of State may either quash or affirm the enforcement notice and, if he affirms it, may do so either in its original form or with such modifications as he may in the circumstances think fit.

(2F) Subject to subsection (2G) below, where an appeal is brought by virtue of subsection (1)(c) above against a decision—

(a) to revoke a discharge consent,

(b) to modify the conditions of any such consent, or

(c) to provide that any such consent which was unconditional shall be subject to conditions,

the revocation, modification or provision shall not take effect pending the final determination or the withdrawal of the appeal.

(2G) Subsection (2F) above shall not apply to a decision in the case of which the notice affecting the revocation, modification or provision in question includes a statement that in the opinion of the Agency it is necessary for the purpose of preventing or, where that is not practicable, minimising—

    (a) the entry into controlled waters of any poisonous, noxious or polluting matter or any solid waste matter, or

    (b) harm to human health,

that that subsection should not apply.

(2H) Where the decision under appeal is one falling within subsection (2G) above, if, on the application of the holder or former holder of the consent, the Secretary of State or other person determining the appeal determines that the Agency acted unreasonably in excluding the application of subsection (2F) above, then—

    (a) if the appeal is still pending at the end of the day on which the determination is made, subsection (2F) above shall apply to the decision from the end of that day; and

    (b) the holder or former holder of the consent shall be entitled to recover compensation from the Agency in respect of any loss suffered by him in consequence of the exclusion of the application of that subsection;

and any dispute as to a person's entitlement to such compensation or as to the amount of it shall be determined by arbitration.

(2J) Where an appeal is brought under this section against an enforcement notice, the bringing of the appeal shall not have the effect of suspending the operation of the notice.

(2K) Provision may be made by the Secretary of State by regulations with respect to appeals under this section and in particular—

    (a) as to the period within which and the manner in which appeals are to be brought; and

    (b) as to the manner in which appeals are to be considered.]

(3) [. . .]

(8) In this section 'discharge consent' means such a consent under this Chapter for any discharges or description of discharges as is given for the purposes of section 88(1)(a) above either on an application for a consent or, by virtue of paragraph [6] of Schedule 10 to this Act, without such an application having been made.

[CHAPTER IIA   ABANDONED MINES

91A Introductory

(1) For the purposes of this Chapter, 'abandonment', in relation to a mine,—

    (a) subject to paragraph (b) below, includes—

        (i) the discontinuance of any or all of the operations for the removal of water from the mine;

        (ii) the cessation of working of any relevant seam, vein or vein-system;

        (iii) the cessation of use of any shaft or outlet of the mine;

        (iv) in the case of a mine in which activities other than mining activities are carried on (whether or not mining activities are also carried on in the mine)—

            (A) the discontinuance of some or all of those other activities in the mine; and

            (B) any substantial change in the operations for the removal of water from the mine; but

    (b) does not include—

        (i) any disclaimer under section 178 or 315 of the Insolvency Act 1986 (power of liquidator, or trustee of a bankrupt's estate, to disclaim onerous property) by the official receiver acting in a compulsory capacity; or

(ii) the abandonment of any rights, interests or liabilities by the Accountant in Bankruptcy acting as permanent or interim trustee in a sequestration (within the meaning of the Bankruptcy (Scotland) Act 1985);

and cognate expressions shall be construed accordingly.

(2) In this Chapter, except where the context otherwise requires—

'the 1954 Act' means the Mines and Quarries Act 1954;

'acting in a compulsory capacity', in the case of the official receiver, means acting as—

(a) liquidator of a company;

(b) receiver or manager of a bankrupt's estate, pursuant to section 287 of the Insolvency Act 1986;

(c) trustee of a bankrupt's estate;

(d) liquidator of an insolvent partnership;

(e) trustee of an insolvent partnership;

(f) trustee, or receiver or manager, of the insolvent estate of a deceased person;

'mine' has the same meaning as in the 1954 Act;

'the official receiver' has the same meaning as it has in the Insolvency Act 1986 by virtue of section 399(1) of that Act;

'prescribed' means prescribed in regulations;

'regulations' means regulations made by the Secretary of State;

'relevant seam, vein or vein-system', in the case of any mine, means any seam, vein or vein-system for the purpose of, or in connection with, whose working any excavation constituting or comprised in the mine was made.

91B   Mine operators to give the Agency six months' notice of any proposed abandonment

(1) If, in the case of any mine, there is to be an abandonment at any time after the expiration of the initial period, it shall be the duty of the operator of the mine to give notice of the proposed abandonment to the Agency at least six months before the abandonment takes effect.

(2) A notice under subsection (1) above shall contain such information (if any) as is prescribed for the purpose, which may include information about the operator's opinion as to any consequences of the abandonment.

(3) A person who fails to give the notice required by subsection (2) above shall be guilty of an offence and liable—

(a) on summary conviction, to a fine not exceeding the statutory maximum;

(b) on conviction on indictment, to a fine.

(4) A person shall not be guilty of an offence under subsection (3) above if—

(a) the abandonment happens in an emergency in order to avoid danger to life or health; and

(b) notice of the abandonment, containing such information as may be prescribed, is given as soon as reasonably practicable after the abandonment has happened.

(5) Where the operator of a mine is—

(a) the official receiver acting in a compulsory capacity, or

(b) the Accountant in Bankruptcy acting as permanent or interim trustee in a sequestration (within the meaning of the Bankruptcy (Scotland) Act 1985),

he shall not be guilty of an offence under subsection (3) above by reason of any failure to give the notice required by subsection (1) above if, as soon as reasonably practicable (whether before or after the abandonment), he gives to the Agency notice of the abandonment or proposed abandonment, containing such information as may be prescribed.

(6) Where a person gives notice under subsection (1), (4)(b) or (5) above, he shall publish prescribed particulars of, or relating to, the notice in one or more local newspapers circulating in the locality where the mine is situated.

(7) Where the Agency—
  (a) receives notice under this section or otherwise learns of the abandonment or proposed abandonment of any mine, and
  (b) considers that, in consequence of the abandonment or proposed abandonment taking effect, any land has or is likely to become contaminated land, within the meaning of Part IIA of the Environmental Protection Act 1990,
it shall be the duty of the Agency to inform the local authority in whose area that land is situated of the abandonment or proposed abandonment.

(8) In this section—
'the initial period' means the period of six months beginning with the day on which subsection (1) above comes into force;
'local authority' means—
  (a) any unitary authority;
  (b) any district council, so far as it is not a unitary authority;
  (c) the Common Council of the City of London and, as respects the Temples, the Sub-Treasurer of the Inner Temple and the Under-Treasurer of the Middle Temple respectively;
'unitary authority' means—
  (a) the council of a county, so far as it is the council of an area for which there are no district councils;
  (b) the council of any district comprised in an area for which there is no county council;
  (c) the council of a London borough;
  (d) the council of a county borough in Wales.]

CHAPTER III   POWERS TO PREVENT AND CONTROL POLLUTION

92 Requirements to take precautions against pollution

(1) The Secretary of State may by regulations make provision—
  (a) for prohibiting a person from having custody or control of any poisonous, noxious or polluting matter unless prescribed works and prescribed precautions and other steps have been carried out or taken for the purpose of preventing or controlling the entry of the matter into any controlled waters;
  (b) for requiring a person who already has custody or control of, or makes use of, any such matter to carry out such works for that purpose and to take such precautions and other steps for that purpose as may be prescribed.

(2) Without prejudice to the generality of the power conferred by subsection (1) above, regulations under that subsection may—
  (a) confer power on the [Agency]—
    (i) to determine for the purposes of the regulations the circumstances in which a person is required to carry out works or to take any precautions or other steps; and
    (ii) by notice to that person, to impose the requirement and to specify or describe the works, precautions or other steps which that person is required to carry out or take;
  (b) provide for appeals to the Secretary of State against notices served by the [Agency] in pursuance of provision made by virtue of paragraph (a) above; and
  (c) provide that a contravention of the regulations shall be an offence the maximum penalties for which shall not exceed the penalties specified in subsection (6) of section 85 above.

[(3) This section is subject to section 114 of the 1995 Act (delegation or reference of appeals etc).]

93   Water protection zones

(1) Where the Secretary of State considers, after consultation (in the case of an area wholly or partly in England) with the Minister, that subsection (2) below is satisfied in relation to any area, he may by order make provision—

  (a) designating that area as a water protection zone; and
  (b) prohibiting or restricting the carrying on in the designated area of such activities as may be specified or described in the order.

(2) For the purposes of subsection (1) above this subsection is satisfied in relation to any area if (subject to subsection (3) below) it is appropriate, with a view to preventing or controlling the entry of any poisonous, noxious or polluting matter into controlled waters, to prohibit or restrict the carrying on in that area of activities which the Secretary of State considers are likely to result in the pollution of any such waters.

(3) The reference in subsection (2) above to the entry of poisonous, noxious or polluting matter into controlled waters shall not include a reference to the entry of nitrate into controlled waters as a result of, or of anything done in connection with, the use of any land for agricultural purposes.

(4) Without prejudice to the generality of the power conferred by virtue of subsection (1) above, an order under this section may—

  (a) confer power on the [Agency] to determine for the purposes of the order the circumstances in which the carrying on of any activities is prohibited or restricted and to determine the activities to which any such prohibition or restriction applies;
  (b) apply a prohibition or restriction in respect of any activities to cases where the activities are carried on without the consent of the [Agency] or in contravention of any conditions subject to which any such consent is given;
  (c) provide that a contravention of a prohibition or restriction contained in the order or of a condition of a consent given for the purposes of any such prohibition or restriction shall be an offence the maximum penalties for which shall not exceed the penalties specified in subsection (6) of section 85 above;
  (d) provide (subject to any regulations under section 96 below) for anything falling to be determined under the order by the [Agency] to be determined in accordance with such procedure and by reference to such matters and to the opinion of such persons as may be specified in the order;
  (e) make different provision for different cases, including different provision in relation to different persons, circumstances or localities; and
  (f) contain such supplemental, consequential and transitional provision as the Secretary of State considers appropriate.

(5) The power of the Secretary of State to make an order under this section shall be exercisable by statutory instrument subject to annulment in pursuance of a resolution of either House of Parliament; but the Secretary of State shall not make such an order except on an application made by the [Agency] in accordance with Schedule 11 to this Act and otherwise in accordance with that Schedule.

94   Nitrate sensitive areas

(1) Where the relevant Minister considers that it is appropriate to do so with a view to achieving the purpose specified in subsection (2) below in relation to any land, he may by order make provision designating that land, together with any other land to which he considers it appropriate to apply the designation, as a nitrate sensitive area.

(2) The purpose mentioned in subsection (1) above is preventing or controlling the entry of nitrate into controlled waters as a result of, or of anything done in connection with, the use for agricultural purposes of any land.

(3) Where it appears to the relevant Minister, in relation to any area which is or is to be designated by an order under this section as a nitrate sensitive area, that it is appropriate for provision for the imposition of requirements, prohibitions or restrictions to be contained in an order under this section (as well as for him to be able to enter into such agreements as are mentioned in section 95 below), he may, by a subsequent order under this section or, as the case may be, by the order designating that area—

    (a) with a view to achieving the purpose specified in subsection (2) above, require, prohibit or restrict the carrying on, either on or in relation to any agricultural land in that area, of such activities as may be specified or described in the order; and

    (b) provide for such amounts (if any) as may be specified in or determined under the order to be paid by one of the Ministers, to such persons as may be so specified or determined, in respect of the obligations imposed in relation to that area on those persons by virtue of paragraph (a) above.

(4) Without prejudice to the generality of subsection (3) above, provision contained in an order under this section by virtue of that subsection may—

    (a) confer power on either of the Ministers to determine for the purposes of the order the circumstances in which the carrying on of any activities is required, prohibited or restricted and to determine the activities to which any such requirement, prohibition or restriction applies;

    (b) provide for any requirement to carry on any activity not to apply in cases where one of the Ministers has consented to a failure to carry on that activity and any conditions on which the consent has been given are complied with;

    (c) apply a prohibition or restriction in respect of any activities to cases where the activities are carried on without the consent of one of the Ministers or in contravention of any conditions subject to which any such consent is given;

    (d) provide that a contravention of a requirement, prohibition or restriction contained in the order or in a condition of a consent given in relation to or for the purposes of any such requirement, prohibition or restriction shall be an offence the maximum penalties for which shall not exceed the penalties specified in subsection (6) of section 85 above;

    (e) provide for amounts paid in pursuance of any provision contained in the order to be repaid at such times and in such circumstances, and with such interest, as may be specified in or determined under the order; and

    (f) provide (subject to any regulations under section 96 below) for anything falling to be determined under the order by any person to be determined in accordance with such procedure and by reference to such matters and to the opinion of such persons as may be specified in the order.

(5) An order under this section may—

    (a) make different provision for different cases, including different provision in relation to different persons, circumstances or localities; and

    (b) contain such supplemental, consequential and transitional provision as the relevant Minister considers appropriate.

(6) The power of the relevant Minister to make an order under this section shall be exercisable by statutory instrument subject to annulment in pursuance of a resolution of either House of Parliament; but the relevant Minister shall not make such an order except in accordance with any applicable provisions of Schedule 12 to this Act.

(7) In this section and in Schedule 12 to this Act 'the relevant Minister'—

    (a) in relation to the making of an order in relation to an area which is wholly in England or which is partly in England and partly in Wales, means the Ministers; and

    (b) in relation to the making of an order in relation to an area which is wholly in Wales, means the Secretary of State.

95   Agreements in nitrate sensitive areas

(1) Where—

>   (a) any area has been designated as a nitrate sensitive area by an order under section 94 above; and

>   (b) the relevant Minister considers that it is appropriate to do so with a view to achieving the purpose mentioned in subsection (2) of that section,

he may, subject to such restrictions (if any) as may be set out in the order, enter into an agreement falling within subsection (2) below.

(2) An agreement falls within this subsection if it is one under which, in consideration of payments to be made by the relevant Minister—

>   (a) the owner of the freehold interest in any agricultural land in a nitrate sensitive area; or

>   (b) where the owner of the freehold interest in any such land has given his written consent to the agreement being entered into by any person having another interest in that land, that other person,

accepts such obligations with respect to the management of that land or otherwise as may be imposed by the agreement.

(3) An agreement such as is mentioned in subsection (2) above between the relevant Minister and a person having an interest in any land shall bind all persons deriving title from or under that person to the extent that the agreement is expressed to bind that land in relation to those persons.

(4) In this section 'the relevant Minister'—

>   (a) in relation to an agreement with respect to land which is wholly in England, means the Minister;

>   (b) in relation to an agreement with respect to land which is wholly in Wales, means the Secretary of State; and

>   (c) in relation to an agreement with respect to land which is partly in England and partly in Wales, means either of the Ministers.

96   Regulations with respect to consents required by virtue of section 93 or 94

(1) The Secretary of State may, for the purposes of any orders under section 93 above which require the consent of the [Agency] to the carrying on of any activities, by regulations make provision with respect to—

>   (a) applications for any such consent;

>   (b) the conditions of any such consent;

>   (c) the revocation or variation of any such consent;

>   (d) appeals against determinations on any such application;

>   (e) the exercise by the Secretary of State of any power conferred on the [Agency] by the orders;

>   (f) the imposition of charges where such an application has been made, such a consent has been given or anything has been done in pursuance of any such consent; and

>   (g) the registration of any such application or consent.

(2) The Ministers may, for the purposes of any orders under section 94 above which require the consent of either of those Ministers to the carrying on of any activities or to any failure to carry on any activity by regulations make provision with respect to—

>   (a) applications for any such consent;

>   (b) the conditions of any such consent;

>   (c) the revocation or variation of any such consent;

>   (d) the reference to arbitration of disputes about determinations on any such application;

>   (e) the imposition of charges where such an application has been made, such a

consent has been given or there has been any act or omission in pursuance of any such consent; and

(f) the registration of any such application or consent.

(3) Without prejudice to the generality of the powers conferred by the preceding provisions of this section, regulations under subsection (1) above may apply (with or without modifications) any enactment having effect in relation to consents under Chapter II of this Part.

[(4) This section is subject to section 114 of the 1995 Act (delegation or reference of appeals etc).]

97   Codes of good agricultural practice

(1) The Ministers may by order made by statutory instrument approve any code of practice issued (whether by either or both of the Ministers or by another person) for the purpose of—

(a) giving practical guidance to persons engaged in agriculture with respect to activities that may affect controlled waters; and

(b) promoting what appear to them to be desirable practices by such persons for avoiding or minimising the pollution of any such waters,

and may at any time by such an order approve a modification of such a code or withdraw their approval of such a code or modification.

(2) A contravention of a code of practice as for the time being approved under this section shall not of itself give rise to any criminal or civil liability, but the [Agency] shall take into account whether there has been or is likely to be any such contravention in determining when and how it should exercise—

(a) Its power, by giving a notice under subsection (1) of section 86 above, to impose a prohibition under that section; and

(b) any powers conferred on the [Agency] by regulations under section 92 above.

(3) The Ministers shall not make an order under this section unless they have first consulted the [Agency].

CHAPTER IV   SUPPLEMENTAL PROVISIONS WITH RESPECT TO
WATER POLLUTION

100   Civil liability in respect of pollution and savings

Except in so far as this Part expressly otherwise provides and subject to the provisions of section 18 of the Interpretation Act 1978 (which relates to offences under two or more laws), nothing in this Part—

(a) confers a right of action in any civil proceedings (other than proceedings for the recovery of a fine) in respect of any contravention of this Part or any subordinate legislation, consent or other instrument made, given or issued under this Part;

(b) derogates from any right of action or other remedy (whether civil or criminal) in proceedings instituted otherwise than under this Part; or

(c) affects any restriction imposed by or under any other enactment, whether public, local or private.

101   Limitation for summary offences under Part III

Notwithstanding anything in section 127 of the Magistrates' Courts Act 1980 (time limit for summary proceedings), a magistrates' court may try any summary offence under this Part, or under any subordinate legislation made under this Part, if the information is laid not more than twelve months after the commission of the offence.

102   Power to give effect to international obligations
The Secretary of State shall have power by regulations to provide that the water pollution provisions of this Act shall have effect with such modifications as may be prescribed for the purpose of enabling Her Majesty's Government in the United Kingdom to give effect—
> (a) to any Community obligations; or
> (b) to any international agreement to which the United Kingdom is for the time being a party.

103   Transitional pollution provisions
The provisions of this Part shall have effect subject to the provisions of Schedule 13 to this Act (which reproduce transitional provision originally made in connection with the coming into force of provisions of the Water Act 1989).

104   Meaning of 'controlled waters' etc. in Part III
(1) References in this Part to controlled waters are references to waters of any of the following classes—
> (a) relevant territorial waters, that is to say, subject to subsection (4) below, the waters which extend seaward for three miles from the baselines from which the breadth of the territorial sea adjacent to England and Wales is measured;
> (b) coastal waters, that is to say, any waters which are within the area which extends landward from those baselines as far as—
>> (a) the limit of the highest tide; or
>> (b) in the case of the waters of any relevant river or watercourse, the fresh-water limit of the river or watercourse, together with the waters of any enclosed dock which adjoins waters within that area;
> (c) inland freshwaters, that is to say, the waters of any relevant lake or pond or of so much of any relevant river or watercourse as is above the fresh-water limit;
> (d) ground waters, that is to say, any waters contained in underground strata;

and, accordingly, in this Part 'coastal waters', 'controlled waters', 'ground waters', 'inland freshwaters' and 'relevant territorial waters' have the meanings given by this subsection.

(2) In this Part any reference to the waters of any lake or pond or of any river or water-course includes a reference to the bottom, channel or bed of any lake, pond, river or, as the case may be, watercourse which is for the time being dry.

(3) In this section—
'fresh-water limit', in relation to any river or watercourse, means the place for the time being shown as the fresh-water limit of that river or watercourse in the latest map deposited for that river or watercourse under section 192 below;
'miles' means international nautical miles of 1,852 metres;
'lake or pond' includes a reservoir of any description;
'relevant lake or pond' means (subject to subsection (4) below) any lake or pond which (whether it is natural or artificial or above or below ground) discharges into a relevant river or watercourse or into another lake or pond which is itself a relevant lake or pond;
'relevant river or watercourse' means (subject to subsection (4) below) any river or watercourse (including an underground river or watercourse and an artificial river or water-course) which is neither a public sewer nor a sewer or drain which drains into a public sewer.

(4) The Secretary of State may by order provide—
> (a) that any area of the territorial sea adjacent to England and Wales is to be treated as if it were an area of relevant territorial waters for the purposes of this Part and of any other enactment in which any expression is defined by reference to the meanings given by this section;

(b) that any lake or pond which does not discharge into a relevant river or water-course or into a relevant lake or pond is to be treated for those purposes as a relevant lake or pond;

(c) that a lake or pond which does so discharge and is of a description specified in the order is to be treated for those purposes as if it were not a relevant lake or pond;

(d) that a watercourse of a description so specified is to be treated for those purposes as if it were not a relevant river or watercourse.

(5) An order under this section may—

(a) contain such supplemental, consequential and transitional provision as the Secretary of State considers appropriate; and

(b) make different provision for different cases, including different provision in relation to different persons, circumstances or localities.

(6) The power of the Secretary of State to make an order under this section shall be exercisable by statutory instrument subject to annulment in pursuance of a resolution of either House of Parliament.

PART VII   LAND AND WORKS POWERS

CHAPTER I   POWERS OF THE AUTHORITY

161   Anti-pollution works and operations

(1) [Subject to subsections (1A) and (2) below,] where it appears to the [Agency] that any poisonous, noxious or polluting matter or any solid waste matter is likely to enter, or to be or to have been present in, any controlled waters, the [Agency] shall be entitled to carry out the following works and operations, that is to say—

(a) in a case where the matter appears likely to enter any controlled waters, works and operations for the purpose of preventing it from doing so; or

(b) in a case where the matter appears to be or to have been present in any controlled waters, works and operations for the purpose—

(i) of removing or disposing of the matter;

(ii) of remedying or mitigating any pollution caused by its presence in the waters; or

(iii) so far as it is reasonably practicable to do so, of restoring the waters, including any flora and fauna dependent on the aquatic environment of the waters, to their state immediately before the matter became present in the waters

[and, in either case, the Agency shall be entitled to carry out investigations for the purpose of establishing the source of the matter and the identity of the person who has caused or know-ingly permitted it to be present in controlled waters or at a place from which it was likely, in the opinion of the Agency, to enter controlled waters.]

[(1A) Without prejudice to the power of the Agency to carry out investigations under subsection (1) above, the power conferred by that subsection to carry out works and operations shall only be exercisable in a case where—

(a) the Agency considers it necessary to carry out forthwith any works or operations failing within paragraph (a) or (b) of that subsection; or

(b) it appears to the Agency, after reasonable inquiry, that no person can be found on whom to serve a works notice under section 161A below.]

(2) Nothing in subsection (1) above shall entitle the [Agency] to impede or prevent the making of any discharge in pursuance of a consent given under Chapter II of Part III of this Act.

(3) Where the [Agency] carries out any such works [operations or investigations] as are mentioned in subsection (1) above, it shall, subject to subsection (4) below, be entitled to

recover the expenses reasonably incurred in doing so from any person who, as the case may be—

> (a) caused or knowingly permitted the matter in question to be present at the place from which it was likely, in the opinion of the [Agency], to enter any controlled waters; or
>
> (b) caused or knowingly permitted the matter in question to be present in any controlled waters.

(4) No such expenses shall be recoverable from a person for any works [operations or investigations] in respect of water from an abandoned mine [or an abandoned part of a mine] which that person permitted to reach such a place as is mentioned in subsection (3) above or to enter any controlled waters.

[(4A) Subsection (4) above shall not apply to the owner or former operator of any mine or part of a mine if the mine or part in question became abandoned after 31st December 1999.

(4B) Subsections (3B) and (3C) of section 89 above shall apply in relation to subsections (4) and (4A) above as they apply in relation to subsections (3) and (3A) of that section.]

(5) Nothing in this section—

> (a) derogates from any right of action or other remedy (whether civil or criminal) in proceedings instituted otherwise than under this section; or
>
> (b) affects any restriction imposed by or under any other enactment, whether public, local or private.

(6) In this section—

'controlled waters' has the same meaning as in Part III of this Act; and

['expenses' includes costs;]

'mine' has the same meaning as in the Mines and Quarries Act 1954.

[161A   Notices requiring persons to carry out anti-pollution works and operations

(1) Subject to the following provisions of this section, where it appears to the Agency that any poisonous, noxious or polluting matter or any solid waste matter is likely to enter, or to be or to have been present in, any controlled waters, the Agency shall be entitled to serve a works notice on any person who, as the case may be,—

> (a) caused or knowingly permitted the matter in question to be present at the place from which it is likely, in the opinion of the Agency, to enter any controlled waters; or
>
> (b) caused or knowingly permitted the matter in question to be present in any controlled waters.

(2) For the purposes of this section, a 'works notice' is a notice requiring the person on whom it is served to carry out such of the following works or operations as may be specified in the notice, that is to say—

> (a) in a case where the matter in question appears likely to enter any controlled waters, works or operations for the purpose of preventing it from doing so; or
>
> (b) in a case where the matter appears to be or to have been present in any controlled waters, works or operations for the purpose—
>
> > (i) of removing or disposing of the matter;
> >
> > (ii) of remedying or mitigating any pollution caused by its presence in the waters; or
> >
> > (iii) so far as it is reasonably practicable to do so, of restoring the waters, including any flora and fauna dependent on the aquatic environment of the waters, to their state immediately before the matter became present in the waters.

(3) A works notice—

(a) must specify the periods within which the person on whom it is served is required to do each of the things specified in the notice; and

(b) is without prejudice to the powers of the Agency by virtue of section 161(1A)(a) above.

(4) Before serving a works notice on any person, the Agency shall reasonably endeavour to consult that person concerning the works or operations which are to be specified in the notice.

(5) The Secretary of State may by regulations make provision for or in connection with—

(a) the form or content of works notices;

(b) requirements for consultation, before the service of a works notice, with persons other than the person on whom that notice is to be served;

(c) steps to be taken for the purposes of any consultation required under subsection (4) above or regulations made by virtue of paragraph (b) above; or

(d) any other steps of a procedural nature which are to be taken in connection with, or in consequence of, the service of a works notice.

(6) A works notice shall not be regarded as invalid, or as invalidly served, by reason only of any failure to comply with the requirements of subsection (4) above or of regulations made by virtue of paragraph (b) of subsection (5) above.

(7) Nothing in subsection (1) above shall entitle the Agency to require the carrying out of any works or operations which would impede or prevent the making of any discharge in pursuance of a consent given under Chapter II of Part III of this Act.

(8) No works notice shall be served on any person requiring him to carry out any works or operations in respect of water from an abandoned mine or an abandoned part of a mine which that person permitted to reach such a place as is mentioned in subsection (1)(a) above or to enter any controlled waters.

(9) Subsection (8) above shall not apply to the owner or former operator of any mine or part of a mine if the mine or part in question became abandoned after 31st December 1999.

(10) Subsections (3B) and (3C) of section 89 above shall apply in relation to subsections (8) and (9) above as they apply in relation to subsections (3) and (3A) of that section.

(11) Where the Agency—

(a) carries out any such investigations as are mentioned in section 161(1) above, and

(b) serves a works notice on a person in connection with the matter to which the investigations relate,

it shall (unless the notice is quashed or withdrawn) be entitled to recover the costs or expenses reasonably incurred in carrying out those investigations from that person.

(12) The Secretary of State may, if he thinks fit in relation to any person, give directions to the Agency as to whether or how it should exercise its powers under this section.

(13) In this section—

'controlled waters' has the same meaning as in Part III of this Act;

'mine' has the same meaning as in the Mines and Quarries Act 1954.

161B   Grant of, and compensation for, rights of entry etc.

(1) A works notice may require a person to carry out works or operations in relation to any land or waters notwithstanding that he is not entitled to carry out those works or operations.

(2) Any person whose consent is required before any works or operations required by a works notice may be carried out shall grant, or join in granting, such rights in relation to any land or waters as will enable the person on whom the works notice is served to comply with any requirements imposed by the works notice.

(3) Before serving a works notice, the Agency shall reasonably endeavour to consult every person who appears to it—

  (a) to be the owner or occupier of any relevant land, and

  (b) to be a person who might be required by subsection (2) above to grant, or join in granting, any rights,

concerning the rights which that person may be so required to grant.

(4) A works notice shall not be regarded as invalid, or as invalidly served, by reason only of any failure to comply with the requirements of subsection (3) above.

(5) A person who grants, or joins in granting, any rights pursuant to subsection (2) above shall be entitled, on making an application within such period as may be prescribed and in such manner as may be prescribed to such person as may be prescribed, to be paid by the person on whom the works notice in question is served compensation of such amount as may be determined in such manner as may be prescribed.

(6) Without prejudice to the generality of the regulations that may be made by virtue of subsection (5) above, regulations by virtue of that subsection may make such provision in relation to compensation under this section as may be made by regulations by virtue of subsection (4) of section 35A of the Environmental Protection Act 1990 in relation to compensation under that section.

(7) In this section—

'prescribed' means prescribed in regulations made by the Secretary of State;

'relevant land' means—

  (a) any land or waters in relation to which the works notice in question requires, or may require, works or operations to be carried out; or

  (b) any land adjoining or adjacent to that land or those waters; 'works notice' means a works notice under section 161A above.

161C Appeals against works notices

(1) A person on whom a works notice is served may, within the period of twenty-one days beginning with the day on which the notice is served, appeal against the notice to the Secretary of State.

(2) On any appeal under this section the Secretary of State—

  (a) shall quash the notice, if he is satisfied that there is a material defect in the notice; but

  (b) subject to that, may confirm the notice, with or without modification, or quash it.

(3) The Secretary of State may by regulations make provision with respect to—

  (a) the grounds on which appeals under this section may be made; or

  (b) the procedure on any such appeal.

(4) Regulations under subsection (3) above may (among other things)—

  (a) include provisions comparable to those in section 290 of the Public Health Act 1936 (appeals against notices requiring the execution of works);

  (b) prescribe the cases in which a works notice is, or is not, to be suspended until the appeal is decided, or until some other stage in the proceedings;

  (c) prescribe the cases in which the decision on an appeal may in some respects be less favourable to the appellant than the works notice against which he is appealing;

  (d) prescribe the cases in which the appellant may claim that a works notice should have been served on some other person and prescribe the procedure to be followed in those cases;

  (e) make provision as respects—

    (i) the particulars to be included in the notice of appeal;

    (ii) the persons on whom notice of appeal is to be served and the particulars, if any, which are to accompany the notice; or

    (iii) the abandonment of an appeal.

(5) In this section 'works notice' means a works notice under section 161A above.

(6) This section is subject to section 114 of the 1995 Act (delegation or reference of appeals).

161D   Consequences of not complying with a works notice

(1) If a person on whom the Agency serves a works notice falls to comply with any of the requirements of the notice, he shall be guilty of an offence.

(2) A person who commits an offence under subsection (1) above shall be liable—

  (a) on summary conviction, to imprisonment for a term not exceeding three months or to a fine not exceeding £20,000 or to both;

  (b) on conviction on indictment to imprisonment for a term not exceeding two years or to a fine or to both.

(3) If a person on whom a works notice has been served fails to comply with any of the requirements of the notice, the Agency may do what that person was required to do and may recover from him any costs or expenses reasonably incurred by the Agency in doing it.

(4) If the Agency is of the opinion that proceedings for an offence under subsection (1) above would afford an ineffectual remedy against a person who has failed to comply with the requirements of a works notice, the Agency may take proceedings in the High Court for the purpose of securing compliance with the notice.

(5) In this section 'works notice' means a works notice under section 161A above.]

PART VIII   INFORMATION PROVISIONS

190   Pollution control register

(1) It shall be the duty of the [Agency] to maintain, in accordance with regulations made by the Secretary of State, registers containing prescribed particulars of [or relating to]—

  (a) any notices of water quality objectives or other notices served under section 83 above;

  (b) applications made for consents under Chapter II of Part III of this Act;

  (c) consents given under that Chapter and the conditions to which the consents are subject;

  (d) [. . .]

  (e) the following, that is to say—

   (i) samples of water or effluent taken by the [Agency] for the purposes of any of the water pollution provisions of this Act;

   (ii) information produced by analyses of those samples;

   (iii) such information with respect to samples of water or effluent taken by any other person, and the analyses of those samples, as is acquired by the [Agency] from any person under arrangements made by the [Agency] for the purposes of any of those provisions; and

   (iv) the steps taken in consequence of any such information as is mentioned in any of sub-paragraphs (i) to (iii) above;

  [. . .]

  [(g) applications made to the Agency for the variation of discharge consents;

  (h) enforcement notices served under section 90B above;

  (j) revocations, under paragraph 7 of Schedule 10 to this Act, of discharge consents;

  (k) appeals under section 91 above;

  (l) directions given by the Secretary of State in relation to the Agency's functions under the water pollution provisions of this Act;

  (m) convictions, for offences under Part III of this Act, of persons who have the benefit of discharge consents;

(n) information obtained or furnished in pursuance of conditions of discharge consents;

(o) works notices under section 161A above;

(p) appeals under section 161C above;

(q) convictions for offences under section 161D above;

(r) such other matters relating to the quality of water or the pollution of water as may be prescribed by the Secretary of State.

(1A) Where information of any description is excluded from any register by virtue of section 191B below, a statement shall be entered in the register indicating the existence of information of that description.]

(2) It shall be the duty of the [Agency]—

(a) to secure that the contents of registers maintained by the [Agency] under this section are available, at all reasonable times, for inspection by the public free of charge; and

(b) to afford members of the public reasonable facilities for obtaining from the [Agency], on payment of reasonable charges, copies of entries in any of the registers [and, for the purposes of this subsection, places may be prescribed by the Secretary of State at which any such registers or facilities as are mentioned in paragraph (a) or (b) above are to be available or afforded to the public in pursuance of the paragraph in question.]

(3) Section 101 above shall have effect in relation to any regulations under this section as it has effect in relation to any subordinate legislation under Part III of this Act.

[(4) The Secretary of State may give to the Agency directions requiring the removal from any register maintained by it under this section of any specified information which is not prescribed for inclusion under subsection (1) above or which, by virtue of section 191A or 191B below, ought to have been excluded from the register.

(5) In this section 'discharge consent' has the same meaning as in section 91 above.]

[191A   Exclusion from registers of information affecting national security

(1) No information shall be included in a register kept or maintained by the Agency under any provision of this Act if and so long as, in the opinion of the Secretary of State, the inclusion in such a register of that information, or information of that description, would be contrary to the interests of national security.

(2) The Secretary of State may, for the purpose of securing the exclusion from registers of information to which subsection (1) above applies, give to the Agency directions—

(a) specifying information, or descriptions of information, to be excluded from their registers; or

(b) specifying descriptions of information to be referred to the Secretary of State for his determination;

and no information referred to the Secretary of State in pursuance of paragraph (b) above shall be included in any such register until the Secretary of State determines that it should be so included.

(3) The Agency shall notify the Secretary of State of any information it excludes from a register in pursuance of directions under subsection (2) above.

(4) A person may, as respects any information which appears to him to be information to which subsection (1) above may apply, give a notice to the Secretary of State specifying the information and indicating its apparent nature; and, if he does so—

(a) he shall notify the Agency that he has done so; and

(b) no information so notified to the Secretary of State shall be included in any such register until the Secretary of State has determined that it should be so included.

191B   Exclusion from registers of certain confidential information

(1) No information relating to the affairs of any individual or business shall, without the consent of that individual or the person for the time being carrying on that business, be included in a register kept or maintained by the Agency under any provision of this Act, if and so long as the information—

(a) is, in relation to him, commercially confidential; and

(b) is not required to be included in the register in pursuance of directions under subsection (7) below;

but information is not commercially confidential for the purposes of this section unless it is determined under this section to be so by the Agency or, on appeal, by the Secretary of State.

(2) Where information is furnished to the Agency for the purpose of—

(a) an application for a discharge consent or for the variation of a discharge consent,

(b) complying with any condition of a discharge consent, or

(c) complying with a notice under section 202 below,

then, if the person furnishing it applies to the Agency to have the information excluded from any register kept or maintained by the Agency under any provision of this Act, on the ground that it is commercially confidential (as regards himself or another person), the Agency shall determine whether the information is or is not commercially confidential.

(3) A determination under subsection (2) above must be made within the period of fourteen days beginning with the date of the application and if the Agency fails to make a determination within that period it shall be treated as having determined that the information is commercially confidential.

(4) Where it appears to the Agency that any information (other than information furnished in circumstances within subsection (2) above) which has been obtained by the Agency under or by virtue of any provision of any enactment might be commercially confidential, the Agency shall—

(a) give to the person to whom or whose business it relates notice that that information is required to be included in a register kept or maintained by the Agency under any provision of this Act, unless excluded under this section; and

(b) give him a reasonable opportunity—

(i) of objecting to the inclusion of the information on the ground that it is commercially confidential; and

(ii) of making representations to the Agency for the purpose of justifying any such objection;

and, if any representations are made, the Agency shall, having taken the representations into account, determine whether the information is or is not commercially confidential.

(5) Where, under subsection (2) or (4) above, the Agency determines that information is not commercially confidential—

(a) the information shall not be entered on the register until the end of the period of twenty-one days beginning with the date on which the determination is notified to the person concerned; and

(b) that person may appeal to the Secretary of State against the decision;

and, where an appeal is brought in respect of any information, the information shall not be entered on the register until the end of the period of seven days following the day on which the appeal is finally determined or withdrawn.

(6) Subsections (2A), (2C) and (2K) of section 91 above shall apply in relation to appeals under subsection (5) above; but—

(a) subsection (2C) of that section shall have effect for the purposes of this subsection with the substitution for the words from '(which may' onwards of the words '(which must be held in private)'; and

(b) subsection (5) above is subject to section 114 of the 1995 Act (delegation or reference of appeals etc).

(7) The Secretary of State may give to the Agency directions as to specified information, or descriptions of information, which the public interest requires to be included in registers kept or maintained by the Agency under any provision of this Act notwithstanding that the information may be commercially confidential.

(8) Information excluded from a register shall be treated as ceasing to be commercially confidential for the purposes of this section at the expiry of the period of four years beginning with the date of the determination by virtue of which it was excluded; but the person who furnished it may apply to the Agency for the information to remain excluded from the register on the ground that it is still commercially confidential and the Agency shall determine whether or not that is the case.

(9) Subsections (5) and (6) above shall apply in relation to a determination under subsection (8) above as they apply in relation to a determination under subsection (2) or (4) above.

(10) The Secretary of State may by regulations substitute (whether in all cases or in such classes or descriptions of case as may be specified in the regulations) for the period for the time being specified in subsection (3) above such other period as he considers appropriate.

(11) Information is, for the purposes of any determination under this section, commercially confidential, in relation to any individual or person, if its being contained in the register would prejudice to an unreasonable degree the commercial interests of that individual or person.

(12) In this section 'discharge consent' has the same meaning as in section 91 above.]

202 Information and assistance required in connection with the control of pollution

(1) It shall be the duty of the [Agency], if and so far as it is requested to do so by either of the Ministers, to give him all such advice and assistance as appears to it to be appropriate for facilitating the carrying out by him of his functions under the water pollution provisions of this Act.

(2) Subject to subsection (3) below, either of the Ministers or the [Agency] may serve on any person a notice requiring that person to furnish him or, as the case may be, it, within a period or at times specified in the notice and in a form and manner so specified, with such information as is reasonably required by the Minister in question or by the [Agency] for the purpose of carrying out any of his or, as the case may be, its functions under the water pollution provisions of this Act.

(3) Each of the Ministers shall have power by regulations to make provision for restricting the information which may be required under subsection (2) above and for determining the form in which the information is to be so required.

(4) A person who fails without reasonable excuse to comply with the requirements of a notice served on him under this section shall be guilty of an offence and [liable—
 (a) on summary conviction, to a fine not exceeding the statutory maximum;
 (b) on conviction on indictment, to a fine or to imprisonment for a term not exceeding two years, or to both.]

(5) [. . .]

203 Exchange of information with respect to pollution incidents etc

(1) It shall be the duty of the [Agency] to provide a water undertaker with all such information to which this section applies as is in the possession of the [Agency] and is reasonably requested by the undertaker for purposes connected with the carrying out of its functions.

(2) It shall be the duty of every water undertaker to provide the [Agency] with all such information to which this section applies as is in the possession of the undertaker and is reasonably requested by the [Agency] for purposes connected with the carrying out of any of its functions.

(3) Information provided to a water undertaker or to the [Agency] under subsection (1) or (2) above shall be provided in such form and in such manner and at such times as the undertaker or, as the case may be, the [Agency] may reasonably require.

(4) Information provided under subsection (1) or (2) above to a water undertaker or to the [Agency] shall be provided free of charge.

(5) The duties of a water undertaker under subsection (2) above shall be enforceable under section 18 of the Water Industry Act 1991 by the Secretary of State.

(6) This section applies to information—

    (a) about the quality of any controlled waters or of any other waters; or

    (b) about any incident in which any poisonous, noxious or polluting matter or any solid waste matter has entered any controlled waters or other waters.

(7) In this section 'controlled waters' has the same meaning as in Part III of this Act.

204   Restriction on disclosure of information

(1) Subject to the following provisions of this section, no information with respect to any particular business which—

    (a) has been obtained by virtue of any of the provisions of this Act; and

    (b) relates to the affairs of any individual or to any particular business,

shall, during the lifetime of that individual or so long as that business continues to be carried on, be disclosed without the consent of that individual or the person for the time being carrying on that business.

(2) Subsection (1) above does not apply to any disclosure of information which is made—

    (a) for the purpose of facilitating the carrying out by either of the Ministers, [the Agency, . . .], the Director General of Water Services, the Monopolies Commission or a local authority of any of his, its or, as the case may be, their functions by virtue of this Act, any of the other consolidation Acts [the Water Act 1989, Part I or IIA of the Environmental Protection Act 1990 [, the 1995 Act or regulations under section 2 of the Pollution Prevention and Control Act 1999.]

    (b) for the purpose of facilitating the performance by a water undertaker or sewerage undertaker of any of the duties imposed on it by or under this Act, any of the other consolidation Acts or the Water Act 1989;

    (c) in pursuance of any duty imposed by section 197(1)(a) or (2) or 203(1) or (2) above or of any arrangements made by the Director General of Water Services under section 29(6) of the Water Industry Act 1991;

    (d) for the purpose of facilitating the carrying out by any person mentioned in Part I of Schedule 24 to this Act of any of his functions under any of the enactments or instruments specified in Part II of that Schedule;

    (e) for the purpose of enabling or assisting the Secretary of State to exercise any powers conferred on him by the Financial Services Act 1986 or by the enactments relating to companies, insurance companies or insolvency or for the purpose of enabling or assisting any inspector appointed by him under the enactments relating to companies to carry out his functions;

    (f) or the purpose of enabling an official receiver to carry out his functions under the enactments relating to insolvency or for the purpose of enabling or assisting a recognised professional body for the purposes of section 391 of the Insolvency Act 1986 to carry out its functions as such;

    (g) for the purpose of facilitating the carrying out by the Health and Safety Commission or the Health and Safety Executive of any of its functions under any enactment or of facilitating the carrying out by any enforcing authority, within the meaning of Part I of the Health and Safety at Work etc. Act 1974, of any functions under a relevant statutory provision, within the meaning of that Act;

(h) for the purpose of facilitating the carrying out by the Comptroller and Auditor General of any of his functions under any enactment;

(i) in connection with the investigation of any criminal offence or for the purposes of any criminal proceedings;

(j) for the purposes of any civil proceedings brought under or by virtue of this Act, any of the other consolidation Acts, the Water Act 1989 or any of the enactments or instruments specified in Part II of Schedule 24 to this Act, or of any arbitration under this Act, any of the other consolidation Acts or that Act of 1989; or

(k) in pursuance of a Community obligation.

(3) Nothing in subsection (1) above shall be construed—

(a) as limiting the matters which may be included in, or made public as part of, a report of—

(i) the [Agency];

. . .

(ii) the Director General of Water Services;

(iii) a customer service committee maintained under the Water Industry Act 1991; or

(iv) the Monopolies Commission,

under any provision of this Act [, Part I or IIA of the Environmental Protection Act 1990, that Act of 1991 [, the Environment Act 1995 or regulations under section 2 of the Pollution Prevention and Control Act 1999.]

(b) as limiting the matters which may be published under section 201 of that Act [of 1991]; or

(c) as applying to any information which has been made public as part of such a report or has been so published or to any information exclusively of a statistical nature.

(4) Subject to subsection (5) below, nothing in subsection (1) above shall preclude the disclosure of information—

(a) if the disclosure is of information relating to a matter connected with the carrying out of the functions of a water undertaker or sewerage undertaker and is made by one Minister of the Crown or government department to another; or

(b) if the disclosure is for the purpose of enabling or assisting any public or other authority for the time being designated for the purposes of this section by an order made by the Secretary of State to discharge any functions which are specified in the order.

(5) The power to make an order under subsection (4) above shall be exercisable by statutory instrument subject to annulment in pursuance of a resolution of either House of Parliament; and where such an order designates an authority for the purposes of paragraph (b) of that subsection, the order may—

(a) impose conditions subject to which the disclosure of information is permitted by virtue of that paragraph; and

(b) otherwise restrict the circumstances in which disclosure is so permitted.

(6) Any person who discloses any information in contravention of the preceding provisions of this section shall be guilty of an offence and liable—

(a) on summary conviction, to a fine not exceeding the statutory maximum;

(b) on conviction on indictment, to imprisonment for a term not exceeding two years or to a fine or to both.

(7) In this section 'the other consolidation Acts' means the Water Industry Act 1991, the Statutory Water Companies Act 1991, the Land Drainage Act 1991 and the Water Consolidation (Consequential Provisions) Act 1991.

PART IX   MISCELLANEOUS AND SUPPLEMENTAL

209   Evidence of samples and abstractions

(1) [. . .]

(2) [. . .]

(3) Where, in accordance with the provisions contained in a licence in pursuance of paragraph (b) of subsection (2) of section 46 above, or in pursuance of that paragraph as read with subsection (6) of that section, it has been determined what quantity of water is to be taken—

> (a) to have been abstracted during any period from a source of supply by the holder of the licence; or
>
> (b) to have been so abstracted at a particular point or by particular means, or for use for particular purposes,

that determination shall, for the purposes of any proceedings under Chapter II of Part II of this Act or any of the related water resources provisions, be conclusive evidence of the matters to which it relates.

(4) [. . .]

217   Criminal liabilities of directors and other third parties

(1) Where a body corporate is guilty of an offence under this Act and that offence is proved to have been committed with the consent or connivance of, or to be attributable to any neglect on the part of, any director, manager, secretary or other similar officer of the body corporate or any person who was purporting to act in any such capacity, then he, as well as the body corporate, shall be guilty of that offence and shall be liable to be proceeded against and punished accordingly.

(2) Where the affairs of a body corporate are managed by its members, subsection (1) above shall apply in relation to the acts and defaults of a member in connection with his functions of management as if he were a director of the body corporate.

(3) Without prejudice to subsections (1) and (2) above, where the commission by any person of an offence under the water pollution provisions of this Act is due to the act or default of some other person, that other person may be charged with and convicted of the offence whether or not proceedings for the offence are taken against the first-mentioned person.

221   General interpretation

(1) In this Act, except in so far as the context otherwise requires—

['the 1995 Act' means the Environment Act 1995;]

['the Agency' means the Environment Agency;]

. . .

'analyse', in relation to any sample of land, water or effluent, includes subjecting the sample to a test of any description, and cognate expressions shall be construed accordingly;

. . .

'disposal'—

> (a) in relation to land or any interest or right in or over land, includes the creation of such an interest or right and a disposal effected by means of the surrender or other termination of any such interest or right; and
>
> (b) in relation to sewage, includes treatment;

and cognate expressions shall be construed accordingly;

. . .

'effluent' means any liquid, including particles of matter and other substances in suspension in the liquid;

['enforcement notice' has the meaning given by section 90B above;]

. . .

'the Minister' means the Minister of Agriculture, Fisheries and Food;

'the Ministers' means the Secretary of State and the Minister;

. . .

'owner', in relation to any premises, means the person who—

(a) is for the time being receiving the rack-rent of the premises, whether on his own account or as agent or trustee for another person; or

(b) would receive the rack-rent if the premises were let at a rack-rent,

but for the purposes of Schedule 2 to this Act, Chapter II of Part II of this Act and the related water resources provisions does not include a mortgagee not in possession, and cognate expressions shall be construed accordingly;

'prescribed' means prescribed by regulations made by the Secretary of State or, in relation to regulations made by the Minister, by those regulations;

. . .

'public sewer' means a sewer for the time being vested in a sewerage undertaker in its capacity as such, whether vested in that undertaker by virtue of a scheme under Schedule 2 to the Water Act 1989, section 179 of or Schedule 2 to the Water Industry Act 1991 or otherwise;

'records' includes computer records and any other records kept otherwise than in a document;

. . .

'sewage effluent' includes any effluent from the sewage disposal or sewerage works of a sewerage undertaker but does not include surface water;

'sewer' has, subject to subsection (2) below, the same meaning as in the Water Industry Act 1991;

. . .

'surface water' includes water from roofs;

'trade effluent' includes any effluent which is discharged from premises used for carrying on any trade or industry, other than surface water and domestic sewage, and for the purposes of this definition any premises wholly or mainly used (whether for profit or not) for agricultural purposes or for the purposes of fish farming or for scientific research or experiment shall be deemed to be premises used for carrying on a trade;

. . .

'watercourse' includes (subject to sections 72(2) and 113(1) above) all rivers, streams, ditches, drains, cuts, culverts, dykes, sluices, sewers and passages through which water flows, except mains and other pipes which—

(a) belong to the [Agency] or a water undertaker; or

(b) are used by a water undertaker or any other person for the purpose only of providing a supply of water to any premises;

. . .

[222　Crown application

(1) Subject to the provisions of this section, this Act binds the Crown.

(2) No contravention by the Crown of any provision made by or under this Act shall make the Crown criminally liable; but the High Court may, on the application of the Agency, declare unlawful any act or omission of the Crown which constitutes such a contravention.

(3) Notwithstanding anything in subsection (2) above, the provisions of this Act shall apply to persons in the public service of the Crown as they apply to other persons.

(4) If the Secretary of State certifies that it appears to him, as respects any Crown premises and any powers of entry exercisable in relation to them specified in the certificate, that it is requisite or expedient that, in the interests of national security, the powers should not be exercisable in relation to those premises, those powers shall not be exercisable in relation to those premises.

(5) . . .

(6) Nothing in this section shall be taken as in any way affecting Her Majesty in her private capacity; and this subsection shall be construed as if section 38(3) of the Crown Proceedings Act 1947 (interpretation of references to Her Majesty in her private capacity) were contained in this Act.

(7) Nothing in this Act, as read with the other provisions of this section, shall be construed as conferring any power of levying drainage charges in respect of lands below the high-water mark of ordinary spring tides.

(8) Section 74 of the Land Drainage Act 1991 (Crown application), so far as it relates to land in which there is a Crown or Duchy interest, shall apply in relation to the flood defence provisions of this Act as it applies in relation to that Act; but nothing in this subsection shall affect any power conferred by this Act for the purposes both of the Agency's functions under those provisions and of other functions of the Agency.

(9) In this section—

'the appropriate authority' has the same meaning as it has in Part XIII of the Town and Country Planning Act 1990 by virtue of section 293(2) of that Act;

'Crown or Duchy interest' means an interest which belongs to Her Majesty in right of the Crown or of the Duchy of Lancaster, or to the Duchy of Cornwall, or belonging to a government department or held in trust for Her Majesty for the purposes of a government department;

'Crown premises' means premises held by or on behalf of the Crown.

(10) The provisions of subsection (3) of section 293 of the Town and Country Planning Act 1990 (questions relating to Crown application) as to the determination of questions shall apply for the purposes of this section.]

[SCHEDULE 10   DISCHARGE CONSENTS

Application for consent

1.—(1) An application for a consent, for the purposes of section 88(1)(a) of this Act, for any discharges—
    (a) shall be made to the Agency on a form provided for the purpose by the Agency; and
    (b) must be advertised by or on behalf of the applicant in such manner as may be required by regulations made by the Secretary of State.

(2) Regulations made by the Secretary of State may make provision for enabling the Agency to direct or determine that any such advertising of an application as is required under sub-paragraph (1)(b) above may, in any case, be dispensed with if, in that case, it appears to the Agency to be appropriate for that advertising to be dispensed with.

(3) The applicant for such a consent must provide to the Agency, either on, or together with, the form mentioned in sub-paragraph (1) above—
    (a) such information as the Agency may reasonably require; and
    (b) such information as may be prescribed for the purpose by the Secretary of State;
but, subject to paragraph 3(3) below and without prejudice to the effect (if any) of any other contravention of the requirements of this Schedule in relation to an application under this paragraph, a failure to provide information in pursuance of this sub-paragraph shall not invalidate an application.

(4) The Agency may give the applicant notice requiring him to provide it with such further information of any description specified in the notice as it may require for the purpose of determining the application.

(5) An application made in accordance with this paragraph which relates to proposed

discharges at two or more places may be treated by the Agency as separate applications for consents for discharges at each of those places.

Consultation in connection with applications

2.—(1) Subject to sub-paragraph (2) below, the Agency shall give notice of any application under paragraph 1 above, together with a copy of the application, to the persons who are prescribed or directed to be consulted under this paragraph and shall do so within the specified period for notification.

(2) The Secretary of State may, by regulations, exempt any class of application from the requirements of this paragraph or exclude any class of information contained in applications from those requirements, in all cases or as respects specified classes only of persons to be consulted.

(3) Any representations made by the persons so consulted within the period allowed shall be considered by the Agency in determining the application.

(4) For the purposes of sub-paragraph (1) above—

    (a) persons are prescribed to be consulted on any description of application if they are persons specified for the purposes of applications of that description in regulations made by the Secretary of State;

    (b) persons are directed to be consulted on any particular application if the Secretary of State specifies them in a direction given to the Agency;

and the 'specified period for notification' is the period specified in the regulations or in the direction.

(5) Any representations made by any other persons within the period allowed shall also be considered by the Agency in determining the application.

(6) Subject to sub-paragraph (7) below, the period allowed for making representations is—

    (a) in the case of persons prescribed or directed to be consulted, the period of six weeks beginning with the date on which notice of the application was given under sub-paragraph (1) above, and

    (b) in the case of other persons, the period of six weeks beginning with the date on which the making of the application was advertised in pursuance of paragraph 1(1)(b) above.

(7) The Secretary of State may, by regulations, substitute for any period for the time being specified in sub-paragraph (6)(a) or (b) above, such other period as he considers appropriate.

Consideration and determination of applications

3.—(1) On an application under paragraph 1 above the Agency shall be under a duty, if the requirements—

    (a) of that paragraph, and

    (b) of any regulations made under paragraph 1 or 2 above or of any directions under paragraph 2 above,

are complied with, to consider whether to give the consent applied for, either unconditionally or subject to conditions, or to refuse it.

(2) Subject to the following provisions of this Schedule, on an application made in accordance with paragraph 1 above, the applicant may treat the consent applied for as having been refused if it is not given within the period of four months beginning with the day on which the application is received or within such longer period as may be agreed in writing between the Agency and the applicant.

(3) Where any person, having made an application to the Agency for a consent, has failed to comply with his obligation under paragraph 1(3) or (4) above to provide information to the Agency, the Agency may refuse to proceed with the application, or refuse to proceed with it until the information is provided.

(4) The conditions subject to which a consent may be given under this paragraph shall be such conditions as the Agency may think fit and, in particular, may include conditions—

(a) as to the places at which the discharges to which the consent relates may be made and as to the design and construction of any outlets for the discharges;

(b) as to the nature, origin, composition, temperature, volume and rate of the discharges and as to the periods during which the discharges may be made;

(c) as to the steps to be taken, in relation to the discharges or by way of subjecting any substance likely to affect the description of matter discharged to treatment or any other process, for minimising the polluting effects of the discharges on any controlled waters;

(d) as to the provision of facilities for taking samples of the matter discharged and, in particular, as to the provision, maintenance and use of manholes, inspection chambers, observation wells and boreholes in connection with the discharges;

(e) as to the provision, maintenance and testing of meters for measuring or recording the volume and rate of the discharges and apparatus for determining the nature, composition and temperature of the discharges;

(f) as to the keeping of records of the nature, origin, composition, temperature, volume and rate of the discharges and, in particular, of records of readings of meters and other recording apparatus provided in accordance with any other condition attached to the consent; and

(g) as to the making of returns and the giving of other information to the Authority about the nature, origin, composition, temperature, volume and rate of the discharges;

and it is hereby declared that a consent may be given under this paragraph subject to different conditions in respect of different periods.

(5) The Secretary of State may, by regulations, substitute for any period for the time being specified in sub-paragraph (2) above, such other period as he considers appropriate.

4. The Secretary of State may give the Agency a direction with respect to any particular application, or any description of applications, for consent under paragraph 1 above requiring the Agency not to determine or not to proceed with the application or applications of that description until the expiry of any such period as may be specified in the direction, or until directed by the Secretary of State that it may do so, as the case may be.

Reference to Secretary of State of certain applications for consent

5.—(1) The Secretary of State may, either in consequence of representations or objections made to him or otherwise, direct the Agency to transmit to him for determination such applications for consent under paragraph 1 above as are specified in the direction or are of a description so specified.

(2) Where a direction is given to the Agency under this paragraph, the Agency shall comply with the direction and inform every applicant to whose application the direction relates of the transmission of his application to the Secretary of State.

(3) Paragraphs 1(1) and 2 above shall have effect in relation to an application transmitted to the Secretary of State under this paragraph with such modifications as may be prescribed.

(4) Where an application is transmitted to the Secretary of State under this paragraph, the Secretary of State may at any time after the application is transmitted and before it is granted or refused—

(a) cause a local inquiry to be held with respect to the application; or

(b) afford the applicant and the Agency an opportunity of appearing before, and being heard by, a person appointed by the Secretary of State for the purpose.

(5) The Secretary of State shall exercise his power under sub-paragraph (4) above in any

case where a request to be heard with respect to the application is made to him in the prescribed manner by the applicant or by the Agency.

(6) It shall be the duty of the Secretary of State, if the requirements of this paragraph and of any regulations made under it are complied with, to determine an application for consent transmitted to him by the Agency under this paragraph by directing the Agency to refuse its consent or to give its consent under paragraph 3 above (either unconditionally or subject to such conditions as are specified in the direction).

(7) Without prejudice to any of the preceding provisions of this paragraph, the Secretary of State may by regulations make provision for the purposes of, and in connection with, the consideration and disposal by him of applications transmitted to him under this paragraph.

Consents without applications

6.—(1) If it appears to the Agency—
    (a) that a person has caused or permitted effluent or other matter to be discharged in contravention—
        (i) of the obligation imposed by virtue of section 85(3) of this Act; or
        (ii) of any prohibition imposed under section 86 of this Act; and
    (b) that a similar contravention by that person is likely,
the Agency may, if it thinks fit, serve on him an instrument in writing giving its consent, subject to any conditions specified in the instrument, for discharges of a description so specified.

(2) A consent given under this paragraph shall not relate to any discharge which occurred before the instrument containing the consent was served on the recipient of the instrument.

(3) Sub-paragraph (4) of paragraph 3 above shall have effect in relation to a consent given under this paragraph as it has effect in relation to a consent given under that paragraph.

(4) Where a consent has been given under this paragraph, the Agency shall publish notice of the consent in such manner as may be prescribed by the Secretary of State and send copies of the instrument containing the consent to such bodies or persons as may be so prescribed.

(5) It shall be the duty of the Agency to consider any representations or objections with respect to a consent under this paragraph as are made to it in such manner, and within such period, as may be prescribed by the Secretary of State and have not been withdrawn.

(6) Where notice of a consent is published by the Agency under sub-paragraph (4) above, the Agency shall be entitled to recover the expenses of publication from the person on whom the instrument containing the consent was served.

Revocation of consents and alteration and imposition of conditions

7.—(1) The Agency may from time to time review any consent given under paragraph 3 or 6 above and the conditions (if any) to which the consent is subject.

(2) Subject to such restrictions on the exercise of the power conferred by this sub-paragraph as are imposed under paragraph 8 below, where the Agency has reviewed a consent under this paragraph, it may by a notice served on the person making a discharge in pursuance of the consent—
    (a) revoke the consent;
    (b) make modifications of the conditions of the consent; or
    (c) in the case of an unconditional consent, provide that it shall be subject to such conditions as may be specified in the notice.

(3) If on a review under sub-paragraph (1) above it appears to the Agency that no discharge has been made in pursuance of the consent to which the review relates at any time during the preceding twelve months, the Agency may revoke the consent by a notice served on the holder of the consent.

(4) If it appears to the Secretary of State appropriate to do so—

    (a) for the purpose of enabling Her Majesty's Government in the United Kingdom to give effect to any Community obligation or to any international agreement to which the United Kingdom is for the time being a party;

    (b) for the protection of public health or of flora and fauna dependent on an aquatic environment; or

    (c) in consequence of any representations or objections made to him or otherwise,

he may, subject to such restrictions on the exercise of the power conferred by virtue of paragraph (c) above as are imposed under paragraph 8 below, at any time direct the Agency, in relation to a consent given under paragraph 3 or 6 above, to do anything mentioned in sub-paragraph (2)(a) to (c) above.

(5) The Agency shall be liable to pay compensation to any person in respect of any loss or damage sustained by that person as a result of the Agency's compliance with a direction given in relation to any consent by virtue of sub-paragraph (4)(b) above if—

    (a) in complying with that direction the Agency does anything which, apart from that direction, it would be precluded from doing by a restriction imposed under paragraph 8 below; and

    (b) the direction is not shown to have been given in consequence of—

        (i) a change of circumstances which could not reasonably have been fore-seen at the beginning of the period to which the restriction relates; or

        (ii) consideration by the Secretary of State of material information which was not reasonably available to the Agency at the beginning of that period.

(6) For the purposes of sub-paragraph (5) above information is material, in relation to a consent, if it relates to any discharge made or to be made by virtue of the consent, to the interaction of any such discharge with any other discharge or to the combined effect of the matter discharged and any other matter.

Restriction on variation and revocation of consent and previous variation

8.—(1) Each instrument signifying the consent of the Agency under paragraph 3 or 6 above shall specify a period during which no notice by virtue of paragraph 7(2) or (4)(c) above shall be served in respect of the consent except, in the case of a notice doing anything mentioned in paragraph 7(2)(b) or (c), with the agreement of the holder of the consent.

(2) Each notice served by the Agency by virtue of paragraph 7(2) or (4)(c) above (except a notice which only revokes a consent) shall specify a period during which a subsequent such notice which alters the effect of the first-mentioned notice shall not be served except, in the case of a notice doing anything mentioned in paragraph 7(2)(b) or (c) above, with the agreement of the holder of the consent.

(3) The period specified under sub-paragraph (1) or (2) above in relation to any consent shall not, unless the person who proposes to make or makes discharges in pursuance of the consent otherwise agrees, be less than the period of four years beginning—

    (a) in the case of a period specified under sub-paragraph (1) above, with the day on which the consent takes effect; and

    (b) in the case of a period specified under sub-paragraph (2) above, with the day on which the notice specifying that period is served.

(4) A restriction imposed under sub-paragraph (1) or (2) above shall not prevent the service by the Agency of a notice by virtue of paragraph 7(2) or (4)(c) above in respect of a consent given under paragraph 6 above if—

    (a) the notice is served not more than three months after the beginning of the period prescribed under paragraph 6(5) above for the making of representations and objections with respect to the consent; and

    (b) the Agency or, as the case may be, the Secretary of State considers, in consequence of any representations or objections received by it or him within that period, that it is appropriate for the notice to be served.

(5) A restriction imposed under sub-paragraph (1) or (2) above shall not prevent the service by the Agency of a notice by virtue of paragraph 7(2)(b) or (c) or (4)(c) above in respect of a consent given under paragraph 6 above if the holder has applied for a variation under paragraph 10 below.

General review of consents

9.—(1) If it appears appropriate to the Secretary of State to do so he may at any time direct the Agency to review—

(a) the consents given under paragraph 3 or 6 above, or

(b) any description of such consents,

and the conditions (if any) to which those consents are subject.

(2) A direction given by virtue of sub-paragraph (1) above—

(a) shall specify the purpose for which, and

(b) may specify the manner in which,

the review is to be conducted.

(3) After carrying out a review pursuant to a direction given by virtue of sub-paragraph (1) above, the Agency shall submit to the Secretary of State its proposals (if any) for—

(a) the modification of the conditions of any consent reviewed pursuant to the direction, or

(b) in the case of any unconditional consent reviewed pursuant to the direction, subjecting the consent to conditions.

(4) Where the Secretary of State has received any proposals from the Agency under sub-paragraph (3) above in relation to any consent he may, if it appears appropriate to him to do so, direct the Agency to do, in relation to that consent, anything mentioned in paragraph 7(2)(b) or (c) above.

(5) A direction given by virtue of sub-paragraph (4) above may only direct the Agency to do, in relation to any consent,—

(a) any such thing as the Agency has proposed should be done in relation to that consent, or

(b) any such thing with such modifications as appear to the Secretary of State to be appropriate.

Applications for variation

10.—(1) The holder of a consent under paragraph 3 or 6 above may apply to the Agency, on a form provided for the purpose by the Agency, for the variation of the consent.

(2) The provisions of paragraphs 1 to 5 above shall apply (with the necessary modifications) to applications under sub-paragraph (1) above, and to the variation of consents in pursuance of such applications, as they apply to applications for, and the grant of, consents.

Transfer of consents

11.—(1) A consent under paragraph 3 or 6 above may be transferred by the holder to a person who proposes to carry on the discharges in place of the holder.

(2) On the death of the holder of a consent under paragraph 3 or 6 above, the consent shall, subject to sub-paragraph (4) below, be regarded as property forming part of the deceased's personal estate, whether or not it would be so regarded apart from this sub-paragraph, and shall accordingly vest in his personal representatives.

(3) If a bankruptcy order is made against the holder of a consent under paragraph 3 or 6 above, the consent shall, subject to sub-paragraph (4) below, be regarded for the purposes of

any of the Second Group of Parts of the Insolvency Act 1986 (insolvency of individuals; bankruptcy), as property forming part of the bankrupt's estate, whether or not it would be so regarded apart from this sub-paragraph, and shall accordingly vest as such in the trustee in bankruptcy.

(4) Notwithstanding anything in the foregoing provisions of this paragraph, a consent under paragraph 3 or 6 above (and the obligations arising out of, or incidental to, such a consent) shall not be capable of being disclaimed.

(5) A consent under paragraph 3 or 6 above which is transferred to, or which vests in, a person under this section shall have effect on and after the date of the transfer or vesting as if it had been granted to that person under paragraph 3 or 6 above, subject to the same conditions as were attached to it immediately before that date.

(6) Where a consent under paragraph 3 or 6 above is transferred under sub-paragraph (1) above, the person from whom it is transferred shall give notice of that fact to the Agency not later than the end of the period of twenty-one days beginning with the date of the transfer.

(7) Where a consent under paragraph 3 or 6 above vests in any person as mentioned in sub-paragraph (2) or (3) above, that person shall give notice of that fact to the Agency not later than the end of the period of fifteen months beginning with the date of the vesting.

(8) If—
    (a) a consent under paragraph 3 or 6 above vests in any person as mentioned in sub-paragraph (2) or (3) above, but
    (b) that person fails to give the notice required by sub-paragraph (7) above within the period there mentioned,
the consent, to the extent that it permits the making of any discharges, shall cease to have effect.

(9) A person who fails to give a notice which he is required by sub-paragraph (6) or (7) above to give shall be guilty of an offence and liable—
    (a) on summary conviction, to a fine not exceeding the statutory maximum;
    (b) on conviction on indictment, to a fine or to imprisonment for a term not exceeding two years, or to both.]

Section 94   # SCHEDULE 12

NITRATE SENSITIVE AREA ORDERS

PART I   APPLICATIONS BY THE [AGENCY] FOR DESIGNATION ORDERS

Orders made only on application

1.—(1) Subject to sub-paragraphs (2) and (3) below, the relevant Minister shall not make an order under section 94 of this Act by virtue of which any land is designated as land comprised in a nitrate sensitive area, except with the consent of the Treasury and on an application which—
    (a) has been made by the [Agency] in accordance with paragraph 2 below; and
    (b) in identifying controlled waters by virtue of sub-paragraph (2)(a) of that paragraph, identified the controlled waters with respect to which that land is so comprised by the order.

(2) This paragraph shall not apply to an order which reproduces or amends an existing order without adding any land appearing to the relevant Minister to constitute a significant area to the land already comprised in the areas for the time being designated as nitrate sensitive areas.

Procedure for applications

2.—(1) The [Agency] shall not for the purposes of paragraph 1 above apply for the making of any order under section 94 of this Act by which any land would be comprised in the areas for the time being designated as nitrate sensitive areas unless it appears to the [Agency]—

    (a) that pollution is or is likely to be caused by the entry of nitrate into controlled waters as a result of, or of anything done in connection with, the use of particular land in England and Wales for agricultural purposes; and

    (b) that the provisions for the time being in force in relation to those waters and that land are not sufficient, in the opinion of the [Agency], for preventing or controlling such an entry of nitrate into those waters.

  (2) An application under this paragraph shall identify—

    (a) the controlled waters appearing to the [Agency] to be the waters which the nitrate is or is likely to enter; and

    (b) the land appearing to the [Agency] to be the land the use of which for agricultural purposes, or the doing of anything in connection with whose use for agricultural purposes, is resulting or is likely to result in the entry of nitrate into those waters.

  (3) An application under this paragraph shall be made—

    (a) where the land identified in the application is wholly in Wales, by serving a notice containing the application on the Secretary of State; and

    (b) in any other case, by serving such a notice on each of the Ministers.

PART II   ORDERS CONTAINING MANDATORY PROVISIONS

Consideration of objections etc.

6. Without prejudice to [section 53 of the 1995 Act (inquiries and other hearings)], where notices with respect to any proposed order have been published and served in accordance with paragraph 3 above, the Secretary of State or, as the case may be, the Ministers may, if he or they consider it appropriate to do so, hold a local inquiry before deciding whether or not to make the proposed order or to make it with modifications.

Consent of Treasury for payment provisions

7. The consent of the Treasury shall be required for the making of any order under section 94 of this Act the making of which does not require the consent of the Treasury by virtue of paragraph 1 above but which contains any such provision as is authorised by subsection (3)(b) of that section.

Clean Air Act 1993
(1993, c. 11)

PART I   DARK SMOKE

1 Prohibition of dark smoke from chimneys

    (1) Dark smoke shall not be emitted from a chimney of any building, and if, on any day, dark smoke is so emitted, the occupier of the building shall be guilty of an offence.

    (2) Dark smoke shall not be emitted from a chimney (not being a chimney of a building) which serves the furnace of any fixed boiler or industrial plant, and if, on any day, dark smoke is so emitted, the person having possession of the boiler or plant shall be guilty of an offence.

(3) This section does not apply to emissions of smoke from any chimney, in such classes of case and subject to such limitations as may be prescribed in regulations made by the Secretary of State, lasting for not longer than such periods as may be so prescribed.

(4) In any proceedings for an offence under this section, it shall be a defence to prove—

(a) that the alleged emission was solely due to the lighting up of a furnace which was cold and that all practicable steps had been taken to prevent or minimise the emission of dark smoke;

(b) that the alleged emission was solely due to some failure of a furnace, or of apparatus used in connection with a furnace, and that—

(i) the failure could not reasonably have been foreseen, or, if foreseen, could not reasonably have been provided against; and

(ii) the alleged emission could not reasonably have been prevented by action taken after the failure occurred; or

(c) that the alleged emission was solely due to the use of unsuitable fuel and that—

(i) suitable fuel was unobtainable and the least unsuitable fuel which was available was used; and

(ii) all practicable steps had been taken to prevent or minimise the emission of dark smoke as the result of the use of that fuel;

or that the alleged emission was due to the combination of two or more of the causes specified in paragraphs (a) to (c) and that the other conditions specified in those paragraphs are satisfied in relation to those causes respectively.

(5) A person guilty of an offence under this section shall be liable on summary conviction—

(a) in the case of a contravention of subsection (1) as respects a chimney of a private dwelling, to a fine not exceeding level 3 on the standard scale; and

(b) in any other case, to a fine not exceeding level 5 on the standard scale.

(6) This section has effect subject to section 51 (duty to notify offences to occupier or other person liable).

2   Prohibition of dark smoke from industrial or trade premises

(1) Dark smoke shall not be emitted from any industrial or trade premises and if, on any day, dark smoke is so emitted the occupier of the premises and any person who causes or permits the emission shall be guilty of an offence.

(2) This section does not apply—

(a) to the emission of dark smoke from any chimney to which section 1 above applies; or

(b) to the emission of dark smoke caused by the burning of any matter prescribed in regulations made by the Secretary of State, subject to compliance with such conditions (if any) as may be so prescribed.

(3) In proceedings for an offence under this section, there shall be taken to have been an emission of dark smoke from industrial or trade premises in any case where—

(a) material is burned on those premises; and

(b) the circumstances are such that the burning would be likely to give rise to the emission of dark smoke,

unless the occupier or any person who caused or permitted the burning shows that no dark smoke was emitted.

(4) In proceedings for an offence under this section, it shall be a defence to prove—

(a) that the alleged emission was inadvertent; and

(b) that all practicable steps had been taken to prevent or minimise the emission of dark smoke.

(5) A person guilty of an offence under this section shall be liable on summary conviction to a fine not exceeding [£20,000].

(6) In this section 'industrial or trade premises' means—

(a) premises used for any industrial or trade purposes; or

(b) premises not so used on which matter is burnt in connection with any industrial or trade process.

(7) This section has effect subject to section 51 (duty to notify offences to occupier or other person liable).

3   Meaning of 'dark smoke'

(1) In this Act 'dark smoke' means smoke which, if compared in the appropriate manner with a chart of the type known on 5th July 1956 (the date of the passing of the Clean Air Act 1956) as the Ringelmann Chart, would appear to be as dark as or darker than shade 2 on the chart.

(2) For the avoidance of doubt it is hereby declared that in proceedings—

(a) for an offence under section 1 or 2 (prohibition of emissions of dark smoke);

(b) [. . .]

the court may be satisfied that smoke is or is not dark smoke as defined in subsection (1) notwithstanding that there has been no actual comparison of the smoke with a chart of the type mentioned in that subsection.

(3) Without prejudice to the generality of subsections (1) and (2), if the Secretary of State by regulations prescribes any method of ascertaining whether smoke is dark smoke as defined in subsection (1), proof in any such proceedings as are mentioned in subsection (2)—

(a) that that method was properly applied, and

(b) that the smoke was thereby ascertained to be or not to be dark smoke as so defined, shall be accepted as sufficient.

PART II   SMOKE, GRIT, DUST AND FUMES

4   Requirement that new furnaces shall be so far as practicable smokeless

(1) No furnace shall be installed in a building or in any fixed boiler or industrial plant unless notice of the proposal to install it has been given to the local authority.

(2) No furnace shall be installed in a building or in any fixed boiler or industrial plant unless the furnace is so far as practicable capable of being operated continuously without emitting smoke when burning fuel of a type for which the furnace was designed.

(3) Any furnace installed in accordance with plans and specifications submitted to, and approved for the purposes of this section by, the local authority shall be treated as complying with the provisions of subsection (2).

(4) Any person who installs a furnace in contravention of subsection (1) or (2) or on whose instructions a furnace is so installed shall be guilty of an offence and liable on summary conviction—

(a) in the case of a contravention of subsection (1), to a fine not exceeding level 3 on the standard scale; and

(b) in the case of a contravention of subsection (2), to a fine not exceeding level 5 on that scale.

(5) This section does not apply to the installation of domestic furnaces.

(6) This section applies in relation to—

(a) the attachment to a building of a boiler or industrial plant which already contains a furnace; or

(b) the fixing to or installation on any land of any such boiler or plant, as it applies in relation to the installation of a furnace in any fixed boiler or industrial plant.

5   Emission of grit and dust from furnaces

(1) This section applies to any furnace other than a domestic furnace.

(2) The Secretary of State may by regulations prescribe limits on the rates of emission of grit and dust from the chimneys of furnaces to which this section applies.

(3) If on any day grit or dust is emitted from a chimney serving a furnace to which this section applies at a rate exceeding the relevant limit prescribed under sub-section (2), the occupier of any building in which the furnace is situated shall be guilty of an offence.

(4) In proceedings for an offence under subsection (3) it shall be a defence to prove that the best practicable means had been used for minimising the alleged emission.

(5) If, in the case of a building containing a furnace to which this section applies and which is served by a chimney to which there is no limit applicable under subsection (2), the occupier fails to use any practicable means there may be for minimising the emission of grit or dust from the chimney, he shall be guilty of an offence.

(6) A person guilty of an offence under this section shall be liable on summary conviction to a fine not exceeding level 5 on the standard scale.

6   Arrestment plant for new non-domestic furnaces

(1) A furnace other than a domestic furnace shall not be used in a building—

   (a)   to burn pulverised fuel; or
   (b)   to burn, at a rate of 45.4 kilograms or more an hour, any other solid matter; or
   (c)   to burn, at a rate equivalent to 366.4 kilowatts or more, any liquid or gaseous matter,

unless the furnace is provided with plant for arresting grit and dust which has been approved by the local authority or which has been installed in accordance with plans and specifications submitted to and approved by the local authority, and that plant is properly maintained and used.

(2) Subsection (1) has effect subject to any exemptions prescribed or granted under section 7.

(3) The Secretary of State may by regulations substitute for any rate mentioned in subsection (1)(b) or (c) such other rate as he thinks fit: but no regulations shall be made so as to reduce any rate unless a draft of the regulations has been laid before and approved by each House of Parliament.

(4) Regulations under subsection (3) reducing any rate shall not apply to a furnace which has been installed, the installation of which has been begun, or an agreement for the purchase or installation of which has been entered into, before the date on which the regulations come into force.

(5) If on any day a furnace is used in contravention of subsection (1), the occupier of the building shall be guilty of an offence and liable on summary conviction to a fine not exceeding level 5 on the standard scale.

7   Exemptions from section 6

(1) The Secretary of State may by regulations provide that furnaces of any class prescribed in the regulations shall, while used for a purpose so prescribed, be exempted from the operation of section 6(1).

(2) If on the application of the occupier of a building a local authority are satisfied that the emission of grit and dust from any chimney serving a furnace in the building will not be prejudicial to health or a nuisance if the furnace is used for a particular purpose without compliance with section 6(1), they may exempt the furnace from the operation of that subsection while used for that purpose.

(3) If a local authority to whom an application is duly made for an exemption under subsection (2) fail to determine the application and to give a written notice of their decision to the applicant within—

   (a)   eight weeks of receiving the application; or

(b) such longer period as may be agreed in writing between the applicant and the authority,

the furnace shall be treated as having been granted an exemption from the operation of section 6(1) while used for the purpose specified in the application.

(4) If a local authority decide not to grant an exemption under subsection (2), they shall give the applicant a written notification of their decision stating their reasons, and the applicant may within twenty-eight days of receiving the notification appeal against the decision to the Secretary of State.

(5) On an appeal under this section the Secretary of State—

    (a) may confirm the decision appealed against; or

    (b) may grant the exemption applied for or vary the purpose for which the furnace to which the application relates may be used without compliance with section 6(1);

and shall give the appellant a written notification of his decision, stating his reasons for it.

(6) If on any day a furnace which is exempt from the operation of section 6(1) is used for a purpose other than a prescribed purpose or, as the case may be, a purpose for which the furnace may be used by virtue of subsection (2), (3) or (5), the occupier of the building shall be guilty of an offence and liable on summary conviction to a fine not exceeding level 5 on the standard scale.

8 Requirement to fit arrestment plant for burning solid fuel in other cases

(1) A domestic furnace shall not be used in a building—

    (a) to burn pulverised fuel; or

    (b) to burn, at a rate of 1.02 tonnes an hour or more, solid fuel in any other form or solid waste,

unless the furnace is provided with plant for arresting grit and dust which has been approved by the local authority or which has been installed in accordance with plans and specifications submitted to and approved by the local authority, and that plant is properly maintained and used.

(2) If a furnace is used in a building in contravention of subsection (1), the occupier of the building shall be guilty of an offence and liable on summary conviction to a fine not exceeding level 5 on the standard scale.

9 Appeal to Secretary of State against refusal of approval

(1) Where a local authority determine an application for approval under section 6 or 8, they shall give the applicant a written notification of their decision and, in the case of a decision not to grant approval, shall state their reasons for not doing so.

(2) A person who—

    (a) has made such an application to a local authority; or

    (b) is interested in a building with respect to which such an application has been made,

may, if he is dissatisfied with the decision of the authority on the application, appeal within twenty-eight days after he is notified of the decision to the Secretary of State; and the Secretary of State may give any approval which the local authority might have given.

(3) An approval given by the Secretary of State under this section shall have the like effect as an approval of the local authority.

10 Measurement of grit, dust and fumes by occupiers

(1) If a furnace in a building is used—

    (a) to burn pulverised fuel;

    (b) to burn, at a rate of 45.4 kilograms or more an hour, any other solid matter; or

    (c) to burn, at a rate equivalent to 366.4 kilowatts or more, any liquid or gaseous matter, the local authority may, by notice in writing served on the occupier of the building, direct that the provisions of subsection (2) below shall apply to the furnace, and those provisions shall apply accordingly.

(2) In the case of a furnace to which this subsection for the time being applies, the occupier of the building shall comply with such requirements as may be prescribed as to—

    (a) making and recording measurements from time to time of the grit, dust and fumes emitted from the furnace;

    (b) making adaptations for that purpose to the chimney serving the furnace;

    (c) providing and maintaining apparatus for making and recording the measurements; and

    (d) informing the local authority of the results obtained from the measurements or otherwise making those results available to them;

and in this subsection 'prescribed' means prescribed (whether generally or for any class of furnace) by regulations made by the Secretary of State.

(3) If the occupier of the building fails to comply with those requirements, he shall be guilty of an offence and liable on summary conviction—

    (a) to a fine not exceeding level 5 on the standard scale; or

    (b) to cumulative penalties on continuance in accordance with section 50.

(4) The occupier of a building who by virtue of subsection (2) is under a duty to make and record measurements of grit, dust and fumes emitted from a furnace in the building shall permit the local authority to be represented during the making and recording of those measurements.

(5) The Secretary of State may by regulations substitute for any rate mentioned in subsection (1)(b) or (c) such other rate as he thinks fit; but regulations shall not be made under this subsection so as to reduce any rate unless a draft of the regulations has been laid before and approved by each House of Parliament.

(6) Any direction given by a local authority under subsection (1) with respect to a furnace in a building may be revoked by the local authority by a subsequent notice in writing served on the occupier of the building, without prejudice, however, to their power to give another direction under that subsection.

11   Measurement of grit, dust and fumes by local authorities

(1) This section applies to any furnace to which section 10(2) (duty to comply with prescribed requirements) for the time being applies and which is used—

    (a) to burn, at a rate less than 1.02 tonnes an hour, solid matter other than pulverised fuel; or

    (b) to burn, at a rate of less than 8.21 Megawatts, any liquid or gaseous matter.

(2) The occupier of the building in which the furnace is situated may, by notice in writing given to the local authority, request that authority to make and record measurements of the grit, dust and fumes emitted from the furnace.

(3) While a notice is in force under subsection (2)—

    (a) the local authority shall from time to time make and record measurements of the grit, dust and fumes emitted from the furnace; and

    (b) the occupier shall not be under a duty to comply with any requirements of regulations under subsection (2) of section 10 in relation to the furnace, except those imposed by virtue of paragraph (b) of that subsection;

and any such notice given by the occupier of a building may be withdrawn by a subsequent notice in writing given to the local authority by him or any subsequent occupier of that building.

(4) A direction under section 10(1) applying section 10(2) to a furnace which is used as mentioned in subsection (1)(a) or (b) of this section shall contain a statement of the effect of subsections (1) to (3) of this section.

12   Information about furnaces and fuel consumed

(1) For the purpose of enabling the local authority properly to perform their functions under and in connection with sections 5 to 11, the local authority may, by notice in writing served on the occupier of any building, require the occupier to furnish to them, within fourteen days or such longer time as may be limited by the notice, such information as to the furnaces in the building and the fuel or waste burned in those furnaces as they may reasonably require for that purpose.

(2) Any person who, having been duly served with a notice under subsection (1)—

(a) fails to comply with the requirements of the notice within the time limited; or

(b) furnishes any information in reply to the notice which he knows to be false in a material particular,

shall be guilty of an offence and liable on summary conviction to a fine not exceeding level 5 on the standard scale.

13   Grit and dust from outdoor furnaces, etc.

(1) Sections 5 to 12 shall apply in relation to the furnace of any fixed boiler or industrial plant as they apply in relation to a furnace in a building.

(2) References in those sections to the occupier of the building shall, in relation to a furnace falling within subsection (1), be read as references to the person having possession of the boiler or plant.

(3) The reference in section 6(4) (and the reference in paragraph 6(1) and (3) of Schedule 5) to the installation and to the purchase of a furnace shall, in relation to a furnace which is already contained in any fixed boiler or industrial plant, be read as a reference to attaching the boiler or plant to the building or fixing it to or installing it on any land and to purchasing it respectively.

14   Height of chimneys for furnaces

(1) This section applies to any furnace served by a chimney.

(2) An occupier of a building shall not knowingly cause or permit a furnace to be used in the building—

(a) to burn pulverised fuel;

(b) to burn, at a rate of 45.4 kilograms or more an hour, any other solid matter; or

(c) to burn, at a rate equivalent to 366.4 kilowatts or more, any liquid or gaseous matter,

unless the height of the chimney serving the furnace has been approved for the purposes of this section and any conditions subject to which the approval was granted are complied with.

(3) If on any day the occupier of a building contravenes subsection (2), he shall be guilty of an offence.

(4) A person having possession of any fixed boiler or industrial plant, other than an exempted boiler or plant, shall not knowingly cause or permit a furnace of that boiler or plant to be used as mentioned in subsection (2), unless the height of the chimney serving the furnace has been approved for the purposes of this section and any conditions subject to which the approval was granted are complied with.

(5) If on any day a person having possession of any boiler or plant contravenes subsection (3), he shall be guilty of an offence.

(6) A person guilty of an offence under this section shall be liable on summary conviction to a fine not exceeding level 5 on the standard scale.

(7) In this section 'exempted boiler or plant' means a boiler or plant which is used or to be used wholly for any purpose prescribed in regulations made by the Secretary of State; and the height of a chimney is approved for the purposes of this section if approval is granted by the local authority or the Secretary of State under section 15.

15   Applications for approval of height of chimneys of furnaces

(1) This section applies to the granting of approval of the height of a chimney for the purposes of section 14.

(2) Approval shall not be granted by a local authority unless they are satisfied that the height of the chimney will be sufficient to prevent, so far as practicable, the smoke, grit, dust, gases or fumes emitted from the chimney from becoming prejudicial to health or a nuisance having regard to—

(a) the purpose of the chimney;

(b) the position and descriptions of buildings near it;

(c) the levels of the neighbouring ground; and

(d) any other matters requiring consideration in the circumstances.

(3) Approval may be granted without qualification or subject to conditions as to the rate or quality, or the rate and quality, of emissions from the chimney.

(4) If a local authority to whom an application is duly made for approval fail to determine the application and to give a written notification of their decision to the applicant within four weeks of receiving the application or such longer period as may be agreed in writing between the applicant and the authority, the approval applied for shall be treated as having been granted without qualification.

(5) If a local authority decide not to approve the height of a chimney, or to attach conditions to their approval, they shall give the applicant a written notification of their decision which—

(a) states their reasons for that decision; and

(b) in the case of a decision not to approve the height of the chimney, specifies—

(i) the lowest height (if any) which they are prepared to approve without qualification; or

(ii) the lowest height which they are prepared to approve if approval is granted subject to any specified conditions,

or (if they think fit) both.

(6) The applicant may within twenty-eight days of receiving a notification under subsection (5) appeal against the local authority's decision to the Secretary of State.

(7) On an appeal under this section the Secretary of State may confirm the decision appealed against or he may—

(a) approve the height of the chimney without qualification or subject to conditions as to the rate or quality, or the rate and quality, of emissions from the chimney; or

(b) cancel any conditions imposed by the local authority or substitute for any conditions so imposed any other conditions which the authority had power to impose.

(8) The Secretary of State shall give the appellant a written notification of his decision on an appeal under this section which—

(a) states his reasons for the decision; and

(b) in the case of a decision not to approve the height of the chimney, specifies—

(i) the lowest height (if any) which he is prepared to approve without qualification; or

(ii) the lowest height which he is prepared to approve if approval is granted subject to any specified conditions,

or (if he thinks fit) both.

(9) References in this section to 'the applicant' shall, in a case where the original applicant notifies the local authority that his interest in the application has been transferred to another person, be read as references to that other person.

16   Height of other chimneys

(1) This section applies where plans for the erection or extension of a building outside

Greater London or in an outer London borough, other than a building used or to be used wholly for one or more of the following purposes, that is to say—

(a) as a residence or residences;

(b) as a shop or shops; or

(c) as an office or offices,

are in accordance with building regulations deposited with the local authority and the plans show that it is proposed to construct a chimney, other than one serving a furnace, for carrying smoke, grit, dust or gases from the building.

(2) The local authority shall reject the plans unless they are satisfied that the height of the chimney as shown on the plans will be sufficient to prevent, so far as practicable, the smoke, grit, dust or gases from becoming prejudicial to health or a nuisance having regard to—

(a) the purpose of the chimney;

(b) the position and descriptions of buildings near it;

(c) the levels of the neighbouring ground; and

(d) any other matters requiring consideration in the circumstances.

(3) If a local authority reject plans under the authority of this section—

(a) the notice given under section 16(6) of the Building Act 1984 shall specify that the plans have been so rejected; and

(b) any person interested in the building may appeal to the Secretary of State.

(4) On an appeal under subsection (3) the Secretary of State may confirm or cancel the rejection and, where he cancels the rejection, may, if he thinks it necessary, direct that the time for rejecting the plans otherwise than under the authority of this section shall be extended so as to run from the date on which his decision is notified to the local authority.

(5) . . .

PART III   SMOKE CONTROL AREAS

18   Declaration of smoke control area by local authority

(1) A local authority may by order declare the whole or any part of the district of the authority to be a smoke control area; and any order made under this section is referred to in this Act as a 'smoke control order'.

(2) A smoke control order—

(a) may make different provision for different parts of the smoke control area;

(b) may limit the operation of section 20 (prohibition of emissions of smoke) to specified classes of building in the area; and

(c) may exempt specified buildings or classes of building or specified fireplaces or classes of fireplace in the area from the operation of that section, upon such conditions as may be specified in the order;

and the reference in paragraph (c) to specified buildings or classes of building include a reference to any specified, or to any specified classes of, fixed boiler or industrial plant.

(3) A smoke control order may be revoked or varied by a subsequent order.

(4) The provisions of Schedule 1 apply to the coming into operation of smoke control orders.

19   Power of Secretary of State to require creation of smoke control areas

(1) If, after consultation with a local authority, the Secretary of State is satisfied—

(a) that it is expedient to abate the pollution of the air by smoke in the district or part of the district of the authority; and

(b) that the authority have not exercised, or have not sufficiently exercised, their powers under section 18 (power to declare smoke control area) to abate the pollution,

he may direct the authority to prepare and submit to him for his approval, within such period not being less than six months from the direction as may be specified in the direction, proposals for making and bringing into operation one or more smoke control orders within such period or periods as the authority think fit.

(2) Any proposals submitted by a local authority in pursuance of a direction under subsection (1) may be varied by further proposals submitted by the authority within the period specified for the making of the original proposals or such longer period as the Secretary of State may allow.

(3) The Secretary of State may reject any proposals submitted to him under this section or may approve them in whole or in part, with or without modifications.

(4) Where a local authority to whom a direction under subsection (1) has been given—

(a) fail to submit proposals to the Secretary of State within the period specified in the direction; or

(b) submit proposals which are rejected in whole or in part,

the Secretary of State may make an order declaring them to be in default and directing them for the purposes of removing the default to exercise their powers under section 18 in such manner and within such period as may be specified in the order.

(5) An order made under subsection (4) may be varied or revoked by a subsequent order so made.

(6) While proposals submitted by a local authority and approved by the Secretary of State under this section are in force, it shall be the duty of the authority to make such order or orders under section 18 as are necessary to carry out the proposals.

20   Prohibition on emission of smoke in smoke control area

(1) If, on any day, smoke is emitted from a chimney of any building within a smoke control area, the occupier of the building shall be guilty of an offence.

(2) If, on any day, smoke is emitted from a chimney (not being a chimney of a building) which serves the furnace of any fixed boiler or industrial plant within a smoke control area, the person having possession of the boiler or plant shall be guilty of an offence.

(3) Subsections (1) and (2) have effect—

(a) subject to any exemptions for the time being in force under section 18, 21 or 22;

(b) subject to section 51 (duty to notify offences to occupier or other person liable).

(4) In proceedings for an offence under this section it shall be a defence to prove that the alleged emission was not caused by the use of any fuel other than an authorised fuel.

(5) A person guilty of an offence under this section shall be liable on summary conviction to a fine not exceeding level 3 on the standard scale.

(6) In this Part 'authorised fuel' means a fuel declared by regulations of the Secretary of State to be an authorised fuel for the purposes of this Part.

21   Power by order to exempt certain fireplaces

The Secretary of State may by order exempt any class of fireplace, upon such conditions as may be specified in the order, from the provisions of section 20 (prohibition of smoke emissions in smoke control area), if he is satisfied that such fireplaces can be used for burning fuel other than authorised fuels without producing any smoke or a substantial quantity of smoke.

22   Exemptions relating to particular areas

(1) The Secretary of State may, if it appears to him to be necessary or expedient so to do, by order suspend or relax the operation of section 20 (prohibition of smoke emissions in smoke control area) in relation to the whole or any part of a smoke control area.

(2) Before making an order under subsection (1) the Secretary of State shall consult with the local authority unless he is satisfied that, on account of urgency, such consultation is impracticable.

(3) As soon as practicable after the making of such an order the local authority shall take such steps as appear to them suitable for bringing the effect of the order to the notice of persons affected.

23 Acquisition and sale of unauthorised fuel in a smoke control area

(1) Any person who
- (a) acquires any solid fuel for use in a building in a smoke control area otherwise than in a building or fireplace exempted from the operation of section 20 (prohibition of smoke emissions in smoke control area);
- (b) acquires any solid fuel for use in any fixed boiler or industrial plant in a smoke control area, not being a boiler or plant so exempted; or
- (c) sells by retail any solid fuel for delivery by him or on his behalf to—
   - (i) a building in a smoke control area; or
   - (ii) premises in such an area in which there is any fixed boiler or industrial plant,

shall be guilty of an offence and liable on summary conviction to a fine not exceeding level 3 on the standard scale.

(2) In subsection (1), 'solid fuel' means any solid fuel other than an authorised fuel.

(3) Subsection (1) shall, in its application to a smoke control area in which the operation of section 20 is limited by a smoke control order to specified classes of buildings, boilers or plant, have effect as if references to a building, boiler or plant were references to a building, boiler or plant of a class specified in the order.

(4) The power of the Secretary of State under section 22 (exemptions relating to particular areas) to suspend or relax the operation of section 20 in relation to the whole or any part of a smoke control area includes power to suspend or relax the operation of subsection (1) in relation to the whole or any part of such an area.

(5) In proceedings for an offence under this section consisting of the sale of fuel for delivery to a building or premises, it shall be a defence for the person accused to prove that he believed and had reasonable grounds for believing—
- (a) that the building was exempted from the operation of section 20 or, in a case where the operation of that section is limited to specified classes of building, was not of a specified class; or
- (b) that the fuel was acquired for use in a fireplace, boiler or plant so exempted or, in a case where the operation of that section is limited to specified classes of boilers or plant, in a boiler or plant not of a specified class.

PART IV   CONTROL OF CERTAIN FORMS OF AIR POLLUTION

30 Regulations about motor fuel

(1) For the purpose of limiting or reducing air pollution, the Secretary of State may by regulations—
- (a) impose requirements as to the composition and contents of any fuel of a kind used in motor vehicles; and
- (b) where such requirements are in force, prevent or restrict the production, treatment, distribution, import, sale or use of any fuel which in any respect fails to comply with the requirements, and which is for use in the United Kingdom.

(2) It shall be the duty of the Secretary of State, before he makes any regulations under this section, to consult—
- (a) such persons appearing to him to represent manufacturers and users of motor vehicles;
- (b) such persons appearing to him to represent the producers and users of fuel for motor vehicles; and
- (c) such persons appearing to him to be conversant with problems of air pollution,

as he considers appropriate.

(3) Regulations under this section—

    (a) in imposing requirements as to the composition and contents of any fuel, may apply standards, specifications, descriptions or tests laid down in documents not forming part of the regulations; and

    (b) where fuel is subject to such requirements, may, in order that persons to whom the fuel is supplied are afforded information as to its composition or contents, impose requirements for securing that the information is displayed at such places and in such manner as may be prescribed by the regulations.

(4) It shall be duty of every local weights and measures authority to enforce the provisions of regulations under this section within its area; and subsections (2) and (3) of section 26 of the Trade Descriptions Act 1968 (reports and inquiries) shall apply as respects those authorities' functions under this subsection as they apply to their functions under that Act.

(5) The following provisions of the Trade Descriptions Act 1968 shall apply in relation to the enforcement of regulations under this section as they apply to the enforcement of that Act, that is to say—

section 27 (power to make test purchases);

section 28 (power to enter premises and inspect and seize goods and documents);

section 29 (obstruction of authorised officers);

section 30 (notice of test);

and section 33 of that Act shall apply to the exercise of powers under section 28 as applied by this subsection.

References to an offence under that Act in those provisions as applied by this subsection, except the reference in section 30(2) to an offence under section 28(5) or 29 of that Act, shall be construed as references to an offence under section 32 of this Act (provisions supplementary to this section) relating to regulations under this section.

31 Regulations about sulphur content of oil fuel for furnaces or engines

(1) For the purpose of limiting or reducing air pollution, the Secretary of State may by regulations impose limits on the sulphur content of oil fuel which is used in furnaces or engines.

(2) It shall be the duty of the Secretary of State, before he makes any regulations in pursuance of this section, to consult—

    (a) such persons appearing to him to represent producers and users of oil fuel;

    (b) such persons appearing to him to represent manufacturers and users of plant and equipment for which oil fuel is used; and

    (c) such persons appearing to him to be conversant with problems of air pollution,

as he considers appropriate.

(3) Regulations under this section may—

    (a) prescribe the kinds of oil fuel, and the kinds of furnaces and engines, to which the regulations are to apply;

    (b) apply standards, specifications, descriptions or tests laid down in documents not forming part of the regulations; and

    (c) without prejudice to the generality of section 63(1)(a), make different provision for different areas.

(4) It shall be the duty—

    (a) of every local authority to enforce the provisions of regulations under this section within its area, except in relation to a furnace which is

        [(i)] part of a process subject to Part I of the Environmental Protection Act 1990, or

        (ii) part of an installation subject to regulation by the Environment Agency under regulations made under section 2 of the Pollution Prevention and Control Act 1999; and]

(b) of the inspectors appointed under that Part to enforce those provisions in relation to [furnaces within sub-paragraph (i) of paragraph (a) above and of the Environment Agency to enforce those provisions in relation to furnaces within sub-paragraph (ii) of that paragraph]

. . .

(5) In this section 'oil fuel' means any liquid petroleum product produced in a refinery.

32 Provisions supplementary to sections 30 and 31

(1) Regulations under section 30 or 31 (regulation of content of motor fuel and fuel oil) may authorise the Secretary of State to confer exemptions from any provision of the regulations.

(2) A person who contravenes or fails to comply with any provision of regulations under section 30 or 31 shall be guilty of an offence and liable—

(a) on conviction on indictment, to a fine; and

(b) on summary conviction, to a fine not exceeding the statutory maximum; but the regulations may in any case exclude liability to conviction on indictment or reduce the maximum fine on summary conviction.

(3) Regulations under section 30 or 31 shall, subject to any provision to the contrary in the regulations, apply to fuel used for, and to persons in, the public service of the Crown as they apply to fuel used for other purposes and to other persons.

(4) A local authority shall not be entitled by virtue of subsection (3) to exercise, in relation to fuel used for and persons in that service, any power conferred on the authority by virtue of sections 56 to 58 (rights of entry and inspection and other local authority powers).

33 Cable burning

(1) A person who burns insulation from a cable with a view to recovering metal from the cable shall be guilty of an offence unless the burning is part of a process subject to Part I of the Environmental Protection Act 1990 [or or an activity subject to regulations under section 2 of the Pollution Prevention and Control Act 1999.]

(2) A person guilty of an offence under this section shall be liable on summary conviction to a fine not exceeding level 5 on the standard scale.

PART V   INFORMATION ABOUT AIR POLLUTION

38 Regulations about local authority functions under sections 34, 35 and 36

(1) The Secretary of State shall by regulations prescribe the manner in which, and the methods by which, local authorities are to perform their functions under sections 34(1)(a) and (b), 35 and 36 (investigation and research etc. into, and the obtaining of information about, air pollution).

(2) It shall be the duty of the Secretary of State, before he makes regulations under this section, to consult—

(a) such persons appearing to him to represent local authorities;

(b) such persons appearing to him to represent industrial interests; and

(c) such persons appearing to him to be conversant with problems of air pollution, as he considers appropriate.

(3) Regulations under this section may in particular—

(a) prescribe the kinds of emissions to which notices under section 36 (power to require information about air pollution) may relate;

(b) prescribe the kinds of information which may be required by those notices;

(c) prescribe the manner in which any such notice is to be given, and the evidence which is to be sufficient evidence of its having been given, and of its contents and authenticity;

    (d) require each local authority to maintain in a prescribed form a register containing—
- (i) information obtained by the authority by virtue of section 35(1) (powers of local authorities to obtain information), other than information as to which a direction under section 37(2) (appeals against notices under section 36) provides that the information is not to be disclosed to the public; and
- (ii) such information (if any) as the Secretary of State may determine, or as may be determined by or under regulations, with respect to any appeal under section 37 against a notice served by the authority which the Secretary of State did not dismiss;

    (e) specify the circumstances in which local authorities may enter into arrangements with owners or occupiers of premises under which they will record and measure emissions on behalf of the local authorities; and

    (f) specify the kinds of apparatus which local authorities are to have power to provide and use for measuring and recording emissions, and for other purposes.

  (4) Regulations made by virtue of subsection (3)(b) may in particular require returns of—

    (a) the total volume of gases, whether pollutant or not, discharged from the premises in question over any period;

    (b) the concentration of pollutant in the gases discharged;

    (c) the total of the pollutant discharged over any period;

    (d) the height or heights at which discharges take place;

    (e) the hours during which discharges take place; or

    (f) the concentration of pollutants at ground level.

  (5) A register maintained by a local authority in pursuance of regulations made by virtue of subsection (3)(d) shall be open to public inspection at the principal office of the authority free of charge at all reasonable hours, and the authority shall afford members of the public reasonable facilities for obtaining from the authority, on payment of reasonable charges, copies of entries in the register.

39 Provision by local authorities of information for Secretary of State

  (1) The Secretary of State may, for the purpose of obtaining information about air pollution, direct a local authority to make such arrangements as may be specified in the direction—

    (a) for the provision, installation, operation and maintenance by the local authority of apparatus for measuring and recording air pollution; and

    (b) for transmitting the information so obtained to the Secretary of State; but before giving the direction under this section the Secretary of State shall consult the local authority.

  (2) Where apparatus is provided in pursuance of a direction under this section, the Secretary of State shall defray the whole of the capital expenditure incurred by the local authority in providing and installing the apparatus.

  (3) It shall be the duty of the local authority to comply with any direction given under this section.

40 Interpretation of Part V

In this Part—

    (a) references to the emission of substances into the atmosphere are to be construed as applying to substances in a gaseous or liquid or solid state, or any combination of those states; and

    (b) any reference to measurement includes a reference to the taking of samples.

PART VI   SPECIAL CASES

41   Relation to Environmental Protection Act 1990

(1) Parts I to III shall not apply to any process which is a prescribed process as from the date which is the determination date for that process.

(2) The 'determination date' for a prescribed process is—

    (a) in the case of a process for which an authorisation is granted, the date on which the enforcing authority grants it, whether in pursuance of the application or, on an appeal, of a direction to grant it, and

    (b) in the case of a process for which an authorisation is refused, the date of the refusal or, on an appeal, of the affirmation of the refusal.

(3) In this section 'authorisation', 'enforcing authority' and 'prescribed process' have the meaning given in section 1 of the Environmental Protection Act 1990 and the reference to an appeal is a reference to an appeal under section 15 of that Act.

[**41A**   (1) Where an activity is subject to regulations under section 2 of the Pollution Prevention and Control Act 1999 (regulation of polluting activities), Parts I to III of this Act shall not apply as from the determination date for the activity in question.

(2) The 'determination date', for an activity, is—

    (a) in the case of an activity for which a permit is granted, the date on which it is granted, whether in pursuance of the application, or on an appeal, of a direction to grant it;

    (b) in the case of an activity for which a permit is refused, the date of refusal or, on appeal, of the affirmation of the refusal.

(3) In subsection (2) 'permit' means a permit under regulations under section 2 of the Pollution Prevention and Control Act 1999 and the reference to an appeal is a reference to an appeal under those regulations.]

42   Colliery spoilbanks

(1) This section applies to any mine or quarry from which coal or shale has been, is being or is to be got.

(2) The owner of a mine or quarry to which this section applies shall employ all practicable means—

    (a) for preventing combustion of refuse deposited from the mine or quarry; and

    (b) for preventing or minimising the emission of smoke and fumes from such refuse;

and, if he fails to do so, he shall be guilty of an offence.

(3) A person guilty of an offence under subsection (2) shall be liable on summary conviction—

    (a) to a fine not exceeding level 5 on the standard scale; or

    (b) to cumulative penalties on continuance in accordance with section 50.

(4) Neither the provisions of Part III of the Environmental Protection Act 1990 nor any provision of Parts I to III of this Act shall apply in relation to smoke, grit or dust from the combustion of refuse deposited from any mine or quarry to which this section applies.

(5) [. . .]

(6) In this section section, 'mine', 'quarry' and 'owner' have the same meaning as in the Mines and Quarries Act 1954.

43   Railway engines

(1) Section 1 (prohibition of emissions of dark smoke) shall apply in relation to railway locomotive engines as it applies in relation to buildings.

(2) In the application of section 1 to such engines, for the reference in subsection (1) of that section to the occupier of the building there shall be substituted a reference to the owner of the engine.

(3) The owner of any railway locomotive engine shall use any practicable means there may be for minimising the emission of smoke from the chimney on the engine and, if he fails to do so, he shall, if smoke is emitted from that chimney, be guilty of an offence.

(4) A person guilty of an offence under subsection (3) shall be liable on summary conviction—

(a) to a fine not exceeding level 5 on the standard scale; or

(b) to cumulative penalties on continuance in accordance with section 50.

(5) Except as provided in this section, nothing in Parts I to III applies to smoke, grit or dust from any railway locomotive engine.

44 Vessels

(1) Section 1 (prohibition of emissions of dark smoke) shall apply in relation to vessels in waters to which this section applies as it applies in relation to buildings.

(2) In the application of section 1 to a vessel—

(a) for the reference in subsection (1) of that section to the occupier of the building there shall be substituted a reference to the owner of, and to the master or other officer or person in charge of, the vessel;

(b) for the references to a furnace shall be read as including references to an engine of the vessel; and

(c) subsection (5) of that section shall be omitted;

and a person guilty of an offence under that section in relation to a vessel shall be liable on summary conviction to a fine not exceeding level 5 on the standard scale.

(3) For the purposes of this Act a vessel in any waters to which this section applies which are not within the district of any local authority shall be deemed to be within the district of the local authority whose district includes that point on land which is nearest to the spot where the vessel is.

(4) The waters to which this section applies are—

(a) all waters not navigable by sea-going ships; and

(b) all waters navigable by sea-going ships which are within the seaward limits of the territorial waters of the United Kingdom and are contained within any port, harbour, river, estuary, haven, dock, canal or other place so long as a person or body of persons is empowered by or under any Act to make charges in respect of vessels entering it or using facilities in it.

(5) In subsection (4) 'charges' means any charges with the exception of light dues, local light dues and any other charges payable in respect of lighthouses, buoys or beacons and of charges in respect of pilotage.

(6) Except as provided in this section, nothing in Parts I to III applies to smoke, grit or dust from any vessel.

45 Exemption for purposes of investigations and research

(1) If the local authority are satisfied, on the application of any person interested, that it is expedient to do so for the purpose of enabling investigations or research relevant to the problem of the pollution of the air to be carried out without rendering the applicant liable to proceedings brought under or by virtue of any of the provisions of this Act or the Environmental Protection Act 1990 mentioned below, the local authority may by notice in writing given to the applicant exempt, wholly or to a limited extent,—

(a) any chimney from the operation of sections 1 (dark smoke), 5 (grit and dust), 20 (smoke in smoke control area) and 43 (railway engines) of this Act and Part III of the Environmental Protection Act 1990 (statutory nuisances);

(b) any furnace, boiler or industrial plant from the operation of section 4(2) (new furnaces to be as far as practicable smokeless);

(c) any premises from the operation of section 2 (emissions of dark smoke);

(d) any furnace from the operation of sections 6 or 8 (arrestment plant) and 10 (measurement of grit, dust and fumes by occupier), and

(e) the acquisition or sale of any fuel specified in the notice from the operation of section 23 (acquisition and sale of unauthorised fuel in smoke control area),

in each case subject to such conditions, if any, and for such period as may be specified in the notice.

(2) Any person who has applied to the local authority for an exemption under this section may, if he is dissatisfied with the decision of the authority on the application, appeal to the Secretary of State; and the Secretary of State may, if he thinks fit, by notice in writing given to the applicant and the local authority, give any exemption which the authority might have given or vary the terms of any exemption which they have given.

46 Crown premises, etc.

(1) It shall be part of the functions of the local authority, in cases where it seems to them proper to do so, to report to the responsible Minister any cases of—

(a) emissions of dark smoke, or of grit or dust, from any premises which are under the control of any Government department and are occupied for the public service of the Crown or for any of the purposes of any Government department;

(b) emissions of smoke, whether dark smoke or not, from any such premises which are within a smoke control area;

(c) emissions of smoke, whether dark smoke or not, from any such premises which appear to them to constitute a nuisance to the inhabitants of the neighbour-hood; or

(d) emissions of dark smoke from any vessel of Her Majesty's navy, or any Government ship in the service of the Secretary of State while employed for the purposes of Her Majesty's navy, which appear to them to constitute a nuisance to the inhabitants of the neighbourhood,

and on receiving any such report the responsible Minister shall inquire into the circumstances and, if his inquiry reveals that there is cause for complaint, shall employ all practicable means for preventing or minimising the emission of the smoke, grit or dust or for abating the nuisance and preventing a recurrence of it, as the case may be.

(2) Subsection (1) shall apply to premises occupied for the purposes of the Duchy of Lancaster or the Duchy of Cornwall as it applies to premises occupied for the public service of the Crown which are under the control of a Government department, with the substitution, in the case of the Duchy of Cornwall, for references to the responsible Minister of references to such person as the Duke of Cornwall or the possessor for the time being of the Duchy of Cornwall appoints.

(3) The fact that there subsists in any premises an interest belonging to Her Majesty in right of the Crown or of the Duchy of Lancaster, or to the Duchy of Cornwall, or belonging to a Government department or held in trust for Her Majesty for the purposes of a Government department, shall not affect the application of this Act to those premises so long as that interest is not the interest of the occupier of the premises, and this Act shall have effect accordingly in relation to the premises and that and all other interests in the premises.

(4) Section 44 (vessels) shall, with the omission of the reference in subsection (2) of that section to the owner, apply to vessels owned by the Crown, except that it shall not apply to vessels of Her Majesty's navy or to Government ships in the service of the Secretary of State while employed for the purposes of Her Majesty's navy.

(5) This Act (except Parts IV and V) shall have effect in relation to premises occupied for the service of a visiting force as if the premises were occupied for the public service of the Crown and were under the control of the Government department by arrangement with whom the premises are occupied.

(6) In this section—

'Government ship' has the same meaning as in section 80 of the Merchant Shipping Act 1906; and

'visiting force' means any such body, contingent or detachment of the forces of any country as is a visiting force for the purposes of any of the provisions of the Visiting Forces Act 1952.

PART VII   MISCELLANEOUS AND GENERAL

47   Application to fumes and gases of certain provisions as to grit, dust and smoke

(1) The Secretary of State may by regulations—

    (a) apply all or any of the provisions of sections 5, 6, 7, 42(4) 43(5) 44(6) and 46(1) to fumes or prescribed gases or both as they apply to grit and dust;

    (b) apply all or any of the provisions of section 4 to fumes or prescribed gases or both as they apply to smoke; and

    (c) apply all or any of the provisions of section 11 to prescribed gases as they apply to grit and dust,

subject, in each case, to such exceptions and modifications as he thinks expedient.

(2) No regulations shall be made under this section unless a draft of the regulations has been laid before and approved by each House of Parliament.

(3) In the application of any provision of this Act to prescribed gases by virtue of regulations under this section, any reference to the rate of emission of any substance shall be construed as a reference to the percentage by volume or by mass of the gas which may be emitted during a period specified in the regulations.

(4) In this section—

'gas' includes vapour and moisture precipitated from vapour; and

'prescribed' means prescribed in regulations under this section.

48   Power to give effect to international agreements

The Secretary of State may by regulations provide that any provision of Parts IV and V, or of this Part (apart from this section) so far as relating to those Parts, shall have effect with such modifications as are prescribed in the regulations with a view to enabling the Government of the United Kingdom to give effect to any provision made by or under any international agreement to which the Government is for the time being a party.

49   Unjustified disclosures of information

(1) If a person discloses any information relating to any trade secret used in carrying on any particular undertaking which has been given to him or obtained by him by virtue of this Act, he shall, subject to subsection (2), be guilty of an offence and liable on summary conviction to a fine not exceeding level 5 on the standard scale.

(2) A person shall not be guilty of an offence under subsection (1) by reason of the disclosure of any information if the disclosure is made—

    (a) in the performance of his duty;

    (b) in pursuance of section 34(1)(b); or

    (c) with the consent of a person having a right to disclose the information.

50   Cumulative penalties on continuance of certain offences

(1) Where—

    (a) a person is convicted of an offence which is subject to cumulative penalties on continuance in accordance with this section; and

    (b) it is shown to the satisfaction of the court that the offence was substantially a repetition or continuation of an earlier offence by him after he had been convicted of the earlier offence,

the penalty provided by subsection (2) shall apply instead of the penalty otherwise specified for the offence.

(2) Where this subsection applies the person convicted shall be liable on summary conviction to a fine not exceeding—

(a) level 5 on the standard scale; or

(b) £50 for every day on which the earlier offence has been so repeated or continued by him within the three months next following his conviction of that offence,

whichever is the greater.

(3) Where an offence is subject to cumulative penalties in accordance with this section—

(a) the court by which a person is convicted of the original offence may fix a reasonable period from the date of conviction for compliance by the defendant with any directions given by the court; and

(b) where a court has fixed such a period, the daily penalty referred to in subsection (2) is not recoverable in respect of any day before the end of that period.

51   Duty to notify occupiers of offences

(1) If, in the opinion of an authorised officer of the local authority—

(a) an offence is being or has been committed under section 1, 2 or 20 (prohibition of certain emissions of smoke);

(b) [. . .]

he shall, unless he has reason to believe that notice of it has already been given by or on behalf of the local authority, as soon as may be notify the appropriate person, and, if his notification is not in writing, shall before the end of the four days next following the day on which he became aware of the offence, confirm the notification in writing.

(2) For the purposes of subsection (1), the appropriate person to notify is the occupier of the premises, the person having possession of the boiler or plant, the owner of the railway locomotive engine or the owner or master or other officer or person in charge of the vessel concerned, as the case may be.

(3) In any proceedings for an offence under section 1, 2 or 20 it shall be a defence to prove that the provisions of subsection (1) have not been complied with in the case of the offence; and if no such notification as is required by that subsection has been given before the end of the four days next following the day of the offence, that subsection shall be taken not to have been complied with unless the contrary is proved.

52   Offences committed by bodies corporate

(1) Where an offence under this Act which has been committed by a body corporate is proved to have been committed with the consent or connivance of, or to be attributable to any neglect on the part of, any director, manager, secretary or other similar officer of the body corporate or any person who was purporting to act in any such capacity, he as well as the body corporate shall be guilty of that offence and be liable to be proceeded against and punished accordingly.

(2) Where the affairs of a body corporate are managed by its members this section shall apply in relation to the acts and defaults of a member in connection with his functions of management as if he were a director of the body corporate.

53   Offence due to act or default of another

(1) Where the commission by any person of an offence under this Act is due to the act or default of some other person, that other person shall be guilty of the offence.

(2) A person may be charged with and convicted of an offence by virtue of this section whether or not proceedings for the offence are taken against any other person.

54   Power of county court to authorise works and order payments

(1) If works are reasonably necessary in or in connection with a building in order to enable the building to be used for some purpose without contravention of any of the provisions of this Act (apart from Parts IV and V), the occupier of the building—

(a) may, if by reason of a restriction affecting his interest in the building he is unable to carry out the works without the consent of the owner of the building or some other person interested in the building and is unable to obtain that consent, apply to the county court for an order to enable the works to be carried out by him; and

(b) may, if he considers that the whole or any proportion of the cost of carrying out the works should be borne by the owner of the building or some other person interested in the building, apply to the county court for an order directing the owner or other person to indemnify him, either wholly or in part, in respect of that cost;

and on an application under paragraph (a) or (b) the court may make such order as may appear to the court to be just.

(2) . . .

55   General provisions as to enforcement

(1) It shall be the duty of the local authority to enforce—

(a) the provisions of Parts I to III, section 33 and Part VI; and

(b) the provisions of this Part so far as relating to those provisions;

but nothing in this section shall be taken as extending to the enforcement of any building regulations.

(2) A local authority in England and Wales may institute proceedings for an offence under section 1 or 2 (prohibition of emissions of dark smoke) in the case of any smoke which affects any part of their district notwithstanding, in the case of an offence under section 1, that the smoke is emitted from a chimney outside their district and, in the case of an offence under section 2, that the smoke is emitted from premises outside their district.

(3) . . .

56   Rights of entry and inspection etc

(1) Any person authorised in that behalf by a local authority may at any reasonable time—

(a) enter upon any land or vessel for the purpose of—

(i) performing any function conferred on the authority or that person by virtue of this Act,

(ii) determining whether, and if so in what manner, such a function should be performed, or

(iii) determining whether any provision of this Act or of an instrument made under this Act is being complied with; and

(b) carry out such inspections, measurements and tests on the land or vessel or of any articles on it and take away such samples of the land or articles as he considers appropriate for such a purpose.

(2) Subsection (1) above does not, except in relation to work under section 24(1) (adaptations to dwellings in smoke control area), apply in relation to a private dwelling.

(3) If it is shown to the satisfaction of a justice of the peace on sworn information in writing—

(a) that admission to any land or vessel which a person is entitled to enter in pursuance of subsection (1) has been refused to that person or that refusal is apprehended or that the land or vessel is unoccupied or that the occupier is temporarily absent or that the case is one of emergency or that an application for admission would defeat the object of the entry; and

(b) that there is reasonable ground for entry upon the land or vessel for the purpose for which entry is required,

then, subject to subsection (4), the justice may by warrant under his hand authorise that person to enter the land or vessel, if need be by force.

(4) A justice of the peace shall not issue a warrant in pursuance of subsection (3) in respect of any land or vessel unless he is satisfied—

(a) that admission to the land or vessel in pursuance of subsection (1) was sought after not less than seven days' notice of the intended entry had been served on the occupier; or

(b) that admission to the land or vessel in pursuance of that subsection was sought in an emergency and was refused by or on behalf of the occupier; or

(c) that the land or vessel is unoccupied; or

(d) that an application for admission to the land or vessel would defeat the object of the entry.

(5) A warrant issued in pursuance of this section shall continue in force until the purpose for which the entry is required has been satisfied.

(6) . . .

57   Provisions supplementary to section 56

(1) A person authorised to enter upon any land or vessel in pursuance of section 56 shall, if so required, produce evidence of his authority before he enters upon the land or vessel.

(2) A person so authorised may take with him on to the land or vessel in question such other persons and such equipment as may be necessary.

(3) Admission to any land or vessel used for residential purposes and admission with heavy equipment to any other land or vessel shall not, except in an emergency or in a case where the land or vessel is unoccupied, be demanded as of right in pursuance of section 56(1) unless notice of the intended entry has been served on the occupier not less than seven days before the demand.

(4) A person who, in the exercise of powers conferred on him by virtue of section 56 or this section, enters upon any land or vessel which is unoccupied or of which the occupier is temporarily absent shall leave the land or vessel as effectually secured against unauthorised entry as he found it.

(5) It shall be the duty of a local authority to make full compensation to any person who has sustained damage by reason of—

(a) the exercise by a person authorised by the authority of any of the powers conferred on the person so authorised by virtue of section 56 or this section; or

(b) the failure of a person so authorised to perform the duty imposed on him by subsection (4),

except where the damage is attributable to the default of the person who sustained it; and any dispute as to a person's entitlement to compensation in pursuance of this subsection or as to the amount of the compensation shall be determined by arbitration.

(6) A person who wilfully obstructs another person acting in the exercise of any powers conferred on the other person by virtue of section 56 or this section shall be guilty of an offence and liable on summary conviction to a fine not exceeding level 3 on the standard scale.

(7) In section 56 and this section any reference to an emergency is a reference to a case where a person requiring entry to any land or vessel has reasonable cause to believe that circumstances exist which are likely to endanger life or health and that immediate entry to the land or vessel is necessary to verify the existence of those circumstances or to ascertain their cause or to effect a remedy.

58   Power of local authorities to obtain information

(1) A local authority may serve on any person a notice requiring him to furnish to the authority, within a period or at times specified in the notice and in a form so specified, any information so specified which the authority reasonably considers that it needs for the purposes of any function conferred on the authority by Part IV or V of this Act (or by this Part of this Act so far as relating to those Parts).

(2) The Secretary of State may by regulations provide for restricting the information which may be required in pursuance of subsection (1) and for determining the form in which the information is to be so required.

(3) Any person who—

  (a) fails without reasonable excuse to comply with the requirements of a notice served on him in pursuance of this section; or

  (b) in furnishing any information in compliance with such a notice, makes any statement which he knows to be false in a material particular or recklessly makes any statement which is false in a material particular,

shall be guilty of an offence and liable on summary conviction to a fine not exceeding level 5 on the standard scale.

59 [Inquiries]

(1) The Secretary of State may cause [an inquiry] to be held in any case in which he considers it appropriate for [an inquiry] to be held either in connection with a provision of this Act or with a view to preventing or dealing with air pollution at any place.

(2) Subsections (2) to (5) of section 250 of the Local Government Act 1972 (which contains supplementary provisions with respect to local inquiries held in pursuance of that section) shall, without prejudice to the generality of subsection (1) of that section, apply to inquiries in England and Wales in pursuance of subsection (1) as they apply to inquiries in pursuance of that section.

(3) . . .

60 Default powers

(1) Of the Secretary of State is satisfied that any local authority (in this section referred to as the 'defaulting authority') have failed to perform any functions which they ought to have performed, he may make an order—

  (a) declaring the authority to be in default; and

  (b) directing the authority to perform such of their functions as are specified in the order;

and he may specify the manner in which and the time or times within which those functions are to be performed by the authority.

(2) If the defaulting authority fails to comply with any direction contained in such an order, the Secretary of State may, instead of enforcing the order by mandamus, make an order transferring to himself such of the functions of the authority as he thinks fit.

(3) Where any functions of the defaulting authority are transferred in pursuance of subsection (2) above, the amount of any expenses which the Secretary of State certifies were incurred by him in performing those functions shall on demand be paid to him by the defaulting authority.

(4) Where any expenses are in pursuance of subsection (3) required to be paid by the defaulting authority in respect of any functions transferred in pursuance of this section—

  (a) the expenses shall be defrayed by the authority in the like manner, and shall be debited to the like account, as if the functions had not been transferred and the expenses had been incurred by the authority in performing them; and

  (b) the authority shall have the like powers for the purpose of raising any money required for the purpose of paragraph (a) as the authority would have had for the purpose of raising money required for defraying expenses incurred for the purposes of the functions in question.

(5) An order transferring any functions of the defaulting authority in pursuance of subsection (2) may provide for the transfer to the Secretary of State of such of the property, rights, liabilities and obligations of the authority as he considers appropriate; and where such an order is revoked the Secretary of State may, by the revoking order or a subsequent order, make

such provision as he considers appropriate with respect to any property, rights, liabilities and obligations held by him for the purposes of the transferred functions.

(6) An order made under this section may be varied or revoked by a subsequent order so made.

(7) This section does not apply to a failure by a local authority—

(a) to discharge their functions under section 18 (declaration of smoke control areas);

(b) to submit proposals to the Secretary of State in pursuance of a direction under subsection (1) of section 19 (Secretary of State's power to require creation of smoke control area); or

(c) to perform a duty imposed on them by or by virtue of subsection (4) or (6) of that section.

(8) In this section 'functions', in relation to an authority, means functions conferred on the authority by virtue of this Act.

61 Joint exercise of local authority functions

(1) Sections 6, 7, 9 and 10 of the Public Health Act 1936 (provisions relating to joint boards) shall, so far as applicable, have effect in relation to this Act as if the provisions of this Act were provisions of that Act.

(2) . . .

(3) Without prejudice to subsections (1) and (2), any two or more local authorities may combine for the purpose of declaring an area to be a smoke control area and in that event—

(a) the smoke control area may be the whole of the districts of those authorities or any part of those districts;

(b) the references in section 18, Schedule 1 and paragraph 1 of Schedule 2 to the local authority shall be read as references to the local authorities acting jointly;

(c) the reference in paragraph 1 of Schedule 1 to a place in the district of the local authority shall be construed as a reference to a place in each of the districts of the local authorities;

but, except as provided in this subsection, references in this Act to the local authority shall, in relation to a building or dwelling, or to a boiler or industrial plant, in the smoke control area, be read as references to that one of the local authorities within whose district the building, dwelling, boiler or plant is situated.

(4) For the avoidance of doubt it is hereby declared that where a port health authority or joint board has functions, rights or liabilities under this Act—

(a) any reference in this Act to a local authority or its district includes, in relation to those functions, rights or liabilities, a reference to the port health authority or board or its district;

(b) for the purposes of this Act, no part of the district of any such port health authority or board is to be treated, in relation to any matter falling within the competence of the authority or board, as forming part of the district of any other authority.

(5) Any premises which extend into the districts of two or more authorities shall be treated for the purposes of this Act as being wholly within such one of those districts—

(a) in England and Wales, as may from time to time be agreed by those authorities; or

(b) . . .

62 Application of certain provisions of Part XII of Public Health Act 1936

(1) In the application of this Act to England and Wales, the following provisions of Part XII of the Public Health Act 1936 shall have effect in relation to the provisions of this Act (apart from Parts IV and V) as if those provisions were provisions of that Act—

section 275 (power of local authority to execute works);

section 276 (power of local authority to sell materials);

section 278 (compensation to individuals for damage resulting from exercise of powers under Act);

section 283 (form of notices);

section 284 (authentication of documents);

section 285 (service of notices);

section 289 (power to require occupier to permit works to be executed by owner);

section 291 (expenses to be a charge on the premises);

section 293 (recovery of expenses);

section 294 (limitation of liability of certain owners);

section 299 (inclusion of several sums in one complaint, etc.);

section 305 (protection of members and officers of local authorities from personal liability).

(2) . . .

64   General provisions as to interpretation

(1) In this Act, except so far as the context otherwise requires,—

'authorised officer' means any officer of a local authority authorised by them in writing, either generally or specially, to act in matters of any specified kind or in any specified matter;
. . .

'caravan' means a caravan within the meaning of Part 1 of the Caravan Sites and Control of Development Act 1960, disregarding the amendment made by section 13(2) of the Caravan Sites Act 1968, which usually and for the time being is situated on a caravan site within the meaning of that Act;

'chimney' includes structures and openings of any kind from or through which smoke, grit, dust or fumes may be emitted, and, in particular, includes flues, and references to a chimney of a building include references to a chimney which serves the whole or a part of a building but is structurally separate from the building;

'dark smoke' has the meaning given by section 3(1);

'day' means a period of twenty-four hours beginning at midnight;

'domestic furnace' means any furnace which is—

(a) designed solely or mainly for domestic purposes, and

(b) used for heating a boiler with a maximum heating capacity of less than 16.12 kilowatts;

'fireplace' includes any furnace, grate or stove, whether open or closed;

'fixed boiler or industrial plant' means any boiler or industrial plant which is attached to a building or is for the time being fixed to or installed on any land;

'fumes' means any airborne solid matter smaller than dust;

'industrial plant' includes any still, melting pot or other plant used for any industrial or trade purposes, and also any incinerator used for or in connection with any such purposes;

'local authority' means—

(a) in England and Wales, the council of a district or a London borough, the Common Council of the City of London, the Sub-Treasurer of the Inner Temple and the Under Treasurer of the Middle Temple; and

(b) . . .

'owner', in relation to premises—

(a) as respects England and Wales, means the person for the time being receiving the rackrent of the premises, whether on his own account or as agent or trustee for another person, or who would so receive the rackrent if the premises were let at a rackrent; and

(b) . . .

'practicable' means reasonably practicable having regard, amongst other things, to local conditions and circumstances, to the financial implications and to the current state of technical knowledge, and 'practicable means' includes the provision and maintenance of plant and its proper use;

'premises' includes land;

'smoke', includes soot, ash, grit and gritty particles emitted in smoke; and

'vessel' has the same meaning as in the Merchant Shipping Act 1894.

(2) Any reference in this Act to the occupier of a building shall, in relation to any building different parts of which are occupied by different persons, be read as a reference to the occupier or other person in control of the part of the building in which the relevant fireplace is situated.

(3) In this Act any reference to the rate of emission of any substance or any reference which is to be understood as such a reference shall, in relation to any regulations or conditions, be construed as a reference to the quantities of that substance which may be emitted during a period specified in the regulations or conditions.

(4) In this Act, except so far as the context otherwise requires, 'private dwelling' means any building or part of a building used or intended to be used as such, and a building or part of a building is not to be taken for the purposes of this Act to be used or intended to be used otherwise than as a private dwelling by reason that a person who resides or is to reside in it is or is to be required or permitted to reside in it in consequence of his employment or of holding an office.

(5) In considering for the purposes of this Act whether any and, if so, what works are reasonably necessary in order to make suitable provision for heating and cooking in the case of a dwelling or are reasonably necessary in order to enable a building to be used for a purpose without contravention of any of the provisions of this Act, regard shall be had to any difficulty there may be in obtaining, or in obtaining otherwise than at a high price, any fuels which would have to be used but for the execution of the works.

(6) Any furnaces which are in the occupation of the same person and are served by a single chimney shall, for the purposes of sections 5 to 12, 14 and 15, be taken to be one furnace.

Noise and Statutory Nuisance Act 1993
(1993, c. 40)

8   Consent of local authorities to the operation of loudspeakers in streets or roads

(1) A local authority may resolve that Schedule 2 is to apply to its area.

(2) If a local authority does so resolve, Schedule 2 shall come into force in its area on such date as may be specified for that purpose in the resolution, being a date at least one month after the date on which the resolution is passed.

(3) Where a local authority has passed a resolution under this section, the authority shall cause a notice to be published, in two consecutive weeks before the Schedule comes into force in its area, in a local newspaper circulating in the area.

(4) The notice shall—
  (a) state that the resolution has been passed, and
  (b) set out the general effect of Schedule 2 and, in particular, the procedure for applying for a consent under that Schedule.

(5) In this section 'local authority' means—
  (a) in relation to England and Wales—
    (i)   the council of a district,

(ii) the council of a London borough,

(iii) the Common Council of the City of London,

(iv) the Sub-Treasurer of the Inner Temple, or

(v) the Under Treasurer of the Middle Temple, and

(b) . . .

9   Audible intruder alarms

(1) A local authority may, after consulting the chief officer of police, resolve that Schedule 3 is to apply to its area.

(2) If a local authority does so resolve—

(a) Schedule 3 (other than paragraph 4) shall come into force in its area on such date as may be specified for that purpose in the resolution ('the first appointed day'), and

(b) paragraph 4 of Schedule 3 shall come into force in its area, and accordingly paragraphs 2 and 3 of that Schedule shall cease to have effect in its area, on such later date as may be so specified ('the second appointed day').

(3) The first appointed day shall be at least four months after the date on which the resolution is passed.

(4) The second appointed day shall be at least nine months after the first appointed day.

(5) Where a local authority has passed a resolution under this section, the authority shall cause a notice to be published, in two consecutive weeks ending at least three months before the first appointed day, in a local newspaper circulating in its area.

(6) The notice shall—

(a) state that the resolution has been passed,

(b) state the first and second appointed days, and

(c) Set out the general effect of Schedule 3 as it will apply from each of those days.

(7) In this section—

'chief officer of police', in relation to a local authority, means—

(a) the chief officer of police for the police area in which the area of the local authority is situated, or

(b) where part of the local authority's area is situated in one police area and part in another, the chief officer of police for each police area in which a part of the local authority's area is situated;

'local authority' means—

(a) in relation to England and Wales, the council of a district, and

(b) . . .

12   Commencement

(1) Subject to subsection (2), this Act shall come into force at the end of the period of two months beginning with the day on which it is passed.

(2) Section 9 and Schedule 3 shall come into force on such day as the Secretary of State may by order made by statutory instrument appoint; and different days may be so appointed in respect of different areas.

Section 8   SCHEDULE 2

CONSENT TO THE OPERATION OF LOUDSPEAKERS IN STREETS OR ROADS

Local authority consent

1.—(1) Subject to sub-paragraph (2), on an application made by any person, the local authority may consent to the operation in its area of a loudspeaker in contravention of section 62(1) of the 1974 Act.

(2) A consent shall not be given to the operation of a loudspeaker in connection with any election or for the purpose of advertising any entertainment, trade or business.

2.   A consent may be granted subject to such conditions as the local authority considers appropriate.

Procedure

3.   An application for a consent shall be made in writing and shall contain such information as the local authority may reasonably require.

4.—(1) Where an application is duly made to the local authority for a consent the authority shall determine the application and notify the applicant in writing of its decision within the period of twenty-one days beginning with the day on which the application is received by the authority.

(2) In a case where a consent is granted, the notification under sub-paragraph (1) shall specify the conditions, if any, subject to which the consent is granted.

5.   An applicant for a consent shall pay such reasonable fee in respect of his application as the local authority may determine.

Publication of consent

6.   Where the local authority grants a consent, the authority may cause a notice giving details of that consent to be published in a local newspaper circulating in its area.

Interpretation

7.   In this Schedule 'a consent' means a consent under paragraph 1.

Section 9   SCHEDULE 3

AUDIBLE INTRUDER ALARMS

Installation of new alarms

1.—(1) A person who installs an audible intruder alarm on or in any premises shall ensure—
- (a) that the alarm complies with any prescribed requirements, and
- (b) that the local authority is notified within 48 hours of the installation.

(2) A person who without reasonable excuse contravenes sub-paragraph (1) shall be guilty of an offence and liable on summary conviction—
- (a) where the alarm does not comply with any prescribed requirements, to a fine not exceeding level 5 on the standard scale, and
- (b) in any other case, to a fine not exceeding level 2 on the standard scale.

Operation of alarms before second appointed day

2.—(1) A person who is the occupier of any premises when (on or after the first appointed day) an audible intruder alarm is installed on or in the premises shall not permit the alarm to be operated unless paragraph 5 is satisfied.

(2) A person who without reasonable excuse contravenes sub-paragraph (1) shall be guilty of an offence and liable on summary conviction—
- (a) where the alarm does not comply with any prescribed requirements, to a fine not exceeding level 5 on the standard scale, and
- (b) in any other case, to a fine not exceeding level 2 on the standard scale.

3.—(1) A person who (on or after the first appointed day) becomes the occupier of any premises on or in which an audible intruder alarm has been installed, shall not permit the alarm to be operated unless paragraph 5 is satisfied.

(2) A person who without reasonable excuse contravenes sub-paragraph (1) shall be guilty of an offence and liable on summary conviction—

- (a) where the alarm does not comply with any prescribed requirements, to a fine not exceeding level 4 on the standard scale, and
- (b) in any other case, to a fine not exceeding level 2 on the standard scale.

Operation of alarms on or after second appointed day

4.—(1) The occupier of any premises shall not permit any audible intruder alarm installed on or in those premises to be operated unless paragraph 5 is satisfied.

(2) A person who without reasonable excuse contravenes sub-paragraph (1) shall be guilty of an offence and liable on summary conviction—

- (a) where the alarm does not comply with any prescribed requirements, to a fine not exceeding level 5 on the standard scale, and
- (b) in any other case, to a fine not exceeding level 2 on the standard scale.

Requirements for operation of alarms

5.—(1) This paragraph is satisfied if—

- (a) the alarm complies with any prescribed requirements,
- (b) the police have been notified in writing of the names, addresses and telephone numbers of the current key-holders, and
- (c) the local authority has been informed of the address of the police station to which notification has been given under paragraph (b).

(2) Notification under sub-paragraph (1)(b) may be given to the police at any police station in the local authority's area.

Entry to premises

6.—(1) Where—

- (a) an intruder alarm installed on or in any premises is operating audibly more than one hour after it was activated, and
- (b) the audible operation of the alarm is such as to give persons living or working in the vicinity of the premises reasonable cause for annoyance,

an officer of the local authority who has been authorised (whether generally or specially) for that purpose may, on production (if so required) of his authority, enter the premises to turn off the alarm.

(2) An officer may not enter premises by force under this paragraph.

7.—(1) If, on an application made by an officer of the local authority who has been authorised (whether generally or specially) for that purpose, a justice of the peace is satisfied—

- (a) that an intruder alarm installed on or in any premises is operating audibly more than one hour after it was activated, and
- (b) that the audible operation of the alarm is such as to give persons living or working in the vicinity of the premises reasonable cause for annoyance,
- (c) where notification of any current key-holders has been given in accordance with paragraph 5(1)(b), that the officer has taken steps to obtain access to the premises with their assistance, and
- (d) that the officer has been unable to obtain access to the premises without the use of force,

the justice may issue a warrant authorising the officer to enter the premises, if need be by force.

(2) Before applying for such a warrant, an officer shall leave a notice at the premises stating—

(a) that the audible operation of the alarm is such as to give persons living or working in the vicinity reasonable cause for annoyance, and

(b) that an application is to be made to a justice of the peace for a warrant authorising the officer to enter the premises and turn off the alarm.

(3) An officer shall not enter premises by virtue of this paragraph unless he is accompanied by a constable.

(4) A warrant under this paragraph shall continue in force until the alarm has been turned off and the officer has complied with paragraph 10.

8.   An officer who enters premises by virtue of paragraph 6 or 7 may take with him such other persons and such equipment as may be necessary to turn off the alarm.

9.   A person who enters premises by virtue of paragraph 6, 7 or 8 shall not cause more damage or disturbance than is necessary.

10.   An officer who has entered premises by virtue of paragraph 6 or 7 which are unoccupied or from which the occupier is temporarily absent shall—

(a) after the alarm has been turned off, re-set it if reasonably practicable,

(b) leave a notice at the premises stating what action has been taken on the premises under this Schedule, and

(c) leave the premises, so far as reasonably practicable, as effectually secured against trespassers as he found them.

Recovery of expenses

11.   Where any premises are entered by virtue of paragraph 6 or 7 in a case where the occupier of those premises has committed an offence under paragraph 2, 3 or 4, any expenses reasonably incurred by the local authority in connection with the entry, turning off the alarm or complying with paragraph 10 may be recovered by the authority from that occupier.

Protection from personal liability

12.   Nothing done by, or by a member of, a local authority or by an officer of or another person authorised by a local authority shall, if done in good faith for the purposes of this Schedule, subject them or any of them personally to any action, liability, claim or demand whatsoever, other than any liability under section 19 or 20 of the Local Government Finance Act 1982 (powers of district auditor and court).

Interpretation

13.—(1) In this Schedule references to the first appointed day or the second appointed day are to be read in accordance with section 9(2).

(2) In this Schedule—

. . .

'key-holders', in relation to an alarm, means—

(a) two persons, other than the occupier of the premises on or in which the alarm is installed, each of whom holds keys sufficient to obtain access to those premises, or

(b) a company which holds keys sufficient to obtain access to those premises, from which those keys can be obtained at any time and the business of which consists of or includes the service of holding keys for occupiers of premises;

'occupier'—

(a) in relation to premises that are unoccupied, means any person entitled to occupy the premises, and

(b) in relation to premises comprising a building that is being erected, constructed, altered, improved, maintained, cleaned or repaired, does not include a person whose occupancy—

(i) is connected with the erection, construction, alteration, improvement, maintenance, cleaning or repair, and

(ii) is by virtue of a licence granted for less than four weeks;

'prescribed' means prescribed in regulations made by the Secretary of State for the purposes of this Schedule.

(3) The Secretary of State's power to make such regulations shall be exercisable by statutory instrument, and an instrument containing such regulations shall be subject to annulment in pursuance of a resolution of either House of Parliament.

(4) Such regulations may make different provision for different cases, circumstances or areas.

(5) Nothing in this Schedule applies to an audible intruder alarm installed on or in a vehicle.

Environment Act 1995
(1995, c. 25)

PART I   THE ENVIRONMENT AGENCY AND THE SCOTTISH ENVIRONMENT PROTECTION AGENCY

CHAPTER I   THE ENVIRONMENT AGENCY

Establishment of the Agency

1   The Environment Agency

(1) There shall be a body corporate to be known as the Environment Agency or, in Welsh, Asiantaeth yr Amgylchedd (in this Act referred to as 'the Agency'), for the purpose of carrying out the functions transferred or assigned to it by or under this Act.

(2) The Agency shall consist of not less than eight nor more than fifteen members of whom—

(a) three shall be appointed by the Minister; and

(b) the others shall be appointed by the Secretary of State.

(3) The Secretary of State shall designate—

(a) one of the members as the chairman of the Agency, and

(b) another of them as the deputy chairman of the Agency.

(4) In appointing a person to be a member of the Agency, the Secretary of State or, as the case may be, the Minister shall have regard to the desirability of appointing a person who has experience of, and has shown capacity in, some matter relevant to the functions of the Agency.

(5) Subject to the provisions of section 36 below, the Agency shall not be regarded—

(a) as the servant or agent of the Crown, or as enjoying any status, immunity or privilege of the Crown; or

(b) by virtue of any connection with the Crown, as exempt from any tax, duty, rate, levy or other charge whatsoever, whether general or local;

and the Agency's property shall not be regarded as property of, or property held on behalf of, the Crown.

(6) . . .

Transfer of functions, property etc. to the Agency

2   Transfer of functions to the Agency

(1) On the transfer date there shall by virtue of this section be transferred to the Agency—

(a) the functions of the National Rivers Authority, that is to say—

(i) its functions under or by virtue of Part II (water resources management) of the Water Resources Act 1991 (in this Part referred to as 'the 1991 Act');

(ii) its functions under or by virtue of Part III of that Act (control of pollution of water resources);

(iii) its functions under or by virtue of Part IV of that Act (flood defence) and the Land Drainage Act 1991 and the functions transferred to the Authority by virtue of section 136(8) of the Water Act 1989 and paragraph 1(3) of Schedule 15 to that Act (transfer of land drainage functions under local statutory provisions and subordinate legislation);

(iv) its functions under or by virtue of Part VII of the 1991 Act (land and works powers);

(v) its functions under or by virtue of the Diseases of Fish Act 1937, the Sea Fisheries Regulation Act 1966, the Salmon and Freshwater Fisheries Act 1975, Part V of the 1991 Act or any other enactment relating to fisheries;

(vi) the functions as a navigation authority, harbour authority or conservancy authority which were transferred to the Authority by virtue of Chapter V of Part III of the Water Act 1989 or paragraph 23(3) of Schedule 13 to that Act or which have been transferred to the Authority by any order or agreement under Schedule 2 to the 1991 Act;

(vii) its functions under Schedule 2 to the 1991 Act;

(viiii) the functions assigned to the Authority by or under any other enactment, apart from this Act;

(b) the functions of waste regulation authorities, that is to say, the functions conferred or imposed on them by or under—

 (i) the Control of Pollution (Amendment) Act 1989, or

 (ii) Part II of the Environmental Protection Act 1990 (in this Part referred to as 'the 1990 Act'),

or assigned to them by or under any other enactment, apart from this Act;

(c) the functions of disposal authorities under or by virtue of the waste regulation provisions of the Control of Pollution Act 1974;

(d) the functions of the chief inspector for England and Wales constituted under section 16(3) of the 1990 Act, that is to say, the functions conferred or imposed on him by or under Part I of that Act or assigned to him by or under any other enactment, apart from this Act;

(e) the functions of the chief inspector for England and Wales appointed under section 4(2)(a) of the Radioactive Substances Act 1993, that is to say, the functions conferred or imposed on him by or under that Act or assigned to him by or under any other enactment, apart from this Act;

(f) the functions conferred or imposed by or under the Alkali, &c, Works Regulation Act 1906 (in this section referred to as 'the 1906 Act') on the chief, or any other, inspector (within the meaning of that Act), so far as exercisable in relation to England and Wales;

(g) so far as exercisable in relation to England and Wales, the functions in relation to improvement notices and prohibition notices under Part I of the Health and Safety at Work etc. Act 1974 (in this section referred to as 'the 1974 Act') of inspectors appointed under section 19 of that Act by the Secretary of State in his capacity as the enforcing authority responsible in relation to England and Wales for the enforcement of the 1906 Act and section 5 of the 1974 Act; and

(h) the functions of the Secretary of State specified in subsection (2) below.

(2) The functions of the Secretary of State mentioned in subsection (1)(h) above are the following, that is to say—

(a) so far as exercisable in relation to England and Wales, his functions under section 30(1) of the Radioactive Substances Act 1993 (power to dispose of radioactive waste);

(b) his functions under Chapter III of Part IV of the Water Industry Act 1991 in relation to special category effluent, within the meaning of that Chapter, other than any function of making regulations or of making orders under section 139 of that Act;

(c) so far as exercisable in relation to England and Wales, the functions conferred or imposed on him by virtue of his being, for the purposes of Part I of the 1974 Act, the authority which is by any of the relevant statutory provisions made responsible for the enforcement of the 1906 Act and section 5 of the 1974 Act;

(d) so far as exercisable in relation to England and Wales, his functions under, or under regulations made by virtue of, section 9 of the 1906 Act (registration of works), other than any functions of his as an appellate authority or any function of making regulations;

(e) so far as exercisable in relation to England and Wales, his functions under regulations 7(1) and 8(2) of, and paragraph 2(2)(c) of Schedule 2 to, the Sludge (Use in Agriculture) Regulations 1989 (which relate to the provision of information and the testing of soil).

(3) The National Rivers Authority and the London Waste Regulation Authority are hereby abolished.

3   Transfer of property, rights and liabilities to the Agency

(1) On the transfer date—

(a) the property, rights and liabilities—

(i) of the National Rivers Authority, and

(ii) of the London Waste Regulation Authority,

shall, by virtue of this paragraph, be transferred to and vested in the Agency;

(b) any property, rights or liabilities which are the subject of—

(i) a scheme made under the following provisions of this section by the Secretary of State, or

(ii) a scheme made under those provisions by a body which is a waste regulation authority and approved (with or without modifications) under those provisions by the Secretary of State,

shall be transferred to and vested in the Agency by and in accordance with the scheme.

(2) The Secretary of State may, before the transfer date, make a scheme for the transfer to the Agency of such of—

(a) his property, rights and liabilities, or

(b) the property, rights and liabilities of any of the inspectors or chief inspectors mentioned in subsection (1) of section 2 above,

as appear to the Secretary of State appropriate to be so transferred in consequence of the transfer of any functions to the Agency by virtue of any of paragraphs (d) to (h) of that subsection.

(3) It shall be the duty of every body which is a waste regulation authority, other than the London Waste Regulation Authority—

(a) to make a scheme, after consultation with the Agency, for the transfer to the Agency of such of the body's property, rights and liabilities as appear to the body appropriate to be so transferred in consequence of the transfer of any functions to the Agency by virtue of section 2(1)(b) or (c) above; and

(b) to submit that scheme to the Secretary of State for his approval before such date as he may direct.

(4) Any body preparing a scheme in pursuance of subsection (3) above shall take into account any guidance given by the Secretary of State as to the provisions which he regards as appropriate for inclusion in the scheme.

(5) Where a scheme under subsection (3) above is submitted to the Secretary of State, he may—

(a) approve the scheme;

(b) approve the scheme subject to such modifications as he considers appropriate; or

(c) reject the scheme; but the power conferred on the Secretary of State by paragraph (b) above shall only be exercisable after consultation with the body which submitted the scheme to him and with the Agency.

(6) The Secretary of State may, in the case of any body which is required to make a scheme under subsection (3) above, himself make a scheme for the transfer to the Agency of such of the body's property, rights or liabilities as appear to him appropriate to be so transferred in consequence of the transfer of any functions to the Agency by virtue of section 2(l)(b) or (c) above, if—

(a) the body fails to submit a scheme under subsection (3) above to him for approval before the due date; or

(b) the Secretary of State rejects a scheme under that subsection submitted to him by that body;

but nothing in this subsection shall prevent the Secretary of State from approving any scheme which may be submitted to him after the due date.

(7) The Secretary of State may, at any time before the transfer date, modify any scheme made or approved by him under this section but only after consultation with the Agency and, in the case of a scheme which was approved by him (with or without modifications), after consultation with the body which submitted the scheme to him for approval.

(8) . . .

4 Principal aim and objectives of the Agency

(1) It shall be the principal aim of the Agency (subject to and in accordance with the provisions of this Act or any other enactment and taking into account any likely costs) in discharging its functions so to protect or enhance the environment, taken as a whole, as to make the contribution towards attaining the objective of achieving sustainable development mentioned in subsection (3) below.

(2) The Ministers shall from time to time give guidance to the Agency with respect to objectives which they consider it appropriate for the Agency to pursue in the discharge of its functions.

(3) The guidance given under subsection (2) above must include guidance with respect to the contribution which, having regard to the Agency's responsibilities and resources, the Ministers consider it appropriate for the Agency to make, by the discharge of its functions, towards attaining the objective of achieving sustainable development.

(4) In discharging its functions, the Agency shall have regard to guidance given under this section.

(5) The power to give guidance to the Agency under this section shall only be exercisable after consultation with the Agency and such other bodies or persons as the Ministers consider it appropriate to consult in relation to the guidance in question.

(6) A draft of any guidance proposed to be given under this section shall be laid before each House of Parliament and the guidance shall not be given until after the period of 40 days beginning with the day on which the draft was so laid or, if the draft is laid on different days, the later of the two days.

(7) If, within the period mentioned in subsection (6) above, either House resolves that the guidance, the draft of which was laid before it, should not be given, the Ministers shall not give that guidance.

(8) In reckoning any period of 40 days for the purposes of subsection (6) or (7) above, no account shall be taken of any time during which Parliament is dissolved or prorogued or during which both Houses are adjourned for more than four days.

(9) The Ministers shall arrange for any guidance given under this section to be published in such manner as they consider appropriate.

5   General functions with respect to pollution control

(1) The Agency's pollution control powers shall be exercisable for the purpose of preventing or minimising, or remedying or mitigating the effects of, pollution of the environment.

(2) The Agency shall, for the purpose—
- (a) of facilitating the carrying out of its pollution control functions, or
- (b) of enabling it to form an opinion of the general state of pollution of the environment,

compile information relating to such pollution (whether the information is acquired by the Agency carrying out observations or is obtained in any other way).

(3) If required by either of the Ministers to do so, the Agency shall—
- (a) carry out assessments (whether generally or for such particular purpose as may be specified in the requirement) of the effect, or likely effect, on the environment of existing or potential levels of pollution of the environment and report its findings to that Minister; or
- (b) prepare and send to that Minister a report identifying—
  - (i) the options which the Agency considers to be available for preventing or minimising, or remedying or mitigating the effects of, pollution of the environment, whether generally or in cases or circumstances specified in the requirement; and
  - (ii) the costs and benefits of such options as are identified by the Agency pursuant to sub-paragraph (i) above.

(4) The Agency shall follow developments in technology and techniques for preventing or minimising, or remedying or mitigating the effects of, pollution of the environment.

(5) In this section, 'pollution control powers' and 'pollution control functions', in relation to the Agency, mean respectively its powers or its functions under or by virtue of the following enactments, that is to say—
- (a) the Alkali, &c, Works Regulation Act 1906;
- (b) Part I of the Health and Safety at Work etc. Act 1974;
- (c) Part I of the Control of Pollution Act 1974;
- (d) the Control of Pollution (Amendment) Act 1989;
- (e) Parts I, II and IIA of the 1990 Act (integrated pollution control etc, waste on land and contaminated land);
- (f) Chapter III of Part IV of the Water Industry Act 1991 (special category effluent);
- (g) Part III and sections 161 to 161D of the 1991 Act (control of pollution of water resources);
- (h) the Radioactive Substances Act 1993;
- (i) regulations under section 2 of the Pollution Prevention and Control Act 1999;]
- (j) regulations made by virtue of section 2(2) of the European Communities Act 1972, to the extent that the regulations relate to pollution.

6   General provisions with respect to water

(1) It shall be the duty of the Agency, to such extent as it considers desirable, generally to promote—
- (a) the conservation and enhancement of the natural beauty and amenity of inland and coastal waters and of land associated with such waters;

(b) the conservation of flora and fauna which are dependent on an aquatic environment; and

(c) the use of such waters and land for recreational purposes;

and it shall be the duty of the Agency, in determining what steps to take in performance of the duty imposed by virtue of paragraph (c) above, to take into account the needs of persons who are chronically sick or disabled.

This subsection is without prejudice to the duties of the Agency under section 7 below.

(2) It shall be the duty of the Agency to take all such action as it may from time to time consider, in accordance with any directions given under section 38 below, to be necessary or expedient for the purpose—

(a) of conserving, redistributing or otherwise augmenting water resources in England and Wales; and

(b) of securing the proper use of water resources in England and Wales;

but nothing in this subsection shall be construed as relieving any water undertaker of the obligation to develop water resources for the purpose of performing any duty imposed on it by virtue of section 37 of the Water Industry Act 1991 (general duty to maintain water supply system).

(3) The provisions of the 1991 Act relating to the functions of the Agency under Chapter II of Part II of that Act and the related water resources provisions so far as they relate to other functions of the Agency shall not apply to so much of any inland waters as—

(a) are part of the River Tweed;

(b) are part of the River Esk or River Sark at a point where either of the banks of the river is in Scotland; or

(c) are part of any tributary stream of the River Esk or the River Sark at a point where either of the banks of the tributary stream is in Scotland.

(4) Subject to section 106 of the 1991 Act (obligation to carry out flood defence functions through committees), the Agency shall in relation to England and Wales exercise a general supervision over all matters relating to flood defence.

(5) The Agency's flood defence functions shall extend to the territorial sea adjacent to England and Wales in so far as—

(a) the area of any regional flood defence committee includes any area of that territorial sea; or

(b) section 165(2) or (3) of the 1991 Act (drainage works for the purpose of defence against sea water or tidal water, and works etc to secure an adequate outfall for a main river) provides for the exercise of any power in the territorial sea.

(6) It shall be the duty of the Agency to maintain, improve and develop salmon fisheries, trout fisheries, freshwater fisheries and eel fisheries.

(7) The area in respect of which the Agency shall carry out its functions relating to fisheries shall be the whole of England and Wales, together with—

(a) such part of the territorial sea adjacent to England and Wales as extends for six miles from the baselines from which the breadth of that sea is measured, and

(b) in the case of—

(i) the Diseases of Fish Act 1937,

(ii) the Salmon and Freshwater Fisheries Act 1975,

(iii) Part V of the 1991 Act (general control of fisheries), and

(iv) subsection (6) above,

so much of the River Esk, with its banks and tributary streams up to their source, as is situated in Scotland, and

(c) in the case of sections 31 to 34 and 36(2) of the Salmon and Freshwater Fisheries Act 1975 as applied by section 39(1B) of that Act, so much of the catchment area of the River Esk as is situated in Scotland, but, in the case of the enactments specified in paragraph (b) above, excluding the River Tweed.

(8) In this section—

'miles' means international nautical miles of 1,852 metres;

'the related water resources provisions' has the same meaning as it has in the 1991 Act;

'the River Tweed' means 'the river' within the meaning of the Tweed Fisheries Amendment Act 1859 as amended by byelaws.

7   General environmental and recreational duties

(1) It shall be the duty of each of the Ministers and of the Agency, in formulating or considering—

  (a) any proposals relating to any functions of the Agency other than its pollution control functions, so far as may be consistent—

    (i) with the purposes of any enactment relating to the functions of the Agency,

    (ii) in the case of each of the Ministers, with the objective of achieving sustainable development,

    (iii) in the case of the Agency, with any guidance under section 4 above,

    (iv) in the case of the Secretary of State, with his duties under section 2 of the Water Industry Act 1991,

so to exercise any power conferred on him or it with respect to the proposals as to further the conservation and enhancement of natural beauty and the conservation of flora, fauna and geological or physiographical features of special interest;

  (b) any proposals relating to pollution control functions of the Agency, to have regard to the desirability of conserving and enhancing natural beauty and of conserving flora, fauna and geological or physiographical features of special interest;

  (c) any proposal relating to any functions of the Agency—

    (i) to have regard to the desirability of protecting and conserving buildings, sites and objects of archaeological, architectural, engineering or historic interest;

    (ii) to take into account any effect which the proposals would have on the beauty or amenity of any rural or urban area or on any such flora, fauna, features, buildings, sites or objects; and

    (iii) to have regard to any effect which the proposals would have on the economic and social well-being of local communities in rural areas.

(2) Subject to subsection (1) above, it shall be the duty of each of the Ministers and of the Agency, in formulating or considering any proposals relating to any functions of the Agency,—

  (a) to have regard to the desirability of preserving for the public any freedom of access to areas of woodland, mountains, moor, heath, down, cliff or foreshore and other places of natural beauty;

  (b) to have regard to the desirability of maintaining the availability to the public of any facility for visiting or inspecting any building, site or object of archaeological, architectural, engineering or historic interest; and

  (c) to take into account any effect which the proposals would have on any such freedom of access or on the availability of any such facility.

(3) Subsections (1) and (2) above shall apply so as to impose duties on the Agency in relation to—

  (a) any proposals relating to the functions of a water undertaker or sewerage undertaker,

  (b) any proposals relating to the management, by the company holding an appointment as such an undertaker, of any land for the time being held by that company for any purpose whatever (whether or not connected with the carrying out of the functions of a water undertaker or sewerage undertaker), and

(c) any proposal which by virtue of section 156(7) of the Water Industry Act 1991 (disposals of protected land) falls to be treated for the purposes of section 3 of that Act as a proposal relating to the functions of a water undertaker or sewerage undertaker,

as they apply in relation to proposals relating to the Agency's own functions, other than its pollution control functions.

(4) Subject to obtaining the consent of any navigation authority, harbour authority or conservancy authority before doing anything which causes obstruction of, or other interference with, navigation which is subject to the control of that authority, it shall be the duty of the Agency to take such steps as are—

(a) reasonably practicable, and

(b) consistent with the purposes of the enactments relating to the functions of the Agency,

for securing, so long as the Agency has rights to the use of water or land associated with water, that those rights are exercised so as to ensure that the water or land is made available for recreational purposes and is so made available in the best manner.

(5) It shall be the duty of the Agency, in determining what steps to take in performance of any duty imposed by virtue of subsection (4) above, to take into account the needs of persons who are chronically sick or disabled.

(6) Nothing in this section, the following provisions of this Act or the 1991 Act shall require recreational facilities made available by the Agency to be made available free of charge.

(7) In this section—

'building' includes structure;

'pollution control functions', in relation to the Agency, has the same meaning as in section 5 above.

8   Environmental duties with respect to sites of special interest

(1) Where the Nature Conservancy Council for England or the Countryside Council for Wales is of the opinion that any area of land in England or, as the case may be, in Wales—

(a) is of special interest by reason of its flora, fauna or geological or physiographical features, and

(b) may at any time be affected by schemes, works, operations or activities of the Agency or by an authorisation given by the Agency,

that Council shall notify the fact that the land is of special interest for that reason to the Agency.

(2) Where a National Park authority or the Broads Authority is of the opinion that any area of land in a National Park or in the Broads—

(a) is land in relation to which the matters for the purposes of which sections 6(1) and 7 above (other than section 7(1)(c)(iii) above) have effect are of particular importance, and

(b) may at any time be affected by schemes, works, operations or activities of the Agency or by an authorisation given by the Agency,

the National Park authority or Broads Authority shall notify the Agency of the fact that the land is such land, and of the reasons why those matters are of particular importance in relation to the land.

(3) Where the Agency has received a notification under subsection (1) or (2) above with respect to any land, it shall consult the notifying body before carrying out or authorising any works, operations or activities which appear to the Agency to be likely—

(a) to destroy or damage any of the flora, fauna, or geological or physiographical features by reason of which the land is of special interest; or

(b) significantly to prejudice anything the importance of which is one of the reasons why the matters mentioned in subsection (2) above are of particular importance in relation to that land.

(4) Subsection (3) above shall not apply in relation to anything done in an emergency where particulars of what is done and of the emergency are notified to the Nature Conservancy Council for England, the Countryside Council for Wales, the National Park authority in question or, as the case may be, the Broads Authority as soon as practicable after that thing is done.

(5) In this section—

'authorisation' includes any consent or licence;

'the Broads' has the same meaning as in the Norfolk and Suffolk Broads Act 1988; and

'National Park authority', [. . .] means a National Park authority established under section 60 below which has become the local planning authority for the National Park in question.

(6) [. . .]

9   Codes of practice with respect to environmental and recreational duties

(1) Each of the Ministers shall have power by order to approve any code of practice issued (whether by him or by another person) for the purpose of—

(a) giving practical guidance to the agency with respect to any of the matters for the purposes of which sections 6(1), 7 and 8 above have effect, and

(b) promoting what appear to him to be desirable practices by the Agency with respect to those matters,

and may at any time by such an order approve a modification of such a code or withdraw his approval of such a code or modification.

(2) In discharging its duties under section 6(1), 7 or 8 above, the Agency shall have regard to any code of practice, and any modifications of a code of practice, for the time being approved under this section.

(3) Neither of the Ministers shall make an order under this section unless he has first consulted—

(a) the Agency;

(b) the Countryside Commission, the Nature Conservancy Council for England and the Countryside Council for Wales;

(c) the Historic Buildings and Monuments Commission for England;

(d) the Sports Council and the Sports Council for Wales; and

(e) such other persons as he considers it appropriate to consult.

(4) The power of each of the Ministers to make an order under this section shall be exercisable by statutory instrument; and any statutory instrument containing such an order shall be subject to annulment in pursuance of a resolution of either House of Parliament.

10   Incidental functions of the Agency

(1) This section has effect—

(a) for the purposes of section 35(1) below, as it applies in relation to the Agency; and

(b) for the construction of any other enactment which, by reference to the functions of the Agency, confers any power on or in relation to the Agency;

and any reference in this section to 'the relevant purposes' is a reference to the purposes described in paragraphs (a) and (b) above.

(2) For the relevant purposes, the functions of the Agency shall be taken to include the protection against pollution of—

(a) any waters, whether on the surface or underground, which belong to the Agency or any water undertaker or from which the Agency or any water undertaker is authorised to take water;

(b) without prejudice to paragraph (a) above, any reservoir which belongs to or is operated by the Agency or any water undertaker or which the Agency or any water

undertaker is proposing to acquire or construct for the purpose of being so operated; and

(c) any underground strata from which the Agency or any water undertaker is for the time being authorised to abstract water in pursuance of a licence under Chapter II of Part II of the 1991 Act (abstraction and impounding).

(3) For the relevant purposes, the functions of the Agency shall be taken to include joining with or acting on behalf of one or more relevant undertakers for the purpose of carrying out any works or acquiring any land which at least one of the undertakers with which it joins, or on whose behalf it acts, is authorised to carry out or acquire for the purposes of—

(a) any function of that undertaker under any enactment; or

(b) any function which is taken to be a function of that undertaker for the purposes to which section 217 of the Water Industry Act 1991 applies.

(4) For the relevant purposes, the functions of the Agency shall be taken to include the provision of supplies of water in bulk, whether or not such supplies are provided for the purposes of, or in connection with, the carrying out of any other function of the Agency.

(5) For the relevant purposes, the functions of the Agency shall be taken to include the provision of houses and other buildings for the use of persons employed by the Agency and the provision of recreation grounds for persons so employed.

(6) In this section—

'relevant undertaker' means a water undertaker or sewerage undertaker; and

'supply of water in bulk' means a supply of water for distribution by a water undertaker taking the supply.

Advisory committees

11   Advisory committee for Wales

(1) The Secretary of State shall establish and maintain a committee for advising him with respect to matters affecting, or otherwise connected with, the carrying out in Wales of the Agency's functions.

(2) The committee shall consist of such persons as may from time to time be appointed by the Secretary of State.

(3) The committee shall meet at least once a year.

(4) The Secretary of State may pay to the members of the committee such sums by way of reimbursement (whether in whole or in part) for loss of remuneration, for travelling expenses and for other out-of-pocket expenses as he may determine.

12   Environment protection advisory committees

(1) It shall be the duty of the Agency—

(a) to establish and maintain advisory committees, to be known as Environment Protection Advisory Committees, for the different regions of England and Wales;

(b) to consult the advisory committee for any region as to any proposals of the Agency relating generally to the manner in which the Agency carries out its functions in that region; and

(c) to consider any representations made to it by the advisory committee for any region (whether in response to consultation under paragraph (b) above or otherwise) as to the manner in which the Agency carries out its functions in that region.

(2) The advisory committee for any region shall consist of—

(a) a chairman appointed by the Secretary of State; and

(b) such other members as the Agency may appoint in accordance with the provisions of the approved membership scheme for that region.

(3) In appointing the chairman of any advisory committee, the Secretary of State shall

have regard to the desirability of appointing a person who has experience of, and has shown capacity in, some matter relevant to the functions of the committee.

(4) The members of advisory committees appointed by virtue of subsection (2)(b) above—

(a) must not be members of the Agency; but

(b) must be persons who appear to the Agency to have a significant interest in matters likely to be affected by the manner in which the Agency carries out any of its functions in the region of the advisory committee in question.

(5) The duty imposed by subsection (1)(a) above to establish and maintain advisory committees is a duty to establish and maintain an advisory committee for each area which the Agency considers it appropriate for the time being to regard as a region of England and Wales for the purposes of this section.

(6) It shall be the duty of the Agency, in determining the regions for which advisory committees are established and maintained under this section, to ensure that one of those regions consists wholly or mainly of, or of most of, Wales.

(7) For the purposes of this section, functions of the Agency which are carried out in any area of Scotland, or of the territorial sea which is adjacent to any region for which an advisory committee is maintained, shall be regarded as carried out in that region.

(8) Schedule 3 to this Act shall have effect with respect to advisory committees.

(9) In this section—

'advisory committee' means an advisory committee under this section;

'approved membership scheme' means a scheme, as in force for the time being, prepared by the Agency and approved (with or without modification) by the Secretary of State under Schedule 3 to this Act which makes provision with respect to the membership of the advisory committee for a region.

13 Regional and local fisheries advisory committees

(1) It shall be the duty of the Agency—

(a) to establish and maintain advisory committees of persons who are not members of the Agency but appear to it to be interested in salmon fisheries, trout fisheries, freshwater fisheries or eel fisheries in the different parts of the controlled area; and

(a) to consult those committees as to the manner in which the Agency is to perform its duty under section 6(6) above.

(2) If the Agency, with the consent of the Ministers, so determines, it shall also be under a duty to consult those committees, or such of them as may be specified or described in the determination, as to—

(a) the manner in which it is to perform its duties under or by virtue of such of the enactments relating to recreation, conservation or navigation as may be the subject of the determination, or

(b) such matters relating to recreation, conservation or navigation as may be the subject of the determination.

(3) Where, by virtue of subsection (2) above, the Agency is under a duty to consult those committees or any of them, there may be included among the members of the committees in question persons who are not members of the Agency but who appear to it to be interested in matters—

(a) likely to be affected by the manner in which it performs the duties to which the determination in question relates, or

(b) which are the subject of the determination, if the Ministers consent to the inclusion of persons of that description.

(4) The duty to establish and maintain advisory committees imposed by subsection (1) above is a duty to establish and maintain—

(a) a regional advisory committee for each such region of the controlled area as the Agency considers it appropriate for the time being to regard as a region of that area for the purposes of this section; and

(b) such local advisory committees as the Agency considers necessary to represent—

(i)   the interests referred to in subsection (1)(a) above, and

(ii) where persons may be appointed members of those committees by virtue of subsection (3) above by reference to any such interests as are mentioned in that subsection, the interests in question,

in the different parts of each such region.

(5) It shall be the duty of the Agency in determining the regions for which regional advisory committees are established and maintained under this section to ensure that one of those regions consists (apart from territorial waters) wholly or mainly of, or of most of, Wales.

(6) In addition to any members appointed under the foregoing provisions of this section, there shall, in the case of each regional advisory committee established and maintained under this section, also be a chairman appointed—

(a) by the Secretary of State, in the case of the committee established and maintained for the region described in subsection (5) above; or

(b) by the Minister, in any other case.

(7) There shall be paid by the Agency—

(a) to the chairman of any regional or local advisory committee established and maintained under this section such remuneration and such travelling and other allowances; and

(b) to any other members of that committee such sums by way of reimbursement (whether in whole or in part) for loss of remuneration, for travelling expenses or for any other out-of-pocket expenses,

as may be determined by one of the Ministers.

(8) In this section 'the controlled area' means the area specified in section 6(7) above in respect of which the Agency carries out functions under section 6(6) above and Part V of the 1991 Act.

Flood defence committees

14   Regional flood defence committees

(1) There shall be committees, known as regional flood defence committees, for the purpose of carrying out the functions which fall to be carried out by such committees by virtue of this Act and the 1991 Act.

(2) Subject to Schedule 4 to this Act (which makes provision for the alteration of the boundaries of and the amalgamation of the areas of regional flood defence committees)—

(a) there shall be a regional flood defence committee for each of the areas for which there was an old committee immediately before the transfer date; but

(b) where under section 165(2) or (3) of the 1991 Act any function of the Agency falls to be carried out at a place beyond the seaward boundaries of the area of any regional flood defence committee, that place shall be assumed for the purposes of this Act and the 1991 Act to be within the area of the regional flood defence committee to whose area the area of sea where that place is situated is adjacent.

(3) The Agency shall maintain a principal office for the area of each regional flood defence committee.

(4) In this section 'old committee' means a regional flood defence committee for the purposes of section 9 of the 1991 Act.

CHAPTER III   MISCELLANEOUS, GENERAL AND SUPPLEMENTAL PROVISIONS
RELATING TO THE NEW AGENCIES

Additional general powers and duties

37   Incidental general functions

(1) Each new Agency (that is to say, in this Part, the Agency or SEPA)—

    (a) may do anything which, in its opinion, is calculated to facilitate, or is conducive or incidental to, the carrying out of its functions; and

    (b) without prejudice to the generality of that power, may, for the purposes of, or in connection with, the carrying out of those functions, acquire and dispose of land and other property and carry out such engineering or building operations as it considers appropriate;

and the Agency may institute criminal proceedings in England and Wales.

(2) It shall be the duty of each new Agency to provide the Secretary of State or the Minister with such advice and assistance as he may request.

(3) Subject to subsection (4) below, each new Agency may provide for any person, whether in or outside the United Kingdom, advice or assistance, including training facilities, as respects any matter in which that new Agency has skill or experience.

(4) Without prejudice to any power of either new Agency apart from subsection (3) above to provide advice or assistance of the kind mentioned in that subsection, the power conferred by that subsection shall not be exercised in a case where the person for whom the advice or assistance is provided is outside the United Kingdom, except with the consent in writing of the appropriate Minister which consent may be given subject to such conditions as the Minister giving it thinks fit.

(5) Each new Agency—

    (a) shall make arrangements for the carrying out of research and related activities (whether by itself or by others) in respect of matters to which its functions relate; and

    (b) may make the results of any such research or related activities available to any person in return for payment of such fee as it considers appropriate.

(6) Subsection (5) above shall not be taken as preventing a new Agency from making the results of any research available to the public free of charge whenever it considers it appropriate to do so.

(7) Each new Agency may by agreement with any person charge that person a fee in respect of work done, or services or facilities provided, as a result of a request made by him for advice or assistance, whether of a general or specific character, in connection with any matter involving or relating to environmental licences.

(8) Subsection (7) above—

    (a) is without prejudice to the generality of the powers of either new Agency to make charges; but

    (b) is subject to any such express provision with respect to charging by the new Agency in question as is contained in the other provisions of this Part or in any other enactment.

(9) In this section 'engineering or building operations', without prejudice to the generality of that expression, includes—

    (a) the construction, alteration, improvement, maintenance or demolition of any building or structure or of any reservoir, watercourse, dam, weir, well, borehole or other works; and

    (b) the installation, modification or removal of any machinery or apparatus.

38   Delegation of functions by Ministers etc. to the new Agencies

(1) Agreements may be made between—

    (a) any Minister of the Crown, and

(b) a new Agency, authorising the new Agency (or any of its employees) to exercise on behalf of that Minister, with or without payment, any eligible function of his.

(2) An agreement under subsection (1) above shall not authorise the new Agency (or any of its employees) to exercise on behalf of a Minister of the Crown any function which consists of a power to make regulations or other instruments of a legislative character or a power to fix fees or charges.

(3) An agreement under this section may provide for any eligible function to which it relates to be exercisable by the new Agency in question (or any of its employees)—

(a) either wholly or to such extent as may be specified in the agreement;

(b) either generally or in such cases or areas as may be so specified; or

(c) either unconditionally or subject to the fulfilment of such conditions as may be so specified.

(4) Subsection (5) below applies where, by virtue of an agreement under this section, a new Agency (or any of its employees) is authorised to exercise any function of a Minister of the Crown.

(5) Subject to subsection (6) below, anything done or omitted to be done by the new Agency (or an employee of the new Agency) in, or in connection with, the exercise or purported exercise of the function shall be treated for all purposes as done or omitted to be done by that Minister in his capacity as such.

(6) Subsection (5) above shall not apply—

(a) for the purposes of so much of any agreement made between that Minister and the new Agency as relates to the exercise of the function; or

(b) for the purposes of any criminal proceedings brought in respect of anything done or omitted to be done as mentioned in that subsection.

(7) An agreement under this section shall not prevent a Minister of the Crown exercising any function to which the agreement relates.

(8) Where a Minister of the Crown has power to include, in any arrangements which he makes in relation to the performance by him of an eligible function, provision for the making of payments to him—

(a) by other parties to the arrangements, or

(b) by persons who use any facilities or services provided by him pursuant to the arrangements or in relation to whom the function is otherwise exercisable,

he may include in any such arrangements provision for the making of such payments to him or a new Agency in cases where the new Agency (or any of its employees) acts on his behalf by virtue of an agreement under this section.

(9) The power conferred on a Minister of the Crown by subsection (1) above is in addition to any other power by virtue of which functions of his may be exercised by other persons on his behalf.

(10) In this section—

'eligible function' means any function of a Minister of the Crown which the Secretary of State, having regard to the functions conferred or imposed upon the new Agency in question under or by virtue of this Act or any other enactment, considers can appropriately be exercised by that new Agency (or any of its employees) on behalf of that Minister;

'Minister of the Crown' has the same meaning as in the Ministers of the Crown Act 1975.

39 General duty of the new Agencies to have regard to costs and benefits in exercising powers

(1) Each new Agency—

(a) in considering whether or not to exercise any power conferred upon it by or under any enactment, or

(b) in deciding the manner in which to exercise any such power,

shall, unless and to the extent that it is unreasonable for it to do so in view of the nature or purpose of the power or in the circumstances of the particular case, take into account the likely costs and benefits of the exercise or non-exercise of the power or its exercise in the manner in question.

(2) The duty imposed upon a new Agency by subsection (1) above does not affect its obligation, nevertheless, to discharge any duties, comply with any requirements, or pursue any objectives, imposed upon or given to it otherwise than under this section.

40 Ministerial directions to the new Agencies

(1) The appropriate Minister may give a new Agency directions of a general or specific character with respect to the carrying out of any of its functions.

(2) The appropriate Minister may give a new Agency such directions of a general or specific character as he considers appropriate for the implementation of—

(a) any obligations of the United Kingdom under the Community Treaties, or

(b) any international agreement to which the United Kingdom is for the time being a party.

(3) Any direction under subsection (2) above shall be published in such manner as the Minister giving it considers appropriate for the purpose of bringing the matters to which it relates to the attention of persons likely to be affected by them; and—

(a) copies of the direction shall be made available to the public; and

(b) notice shall be given—

(i) in the case of a direction given to the Agency, in the London Gazette, or

(ii) ... of the giving of the direction and of where a copy of the direction may be obtained.

(4) The provisions of subsection (3) above shall have effect in relation to any direction given to a new Agency under an enactment other than subsection (2) above for the implementation of—

(a) any obligations of the United Kingdom under the Community Treaties, or

(b) any international agreement to which the United Kingdom is for the time being a party,

as those provisions have effect in relation to a direction given under subsection (2) above.

(5) In determining—

(a) any appeal against, or reference or review of, a decision of a new Agency, or

(b) any application transmitted from a new Agency,

the body or person making the determination shall be bound by any direction given by a Minister of the Crown to the new Agency to the same extent as the new Agency.

(6) Any power to give a direction under this section shall be exercisable, except in an emergency, only after consultation with the new Agency concerned.

(7) Any power of the appropriate Minister to give directions to a new Agency otherwise than by virtue of this section shall be without prejudice to any power to give directions conferred by this section.

(8) It is the duty of a new Agency to comply with any direction which is given to that new Agency by a Minister of the Crown under this section or any other enactment.

Charging schemes

41 Power to make schemes imposing charges

(1) Subject to the following provisions of this section and section 40 below—

(a) in the case of any particular licence under Chapter II of Part II of the 1991 Act (abstraction and impounding), the Agency may require the payment to it of such charges as may from time to time be prescribed;

(b) in relation to other environmental licences, there shall be charged by and paid to a new Agency such charges as may from time to time be prescribed; and

(c) as a means of recovering costs incurred by it in performing functions conferred by regulations under section 62 of the 1990 Act (dangerous or intractable waste) each of the new Agencies may require the payment to it of such charges as may from time to time be prescribed;

and in this section 'prescribed' means specified in, or determined under, a scheme (in this section referred to as a 'charging scheme') made under this section by the new Agency in question.

(2) As respects environmental licences, charges may be prescribed in respect of—

(a) the grant or variation of an environmental licence, or any application for, or for a variation of, such a licence;

(b) the subsistence of an environmental licence;

(c) the transfer (where permitted) of an environmental licence to another person, or any application for such a transfer;

(d) the renewal (where permitted) of an environmental licence, or any application for such a renewal;

(e) the surrender (where permitted) of an environmental licence, or any application for such a surrender; or

(f) any application for the revocation (where permitted) of an environmental licence.

(3) A charging scheme may, for the purposes of subsection (2)(b) above, impose—

(a) a single charge in respect of the whole of any relevant licensed period;

(b) separate charges in respect of different parts of any such period; or

(c) both such a single charge and such separate charges,

and in this subsection 'relevant licensed period' means the period during which an environmental licence is in force or such part of that period as may be prescribed.

(4) Without prejudice to subsection (7)(a) below, a charging scheme may, as respects environmental licences, provide for different charges to be payable according to—

(a) the description of environmental licence in question;

(b) the description of authorised activity in question;

(c) the scale on which the authorised activity in question is carried on;

(d) the description or amount of the substance to which the authorised activity in question relates;

(e) the number of different authorised activities carried on by the same person.

(5) A charging scheme—

(a) shall specify, in relation to any charge prescribed by the scheme, the description of person who is liable to pay the charge; and

(b) may provide that it shall be a condition of an environmental licence of any particular description that any charge prescribed by a charging scheme in relation to an environmental licence of that description is paid in accordance with the scheme.

(6) Without prejudice to subsection (5)(b) above, if it appears to a new Agency that any charges due and payable to it in respect of the subsistence of an environmental licence have not been paid, it may, in accordance with the appropriate procedure, suspend or revoke the environmental licence to the extent that it authorises the carrying on of an authorised activity.

(7) A charging scheme may—

(a) make different provision for different cases, including different provision in relation to different persons, circumstances or localities;

(b) provide for the times at which, and the manner in which, the charges prescribed by the scheme are to be paid;

(c) revoke or amend any previous charging scheme;

(d) contain supplemental, incidental, consequential or transitional provision for the purposes of the scheme.

(8) If and to the extent that a charging scheme relates to licences under Chapter II of Part II of the 1991 Act (abstraction and impounding), the scheme shall have effect subject to any provision made by or under sections 125 to 130 of that Act (exemption from charges, imposition of special charges for spray irrigation, and charges in respect of abstraction from waters of the British Waterways Board).

(9) A new Agency shall not make a charging scheme unless the provisions of the scheme have been approved by the Secretary of State under section 42 below.

(10) In this section—

'the appropriate procedure' means such procedure as may be specified or described in regulations made for the purpose by the Secretary of State;

'authorised activity' means any activity to which an environmental licence relates.

(11) Any power to make regulations under this section shall be exercisable by statutory instrument; and a statutory instrument containing any such regulations shall be subject to annulment pursuant to a resolution of either House of Parliament.

42 Approval of charging schemes

(1) Before submitting a proposed charging scheme to the Secretary of State for his approval, a new Agency shall, in such manner as it considers appropriate for bringing it to the attention of persons likely to be affected by the scheme, publish a notice—

(a) setting out its proposals; and

(b) specifying the period within which representations or objections with respect to the proposals may be made to the Secretary of State.

(2) Where any proposed charging scheme has been submitted to the Secretary of State for his approval, he shall, in determining whether or not to approve the scheme or to approve it subject to modifications,—

(a) consider any representations or objections duly made to him and not withdrawn; and

(b) have regard to the matter specified in subsection (3) below.

(3) The matter mentioned in subsection (2)(b) above is the desirability of ensuring that, in the case of each of the descriptions of environmental licence specified in the paragraphs of the definition of that expression in section 56 below, the amounts recovered by the new Agency in question by way of charges prescribed by charging schemes are the amounts which, taking one year with another, need to be recovered by that new Agency to meet such of the costs and expenses (whether of a revenue or capital nature)—

(a) which it incurs in carrying out its functions,

(b) in the case of environmental licences which are authorisations under section 13(1) of the Radioactive Substances Act 1993—

(i) which the Minister incurs in carrying out his functions under or in consequence of that Act, and

(ii) which the Secretary of State incurs under that Act in carrying out in relation to ... Wales such of his functions under or in consequence of that Act as are exercised by the Minister in relation to England,

as the Secretary of State may consider it appropriate to attribute to the carrying out of those functions in relation to activities to which environmental licences of the description in question relate.

(4) Without prejudice to the generality of the expression 'costs and expenses', in determining for the purposes of subsection (3) above the amounts of the costs and expenses which the Secretary of State considers it appropriate to attribute to the carrying out of a

new Agency's or the Minister's or the Secretary of State's functions in relation to the activities to which environmental licences of any particular description relate, the Secretary of State—

(a) shall take into account any determination of the new Agency's financial duties under section 44 below; and

(b) may include amounts in respect of the depreciation of, and the provision of a return on, such assets as are held by the new Agency, the Minister or the Secretary of State, as the case may be, for purposes connected with the carrying out of the functions in question.

(5) If and to the extent that a charging scheme relates to any licence under Chapter II of Part II of the 1991 Act (abstraction and impounding), the Secretary of State may consider it appropriate to attribute to the carrying out of the Agency's functions in relation to activities to which such a licence relates any costs and expenses incurred by the Agency in carrying out any of its functions under Part II of that Act or under section 6(2) above.

(6) Subsection (5) above is without prejudice to what costs and expenses the Secretary of State may consider it appropriate to attribute to the carrying out of any functions of a new Agency, the Minister or the Secretary of State in relation to activities to which environmental licences of any particular description relate.

(7) The consent of the Treasury shall be required for the giving of approval to a charging scheme and, if and to the extent that the scheme relates to authorisations by the Agency under section 13 of the Radioactive Substances Act 1993 (disposal of radioactive waste), the consent of the Minister shall also be required.

(8) It shall be the duty of a new Agency to take such steps as it considers appropriate for bringing the provisions of any charging scheme made by it which is for the time being in force to the attention of persons likely to be affected by them.

(9) If and to the extent that any sums recovered by a new Agency by way of charges prescribed by charging schemes may fairly be regarded as so recovered for the purpose of recovering the amount required to meet (whether in whole or in part—

(a) such of the costs and expenses incurred by the Secretary of State as fall within subsection (3) above, or

(b) such of the costs and expenses incurred by the Minister as fall within that sub-section,

those sums shall be paid by that new Agency to the Secretary of State or, as the case may be, to the Minister.

(10) For the purposes of subsection (9) above, any question as to the extent to which any sums may fairly be regarded as recovered for the purpose of recovering the amount required to meet the costs and expenses falling within paragraph (a) or paragraph (b) of that subsection shall be determined—

(a) in the case of costs and expenses falling within paragraph (a) of that subsection, by the Secretary of State; and

(b) in the case of costs and expenses falling within paragraph (b) of that subsection, by the Secretary of State and the Minister.

(11) In this section 'charging scheme' has the same meaning as in section 39 above.

Incidental power to impose charges

43   Incidental power of the new Agencies to impose charges

Without prejudice to the generality of its powers by virtue of section 37(1)(a) above and subject to any such express provision with respect to charging by a new Agency as is contained in the preceding provisions of this Chapter or any other enactment, each new Agency shall have the power to fix and recover charges for services and facilities provided in the course of carrying out its functions.

General financial provisions

44   General financial duties

(1) The appropriate Ministers may—

(a) after consultation with a new Agency, and

(b) with the approval of the Treasury, determine the financial duties of that new Agency; and different determinations may be made for different functions and activities of the new Agency.

(2) The appropriate Ministers shall give a new Agency notice of every determination of its financial duties under this section, and such a determination may—

(a) relate to a period beginning before, on, or after, the date on which it is made;

(b) contain supplemental provisions; and

(c) be varied by a subsequent determination.

(3) The appropriate Minister may, after consultation with the Treasury and a new Agency, give a direction to that new Agency requiring it to pay to him an amount equal to the whole or such part as may be specified in the direction of any sum, or any sum of a description, so specified which is or has been received by that new Agency.

(4) Where it appears to the appropriate Minister that a new Agency has a surplus, whether on capital or revenue account, he may, after consultation with the Treasury and the new Agency, direct the new Agency to pay to him such amount not exceeding the amount of that surplus as may be specified in the direction.

(5) In the case of the Agency—

(a) subsection (1) above is subject to section 118 of the 1991 Act (special duties with respect to flood defence revenue);

(b) subsection (3) above is subject to sections 118(1)(a) and 119(1) of the 1991 Act (special duties with respect to flood defence revenue and funds raised for fishery purposes under local enactments); and

(c) subsection (4) above is subject to sections 118(1)(b) and 119(2) of the 1991 Act (which provide for flood defence revenue and certain funds raised under local enactments to be disregarded in determining whether there is a surplus).

45   Accounts and records

(1) Each new Agency shall—

(a) keep proper accounts and proper accounting records; and

(b) prepare in respect of each accounting year a statement of accounts giving a true and fair view of the state of affairs and the income and expenditure of the new Agency.

(2) Every statement of accounts prepared by a new Agency in accordance with this section shall comply with any requirement which the appropriate Ministers have, with the consent of the Treasury, notified in writing to the new Agency and which relates to any of the following matters, namely—

(a) the information to be contained in the statement;

(b) the manner in which that information is to be presented;

(c) the methods and principles according to which the statement is to be prepared.

(3) In this section—

'accounting records', in the case of a new Agency, includes all books, papers and other records of the new Agency relating to, or to matters dealt with in, the accounts required to be kept by virtue of this section;

'accounting year', subject to subsection (4) below, means, in relation to a new Agency, a financial year.

(4) . . .

Information

51   Provision of information by the new Agencies

(1) A new Agency shall furnish the appropriate Minister with all such information as he may reasonably require relating to—

(a) the new Agency's property;

(b) the carrying out and proposed carrying out of its functions; and

(c) its responsibilities generally.

(2) Information required under this section shall be furnished in such form and manner, and be accompanied or supplemented by such explanations, as the appropriate Minister may reasonably require.

(3) The information which a new Agency may be required to furnish to the appropriate Minister under this section shall include information which, although it is not in the possession of the new Agency or would not otherwise come into the possession of the new Agency, is information which it is reasonable to require the new Agency to obtain.

(4) A requirement for the purposes of this section shall be contained in a direction which—

(a) may describe the information to be furnished in such manner as the Minister giving the direction considers appropriate; and

(b) may require the information to be furnished on a particular occasion, in particular circumstances or from time to time.

(5) For the purposes of this section a new Agency shall—

(a) permit any person authorised for the purpose by the appropriate Minister to inspect and make copies of the contents of any accounts or other records of the new Agency; and

(b) give such explanation of them as that person or the appropriate Minister may reasonably require.

52   Annual report

(1) As soon as reasonably practicable after the end of each financial year, each new Agency shall prepare a report on its activities during that year and shall send a copy of that report to each of the appropriate Ministers.

(2) Every such report shall set out any directions under section 40 above which have been given to the new Agency in question during the year to which the report relates, other than directions given under subsection (1) of that section which are identified to that new Agency in writing by the appropriate Minister as being directions the disclosure of which would, in his opinion, be contrary to the interests of national security.

(3) The Secretary of State shall lay a copy of every such report before each House of Parliament and shall arrange for copies of every such report to be published in such manner as he considers appropriate.

(4) A new Agency's annual report shall be in such form and contain such information as may be specified in any direction given to the new Agency by the appropriate Ministers.

Supplemental provisions

53   Inquiries and other hearings

(1) Without prejudice to any other provision of this Act or any other enactment by virtue of which an inquiry or other hearing is authorised or required to be held, the appropriate Minister may cause an inquiry or other hearing to be held if it appears to him expedient to do so—

(a) in connection with any of the functions of a new Agency; or

(b) in connection with any of his functions in relation to a new Agency.

(2) Subsections (2) to (5) of section 250 of the Local Government Act 1972 (which

contain supplementary provisions with respect to local inquiries held in pursuance of that section) shall apply to inquiries or other hearings under this section or any other enactment—

(a) in connection with any of the functions of the Agency, or

(b) in connection with any functions of the Secretary of State or the Minister in relation to the Agency,

as they apply to inquiries under that section, but taking the reference in subsection (4) of that section to a local authority as including a reference to the Agency.

(3) . . .

54 Appearance in legal proceedings

In England and Wales, a person who is authorised by the Agency to prosecute on its behalf in proceedings before a magistrates' court shall be entitled to prosecute in any such proceedings although not of counsel or a solicitor.

55 Continuity of exercise of functions: the new Agencies

(1) The abolition of—

(a) the National Rivers Authority,

(b) the London Waste Regulation Authority, or

(c) . . .,

shall not affect the validity of anything done by that Authority . . . before the transfer date.

(2) Anything which, at the transfer date, is in the process of being done by or in relation to a transferor in the exercise of, or in connection with, any of the transferred functions may be continued by or in relation to the transferee.

(3) Anything done by or in relation to a transferor before the transfer date in the exercise of, or otherwise in connection with, any of the transferred functions, shall, so far as is required for continuing its effect on and after that date, have effect as if done by or in relation to the transferee.

(4) Subsection (3) above applies in particular to—

(a) any decision, determination, declaration, designation, agreement or instrument made by a transferor;

(b) any regulations or byelaws made by a transferor;

(c) any licence, permission, consent, approval, authorisation, exemption, dispensation or relaxation granted by or to a transferor;

(d) any notice, direction or certificate given by or to a transferor;

(e) any application, request, proposal or objection made by or to a transferor;

(f) any condition or requirement imposed by or on a transferor;

(g) any fee or charge paid by or to a transferor;

(h) any appeal allowed by or in favour of or against a transferor;

(j) any proceedings instituted by or against a transferor.

(5) Any reference in the foregoing provisions of this section to anything done by or in relation to a transferor includes a reference to anything which, by virtue of any enactment, is treated as having been done by or in relation to that transferor.

(6) Any reference to a transferor in any document constituting or relating to anything to which the foregoing provisions of this section apply shall, so far as is required for giving effect to those provisions, be construed as a reference to the transferee.

(7) The foregoing provisions of this section—

(a) are without prejudice to any provision made by this Act in relation to any particular functions; and

(b) shall not be construed as continuing in force any contract of employment made by a transferor;

and the Secretary of State may, in relation to any particular functions, by order exclude, modify or supplement any of the foregoing provisions of this section or make such other transitional provisions as he thinks necessary or expedient.

(8) . . .

(9) The power to make an order under subsection (7) above shall be exercisable by statutory instrument; and any statutory instrument containing such an order shall be subject to annulment pursuant to a resolution of either House of Parliament.

(10) In this section—

'the transferee', in the case of any transferred functions, means the new Agency whose functions they become by virtue of any provision made by or under this Act;

'transferred functions' means any functions which, by virtue of any provision made by or under this Act, become functions of a new Agency; and

'transferor' means any body or person any or all of whose functions become, by virtue of any provision made by or under this Act, functions of a new Agency.

56 Interpretation of Part I

(1) In this Part of this Act, except where the context otherwise requires—

. . .

'the 1990 Act' means the Environmental Protection Act 1990;

'the 1991 Act' means the Water Resources Act 1991;

'the appropriate Minister'—

   (a) in the case of the Agency, means the Secretary of State or the Minister; and

   (b) . . .

'the appropriate Ministers'—

   (a) in the case of the Agency, means the Secretary of State and the Minister; and

   (b) . . .

'conservancy authority' has the meaning given by section 221 (1) of the 1991 Act; 'costs' includes—

   (a) costs to any person; and

   (b) costs to the environment;

'disposal authority'—

   (a) in the application of this Part in relation to the Agency, has the same meaning as it has in Part I of the Control of Pollution Act 1974 by virtue of section 30(1) of that Act; and

   (b) . . .

['the environment' means all, or any, of the following media, namely, the air, water and land (and the medium of air includes the air within buildings and the air within other natural or man-made structures above or below ground);]

'environmental licence', in the application of this Part in relation to the Agency, means any of the following—

   (a) registration of a person as a carrier of controlled waste under section 2 of the Control of Pollution (Amendment) Act 1989,

   [(aa) a permit granted by the Agency under regulations under section 2 of the Pollution Prevention and Control Act 1999;]

   (b) an authorisation under Part I of the 1990 Act, other than any such authorisation granted by a local enforcing authority,

   (c) a waste management licence under Part II of that Act,

   (d) a licence under Chapter II of Part II of the 1991 Act,

   (e) a consent for the purposes of section 88(1)(a), 89(4)(a) or 90 of that Act,

   (f) registration under the Radioactive Substances Act 1993,

   (g) an authorisation under that Act,

   (h) registration of a person as a broker of controlled waste under the Waste Management Licensing Regulations 1994,

(j) registration in respect of an activity falling within paragraph 45(1) or (2) of Schedule 3 to those Regulations,

so far as having effect in relation to England and Wales;

. . .

'flood defence functions', in relation to the Agency, has the same meaning as in the 1991 Act;

'harbour authority' has the meaning given by section 221(1) of the 1991 Act;

. . .

'the Minister' means the Minister of Agriculture, Fisheries and Food;

'the Ministers' means the Secretary of State and the Minister;

'navigation authority' has the meaning given by section 221(1) of the 1991 Act;

'new Agency' means the Agency . . .

. . .

. . .

'the transfer date' means such date as the Secretary of State may by order made by statutory instrument appoint as the transfer date for the purposes of this Part; and different dates may be appointed for the purposes of this Part—

(i) as it applies for or in connection with transfers under or by virtue of Chapter I above, and

(ii) . . .

'waste regulation authority'—

(a) in the application of this Part in relation to the Agency, means any authority in England or Wales which, by virtue of section 30(1) of the 1990 Act, is a waste regulation authority for the purposes of Part II of that Act; and

(b) . . .

(2) . . .

(3) Where by virtue of any provision of this Part any function of a Minister of the Crown is exercisable concurrently by different Ministers, that function shall also be exercisable jointly by any two or more of those Ministers.

PART III   NATIONAL PARKS

Establishment of National Park authorities

63   Establishment of National Park authorities

(1) The Secretary of State may—

(a) in the case of any National Park for which there is an existing authority, or

(b) in connection with the designation of any area as a new such Park,

by order establish an authority (to be known as 'a National Park authority') to carry out in relation to that Park the functions conferred on such an authority by or under this Part.

(2) An order under this section may provide, in relation to any National Park for which there is an existing authority—

(a) for the existing authority to cease to have any functions in relation to that Park as from the time when a National Park authority becomes the local planning authority, for that Park;

(b) for such (if any) of the functions of the existing authority as, by virtue of this Part, are not as from that time to be functions of the National Park authority for that Park to become functions of the person on whom they would be conferred if the area in question were not in a National Park; and

(c) for the winding up of the existing authority and for that authority to cease to exist, or to be dissolved, as from such time as may be specified in the order.

(3) Subject to any order under subsection (4) below, where there is a variation of the area of a National Park for which there is or is to be a National Park authority, the Park for which that authority is or is to be the authority shall be deemed, as from the time when the variation takes effect, to be that area as varied.

(4) Where provision is made for the variation of the area of a National Park for which there is or is to be a National Park authority, the Secretary of State may by order make such transitional provision as he thinks fit with respect to—

(a) any functions which, in relation to any area that becomes part of the National Park, are by virtue of the variation to become functions of that authority; and

(b) any functions which, in relation to any area that ceases to be part of the National Park, are by virtue of the variation to become functions of a person other than that authority.

(5) Schedule 7 to this Act shall have effect with respect to National Park authorities.

Functions of National Park authorities

65 General purposes and powers

(1) This Part so far as it relates to the establishment and functions of National Park authorities shall have effect for the purposes specified in section 5(1) of the National Parks and Access to the Countryside Act 1949 (purposes of conserving and enhancing the natural beauty, wildlife and cultural heritage of National Parks and of promoting opportunities for the understanding and enjoyment of the special qualities of those Parks by the public).

(2) Sections 37 and 38 of the Countryside Act 1968 (general duties as to the protection of interests of the countryside and the avoidance of pollution) shall apply to National Park authorities as they apply to local authorities.

(3) The functions of a National Park authority in the period (if any) between the time when it is established and the time when it becomes the local planning authority for the relevant Park shall be confined to the taking of such steps as the authority, after consultation with the Secretary of State and any existing authority for that Park, considers appropriate for securing that it is able properly to carry out its functions after that time.

(4) In the application of subsection (3) above in the case of a National Park authority established in relation to a National Park in Wales, the reference to any existing authority for that Park shall have effect as respects consultation carried out during so much of that period as falls before 1st April 1996 as including a reference to any principal council whose area is wholly or partly comprised in that Park.

(5) The powers of a National Park authority shall include power to do anything which, in the opinion of that authority, is calculated to facilitate, or is conducive or incidental to—

(a) the accomplishment of the purposes mentioned in subsection (1) above; or

(b) the carrying out of any functions conferred on it by virtue of any other enactment.

(6) The powers conferred on a National Park authority by subsection (5) above shall not include either—

(a) power to do anything in contravention of any restriction imposed by virtue of this Part in relation to any express power of the authority; or

(b) a power to raise money (whether by borrowing or otherwise) in a manner which is not authorised apart from that subsection;

but the things that may be done in exercise of those powers shall not be treated as excluding anything by reason only that it involves the expenditure, borrowing or lending of money or the acquisition or disposal of any property or rights.

(7) Schedule 8 to this Act shall have effect with respect to the supplemental and incidental powers of a National Park authority.

66   National Park Management Plans

(1) Subject to subsection (2) below, every National Park authority shall, within three years after its operational date, prepare and publish a plan, to be known as a National Park Management Plan, which formulates its policy for the management of the relevant Park and for the carrying out of its functions in relation to that Park.

(2) A National Park authority for a Park wholly or mainly comprising any area which, immediately before the authority's operational date, was or was included in an area for which there was a National Park Plan prepared and published under paragraph 18 of Schedule 17 to the 1972 Act (National Park plans) shall not be required to prepare a Management Plan under subsection (1) above if, within six months of that date, it adopts the existing National Park Plan as its Management Plan and publishes notice that it has done so.

(3) Where a National Park authority is proposing to adopt a plan under subsection (2) above, it may review the plan before adopting it and shall do so if the plan would have fallen to be reviewed under paragraph 18 of Schedule 17 to the 1972 Act in the period of twelve months beginning with the authority's operational date.

(4) A National Park authority shall review its National Park Management Plan within the period of five years of its operational date and, after the first review, at intervals of not more than five years.

(5) Where a National Park authority has adopted a plan under subsection (2) above as its National Park Management Plan and has not reviewed that Plan before adopting it, the first review of that Plan under subsection (4) above shall take place no later than the time when the adopted plan would otherwise have fallen to be reviewed under paragraph 18 of Schedule 17 to the 1972 Act.

(6) Where a National Park authority reviews any plan under this section, it shall—

    (a) determine on that review whether it would be expedient to amend the plan and what (if any) amendments would be appropriate;

    (b) make any amendments that it considers appropriate; and

    (c) publish a report on the review specifying any amendments made.

(7) A National Park authority which is proposing to publish, adopt or review any plan under this section shall—

    (a) give notice of the proposal to every principal council whose area is wholly or partly comprised in the relevant Park and, according to whether that Park is in England or in Wales, to the Countryside Commission and the Nature Conservancy Council for England or to the Countryside Council for Wales;

    (b) send a copy of the plan, together (where appropriate) with any proposed amendments of the plan, to every body to which notice of the proposal is required to be given by paragraph (a) above; and

    (c) take into consideration any observations made by any such body.

(8) A National Park authority shall send to the Secretary of State a copy of every plan, notice or report which it is required to publish under this section.

(9) In this section 'operational date', in relation to a National Park authority, means the date on which the authority becomes the local planning authority for the relevant Park.

67   National Park authority to be local planning authority

(1) After section 4 of the Town and Country Planning Act 1990 (National Parks) there shall be inserted—

. . .

(2) The Secretary of State may by order make provision—

    (a) for applying Chapter I of Part II of that Act of 1990 (unitary development plans), instead of provisions of Chapter II of that Part (structure and local plans), in relation to the area of any National Park; or

  (b) for applying Chapter II of that Part in relation to the area of such a Park—

    (i) as if functions under that Chapter of a planning authority of any description were functions of such public authority as may be specified in the order (and not of the National Park authority); and

    (ii) as if that Part had effect with such other modifications as may be so specified in relation to the carrying out of those functions by an authority so specified.

  (3) Without prejudice to any power conferred by virtue of section 75 below, the Secretary of State shall have power by order, for the purposes of any provision made by virtue of this section, to modify the provisions of Part II of that Act of 1990 (development plans) in relation to any such area of a local planning authority as, but for any exclusion by virtue of section 4A of that Act, would include the whole or any part of a National Park.

  (4) References in this section to provisions of Part II of that Act of 1990 include references to any provisions for modifying those provisions which are contained in any enactment passed after this Act.

. . .

69 Planning authority functions under the Wildlife and Countryside Act 1981

  (1) A National Park authority which is the local planning authority for any National Park, and not any other authority, shall have all the functions under the Wildlife and Countryside Act 1981 which are conferred as respects that Park on a planning authority of any description.

  (2) Accordingly—

  (a) a National Park authority shall be the relevant authority for the purposes of sections 39, 41 and 50 of that Act (management agreements and duties of agriculture Ministers in relation to the countryside) as respects any land in any National Park for which that authority is the local planning authority; and

  (b) section 52(2) of that Act (construction of references to a local planning authority) shall not apply as respects any National Park for which a National Park authority is the local planning authority.

  (3) Section 43 of that Act (maps of National Parks) shall have effect in accordance with the preceding provisions of this section—

  (a) in the case of a National Park designated after the commencement of this section, as if the relevant date for the purposes of that section were the date on which a National Park authority becomes the local planning authority for the Park; and

  (b) in any other case, as if the function of reviewing and revising any map of a part of the Park in question included a power, in pursuance of the review and revisions, to consolidate that map with other maps prepared under that section as respects other parts of that Park.

  (4) In section 44 of that Act (grants and loans for purposes of National Parks), after subsection (1) there shall be inserted the following subsection—

'(1A) Subsection (1) above shall not apply in relation to any National Park for which a National Park authority is the local planning authority; but the National Park authority for such a Park may give financial assistance by way of grant or loan, or partly in one way and partly in the other, to any person in respect of expenditure incurred by him in doing anything which, in the opinion of the authority, is conducive to the attainment in the Park in question of any of the purposes mentioned in section 5(1) of the 1949 Act (purposes of conserving and enhancing the natural beauty, wildlife and cultural heritage of National Parks and of promoting opportunities for the understanding and enjoyment of the special qualities of those Parks by the public).'

PART IV   AIR QUALITY

80   National air quality strategy

(1) The Secretary of State shall as soon as possible prepare and publish a statement (in this Part referred to as 'the strategy') containing policies with respect to the assessment or management of the quality of air.

(2) The strategy may also contain policies for implementing—

    (a) obligations of the United Kingdom under the Community Treaties, or

    (b) international agreements to which the United Kingdom is for the time being a party,

so far as relating to the quality of air.

(3) The strategy shall consist of or include—

    (a) a statement which relates to the whole of Great Britain; or

    (b) two or more statements which between them relate to every part of Great Britain.

(4) The Secretary of State—

    (a) shall keep under review his policies with respect to the quality of air; and

    (b) may from time to time modify the strategy.

(5) Without prejudice to the generality of what may be included in the strategy, the strategy must include statements with respect to—

    (a) standards relating to the quality of air;

    (b) objectives for the restriction of the levels at which particular substances are present in the air; and

    (c) measures which are to be taken by local authorities and other persons for the purpose of achieving those objectives.

(6) In preparing the strategy or any modification of it, the Secretary of State shall consult—

    (a) the appropriate new Agency;

    (b) such bodies or persons appearing to him to be representative of the interests of local government as he may consider appropriate;

    (c) such bodies or persons appearing to him to be representative of the interests of industry as he may consider appropriate; and

    (d) such other bodies or persons as he may consider appropriate.

(7) Before publishing the strategy or any modification of it, the Secretary of State—

    (a) shall publish a draft of the proposed strategy or modification, together with notice of a date before which, and an address at which, representations may be made to him concerning the draft so published; and

    (b) shall take into account any such representations which are duly made and not withdrawn.

81   Functions of the new Agencies

(1) In discharging its pollution control functions, each new Agency shall have regard to the strategy.

(2) In this section 'pollution control functions', in relation to a new Agency, means—

    (a) in the case of the Agency, the functions conferred on it by or under the enactments specified in section 5(5) above; or

    (b) . . .

82   Local authority reviews

(1) Every local authority shall from time to time cause a review to be conducted of the quality for the time being, and the likely future quality within the relevant period, of air within the authority's area.

(2) Where a local authority causes a review under subsection (1) above to be conducted, it shall also cause an assessment to be made of whether air quality standards and objectives are

being achieved, or are likely to be achieved within the relevant period, within the authority's area.

(3) If, on an assessment under subsection (2) above, it appears that any air quality standards or objectives are not being achieved, or are not likely within the relevant period to be achieved, within the local authority's area, the local authority shall identify any parts of its area in which it appears that those standards or objectives are not likely to be achieved within the relevant period.

83   Designation of air quality management areas

(1) Where, as a result of an air quality review, it appears that any air quality standards or objectives are not being achieved, or are not likely within the relevant period to be achieved, within the area of a local authority, the local authority shall by order designate as an air quality management area (in this Part referred to as a 'designated area') any part of its area in which it appears that those standards or objectives are not being achieved, or are not likely to be achieved within the relevant period.

(2) An order under this section may, as a result of a subsequent air quality review,—

   (a) be varied by a subsequent order; or
   (b) be revoked by such an order, if it appears on that subsequent air quality review that the air quality standards and objectives are being achieved, and are likely throughout the relevant period to be achieved, within the designated area.

84   Duties of local authorities in relation to designated areas

(1) Where an order under section 83 above comes into operation, the local authority which made the order shall, for the purpose of supplementing such information as it has in relation to the designated area in question, cause an assessment to be made of—

   (a) the quality for the time being, and the likely future quality within the relevant period, of air within the designated area to which the order relates; and
   (b) the respects (if any) in which it appears that air quality standards or objectives are not being achieved, or are not likely within the relevant period to be achieved, within that designated area.

(2) A local authority which is required by subsection (1) above to cause an assessment to be made shall also be under a duty—

   (a) to prepare, before the expiration of the period of twelve months beginning with the coming into operation of the order mentioned in that subsection, a report of the results of that assessment; and
   (b) to prepare, in accordance with the following provisions of this Part, a written plan (in this Part referred to as an 'action plan') for the exercise by the authority, in pursuit of the achievement of air quality standards and objectives in the designated area, of any powers exercisable by the authority.

(3) An action plan shall include a statement of the time or times by or within which the local authority in question proposes to implement each of the proposed measures comprised in the plan.

(4) A local authority may from time to time revise an action plan.

(5) This subsection applies in any case where the local authority preparing an action plan or a revision of an action plan is the council of a district in England which is comprised in an area for which there is a county council; and if, in a case where this subsection applies, the county council disagrees with the authority about the contents of the proposed action plan or revision of the action plan—

   (a) either of them may refer the matter to the Secretary of State;
   (b) on any such reference the Secretary of State may confirm the authority's proposed action plan or revision of the action plan, with or without modifications (whether or not proposed by the county council) or reject it and, if he rejects it, he may also exercise any powers of his under section 85 below; and

(c) the authority shall not finally determine the content of the action plan, or the revision of the action plan, except in accordance with his decision on the reference or in pursuance of directions under section 85 below.

85   Reserve powers of the Secretary of State or SEPA

(1) In this section, 'the appropriate authority' means—
   (a) in relation to England and Wales, the Secretary of State; and
   (b) . . .

(2) The appropriate authority may conduct or make, or cause to be conducted or made,—
   (a) a review of the quality for the time being, and the likely future quality within the relevant period, of air within the area of any local authority;
   (b) an assessment of whether air quality standards and objectives are being achieved, or are likely to be achieved within the relevant period, within the area of a local authority;
   (c) an identification of any parts of the area of a local authority in which it appears that those standards or objectives are not likely to be achieved within the relevant period; or
   (d) an assessment of the respects (if any) in which it appears that air quality standards or objectives are not being achieved, or are not likely within the relevant period to be achieved, within the area of a local authority or within a designated area.

(3) If it appears to the appropriate authority—
   (a) that air quality standards or objectives are not being achieved, or are not likely within the relevant period to be achieved, within the area of a local authority,
   (b) that a local authority has failed to discharge any duty imposed on it under or by virtue of this Part,
   (c) that the actions, or proposed actions, of a local authority in purported compliance with the provisions of this Part are inappropriate in all the circumstances of the case, or
   (d) that developments in science or technology, or material changes in circumstances, have rendered inappropriate the actions or proposed actions of a local authority in pursuance of this Part,
the appropriate authority may give directions to the local authority requiring it to take such steps as may be specified in the directions.

(4) Without prejudice to the generality of subsection (3) above, directions under that subsection may, in particular, require a local authority—
   (a) to cause an air quality review to be conducted under section 82 above in accordance with the directions;
   (b) to cause an air quality review under section 82 above to be conducted afresh, whether in whole or in part, or to be so conducted with such differences as may be specified or described in the directions;
   (c) to make an order under section 83 above designating as an air quality management area an area specified in, or determined in accordance with, the directions;
   (d) to revoke, or modify in accordance with the directions, any order under that section;
   (e) to prepare in accordance with the directions an action plan for a designated area;
   (f) to modify, in accordance with the directions, any action plan prepared by the authority; or
   (g) to implement, in accordance with the directions, any measures in an action plan.

(5) The Secretary of State shall also have power to give directions to local authorities requiring them to take such steps specified in the directions as he considers appropriate for the implementation of—

(a) any obligations of the United Kingdom under the Community Treaties, or

(b) any international agreement to which the United Kingdom is for the time being a party,

so far as relating to the quality of air.

(6) Any direction given under this section shall be published in such manner as the body or person giving it considers appropriate for the purpose of bringing the matters to which it relates to the attention of persons likely to be affected by them; and—

(a) copies of the direction shall be made available to the public; and

(b) notice shall be given—

    (i) in the case of a direction given to a local authority in England and Wales, in the London Gazette, or

    (ii) ... of the giving of the direction and of where a copy of the direction may be obtained.

(7) It is the duty of a local authority to comply with any direction given to it under or by virtue of this Part.

86 Functions of county councils for areas for which there are district councils

(1) This section applies in any case where a district in England for which there is a district council is comprised in an area for which there is a county council; and in this paragraph—

(a) any reference to the county council is a reference to the council of that area; and

(b) any reference to a district council is a reference to the council of a district comprised in that area.

(2) The county council may make recommendations to a district council with respect to the carrying out of—

(a) any particular air quality review,

(b) any particular assessment under section 82 or 84 above, or

(c) the preparation of any particular action plan or revision of an action plan, and the district council shall take into account any such recommendations.

(3) Where a district council is preparing an action plan, the county council shall, within the relevant period, submit to the district council proposals for the exercise (so far as relating to the designated area) by the county council, in pursuit of the achievement of air quality standards and objectives, of any powers exercisable by the county council.

(4) Where the county council submits proposals to a district council in pursuance of subsection (3) above, it shall also submit a statement of the time or times by or within which it proposes to implement each of the proposals.

(5) An action plan shall include a statement of—

(a) any proposals submitted pursuant to subsection (3) above; and

(b) any time or times set out in the statement submitted pursuant to subsection (4) above.

(6) If it appears to the Secretary of State—

(a) that air quality standards or objectives are not being achieved, or are not likely within the relevant period to be achieved, within the area of a district council,

(b) that the county council has failed to discharge any duty imposed on it under or by virtue of this Part,

(c) that the actions, or proposed actions, of the county council in purported compliance with the provisions of this Part are inappropriate in all the circumstances of the case, or

(d) that developments in science or technology, or material changes in circumstances, have rendered inappropriate the actions or proposed actions of the county council in pursuance of this Part, the Secretary of State may give directions to the county council requiring it to take such steps as may be specified in the directions.

(7) Without prejudice to the generality of subsection (6) above, directions under that subsection may, in particular, require the county council—

(a) to submit, in accordance with the directions, proposals pursuant to subsection (3) above or a statement pursuant to subsection (4) above;

(b) to modify, in accordance with the directions, any proposals or statement submitted by the county council pursuant to subsection (3) or (4) above;

(c) to submit any proposals or statement so modified to the district council in question pursuant to subsection (3) or (4) above; or

(d) to implement, in accordance with the directions, any measures included in an action plan.

(8) The Secretary of State shall also have power to give directions to county councils for areas for which there are district councils requiring them to take such steps specified in the directions as he considers appropriate for the implementation of—

(a) any obligations of the United Kingdom under the Community Treaties, or

(b) any international agreement to which the United Kingdom is for the time being a party,

so far as relating to the quality of air.

(9) Any direction given under this section shall be published in such manner as the Secretary of State considers appropriate for the purpose of bringing the matters to which it relates to the attention of persons likely to be affected by them; and—

(a) copies of the direction shall be made available to the public; and

(b) notice of the giving of the direction, and of where a copy of the direction may be obtained, shall be given in the London Gazette.

(10) It is the duty of a county council for an area for which there are district councils to comply with any direction given to it under or by virtue of this Part.

87 Regulations for the purposes of Part IV

(1) Regulations may make provision—

(a) for, or in connection with, implementing the strategy;

(b) for, or in connection with, implementing—

(i) obligations of the United Kingdom under the Community Treaties, or

(ii) international agreements to which the United Kingdom is for the time being a party,

so far as relating to the quality of air; or

(c) otherwise with respect to the assessment or management of the quality of air

(2) Without prejudice to the generality of subsection (1) above, regulations under that subsection may make provision—

(a) prescribing standards relating to the quality of air;

(b) prescribing objectives for the restriction of the levels at which particular substances are present in the air;

(c) conferring powers or imposing duties on local authorities;

(d) for or in connection with—

(i) authorising local authorities (whether by agreements or otherwise) to exercise any functions of a Minister of the Crown on his behalf,

(ii) directing that functions of a Minister of the Crown shall be exercisable concurrently with local authorities; or

(iii) transferring functions of a Minister of the Crown to local authorities;

(e) prohibiting or restricting, or for or in connection with prohibiting or restricting,—

    (i) the carrying on of prescribed activities, or

    (ii) the access of prescribed vehicles or mobile equipment to prescribed areas,

    whether generally or in prescribed circumstances;

(f) for or in connection with the designation of air quality management areas by orders made by local authorities in such cases or circumstances not falling within section 83 above as may be prescribed;

(g) for the application, with or without modifications, of any provisions of this Part in relation to areas designated by virtue of paragraph (f) above or in relation to orders made by virtue of that paragraph;

(h) with respect to—

    (i) air quality reviews;

    (ii) assessments under this Part;

    (iii) orders designating air quality management areas; or

    (iv) action plans;

(j) prescribing measures which are to be adopted by local authorities (whether in action plans or otherwise) or other persons in pursuance of the achievement of air quality standards or objectives;

(k) for or in connection with the communication to the public of information relating to quality for the time being, or likely future quality, of the air;

(l) for or in connection with the obtaining by local authorities from any person of information which is reasonably necessary for the discharge of functions conferred or imposed on them under or by virtue of this Part;

(m) for or in connection with the recovery by a local authority from prescribed persons in prescribed circumstances, and in such manner as may be prescribed, of costs incurred by the authority in discharging functions conferred or imposed on the authority under or by virtue of this Part;

(n) for a person who contravenes, or fails to comply with, any prescribed provision of the regulations to be guilty of an offence and liable on summary conviction to a fine not exceeding level 5 on the standard scale or such lower level on that scale as may be prescribed in relation to the offence;

(o) for or in connection with arrangements under which a person may discharge any liability to conviction for a prescribed offence by payment of a penalty of a prescribed amount;

(p) for or in connection with appeals against determinations or decisions made, notices given or served, or other things done under or by virtue of the regulations.

(3) Without prejudice to the generality of paragraph (h) of subsection (2) above, the provision that may be made by virtue of that paragraph includes provision for or in connection with any of the following, that is to say—

(a) the scope or form of a review or assessment;

(b) the scope, content or form of an action plan;

(c) the time at which, period within which, or manner in which a review or assessment is to be carried out or an action plan is to be prepared;

(d) the methods to be employed—

    (i) in carrying out reviews or assessments; or

    (ii) in monitoring the effectiveness of action plans;

(e) the factors to be taken into account in preparing action plans;

(f) the actions which must be taken by local authorities or other persons in consequence of reviews, assessments or action plans;

(g) requirements for consultation;

(h) the treatment of representations or objections duly made;

(j) the publication of, or the making available to the public of, or of copies of,—

      (i)   the results, or reports of the results, of reviews or assessments; or

      (ii) orders or action plans;

   (k) requirements for—

      (i)   copies of any such reports, orders or action plans, or

      (ii) prescribed information, in such form as may be prescribed, relating to reviews or assessments,

    to be sent to the Secretary of State or to the appropriate new Agency.

  (4) In determining—

   (a) any appeal against, or reference or review of, a decision of a local authority under or by virtue of regulations under this Part, or

   (b) any application transmitted from a local authority under or by virtue of any such regulations,

the body or person making the determination shall be bound by any direction given by a Minister of the Crown ... to the local authority to the same extent as the local authority.

  (5) The provisions of any regulations under this Part may include—

   (a) provision for anything that may be prescribed by the regulations to be determined under the regulations and for anything falling to be so determined to be determined by such persons, in accordance with such procedure and by reference to such matters, and to the opinion of such persons, as may be prescribed;

   (b) different provision for different cases, including different provision in relation to different persons, circumstances, areas or localities; and

   (c) such supplemental, consequential, incidental or transitional provision (including provision amending any enactment or any instrument made under any enactment) as the Secretary of State considers appropriate.

  (6) Nothing in regulations under this Part shall authorise any person other than a constable in uniform to stop a vehicle on any road.

  (7) Before making any regulations under this Part, the Secretary of State shall consult—

   (a) the appropriate new Agency;

   (b) such bodies or persons appearing to him to be representative of the interests of local government as he may consider appropriate;

   (c) such bodies or persons appearing to him to be representative of the interests of industry as he may consider appropriate; and

   (d) such other bodies or persons as he may consider appropriate.

  (8) Any power conferred by this Part to make regulations shall be exercisable by statutory instrument; and no statutory instrument containing regulations under this Part shall be made unless a draft of the instrument has been laid before, and approved by a resolution of, each House of Parliament.

  (9) If, apart from this subsection, the draft of an instrument containing regulations under this Part would be treated for the purposes of the Standing Orders of either House of Parliament as a hybrid instrument, it shall proceed in that House as if it were not such an instrument.

88 Guidance for the purposes of Part IV

  (1) The Secretary of State may issue guidance to local authorities with respect to, or in connection with, the exercise of any of the powers conferred, or the discharge of any of the duties imposed, on those authorities by or under this Part.

  (2) A local authority, in carrying out any of its functions under or by virtue of this Part, shall have regard to any guidance issued by the Secretary of State under this Part.

  (3) This section shall apply in relation to county councils for areas for which there are district councils as it applies in relation to local authorities.

89 ...

90 Supplemental provisions
Schedule 11 to this Act shall have effect.

91 Interpretation of Part IV
(1) In this Part—
'action plan' shall be construed in accordance with section 84(2)(b) above;
'air quality objectives' means objectives prescribed by virtue of section 87(2)(b) above;
'air quality review' means a review under section 82 or 85 above;
'air quality standards' means standards prescribed by virtue of section 87(2)(a) above;
'the appropriate new Agency' means—

(a) in relation to England and Wales, the Agency;

(b) ...

'designated area' has the meaning given by section 83(1) above;
'local authority', in relation to England and Wales, means—

(a) any unitary authority,

(b) any district council, so far as it is not a unitary authority,

(c) the Common Council of the City of London and, as respects the Temples, the Sub-Treasurer of the Inner Temple and the Under-Treasurer of the Middle Temple respectively, . . .;

'new Agency' means the Agency . . .;
'prescribed' means prescribed, or of a description prescribed, by or under regulations;
'regulations' means regulations made by the Secretary of State;
'the relevant period', in the case of any provision of this Part, means such period as may be prescribed for the purposes of that provision;
'the strategy' has the meaning given by section 80(1) above;
'unitary authority' means—

(a) the council of a county, so far as it is the council of an area for which there are no district councils;

(b) the council of any district comprised in an area for which there is no county council;

(c) the council of a London borough;

(d) the council of a county borough in Wales.

(2) Any reference in this Part to it appearing that any air quality standards or objectives are not likely within the relevant period to be achieved includes a reference to it appearing that those standards or objectives are likely within that period not to be achieved.

PART V   MISCELLANEOUS, GENERAL AND SUPPLEMENTAL PROVISIONS

Waste

93 Producer responsibility: general
(1) For the purpose of promoting or securing an increase in the re-use, recovery or recycling of products or materials, the Secretary of State may by regulations make provision for imposing producer responsibility obligations on such persons, and in respect of such products or materials, as may be prescribed.

(2) The power of the Secretary of State to make regulations shall be exercisable only after consultation with bodies or persons appearing to him to be representative of bodies or persons whose interests are, or are likely to be, substantially affected by the regulations which he proposes to make.

(3) Except in the case of regulations for the implementation of—

    (a) any obligations of the United Kingdom under the Community Treaties, or

    (b) any international agreement to which the United Kingdom is for the time being a party,

the power to make regulations shall be exercisable only where the Secretary of State, after such consultation as is required by subsection (2) above, is satisfied as to the matters specified in subsection (6) below.

(4) The powers conferred by subsection (1) above shall also be exercisable, in a case falling within paragraph (a) or (b) of subsection (3) above, for the purpose of sustaining at least a minimum level of (rather than promoting or securing an increase in) re-use, recovery or recycling of products or materials.

(5) In making regulations by virtue of paragraph (a) or (b) of subsection (3) above, the Secretary of State shall have regard to the matters specified in subsection (6) below; and in its application in relation to the power conferred by virtue of subsection (4) above, subsection (6) below shall have effect as if—

    (a) any reference to an increase in the re-use, recovery or recycling of products or materials were a reference to the sustaining of at least a minimum level of re-use, recovery or recycling of the products or materials in question, and

    (b) any reference to the production of environmental or economic benefits included a reference to the sustaining of at least a minimum level of any such existing benefits,

and any reference in this section or section 94 below to securing or achieving any such benefits shall accordingly include a reference to sustaining at least a minimum level of any such existing benefits.

(6) The matters mentioned in subsections (3) and (5) above are—

    (a) that the proposed exercise of the power would be likely to result in an increase in the re-use, recovery or recycling of the products or materials in question;

    (b) that any such increase would produce environmental or economic benefits;

    (c) that those benefits are significant as against the likely costs resulting from the imposition of the proposed producer responsibility obligation;

    (d) that the burdens imposed on businesses by the regulations are the minimum necessary to secure those benefits; and

    (e) that those burdens are imposed on persons most able to make a contribution to the achievement of the relevant targets—

        (i) having regard to the desirability of acting fairly between persons who manufacture, process, distribute or supply products or materials; and

        (ii) taking account of the need to ensure that the proposed producer responsibility obligation is so framed as to be effective in achieving the purposes for which it is to be imposed;

but nothing in sub-paragraph (i) of paragraph (e) above shall be taken to prevent regulations imposing a producer responsibility obligation on any class or description of person to the exclusion of any others.

(7) The Secretary of State shall have a duty to exercise the power to make regulations in the manner which he considers best calculated to secure that the exercise does not have the effect of restricting, distorting or preventing competition or, if it is likely to have any such effect, that the effect is no greater than is necessary for achieving the environmental or economic benefits mentioned in subsection (6) above.

(8) In this section—

'prescribed' means prescribed in regulations;

'product' and 'material' include a reference to any product or material (as the case may be) at a time when it becomes, or has become, waste;

'producer responsibility obligation' means the steps which are required to be taken by relevant persons of the classes or descriptions to which the regulations in question apply in order to secure attainment of the targets specified or described in the regulations;

'recovery', in relation to products or materials, includes—

(a) composting, or any other form of transformation by biological process, of products or materials; or

(b) the obtaining, by any means, of energy from products or materials; 'regulations' means regulations under this section;

'relevant persons', in the case of any regulations or any producer responsibility obligation, means persons of the class or description to which the producer responsibility obligation imposed by the regulations applies;

'relevant targets' means the targets specified or described in the regulations imposing the producer responsibility obligation in question;

and regulations may prescribe, in relation to prescribed products or materials, activities, or the activities, which are to be regarded for the purposes of this section and sections 94 and 95 below or any regulations as re-use, recovery or recycling of those products or materials.

(9) The power to make regulations shall be exercisable by statutory instrument.

(10) Subject to the following provisions of this section, a statutory instrument containing regulations shall not be made unless a draft of the instrument has been laid before and approved by a resolution of each House of Parliament.

(11) Subsection (10) above shall not apply to a statutory instrument by reason only that it contains regulations varying any relevant targets.

(12) A statutory instrument which, by virtue of subsection (11) above, is not subject to any requirement that a draft of the instrument be laid before and approved by a resolution of each House of Parliament shall be subject to annulment in pursuance of a resolution of either House of Parliament.

94   Producer responsibility: supplementary provisions

(1) Without prejudice to the generality of section 93 above, regulations may, in particular, make provision for or with respect to—

(a) the classes or descriptions of person to whom the producer responsibility obligation imposed by the regulations applies;

(b) the classes or descriptions of products or materials in respect of which the obligation applies;

(c) the targets which are to be achieved with respect to the proportion (whether by weight, volume or otherwise) of the products or materials in question which are to be re-used, recovered or recycled, whether generally or in any prescribed way;

(d) particulars of the obligation imposed by the regulations;

(e) the registration of persons who are subject to a producer responsibility obligation and who are not members of registered exemption schemes, the imposition of requirements in connection with such registration, the variation of such requirements, the making of applications for such registration, the period for which any such registration is to remain in force and the cancellation of any such registration;

(f) the approval, or withdrawal of approval, of exemption schemes by the Secretary of State;

(g) the imposition of requirements on persons who are not members of registered exemption schemes to furnish certificates of compliance to the appropriate Agency;

(h) the approval of persons by the appropriate Agency for the purpose of issuing certificates of compliance;

   (j) the registration of exemption schemes, the imposition of conditions in connection with such registration, the variation of such conditions, the making of applications for such registration and the period for which any such registration is to remain in force;

   (k) the requirements which must be fulfilled, and the criteria which must be met, before an exemption scheme may be registered;

   (l) the powers of the appropriate Agency in relation to applications received by it for registration of exemption schemes;

   (m) the cancellation of the registration of an exemption scheme;

   (n) competition scrutiny of registered exemption schemes or of exemption schemes in whose case applications for registration have been received by the appropriate Agency;

   (o) the exclusion or modification of any provision of the Restrictive Trade Practices Acts 1976 and 1977 in relation to exemption schemes or in relation to agreements where at least one of the parties is an operator of an exemption scheme;

   (p) the fees, or the method of determining the fees, which are to be paid to the appropriate Agency—

      (i) in respect of the approval of persons for the purpose of issuing certificates of compliance;

      (ii) on the making of an application for registration of an exemption scheme;

      (iii) in respect of the subsistence of the registration of that scheme;

      (iv) on submission to the appropriate Agency of a certificate of compliance;

      (v) on the making of an application for, or for the renewal of, registration of a person required to register under the regulations,

      (vi) in respect of the renewal of the registration of that person;

   (q) appeals against the refusal of registration, the imposition of conditions in connection with registration, or the cancellation of the registration, of any exemption scheme;

   (r) the procedure on any such appeal;

   (s) cases, or classes of case,—

      (i) in which an exemption scheme is, or is not, to be treated as registered, or

      (ii) in which a person is, or is not, to be treated as a member of a registered exemption scheme,

      pending the determination or withdrawal of an appeal, and otherwise with respect to the position of persons and exemption schemes pending such determination or withdrawal;

   (t) the imposition on the appropriate Agency of a duty to monitor compliance with any of the obligations imposed by the regulations;

   (u) the imposition on prescribed persons of duties to maintain records, and furnish to the Secretary of State or to the appropriate Agency returns, in such form as may be prescribed of such information as may be prescribed for any purposes of, or for any purposes connected with, or related to, sections 93 to 95 of this Act or any regulations;

   (w) the imposition on the appropriate Agency of a duty to maintain, and make available for inspection by the public, a register containing prescribed information relating to registered exemption schemes or persons required to register under the regulations;

   (y) the powers of entry and inspection which are exercisable by a new Agency for the purposes of its functions under the regulations.

   (ya) the conferring on prescribed persons of power to require, for the purposes of or otherwise in connection with competition scrutiny, the provision by any person of any information which he has, or which he may at any future time acquire, relating to any exemption scheme or to any acts or omissions of an operator of such a scheme or of any person dealing with such an operator.

(2) If it appears to the Secretary of State—

(a) that any action proposed to be taken by the operator of a registered exemption scheme would be incompatible with—

(i) any obligations of the United Kingdom under the Community Treaties, or

(ii) any international agreement to which the United Kingdom is for the time being a party, or

(b) that any action which the operator of such a scheme has power to take is required for the purpose of implementing any such obligations or agreement,

he may direct that operator not to take or, as the case may be, to take the action in question.

(3) Regulations may make provision as to which of the new Agencies is the appropriate Agency for the purposes of any function conferred or imposed by or under this section or section 93 above, or for the purposes of the exercise of that function in relation to the whole or a prescribed part of Great Britain, and may make provision for things done or omitted to be done by either new Agency in relation to any part of Great Britain to be treated for prescribed purposes as done or omitted to be done by the other of them in relation to some other part of Great Britain.

(4) Persons issuing certificates of compliance shall act in accordance with guidance issued for the purpose by the appropriate Agency, which may include guidance as to matters which are, or are not, to be treated as evidence of compliance or as evidence of non-compliance.

(5) In making any provision in relation to fees, regard shall be had to the desirability of securing that the fees received by each new Agency under the regulations are sufficient to meet the costs and expenses incurred by that Agency in the performance of its functions under the regulations.

(6) In this section—

'the appropriate Agency', subject to regulations made by virtue of subsection (3) above, means—

(a) in relation to England and Wales, the Agency;

(b) . . .

'certificate of compliance' means a certificate issued by a person approved for the purpose by the appropriate Agency to the effect that that person is satisfied that the person in respect of whom the certificate is issued is complying with any producer responsibility obligation to which he is subject;

'competition scrutiny', in the case of any scheme, means scrutiny of the scheme for the purpose of enabling the Secretary of State to satisfy himself—

(i) whether or not the scheme has or is likely to have the effect of restricting, distorting or preventing competition or, if it appears to him that the scheme has or is likely to have any such effect, that the effect is or is likely to be no greater than is necessary for achieving the environmental or economic benefits mentioned in section 93(6) above; or

(ii) whether or not the scheme leads or is likely to lead to an abuse of market power;

'exemption scheme' means a scheme which is (or, if it were to be registered in accordance with the regulations, would be) a scheme whose members for the time being are, by virtue of the regulations and their membership of that scheme, exempt from the requirement to comply with the producer responsibility obligation imposed by the regulations;

'new Agency' means the Agency . . .;

'operator', in relation to an exemption scheme, includes any person responsible for establishing, maintaining or managing the scheme;

'registered exemption scheme' means an exemption scheme which is registered pursuant to regulations;

and expressions used in this section and in section 93 above have the same meaning in this section as they have in that section.

(7) Regulations—

(a) may make different provision for different cases;

(b) without prejudice to the generality of paragraph (a) above, may impose different producer responsibility obligations in respect of different classes or descriptions of products or materials and for different classes or descriptions of person or exemption scheme;

(c) may include incidental, consequential, supplemental or transitional provision.

(8) Any direction under this section—

(a) may include such incidental, consequential, supplemental or transitional provision as the Secretary of State considers necessary or expedient; and

(b) shall, on the application of the Secretary of State, be enforceable by injunction. . . .

95 Producer responsibility: offences

(1) Regulations may make provision for a person who contravenes a prescribed requirement of the regulations to be guilty of an offence and liable—

(a) on summary conviction, to a fine not exceeding the statutory maximum;

(b) on conviction on indictment, to a fine.

(2) Where an offence under any provision of the regulations committed by a body corporate is proved to have been committed with the consent or connivance of, or to have been attributable to any neglect on the part of, any director, manager, secretary or other similar officer of the body corporate or a person who was purporting to act in any such capacity, he as well as the body corporate shall be guilty of that offence and shall be liable to be proceeded against and punished accordingly.

(3) Where the affairs of a body corporate are managed by its members, subsection (2) above shall apply in relation to the acts or defaults of a member in connection with his functions of management as if he were a director of the body corporate.

(4) Where the commission by any person of an offence under the regulations is due to the act or default of some other person, that other person may be charged with and convicted of the offence by virtue of this section whether or not proceedings for the offence are taken against the first-mentioned person.

(5) Expressions used in this section and in section 93 or 94 above have the same meaning in this section as they have in that section.

Hedgerows etc.

97 Hedgerows

(1) The appropriate Ministers may by regulations make provision for, or in connection with, the protection of important hedgerows in England or Wales.

(2) The question whether a hedgerow is or is not 'important' for the purposes of this section shall be determined in accordance with prescribed criteria.

(3) For the purpose of facilitating the protection of important hedgerows, regulations under subsection (1) above may also make provision in relation to other hedgerows in England or Wales.

(4) Without prejudice to the generality of subsections (1) to (3) above, regulations under subsection (1) above may provide for the application (with or without modifications) of, or include provision comparable to, any provision contained in the planning Acts and may, in particular, make provision—

(a) prohibiting, or for prohibiting, the removal of, or the carrying out of prescribed acts in relation to, a hedgerow except in prescribed cases;

(b) for or with respect to appeals against determinations or decisions made, or notices given or served, under or by virtue of the regulations, including provision authorising or requiring any body or person to whom an appeal lies to consult prescribed persons with respect to the appeal in prescribed cases;

(c) for a person who contravenes, or fails to comply with, any prescribed provision of the regulations to be guilty of an offence;

(d) for a person guilty of an offence by virtue of paragraph (c) above which consists of the removal, in contravention of the regulations, of a hedgerow of a description prescribed for the purposes of this paragraph to be liable—

(i) on summary conviction, to a fine not exceeding the statutory maximum, or

(ii) on conviction on indictment, to a fine;

(e) for a person guilty of any other offence by virtue of paragraph (c) above to be liable on summary conviction to a fine not exceeding such level on the standard scale as may be prescribed.

(5) Regulations under this section may make different provision for different cases, including different provision in relation to different descriptions of hedgerow, different descriptions of person, different areas or localities or different circumstances.

(6) Before making any regulations under this section the appropriate Ministers shall consult—

(a) such bodies appearing to them to be representative of persons whose business interests are likely to be affected by the proposed regulations,

(b) such bodies appearing to them to be representative of the interests of owners or occupiers of land,

(c) such bodies appearing to them to be representative of the interests of local authorities,

(d) such bodies whose statutory functions include the provision to Ministers of the Crown of advice concerning matters relating to environmental conservation, and

(e) such bodies not falling within paragraphs (a) to (d) above,

as the appropriate Ministers may consider appropriate.

(7) No statutory instrument containing regulations under this section shall be made unless a draft of the instrument has been laid before, and approved by a resolution of, each House of Parliament.

(8) In this section—

'the appropriate Ministers' means—

(a) as respects England, the Secretary of State and the Minister of Agriculture, Fisheries and Food;

(b) as respects Wales, the Secretary of State;

'environmental conservation' means conservation—

(a) of the natural beauty or amenity, or flora or fauna, of England or Wales; or

(b) of features of archaeological or historic interest in England or Wales; 'hedgerow' includes any stretch of hedgerow;

'local authority' means—

(a) the council of a county, county borough, district, London borough, parish or community;

(b) the Common Council of the City of London;

(c) the Council of the Isles of Scilly; 'the planning Acts' has the same meaning as it has in the Town and Country Planning Act 1990 by virtue of section 336(1) of that Act;

'prescribed' means specified, or of a description specified, in regulations;

'regulations' means regulations made by statutory instrument;

'remove', in relation to a hedgerow, means uproot or otherwise destroy, and cognate expressions shall be construed accordingly;

'statutory functions' means functions conferred or imposed by or under any enactment.

(9) Any reference in this section to removing, or carrying out an act in relation to, a hedgerow includes a reference to causing or permitting another to remove, or (as the case may be) carry out an act in relation to, a hedgerow.

Powers of entry

108   Powers of enforcing authorities and persons authorised by them

(1) A person who appears suitable to an enforcing authority may be authorised in writing by that authority to exercise, in accordance with the terms of the authorisation, any of the powers specified in subsection (4) below for the purpose—

   (a) of determining whether any provision of the pollution control enactments in the case of that authority is being, or has been, complied with;

   (b) of exercising or performing one or more of the pollution control functions of that authority; or

   (c) of determining whether and, if so, how such a function should be exercised or performed.

(2) A person who appears suitable to the Agency . . . may be authorised in writing by the Agency . . . to exercise, in accordance with the terms of the authorisation, any of the powers specified in subsection (4) below for the purpose of enabling the Agency . . . to carry out any assessment or prepare any report which the Agency . . . is required to carry out or prepare under section 5(3) or 33(3) above.

(3) Subsection (2) above only applies where the Minister who required the assessment to be carried out, or the report to be prepared, has, whether at the time of making the requirement or at any later time, notified the Agency . . . that the assessment or report appears to him to relate to an incident or possible incident involving or having the potential to involve—

   (a) serious pollution of the environment,

   (b) serious harm to human health, or

   (c) danger to life or health.

(4) The powers which a person may be authorised to exercise under subsection (1) or (2) above are—

   (a) to enter at any reasonable time (or, in an emergency, at any time and, if need be, by force) any premises which he has reason to believe it is necessary for him to enter;

   (b) on entering any premises by virtue of paragraph (a) above, to take with him—

      (i) any other person duly authorised by the enforcing authority and, if the authorised person has reasonable cause to apprehend any serious obstruction in the execution of his duty, a constable; and

      (ii) any equipment or materials required for any purpose for which the power of entry is being exercised;

   (c) to make such examination and investigation as may in any circumstances be necessary;

   (d) as regards any premises which he has power to enter, to direct that those premises or any part of them, or anything in them, shall be left undisturbed (whether generally or in particular respects) for so long as is reasonably necessary for the purpose of any examination or investigation under paragraph (c) above;

   (e) to take such measurements and photographs and make such recordings as he considers necessary for the purpose of any examination or investigation under paragraph (c) above;

(f) to take samples, or cause samples to be taken, of any articles or substances found in or on any premises which he has power to enter, and of the air, water or land in, on, or in the vicinity of, the premises;

(g) in the case of any article or substance found in or on any premises which he has power to enter, being an article or substance which appears to him to have caused or to be likely to cause pollution of the environment or harm to human health, to cause it to be dismantled or subjected to any process or test (but not so as to damage or destroy it, unless that is necessary);

(h) in the case of any such article or substance as is mentioned in paragraph (g) above, to take possession of it and detain it for so long as is necessary for all or any of the following purposes, namely—

   (i) to examine it, or cause it to be examined, and to do, or cause to be done, to it anything which he has power to do under that paragraph;

   (ii) to ensure that it is not tampered with before examination of it is completed;

   (iii) to ensure that it is available for use as evidence in any proceedings for an offence under the pollution control enactments in the case of the enforcing authority under whose authorisation he acts or in any other proceedings relating to a variation notice, enforcement notice or prohibition notice under those enactments;

(j) to require any person whom he has reasonable cause to believe to be able to give any information relevant to any examination or investigation under paragraph (c) above to answer (in the absence of persons other than a person nominated by that person to be present and any persons whom the authorised person may allow to be present) such questions as the authorised person thinks fit to ask and to sign a declaration of the truth of his answers;

(k) to require the production of, or where the information is recorded in computerised form, the furnishing of extracts from, any records—

   (i) which are required to be kept under the pollution control enactments for the enforcing authority under whose authorisation he acts, or

   (ii) which it is necessary for him to see for the purposes of an examination or investigation under paragraph (c) above,

and to inspect and take copies of, or of any entry in, the records;

(l) to require any person to afford him such facilities and assistance with respect to any matters or things within that person's control or in relation to which that person has responsibilities as are necessary to enable the authorised person to exercise any of the powers conferred on him by this section;

(m) any other power for—

   (i) a purpose falling within any paragraph of subsection (1) above, or

   (ii) any such purpose as is mentioned in subsection (2) above, which is conferred by regulations made by the Secretary of State.

(5) The powers which by virtue of subsections (1) and (4) above are conferred in relation to any premises for the purpose of enabling an enforcing authority to determine whether any provision of the pollution control enactments in the case of that authority is being, or has been, complied with shall include power, in order to obtain the information on which that determination may be made,—

   (a) to carry out experimental borings or other works on those premises; and

   (b) to install, keep or maintain monitoring and other apparatus there.

(6) Except in an emergency, in any case where it is proposed to enter any premises used for residential purposes, or to take heavy equipment on to any premises which are to be entered, any entry by virtue of this section shall only be effected—

(a) after the expiration of at least seven days' notice of the proposed entry given to a person who appears to the authorised person in question to be in occupation of the premises in question, and

(b) either—

(i) with the consent of a person who is in occupation of those premises; or

(ii) under the authority of a warrant by virtue of Schedule 18 to this Act.

(7) Except in an emergency, where an authorised person proposes to enter any premises and—

(a) entry has been refused and he apprehends on reasonable grounds that the use of force may be necessary to effect entry, or

(b) he apprehends on reasonable grounds that entry is likely to be refused and that the use of force may be necessary to effect entry,

any entry on to those premises by virtue of this section shall only be effected under the authority of a warrant by virtue of Schedule 18 to this Act.

(8) In relation to any premises belonging to or used for the purposes of the United Kingdom Atomic Energy Authority, subsections (1) to (4) above shall have effect subject to section 6(3) of the Atomic Energy Authority Act 1954 (which restricts entry to such premises where they have been declared to be prohibited places for the purposes of the Official Secrets Act 1911).

(9) The Secretary of State may by regulations make provision as to the procedure to be followed in connection with the taking of, and the dealing with, samples under subsection (4)(f) above.

(10) Where an authorised person proposes to exercise the power conferred by subsection (4)(g) above in the case of an article or substance found on any premises, he shall, if so requested by a person who at the time is present on and has responsibilities in relation to those premises, cause anything which is to be done by virtue of that power to be done in the presence of that person.

(11) Before exercising the power conferred by subsection (4)(g) above in the case of any article or substance, an authorised person shall consult—

(a) such persons having duties on the premises where the article or substance is to be dismantled or subjected to the process or test, and

(b) such other persons,

as appear to him appropriate for the purpose of ascertaining what dangers, if any, there may be in doing anything which he proposes to do or cause to be done under the power.

(12) No answer given by a person in pursuance of a requirement imposed under subsection (4)(j) above shall be admissible in evidence in England and Wales against that person in any proceedings . . .

(13) Nothing in this section shall be taken to compel the production by any person of a document of which he would on grounds of legal professional privilege be entitled to withhold production on an order for discovery in an action in the High Court . . .

(14) Schedule 18 to this Act shall have effect with respect to the powers of entry and related powers which are conferred by this section.

(15) In this section—

'authorised person' means a person authorised under subsection (1) or (2) above;

'emergency' means a case in which it appears to the authorised person in question—

(a) that there is an immediate risk of serious pollution of the environment or serious harm to human health, or

(b) that circumstances exist which are likely to endanger life or health,

and that immediate entry to any premises is necessary to verify the existence of that risk or those circumstances or to ascertain the cause of that risk or those circumstances or to effect a remedy;

'enforcing authority' means—

(a) the Secretary of State;

(b) the Agency;

(c) ... or

(d) a local enforcing authority;

'local enforcing authority' means—

(a) a local enforcing authority, within the meaning of Part I of the Environmental Protection Act 1990;

(b) a local authority, within the meaning of Part IIA of that Act, in its capacity as an enforcing authority for the purposes of that Part;

(c) a local authority for the purposes of Part IV of this Act or regulations under that Part;

[(d) a local authority for the purposes of regulations under section 2 of the Pollution Prevention and Control Act 1999 extending to England and Wales;]

'mobile plant' means plant which is designed to move or to be moved whether on roads or otherwise;

'pollution control enactments', in relation to an enforcing authority, means the enactments and instruments relating to the pollution control functions of that authority;

'pollution control functions', in relation to the Agency ... means the functions conferred on it by or under—

(a) the Alkali, &c, Works Regulation Act 1906;

(b) ...

(c) ...

(d) Part I of the Health and Safety at Work etc Act 1974;

(e) Parts I, IA and II of the Control of Pollution Act 1974;

(f) the Control of Pollution (Amendment) Act 1989;

(g) Parts I, II and IIA of the Environmental Protection Act 1990 (integrated pollution control, waste on land and contaminated land);

(h) Chapter III of Part IV of the Water Industry Act 1991 (special category effluent);

(j) Part III and sections 161 to 161D of the Water Resources Act 1991;

(k) section 19 of the Clean Air Act 1993;

(l) the Radioactive Substances Act 1993;

(m) regulations made by virtue of section 2(2) of the European Communities Act 1972, to the extent that the regulations relate to pollution;

[and, in relation to the Agency, includes the functions conferred or imposed on, or transferred to, it under section 2 of the Pollution Prevention and Control Act 1999;]

'pollution control functions', in relation to a local enforcing authority, means the functions conferred or imposed on, or transferred to, that authority—

(a) by or under Part I or IIA of the Environmental Protection Act 1990;

(b) by or under regulations made by virtue of Part IV of this Act; or

(c) by or under regulations made by virtue of section 2(2) of the European Communities Act 1972, to the extent that the regulations relate to pollution;

[and, in relation to an authority in England or Wales, includes the functions conferred or imposed on, or transferred to, that authority under section 2 of the Pollution Prevention and Control Act 1999;]

'pollution control functions', in relation to the Secretary of State, means any functions which are conferred or imposed upon him by or under any enactment or instrument and which relate to the control of pollution;

'premises' includes any land, vehicle, vessel or mobile plant.

(16) Any power to make regulations under this section shall be exercisable by statutory instrument; and a statutory instrument containing any such regulations shall be subject to annulment pursuant to a resolution of either House of Parliament.

109   Power to deal with cause of imminent danger of serious pollution etc.

(1) Where, in the case of any article or substance found by him on any premises which he has power to enter, an authorised person has reasonable cause to believe that, in the circumstances in which he finds it, the article or substance is a cause of imminent danger of serious pollution of the environment or serious harm to human health, he may seize it and cause it to be rendered harmless (whether by destruction or otherwise).

(2) As soon as may be after any article or substance has been seized and rendered harmless under this section, the authorised person shall prepare and sign a written report giving particulars of the circumstances in which the article or substance was seized and so dealt with by him, and shall—

(a) give a signed copy of the report to a responsible person at the premises where the article or substance was found by him; and

(b) unless that person is the owner of the article or substance, also serve a signed copy of the report on the owner;

and if, where paragraph (b) above applies, the authorised person cannot after reasonable inquiry ascertain the name or address of the owner, the copy may be served on him by giving it to the person to whom a copy was given under paragraph (a) above.

(3) In this section, 'authorised person' has the same meaning as in section 108 above.

110   Offences

(1) It is an offence for a person intentionally to obstruct an authorised person in the exercise or performance of his powers or duties.

(2) It is an offence for a person, without reasonable excuse,—

(a) to fail to comply with any requirement imposed under section 108 above;

(b) to fail or refuse to provide facilities or assistance or any information or to permit any inspection reasonably required by an authorised person in the execution of his powers or duties under or by virtue of that section; or

(c) to prevent any other person from appearing before an authorised person, or answering any question to which an authorised person may require an answer, pursuant to subsection (4) of that section.

(3) It is an offence for a person falsely to pretend to be an authorised person.

(4) A person guilty of an offence under subsection (1) above shall be liable—

(a) in the case of an offence of obstructing an authorised person in the execution of his powers under section 109 above—

(i) on summary conviction, to a fine not exceeding the statutory maximum;

(ii) on conviction on indictment, to a fine or to imprisonment for a term not exceeding two years, or to both;

(b) in any other case, on summary conviction, to a fine not exceeding level 5 on the standard scale.

(5) A person guilty of an offence under subsection (2) or (3) above shall be liable on summary conviction to a fine not exceeding level 5 on the standard scale.

(6) In this section — 'authorised person' means a person authorised under section 108 above and includes a person designated under paragraph 2 of Schedule 18 to this Act; 'powers and duties' includes powers or duties exercisable by virtue of a warrant under Schedule 18 to this Act.

Evidence

111   Evidence in connection with certain pollution offences

(1) The following provisions (which restrict the admissibility in evidence of information obtained from samples) shall cease to have effect—

(a) . . .

(b) . . .

    (c) section 171(4) and (5) of the Water Industry Act 1991; and
    (d) section 209(1), (2) and (4) of the Water Resources Act 1991.
    (2) Information provided or obtained pursuant to or by virtue of a condition of a relevant licence (including information so provided or obtained, or recorded, by means of any apparatus) shall be admissible in evidence in any proceedings, whether against the person subject to the condition or any other person.
    (3) For the purposes of subsection (2) above, apparatus shall be presumed in any proceedings to register or record accurately, unless the contrary is shown or the relevant licence otherwise provides.
    (4) Where—
    (a) by virtue of a condition of a relevant licence, an entry is required to be made in any record as to the observance of any condition of the relevant licence, and
    (b) the entry has not been made, that fact shall be admissible in any proceedings as evidence that that condition has not been observed.
    (5) In this section—
'apparatus' includes any meter or other device for measuring, assessing, determining, recording or enabling to be recorded, the volume, temperature, radioactivity, rate, nature, origin, composition or effect of any substance, flow, discharge, emission, deposit or abstraction;
'condition of a relevant licence' includes any requirement to which a person is subject under, by virtue of or in consequence of a relevant licence; 'environmental licence' has the same meaning as it has in Part I above as it applies in relation to the Agency . . .;
'relevant licence' means—
    (a) any environmental licence;
    (b) . . .
    (c) . . .
    (d) any consent under Chapter III of Part IV of the Water Industry Act 1991 to make discharges of special category effluent; or
    (e) any agreement under section 129 of that Act with respect to, or to any matter connected with, the reception or disposal of such effluent.

Information

113   Disclosure of information

    (1) Notwithstanding any prohibition or restriction imposed by or under any enactment or rule of law, information of any description may be disclosed—
    (a) by a new Agency to a Minister of the Crown, the other new Agency or a local enforcing authority,
    (b) by a Minister of the Crown to a new Agency, another Minister of the Crown or a local enforcing authority, or
    (c) by a local enforcing authority to a Minister of the Crown, a new Agency or another local enforcing authority,
for the purpose of facilitating the carrying out by either of the new Agencies of any of its functions, by any such Minister of any of his environmental functions or by any local enforcing authority of any of its relevant functions; and no person shall be subject to any civil or criminal liability in consequence of any disclosure made by virtue of this subsection.
    (2) Nothing in this section shall authorise the disclosure to a local enforcing authority by a new Agency or another local enforcing authority of information—
    (a) disclosure of which would, in the opinion of a Minister of the Crown, be contrary to the interests of national security; or

(b) which was obtained under or by virtue of the Statistics of Trade Act 1947 and which was disclosed to a new Agency or any of its officers by the Secretary of State.

(3) No information disclosed to any person under or by virtue of this section shall be disclosed by that person to any other person otherwise than in accordance with the provisions of this section, or any provision of any other enactment which authorises or requires the disclosure, if that information is information—

(a) which relates to a trade secret of any person or which otherwise is or might be commercially confidential in relation to any person; or

(b) whose disclosure otherwise than under or by virtue of this section would, in the opinion of a Minister of the Crown, be contrary to the interests of national security.

(4) Any authorisation by or under this section of the disclosure of information by or to any person shall also be taken to authorise the disclosure of that information by or, as the case may be, to any officer of his who is authorised by him to make the disclosure or, as the case may be, to receive the information.

(5) In this section—

'new Agency' means the Agency . . .;

'the environment' means all, or any, of the following media, namely, the air, water and land (and the medium of air includes the air within buildings and the air within other natural or man-made structures above or below ground);] 'environmental functions', in relation to a Minister of the Crown, means any function of that Minister, whether conferred or imposed under or by virtue of any enactment or otherwise, relating to the environment; and

'local enforcing authority' means—

(a) any local authority within the meaning of Part IIA of the Environmental Protection Act 1990, and the 'relevant functions' of such an authority are its functions under or by virtue of that Part;

[(aa) in relation to England and Wales, any local authority within the meaning of regulations under section 2 of the Pollution Prevention and Control Act 1999;]

(b) any local authority within the meaning of Part IV of this Act, and the 'relevant functions' of such an authority are its functions under or by virtue of that Part; [or]

(c) in relation to England, any county council for an area for which there are district councils, and the 'relevant functions' of such a county council are its functions under or by virtue of Part IV of this Act; or

(d) in relation to England and Wales, any local enforcing authority within the meaning of section 1(7) of the Environmental Protection Act 1990, and the 'relevant functions' of such an authority are its functions under or by virtue of Part I of that Act.

Appeals

114 Power of Secretary of State to delegate his functions of determining, or to refer matters involved in, appeals

(1) The Secretary of State may—

(a) appoint any person to exercise on his behalf, with or without payment, any function to which this paragraph applies; or

(b) refer any item to which this paragraph applies to such person as the Secretary of State may nominate for the purpose, with or without payment.

(2) The functions to which paragraph (a) of subsection (1) above applies are any of the Secretary of State's functions of determining—

(a) an appeal under—

(i) section 31A(2)(b), 42B(5) or 49B of the Control of Pollution Act 1974,

(ii) section 4 of the Control of Pollution (Amendment) Act 1989,

(iii) section 15, 22(5), 43, 62(3)(c), 66(5) or 78G of the Environmental Protection Act 1990,

(iv) . . .

(v) section 43, 91, 92, 96, 161C or 191B(5) of the Water Resources Act 1991,

(vi) . . .

(vii) paragraph 6 of Schedule 5 to the Waste Management Licensing Regulations 1994,

[(viii) regulations under section 2 of the Pollution Prevention and Control Act 1999 extending to England and Wales,]

or any matter involved in such an appeal;

(b) the questions, or any of the questions, which fall to be determined by the Secretary of State under section 39(1) or section 49(4) of the Control of Pollution Act 1974.

(3) The items to which paragraph (b) of subsection (1) above applies are—

(a) any matter involved in an appeal falling within subsection (2)(a) above;

(b) any of the questions which fall to be determined by the Secretary of State under section 39(1) or section 49(4) of the Control of Pollution Act 1974.

(4) Schedule 20 to this Act shall have effect with respect to appointments under subsection (1)(a) above.

Crown application

115 Application of this Act to the Crown

(1) Subject to the provisions of this section, this Act shall bind the Crown.

(2) Part III of this Act and any amendments, repeals and revocations made by other provisions of this Act (other than those made by Schedule 21, which shall bind the Crown) bind the Crown to the extent that the enactments to which they relate bind the Crown.

(3) No contravention by the Crown of any provision made by or under this Act shall make the Crown criminally liable; but the High Court . . . may, on the application of the Agency . . . declare unlawful any act or omission of the Crown which constitutes such a contravention.

(4) Notwithstanding anything in subsection (3) above, any provision made by or under this Act shall apply to persons in the public service of the Crown as it applies to other persons.

(5) If the Secretary of State certifies that it appears to him, as respects any Crown premises and any powers of entry exercisable in relation to them specified in the certificate, that it is requisite or expedient that, in the interests of national security, the powers should not be exercisable in relation to those premises, those powers shall not be exercisable in relation to those premises; and in this subsection 'Crown premises' means premises held or used by or on behalf of the Crown.

(6) Nothing in this section shall be taken as in any way affecting Her Majesty in her private capacity; and this subsection shall be construed as if section 38(3) of the Crown Proceedings Act 1947 (interpretation of references to Her Majesty in her private capacity) were contained in this Act.

Section 90	SCHEDULE 11

AIR QUALITY: SUPPLEMENTAL PROVISIONS

Consultation requirements

1.—(1) A local authority in carrying out its functions in relation to—

(a) any air quality review,

(b) any assessment under section 82 or 84 of this Act, or

(c) the preparation of an action plan or any revision of an action plan, shall consult such other persons as fall within sub-paragraph (2) below.

(2) Those persons are—

(a) the Secretary of State;

(b) the appropriate new Agency;

(c) in England and Wales, the highway authority for any highway in the area to which the review or, as the case may be, the action plan or revision relates;

(d) every local authority whose area is contiguous to the authority's area;

(e) any county council in England whose area consists of or includes the whole or any part of the authority's area;

(f) any National Park authority for a National Park whose area consists of or includes the whole or any part of the authority's area;

(g) such public authorities exercising functions in, or in the vicinity of, the authority's area as the authority may consider appropriate;

(h) such bodies appearing to the authority to be representative of persons with business interests in the area to which the review or action plan in question relates as the authority may consider appropriate;

(j) such other bodies or persons as the authority considers appropriate.

(3) In this paragraph 'National Park authority', [. . .] means a National Park authority established under section 63 of this Act which has become the local planning authority for the National Park in question.

(4) [. . .]

Exchange of information with county councils in England

2.—(1) This paragraph applies in any case where a district in England for which there is a district council is comprised in an area for which there is a county council; and in this paragraph—

(a) any reference to the county council is a reference to the council of that area; and

(b) any reference to a district council is a reference to the council of a district comprised in that area.

(2) It shall be the duty of the county council to provide a district council with all such information as is reasonably requested by the district council for purposes connected with the carrying out of its functions under or by virtue of this Part.

(3) It shall be the duty of a district council to provide the county council with all such information as is reasonably requested by the county council for purposes connected with the carrying out of any of its functions relating to the assessment or management of the quality of air.

(4) Information provided to a district council or county council under sub-paragraph (2) or (3) above shall be provided in such form and in such manner and at such times as the district council or, as the case may be, the county council may reasonably require.

(5) A council which provides information under sub-paragraph (2) or (3) above shall be entitled to recover the reasonable cost of doing so from the council which requested the information.

(6) The information which a council may be required to provide under this paragraph shall include information which, although it is not in the possession of the council or would not otherwise come into the possession of the council, is information which it is reasonable to require the council to obtain.

Joint exercise of local authority functions

3.—(1) The appropriate authority may give directions to any two or more local authorities requiring them to exercise the powers conferred by—

(a) section 101(5) of the Local Government Act 1972 (power of two or more local authorities to discharge functions jointly), or

(b) . . .

in relation to functions under or by virtue of this Part in accordance with the directions.

(2) The appropriate authority may give directions to a local authority requiring it—

(a) not to exercise those powers, or

(b) not to exercise those powers in a manner specified in the directions, in relation to functions under or by virtue of this Part.

(3) Where two or more local authorities have exercised those powers in relation to functions under or by virtue of this Part, the appropriate authority may give them directions requiring them to revoke, or modify in accordance with the directions, the arrangements which they have made.

(4) In this paragraph, 'the appropriate authority' means—

(a) in relation to England and Wales, the Secretary of State; and

(b) . . .

Public access to information about air quality

4.—(1) It shall be the duty of every local authority—

(a) to secure that there is available at all reasonable times for inspection by the public free of charge a copy of each of the documents specified in sub-paragraph (2) below; and

(b) to afford to members of the public facilities for obtaining copies of those documents on payment of a reasonable charge.

(2) The documents mentioned in sub-paragraph (1)(a) above are—

(a) a report of the results of any air quality review which the authority has caused to be conducted;

(b) a report of the results of any assessment which the authority has caused to be made under section 82 or 84 of this Act;

(c) any order made by the authority under section 83 of this Act;

(d) any action plan prepared by the authority;

(e) any proposals or statements submitted to the authority pursuant to subsection (3) or (4) of section 86 of this Act;

(f) any directions given to the authority under this Part;

(g) in a case where section 86 of this Act applies, any directions given to the county council under this Part.

Fixed penalty offences

5.—(1) Without prejudice to the generality of paragraph (o) of subsection (2) of section 87 of this Act, regulations may, in particular, make provision—

(a) for the qualifications, appointment or authorisation of persons who are to issue fixed penalty notices;

(b) for the offences in connection with which, the cases or circumstances in which, the time or period at or within which, or the manner in which fixed penalty notices may be issued;

(c) prohibiting the institution, before the expiration of the period for paying the fixed penalty, of proceedings against a person for an offence in connection with which a fixed penalty notice has been issued;

(d) prohibiting the conviction of a person for an offence in connection with which a fixed penalty notice has been issued if the fixed penalty is paid before the expiration of the period for paying it;

(e) entitling, in prescribed cases, a person to whom a fixed penalty notice is issued to give, within a prescribed period, notice requesting a hearing in respect of the offence to which the fixed penalty notice relates;

(f) for the amount of the fixed penalty to be increased by a prescribed amount in any case where the person liable to pay the fixed penalty fails to pay it before the expiration of the period for paying it, without having given notice requesting a hearing in respect of the offence to which the fixed penalty notice relates;

(g) for or in connection with the recovery of an unpaid fixed penalty as a fine or as a civil debt or as if it were a sum payable under a county court order;

(h) for or in connection with execution or other enforcement in respect of an unpaid fixed penalty by prescribed persons;

(j) for a fixed penalty notice, and any prescribed proceedings or other prescribed steps taken by reference to the notice, to be rendered void in prescribed cases where a person makes a prescribed statutory declaration, and for the consequences of any notice, proceedings or other steps being so rendered void (including extension of any time limit for instituting criminal proceedings);

(k) for or in connection with the extension, in prescribed cases or circumstances, by a prescribed person of the period for paying a fixed penalty;

(l) for or in connection with the withdrawal, in prescribed circumstances, of a fixed penalty notice, including—
  (i) repayment of any amount paid by way of fixed penalty in pursuance of a fixed penalty notice which is withdrawn; and
  (ii) prohibition of the institution or continuation of proceedings for the offence in connection with which the withdrawn notice was issued;

(m) for or in connection with the disposition of sums received by way of fixed penalty;

(n) for a certificate purporting to be signed by or on behalf of a prescribed person and stating either—
  (i) that payment of a fixed penalty was, or (as the case may be) was not, received on or before a date specified in the certificate, or
  (ii) that an envelope containing an amount sent by post in payment of a fixed penalty was marked as posted on a date specified in the certificate,
  to be received as evidence of the matters so stated and to be treated, without further proof, as being so signed unless the contrary is shown;

(o) requiring a fixed penalty notice to give such reasonable particulars of the circumstances alleged to constitute the fixed penalty offence to which the notice relates as are necessary for giving reasonable information of the offence and to state—
  (i) the monetary amount of the fixed penalty which may be paid;
  (ii) the person to whom, and the address at which, the fixed penalty may be paid and any correspondence relating to the fixed penalty notice may be sent;
  (iii) the method or methods by which payment of the fixed penalty may be made;
  (iv) the period for paying the fixed penalty;
  (v) the consequences of the fixed penalty not being paid before the expiration of that period;

(p) similar to any provision made by section 79 of the Road Traffic Offenders Act 1988 (statements by constables in fixed penalty cases);

(q) for presuming, in any proceedings, that any document of a prescribed description purporting to have been signed by a person to whom a fixed penalty notice has been issued has been signed by that person;

(r) requiring or authorising a fixed penalty notice to contain prescribed information relating to, or for the purpose of facilitating, the administration of the fixed penalty system;

(s) with respect to the giving of fixed penalty notices, including, in particular, provision with respect to—

    (i) the methods by which,

    (ii) the officers, servants or agents by, to or on whom, and

    (iii) the places at which, fixed penalty notices may be given by, or served on behalf of, a prescribed person;

(t) prescribing the method or methods by which fixed penalties may be paid;

(u) for or with respect to the issue of prescribed documents to persons to whom fixed penalty notices are or have been given;

(w) for a fixed penalty notice to be treated for prescribed purposes as if it were an information or summons or any other document of a prescribed description.

(2) The provision that may be made by regulations prescribing fixed penalty offences includes provision for an offence to be a fixed penalty offence—

    (a) only if it is committed in such circumstances or manner as may be prescribed; or

    (b) except if it is committed in such circumstances or manner as may be prescribed.

(3) Regulations may provide for any offence which is a fixed penalty offence to cease to be such an offence.

(4) An offence which, in consequence of regulations made by virtue of sub-paragraph (3) above, has ceased to be a fixed penalty offence shall be eligible to be prescribed as such an offence again.

(5) Regulations may make provision for such exceptions, limitations and conditions as the Secretary of State considers necessary or expedient.

(6) In this paragraph —

'fixed penalty' means a penalty of such amount as may be prescribed (whether by being specified in, or made calculable under, regulations);

'fixed penalty notice' means a notice offering a person an opportunity to discharge any liability to conviction for a fixed penalty offence by payment of a penalty of a prescribed amount;

'fixed penalty offence' means, subject to sub-paragraph (2) above, any offence (whether under or by virtue of this Part or any other enactment) which is for the time being prescribed as a fixed penalty offence;

'the fixed penalty system' means the system implementing regulations made under or by virtue of paragraph (o) of subsection (2) of section 87 of this Act; 'the period for paying', in relation to any fixed penalty, means such period as may be prescribed for the purpose;

'regulations' means regulations under or by virtue of paragraph (o) of subsection (2) of section 87 of this Act.

Section 108   SCHEDULE 18

SUPPLEMENTAL PROVISIONS WITH RESPECT TO POWERS OF ENTRY

Interpretation

1.—(1) In this Schedule—

'designated person' means an authorised person, within the meaning of section 91 of this Act and includes a person designated by virtue of paragraph 2 below; 'relevant power' means a power conferred by section 108 of this Act, including a power exercisable by virtue of a warrant under this Schedule.

(2) Expressions used in this Schedule and in section 108 of this Act have the same meaning in this Schedule as they have in that section.

Issue of warrants

2.—(1) If it is shown to the satisfaction of a justice of the peace . . . on sworn information in writing—
- (a) that there are reasonable grounds for the exercise in relation to any premises of a relevant power; and
- (b) that one or more of the conditions specified in sub-paragraph (2) below is fulfilled in relation to those premises,

the justice . . . may by warrant authorise an enforcing authority to designate a person who shall be authorised to exercise the power in relation to those premises, in accordance with the warrant and, if need be, by force.

(2) The conditions mentioned in sub-paragraph (1)(b) above are—
- (a) that the exercise of the power in relation to the premises has been refused;
- (b) that such a refusal is reasonably apprehended;
- (c) that the premises are unoccupied;
- (d) that the occupier is temporarily absent from the premises and the case is one of urgency; or
- (e) that an application for admission to the premises would defeat the object of the proposed entry.

(3) In a case where subsection (6) of section 108 of this Act applies, a justice of the peace . . . shall not issue a warrant under this Schedule by virtue only of being satisfied that the exercise of a power in relation to any premises has been refused, or that a refusal is reasonably apprehended, unless he is also satisfied that the notice required by that subsection has been given and that the period of that notice has expired.

(4) Every warrant under this Schedule shall continue in force until the purposes for which the warrant was issued have been fulfilled.

Manner of exercise of powers

3.   A person designated as the person who may exercise a relevant power shall produce evidence of his designation and other authority before he exercises the power.

Information obtained to be admissible in evidence

4.—(1) Subject to section 108(12) of this Act, information obtained in consequence of the exercise of a relevant power, with or without the consent of any person, shall be admissible in evidence against that or any other person.

(2) Without prejudice to the generality of sub-paragraph (1) above, information obtained by means of monitoring or other apparatus installed on any premises in the exercise of a relevant power, with or without the consent of any person in occupation of the premises, shall be admissible in evidence in any proceedings against that or any other person.

Duty to secure premises

5.   A person who, in the exercise of a relevant power enters on any premises which are unoccupied or whose occupier is temporarily absent shall leave the premises as effectually secured against trespassers as he found them.

Compensation

6.—(1) Where any person exercises any power conferred by section 108(4)(a) or (b) or (5) of this Act, it shall be the duty of the enforcing authority under whose authorisation he acts to make full compensation to any person who has sustained loss or damage by reason of—

>   (a) the exercise by the designated person of that power; or
>   (b) the performance of, or failure of the designated person to perform, the duty imposed by paragraph 5 above.

(2) Compensation shall not be payable by virtue of sub-paragraph (1) above in respect of any loss or damage if the loss or damage—

>   (a) is attributable to the default of the person who sustained it; or
>   (b) is loss or damage in respect of which compensation is payable by virtue of any other provision of the pollution control enactments.

(3) Any dispute as to a person's entitlement to compensation under this paragraph, or as to the amount of any such compensation, shall be referred to the arbitration of a single arbitrator . . . or, in default of agreement, by the Secretary of State.

(4) A designated person shall not be liable in any civil or criminal proceedings for anything done in the purported exercise of any relevant power if the court is satisfied that the act was done in good faith and that there were reasonable grounds for doing it.

Noise Act 1996
(1996, c. 37)

Summary procedure for dealing with noise at night

1   Adoption of these provisions by local authorities

(1) Sections 2 to 9 only apply to the area of a local authority if the authority have so resolved or an order made by the Secretary of State so provides.

(2) If a local authority resolve to apply those sections to their area—

>   (a) those sections are to have effect there on and after a date specified in the resolution ('the commencement date'), which must be at least three months after the passing of the resolution, and
>   (b) the local authority must cause a notice to be published, in two consecutive weeks ending at least two months before the commencement date, in a local newspaper circulating in their area.

(3) A notice published under subsection (2)(b) must—

>   (a) state that the resolution has been passed,
>   (b) give the commencement date, and
>   (c) set out the general effect of those sections.

(4) An order under this section must not provide for those sections to have effect before the end of the period of three months beginning with the making of the order.

2   Investigation of complaints of noise from a dwelling at night

(1) A local authority must, if they receive a complaint of the kind mentioned in subsection (2), secure that an officer of the authority takes reasonable steps to investigate the complaint.

(2) The kind of complaint referred to is one made by any individual present in a dwelling during night hours (referred to in this Act as 'the complainant's dwelling') that excessive noise is being emitted from another dwelling (referred to in this group of sections as 'the offending dwelling').

(3) A complaint under subsection (2) may be made by any means.

(4) If an officer of the authority is satisfied, in consequence of an investigation under subsection (1), that—

    (a) noise is being emitted from the offending dwelling during night hours, and

    (b) the noise, if it were measured from within the complainant's dwelling, would or might exceed the permitted level,

he may serve a notice about the noise under section 3.

    (5) For the purposes of subsection (4), it is for the officer of the authority dealing with the particular case—

    (a) to decide whether any noise, if it were measured from within the complain-ant's dwelling, would or might exceed the permitted level, and

    (b) for the purposes of that decision, to decide whether to assess the noise from within or outside the complainant's dwelling and whether or not to use any device for measuring the noise.

    (6) In this group of sections, 'night hours' means the period beginning with 11 p.m. and ending with the following 7 a.m.

    (7) Where a local authority receive a complaint under subsection (2) and the offending dwelling is within the area of another local authority, the first local authority may act under this group of sections as if the offending dwelling were within their area, and accordingly may so act whether or not this group of sections applies to the area of the other local authority.

    (8) In this section and sections 3 to 9, 'this group of sections' means this and those sections.

3 Warning notices

    (1) A notice under this section (referred to in this Act as 'a warning notice') must—

    (a) state that an officer of the authority considers—

        (i) that noise is being emitted from the offending dwelling during night hours, and

        (ii) that the noise exceeds, or may exceed, the permitted level, as measured from within the complainant's dwelling, and

    (b) give warning that any person who is responsible for noise which is emitted from the dwelling, in the period specified in the notice, and exceeds the permitted level, as measured from within the complainant's dwelling, may be guilty of an offence.

    (2) The period specified in a warning notice must be a period—

    (a) beginning not earlier than ten minutes after the time when the notice is served and

    (b) ending with the following 7 a.m.

    (3) A warning notice must be served—

    (a) by delivering it to any person present at or near the offending dwelling and appearing to the officer of the authority to be responsible for the noise, or

    (b) if it is not reasonably practicable to identify any person present at or near the dwelling as being a person responsible for the noise on whom the notice may reasonably be served, by leaving it at the offending dwelling.

    (4) A warning notice must state the time at which it is served.

    (5) For the purposes of this group of sections, a person is responsible for noise emitted from a dwelling if he is a person to whose act, default or sufferance the emission of the noise is wholly or partly attributable.

4 Offence where noise exceeds permitted level after service of notice

    (1) If a warning notice has been served in respect of noise emitted from a dwelling, any person who is responsible for noise which—

    (a) is emitted from the dwelling in the period specified in the notice, and

    (b) exceeds the permitted level, as measured from within the complainant's dwelling,

is guilty of an offence.

(2) It is a defence for a person charged with an offence under this section to show that there was a reasonable excuse for the act, default or sufferance in question.

(3) A person guilty of an offence under this section is liable on summary conviction to a fine not exceeding level 3 on the standard scale.

5   Permitted level of noise

(1) For the purposes of this group of sections, the Secretary of State may by directions in writing determine the maximum level of noise (referred to in this group of sections as 'the permitted level') which may be emitted during night hours from any dwelling.

(2) The permitted level is to be a level applicable to noise as measured from within any other dwelling in the vicinity by an approved device used in accordance with any conditions subject to which the approval was given.

(3) Different permitted levels may be determined for different circumstances, and the permitted level may be determined partly by reference to other levels of noise.

(4) The Secretary of State may from time to time vary his directions under this section by further directions in writing.

6   Approval of measuring devices

(1) For the purposes of this group of sections, the Secretary of State may approve in writing any type of device used for the measurement of noise; and references in this group of sections to approved devices are to devices of a type so approved.

(2) Any such approval may be given subject to conditions as to the purposes for which, and the manner and other circumstances in which, devices of the type concerned are to be used.

(3) In proceedings for an offence under section 4, a measurement of noise made by a device is not admissible as evidence of the level of noise unless it is an approved device and any conditions subject to which the approval was given are satisfied.

7   Evidence

(1) In proceedings for an offence under section 4, evidence—
  (a) of a measurement of noise made by a device, or of the circumstances in which it was made, or
  (b) that a device was of a type approved for the purposes of section 6, or that any conditions subject to which the approval was given were satisfied,
may be given by the production of a document mentioned in subsection (2).

(2) The document referred to is one which is signed by an officer of the local authority and which (as the case may be)—
  (a) gives particulars of the measurement or of the circumstances in which it was made, or
  (b) states that the device was of such a type or that, to the best of the knowledge and belief of the person making the statement, all such conditions were satisfied;
and if the document contains evidence of a measurement of noise it may consist partly of a record of the measurement produced automatically by a device.

(3) In proceedings for an offence under section 4, evidence that noise, or noise of any kind, measured by a device at any time was noise emitted from a dwelling may be given by the production of a document—
  (a) signed by an officer of the local authority, and
  (b) stating that he had identified that dwelling as the source at that time of the noise or, as the case may be, the noise of that kind.

(4) For the purposes of this section, a document purporting to be signed as mentioned in subsection (2) or (3)(a) is to be treated as being so signed unless the contrary is proved.

(5) This section does not make a document admissible as evidence in proceedings for an offence unless a copy of it has, not less than seven days before the hearing or trial, been served on the person charged with the offence.

(6) This section does not make a document admissible as evidence of anything other than the matters shown on a record produced automatically by a device if, not less than three days before the hearing or trial or within such further time as the court may in special circumstances allow, the person charged with the offence serves a notice on the prosecutor requiring attendance at the hearing or trial of the person who signed the document.

8 Fixed penalty notices

(1) Where an officer of a local authority who is authorised for the purposes of this section has reason to believe that a person is committing or has just committed an offence under section 4, he may give that person a notice (referred to in this Act as a 'fixed penalty notice') offering him the opportunity of discharging any liability to conviction for that offence by payment of a fixed penalty.

(2) A fixed penalty notice may be given to a person—
  (a) by delivering the notice to him, or
  (b) if it is not reasonably practicable to deliver it to him, by leaving the notice, addressed to him, at the offending dwelling.

(3) Where a person is given a fixed penalty notice in respect of such an offence—
  (a) proceedings for that offence must not be instituted before the end of the period of fourteen days following the date of the notice, and
  (b) he cannot be convicted of that offence if he pays the fixed penalty before the end of that period.

(4) A fixed penalty notice must give such particulars of the circumstances alleged to constitute the offence as are necessary for giving reasonable information of the offence.

(5) A fixed penalty notice must state—
  (a) the period during which, because of subsection (3)(a), proceedings will not be taken for the offence,
  (b) the amount of the fixed penalty, and
  (c) the person to whom and the address at which the fixed penalty may be paid.

(6) Payment of the fixed penalty may (among other methods) be made by pre-paying and posting to that person at that address a letter containing the amount of the penalty (in cash or otherwise).

(7) Where a letter containing the amount of the penalty is sent in accordance with subsection (6), payment is to be regarded as having been made at the time at which that letter would be delivered in the ordinary course of post.

(8) The fixed penalty payable under this section is £100.

9 Section 8: supplementary

(1) If a form for a fixed penalty notice is specified in an order made by the Secretary of State, a fixed penalty notice must be in that form.

(2) If a fixed penalty notice is given to a person in respect of noise emitted from a dwelling in any period specified in a warning notice—
  (a) no further fixed penalty notice may be given to that person in respect of noise emitted from the dwelling during that period, but
  (b) that person may be convicted of a further offence under section 4 in respect of noise emitted, from the dwelling after the fixed penalty notice is given and before the end of that period.

(3) The Secretary of State may from time to time by order amend section 8(8) so as to change the amount of the fixed penalty payable under that section.

(4) Sums received by a local authority under section 8 must be paid to the Secretary of State.

(5) In proceedings for an offence under section 4, evidence that payment of a fixed penalty was or was not made before the end of any period may be given by the production of a certificate which—

(a) purports to be signed by or on behalf of the person having responsibility for the financial affairs of the local authority, and

(b) states that payment of a fixed penalty was made on any date or, as the case may be, was not received before the end of that period.

Seizure, etc. of equipment used to make noise unlawfully

10 Powers of entry and seizure etc.

(1) The power conferred by subsection (2) may be exercised where an officer of a local authority has reason to believe that—

(a) a warning notice has been served in respect of noise emitted from a dwelling, and

(b) at any time in the period specified in the notice, noise emitted from the dwelling has exceeded the permitted level, as measured from within the complainant's dwelling.

(2) An officer of a local authority, or a person authorised by the authority for the purpose, may enter the dwelling from which the noise in question is being or has been emitted and may seize and remove any equipment which it appears to him is being or has been used in the emission of the noise.

(3) A person exercising the power conferred by subsection (2) must produce his authority, if he is required to do so.

(4) If it is shown to a justice of the peace on sworn information in writing that—

(a) a warning notice has been served in respect of noise emitted from a dwelling,

(b) at any time in the period specified in the notice, noise emitted from the dwelling has exceeded the permitted level, as measured from within the complainant's dwelling, and

(c) entry of an officer of the local authority, or of a person authorised by the authority for the purpose, to the dwelling has been refused, or such a refusal is apprehended, or a request by an officer of the authority, or of such a person, for admission would defeat the object of the entry,

the justice may by warrant under his hand authorise the local authority, by any of their officers or any person authorised by them for the purpose, to enter the premises, if need be by force.

(5) A person who enters any premises under subsection (2), or by virtue of a warrant issued under subsection (4), may take with him such other persons and such equipment as may be necessary; and if, when he leaves, the premises are unoccupied, must leave them as effectively secured against trespassers as he found them.

(6) A warrant issued under subsection (4) continues in force until the purpose for which the entry is required has been satisfied.

(7) The power of a local authority under section 81(3) of the Environmental Protection Act 1990 to abate any matter, where that matter is a statutory nuisance by virtue of section 79(1)(g) of that Act (noise emitted from premises so as to be prejudicial to health or a nuisance), includes power to seize and remove any equipment which it appears to the authority is being or has been used in the emission of the noise in question.

(8) A person who wilfully obstructs any person exercising any powers conferred under subsection (2) or by virtue of subsection (7) is liable, on summary conviction, to a fine not exceeding level 3 on the standard scale.

(9) The Schedule to this Act (which makes further provision in relation to anything seized and removed by virtue of this section) has effect.

General

11 Interpretation and subordinate legislation

(1) In this Act, 'local authority' means—

    (a) in Greater London, a London borough council, the Common Council of the City of London and, as respects the Temples, the Sub-Treasurer of the Inner Temple and the Under-Treasurer of the Middle Temple respectively,

    (b) outside Greater London—

        (i) any district council,

        (ii) the council of any county so far as they are the council for any area for which there are no district councils,

        (iii) in Wales, the council of a county borough, and

    (c) the Council of the Isles of Scilly.

  (2) In this Act—

    (a) 'dwelling' means any building, or part of a building, used or intended to be used as a dwelling,

    (b) references to noise emitted from a dwelling include noise emitted from any garden, yard, outhouse or other appurtenance belonging to or enjoyed with the dwelling.

  (3) The power to make an order under this Act is exercisable by statutory instrument which (except in the case of an order under section 14) shall be subject to annulment in pursuance of a resolution of either House of Parliament.

12 Protection from personal liability

  (1) A member of a local authority or an officer or other person authorised by a local authority is not personally liable in respect of any act done by him or by the local authority or any such person if the act was done in good faith for the purpose of executing powers conferred by, or by virtue, of this Act.

  (2) Subsection (1) does not apply to liability under section 19 or 20 of the Local Government Finance Act 1982 (powers of district auditor and court).

13 Expenses

There is to be paid out of money provided by Parliament any increase attributable to this Act in the sums payable out of money so provided under any other enactment.

14 Short title, commencement and extent

  (1) This Act may be cited as the Noise Act 1996.

  (2) This Act is to come into force on such day as the Secretary of State may by order appoint, and different days may be appointed for different purposes.

  (3) . . .

  (4) . . .

Section 10   SCHEDULE

POWERS IN RELATION TO SEIZED EQUIPMENT

Introductory

1 In this Schedule—

    (a) a 'noise offence' means—

        (i) in relation to equipment seized under section 10(2) of this Act, an offence under section 4 of this Act, and

        (ii) in relation to equipment seized under section 81(3) of the Environmental Protection Act 1990 (as extended by section 10(7) of this Act), an offence under section 80(4) of that Act in respect of a statutory nuisance falling within section 79(1)(g) of that Act,

    (b) 'seized equipment' means equipment seized in the exercise of the power of seizure and removal conferred by section 10(2) of this Act or section 81(3) of the Environmental Protection Act 1990 (as so extended),

(c) 'related equipment', in relation to any conviction of or proceedings for a noise offence, means seized equipment used or alleged to have been used in the commission of the offence,

(d) 'responsible local authority', in relation to seized equipment, means the local authority by or on whose behalf the equipment was seized.

Retention

2.—(1) Any seized equipment may be retained—

(a) during the period of twenty-eight days beginning with the seizure, or

(b) if it is related equipment in proceedings for a noise offence instituted within that period against any person, until—

(i) he is sentenced or otherwise dealt with for the offence or acquitted of the offence, or

(ii) the proceedings are discontinued.

(2) Sub-paragraph (1) does not authorise the retention of seized equipment if—

(a) a person has been given a fixed penalty notice under section 8 of this Act in respect of any noise,

(b) the equipment was seized because of its use in the emission of the noise in respect of which the fixed penalty notice was given, and

(c) that person has paid the fixed penalty before the end of the period allowed for its payment.

Forfeiture

3.—(1) Where a person is convicted of a noise offence the court may make an order ('a forfeiture order') for forfeiture of any related equipment.

(2) The court may make a forfeiture order whether or not it also deals with the offender in respect of the offence in any other way and without regard to any restrictions on forfeiture in any enactment.

(3) In considering whether to make a forfeiture order in respect of any equipment a court must have regard—

(a) to the value of the equipment, and

(b) to the likely financial and other effects on the offender of the making of the order (taken together with any other order that the court contemplates making).

(4) A forfeiture order operates to deprive the offender of any rights in the equipment to which it relates.

Consequences of forfeiture

4.—(1) Where any equipment has been forfeited under paragraph 3, a magistrates' court may, on application by a claimant of the equipment (other than the person in whose case the forfeiture order was made) make an order for delivery of the equipment to the applicant if it appears to the court that he is the owner of the equipment.

(2) No application may be made under sub-paragraph (1) by any claimant of the equipment after the expiry of the period of six months beginning with the date on which a forfeiture order was made in respect of the equipment.

(3) Such an application cannot succeed unless the claimant satisfies the court—

(a) that he had not consented to the offender having possession of the equipment, or

(b) that he did not know, and had no reason to suspect, that the equipment was likely to be used in the commission of a noise offence.

(4) Where the responsible local authority is of the opinion that the person in whose case the forfeiture order was made is not the owner of the equipment, it must take reasonable steps to bring to the attention of persons who may be entitled to do so their right to make an application under sub-paragraph (1).

(5) An order under sub-paragraph (1) does not affect the right of any person to take, within the period of six months beginning with the date of the order, proceedings for the recovery of the equipment from the person in possession of it in pursuance of the order, but the right ceases on the expiry of that period.

(6) If on the expiry of the period of six months beginning with the date on which a forfeiture order was made in respect of the equipment no order has been made under sub-paragraph (1), the responsible local authority may dispose of the equipment.

Return etc. of seized equipment

5.   If in proceedings for a noise offence no order for forfeiture of related equipment is made, the court (whether or not a person is convicted of the offence) may give such directions as to the return, retention or disposal of the equipment by the responsible local authority as it thinks fit.

6.—(1) Where in the case of any seized equipment no proceedings in which it is related equipment are begun within the period mentioned in paragraph 2(1)(a)—

> (a) the responsible local authority must return the equipment to any person who—
>> (i)   appears to them to be the owner of the equipment, and
>> (ii) makes a claim for the return of the equipment within the period mentioned in sub-paragraph (2), and
> (b) if no such person makes such a claim within that period, the responsible local authority may dispose of the equipment.

(2) The period referred to in sub-paragraph (1)(a)(ii) is the period of six months beginning with the expiry of the period mentioned in paragraph 2(1)(a).

(3) The responsible local authority must take reasonable steps to bring to the attention of persons who may be entitled to do so their right to make such a claim.

(4) Subject to sub-paragraph (6), the responsible local authority is not required to return any seized equipment under sub-paragraph (1)(a) until the person making the claim has paid any such reasonable charges for the seizure, removal and retention of the equipment as the authority may demand.

(5) If—

> (a) equipment is sold in pursuance of—
>> (i)   paragraph 4(6),
>> (ii) directions under paragraph 5, or
>> (iii) this paragraph, and
> (b) before the expiration of the period of one year beginning with the date on which the equipment is sold any person satisfies the responsible local authority that at the time of its sale he was the owner of the equipment,

the authority is to pay him any sum by which any proceeds of sale exceed any such reasonable charges for the seizure, removal or retention of the equipment as the authority may demand.

(6) The responsible local authority cannot demand charges from any person under sub-paragraph (4) or (5) who they are satisfied did not know, and had no reason to suspect, that the equipment was likely to be used in the emission of noise exceeding the level determined under section 5.

Pollution Prevention and Control Act 1999
(1999, c. 24)

1 General purpose of section 2 and definitions

(1) The purpose of section 2 is to enable provision to be made for or in connection with—

(a) implementing Council Directive 96/61/EC concerning integrated pollution prevention and control;

(b) regulating, otherwise than in pursuance of that Directive, activities which are capable of causing any environmental pollution;

(c) otherwise preventing or controlling emissions capable of causing any such pollution.

(2) In this Act—

'activities' means activities of any nature, whether—

(a) industrial or commercial or other activities, or

(b) carried on on particular premises or otherwise,

and includes (with or without other activities) the depositing, keeping or disposal of any substance;

'environmental pollution' means pollution of the air, water or land which may give rise to any harm; and for the purposes of this definition (but without prejudice to its generality)—

(a) 'pollution' includes pollution caused by noise, heat or vibrations or any other kind of release of energy, and

(b) 'air' includes air within buildings and air within other natural or man-made structures above or below ground.

(3) In the definition of 'environmental pollution' in subsection (2), 'harm' means—

(a) harm to the health of human beings or other living organisms;

(b) harm to the quality of the environment, including—

(i) harm to the quality of the environment taken as a whole,

(ii) harm to the quality of the air, water or land, and

(iii) other impairment of, or interference with, the ecological systems of which any living organisms form part;

(c) offence to the senses of human beings;

(d) damage to property; or

(e) impairment of, or interference with, amenities or other legitimate uses of the environment (expressions used in this paragraph having the same meaning as in Council Directive 96/61/EC).

2 Regulation of polluting activities

(1) The Secretary of State may by regulations make provision for any of the purposes listed in Part I of Schedule 1; and Part II of that Schedule has effect for supplementing Part I.

(2) In accordance with subsection (1) of section 1, the provision which may be made by regulations under this section is provision for or in connection with any of the matters mentioned in paragraphs (a) to (c) of that subsection.

(3) Regulations under this section may—

(a) contain such consequential, incidental, supplementary, transitional or saving provisions (including provisions amending, repealing or revoking enactments) as the Secretary of State considers appropriate; and

(b) make different provision for different cases, including different provision in relation to different persons, circumstances, areas or localities.

(4) Before making any regulations under this section, the Secretary of State shall consult—

    (a) the Environment Agency if the regulations are to apply in relation to England or Wales;

    (b) . . .

    (c) such bodies or persons appearing to him to be representative of the interests of local government, industry, agriculture and small businesses respectively as he may consider appropriate; and

    (d) such other bodies or persons as he may consider appropriate.

(5) Consultation undertaken before the passing of this Act shall constitute as effective compliance with subsection (4) as if undertaken after that passing.

(6) The power to make regulations under this section shall be exercised by statutory instrument.

(7) A statutory instrument containing regulations under this section, if made without a draft having been laid before, and approved by a resolution of, each House of Parliament, shall be subject to annulment in pursuance of a resolution of either House.

(8) No regulations to which this subsection applies shall be made (whether alone or with other regulations) unless a draft of the statutory instrument containing the regulations has been laid before, and approved by a resolution of, each House of Parliament.

(9) Subsection (8) applies to—

    (a) the first regulations to be made under this section which apply in relation to England;

    (b) the first regulations to be made under this section which apply in relation to Wales;

    (c) . . .

    (d) regulations under this section which create an offence or increase a penalty for an existing offence;

    (e) regulations under this section which amend or repeal any provision of an Act.

3 Prevention etc. of pollution after accidents involving offshore installations

(1) The Secretary of State may, in relation to offshore installations, by regulations make provision which, subject to any modifications that he considers appropriate, corresponds or is similar to any provision made by, or capable of being made under, sections 137 to 140 of the Merchant Shipping Act 1995 (powers to prevent and reduce pollution, and the risk of pollution, by oil or other substances following an accident) in relation to ships.

(2) In this section—

'offshore installation' means any structure or other thing (but not a ship) in or under—

    (a) United Kingdom territorial waters, or

    (b) any waters mentioned in section 7(9)(b) or (c),

which is used for the purposes of, or in connection with, the exploration, development or production of petroleum;

'petroleum' has the meaning given by section 1 of the Petroleum Act 1998;

'ship' has the same meaning as in the Merchant Shipping Act 1995.

(3) Regulations under this section may—

    (a) contain such consequential, incidental, supplementary, transitional or saving provisions as the Secretary of State considers appropriate; and

    (b) make different provision for different cases, including different provision in relation to different persons, circumstances, areas or localities.

(4) Before making any regulations under this section, the Secretary of State shall consult—

    (a) the Environment Agency, . . . ;

(b) such bodies or persons appearing to him to be representative of the interests of owners or operators of offshore installations as he may consider appropriate; and

(c) such other bodies or persons as he may consider appropriate.

(5) The power to make regulations under this section shall be exercised by statutory instrument.

(6) No regulations shall be made under this section (whether alone or with other regulations) unless a draft of the statutory instrument containing the regulations has been laid before, and approved by a resolution of, each House of Parliament.

4   Time-limited disposal or waste management licences

(1) Where—

(a) a disposal licence under section 5 of the 1974 Act became a site licence by virtue of section 77(2) of the 1990 Act (conversion, on the appointed day, of existing disposal licence under section 5 of the 1974 Act into a site licence),

(b) the licence has expired at a time ('the time of expiry') falling before the day on which this Act is passed but not earlier than the appointed day,

(c) the licence authorised the carrying on of activities in or on land in England or Wales, and

(d) relevant activities have taken place at a time falling not more than one year before the day on which this Act is passed,

the licence shall (subject to subsection (7)) for all purposes be deemed not to have expired but to have become, at the time of expiry, a site licence continuing in force in accordance with section 35(11) of the 1990 Act.

(2) Subsection (3) applies where—

(a) a disposal licence under section 5 of the 1974 Act expired at a time ('the time of expiry') falling before the appointed day (so that it was not converted into a site licence by section 77(2) of the 1990 Act),

(b) the licence authorised the carrying on of activities in or on land in England or Wales, and

(c) relevant activities have taken place at a time falling not more than one year before the day on which this Act is passed.

(3) The licence shall (subject to subsection (7)) for all purposes be deemed—

(a) not to have expired, and

(b) to have been subsisting on the appointed day and (accordingly) to have become on that day a site licence by virtue of section 77(2) of the 1990 Act,

and the site licence which the licence is deemed to have become on that day shall for all purposes be deemed to have been one that continues in force in accordance with section 35(11) of the 1990 Act.

(4) Where—

(a) a site licence in force immediately before the day on which this Act is passed—

(i) became a site licence by virtue of section 77(2) of the 1990 Act, and

(ii) will expire on or after the day on which this Act is passed (if it has not previously been revoked entirely, or had its surrender accepted, under Part II of the 1990 Act), and

(b) relevant activities have taken place at a time falling not more than one year before that day,

the licence shall for all purposes be deemed to have become at the beginning of that day a site licence continuing in force in accordance with section 35(11) of the 1990 Act.

(5) Where subsection (1), (3) or (4) has effect in relation to a licence, the terms and conditions of the licence as continued in force by that subsection shall, except so far as providing for the expiry of the licence and subject to subsection (6)(b) and (c), be such as were

in force immediately before the relevant time (unless and until varied under Part II of the 1990 Act); and 'the relevant time' means—

    (a) where subsection (1) or (3) has effect in relation to a licence, the time of expiry;

    (b) where subsection (4) has effect in relation to a licence, the beginning of the day on which this Act is passed.

(6) Where subsection (1) or (3) has effect in relation to a licence (but without prejudice to the generality of that subsection)—

    (a) activities carried out during the interim period which (by virtue of subsection (1) or (3)) become authorised by the licence shall be treated as authorised at the time they were carried out (even though at that time their being carried out amounted to a contravention of section 33(1)(a) or (b) of the 1990 Act or section 3(1) of the 1974 Act);

    (b) anything done in relation to the licence before the time of expiry but purporting to take effect after that time (such as the serving of a notice under section 37(4) or 38(12) of the 1990 Act, or in pursuance of section 7 of the 1974 Act, specifying a time falling during or after the interim period) shall be treated as having had (or having) effect as if the licence had not in fact expired;

    (c) anything which during the interim period purported to be done in relation to the licence (such as a modification of the licence or the revocation, suspension, transfer or acceptance of the surrender of the licence or the carrying out of consultation, exercise of functions under section 9 of the 1974 Act or section 42 of the 1990 Act, imposition of requirements during a suspension or bringing or determination of an appeal) shall be treated as having had effect as if the licence had then been in force;

    (d) any fees which (by virtue of subsection (1) or (3)) are treated as having become payable before the passing of this Act shall be taken to have become payable at the time they would have become payable had the licence not in fact expired; and

    (e) the holder of the licence shall be treated as having been, during the interim period, an authorised person for the purposes of section 34(1)(c) of the 1990 Act.

(7) Where subsection (1) or (3) has effect in relation to a licence, a person shall not be guilty of an offence under section 33(6) or 38(10) or (11) of the 1990 Act as a result of anything done or omitted to be done during the interim period becoming (by virtue of subsection (1) or (3)) a contravention of any condition of the licence or (as the case may be) a failure to comply with any requirement imposed under section 38(9) of the 1990 Act.

(8) Nothing in this section affects any criminal proceedings which have been concluded before the passing of this Act.

(9) The waste regulation authority (within the meaning given by section 30(1) of the 1990 Act) shall notify the holder of a licence affected by this section of the fact that the licence is so affected and of how it is so affected.

(10) For the purposes of this section 'relevant activities', in relation to a licence, are—

    (a) any activities authorised by the licence or, in the case of an expired licence, any which would have been authorised by it had it not expired, and

    (b) any precautions or works required by the licence to be taken or carried out in connection with or in consequence of those activities or, in the case of an expired licence, any which would have been so required had the licence not expired.

(11) In this section—

'the 1974 Act' means the Control of Pollution Act 1974;

'the 1990 Act' means the Environmental Protection Act 1990;

'the appointed day', in relation to a licence, means the day which in relation to that licence is (or would have been if the licence had not previously expired) the relevant appointed day for licences (within the meaning of section 77 of the 1990 Act);

'the interim period', in connection with a licence in relation to which subsection (1) or (3) has effect, means the period beginning with the time of expiry and ending immediately before the day on which this Act is passed;

'site licence' has the same meaning as it has in Part II of the 1990 Act by virtue of section 35(12) of that Act.

5   Application to Wales and Scotland

(1) Subsection (2) applies to an Order in Council under section 22 of the Government of Wales Act 1998 (transfer of Ministerial functions) if the Order in Council contains a statement that it makes no provision which is not—

(a) provision about functions under this Act; or

(b) provision in connection with such provision.

(2) An Order in Council to which this subsection applies—

(a) shall not be subject to subsection (4)(a) of that section (affirmative resolution of both Houses of Parliament); but

(b) shall be subject to annulment in pursuance of a resolution of either House of Parliament.

(3) . . .

7   Short title, interpretation, commencement and extent

(1) . . .

(2) In this Act—

'enactment' includes an enactment comprised in subordinate legislation within the meaning of the Interpretation Act 1978;

'modifications' includes additions, alterations and omissions and 'modify' shall be construed accordingly.

(3) . . .

(9) Regulations and orders under this Act may make provision applying in relation to (and to places above and below)—

(a) the territorial waters adjacent to any part of the United Kingdom,

(b) the sea in any designated area within the meaning of the Continental Shelf Act 1964, and

(c) the sea in any area specified under section 10(8) of the Petroleum Act 1998.

SCHEDULE 1

PART I   LIST OF PURPOSES

Preliminary

1.—(1) Establishing standards, objectives or requirements in relation to emissions within the meaning of the regulations.

(2) Authorising the making of plans for—

(a) the setting of overall limits,

(b) the allocation of quotas, or

(c) the progressive improvement of standards or objectives, relating to such emissions.

(3) Authorising the making of schemes for the trading or other transfer of quotas so allocated.

2.—(1) Determining the authorities (whether public or local or the Secretary of State) by whom functions conferred by the regulations—

(a) in relation to permits under the regulations, or

(b) otherwise for or in connection with the prevention or control of environ-mental pollution,

are to be exercisable (in this Schedule referred to as 'regulators').

(2) Specifying any purposes for which any such functions are to be exercisable by regulators.

3. Enabling the Secretary of State to give directions which regulators are to comply with, or guidance which regulators are to have regard to, in exercising functions under the regulations, including—

(a) directions providing for any functions exercisable by one regulator to be instead exercisable by another;

(b) directions given for the purposes of the implementation of any obligations of the United Kingdom under the Community Treaties or under any international agreement to which the United Kingdom is a party;

(c) directions relating to the exercise of any function in a particular case or class of case.

Permits

4. Prohibiting persons from operating any installation or plant of any specified description, or otherwise carrying on any activities of any specified description, except—

(a) under a permit in force under the regulations, and

(b) in accordance with any conditions to which the permit is subject.

5. Specifying restrictions or other requirements in connection with the grant of permits (including provisions for restricting the grant of permits to those who are fit and proper persons within the meaning of the regulations); and otherwise regulating the procedure to be followed in connection with the grant of permits.

6.—(1) Prescribing the contents of permits.

(2) Authorising permits to be granted subject to conditions imposed by regulators.

(3) Securing that permits have effect subject to—

(a) conditions specified in the regulations; or

(b) rules of general application specified in or made under the regulations.

7.—(1) Requiring permits or the conditions to which permits are subject to be reviewed by regulators (whether periodically or in any specified circumstances).

(2) Authorising or requiring the variation of permits or such conditions by regulators (whether on applications made by holders of permits or otherwise).

(3) Regulating the making of changes—

(a) in the operation of the installations or plant to which permits relate, or

(b) in the case of permits for the carrying on of activities otherwise than in the course of operating any installation or plant, in the carrying on of the activities.

8.—(1) Regulating the transfer or surrender of permits.

(2) Authorising the revocation of permits by regulators.

(3) Authorising the imposition by regulators of requirements with respect to the taking of preventive or remedial action (by holders of permits or other persons) in connection with the surrender or revocation of permits.

9. Authorising the Secretary of State to make schemes for the charging by regulators of fees or other charges in respect of, or in respect of an application for—

(a) the grant of a permit,

(b) the variation of a permit or the conditions to which it is subject, or

(c) the transfer or surrender of a permit, or in respect of the subsistence of a permit.

10. Authorising, or authorising a Minister of the Crown to make schemes for, the charging by Ministers of the Crown or public or local authorities of fees or other charges in respect of—

(a) the testing or analysis of substances,

(b) the validating of, or of the results of, any testing or analysis of substances, or

(c) assessing how the environment might be affected by the release into it of any substances, in cases where the testing, analysis, validating or assessing is in any way in anticipation of, or otherwise in connection with, the making of applications for the grant of permits or is carried out in pursuance of conditions to which any permit is subject.

Information, publicity and consultation

11. Enabling persons of any specified description (whether or not they are holders of permits) to be required—
   (a) to compile information—
      (i) on emissions within the meaning of the regulations;
      (ii) on energy consumption and on the efficiency with which energy is used;
      (iii) on waste within the meaning of the regulations and on the destinations of such waste;
   (b) to provide such information in such manner as is specified in the regulations.
12. Securing
   (a) that publicity is given to specified matters;
   (b) that regulators maintain registers of specified matters (but excepting information which under the regulations is, or is determined to be, commercially confidential and subject to any other exceptions specified in the regulations) which are open to public inspection;
   (c) that copies of entries in such registers, or of specified documents, may be obtained by members of the public.
13. Requiring or authorising regulators to carry out consultation in connection with the exercise of any of their functions; and providing for them to take into account representations made to them on consultation.

Enforcement and offences

14.—(1) Conferring on regulators functions with respect to the monitoring and inspection of the carrying on of activities to which permits relate, including—
   (a) power to take samples or to make copies of information;
   (b) power to arrange for preventive or remedial action to be taken at the expense of holders of permits.
   (2) Authorising regulators to appoint suitable persons to exercise any such functions and conferring powers (such as those specified in section 108(4) of the Environment Act 1995) on persons so appointed.
15.—(1) Authorising regulators to serve on holders of permits—
   (a) notices requiring them to take remedial action in respect of contraventions, actual or potential, of conditions to which their permits are subject;
   (b) notices requiring them to provide such financial security as the regulators serving the notices consider appropriate pending the taking of remedial action in respect of any such contraventions;
   (c) notices requiring them to take steps to remove imminent risks of serious environmental pollution (whether or not arising from any such contraventions).
   (2) Providing for the enforcement of such notices by proceedings in the High Court . . .
16. Authorising regulators to suspend the operation of permits so far as having effect to authorise the carrying on of activities to which they relate.
17. The creation of offences and dealing with matters relating to such offences, including—
   (a) the provision of defences; and
   (b) evidentiary matters.

18. Enabling, where a person has been convicted of an offence under the regulations—
   (a) a court dealing with that person for the offence to order the taking of remedial action (in addition to or instead of imposing any punishment); or
   (b) a regulator to arrange for such action to be taken at that person's expense.

Appeals

19. Conferring rights of appeal in respect of decisions made, notices served or other things done (or omitted to be done) under the regulations; and making provision for (or for the determination of) matters relating to the making, considering and determination of such appeals (including provision for or in connection with the holding of inquiries or hearings).

General

20.—(1) Making provision which, subject to any modifications that the Secretary of State considers appropriate, corresponds or is similar to—
   (a) any provision made by or under, or capable of being made under, Part I or II of the Environmental Protection Act 1990 or made by any of sections 157, 158 and 160 of that Act; or
   (b) any provision made, or capable of being made, under section 2(2) of the European Communities Act 1972 in connection with one of the relevant directives.
   (2) In sub-paragraph (1) 'the relevant directives' means—
   (a) Council Directive 96/61/EC concerning integrated pollution prevention and control;
   (b) Council Directive 75/442/EEC on waste, as amended; and
   (c) any other directive of the Council of the European Communities designated by the Secretary of State for the purposes of this paragraph by order made by statutory instrument.
   (3) Making provision about the application of the regulations to the Crown.

PART II   SUPPLEMENTARY PROVISIONS

Particular types of pollution

21. The regulations may provide for specified provisions of the regulations to have effect in relation only to such environmental pollution as is specified.

Determination of matters by regulators

22. The regulations may make provision for anything which, by virtue of paragraphs 5 to 8, could be provided for by the regulations to be determined under the regulations by regulators.

Imposition of conditions

23. In connection with the determination of conditions as mentioned in paragraph 6(3)(a) the regulations may in particular provide—
   (a) for such conditions to be determined in the light of any specified general principles and any directions or guidance given under the regulations;
   (b) for such guidance to include guidance sanctioning reliance by a regulator on any arrangements referred to in the guidance to operate to secure a particular result as an alternative to imposing a condition.

Charging schemes

24. The regulations may—
    (a) require any such scheme as is mentioned in paragraph 9 or 10 to be so framed that the fees and charges payable under the scheme are sufficient, taking one year with another, to cover such expenditure (whether or not incurred by the regulator or other person to whom they are so payable) as is specified;
    (b) authorise any such scheme to make different provision for different cases (and specify particular kinds of such cases).

Offences

25.—(1) The regulations may provide for any such offence as is mentioned in paragraph 17 to be triable—
    (a) only summarily; or
    (b) either summarily or on indictment.
(2) The regulations may provide for such an offence to be punishable—
    (a) on summary conviction by—
        (i) imprisonment for a term not exceeding such period as is specified (which may not exceed six months), or
        (ii) a fine not exceeding such amount as is specified (which may not exceed £20,000),
        or both; or
    (b) on conviction on indictment by—
        (i) imprisonment for a term not exceeding such period as is specified (which may not exceed five years), or
        (ii) a fine, or both.

Interpretation

26. In this Schedule—
'functions' includes powers and duties;
'the regulations' means regulations under section 2;
'specified' means specified in regulations under that section.

Freedom of Information Act 2000
(2000, c. 36)

PART III

GENERAL FUNCTIONS OF SECRETARY OF STATE, LORD CHANCELLOR AND INFORMATION COMMISSIONER

47 General functions of Commissioner
(1) It shall be the duty of the Commissioner to promote the following of good practice by public authorities and, in particular, so to perform his functions under this Act as to promote the observance by public authorities of—
    (a) the requirements of this Act, and
    (b) the provisions of the codes of practice under sections 45 and 46.
(2) The Commissioner shall arrange for the dissemination in such form and manner as he considers appropriate of such information as it may appear to him expedient to give to the public—

    (a) about the operation of this Act,

    (b) about good practice, and

    (c) about other matters within the scope of his functions under this Act,

and may give advice to any person as to any of those matters.

    (3) The Commissioner may, with the consent of any public authority, assess whether that authority is following good practice.

    (4) The Commissioner may charge such sums as he may with the consent of the Secretary of State determine for any services provided by the Commissioner under this section.

    (5) The Commissioner shall from time to time as he considers appropriate—

        (a) consult the Keeper of Public Records about the promotion by the Commissioner of the observance by public authorities of the provisions of the code of practice under section 46 in relation to records which are public records for the purposes of the Public Records Act 1958, and

        (b) ...

    (6) In this section 'good practice', in relation to a public authority, means such practice in the discharge of its functions under this Act as appears to the Commissioner to be desirable, and includes (but is not limited to) compliance with the requirements of this Act and the provisions of the codes of practice under sections 45 and 46.

48 Recommendations as to good practice.

    (1) If it appears to the Commissioner that the practice of a public authority in relation to the exercise of its functions under this Act does not conform with that proposed in the codes of practice under sections 45 and 46, he may give to the authority a recommendation (in this section referred to as a 'practice recommendation') specifying the steps which ought in his opinion to be taken for promoting such conformity.

    (2) A practice recommendation must be given in writing and must refer to the particular provisions of the code of practice with which, in the Commissioner's opinion, the public authority's practice does not conform.

    (3) Before giving to a public authority other than the Public Record Office a practice recommendation which relates to conformity with the code of practice under section 46 in respect of records which are public records for the purposes of the Public Records Act 1958, the Commissioner shall consult the Keeper of Public Records.

    (4) ...

PART VIII

MISCELLANEOUS AND SUPPLEMENTAL

74 Power to make provision relating to environmental information

    (1) In this section 'the Aarhus Convention' means the Convention on Access to Information, Public Participation in Decision-making and Access to Justice in Environmental Matters signed at Aarhus on 25th June 1998.

    (2) For the purposes of this section 'the information provisions' of the Aarhus Convention are Article 4, together with Articles 3 and 9 so far as relating to that Article.

    (3) The Secretary of State may by regulations make such provision as he considers appropriate—

        (a) for the purpose of implementing the information provisions of the Aarhus Convention or any amendment of those provisions made in accordance with Article 14 of the Convention, and

        (b) for the purpose of dealing with matters arising out of or related to the implementation of those provisions or of any such amendment.

    (4) Regulations under subsection (3) may in particular—

        (a) enable charges to be made for making information available in accordance with the regulations,

(b) provide that any obligation imposed by the regulations in relation to the disclosure of information is to have effect notwithstanding any enactment or rule of law,

(c) make provision for the issue by the Secretary of State of a code of practice,

(d) provide for sections 47 and 48 to apply in relation to such a code with such modifications as may be specified,

(e) provide for any of the provisions of Parts IV and V to apply, with such modifications as may be specified in the regulations, in relation to compliance with any requirement of the regulations, and

(f) contain such transitional or consequential provision (including provision modifying any enactment) as the Secretary of State considers appropriate.

(5) . . .

PART III

Statutory Instruments

Town and Country Planning (Use Classes) Order 1987
(SI 1987, No. 764) (as amended)

1   Citation and commencement

This Order may be cited as the Town and Country Planning (Use Classes) Order 1987 and shall come into force in June 1987.

2   Interpretation

In this Order, unless the context otherwise requires:—

'care' means personal care for people in need of such care by reason of old age, disablement, past or present dependence on alcohol or drugs or past or present mental disorder, and in class C2 also includes the personal care of children and medical care and treatment;

'day centre' means premises which are visited during the day for social or recreational purposes or for the purposes of rehabilitation or occupational training, at which care is also provided;

'industrial process' means a process for or incidental to any of the following purposes:—

(a)   the making of any article or part of any article (including a ship or vessel, or a film, video or sound recording);

(b)   the altering, repairing, maintaining, ornamenting, finishing, cleaning, washing, packing, canning, adapting for sale, breaking up or demolition of any article; or

(c)   the getting, dressing or treatment of minerals;

in the course of any trade or business other than agriculture, and other than a use carried out in or adjacent to a mine or quarry;

'Schedule' means the Schedule to this Order;

'site' means the whole area of land within a single unit of occupation.

3   Use classes

(1) Subject to the provisions of this Order, where a building or other land is used for a purpose of any class specified in the Schedule, the use of that building or that other land for any other purpose of the same class shall not be taken to involve development of the land.

(2) References in paragraph (1) to a building include references to land occupied with the building and used for the same purposes.

(3) A use which is included in and ordinarily incidental to any use in a class specified in the Schedule is not excluded from the use to which it is incidental merely because it is specified in the Schedule as a separate use.

(4) Where land on a single site or on adjacent sites used as parts of a single undertaking is used for purposes consisting of or including purposes falling [within classes B1 and B2] in the Schedule, those classes may be treated as a single class in considering the use of that land for the purposes of this Order, so long as the area used for a purpose falling [within class B2] is not substantially increased as a result.

(5) [. . .]

(6) No class specified in the Schedule includes use—
  (a) as a theatre,
  (b) as an amusement arcade or centre, or a funfair,
  [(c) as a launderette,]
  (d) for the sale of fuel for motor vehicles,
  (e) for the sale or display for sale of motor vehicles,
  (f) for a taxi business or business for the hire of motor vehicles,
  (g) as a scrapyard, or a yard for the storage or distribution of minerals or the breaking of motor vehicles.
  [(h) for any work registrable under the Alkali, etc. Works Regulation Act 1906]
  [(i) as a hostel]
  [(j) as a waste disposal installation for the incineration, chemical treatment (as defined in Annex IIA to Directive 75/442/EEC under heading D9) or landfill of waste to which Directive 91/689/EEC applies.]

4   Change of use of part of building or land

In the case of a building used for a purpose within class C3 (dwelling-houses) in the Schedule, the use as a separate dwelling-house of any part of the building or of any land occupied with and used for the same purposes as the building is not, by virtue of this Order, to be taken as not amounting to development.

5   Revocation

The Town and Country Planning (Use Classes) Order 1972 and the Town and Country Planning (Use Classes) (Amendment) Order 1983 are hereby revoked.

SCHEDULE

PART A

Class A1   Shops

Use for all or any of the following purposes—
  (a) for the retail sale of goods other than hot food,
  (b) as a post office,
  (c) for the sale of tickets or as a travel agency,
  (d) for the sale of sandwiches or other cold food for consumption off the premises,
  (e) for hairdressing,
  (f) for the direction of funerals,
  (g) for the display of goods for sale,
  (h) for the hiring out of domestic or personal goods or articles,
  [(i) for the washing or cleaning of clothes or fabrics on the premises,]
  [(j) for the reception of goods to be washed, cleaned or repaired,]
where the sale, display or services is to visiting members of the public.

Class A2   Financial and professional services

Use for the provision of—
  (a) financial services, or
  (b) professional services (other than health or medical services), or
  (c) any other services (including use as a betting office) which it is appropriate to provide in a shopping area,
where the services are provided principally to visiting members of the public.

Class A3   Food and drink

Use for the sale of food or drink for consumption on the premises or of hot food for consumption off the premises.

PART B

Class B1   Business
Use for all or any of the following purposes—
      (a) as an office other than a use within class A2 (financial and professional services),
      (b) for research and development of products or processes, or
      (c) for any industrial process,
being a use which can be carried out in any residential area without detriment to the amenity of that area by reason of noise, vibration, smell, fumes, smoke, soot, ash, dust or grit.

Class B2   General industrial
Use for the carrying on of an industrial process other than one falling within class B1 above [. . .]

Class B3   [. . .]

Class B4   [. . .]

Class B5   [. . .]

Class B6   [. . .]

Class B7   [. . .]

Class B8   Use for storage or distribution
Use for storage or as a distribution centre.

PART C

[Class C1   Hotels
Use as a hotel or as a boarding or guest house where, in each case, no significant element of care is provided.]

Class C2   Residential institutions
Use for the provision of residential accommodation and care to people in need of care (other than a use within class C3 (dwelling houses)).
   Use as a hospital or nursing home.
   Use as a residential school, college or training centre.

Class C3   Dwellinghouses
Use as a dwellinghouse (whether or not as a sole or main residence)—
      (a) by a single person or by people living together as a family, or
      (b) by not more than six residents living together as a single household (including a household where care is provided for residents).

PART D

Class D1   Non-residential institutions
Any use not including a residential use—
      (a) for the provision of any medical or health services except the use of premises attached to the residence of the consultant or practitioner,
      (b) as a crèche, day nursery or day centre,
      (c) for the provision of education,
      (d) for the display of works of art (otherwise than for sale or hire),
      (e) as a museum,
      (f) as a public library or public reading room,

(g) as a public hall or exhibition hall,

(h) for, or in connection with, public worship or religious instruction.

Class D2   Assembly and leisure

Use as—

(a) a cinema,

(b) a concert hall,

(c) a bingo hall or casino,

(d) a dance hall,

(e) a swimming bath, skating rink, gymnasium or area for other indoor or outdoor sports or recreations, not involving motorised vehicles or firearms.

Controlled Waste Regulations 1992
(SI 1992, No. 588) (as amended)

1   Citation, commencement and interpretation

(1) . . .

(2) In these Regulations —

'the Act' means the Environmental Protection Act 1990;

'the 1989 Regulations' means the Sludge (Use in Agriculture) Regulations 1989;

'camp site' means land on which tents are pitched for the purposes of human habitation and land the use of which is incidental to land on which tents are so pitched;

'charity' means any body of persons or trust established for charitable purposes only;

'clinical waste' means

(a) any waste which consists wholly or partly of human or animal tissue, blood or other body fluids, excretions, drugs or other pharmaceutical products, swabs or dressings, or syringes, needles or other sharp instruments, being waste which unless rendered safe may prove hazardous to any person coming into contact with it; and

(b) any other waste arising from medical, nursing, dental, veterinary, pharmaceutical or similar practice, investigation, treatment, care, teaching or research, or the collection of blood for transfusion, being waste which may cause infection to any person coming into contact with it;

'composite hereditament' has the same meaning as in section 64(9) of the Local Government Finance Act 1988;

'construction' includes improvement, repair or alteration;

['Directive waste' has the meaning given by regulation 1(3) of the Waste Management Licensing Regulations 1994;]

. . .

'scrap metal' has the same meaning as in section 9(2) of the Scrap Metal Dealers Act 1964;

'septic tank sludge' and 'sludge' have the same meaning as in regulation 2(1) of the 1989 Regulations; and

'vessel' includes a hovercraft within the meaning of section 4(1) of the Hovercraft Act 1968.

(3) Any reference in these Regulations to a section is, except where the context otherwise requires, a reference to a section of the Act.

(4) References in these Regulations to waste—

(a) do not include waste from any mine or quarry or waste from premises used for agriculture within the meaning of the Agriculture Act 1947 or, in Scotland, the Agriculture (Scotland) Act 1948;

(b) except so far as otherwise provided, do not include sewage (including matter in or from a privy).

2   Waste to be treated as household waste

(1) [Subject to paragraph (2) and regulations 3 and 7A,] waste of the descriptions set out in Schedule 1 shall be treated as household waste for the purposes of Part II of the Act.

(2) Waste of the following descriptions shall be treated as household waste for the purposes only of section 34(2) (household waste produced on domestic property)—

(a) waste arising from works of construction or demolition, including waste arising from work preparatory thereto; and

(b) septic tank sludge.

3   Waste not to be treated as household waste

(1) Waste of the following descriptions shall not be treated as household waste for the purposes of section 33(2) (treatment, keeping or disposal of household waste within the curtilage of a dwelling)—

(a) any mineral or synthetic oil or grease;

(b) asbestos; and

(c) clinical waste.

(2) Scrap metal shall not be treated as household waste for the purposes of section 34 [at any time before [1st October 1995]].

4   Charges for the collection of household waste

The collection of any of the types of household waste set out in Schedule 2 is prescribed for the purposes of section 45(3) as a case in respect of which a charge for collection may be made.

5   Waste to be treated as industrial waste

(1) Subject to paragraph (2) and [regulations 7 and 7A] waste of the descriptions set out in Schedule 3 shall be treated as industrial waste for the purposes of Part II of the Act.

(2) Waste of the following descriptions shall be treated as industrial waste for the purposes of Part II of the Act (except section 34(2))—

(a) waste arising from works of construction or demolition, including waste arising from work preparatory thereto;

(b) septic tank sludge not falling within [regulation 7(1)(a) or (c)].

6   Waste to be treated as commercial waste

Subject to [regulations 7 and 7A] waste of the descriptions set out in Schedule 4 shall be treated as commercial waste for the purposes of Part II of the Act.

7   Waste not to be treated as industrial or commercial waste

(1) Waste of the following descriptions shall not be treated as industrial waste or commercial waste for the purposes of Part II of the Act—

(a) sewage, sludge or septic tank sludge which is treated, kept or disposed of (otherwise than by means of mobile plant) within the curtilage of a sewage treatment works as an integral part of the operation of those works;

(b) sludge which is supplied or used in accordance with the 1989 Regulations;

(c) septic tank sludge which is used [on agricultural land within the meaning of] the 1989 Regulations.

(2) Scrap metal shall not be treated as industrial waste or commercial waste for the purposes of section 34 at any time before [1st October 1995]].

[(3) Animal by-products which are collected and transported in accordance with Schedule 2 to the Animal By-Products Order 1992 shall not be treated as industrial waste or commercial waste for the purposes of section 34 (duty of care etc. as respects waste).

(4) In this regulation, "animal by-products' has the same meaning as in article 3(1) of the Animal By-Products Order 1992.]

[7A   Waste not to be treated as household, industrial or commercial waste
For the purposes of Part II of the Act, waste which is not Directive waste shall not be treated as household waste, industrial waste or commercial waste.]

8   Application of Part II of the Act to litter and refuse
Part II of the Act shall have effect as if—

(a) references to controlled waste included references to litter and refuse to which section 96 applies;

(b) references to controlled waste of a description set out in the first column of Table A below included references to litter and refuse of a description set out in the second column thereof;

(c) references to controlled waste collected under section 45 included references to litter and refuse collected under sections 89(1)(a) and (c) and 92(9); and

(d) references to controlled waste collected under section 45 which is waste of a description set out in the first column of Table B below included references to litter and refuse of a description set out in the second column thereof.

Table A

Description of waste	Description of litter and refuse
Household waste.	Litter and refuse collected under section 89(1)(a), (c) and (f).
Industrial waste.	Litter and refuse collected under section 89(1)(b) and (e).
Commercial waste.	Litter and refuse collected under sections 89(1)(d) and (g), 92(9) and 93.

Table B

Description of waste	Description of litter and refuse
Household waste.	Litter and refuse collected under section 89(1)(a) and (c).
Commercial waste.	Litter and refuse collected under section 92(9).

Regulation 2(1)   SCHEDULE 1

WASTE TO BE TREATED AS HOUSEHOLD WASTE

1.   Waste from a hereditament or premises exempted from local non-domestic rating by virtue of—

(a) in England and Wales, paragraph 11 of Schedule 5 to the Local Government Finance Act 1988 (places of religious worship etc.);

(b) . . .

2.   Waste from premises occupied by a charity and wholly or mainly used for charitable purposes.

3.   Waste from any land belonging to or used in connection with domestic property, a caravan or a residential home.

4.   Waste from a private garage which either has a floor area of 25 square metres or less or is used wholly or mainly for the accommodation of a private motor vehicle.

5.   Waste from private storage premises used wholly or mainly for the storage of articles of domestic use.

6.   Waste from a moored vessel used wholly for the purposes of living accommodation.
7.   Waste from a camp site.
8.   Waste from a prison or other penal institution.
9.   Waste from a hall or other premises used wholly or mainly for public meetings.
10.   Waste from a royal palace.
11.   Waste arising from the discharge by a local authority of its duty under section 89(2).

Regulation 4   SCHEDULE 2

TYPES OF HOUSEHOLD WASTE FOR WHICH A CHARGE FOR COLLECTION MAY BE MADE

1.   Any article of waste which exceeds 25 kilograms in weight.
2.   Any article of waste which does not fit, or cannot be fitted into—
      (a) a receptacle for household waste provided in accordance with section 46; or
      (b) where no such receptacle is provided, a cylindrical container 750 millimetres in diameter and 1 metre in length.
3.   Garden waste.
4.   Clinical waste from a domestic property, a caravan or from a moored vessel used wholly for the purposes of living accommodation.
5.   Waste from a residential hostel, a residential home or from premises forming part of a university, school or other educational establishment or forming part of a hospital or nursing home.
6.   Waste from domestic property or a caravan used in the course of a business for the provision of self-catering holiday accommodation.
7.   Dead domestic pets.
8.   Any substances or articles which, by virtue of a notice served by a collection authority under section 46, the occupier of the premises may not put into a receptacle for household waste provided in accordance with that section.
9.   Litter and refuse collected under section 89(1)(f).
10.   Waste from—
      (a) in England and Wales, domestic property forming part of a composite hereditament;
      (b) . . .
11.   Any mineral or synthetic oil or grease.
12.   Asbestos.
13.   Waste from a caravan which in accordance with any licence or planning permission regulating the use of the caravan site on which the caravan is stationed is not allowed to be used for human habitation throughout the year.
14.   Waste from a camp site, other than from any domestic property on that site.
15.   Waste from premises occupied by a charity and wholly or mainly used for charitable purposes, unless it is waste falling within paragraph 1 of Schedule 1.
16.   Waste from a prison or other penal institution.
17.   Waste from a hall or other premises used wholly or mainly for public meetings.
18.   Waste from a royal palace.

Regulation 5(1)   SCHEDULE 3

WASTE TO BE TREATED AS INDUSTRIAL WASTE

1.   Waste from premises used for maintaining vehicles, vessels or aircraft, not being waste from a private garage to which paragraph 4 of Schedule 1 applies.

2.   Waste from a laboratory.

3.—(1) Waste from a workshop or similar premises not being a factory within the meaning of section 175 of the Factories Act 1961 because the people working there are not employees or because the work there is not carried on by way of trade or for purposes of gain.

(2) In this paragraph, 'workshop' does not include premises at which the principal activities are computer operations or the copying of documents by photographic or lithographic means

4.   Waste from premises occupied by a scientific research association approved by the Secretary of State under section 508 of the Income and Corporation Taxes Act 1988.

5.   Waste from dredging operations.

6.   Waste arising from tunnelling or from any other excavation.

7.   Sewage not falling within a description in regulation 7 which—
 (a) is treated, kept or disposed of in or on land, other than by means of a privy, cesspool or septic tank;
 (b) is treated, kept or disposed of by means of mobile plant; or
 (c) has been removed from a privy or cesspool.

8.   Clinical waste other than—
 (a) clinical waste from a domestic property, caravan, residential home or from a moored vessel used wholly for the purposes of living accommodation;
 (b) . . .
 (c) waste collected under sections 89, 92(9) or 93.

9.   Waste arising from any aircraft, vehicle or vessel which is not occupied for domestic purposes.

10.   Waste which has previously formed part of any aircraft, vehicle or vessel and which is not household waste.

11.   Waste removed from land on which it has previously been deposited and any soil with which such waste has been in contact, other than—
 (a) . . .
 (b) waste collected under sections 89, 92(9) or 93.

12.   Leachate from a deposit of waste.

13.   Poisonous or noxious waste arising from any of the following processes under-taken on premises used for the purposes of a trade or business—
 (a) mixing or selling paints;
 (b) sign writing;
 (c) laundering or dry cleaning;
 (d) developing photographic film or making photographic prints;
 (e) selling petrol, diesel fuel, paraffin, kerosene, heating oil or similar substances; or
 (f) selling pesticides, herbicides or fungicides.

14.   Waste from premises used for the purposes of breeding, boarding, stabling or exhibiting animals.

15.—(1) Waste oil, waste solvent or (subject to regulation 7(2)) scrap metal, other than—
 (a) waste from a domestic property, caravan or residential home;
 (b) waste falling within paragraphs 3 to 6 of Schedule 1.

(2) in this paragraph — 'waste oil' means mineral or synthetic oil which is contaminated, spoiled or otherwise unfit for its original purpose; and

'waste solvent' means solvent which is contaminated, spoiled or otherwise unfit for its original purpose.

16.   Waste arising from the discharge by the Secretary of State of his duty under section 89(2).

17.   Waste imported into Great Britain.

18.—(1) Tank washings or garbage landed in Great Britain.

(2) In this paragraph—

['tank washings' has the same meaning as in paragraph 36 of Schedule 3 to the Waste Management Licensing Regulations 1994;] and

'garbage' has the same meaning as in regulation 1(2) of the Merchant Shipping (Reception Facilities for Garbage) Regulations 1988.

Regulation 6	SCHEDULE 4

WASTE TO BE TREATED AS COMMERCIAL WASTE

1.   Waste from an office or showroom.

2.   Waste from a hotel within the meaning of—

    (a)   in England and Wales, section 1(3) of the Hotel Proprietors Act 1956; and

    (b)   . . .

3.   Waste from any part of a composite hereditament, . . . which is used for the purposes of a trade or business.

4.   Waste from a private garage which either has a floor area exceeding 25 square metres or is not used wholly or mainly for the accommodation of a private motor vehicle.

5.   Waste from premises occupied by a club, society or any association of persons (whether incorporated or not) in which activities are conducted for the benefit of the members.

6.   Waste from premises (not being premises from which waste is by virtue of the Act or of any other provision of these Regulations to be treated as household waste or industrial waste) occupied by—

    (a)   a court;

    (b)   a government department;

    (c)   a local authority;

    (d)   a body corporate or an individual appointed by or under any enactment to discharge any public functions; or

    (e)   a body incorporated by a Royal Charter.

7.   Waste from a tent pitched on land other than a camp site.

8.   Waste from a market or fair.

9.   . . .

Environmental Information Regulations 1992
(SI 1992, No. 3240) (as amended)

1   . . .

2   Construction of Regulations

    (1) These Regulations apply to any information which—

    (a)   relates to the environment;

    (b)   is held by a relevant person in an accessible form and otherwise than for the purposes of any judicial or legislative functions; and

    (c)   is not (apart from these Regulations) either—

        (i)   information which is required, in accordance with any statutory provision, to be provided on request to every person who makes a request; or

        (ii)   information contained in records which are required, in accordance with any statutory provision, to be made available for inspection by every person who wishes to inspect them.

    (2) For the purposes of these Regulations information relates to the environment if, and only if, it relates to any of the following, that is to say—

    (a)   the state of any water or air, the state of any flora or fauna, the state of any soil or the state of any natural site or other land;

(b) any activities or measures (including activities giving rise to noise or any other nuisance) which adversely affect anything mentioned in sub-paragraph (a) above or are likely adversely to affect anything so mentioned;

(c) any activities or administrative or other measures (including any environmental management programmes) which are designed to protect anything so mentioned.

(3) For the purposes of these Regulations the following are relevant persons, that is to say—

(a) all such Ministers of the Crown, Government departments, local authorities and other persons carrying out functions of public administration at a national, regional or local level as, for the purposes of or in connection with their functions, have responsibilities in relation to the environment; and

(b) any body with public responsibilities for the environment which does not fall within sub-paragraph (a) above but is under the control of a person falling within that sub-paragraph.

(4) In these Regulations —

'information' includes anything contained in any records;

'records' includes registers, reports and returns, as well as computer records and other records kept otherwise than in a document; and

'statutory provision' means any provision made by or under any enactment.

3 Obligation to make environmental information available

(1) Subject to the following provisions of these Regulations, a relevant person who holds any information to which these Regulations apply shall make that information available to every person who requests it.

(2) It shall be the duty of every relevant person who holds information to which these Regulations apply to make such arrangements for giving effect to paragraph (1) above as secure—

(a) that every request made for the purposes of that paragraph is responded to as soon as possible;

(b) that no such request is responded to more than two months after it is made; and

(c) that, where the response to such a request contains a refusal to make information available, the refusal is in writing and specifies the reasons for the refusal.

(3) Arrangements made by a relevant person for giving effect to paragraph (1) above may include provision entitling that person to refuse a request for information in cases where a request is manifestly unreasonable or is formulated in too general a manner.

(4) The arrangements made by a relevant person for giving effect to paragraph (1) above may—

(a) include provision for the imposition of a charge on any person in respect of the costs reasonably attributable to the supply of information to that person in pursuance of that paragraph; and

(b) make the supply of any information in pursuance of that paragraph conditional on the payment of such a charge.

(5) The obligation of a relevant person to make information available in pursuance of paragraph (1) above shall not require him to make it available except in such form, and at such times and places, as may be reasonable.

(6) Without prejudice to any remedies available apart from by virtue of this paragraph in respect of any failure by a relevant person to comply with the requirements of these Regulations, the obligation of such a person to make information available in pursuance of paragraph (1) above shall be a duty owed to the person who has requested the information.

(7) Subject to regulation 4 below, where any statutory provision or rule of law imposes any restriction or prohibition on the disclosure of information by any person, that restriction

or prohibition shall not apply to any disclosure of information in pursuance of these Regulations.

4 Exceptions to right to information

(1) Nothing in these Regulations shall—
- (a) require the disclosure of any information which is capable of being treated as confidential; or
- (b) authorise or require the disclosure of any information which must be so treated.

[(2) For the purposes of these Regulations, information is to be capable of being treated as confidential if, and only if, it is information the disclosure of which—
- (a) would affect international relations, national defence or public security;
- (b) would affect matters which are, or have been, an issue in any legal proceedings or in any enquiry (including any disciplinary enquiry), or are the subject-matter of any investigation undertaken with a view to any such proceedings or enquiry;
- (c) would affect the confidentiality of the deliberations of any relevant person;
- (d) would involve the supply of a document or other record which is still in the course of completion, or of any international communication of a relevant person;
- (e) would affect the confidentiality of matters to which any commercial or industrial confidentiality attaches, including intellectual property.]

(3) For the purposes of these Regulations information must be treated as confidential if, and only if, in the case of any request made to a relevant person under regulation 3 above—
- (a) it is capable of being so treated and its disclosure in response to that request would (apart from regulation 3(7) above) contravene any statutory provision or rule of law or would involve a breach of any agreement;
- (b) the information is personal information contained in records held in relation to an individual who has not given his consent to its disclosure;
- (c) the information is held by the relevant person in consequence of having been supplied by a person who—
  - (i) was not under, and could not have been put under, any legal obligation to supply it to the relevant person;
  - (ii) did not supply it in circumstances such that the relevant person is entitled apart from these Regulations to disclose it; and
  - (iii) has not consented to its disclosure;

  or
- (d) the disclosure of the information in response to that request would, in the circumstances, increase the likelihood of damage to the environment affecting anything to which the information relates.

(4) Nothing in this regulation shall authorise a refusal to make available any information contained in the same record as, or otherwise held with, other information which is withheld by virtue of this regulation unless it is incapable of being separated from the other information for the purpose of making it available.

[(5) . . .]

5 Existing rights to information

Where any information which is not information to which these Regulations apply is required under any statutory provision to be made available to any person, the arrangements made by any relevant person for giving effect to the requirements of that provision shall be such as to secure—
- (a) that every request for information relating to the environment which is made for the purposes of that provision is responded to as soon as possible;
- (b) that no such request is responded to more than two months after it is made;

(c) that, where the response to such a request contains a refusal to make information available, the refusal is in writing and specifies the reasons for the refusal; and

(d) that no charge that exceeds a reasonable amount is made for making information relating to the environment available in accordance with that provision.

Waste Management Licensing Regulations 1994
(SI 1994, No. 1056) (as amended)

1 Citation, commencement, interpretation and extent

(1) . . .

(2) . . .

(3) In these Regulations, unless the context otherwise requires—

'the 1990 Act' means the Environmental Protection Act 1990;

'the 1991 Regulations' means the Environmental Protection (Prescribed Processes and Substances) Regulations 1991;

['the 2000 Regulations' means the Pollution Prevention and Control (England and Wales) Regulations 2000;]

'construction work' includes the repair, alteration or improvement of existing works;

'the Directive' means Council Directive 75/442/EEC on waste as amended by Council Directives 91/156/EEC and 91/692/EEC;

'Directive waste' means any substance or object in the categories set out in Part II of Schedule 4 which the producer or the person in possession of it discards or intends or is required to discard but with the exception of anything excluded from the scope of the Directive by Article 2 of the Directive, 'discard' has the same meaning as in the Directive, and 'producer' means anyone whose activities produce Directive waste or who carries out preprocessing, mixing or other operations resulting in a change in its nature or composition;

'disposal' means any of the operations listed in Part III of Schedule 4, and any reference to waste being disposed of is a reference to its being submitted to any of those operations;

'disposal licence' and 'disposal authority' have the meaning given by sections 3(1) and 30(2) to (2D) respectively of the Control of Pollution Act 1974;

'enforcing authority' and 'local enforcing authority' have the meaning given by section 1(7) and (8) of the 1990 Act;

'exempt activity' means any of the activities set out in Schedule 3; 'inland waters'—

(a) in England and Wales, has the meaning given by section 221(1) of the Water Resources Act 1991;

(b) . . .

'operational land' has the meaning given by sections 263 and 264 of the Town and Country Planning Act 1990 . . .

'recovery' means any of the operations listed in Part IV of Schedule 4, and any reference to waste being recovered is a reference to its being submitted to any of those operations;

'scrap metal' has the meaning given by section 9(2) of the Scrap Metal Dealers Act 1964;

['special waste' has the meaning given by regulation 2 of the Special Waste Regulations 1996, except that it does not include radioactive waste within the meaning of the Radioactive Substances Act 1993;]

'waste' means Directive waste;

'waste management licence' has the meaning given by section 35(1) of the 1990 Act, and 'site licence' has the meaning given by section 35(12) of the 1990 Act;

'waste oil' means any mineral-based lubricating or industrial oil which has become unfit for the use for which it was originally intended and, in particular, used combustion engine oil, gearbox oil, mineral lubricating oil, oil for turbines and hydraulic oil;

'waste regulation authority', 'waste disposal authority' and 'waste collection authority' have the meaning given by section 30 of the 1990 Act; and

'work' includes preparatory work.

(4) Any reference in these Regulations to carrying on business as a scrap metal dealer has the meaning given by section 9(1) of the Scrap Metal Dealers Act 1964, . . .

(5) . . .

(6) . . .

[(7) The provisions of section 160 of the 1990 Act shall apply to—

(a) the service or giving of any notice required or authorised by these Regulations to be served on or given to a person; or

(b) the sending or giving of any document required or authorised by these Regulations to be sent or given to a person,

as if the service or giving of any such notice or, as the case may be, the sending or giving of any such document, was required or authorised by or under that Act.]

2   Application for a waste management licence or for the surrender or transfer of a waste management licence

(1) An application for a waste management licence shall be made in writing.

(2) An application for the surrender of a site licence shall be made in writing and shall, subject to paragraphs (3) and (4) below, include the information and be accompanied by the evidence prescribed by Schedule 1.

(3) Nothing in paragraph (2) above shall require the information prescribed by paragraphs 3 to 6 of Schedule 1 to be provided to the waste regulation authority if the information has previously been provided by the applicant to the authority or a predecessor of the authority in connection with a waste management licence, or a disposal licence under section 5 of the Control of Pollution Act 1974, in respect of the site in question or any part of it.

(4) Insofar as the information prescribed by paragraphs 4, 5(a) and 6(a) of Schedule 1 relates to activities carried on, or works carried out, at the site at a time prior to the applicant's first involvement with the site, paragraph (2) above only requires that information to be included in the application so far as it is known to either the applicant or, where the applicant is a partnership or body corporate, to any of the partners or, as the case may be, to any director, manager, secretary or other similar officer of the body corporate.

(5) An application for the transfer of a waste management licence shall be made in writing and shall include the information prescribed by Schedule 2.

3   Relevant offences

An offence is relevant for the purposes of section 74(3)(a) of the 1990 Act if it is an offence under any of the following enactments—

(a) section 22 of the Public Health (Scotland) Act 1897;

(b) section 95(1) of the Public Health Act 1936;

(c) section 3, 5(6), 16(4), 18(2), 31(1), 32(1), 34(5), 78, 92(6) or 93(3) of the Control of Pollution Act 1974;

(d) section 2 of the Refuse Disposal (Amenity) Act 1978;

(e) the Control of Pollution (Special Waste) Regulations 1980;

(f) section 9(1) of the Food and Environment Protection Act 1985;

(g) the Transfrontier Shipment of Hazardous Waste Regulations 1988;

(h) the Merchant Shipping (Prevention of Pollution by Garbage) Regulations 1988;

(i) section 1, 5, 6(9) or 7(3) of the Control of Pollution (Amendment) Act 1989;

(j) section 107, 118(4) or 175(1) of the Water Act 1989;

(k) section 23(1), 33, 34(6), 44, 47(6), 57(5), 59(5), 63(2), 69(9), 70(4), 71(3) or 80(4) of the 1990 Act;

(l) section 85, 202 or 206 of the Water Resources Act 1991;

(m) section 33 of the Clean Air Act 1993. [(n) the Transfrontier Shipment of Waste Regulations 1994]

[(n) the Special Waste Regulations 1996.]

[(o) regulation 30(1) of the 2000 Regulations.]

[(p) regulation 17(1) of the Landfill (England and Wales) Regulations 2002.]

4   Technical competence

(1) Subject to paragraph (2) and regulation 5 below, a person is technically competent for the purposes of section 74(3)(b) of the 1990 Act in relation to a facility of a type listed in Table 1 below if, and only if, he is the holder of one of the certificates awarded by the Waste Management Industry Training and Advisory Board specified in that Table as being a relevant certificate of technical competence for that type of facility.

[Table 1

Type of facility	Relevant certificate of technical competence
A landfill site which receives special waste.	Managing landfill operations: special waste (level 4).
A landfill site which receives biodegradable waste or which for some other reason requires substantial engineering works to protect the environment but which in either case does not receive any special waste.	1. Managing landfill operations biodegradable waste (level 4); or 2. Managing landfill operations: special waste (level 4).
Any other type of landfill site with a total capacity exceeding 50,000 cubic metres.	1. Landfill operations: inert waste (level 3); or 2. Managing landfill operations: biodegradable waste (level 4); or 3. Managing landfill operations: special waste (level 4).
A site on which waste is burned in an incinerator designed to incinerate waste at a rate of more than 50 kilograms per hour but less than 1 tonne per hour.	Managing incinerator operations: special waste (level 4).
A waste treatment plant where clinical or special waste is subjected to a chemical or physical process.	1. Managing treatment operations: clinical or special waste (level 4); or 2. *Managing treatment operations: special waste (level 4) (see note).*
A waste treatment plant where biodegradable waste, but no clinical or special waste, is subjected to a chemical or physical process.	1. Managing treatment operations: biodegradable waste (level 4); or 2. Managing treatment operations: clinical or special waste (level 4); or 3. *Managing treatment operations: special waste (level 4) (see note).*
A waste treatment plant where waste, none of which is biodegradable, clinical or special waste, is subjected to a chemical or physical process.	1. Treatment operations: inert waste (level 3); or 2. Managing treatment operations: biodegradable waste (level 4); or 3. Managing treatment operations: clinical or special waste (level 4); or 4. *Managing treatment operations: special waste (level 4) (see note).*

Type of facility	Relevant certificate of technical competence
A transfer station where— (a) clinical or special waste is dealt with; and (b) the total quantity of waste at the station at any time exceeds 5 cubic metres.	1. Managing transfer operations: clinical or special waste (level 4); or 2. *Managing transfer operations: special waste (level 4) (see note).*
A transfer station where— (a) biodegradable waste, but no clinical or special waste, is dealt with; and (b) the total quantity of waste at the station at any time exceeds 50 cubic metres.	1. Managing transfer operations: biodegradable waste (level 4); or 2. Managing transfer operations: clinical or special waste (level 4); or 3. *Managing transfer operations: special waste (level 4) (see note).*
Any other type of waste transfer station where the total quantity of waste at the station at any time exceeds 50 cubic metres.	1. Transfer operations: inert waste (level 3); or 2. Managing transfer operations: biodegradable waste (level 4); or 3. Managing transfer operations: clinical or special waste (level 4); or 4. *Managing transfer operations: special waste (level 4) (see note).*
A civic amenity site.	1. Civil amenity site operations (level 3); or 2. Managing transfer operations: biodegradable waste (level 4); or 3. Managing transfer operations: clinical or special waste (level 4); or 4. *Managing transfer operations: special waste (level 4) (see note).*

Note: The certificates shown in italics will cease to be awarded on 9th October 1997.]

(2) Paragraph (1) above does not apply in relation to a facility which is used exclusively for the purposes of—

(a) Carrying on business as a scrap metal dealer . . . or

(b) dismantling motor vehicles.

(3) In this regulation —

'civic amenity site' means a place provided under section 1 of the Refuse Disposal (Amenity) Act 1978 or by virtue of section 51(1)(b) of the 1990 Act;

'clinical waste' has the meaning given by regulation 1(2) of the Controlled Waste Regulations 1992; and

['landfill site' does not include a site used only for the burial of dead domestic pets;]

'transfer station' means a facility where waste is unloaded in order to permit its preparation for further transport for treatment, keeping or disposal elsewhere.

5 Technical competence—transitional provisions

(1) [Subject to paragraph (4),] where before 10th August 1994 a person has applied to the Waste Management Industry Training and Advisory Board for a certificate of technical competence and at any time in the 12 months ending on that date he acted as the manager of a facility of a type listed in Table 1 above for which the certificate is a relevant certificate, then, until 10th August 1999, regulation 4 shall not apply to him in relation to either—

(a) any facility of that type; or

(b) a facility of any other type if—

  (i) the certificate is a relevant certificate for that other type of facility; and

  (ii) the entry for that other type of facility appears, in Table 1 above, after the entry in that Table for the type of facility in respect of which he acted as the manager, and he shall be treated as technically competent for the purposes of section 74(3)(b) of the 1990 Act in relation to any such facility.

 (2) [Subject to paragraph (4),] where a person is 55 or over on 10th August 1994 and in the 10 years ending on that date he has had at least 5 years experience as the manager of a facility of a type listed in Table 1 above, then, until 10th August 2004, regulation 4 shall not apply to him in relation to either—

  (a) any facility of that type; or

  (b) a facility of any other type if each certificate which is a relevant certificate for the type of facility in relation to which he has had such experience as manager is also a relevant certificate for that other type of facility,

and he shall be treated as technically competent for the purposes of section 74(3)(b) of the 1990 Act in relation to any such facility.

 (3) A person shall be treated as the manager of a facility for the purposes of paragraph (1) or (2) above if at the relevant time he was the manager of activities which were carried on at that facility and which were authorised by a disposal licence under section 5 of the Control of Pollution Act 1974, a resolution under section 11 of that Act or under section 54 of the 1990 Act, or a waste management licence.

 [(4) Subject to paragraphs (6) and (7), in their application in relation to a person mentioned in paragraph (5), paragraphs (1) and (2) shall apply as if the following dates were substituted for the dates in those paragraphs which are specified—

  (a) in paragraph (1)

   (i) for '10th August 1994', '1st October 1996';

   (ii) for '10th August 1999', '1st October 2001'; and

  (b) in paragraph (2),

   (i) for '10th August 1994', '1st October 1996';

   (ii) for '10th August 2004', '1st October 2006'.

 (5) The person mentioned in paragraph (4) is the manager of a facility at which activities were authorised by a resolution under section 11 of the Control of Pollution Act 1974(a).

 (6) Paragraph (4) does not apply to a person who is to be treated as technically competent by virtue of other provisions than those in that paragraph.

 (7) . . .]

6 Notice of appeal

 (1) A person who wishes to appeal to the Secretary of State under section 43 or 66(5) of the 1990 Act (appeals to the Secretary of State from decisions with respect to waste management licences or from determinations that information is not commercially confidential) shall do so by notice in writing.

 (2) The notice shall be accompanied by—

  (a) a statement of the grounds of appeal;

  (b) where the appeal relates to an application for a waste management licence or for the modification, surrender or transfer of a waste management licence, a copy of the appellant's application and any supporting documents;

  (c) where the appeal relates to a determination under section 66(2) or (4) of the 1990 Act that information is not commercially confidential, the information in question;

  (d) where the appeal relates to an existing waste management licence (including a waste management licence which has been suspended or revoked), a copy of that waste management licence;

  (e) a copy of any correspondence relevant to the appeal;

(f) a copy of any other document relevant to the appeal including, in particular, any relevant consent, determination, notice, planning permission, established use certificate or certificate of lawful use or development; and

(g) a statement indicating whether the appellant wishes the appeal to be in the form of a hearing or to be determined on the basis of written representations.

(3) The appellant shall serve a copy of his notice of appeal on the waste regulation authority together with copies of the documents mentioned in paragraph (2) above.

(4) If the appellant wishes to withdraw an appeal, he shall do so by notifying the Secretary of State in writing and shall send a copy of that notification to the waste regulation authority.

7   Time limit for making an appeal

(1) Subject to paragraph (2) below, notice of appeal shall be given—

(a) in the case of an appeal under section 43 of the 1990 Act, before the expiry of the period of 6 months beginning with—

(i) the date of the decision which is the subject of the appeal; or

(ii) the date on which the waste regulation authority is deemed by section 36(9), 37(6), 39(10) or 40(6) of the 1990 Act to have rejected the application;

(b) in the case of an appeal under section 66(5) of the 1990 Act, before the expiry of the period of 21 days beginning with the date on which the determination which is the subject of the appeal is notified to the person concerned.

(2) The Secretary of State may in relation to an appeal under section 43 of the 1990 Act at any time allow notice of appeal to be given after the expiry of the period mentioned in paragraph (1)(a) above.

8   Reports of hearings

The person hearing an appeal under section 43(2)(c) of the 1990 Act shall, unless he has been appointed to determine the appeal under [section 114(1)(a) of the Environment Act 1995], make a written report to the Secretary of State which shall include his conclusions and recommendations or his reasons for not making any recommendations.

9   Notification of determination

(1) The Secretary of State or other person determining an appeal shall notify the appellant in writing of his decision and of his reasons.

(2) If the Secretary of State determines an appeal after a hearing under section 43(2)(c) of the 1990 Act, he shall provide the appellant with a copy of any report made to him under regulation 8.

(3) The Secretary of State or other person determining an appeal shall, at the same time as notifying the appellant of his decision, send the waste regulation authority a copy of any document sent to the appellant under this regulation.

10   Particulars to be entered in public registers

(1) Subject to sections 65 and 66 of the 1990 Act and regulation 11, a register maintained by a waste regulation authority under section 64(1) of the 1990 Act shall contain full particulars of—

(a) current or recently current waste management licences ('licences') granted by the authority and any associated working plans;

(b) current or recently current applications to the authority for licences, or for the transfer or modification of licences, including details of—

(i) documents submitted by applicants containing supporting information;

(ii) written representations considered by the authority under section 36(4)(b), (6)(b) or (7)(b) or 37(5) of the 1990 Act;

(iii) decisions of the Secretary of State under section 36(5) . . . of the 1990

(iv) notices by the authority rejecting applications;

(v) emergencies resulting in the postponement of references under section 37(5)(a) of the 1990 Act;

(c) notices issued by the authority under section 37 of the 1990 Act effecting the modification of licences;

(d) notices issued by the authority under section 38 of the 1990 Act effecting the revocation or suspension of licences or imposing requirements on the holders of licences;

(e) notices of appeal under section 43 of the 1990 Act relating to decisions of the authority and other documents relating to such appeals served on or sent to the authority under regulation 6(3) or (4) or 9(3);

(f) convictions of holders of licences granted by the authority for any offence under Part II of the 1990 Act (whether or not in relation to a licence) [or regulation 17(1) of the Landfill (England and Wales) Regulations 2002] including the name of the offender, the date of conviction, the penalty imposed and the name of the Court;

(g) reports produced by the authority in discharge of any functions under section 42 of the 1990 Act, including details of—

(i) any correspondence with the [Agency . . .] as a result of section 42(2) of the 1990 Act;

(ii) remedial or preventive action taken by the authority under section 42(3) of the 1990 Act;

(iii) notices issued by the authority under section 42(5) of the 1990 Act;

(h) any monitoring information relating to the carrying on of any activity under a licence granted by the authority which was obtained by the authority as a result of its own monitoring or was furnished to the authority in writing by virtue of any condition of the licence or section 71(2) of the 1990 Act;

(i) directions given by the Secretary of State to the authority under section 35(7), 37(3), 38(7), 42(8), 50(9), 54(11) or (15), 58 or 66(7) of the 1990 Act;

(j) any summary prepared by the authority of the amount of special waste produced or disposed of in their area;

(k) registers and records provided to the authority under regulation 13(5) or 14(1) of the Control of Pollution (Special Waste) Regulations 1980 [or regulation 15(5) or 16(1) of the Special Waste Regulations 1996];

(l) applications to the authority under section 39 of the 1990 Act for the surrender of licences, including details of—

(i) documents submitted by applicants containing supporting information and evidence;

(ii) information and evidence obtained under section 39(4) of the 1990 Act;

(iii) written representations considered by the authority under section 39(7)(b) or (8)(b) of the 1990 Act;

(iv) decisions by the Secretary of State under section 39(7) or (8) of the 1990 Act; and

(v) notices of determination and certificates of completion issued under section 39(9) of the 1990 Act;

(m) written reports under section 70(3) of the 1990 Act by inspectors appointed by the authority [or written reports under section 109(2) of the Environment Act 1995 by persons authorised by the authority under section 108(1) or (2) of that Act where the articles or substances seized and rendered harmless are waste];

(n) . . .

(o) . . .

[(p) all particulars of any site conditioning plan or notice submitted to the authority under paragraph 1(3) or (5) of Schedule 4 to the Landfill (England and Wales) Regulations 2002;

(q) all particulars of any notice of a decision under paragraph 1(6) of Schedule 4 to the Landfill (England and Wales) Regulations 2002;

(r) all particulars of any notification or report required before definitive closure of a landfill under regulation 15(4) of the Landfill (England and Wales) Regulations 2002.]

(2) The register shall also contain the following—

(a) where an inspector appointed by the authority exercises any power under section 69(3) of the 1990 Act, a record showing when the power was exercised and indicating what information was obtained, and what action was taken, on that occasion;

[(aa) where a person authorised by the authority exercises any power under section 108(4) of the Environment Act 1995 in connection with the authority's functions under Part II of the Environmental Protection Act 1990, a record showing when the power was exercised and indicating what information was obtained, and what action was taken, on that occasion;]

(b) where any information is excluded from the register by virtue of section 66 of the 1990 Act and the information shows whether or not there is compliance with any condition of a waste management licence, a statement based on that information indicating whether or not there is compliance with that condition.

(3) A register maintained under section 64(4) of the 1990 Act by a waste collection authority in England [or Wales] ... shall contain full particulars of the following information contained in any register maintained under section 64(1) of the 1990 Act, to the extent that it relates to the treatment, keeping or disposal of controlled waste in the area of the authority—

(a) current or recently current waste management licences;

(b) notices issued under section 37 of the 1990 Act effecting the modification of waste management licences;

(c) notices issued under section 38 of the 1990 Act effecting the revocation or suspension of waste management licences;

(d) certificates of completion issued under section 39(9) of the 1990 Act.

[(3A) A register maintained under section 64(4) of the 1990 Act by a waste collection authority in England and Wales shall also contain full particulars of the following information contained in any register maintained by the Environment Agency under regulation 29 of the 2000 Regulations to the extent that it relates to a specified waste management activity (within the meaning of those Regulations) carried out in the area of the authority—

(a) current or recently current permits granted under the 2000 Regulations;

(b) variation notices under regulation 17 of the 2000 Regulations varying such permits;

(c) revocation notices under regulation 21 of those Regulations and suspension notices under regulation 25 of those Regulations issued in relation to such permits;

(d) notices of determination issued under regulation 19 of those Regulations in relation to applications made to surrender such permits.]

(4) For the purposes of this regulation, waste management licences [and permits granted under the 2000 Regulations] are 'recently' current for the period of twelve months after they cease to be in force, and applications for waste management licences, or for the transfer or modification of such licences, are 'recently' current if they relate to a waste management licence which is current or recently current or, in the case of an application which is rejected, for the period of twelve months beginning with the date on which the waste regulation

authority gives notice of rejection or, as the case may be, on which the application is deemed by section 36(9), 37(6) or 40(6) of the 1990 Act to have been rejected.

[(5) The Environment Agency shall furnish waste collection authorities with the particulars necessary to enable them to discharge their duty under paragraph (3A).]

11   Information to be excluded or removed from a register
(1) Nothing in regulation 10(1)(g) or (m) or (2) shall require a register maintained by a waste regulation authority under section 64(1) of the 1990 Act to contain information relating to, or to anything which is the subject-matter of, any criminal proceedings (including prospective proceedings) at any time before those proceedings are finally disposed of.

(2) Nothing in regulation 10 shall require a register maintained by a waste regulation authority or waste collection authority under section 64 of the 1990 Act to contain—

    (a) any such monitoring information as is mentioned in regulation 10(1)(h) after 4 years have elapsed from that information being entered in the register; or

    (b) any information which has been superseded by later information after 4 years have elapsed from that later information being entered in the register.

[(3) Nothing in regulation 10(3A) shall require a register maintained by a waste collection authority under that regulation to contain any information which has been superseded by later information after 4 years have elapsed from that later information being entered in the register.]

[12   Mobile plant
(1) Plant of the following descriptions, if it is designed to move or be moved by any means from place to place with a view to being used at each such place or, if not so designed, is readily capable of so moving or being so moved, but no other plant, shall be treated as being mobile plant for the purposes of Part II of the 1990 Act—

    (a) an incinerator which is an exempt incinerator for the purposes of Section 5.1 of Schedule 1 to the 1991 Regulations;

    (b) plant for—

        (i) the recovery, by filtration or heat treatment, of waste oil from electrical equipment; [. . .]

        (ii) the destruction by dechlorination of waste polychlorinated biphenyls or terphenyls (PCBs or PCTs);

        [(iii) the collection or storage of a controlled substance from any waste product, installation or equipment.]

    (c) plant for the vitrification of waste;

    (d) plant for the treatment by microwave of clinical waste.

    [(e) plant for the treatment of waste soil.]

[(1A) For the purposes of paragraph (1)(b)(iii) above, 'controlled substance' means any one of the following:

chlorofluorocarbons, other fully halogenated chlorofluorocarbons, halons, carbon tetrachloride, 1,1,1-trichloroethane, methyl bromide, hydrobromofluorocarbons, hydro-chlorofluorocarbons.]

(2) For the purposes of paragraph (1)(d) above, 'clinical waste' has the meaning given by regulation 1(2) of the Controlled Waste Regulations 1992.]

13   Health at work
No conditions shall be imposed in any waste management licence for the purpose only of securing the health of persons at work (within the meaning of Part I of the Health and Safety at Work etc. Act 1974).

14   Waste oils
(1) Where a waste management licence or disposal licence authorises the regeneration of waste oil, it shall include conditions which ensure that base oils derived from regeneration

do not constitute a toxic and dangerous waste and do not contain PCBs or PCTs at all or do not contain them in concentrations beyond a specified maximum limit which in no case is to exceed 50 parts per million.

(2) Where a waste management licence or disposal licence authorises the keeping of waste oil, it shall include conditions which ensure that it is not mixed with toxic and dangerous waste or PCBs or PCTs.

(3) In this regulation—

'PCBs or PCTs' means polychlorinated biphenyls, polychlorinated terphenyls and mixtures containing one or both of such substances; and

'toxic and dangerous waste' has the meaning given by Article 1(b) of Council Directive 78/319/EEC.

15   Groundwater

(1) Where a waste regulation authority proposes to issue a waste management licence authorising—

(a) any disposal or tipping for the purpose of disposal of a substance in list I which might lead to an indirect discharge into groundwater of such a substance;

(b) any disposal or tipping for the purpose of disposal of a substance in list II which might lead to an indirect discharge into groundwater of such a substance;

(c) a direct discharge into groundwater of a substance in list I; or

(d) a direct discharge into groundwater of a substance in list II, the authority shall ensure that the proposed activities are subjected to prior investigation.

(2) The prior investigation referred to in paragraph (1) above shall include examination of the hydrogeological conditions of the area concerned, the possible purifying powers of the soil and sub-soil and the risk of pollution and alteration of the quality of the groundwater from the discharge and shall establish whether the discharge of substances into groundwater is a satisfactory solution from the point of view of the environment.

(3) A waste management licence shall not be issued in any case within paragraph (1) above until the waste regulation authority has checked that the groundwater, and in particular its quality, will undergo the requisite surveillance.

(4) In a case within paragraph (1)(a) or (c) above—

(a) where the waste regulation authority is satisfied, in the light of the investigation, that the groundwater which may be affected by a direct or indirect discharge of a substance in list I is permanently unsuitable for other uses, especially domestic and agricultural, the waste management licence may only be issued if the authority is also satisfied that—

(i) the presence of that substance once discharged into groundwater will not impede exploitation of ground resources; and

(ii) all technical precautions will be taken to ensure that no substance in list I can reach other aquatic systems or harm other ecosystems; and

(b) where the waste regulation authority is not satisfied, in the light of the investigation, that the groundwater which may be affected by such a discharge is permanently unsuitable for other uses, especially domestic and agricultural, a waste management licence may only be issued if it is made subject to such conditions as the authority, in the light of the investigations, is satisfied will ensure the observance of all technical precautions necessary to prevent any discharges into groundwater of substances in list I.

(5) In a case within paragraph (1)(b) or (d) above, if a waste management licence is issued, it shall be issued subject to such conditions as the waste regulation authority, in the light of the investigation, is satisfied will ensure the observance of all technical precautions for preventing groundwater pollution by substances in list II.

(6) Where a waste management licence is granted in any case within paragraph (1)(a) or (b) above, the licence shall be granted on such terms and subject to such conditions as specify—

    (a) the place where any disposal or tipping which might lead to a discharge into groundwater of any substances in list I or II is to be done;

    (b) the methods of disposal or tipping which may be used;

    (c) the essential precautions which must be taken, paying particular attention to the nature and concentration of the substances present in the matter to be disposed of or tipped, the characteristics of the receiving environment and the proximity of the water catchment areas, in particular those for drinking, thermal and mineral water;

    (d) the maximum quantity permissible, during one or more specified periods of time, of matter containing substances in list I or II and, where possible, of those substances themselves, to be disposed of or tipped and the appropriate requirements as to the concentration of those substances;

    (e) the technical precautions required by paragraph (4)(b) or (5) above;

    (f) if necessary, the measures for monitoring the groundwater, and in particular its quality.

(7) Where a waste management licence is granted in any case within paragraph (1)(c) or (d) above, the licence shall be granted on such terms and subject to such conditions as specify—

    (a) the place where any substances in list I or II are to be discharged into groundwater;

    (b) the method of discharge which may be used;

    (c) the essential precautions which must be taken, paying particular attention to the nature and concentration of the substances present in the effluents, the characteristics of the receiving environment and the proximity of the water catchment areas, in particular those for drinking, thermal and mineral water;

    (d) the maximum quantity of a substance in list I or II permissible in an effluent during one or more specified periods of time and the appropriate requirements as to the concentration of those substances;

    (e) the arrangements enabling effluents discharged into groundwater to be monitored;

    (f) if necessary, the measures for monitoring the groundwater, and in particular its quality.

(8) Any authorisation granted by a waste management licence for an activity within paragraph (1) above shall be granted for a limited period only.

(9) Any authorisation granted by a waste management licence for an activity within paragraph (1) above shall be reviewed at least every 4 years.

(10) Waste regulation authorities shall review all waste management licences current on 1st May 1994 which authorise any activity within paragraph (1) above and shall, so far as may be necessary to give effect to Council Directive 80/68/EEC, exercise their powers under sections 37 and 38 of the 1990 Act (variation and revocation etc. of waste management licences) in relation to any such authorisation.

(11) . . .

(12) Expressions used both in this regulation and in Council Directive 80/68/EEC have for the purposes of this regulation the same meaning as in that Directive.

16   Exclusion of activities under other control regimes from waste management licensing

(1) Subject to paragraph (2) below, section 33(1)(a), (b) and (c) of the 1990 Act shall not apply in relation to the carrying on of any of the following activities—

    (a) the [deposit in or on land,] recovery or disposal of waste under an authorisation granted under Part I of the 1990 Act where the activity is or forms part of a process designated for central control under section 2(4) of the 1990 Act;

(b) the disposal of waste under an authorisation granted under Part I of the 1990 Act where the activity is or forms part of a process within paragraph (a) of Part B of Section 5.1 (incineration) of Schedule 1 to the 1991 Regulations insofar as the activity results in releases of substances into the air;

[(ba) the deposit in or on land, recovery or disposal of waste under a permit granted under the 2000 Regulations to operate a Part A(1) installation;

(bb) the disposal of waste under a permit granted under the 2000 Regulations where the activity is or forms part of an activity within paragraph (a) or (b) of Part B of Section 5.1 (incineration) of Part 1 of Schedule 1 to those Regulations in so far as the activity results in the release of substances into the air;]

(c) the disposal of liquid waste under a consent under Chapter II of Part III of the Water Resources Act 1991 or under Part II of the Control of Pollution Act 1974; and

(d) the recovery or disposal of waste where the activity is or forms part of an operation which is for the time being either—

(i) the subject of a licence under Part II of the Food and Environment Protection Act 1985; or

(ii) carried on in circumstances where such a licence would be required but for an order under section 7 of that Act.

(2) Paragraph (1)(a) [, (b) and (bb)] above does not apply insofar as the activity involves the final disposal of waste by deposit in or on land.

[(3) In paragraph (1)(ba) 'Part A(1) installation' has the meaning given by regulation 2(1) of the 2000 Regulations.]

17   Exemptions from waste management licensing

(1) Subject to the following provisions of this regulation and to any conditions or limitations in Schedule 3, section 33(1)(a) and (b) of the 1990 Act shall not apply in relation to the carrying on of any exempt activity set out in that Schedule.

[(1A) Paragraph (1) above does not apply to the carrying on of an exempt activity falling within paragraph 45(1), (2) or (5) of Schedule 3 where the carrying on of that activity is authorised by a waste management licence granted upon an application made after 31st March 1995 under section 36 of the 1990 Act.]

(2) In the case of an exempt activity set out in paragraph 4, 7, 9, 11, 13, 14, 15, 17, 18, 19, 25, 37, [40, 41 or 45] of Schedule 3, paragraph (1) above only applies if—

(a) the exempt activity is carried on by or with the consent of the occupier of the land where the activity is carried on; or

(b) the person carrying on the exempt activity is otherwise entitled to do so on that land.

(3) Unless otherwise indicated in Schedule 3, paragraph (1) above does not apply to the carrying on of an exempt activity insofar as it involves special waste.

[(3A) Paragraph (1) does not apply to the carrying on of an exempt activity insofar as it involves the carrying out, by an establishment or undertaking, of their own waste disposal at the place of production if the waste being disposed of is special waste.]

(4) Paragraph (1) above only applies in relation to an exempt activity involving the disposal or recovery of waste by an establishment or undertaking if the type and quantity of waste submitted to the activity, and the method of disposal or recovery, are consistent with the need to attain the objectives mentioned in paragraph 4(1)(a) of Part I of Schedule 4.

(5) For the purposes of Schedule 3, a container, lagoon or place is secure in relation to waste kept in it if all reasonable precautions are taken to ensure that the waste cannot escape from it and members of the public are unable to gain access to the waste, and any reference to secure storage means storage in a secure container, lagoon or place.

18   Registration in connection with exempt activities

(1) Subject to [paragraphs (1A), (1B) and (7)] below, it shall be an offence for an establishment or undertaking to carry on, after 31st December 1994, an exempt activity involving the recovery or disposal of waste without being registered with the appropriate registration authority.

[(1A) In the case of an exempt activity falling within paragraph 45(1) or (2) of Schedule 3, paragraph (1) above shall have effect as if '30th September 1995' were substituted for '31st December 1994'.

(1B) Paragraph (1) above shall not apply in the case of an exempt activity to which a resolution under section 54 of the 1990 Act relates and which is carried on in accordance with the conditions, specified in the resolution, which relate to it.]

(2) It shall be the duty of each appropriate registration authority to establish and maintain a register for the purposes of paragraph (1) above of establishments and undertakings carrying on exempt activities involving the recovery or disposal of waste in respect of which it is the appropriate registration authority.

(3) Subject to paragraph (4) below, the register shall contain the following particulars in relation to each such establishment or undertaking—

    (a) the name and address of the establishment or undertaking;

    (b) the activity which constitutes the exempt activity; and

    (c) the place where the activity is carried on.

(4) [Subject to paragraphs (4A) and (4B) below,] the appropriate registration authority shall enter the relevant particulars in the register in relation to an establishment or undertaking if it receives notice of them in writing or otherwise becomes aware of those particulars.

[(4A) Paragraph (4) above shall not apply in the case of an exempt activity falling within paragraph 45(1) or (2) of Schedule 3 and, in such a case, the appropriate registration authority shall enter the relevant particulars in the register in relation to an establishment or undertaking only if—

    (a) it receives notice of them in writing;

    (b) that notice is provided to it by that establishment or undertaking;

    (c) that notice is accompanied by a plan of each place at which any such exempt activity is carried on showing—

        (i)   the boundaries of that place;

        (ii) the locations within that place at which the exempt activity is to be carried on;

        (iii) the location and specifiations of any such impermeable pavements, drainage systems or hardstandings as are mentioned in paragraph 45(1)(c) or (2)(f) or (g) of Schedule 3; and

        (iv) the location of any such secure containers as are mentioned in paragraph 45(2)(e) of Schedule 3;

    and

    (d) that notice is also accompanied by payment of [the charge prescribed for the purpose by a charging scheme under section 41 of the Environment Act 1995] in respect of each place where any such exempt activity is carried on.

(4B) Where any fee payable under paragraph 45(3)(d) of Schedule 3 is not received by the appropriate registration authority within 2 months of the due date for its payment as ascertained in accordance with paragraph 45(4) of Schedule 3—

    (a) in a case where the establishment or undertaking is registered for exempt activities falling within paragraph 45(1) or (2) in respect of only one place, or where it is so registered in respect of more than one place and the fee in respect of each such place is then unpaid, the registration of the establishment or undertaking shall be cancelled and the authority shall remove from its register the relevant entry in respect of the establishment or undertaking;

(b) in any other case, the registration of the establishment or undertaking in respect of those activities shall be cancelled insofar as it relates to any place in respect of which the fee is then unpaid and the authority shall amend the relevant entry in its register accordingly,

and where the authority removes or amends an entry from or in its register by virtue of this paragraph it shall notify the establishment or undertaking in writing of the removal or amendment.]

(5) For the purposes of paragraph (4) above, the appropriate registration authority shall be taken to be aware of the relevant particulars in relation to an exempt activity mentioned in paragraph (10)(a), (b) or (c) below.

(6) A person guilty of an offence under paragraph (1) above shall be liable on summary conviction to a fine [not exceeding—

(a) in the case of an exempt activity falling within paragraph 45(1) or (2) of Schedule 3, level 2 on the standard scale; and

(b) in any other case, £10.]

(7) The preceding provisions of this regulation shall not apply in the case of an exempt activity to which paragraph 7(3)(c) of Schedule 3 applies, but the appropriate registration authority shall enter in its register the particulars furnished to it pursuant to that provision.

(8) Each appropriate registration authority shall secure that any register maintained by it under this regulation is open to inspection . . . by members of the public free of charge at all reasonable hours and shall afford to members of the public reasonable facilities for obtaining, on payment of reasonable charges, copies of entries in the register.

(9) Registers under this regulation may be kept in any form.

(10) For the purposes of this regulation, the appropriate registration authority is—

(a) in the case of an exempt activity falling within—
   (i) paragraph 1, 2, 3 or 24 of Schedule 3 [and carried out under an authorisation granted under Part I of the 1990 Act];
   (ii) paragraph 4 of Schedule 3 if it involves the coating or spraying of metal containers as or as part of a process within Part B of Section 6.5 (coating processes and printing) of Schedule 1 to the 1991 Regulations and the process is for the time being the subject of an authorisation granted under Part I of the 1990 Act, or if it involves storage related to that process; or
   (iii) paragraph 12 of Schedule 3 if it involves the composting of biodegradable waste as or as part of a process within paragraph (a) of Part B of Section 6.9 (treatment or processing of animal or vegetable matter) of Schedule 1 to the 1991 Regulations, the compost is to be used for the purpose of cultivating mushrooms and the process is for the time being the subject of an authorisation granted under Part I of the 1990 Act, or if it involves storage related to that process,
   the local enforcing authority responsible for granting the authorisation under Part I of the 1990 Act for the prescribed process involving the exempt activity, or to which the exempt activity relates;

[(aa) in the case of an exempt activity falling within—
   (i) paragraph 1A, 2A, 3 or 24 of Schedule 3 and carried out under a permit under the 2000 Regulations;
   (ii) paragraph 4 of Schedule 3 if it involves the coating or spraying of metal containers as or as part of an activity within Part B of Section 6.4 (coating activities and printing) of Part 1 of Schedule 1 to the 2000 Regulations and the activity is for the time being the subject of a permit granted under those Regulations, or if it involves storage related to that activity; or

(iii) paragraph 12 of Schedule 3 if it involves the composting of biodegradable waste as or as part of an activity within paragraph (a) of Part B of Section 6.8 (treatment of animal and vegetable matter) of Part 1 of Schedule 1 to the 2000 Regulations, the compost is to be used for the purpose of cultivating mushrooms and the activity is for the time being the subject of a permit granted under those Regulations, or if it involves storage related to that activity,

the local authority regulator responsible for granting the permit under the 2000 Regulations authorising the exempt activity;]

(b) in a case falling within paragraph 16 of Schedule 3, the issuing authority responsible for granting the licence under article 7 or 8 of the Diseases of Animals (Waste Food) Order 1973 under which the exempt activity is carried on;

(c) in a case falling within paragraph 23 of Schedule 3—

  (i) where the exempt activity is carried on by virtue of a licence under article 5(2)(c) or 6(2)(d), or an approval under article 8, of the Animal By-Products Order 1992, the Minister;

  (ii) where the exempt activity is carried on by virtue of a registration under article 9 or 10 of that Order, the appropriate Minister;

  (iii) where the exempt activity is carried on at a knacker's yard in respect of which the occupier holds a licence under section 1 of the Slaughterhouses Act 1974 authorising the use of that yard as a knacker's yard . . . the local authority;

  and in this sub-paragraph 'the Minister' and 'the appropriate Minister' have the meaning given by section 86(1) of the Animal Health Act 1981, and 'knacker's yard' and 'local authority' have the meaning given by section 34 of the Slaughterhouses Act 1974 . . . ;

(d) in any other case, the waste regulation authority for the area in which the exempt activity is carried on.

19 Waste framework directive

Schedule 4 (which implements certain provisions of Council Directive 75/442/EEC on waste) shall have effect.

20 Registration of brokers

(1) Subject to paragraphs (2) to (4) below, it shall be an offence for an establishment or undertaking after 31st December 1994 to arrange (as dealer or broker) for the disposal or recovery of controlled waste on behalf of another person unless it is a registered broker of controlled waste.

(2) Paragraph (1) above shall not apply in relation to an arrangement under which an establishment or undertaking will itself carry out the disposal or recovery of the waste and either—

(a) it is authorised to carry out the disposal or recovery of the waste by a waste management licence, an authorisation under Part I of the 1990 Act, [a permit under the 2000 Regulations,] a consent under Chapter II of Part III of the Water Resources Act 1991 or under Part II of the Control of Pollution Act 1974 or a licence under Part II of the Food and Environment Protection Act 1985; or

(b) the recovery of the waste is covered by an exemption conferred by—

  (i) regulation 17(1) of, and Schedule 3 to, these Regulations; or

  (ii) article 3 of the Deposits in the Sea (Exemptions) Order 1985.

(3) Paragraph (1) above shall not apply in relation to an arrangement for the disposal or recovery of controlled waste made by a person who is registered as a carrier of controlled waste, or who is registered for the purposes of paragraph 12(1) of Part I of Schedule 4, if as part of the arrangement he transports the waste to or from any place in Great Britain.

(4) Paragraph (1) above shall not apply to an establishment or undertaking which—

(a) is a charity;
(b) is a voluntary organisation within the meaning of section 48(11) of the Local Government Act 1985 or section 83(2D) of the Local Government (Scotland) Act 1973;
(c) is an authority which is a waste collection authority, waste disposal authority or waste regulation authority; or
(d) applies before 1st January 1995 in accordance with Schedule 5 for registration as a broker of controlled waste but only whilst its application is pending (and paragraph 1(4) and (5) of Part I of Schedule 5 shall apply for the purpose of determining whether an application is pending).

(5) A person guilty of an offence under this section shall be liable on summary conviction to a fine not exceeding level 5 on the standard scale.

(6) Section 157 of the 1990 Act shall apply in relation to an offence under this section as it applies in relation to an offence under that Act.

(7) Schedule 5 (which makes provision for the registration of brokers of controlled waste) shall have effect.

(8) Sections 68(3) to (5), 69 and 71(2) and (3) of the 1990 Act (power to appoint inspectors, powers of entry and power to obtain information) shall have effect as if the provisions of this regulation and Schedule 5 were provisions of Part II of that Act.

Regulation 2(2), (3) and (4)   SCHEDULE 1

INFORMATION AND EVIDENCE REQUIRED IN RELATION TO AN APPLICATION FOR THE SURRENDER OF A SITE LICENCE

1.   The full name, address and daytime telephone, fax and telex number (if any) of the holder of the site licence and, where the holder employs an agent in relation to the application, of that agent.

2.   The number (if any) of the site licence, and the address or a description of the location of the site.

3.   A map or plan—
(a) showing the location of the site;
(b) indicating whereabouts on the site the different activities mentioned in paragraph 4 were carried on; and
(c) indicating relevant National Grid references.

4.   A description of the different activities involving the treatment, keeping or disposal of controlled waste which were carried on at the site (whether or not in pursuance of the licence), an indication of when those activities were carried on and an estimate of the total quantities of the different types of waste which were dealt with at the site.

5.   Where the site is a landfill or lagoon—
(a) particulars of all significant engineering works carried out for the purpose of preventing or minimising pollution of the environment or harm to human health as a result of activities carried on at the site, including—
  (i) an indication of when those works were carried out and a copy of all relevant plans or specifications; and
  (ii) details of works of restoration carried out after completion of operations at the site;
(b) geological, hydrological and hydrogeological information relating to the site and its surrounds, including information about the flows of groundwater;
(c) monitoring data on the quality of surface water or groundwater which could be affected by the site and on the production of any landfill gas or leachate at the site and information about the physical stability of the site; and

(d) where special waste has been deposited at the site, a copy of the records and plans relating to the deposits kept under regulation 14 of the Control of Pollution (Special Waste) Regulations 1980;

and any estimate under paragraph 4 of the total quantities of the different types of waste dealt with at the site shall, in particular, differentiate between biodegradable waste, non-biodegradable waste and special waste.

6.   Where the site is not a landfill or lagoon—

(a) details of the contaminants likely to be present at the site having regard to—

(i) the different activities involving the treatment, keeping or disposal of controlled waste carried on at the site (whether or not in pursuance of the licence); and

(ii) the nature of the different types of waste dealt with at the site; and

(b) a report which—

(i) records the results of the analysis of samples taken in such numbers, and at such locations at the site, that they provide a reliable indication of the locations where contaminants are likely to be present in high concentrations; and

(ii) shows how many (and from where) samples were taken.

7.   Any other information which the applicant wishes the waste regulation authority to take into account.

Regulations 1(3) and 19   SCHEDULE 4

WASTE FRAMEWORK DIRECTIVE ETC.
PART I   GENERAL

1   Interpretation of Schedule 4
In this Schedule, unless the context otherwise requires—

'competent authority' has the meaning given by paragraph 3;

'development', 'development plan', 'government department' and 'planning permission' have the same meaning as in the Town and Country Planning Act 1990 . . . ;

'licensing authority' and 'the Ministers' have the meaning given by section 24(1) of the Food and Environment Protection Act 1985;

'local planning authority' and 'the planning Acts' have the same meaning as in the Town and Country Planning Act 1990;

'permit' means a waste management licence, a disposal licence, an authorisation under Part I of the 1990 Act, [a permit under the 2000 Regulations,] a resolution under section 54 of the 1990 Act, a licence under Part II of the Food and Environment Protection Act 1985 or a consent under Chapter II of Part III of the Water Resources Act 1991 or under Part II of the Control of Pollution Act 1974 (and, in relation to a permit, 'grant' includes give, issue or pass, 'modify' includes vary, and cognate expressions shall be construed accordingly);

'plan-making provisions' means paragraph 5 below, section 50 of the 1990 Act . . . Part II of the Town and Country Planning Act 1990 [and section 44A of the Environmental Protection Act 1990 . . .]

'planning authority' means the local planning authority, the person appointed under paragraph 1 of Schedule 6 to the Town and Country Planning Act 1990 or, as the case may be, the government department responsible for discharging a function under the planning Acts . . . and the Secretary of State shall be treated as a planning authority in respect of his functions under the planning Acts . . .

'pollution control authority' means any competent authority other than a planning authority;

. . .

'specified action' means any of the following—
- (a) determining—
  - (i) an application for planning permission; or
  - (ii) an appeal made under section 78 of the Town and Country Planning Act 1990 . . . in respect of such an application;
- (b) deciding whether to take any action under section 141(2) or (3) or 177(1)(a) or (b) of the Town and Country Planning Act 1990, or under section 196(5) of that Act as originally enacted, or under section 35(5) of the Planning (Listed Buildings and Conservation Areas) Act 1990 . . .
- (c) deciding whether to direct under section 90(1), (2) or (2A) of the Town and Country Planning Act 1990 or . . . or paragraph 7(1) of Schedule 8 to the Electricity Act 1989, that planning permission shall be deemed to be granted;
- (d) deciding whether—
  - (i) in making or confirming a discontinuance order, to include in the order any grant of planning permission; or
  - (ii) to confirm (with or without modifications) a discontinuance order insofar as it grants planning permission,

  and, for the purposes of this sub-paragraph, 'discontinuance order' means an order under section 102 of the Town and Country Planning Act 1990 (including an order made under that section by virtue of section 104 of that Act), or under paragraph 1 of Schedule 9 to that Act (including an order made under that paragraph by virtue of paragraph 11 of that Schedule) . . .
- (e) discharging functions under Part II of the Town and Country Planning Act 1990 . . .

2 Duties of competent authorities

(1) Subject to the following provisions of this paragraph, the competent authorities shall discharge their specified functions, insofar as they relate to the recovery or disposal of waste, with the relevant objectives.

(2) Nothing in sub-paragraph (1) above requires a planning authority to deal with any matter which the relevant pollution control authority has power to deal with.

(3) In a case where the recovery or disposal of waste is or forms part of a prescribed process designated for local control under Part I of the 1990 Act, and either requires a waste management licence or is covered by an exemption conferred by regulation 17(1) of, and Schedule 3 to, these Regulations, nothing in sub-paragraph (1) above shall require a competent authority to discharge its functions under—
- (a) Part I of the 1990 Act in order to control pollution of the environment due to the release of substances into any environmental medium other than the air; or
- (b) Part II of the 1990 Act in order to control pollution of the environment due to the release of substances into the air resulting from the carrying on of the prescribed process.

(4) In sub-paragraph (3) above, 'prescribed process', 'designated for local control', 'pollution of the environment due to the release of substances into the air' and 'pollution of the environment due to the release of substances into any environmental medium other than the air' have the meaning which they have in Part I of the 1990 Act.

[(5) In a case where the recovery or disposal of waste is or forms part of an activity carried out at a Part B installation and requires a waste management licence, nothing in sub-paragraph (1) shall require a competent authority to discharge its functions under—
- (a) the 2000 Regulations for any purpose other than preventing or, where that is not practicable, reducing emissions into the air;
- (b) Part II of the 1990 Act for the purpose of preventing or reducing emissions into the air.

(6) In sub-paragraph (5), 'Part B installation' has the meaning given by regulation 2(1) of the 2000 Regulations.]

3   Meaning of 'competent authority' etc.

(1) For the purposes of this Schedule, 'competent authority' means any of the persons or bodies listed in column (1) of Table 5 below and, subject to sub-paragraph (2) below, in relation to a competent authority 'specified function' means any function of that authority listed in column (2) of that Table opposite the entry for that authority.

Table 5

Competent authorities (1)	Specified functions (2)
Any planning authority.	The taking of any specified action.
A waste regulation authority, the Secretary of State or a person appointed under [section 114(1)(a) of the Environment Act 1995].	Their respective functions under Part II of the 1990 Act in relation to waste management licences, including preparing plans or modifications of them under section 50 of the 1990 Act [and preparing the strategy, or any modification of it, under section 44A . . . of that Act].
. . .	. . .
A licensing authority or the Ministers.	Their respective functions under Part II of the Food and Environment Protection Act 1985, or under paragraph 5 below.
An enforcing authority, the Secretary of State or a person appointed under [section 114(1)(a) of the Environment Act 1995].	Their respective functions under Part I of the 1990 Act in relation to prescribed processes except when— (a) the process is designated for local control; and (b) it is an exempt activity carried out subject to the conditions and limitations specified in Schedule 3.
[The Environment Agency] or the Secretary of State.]	Their respective functions in relation to [— (a) consents under Chapter II of Part III of the Water Resources Act 1991 (offences in relation to pollution of water resources) for any discharge of waste in liquid form other than waste waters; (b) authorisations under regulation 18 of the Groundwater Regulations 1998 (disposal or tipping of substances in list I or II); and (c) notices under regulation 19 of the Groundwater Regulations 1998 (prohibition or authorisation of activities which may result in indirect discharges of substances in list I or II).]
. . .	. . .
[A regulator (within the meaning of regulation 2(1) of the 2000 Regulations), the Secretary of State or a person appointed under section 114(1)(a) of the Environment Act 1995.	Their respective functions in relation to permits under the 2000 Regulations except in relation to the carrying out of an exempt activity under such permits.]

(2) In Table 5 above, references to functions do not include functions of making, revoking, amending, revising or re-enacting orders, regulations or schemes where those functions are required to be discharged by statutory instrument.

4   Relevant objectives

(1) For the purposes of this Schedule, the following objectives are relevant objectives in relation to the disposal or recovery of waste—

  (a) ensuring that waste is recovered or disposed of without endangering human health and without using processes or methods which could harm the environment and in particular without—

  (i)   risk to water, air, soil, plants or animals; or

  (ii) causing nuisance through noise or odours; or

  (iii) adversely affecting the countryside or places of special interest;

  (b) implementing, so far as material, any plan made under the plan-making provisions.

(2) The following additional objectives are relevant objectives in relation to the disposal of waste—

  (a) establishing an integrated and adequate network of waste disposal installations, taking account of the best available technology not involving excessive costs; and

  (b) ensuring that the network referred to at paragraph (a) above enables—

  (i) the European Community as a whole to become self-sufficient in waste disposal, and the Member States individually to move towards that aim, taking into account geographical circumstances or the need for specialized installations for certain types of waste; and

  (ii) waste to be disposed of in one of the nearest appropriate installations, by means of the most appropriate methods and technologies in order to ensure a high level of protection for the environment and public health.

(3) The following further objectives are relevant objectives in relation to functions under the plan-making provisions—

  (a) encouraging the prevention or reduction of waste production and its harmfulness, in particular by—

  (i)   the development of clean technologies more sparing in their use of natural resources;

  (ii) the technical development and marketing of products designed so as to make no contribution or to make the smallest possible contribution, by the nature of their manufacture, use or final disposal, to increasing the amount or harmfulness of waste and pollution hazards; and

  (iii) the development of appropriate techniques for the final disposal of dangerous substances contained in waste destined for recovery; and

  (b) encouraging—

  (i) the recovery of waste by means of recycling, reuse or reclamation or any other process with a view to extracting secondary raw materials; and

  (ii) the use of waste as a source of energy.

5   Preparation of offshore waste management plan

(1) Subject to sub-paragraph (2) below, it shall be the duty of a licensing authority to prepare a statement ('the plan') containing the authority's policies in relation to the recovery or disposal of waste for attaining the relevant objectives in those parts of United Kingdom waters and United Kingdom controlled waters for which the authority is the licensing authority.

(2) Two or more licensing authorities may join together to prepare a single statement covering the several parts of United Kingdom waters and United Kingdom controlled waters for which they are the licensing authorities.

(3) The plan shall relate in particular to—

    (a) the type, quantity and origin of waste to be recovered or disposed of;

    (b) general technical requirements;

    (c) any special arrangements for particular wastes; and

    (d) suitable disposal sites or installations.

(4) The licensing authority shall make copies of the plan available to the public on payment of reasonable charges.

(5) In this paragraph, 'United Kingdom waters' and 'United Kingdom controlled waters' have the meaning given by section 24(1) of the Food and Environment Protection Act 1985.

6 Matters to be covered by permits

When a pollution control authority grants or modifies a permit, and the activities authorised by the permit include the disposal of waste, the pollution control authority shall ensure that the permit covers—

    (a) the types and quantities of waste,

    (b) the technical requirements,

    (c) the security precautions to be taken,

    (d) the disposal site, and

    (e) the treatment method.

7 Modifications of provisions relating to development plans

(1) Subject to sub-paragraph (2) below, sections 12(3A), 31(3) and 36(3) of the Town and Country Planning Act 1990 . . . shall have effect as if the policies referred to in those sections also included policies in respect of suitable waste disposal sites or installations.

(2) In the case of the policies referred to in section 36(3) of the Town and Country Planning Act 1990, sub-paragraph (1) above shall have effect subject to the provisions of section 36(5) of that Act.

(3) Section 38(1) of the Town and Country Planning Act 1990 shall have effect as if the definition of waste policies included detailed policies in respect of suitable disposal sites or installations for the carrying on of such development as is referred to in that definition.

8 Modifications of Part I of the Environmental Protection Act 1990

(1) Subject to section 28(1) of the 1990 Act, Part I of the 1990 Act shall have effect in relation to prescribed processes involving the disposal or recovery of waste with such modifications as are needed to allow an enforcing authority to exercise its functions under that Part for the purpose of achieving the relevant objectives.

(2) Nothing in sub-paragraph (1) above requires an enforcing authority granting an authorisation in relation to such a process to take account of the relevant objectives insofar as they relate to the prevention of detriment to the amenities of the locality in which the process is (or is to be) carried on if planning permission, resulting from the taking of a specified action by a planning authority after 30th April 1994, is or, before the process is carried on, will be in force.

9 Modifications of Part II of the Environmental Protection Act 1990

(1) Part II of the 1990 Act shall have effect subject to the following modifications.

(2) Any reference to waste shall include a reference to Directive waste.

(3) In sections 33(1)(a) and (5), 54(1)(a), (2), (3) and (4)(d) and 69(2), any reference to the deposit of waste in or on land shall include a reference to any operation listed in Part III or IV of this Schedule involving such a deposit.

(4) In sections 33(1)(b), 54(1)(b), (2), (3) and (4)(d) and 69(2), any reference to the treatment or disposal, or to the treatment, keeping or disposal, of controlled waste shall be taken to be a reference to submitting controlled waste to any of the operations listed in Part III or IV of this Schedule other than an operation mentioned in sub-paragraph (3) above.

(5) In sections 33(1)(c) and 35, any reference to the treatment or disposal, or to the treatment, keeping or disposal, of controlled waste shall include a reference to submitting controlled waste to any of the operations listed in Part III or Part IV of this Schedule.

(6) Section 33(2) shall not apply to the treatment, keeping or disposal of household waste by an establishment or undertaking.

(7) In section 36(3), the reference to planning permission shall be taken to be a reference to planning permission resulting from the taking of a specified action by a planning authority after 30th April 1994.

(8) In section 50(3), any reference to the disposal of waste shall include a reference to the recovery of waste.

[(9) In subsection (1) of section 62, any reference to the treatment, keeping or disposal of such waste as is referred to in that subsection shall include a reference to submitting such waste to any of the operations listed in Part III or IV of this Schedule.

(10) In subsection (2) of section 62, any reference to the treatment, keeping or disposal of special waste shall include a reference to submitting special waste to any of the operations listed in Part III or IV of this Schedule.]

10 . . .

11   References to 'waste' in Planning and Water legislation
In the Town and Country Planning Act 1990, . . . and Chapter II of Part III of the Water Resources Act 1991, any reference to 'waste' shall include a reference to Directive waste.

12   Registration by professional collectors and transporters of waste, and by dealers and brokers
(1) Subject to sub-paragraph (3) below, it shall be an offence for an establishment or undertaking falling within sub-paragraph (a), (c), (f) or (g) of regulation 2(1) of the Controlled Waste (Registration of Carriers and Seizure of Vehicles) Regulations 1991 after 31st December 1994 to collect or transport waste on a professional basis unless it is registered in accordance with the provisions of this paragraph.

(2) Subject to sub-paragraph (3) below, it shall be an offence for an establishment or undertaking falling within sub-paragraph (a), (b) or (c) of regulation 20(4) after 31st December 1994 to arrange for the recovery or disposal of waste on behalf of another person unless it is registered in accordance with the provisions of this paragraph.

(3) Sub-paragraphs (1) and (2) above do not apply in cases where the establishment or undertaking is carrying on the activities therein mentioned pursuant to, and in accordance with the terms and conditions of, a permit.

(4) An establishment or undertaking shall register with the waste regulation authority in whose area its principal place of business in Great Britain is located or, where it has no place of business in Great Britain, with any waste regulation authority.

(5) Each waste regulation authority shall establish and maintain a register of establishments and undertakings registering with it under the provisions of this paragraph.

(6) The register shall contain the following particulars in relation to each such establishment or undertaking—
  (a) the name of the establishment or undertaking;
  (b) the address of its principal place of business; and
  (c) the address of any place at or from which it carries on its business.

(7) The waste regulation authority shall enter the relevant particulars in the register in relation to an establishment or undertaking if it receives notice of them in writing or otherwise becomes aware of those particulars.

(8) A person guilty of an offence under sub-paragraph (1) or (2) above shall be liable on summary conviction to a fine not exceeding level 2 on the standard scale.

(9) Each waste regulation authority shall secure that any register maintained by it under this paragraph is open to inspection . . . by members of the public free of charge at all

reasonable hours and shall afford to members of the public reasonable facilities for obtaining, on payment of reasonable charges, copies of entries in the register.

(10) Registers under this paragraph may be kept in any form.

(11) In this paragraph, 'registered carrier' and 'controlled waste' have the same meaning as they have in the Control of Pollution (Amendment) Act 1989, 'registered broker' has the same meaning as in regulation 20 and Schedule 5, and 'collect' and 'transport' have the same meaning as they have in Article 12 of the Directive.

13   Duty to carry out appropriate periodic inspections

(1) [Subject to sub-paragraphs (3) to (5) below,] any establishment or undertaking which carries out the recovery or disposal of controlled waste, or which collects or transports controlled waste on a professional basis, or which arranges for the recovery or disposal of controlled waste on behalf of others (dealers or brokers), [and producers of special waste,] shall be subject to appropriate periodic inspections by the competent authorities.

(2) [Section] 71(2) and (3) of the 1990 Act (. . . power to obtain information) shall have effect as if the provisions of this paragraph were provisions of Part II of that Act and as if, in those sections, references to a waste regulation authority were references to a competent authority.

[(2A) Section 108 of the Environment Act 1995 (powers of entry) shall apply as if the competent authority was an enforcing authority and its functions under this paragraph were pollution control functions.]

[(3) Subject to sub-paragraph (4) below, in a case where an establishment or undertaking is carrying on an exempt activity in reliance upon an exemption conferred by regulation 17(1) of, and paragraph 45(1) or (2) of Schedule 3 to, these Regulations, a competent authority which is a waste regulation authority shall discharge its duty under sub-paragraph (1) in respect of any place where such an activity is so carried on by—

(a)   carrying out an initial inspection of that place within two months of having received in respect of that place the notice, plan and fee referred to in regulation 18(4A); and

(b)   thereafter carrying out periodic inspections of that place at intervals not exceeding 12 months.

(4)   Where the notice, plan and fee referred to in paragraph (a) of sub-paragraph (3) above are received by the authority before 1st October 1995, that paragraph shall have effect as if for the reference to carrying out an initial inspection within two months of the receipt of such notice, plan and fee there were substituted a reference to carrying out such an inspection within nine months of their receipt.

(5)   In the case of any such place as is mentioned in sub-paragraph (3) above, but without prejudice to any duties of waste regulation authorities imposed otherwise than by this paragraph, sub-paragraph (1) above does not require (but does permit) a competent authority which is a waste regulation authority to carry out the periodic inspections referred to in sub-paragraph (3)(b) above at intervals of less than 10 months.]

14   Record keeping

(1) Subject to [paragraph 45(3)(b) of Schedule 3 and] sub-paragraph (2) below, an establishment or undertaking which carries out the disposal or recovery of controlled waste shall—

(a)   keep a record of the quantity, nature, origin and, where relevant, the destination, frequency of collection, mode of transport and treatment method of any waste which is disposed of or recovered; and

(b)   make that information available, on request, to the competent authorities [or, in the case of special waste, to a previous holder; and for this purpose 'holder', in respect of any such waste, means the producer or the person in possession of it].

[(1A) Where special waste is recovered or disposed of by an establishment or undertaking, it shall keep a record of the carrying out and supervision of the operation and, in the case of a disposal operation, of the after-care of the disposal site.]

(2) [Subject to sub-paragraph (3) below,] sub-paragraph (1) above does not apply where the disposal or recovery of the waste is covered by an exemption conferred by—

(a) regulation 17(1) of, and Schedule 3 to, these Regulations; or

(b) article 3 of the Deposits in the Sea (Exemptions) Order 1985

[(3) Sub-paragraph (1) above does apply to an activity subject to an exemption conferred by regulation 17(1) of, and paragraph 45(1) or (2) of Schedule 3 to, these Regulations.]

[(4) Subject to sub-paragraph (5) below, it shall be an offence for an establishment or undertaking to fail to comply with any of the foregoing provisions of this paragraph insofar as that provision imposes any requirement or obligation upon it.

(5) Paragraph (2) of regulation 18 of the Special Waste Regulations 1996 (defence in cases of emergency etc.) shall apply to a person charged with an offence under sub-paragraph (4) above as it applies to a person charged with an offence under paragraph (1) of that regulation.

(6) A person who, in purported compliance with a requirement to furnish any information imposed by or under any of the provisions of this paragraph, makes a statement which he knows to be false or misleading in a material particular, commits an offence.

(7) A person who intentionally makes a false entry in any record required to be kept by virtue of any of the provisions of this paragraph commits an offence.

(8) Paragraphs (5) to (9) regulation 18 of the Special Waste Regulations 1996 (offence where act or default causes offence by another, offences by bodies coporate and penalties) shall apply to an offence under this paragraph as they apply to an offence under that regulation.]

PART II   SUBSTANCES OR OBJECTS WHICH ARE WASTE WHEN DISCARDED ETC.

1. Production or consumption residues not otherwise specified in this Part of this Schedule (Q1).

2. Off-specification products (Q2).

3. Products whose date for appropriate use has expired (Q3).

4. Materials spilled, lost or having undergone other mishap, including any materials, equipment, etc., contaminated as a result of the mishap (Q4).

5. Materials contaminated or soiled as a result of planned actions (e.g. residues from cleaning operations, packing materials, containers, etc.) (Q5).

6. Unusable parts (e.g. reject batteries, exhausted catalysts, etc.) (Q6).

7. Substances which no longer perform satisfactorily (e.g. contaminated acids, contaminated solvents, exhausted tempering salts, etc.) (Q7).

8. Residues of industrial processes (e.g. slags, still bottoms, etc.) (Q8).

9. Residues from pollution abatement processes (e.g. scrubber sludges, baghouse dusts, spent filters, etc.) (Q9).

10. Machining or finishing residues (e.g. lathe turnings, mill scales, etc.) (Q10).

11. Residues from raw materials extraction and processing (e.g. mining residues, oil field slops, etc.) (Q11).

12. Adulterated materials (e.g. oils contaminated with PCBs, etc.) (Q12).

13. Any materials, substances or products whose use has been banned by law (Q13).

14. Products for which the holder has no further use (e.g. agricultural, household, office, commercial and shop discards, etc.) (Q14).

15. Contaminated materials, substances or products resulting from remedial action with respect to land (Q15).

16. Any materials, substances or products which are not contained in the above categories (Q16).

(Note: — the reference in brackets at the end of each paragraph of this Part of this Schedule is the number of the corresponding paragraph in Annex I to the Directive.)

PART III   WASTE DISPOSAL OPERATIONS

1. Tipping of waste above or underground (e.g. landfill, etc.) (D1).

2. Land treatment of waste (e.g. biodegradation of liquid or sludge discards in soils, etc.) (D2).

3. Deep injection of waste (e.g. injection of pumpable discards into wells, salt domes or naturally occurring repositories, etc.) (D3).

4. Surface impoundment of waste (e.g. placement of liquid or sludge discards into pits, ponds or lagoons, etc.) (D4).

5. Specially engineered landfill of waste (e.g. placement of waste into lined discrete cells which are capped and isolated from one another and the environment, etc.) (D5).

6. Release of solid waste into a water body except seas or oceans (D6).

7. Release of waste into seas or oceans including seabed insertion (D7).

8. Biological treatment of waste not listed elsewhere in this Part of this Schedule which results in final compounds or mixtures which are disposed of by means of any of the operations listed in this Part of this Schedule (D8).

9. Physico-chemical treatment of waste not listed elsewhere in this Part of this Schedule which results in final compounds or mixtures which are disposed of by means of any of the operations listed in this Part of this Schedule (e.g. evaporation, drying, calcination, etc.) (D9).

10. Incineration of waste on land (D10).

11. Incineration of waste at sea (D11).

12. Permanent storage of waste (e.g. emplacement of containers in a mine, etc.) (D12).

13. Blending or mixture of waste prior to the waste being submitted to any of the operations listed in this Part of this Schedule (D13).

14. Repackaging of waste prior to the waste being submitted to any of the operations listed in this Part of this Schedule (D14).

15. Storage of waste pending any of the operations listed in this Part of this Schedule, but excluding temporary storage, pending collection, on the site where the waste is produced (D15).

(Note:—the reference in brackets at the end of each paragraph of this Part of this Schedule is the number of the corresponding paragraph in Annex IIA to the Directive.)

PART IV   WASTE RECOVERY OPERATIONS

1. Reclamation or regeneration of solvents (R1).

2. Recycling or reclamation of organic substances which are not used as solvents (R2).

3. Recycling or reclamation of metals and metal compounds (R3).

4. Recycling or reclamation of other inorganic materials (R4).

5. Regeneration of acids or bases (R5).

6. Recovery of components used for pollution abatement (R6).

7. Recovery of components from catalysts (R7).

8. Re-refining, or other reuses, of oil which is waste (R8).

9. Use of waste principally as a fuel or for other means of generating energy (R9).

10. Spreading of waste on land resulting in benefit to agriculture or ecological improvement, including composting and other biological transformation processes, except in the case of waste excluded under Article 2(1)(b)(iii) of the Directive (R10).

11.   Use of wastes obtained from any of the operations listed in paragraphs 1 to 10 of this Part of this Schedule (R11).

12.   Exchange of wastes for submission to any of the operations listed in paragraphs 1 to 11 of this Part of this Schedule (R12).

13.   Storage of waste consisting of materials intended for submission to any operation listed in this Part of this Schedule, but excluding temporary storage, pending collection, on the site where it is produced (R13).

(Note:—the reference in brackets at the end of each paragraph of this Part of this Schedule is the number of the corresponding paragraph in Annex IIB to the Directive.)

Conservation (Natural Habitats, etc.) Regulations 1994
(SI 1994, No. 2716) (as amended)

PART I   INTRODUCTORY PROVISIONS

1   Citation and commencement

(1) These Regulations may be cited as the Conservation (Natural Habitats, &c.) Regulations 1994.

(2) These Regulations shall come into force on the tenth day after that on which they are made.

2   Interpretation and application

(1) In these Regulations—

'agriculture Minister' means the Minister of Agriculture, Fisheries and Food or the Secretary of State;

'competent authority' shall be construed in accordance with regulation 6;

'destroy', in relation to an egg, includes doing anything to the egg which is calculated to prevent it from hatching, and 'destruction' shall be construed accordingly;

'enactment' includes a local enactment and an enactment contained in subordinate legislation within the meaning of the Interpretation Act 1978;

'European site' has the meaning given by regulation 10 and 'European marine site' means a European site which consists of, or so far as it consists of, marine areas;

'functions' includes powers and duties;

['the Habitats Directive' means Council Directive 92/43/EEC on the conservation of natural habitats and of wild fauna and flora as amended by the Act of Accession to the European Union of Austria, Finland and Sweden and by Council Directive 97/62/EC);]

'land' includes land covered by water and as respects Scotland includes salmon fishings;

'livestock' includes any animal which is kept—

    (a)   for the provision of food, skins or fur,

    (b)   for the purpose of its use in the carrying on of any agricultural activity, or

    (c)   for the provision or improvement of shooting or fishing;

'local planning authority' means—

    (a)   in England and Wales, except as otherwise provided, any authority having any function as a local planning authority or mineral planning authority under the Town and Country Planning Act 1990, and

    (b) . . .

'management agreement' means an agreement entered into, or having effect as if entered into, under regulation 16;

'marine area' means any land covered (continuously or intermittently) by tidal waters or any part of the sea in or adjacent to Great Britain up to the seaward limit of territorial waters;

'Natura 2000' means the European network of special areas of conservation, and special protection areas under the Wild Birds Directive, provided for by Article 3(1) of the Habitats Directive;

'nature conservation body', and 'appropriate nature conservation body' in relation to England, Wales or Scotland, have the meaning given by regulation 4;

'occupier', for the purposes of Part III (protection of species), includes, in relation to any land other than the foreshore, any person having any right of hunting, shooting, fishing or taking game or fish;

. . .

'the register' means the register of European sites in Great Britain provided for by regulation 11;

'relevant authorities', in relation to marine areas and European marine sites, shall be construed in accordance with regulation 5;

'statutory undertaker' has the same meaning as in the National Parks and Access to the Countryside Act 1949;

'the Wild Birds Directive' means Council Directive 79/409/EEC on the conservation of wild birds.

(2) Unless the context otherwise requires, expressions used in these Regulations and in the Habitats Directive have the same meaning as in that Directive.

The following expressions, in particular, are defined in Article 1 of that Directive—

'priority natural habitat types' and 'priority species';

'site' and 'site of Community importance'; and

'special area of conservation'.

(3) In these Regulations, unless otherwise indicated—

    (a) any reference to a numbered regulation or Schedule is to the regulation or Schedule in these Regulations which bears that number, and

    (b) any reference in a regulation or Schedule to a numbered paragraph is to the paragraph of that regulation or Schedule which bears that number.

(4) Subject to regulation 68 (which provides for Part IV to be construed as one with the Town and Country Planning Act 1990), these Regulations apply to the Isles of Scilly as if the Isles were a county and the Council of the Isles were a county council.

(5) For the purposes of these Regulations the territorial waters of the United Kingdom adjacent to Great Britain shall be treated as part of Great Britain and references to England, Wales and Scotland shall be construed as including the adjacent territorial waters.

For the purposes of this paragraph—

    (a) territorial waters include any waters landward of the baselines from which the breadth of the territorial sea is measured; and

    (b) any question as to whether territorial waters are to be treated as adjacent to England, Wales or Scotland shall be determined by the Secretary of State or, for any purpose in relation to which the Minister of Agriculture, Fisheries and Food has responsibility, by the Secretary of State and that Minister acting jointly.

3   Implementation of Directive

(1) These Regulations make provision for the purpose of implementing, for Great Britain, ['the Habitats Directive'].

(2) The Secretary of State, the Minister of Agriculture, Fisheries and Food and the nature conservation bodies shall exercise their functions under the enactments relating to nature conservation so as to secure compliance with the requirements of the Habitats Directive.

Those enactments include—

Part III of the National Parks and Access to the Countryside Act 1949, section 49A of the Countryside (Scotland) Act 1967 (management agreements), section 15 of the Countryside Act 1968 (areas of special scientific interest), Part I and sections 28 to 38 of the Wildlife and Countryside Act 1981, sections 131 to 134 of the Environmental Protection Act 1990, sections 2, 3, 5, 6, 7 and 11 of the Natural Heritage (Scotland) Act 1991 and these Regulations.

(3) In relation to marine areas any competent authority having functions relevant to marine conservation shall exercise those functions so as to secure compliance with the requirements of the Habitats Directive.

This applies, in particular, to functions under the following enactments—

the Sea Fisheries Acts within the meaning of section 1 of the Sea Fisheries (Wildlife Conservation) Act 1992,

the Dockyard Ports Regulation Act 1865,

section 2(2) of the Military Lands Act 1900 (provisions as to use of sea, tidal water or shore),

the Harbours Act 1964,

Part II of the Control of Pollution Act 1974,

sections 36 and 37 of the Wildlife and Countryside Act 1981 (marine nature reserves),

sections 120 to 122 of the Civic Government (Scotland) Act 1982 (control of the seashore, adjacent waters and inland waters),

the Water Resources Act 1991,

the Land Drainage Act 1991, and

these Regulations.

(4) Without prejudice to the preceding provisions, every competent authority in the exercise of any of their functions, shall have regard to the requirements of the Habitats Directive so far as they may be affected by the exercise of those functions.

4 Nature conservation bodies

In these Regulations 'nature conservation body' means the Nature Conservancy Council for England, the Countryside Council for Wales or Scottish Natural Heritage; and references to 'the appropriate nature conservation body', in relation to England, Wales or Scotland, shall be construed accordingly.

5 Relevant authorities in relation to marine areas and European marine sites

For the purposes of these Regulations the relevant authorities, in relation to a marine area or European marine site, are such of the following as have functions in relation to land or waters within or adjacent to that area or site—

(a) a nature conservation body;

(b) a county council, district council, London borough council or, in Scotland, a regional, islands or district council;

(c) the [the Agency,] a water undertaker or sewerage undertaker, or an internal drainage board;

(d) a navigation authority within the meaning of the Water Resources Act 1991;

(e) a harbour authority within the meaning of the Harbours Act 1964;

(f) a lighthouse authority;

(g) a river purification board or a district salmon fishery board;

(h) a local fisheries committee constituted under the Sea Fisheries Regulation Act 1966 or any authority exercising the powers of such a committee.

6 Competent authorities generally

(1) For the purposes of these Regulations the expression 'competent authority' includes any Minister, government department, public or statutory undertaker, public body of any description or person holding a public office.

The expression also includes any person exercising any function of a competent authority in the United Kingdom.

(2) In paragraph (1)—

(a) 'public body' includes any local authority, joint board or joint committee; and
(b) 'public office' means—
   (a) an office under Her Majesty,
   (b) an office created or continued in existence by a public general Act of Parliament, or
   (c) an office the remuneration in respect of which is paid out of money provided by Parliament.
(3) In paragraph (2)(a)—
'local authority'—
   (a) in relation to England, means a county council, district council or London borough council, the Common Council of the City of London, the sub-treasurer of the Inner Temple, the under-treasurer of the Middle Temple or a parish council,
   (b) in relation to Wales, means a county council, district council or community council, and
   (c) in relation to Scotland, means a regional, islands or district council;
'joint board' and 'joint committee' in relation to England and Wales mean—
   (a) a joint or special planning board constituted for a National Park by order under paragraph 1 or 3 of Schedule 17 to the Local Government Act 1972 or a joint planning board within the meaning of section 2 of the Town and Country Planning Act 1990, and
   (b) a joint committee appointed under section 102(1)(b) of the Local Government Act 1972,
and in relation to Scotland have the same meaning as in the Local Government (Scotland) Act 1973.

PART II   CONSERVATION OF NATURAL HABITATS AND HABITATS OF SPECIES

European sites

7   Selection of sites eligible for identification as of Community importance

(1) On the basis of the criteria set out in Annex III (Stage 1) to the Habitats Directive, and relevant scientific information, the Secretary of State shall propose a list of sites indicating with respect to each site—
   (a) which natural habitat types in Annex I to the Directive the site hosts, and
   (b) which species in Annex II to the Directive that are native to Great Britain the site hosts.

(2) For animal species ranging over wide areas these sites shall correspond to the places within the natural range of such species which present the physical or biological factors essential to their life and reproduction.

For aquatic species which range over wide areas, such sites shall be proposed only where there is a clearly identifiable area representing the physical and biological factors essential to their life and reproduction.

(3) Where appropriate the Secretary of State may propose modification of the list in the light of the results of the surveillance referred to in Article 11 of the Habitats Directive.

(4) The list shall be transmitted to the Commission on or before 5th June 1995, together with information on each site including—
   (a) a map of the site,
   (b) its name, location and extent, and
   (c) the data resulting from application of the criteria specified in Annex III (Stage 1), provided in a format established by the Commission.

8   Adoption of list of sites: designation of special areas of conservation

(1) Once a site of Community importance in Great Britain has been adopted in accordance with the procedure laid down in paragraph 2 of Article 4 of the Habitats Directive, the Secretary of State shall designate that site as a special area of conservation as soon as possible and within six years at most.

(2) The Secretary of State shall establish priorities for the designation of sites in the light of—

(a) the importance of the sites for the maintenance or restoration at a favourable conservation status of—

(i) a natural habitat type in Annex I to the Habitats Directive, or

(ii) a species in Annex II to the Directive, and for the coherence of Natura 2000; and

(b) the threats of degradation or destruction to which those sites are exposed.

9   Consultation as to inclusion of site omitted from the list

If consultation is initiated by the Commission in accordance with Article 5(1) of the Habitats Directive with respect to a site in Great Britain hosting a priority natural habitat type or priority species and—

(a) the Secretary of State agrees that the site should be added to the list transmitted in accordance with regulation 7, or

(b) the Council, acting on a proposal from the Commission in pursuance of paragraph 2 of Article 5 of the Habitats Directive, so decides,

the site shall be treated as added to the list as from the date of that agreement or decision.

10   Meaning of 'European site' in these Regulations

(1) In these Regulations a 'European site' means—

(a) a special area of conservation,

(b) a site of Community importance which has been placed on the list referred to in the third sub-paragraph of Article 4(2) of the Habitats Directive,

(c) a site hosting a priority natural habitat type or priority species in respect of which consultation has been initiated under Article 5(1) of the Habitats Directive, during the consultation period or pending a decision of the Council under Article 5(3),

(d) an area classified pursuant to Article 4(1) or (2) of the Wild Birds Directive, [or

(e) a site in England included in the list of sites which has been proposed by the Secretary of State and transmitted to the Commission under regulation 7 until such time as—

(i) the draft list of sites of Community importance is established under the first sub-paragraph of Article 4(2) of the Habitats Directive where in any case the site is not included in that list, or

(ii) the list of sites referred to in the third sub-paragraph of Article 4(2) of the Habitats Directive is adopted by the Commission in accordance with that sub-paragraph].

(2) Sites which are European sites by virtue only of paragraph (1)(c) are not within regulations 20(1) and (2), 24 and 48 (which relate to the approval of certain plans and projects); but this is without prejudice to their protection under other provisions of these Regulations.

Register of European sites

11   Duty to compile and maintain register of European sites

(1) The Secretary of State shall compile and maintain, in such form as he thinks fit, a register of European sites in Great Britain.

(2) He shall include in the register—

(a) special areas of conservation, as soon as they are designated by him;

(b) sites of Community importance as soon as they are placed on the list referred to in the third sub-paragraph of Article 4(2) of the Habitats Directive, until they are designated as special areas of conservation;

(c) any site hosting a priority natural habitat type or priority species in respect of which consultation is initiated under Article 5(1) of the Habitats Directive, during the consultation period or pending a Council decision under Article 5(3);

(d) areas classified by him pursuant to Article 4(1) or (2) of the Wild Birds Directive, as soon as they are so classified or, if they have been classified before the commencement of these Regulations, as soon as practicable after commencement [; and

(e) any site in England included in the list of sites which has been proposed by the Secretary of State and transmitted to the Commission under regulation 7 until such time as paragraph (i) or paragraph (ii) of regulation 10(1)(e) applies.]

(3) He may, if appropriate, amend the entry in the register relating to a European site.

(4) He shall remove the relevant entry—

(a) if a special area of conservation is declassified by the Commission under Article 9 of the Habitats Directive; or

(b) if a site otherwise ceases to fall within any of the categories listed in paragraph (2) above.

(5) He shall keep a copy of the register available for public inspection at all reasonable hours and free of charge.

12   Notification to appropriate nature conservation body

(1) The Secretary of State shall notify the appropriate nature conservation body as soon as may be after including a site in the register, amending an entry in the register or removing an entry from the register.

(2) Notification of the inclusion of a site in the register shall be accompanied by a copy of the register entry.

(3) Notification of the amendment of an entry in the register shall be accompanied by a copy of the amended entry.

(4) Each nature conservation body shall keep copies of the register entries relating to European sites in their area available for public inspection at all reasonable hours and free of charge.

13   Notice to landowners, relevant authorities, &c.

(1) As soon as practicable after a nature conservation body receive notification under regulation 12 they shall give notice to—

(a) every owner or occupier of land within the site,

(b) every local planning authority in whose area the site, or any part of it, is situated, and

(c) such other persons or bodies as the Secretary of State may direct.

(2) Notice of the inclusion of a site in the register, or of the amendment of an entry in the register, shall be accompanied by a copy of so much of the relevant register entry as relates to land owned or occupied by or, as the case may be, to land within the area of, the person or authority to whom the notice is given.

(3) The Secretary of State may give directions as to the form and content of notices to be given under this regulation.

14   Local registration: England and Wales

An entry in the register relating to a European site in England and Wales is a local land charge.

. . .

Management agreements

16 Management agreements

(1) The appropriate nature conservation body may enter into an agreement (a 'management agreement') with every owner, lessee and occupier of land forming part of a European site, or land adjacent to such a site, for the management, conservation, restoration or protection of the site, or any part of it.

(2) A management agreement may impose such restrictions as may be expedient for the purposes of the agreement on the exercise of rights over the land by the persons who can be bound by the agreement.

(3) A management agreement—

(a) may provide for the management of the land in such manner, the carrying out thereon of such work and the doing thereon of such other things as may be expedient for the purposes of the agreement;

(b) may provide for any of the matters mentioned in sub-paragraph (a) being carried out, or for the costs thereof being defrayed, either by the said owner or other persons or by the appropriate nature conservation body, or partly in one way and partly in another;

(c) may contain such other provisions as to the making of payments by the appropriate nature conservation body, and in particular for the payment by them of compensation for the effect of the restrictions mentioned in paragraph (2), as may be specified in the agreement.

(4) Where land in England and Wales is subject to a management agreement, the appropriate nature conservation body shall, as respects the enforcement of the agreement against persons other than the original contracting party, have the like rights as if—

(a) they had at all material times been the absolute owners in possession of ascertained land adjacent to the land subject to the agreement and capable of being benefited by the agreement, and

(b) the management agreement had been expressed to be for the benefit of that adjacent land;

and section 84 of the Law of Property Act 1925 (which enables the Lands Tribunal to discharge or modify restrictive covenants) shall not apply to the agreement.

(5) . . .

17 Continuation in force of existing agreement, etc.

(1) Any agreement previously entered into under—

(a) section 16 of the National Parks and Access to the Countryside Act 1949 (nature reserves),

(b) section 15 of the Countryside Act 1968 (areas of special scientific interest),

(c) section 49A of the Countryside (Scotland) Act 1967 (management agreements),

in relation to land which on or after the commencement of these Regulations becomes land within a European site or adjacent to such a site, shall have effect as if entered into under regulation 16 above.

Regulation 32(1)(b) (power of compulsory acquisition in case of breach of agreement) shall apply accordingly.

(2) Any other thing done or deemed to have been done under any provision of Part III or VI of the National Parks and Access to the Countryside Act 1949, or under section 49A of the Countryside (Scotland) Act 1967, in respect of any land prior to that land becoming land within a European site, or adjacent to such a site, shall continue to have effect as if done under the corresponding provision of these Regulations.

For the purposes of this paragraph Part III of the 1949 Act shall be deemed to include section 15 of the Countryside Act 1968 and anything done or deemed to be done under that section and to which this paragraph applies shall have effect as if done or deemed to be done under section 16 of the 1949 Act.

(3) Any reference in an outlying enactment to a nature reserve within the meaning of section 15 of the National Parks and Access to the Countryside Act 1949 shall be construed as including a European site.

For this purpose an 'outlying enactment' means an enactment not contained in, or in an instrument made under, the National Parks and Access to the Countryside Act 1949 or the Wildlife and Countryside Act 1981.

Control of potentially damaging operations

18   Notification of potentially damaging operations

(1) Any notification in force in relation to a European site under section 28 of the Wildlife and Countryside Act 1981 (areas of special scientific interest) specifying—
  (a) the flora, fauna, or geological or physiographical features by reason of which the land is of special interest, and
  (b) any operations appearing to the appropriate nature conservation body to be likely to damage that flora or fauna or those features,
shall have effect for the purposes of these Regulations.

(2) The appropriate nature conservation body may, for the purpose of securing compliance with the requirements of the Habitats Directive, at any time amend the notification with respect to any of the matters mentioned in paragraph (1)(a) or (b).

(3) Notice of any amendment shall be given—
  (a) to every owner and occupier of land within the site who in the opinion of the appropriate nature conservation body may be affected by the amendment, and
  (b) to the local planning authority;
and the amendment shall come into force in relation to an owner or occupier upon such notice being given to him.

(4) The provisions of—
  (a) section 28(11) of the Wildlife and Countryside Act 1981 (notification to be local land charge in England and Wales), and
  (b) section 28(12) to (12B) of that Act (local registration of notification in Scotland),
apply, with the necessary modifications, in relation to an amendment of a notification under this regulation as in relation to the original notification.

19   Restriction on carrying out operations specified in notification

(1) The owner or occupier of any land within a European site shall not carry out, or cause or permit to be carried out, on that land any operation specified in a notification in force in relation to the site under regulation 18, unless—
  (a) one of them has given the appropriate nature conservation body written notice of a proposal to carry out the operation, specifying its nature and the land on which it is proposed to carry it out, and
  (b) one of the conditions specified in paragraph (2) is fulfilled.

(2) Those conditions are—
  (a) that the operation is carried out with the written consent of the appropriate nature conservation body;
  (b) that the operation is carried out in accordance with the terms of a management agreement;
  (c) that four months have expired from the giving of the notice under paragraph (1)(a).

(3) A person who, without reasonable excuse, contravenes paragraph (1) commits an offence and is liable on summary conviction to a fine not exceeding level 4 on the standard scale.

(4) For the purposes of paragraph (3) it is a reasonable excuse for a person to carry out an operation—

(a) that the operation was an emergency operation particulars of which (including details of the emergency) were notified to the appropriate nature conservation body as soon as practicable after the commencement of the operation; or

(b) that the operation was authorised by a planning permission granted on an application under Part III of the Town and Country Planning Act 1990 or Part III of the Town and Country Planning (Scotland) Act 1972.

(5) The appropriate nature conservation body has power to enforce this regulation; but nothing in this paragraph shall be construed as authorising the institution of proceedings in Scotland for an offence.

(6) Proceedings in England and Wales for an offence under this regulation shall not, without the consent of the Director of Public Prosecutions, be taken by a person other than the appropriate nature conservation body.

20   Supplementary provisions as to consents

(1) Where it appears to the appropriate nature conservation body that an application for consent under regulation 19(2)(a) relates to an operation which is or forms part of a plan or project which—

(a) is not directly connected with or necessary to the management of the site, and

(b) is likely to have a significant effect on the site (either alone or in combination with other plans or projects),

they shall make an appropriate assessment of the implications for the site in view of that site's conservation objectives.

(2) In the light of the conclusions of the assessment, they may give consent for the operation only after having ascertained that the plan or project will not adversely affect the integrity of the site.

(3) The above provisions do not apply in relation to a site which is a European site by reason only of regulation 10(1)(c) (site protected in accordance with Article 5(4)).

(4) Where in any case, whether in pursuance of this regulation or otherwise, the appropriate nature conservation body have not given consent for an operation, but they consider that there is a risk that the operation may nevertheless be carried out, they shall notify the Secretary of State.

(5) They shall take such steps as are requisite to secure that any such notification is given at least one month before the expiry of the period mentioned in regulation 19(2)(c) (period after which operation may be carried out in absence of consent).

21   Provision as to existing notices and consents

(1) Any notice or consent previously given under section 28(5)(a) or (6)(a) of the Wildlife and Countryside Act 1981 in relation to land which on or after the commencement of these Regulations becomes land within a European site shall have effect, subject as follows, as if given under regulation 19(1)(a) or (2)(a) above.

(2) The appropriate nature conservation body shall review any such consent as regards its compatibility with the conservation objectives of the site, and may modify or withdraw it.

(3) Notice of any such modification or withdrawal of consent shall be given to every owner and occupier of land within the site who in the opinion of the appropriate nature conservation body may be affected by it; and the modification or withdrawal shall come into force in relation to an owner or occupier upon such notice being given to him.

(4) The modification or withdrawal of a consent shall not affect anything done in reliance on the consent before the modification or withdrawal takes effect.

(5) Where or to the extent that an operation ceases to be covered by a consent by reason of the consent being modified or withdrawn, the period after which in accordance with

regulation 19(2)(c) the operation may be carried out in the absence of consent shall be four months from the giving of notice of the modification or withdrawal under paragraph (3) above.

(6) Regulation 20(4) and (5) (provisions as to notification of Secretary of State) apply in such a case, with the following modifications—

(a) for the reference to consent not having been given substitute a reference to consent being modified or withdrawn;

(b) for the reference to the period specified in regulation 19(2)(c) substitute a reference to the period specified in paragraph (5) above.

Special nature conservation orders

22   Power to make special nature conservation order

(1) The Secretary of State may, after consultation with the appropriate nature conservation body, make in respect of any land within a European site an order (a 'special nature conservation order') specifying operations which appear to him to be likely to destroy or damage the flora, fauna, or geological or physiographical features by reason of which the land is a European site.

(2) A special nature conservation order may be amended or revoked by a further order.

(3) Schedule 1 has effect with respect to the making, confirmation and coming into operation of special nature conservation orders and amending or revoking orders.

(4) A special nature conservation order in relation to land in England and Wales is a local land charge.

(5) . . .

(6) A report submitted by a nature conservation body to the Secretary of State under paragraph 20 of Schedule 6 to the Environmental Protection Act 1990 or section 10(2) of the Natural Heritage (Scotland) Act 1991 shall set out particulars of any land in their area as respects which a special nature conservation order has come into operation during the year to which the report relates.

23   Restriction on carrying out operations specified in order

(1) No person shall carry out on any land within a European site in respect of which a special nature conservation order is in force any operation specified in the order unless the operation is carried out, or caused or permitted to be carried out, by the owner or occupier of the land and—

(a) one of them has, after the making of the order, given the appropriate nature conservation body written notice of a proposal to carry out the operation specifying its nature and the land on which it is proposed to carry it out, and

(b) one of the conditions specified in paragraph (2) is fulfilled.

(2) Those conditions are—

(a) that the operation is carried out with the written consent of the appropriate nature conservation body;

(b) that the operation is carried out in accordance with the terms of a management agreement.

(3) A person who, without reasonable excuse, contravenes paragraph (1) commits an offence and is liable—

(a) on summary conviction, to a fine not exceeding the statutory maximum;

(b) on conviction on indictment, to a fine.

(4) For the purposes of paragraph (3) it is a reasonable excuse for a person to carry out an operation—

(a) that the operation was an emergency operation particulars of which (including details of the emergency) were notified to the appropriate nature conservation body as soon as practicable after the commencement of the operation; or

(b) that the operation was authorised by a planning permission granted on an application under Part III of the Town and Country Planning Act 1990 or Part III of the Town and Country Planning (Scotland) Act 1972.

24 Supplementary provisions as to consents

(1) Where it appears to the appropriate nature conservation body that an application for consent under regulation 23(2)(a) relates to an operation which is or forms part of a plan or project which—

(a) is not directly connected with or necessary to the management of the site, and

(b) is likely to have a significant effect on the site (either alone or in combination with other plans or projects),

they shall make an appropriate assessment of the implications for the site in view of that site's conservation objectives.

(2) In the light of the conclusions of the assessment, they may give consent for the operation only after having ascertained that the plan or project will not adversely affect the integrity of the site.

(3) Where the appropriate nature conservation body refuse consent in accordance with paragraph (2) they shall give reasons for their decision.

(4) The owner or occupier of the land in question may—

(a) within two months of receiving notice of the refusal of consent, or

(b) if no notice of a decision is received by him within three months of an application for consent being made,

by notice in writing to the appropriate nature conservation body require them to refer the matter forthwith to the Secretary of State.

(5) If on the matter being referred to the Secretary of State he is satisfied that, there being no alternative solutions, the plan or project must be carried out for imperative reasons of overriding public interest (which, subject to paragraph (6), may be of a social or economic nature), he may direct the appropriate nature conservation body to give consent to the operation.

(6) Where the site concerned hosts a priority natural habitat type or a priority species, the reasons referred to in paragraph (5) must be either—

(a) reasons relating to human health, public safety or beneficial consequences of primary importance to the environment, or

(b) other reasons which in the opinion of the European Commission are imperative reasons of overriding public interest.

(7) Where the Secretary of State directs the appropriate nature conservation body to give consent under this regulation, he shall secure that such compensatory measures are taken as are necessary to ensure that the overall coherence of Natura 2000 is protected.

(8) This regulation does not apply in relation to a site which is a European site by reason only of regulation 10(1)(c) (site protected in accordance with Article 5(4)).

25 Compensation for effect of order

(1) Where a special nature conservation order is made, the appropriate nature conservation body shall pay compensation to any person having at the time of the making of the order an interest in land comprised in an agricultural unit comprising land to which the order relates who, on a claim made to the appropriate nature conservation body within the time and in the manner prescribed by regulations, shows that the value of his interest is less than it would have been if the order had not been made.

(2) For this purpose an 'agricultural unit' means land which is occupied as a unit for agricultural purposes, including any dwelling-house or other building occupied by the same person for the purpose of farming the land.

(3) No claim for compensation shall be made under this regulation in respect of an order unless the Secretary of State has given notice under paragraph 6(1) or (2) of Schedule 1 of his decision in respect of the order.

26 Restoration where order contravened

(1) Where a person is convicted of an offence under regulation 23, the court by which he is convicted may, in addition to dealing with him in any other way, make an order requiring him to carry out, within such period as may be specified in the order, such operations for the purpose of restoring the land to its former condition as may be so specified.

(2) An order under this regulation made on conviction on indictment shall be treated for the purposes of section 30 of the Criminal Appeal Act 1968; (effect of appeals on orders for the restitution of property) as an order for the restitution of property.

(3) In the case of an order under this regulation made by a magistrates' court the period specified in the order shall not begin to run—

(a) in any case until the expiration of the period for the time being prescribed by law for the giving of notice of appeal against a decision of a magistrates' court;

(b) where notice of appeal is given within the period so prescribed, until determination of the appeal.

(4) At any time before an order under this regulation has been complied with or fully complied with, the court by which it was made may, on the application of the person against whom it was made, discharge or vary the order if it appears to the court that a change in circumstances has made compliance or full compliance with the order impracticable or unnecessary.

(5) If a person fails without reasonable excuse to comply with an order under this regulation, he commits an offence and is liable on summary conviction to a fine not exceeding level 5 on the standard scale; and if the failure continues after conviction, he may be proceeded against for a further offence from time to time until the order is complied with.

(6) If, within the period specified in an order under this regulation, any operations specified in the order have not been carried out, the appropriate nature conservation body may enter the land and carry out those operations and recover from the person against whom the order was made any expenses reasonably incurred by them in doing so.

(7) ...

27 Continuation in force of existing orders, etc

(1) Where an order is in force under section 29 of the Wildlife and Countryside Act 1981 (special protection for certain areas of special scientific interest) in relation to land which on or after the commencement of these Regulations becomes land within a European site, the order shall have effect as if made under regulation 22 above.

(2) Any notice previously given under section 29(4)(a) (notice by owner or occupier of proposal to carry out operation) shall have effect as if given under regulation 23(1)(a) and, if the appropriate nature conservation body have neither given nor refused consent, shall be dealt with under these Regulations.

(3) Any consent previously given under section 29(5)(a) shall be reviewed by the appropriate nature conservation body as regards its compatibility with the conservation objectives of the site, and may be modified or withdrawn.

(4) Notice of any such modification or withdrawal of consent shall be given to every owner and occupier of land within the site who in the opinion of the appropriate nature conservation body may be affected by it; and the modification or withdrawal shall come into force in relation to an owner or occupier upon such notice being given to him.

(5) The modification or withdrawal of a consent shall not affect anything done in reliance on the consent before the modification or withdrawal takes effect.

(6) Section 29(5)(c), (6) and (7) shall cease to apply and the carrying out, or continuation, of any operation on land within a European site which is not otherwise authorised in accordance with these Regulations shall be subject to the prohibition in regulation 23(1).

Byelaws

28 Power to make byelaws

(1) The appropriate nature conservation body may make byelaws for the protection of a European site under section 20 of the National Parks and Access to the Countryside Act 1949 (byelaws for protection of nature reserves).

(2) Without prejudice to the generality of paragraph (1), byelaws under that section as it applies by virtue of this regulation may make provision of any of the following kinds.

(3) They may—

    (a) provide for prohibiting or restricting the entry into, or movement within, the site of persons, vehicles, boats and animals;

    (b) prohibit or restrict the killing, taking, molesting or disturbance of living creatures of any description in the site, the taking, destruction or disturbance of eggs of any such creature, the taking of, or interference with, vegetation of any description in the site, or the doing of anything in the site which will interfere with the soil or damage any object in the site;

    (c) contain provisions prohibiting the depositing of rubbish and the leaving of litter in the site;

    (d) prohibit or restrict, or provide for prohibiting or restricting, the lighting of fires in the site or the doing of anything likely to cause a fire in the site.

(4) They may prohibit or restrict any activity referred to in paragraph (3) within such area surrounding or adjoining the site as appears to the appropriate nature conservation body requisite for the protection of the site.

(5) They may provide for the issue, on such terms and subject to such conditions as may be specified in the byelaws, of permits authorising—

    (a) entry into the site or any such surrounding or adjoining area as mentioned in paragraph (4), or

    (b) the doing of anything within the site, or any such surrounding or adjoining area, where such entry, or doing that thing, would otherwise be unlawful under the byelaws.

(6) They may be made so as to relate either to the whole or to any part of the site, or of any such surrounding or adjoining area as is mentioned in paragraph (4), and may make different provision for different parts thereof.

(7) This regulation does not apply in relation to a European marine site (but see regulation 36).

29 Byelaws: limitation on effect

Byelaws under section 20 of the National Parks and Access to the Countryside Act 1949 as it applies by virtue of regulation 28 shall not interfere with—

    (a) the exercise by any person of a right vested in him as owner, lessee or occupier of land in the European site, or in any such surrounding or adjoining area as is mentioned in paragraph (4) of that regulation;

    (b) the exercise of any public right of way;

    (c) the exercise of any functions of statutory undertakers;

    (d) the exercise of any functions of an internal drainage board, a district salmon fishery board or the Commissioners appointed under the Tweed Fisheries Act 1969; or

    (e) the running of a telecommunications code system or the exercise of any right conferred by or in accordance with the telecommunications code on the operator of any such system.

30 Compensation for effect of byelaws

Where the exercise of any right vested in a person, whether by reason of his being entitled to any interest in land or by virtue of a licence or agreement, is prevented or hindered by the coming into operation of byelaws under section 20 of the National Parks and Access to the

Countryside Act 1949 as it applies by virtue of regulation 28, he shall be entitled to receive from the appropriate nature conservation body compensation in respect thereof.

31 Continuation in force of existing byelaws

Any byelaws in force under section 20 of the National Parks and Access to the Countryside Act 1949 in relation to land which on or after the commencement of these Regulations becomes land within a European site, or adjacent to such a site, shall have effect as if made under the said section 20 as it applies by virtue of regulation 28 and shall be construed as if originally so made.

Powers of compulsory acquisition

32 Powers of compulsory acquisition

(1) Where the appropriate nature conservation body are satisfied—

    (a) that they are unable, as respects any interest in land within a European site, to conclude a management agreement on terms appearing to them to be reasonable, or

    (b) where they have entered into a management agreement as respects such an interest, that a breach of the agreement has occurred which prevents or impairs the satisfactory management of the European site,

they may acquire that interest compulsorily.

(2) Such a breach as is mentioned in paragraph (1)(b) shall not be treated as having occurred by virtue of any act or omission capable of remedy unless there has been default in remedying it within a reasonable time after notice given by the appropriate nature conservation body requiring the remedying thereof.

(3) Any dispute arising whether there has been such a breach of a management agreement shall be determined—

    (a) in the case of land in England and Wales, by an arbitrator appointed by the Lord Chancellor;

    (b) . . .

Special provisions as to European marine sites

33 Marking of site and advice by nature conservation bodies

(1) The appropriate nature conservation body may install markers indicating the existence and extent of a European marine site.

This power is exercisable subject to the obtaining of any necessary consent under section 34 of the Coast Protection Act 1949 (restriction of works detrimental to navigation).

(2) As soon as possible after a site becomes a European marine site, the appropriate nature conservation body shall advise other relevant authorities as to—

    (a) the conservation objectives for that site, and

    (b) any operations which may cause deterioration of natural habitats or the habitats of species, or disturbance of species, for which the site has been designated.

34 Management scheme for European marine site

(1) The relevant authorities, or any of them, may establish for a European marine site a management scheme under which their functions (including any power to make byelaws) shall be exercised so as to secure in relation to that site compliance with the requirements of the Habitats Directive.

(2) Only one management scheme may be made for each European marine site.

(3) A management scheme may be amended from time to time.

(4) As soon as a management scheme has been established, or is amended, a copy of it shall be sent by the relevant authority or authorities concerned to the appropriate nature conservation body.

35   Direction to establish or amend management scheme

(1) The relevant Minister may give directions to the relevant authorities, or any of them, as to the establishment of a management scheme for a European marine site.

(2) Directions may, in particular—

(a) require conservation measures specified in the direction to be included in the scheme;

(b) appoint one of the relevant authorities to co-ordinate the establishment of the scheme;

(c) set time limits within which any steps are to be taken;

(d) provide that the approval of the Minister is required before the scheme is established; and

(e) require any relevant authority to supply to the Minister such information concerning the establishment of the scheme as may be specified in the direction.

(3) The relevant Minister may give directions to the relevant authorities, or any of them, as to the amendment of a management scheme for a European marine site, either generally or in any particular respect.

(4) Any direction under this regulalion shall be in writing and may be varied or revoked by a further direction.

(5) In this regulation 'the relevant Minister' means, in relation to a site in England, the Secretary of State and the Minister of Agriculture, Fisheries and Food acting jointly and in any other case the Secretary of State.

36   Byelaws for protection of European marine site

(1) The appropriate nature conservation body may make byelaws for the protection of a European marine site under section 37 of the Wildlife and Countryside Act 1981 (byelaws for protection of marine nature reserves).

(2) The provisions of subsections (2) to (11) of that section apply in relation to byelaws made by virtue of this regulation with the substitution for the references to marine nature reserves of references to European marine sites.

(3) Nothing in byelaws made by virtue of this regulation shall interfere with the exercise of any functions of a relevant authority, any functions conferred by or under an enactment (whenever passed) or any right of any person (whenever vested).

Miscellaneous

37   Nature conservation policy in planning contexts

(1) For the purposes of the planning enactments mentioned below, policies in respect of the conservation of the natural beauty and amenity of the land shall be taken to include policies encouraging the management of features of the landscape which are of major importance for wild flora and fauna.

Such features are those which, by virtue of their linear and continuous structure (such as rivers with their banks or the traditional systems of marking field boundaries) or their function as stepping stones (such as ponds or small woods), are essential for the migration, dispersal and genetic exchange of wild species.

(2) The enactments referred to in paragraph (1) are—

(a) in the Town and Country Planning Act 1990, section 12(3A) (unitary development plans), section 31(3) (structure plans) and section 36(3) (local plans);

(b) . . .

PART III   PROTECTION OF SPECIES

Protection of animals

38   European protected species of animals

The species of animals listed in Annex IV(a) to the Habitats Directive whose natural range includes any area in Great Britain are listed in Schedule 2 to these Regulations.

References in these Regulations to a 'European protected species' of animal are to any of those species.

39   Protection of wild animals of European protected species

(1) It is an offence—
- (a) deliberately to capture or kill a wild animal of a European protected species;
- (b) deliberately to disturb any such animal;
- (c) deliberately to take or destroy the eggs of such an animal; or
- (d) to damage or destroy a breeding site or resting place of such an animal.

(2) It is an offence to keep, transport, sell or exchange, or offer for sale or exchange, any live or dead wild animal of a European protected species, or any part of, or anything derived from, such an animal.

(3) Paragraphs (1) and (2) apply to all stages of the life of the animals to which they apply.

(4) A person shall not be guilty of an offence under paragraph (2) if he shows—
- (a) that the animal had not been taken or killed, or had been lawfully taken or killed, or
- (b) that the animal or other thing in question had been lawfully sold (whether to him or any other person).

For this purpose 'lawfully' means without any contravention of these Regulations or Part I of the Widlife and Countryside Act 1981.

(5) In any proceedings for an offence under this regulation, the animal in question shall be presumed to have been a wild animal unless the contrary is shown.

(6) A person guilty of an offence under this regulation is liable on summary conviction to a fine not exceeding level 5 on the standard scale.

40   Exceptions from regulation 39

(1) Nothing in regulation 39 shall make unlawful—
- (a) anything done in pursuance of a requirement by the agriculture Minister under section 98 of the Agriculture Act 1947 or section 39 of the Agriculture (Scotland) Act 1948 (prevention of damage by pests); or
- (b) anything done under, or in pursuance of an order made under, the Animal Health Act 1981.

(2) Nothing in regulation 39(1)(b) or (d) shall make unlawful anything done within a dwelling-house.

(3) Notwithstanding anything in regulation 39, a person shall not be guilty of an offence by reason of—
- (a) the taking of a wild animal of a European protected species if he shows that the animal had been disabled otherwise than by his unlawful act and was taken solely for the purpose of tending it and releasing it when no longer disabled;
- (b) the killing of such an animal if he shows that the animal has been so seriously disabled otherwise than by his unlawful act that there was no reasonable chance of its recovering; or
- (c) any act made unlawful by that regulation if he shows that the act was the incidental result of a lawful operation and could not reasonably have been avoided.

(4) A person shall not be entitled to rely on the defence provided by paragraph (2) or (3)(c) as respects anything done in relation to a bat otherwise than in the living area of a dwelling-house unless he had notified the appropriate nature conservation body of the proposed action or operation and allowed them a reasonable time to advise him as to whether it should be carried out and, if so, the method to be used.

(5) Notwithstanding anything in regulation 39 a person—

(a) being the owner or occupier, or any person authorised by the owner or occupier, of the land on which the action authorised is taken, or

(b) authorised by the local authority for the area within which the action authorised is taken,

shall not be guilty of an offence by reason of the killing or disturbing of an animal of a European protected species if he shows that his action was necessary for the purpose of preventing, serious damage to livestock, foodstuffs, crops, vegetables, fruit, growing timber or any other form of property or fisheries.

(6) A person may not rely on the defence provided by paragraph (5) as respects action taken at any time if it had become apparent before that time that the action would prove necessary for the purpose mentioned in that paragraph and either—

(a) a licence under regulation 44 authorising that action had not been applied for as soon as reasonably practicable after that fact had become apparent, or

(b) an application for such a licence had been determined.

(7) In paragraph (5) 'local authority' means—

(a) in relation to England and Wales, a county, district or London borough council and includes the Common Council of the City of London, and

(b) . . .

41 Prohibition of certain methods of taking or killing wild animals

(1) This regulation applies in relation to the taking or killing of a wild animal—

(a) of any of the species listed in Schedule 3 to these Regulations (which shows the species listed in Annex V(a) to the Habitats Directive, and to which Article 15 applies, whose natural range includes any area of Great Britain), or

(b) of a European protected species, where the taking or killing of such animals is permitted in accordance with these Regulations.

(2) It is an offence to use for the purpose of taking or killing any such wild animal—

(a) any of the means listed in paragraph (3) or (4) below, or

(b) any form of taking or killing from the modes of transport listed in paragraph (5) below.

(3) The prohibited means of taking or killing of mammals are—

(a) blind or mutilated animals used as live decoys;

(b) tape recorders;

(c) electrical and electronic devices capable of killing or stunning;

(d) artificial light sources;

(e) mirrors and other dazzling devices;

(f) devices for illuminating targets;

(g) sighting devices for night shooting comprising an electronic image magnifier or image converter;

(h) explosives;

(i) nets which are non-selective according to their principle or their conditions of use;

(j) traps which are non-selective according to their principle or their conditions of use;

(k) crossbows;

(l) poisons and poisoned or anaesthetic bait;

(m) gassing or smoking out;

(n) semi-automatic or automatic weapons with a magazine capable of holding more than two rounds of ammunition.

(4) The prohibited means of taking or killing fish are—

(a) poison;

(b) explosives.

(5) The prohibited modes of transport are—

(a) aircraft;

(b) moving motor vehicles

(6) A person guilty of an offence under this regulation is liable on summary conviction to a fine not exceeding level 5 on the standard scale.

Protection of plants

42   European protected species of plants

The species of plants listed in Annex IV(b) to the Habitats Directive whose natural range includes any area in Great Britain are listed in Schedule 4 to these Regulations.

References in these Regulations to a 'European protected species' of plant are to any of those species.

43   Protection of wild plants of European protected species

(1) It is an offence deliberately to pick, collect, cut, uproot or destroy a wild plant of a European protected species.

(2) It is an offence to keep, transport, sell or exchange, or offer for sale or exchange, any live or dead wild plant of a European protected species, or any part of, or anything derived from, such a plant.

(3) Paragraphs (1) and (2) apply to all stages of the biological cycle of the plants to which they apply.

(4) A person shall not be guilty of an offence under paragraph (1), by reason of any act made unlawful by that paragraph if he shows that the act was an incidental result of a lawful operation and could not reasonably have been avoided.

(5) A person shall not be guilty of an offence under paragraph (2) if he shows that the plant or other thing in question had been lawfully sold (whether to him or any other person).

For this purpose 'lawfully' means without any contravention of these Regulations or Part I of the Wildlife and Countryside Act 1981.

(6) In any proceedings for an offence under this regulation, the plant in question shall be presumed to have been a wild plant unless the contrary is shown.

(7) A person guilty of an offence under this section is liable on summary conviction to a fine not exceeding level 4 on the standard scale.

Power to grant licences

44   Grant of licences for certain purposes

(1) Regulations 39, 41 and 43 do not apply to anything done for any of the following purposes under and in accordance with the terms of a licence granted by the appropriate authority.

(2) The purposes referred to in paragraph (1) are—

(a) scientific or educational purposes;

(b) ringing or marking, or examining any ring or mark on, wild animals;

(c) conserving wild animals or wild plants or introducing them to particular areas;

(d) protecting any zoological or botanical collection;

    (e) preserving public health or public safety or other imperative reasons of overriding public interest including those of a social or economic nature and beneficial consequences of primary importance for the environment;

    (f) preventing the spread of disease; or

    (g) preventing serious damage to livestock, foodstuffs for livestock, crops, vegetables, fruit, growing timber or any other form of property or to fisheries.

(3) The appropriate authority shall not grant a licence under this regulation unless they are satisfied—

    (a) that there is no satisfactory alternative, and

    (b) that the action authorised will not be detrimental to the maintenance of the population of the species concerned at a favourable conservation status in their natural range.

(4) For the purposes of this regulation 'the appropriate authority' means—

    (a) in the case of a licence under any of sub-paragraphs (a) to (d) of paragraph (2), the appropriate nature conservation body; and

    (b) in the case of a licence under any of sub-paragraphs (e) to (g) of that paragraph, the agriculture Minister.

(5) The agriculture Minister shall from time to time consult with the nature conservation bodies as to the exercise of his functions under this regulation; and he shall not grant a licence of any description unless he has been advised by the appropriate nature conservation body as to the circumstances in which, in their opinion, licences of that description should be granted.

45 Licences: supplementary provisions

(1) A licence under regulation 44—

    (a) may be, to any degree, general or specific;

    (b) may be granted either to persons of a class or to a particular person; and

    (c) may be subject to compliance with any specified conditions.

(2) For the purposes of a licence under regulation 44 the definition of a class of persons may be framed by reference to any circumstances whatever including, in particular, their being authorised by any other person.

(3) A licence under regulation 44 may be modified or revoked at any time by the appropriate authority; but otherwise shall be valid for the period stated in the licence.

(4) A licence under regulation 44 which authorises any person to kill wild animals shall specify the area within which and the methods by which the wild animals may be killed and shall not be granted for a period of more than two years.

(5) It shall be a defence in proceedings for an offence under section 8(b) of the Protection of Animals Act 1911 or section 7(b) of the Protection of Animals (Scotland) Act 1912 (which restrict the placing on land of poison and poisonous substances) to show that—

    (a) the act alleged to constitute the offence was done under and in accordance with the terms of a licence under regulation 44, and

    (b) any conditions specified in the licence were complied with.

(6) The appropriate authority may charge for a licence under regulation 44 such reasonable sum (if any) as they may determine.

46 False statements made for obtaining licence

(1) A person commits an offence who, for the purposes of obtaining, whether for himself or another, the grant of a licence under regulation 44—

    (a) makes a statement or representation, or furnishes a document or information, which he knows to be false in a material particular, or

    (b) recklessly makes a statement or representation, or furnishes a document or information, which is false in a material particular.

(2) A person guilty of an offence under this regulation is liable on summary conviction to a fine not exceeding level 4 on the standard scale.

PART IV   ADAPTATION OF PLANNING AND OTHER CONTROLS

Introductory

47   Application of provisions of this Part

(1) The requirements of—
- (a) regulations 48 and 49 (requirement to consider effect on European sites), and
- (b) regulations 50 and 51 (requirement to review certain existing decisions and consents, etc.),

apply, subject to and in accordance with the provisions of regulations 54 to 85, in relation to the matters specified in those provisions.

(2) Supplementary provision is made by—
- (a) regulation 52 (co-ordination where more than one competent authority involved), and
- (b) regulation 53 (compensatory measures where plan or project is agreed to notwithstanding a negative assessment of the implications for a European site).

General provisions for protection of European sites

48   Assessment of implications for European site

(1) A competent authority, before deciding to undertake, or give any consent, permission or other authorisation for, a plan or project which—
- (a) is likely to have a significant effect on a European site in Great Britain (either alone or in combination with other plans or projects), and
- (b) is not directly connected with or necessary to the management of the site, shall make an appropriate assessment of the implications for the site in view of that site's conservation objectives.

(2) A person applying for any such consent, permission or other authorisation shall provide such information as the competent authority may reasonably require for the purposes of the assessment.

(3) The competent authority shall for the purposes of the assessment consult the appropriate nature conservation body and have regard to any representations made by that body within such reasonable time as the authority may specify.

(4) They shall also, if they consider it appropriate, take the opinion of the general public; and if they do so, they shall take such steps for that purpose as they consider appropriate.

(5) In the light of the conclusions of the assessment, and subject to regulation 49, the authority shall agree to the plan or project only after having ascertained that it will not adversely affect the integrity of the European site.

(6) In considering whether a plan or project will adversely affect the integrity of the site, the authority shall have regard to the manner in which it is proposed to be carried out or to any conditions or restrictions subject to which they propose that the consent, permission or other authorisation should be given.

(7) This regulation does not apply in relation to a site which is a European site by reason only of regulation 10(1)(c) (site protected in accordance with Article 5(4)).

49   Considerations of overriding public interest

(1) If they are satisfied that, there being no alternative solutions, the plan or project must be carried out for imperative reasons of overriding public interest (which, subject to paragraph

(2), may be of a social or economic nature), the competent authority may agree to the plan or project notwithstanding a negative assessment of the implications for the site.

(2) Where the site concerned hosts a priority natural habitat type or a priority species, the reasons referred to in paragraph (1) must be either—

    (a) reasons relating to human health, public safety or beneficial consequences of primary importance to the environment, or

    (b) other reasons which in the opinion of the European Commission are imperative reasons of overriding public interest.

(3) Where a competent authority other than the Secretary of State desire to obtain the opinion of the European Commission as to whether reasons are to be considered imperative reasons of overriding public interest, they shall submit a written request to the Secretary of State—

    (a) identifying the matter on which an opinion is sought, and

    (b) accompanied by any documents or information which may be required.

(4) The Secretary of State may thereupon, if he thinks fit, seek the opinion of the Commission; and if he does so, he shall upon receiving the Commission's opinion transmit it to the authority.

(5) Where an authority other than the Secretary of State propose to agree to a plan or project under this regulation notwithstanding a negative assessment of the implications for a European site, they shall notify the Secretary of State.

Having notified the Secretary of State, they shall not agree to the plan or project before the end of the period of 21 days beginning with the day notified to them by the Secretary of State as that on which their notification was received by him, unless the Secretary of State notifies them that they may do so.

(6) In any such case the Secretary of State may give directions to the authority prohibiting them from agreeing to the plan or project, either indefinitely or during such period as may be specified in the direction.

This power is without prejudice to any other power of the Secretary of State in relation to the decision in question.

50   Review of existing decisions and consents, etc.

(1) Where before the date on which a site becomes a European site or, if later, the commencement of these Regulations, a competent authority have decided to under-take, or have given any consent, permission or other authorisation for, a plan or project to which regulation 48(1) would apply if it were to be reconsidered as of that date, the authority shall as soon as reasonably practicable, review their decision or, as the case may be, the consent, permission or other authorisation, and shall affirm, modify or revoke it.

(2) They shall for that purpose make an appropriate assessment of the implications for the site in view of that site's conservation objectives; and the provisions of regulation 48(2) to (4) shall apply, with the appropriate modifications, in relation to such a review.

(3) Subject to the following provisions of this Part, any review required by this regulation shall be carried out under existing statutory procedures where such procedures exist, and if none exist the Secretary of State may give directions as to the procedure to be followed.

(4) Nothing in this regulation shall affect anything done in pursuance of the decision, or the consent, permission or other authorisation, before the date mentioned in paragraph (1).

51   Consideration on review

(1) The following provisions apply where a decision, or a consent, permission or other authorisation, falls to be reviewed under regulation 50.

(2) Subject as follows, the provisions of regulation 48(5) and (6) and regulation 49 shall apply, with the appropriate modifications, in relation to the decision on the review.

(3) The decision, or the consent, permission or other authorisation, may be affirmed if it appears to the authority reviewing it that other action taken or to be taken by them, or by

another authority, will secure that the plan or project does not adversely affect the integrity of the site.

Where that object may be attained in a number of ways, the authority or authorities concerned shall seek to secure that the action taken is the least onerous to those affected.

(4) The Secretary of State may issue guidance to authorities for the purposes of paragraph (3) as to the manner of determining which of different ways should be adopted for securing that the plan or project does not have any such effect, and in particular—

    (a) the order of application of different controls, and

    (b) the extent to which account should be taken of the possible exercise of other powers;

and the authorities concerned shall have regard to any guidance so issued in discharging their functions under that paragraph.

(5) Any modification or revocation effected in pursuance of this regulation shall be carried out under existing statutory procedures where such procedures exist.

If none exist, the Secretary of State may give directions as to the procedure to be followed.

52   Co-ordination where more than one competent authority involved

    (1) The following provisions apply where a plan or project—

    (a) is undertaken by more than one competent authority,

    (b) requires the consent, permission or other authorisation of more than one competent authority, or

    (c) is undertaken by one or more competent authorities and requires the consent, permission or other authorisation of one or more other competent authorities.

(2) Nothing in regulation 48(1) or 50(2) requires a competent authority to assess any implications of a plan or project which would be more appropriately assessed under that provision by another competent authority.

(3) The Secretary of State may issue guidance to authorities for the purposes of regulations 48 to 51 as to the circumstances in which an authority may or should adopt the reasoning or conclusions of another competent authority as to whether a plan or project—

    (a) is likely to have a significant effect on a European site, or

    (b) will adversely affect the integrity of a European site;

and the authorities involved shall have regard to any guidance so issued in discharging their functions under those regulations.

(4) In determining whether a plan or project should be agreed to under regulation 49(1) (considerations of overriding public interest) a competent authority other than the Secretary of State shall seek and have regard to the views of the other competent authority or authorities involved.

53   Compensatory measures

Where in accordance with regulation 49 (considerations of overriding public interest)—

    (a) a plan or project is agreed to, notwithstanding a negative assessment of the implications for a European site, or

    (b) a decision, or a consent, permission or other authorisation, is affirmed on review, notwithstanding such an assessment,

the Secretary of State shall secure that any necessary compensatory measures are taken to ensure that the overall coherence of Natura 2000 is protected.

Planning

54   Grant of planning permission

    (1) Regulations 48 and 49 (requirement to consider effect on European site) apply, in England and Wales, in relation to—

(a) granting planning permission on an application under Part III of the Town and Country Planning Act 1990;

(b) granting planning permission, or upholding a decision of the local planning authority to grant planning permission (whether or not subject to the same conditions and limitations as those imposed by the local planning authority), on determining an appeal under section 78 of that Act in respect of such an application;

(c) granting planning permission under—

    (i) section 141(2)(a) of that Act (action by Secretary of State in relation to purchase notice),

    (ii) section 177(1)(a) of that Act (powers of Secretary of State on appeal against enforcement notice), or

    (iii) section 196(5) of that Act as originally enacted (powers of Secretary of State on reference or appeal as to established use certificate);

(d) directing under section 90(1), (2) or (2A) of that Act (development with government authorisation), or under section 5(1) of the Pipe-lines Act 1962, that planning permission shall be deemed to be granted;

(e) making—

    (i) an order under section 102 of that Act (order requiring discontinuance of use or removal of buildings or works), including an order made under that section by virtue of section 104 (powers of Secretary of State), which grants planning permission, or

    (ii) an order under paragraph 1 of Schedule 9 to that Act (order requiring discontinuance of mineral working), including an order made under that paragraph by virtue of paragraph 11 of that Schedule (default powers of Secretary of State), which grants planning permission,

or confirming any such order under section 103 of that Act;

(f) directing under—

    (i) section 141(3) of that Act (action by Secretary of State in relation to purchase notice), or

    (ii) section 35(5) of the Planning (Listed Buildings and Conservation Areas) Act 1990 (action by Secretary of State in relation to listed building purchase notice), that if an application is made for planning permission it shall be granted.

(2) Regulations 48 and 49 (requirement to consider effect on European site) apply, in Scotland, in relation to—

(a) . . .

(b) granting planning permission, or upholding a decision of the planning authority to grant planning permission (whether or not subject to the same conditions and limitations as those imposed by the local planning authority), on determining an appeal under section 33 (appeals) of that Act in respect of such an application;

(c) granting planning permission under—

    (i) section 172(2) of that Act (action by Secretary of State in relation to purchase notice),

    (ii) section 85(5) of that Act (powers of Secretary of State on appeal against enforcement notice), or

    (iii) section 91(3) of that Act as originally enacted (powers of Secretary of State on reference or appeal as to established use certificate);

(d) directing under section 37(1) (development with government authorisation) of that Act, or under section 5(1) of the Pipe-lines Act 1962 or paragraph 7 of Schedule 8 to the Electricity Act 1989, that planning permission shall be deemed to be granted;

(e) making an order under section 49 of that Act (order requiring discontinuance of use or removal of buildings or works), including an order made under that section by virtue of section 260 (default powers of Secretary of State), which grants planning permission, or confirming any such order;

(f) directing under—

(i) section 172(3) of that Act (powers of Secretary of State in relation to purchase notice), or

(ii) paragraph 2(6) of Schedule 17 to that Act (powers of Secretary of State in relation to listed building purchase notice), that if an application is made for planning permission it shall be granted.

(3) Where regulations 48 and 49 apply, the competent authority may, if they consider that any adverse effects of the plan or project on the integrity of a European site would be avoided if the planning permission were subject to conditions or limitations, grant planning permission or, as the case may be, take action which results in planning permission being granted or deemed to be granted subject to those conditions or limitations.

(4) Where regulations 48 and 49 apply, outline planning permission shall not be granted unless the competent authority are satisfied (whether by reason of the conditions and limitations to which the outline planning permission is to be made subject, or otherwise) that no development likely adversely to affect the integrity of a European site could be carried out under the permission, whether before or after obtaining approval of any reserved matters.

In this paragraph 'outline planning permission' and 'reserved matters' have the same meaning as in section 92 of the Town and Country Planning Act 1990 or section 39 of the Town and Country Planning (Scotland) Act 1972.

55 Planning permission: duty to review

(1) Subject to the following provisions of this regulation, regulations 50 and 51 (requirement to review certain decisions and consents, &c.) apply to any planning permission or deemed planning permission, unless—

(a) the development to which it related has been completed, or

(b) it was granted subject to a condition as to the time within which the development to which it related was to be begun and that time has expired without the development having been begun, or

(c) it was granted for a limited period and that period has expired.

(2) Regulations 50 and 51 do not apply to planning permission granted or deemed to have been granted—

(a) by a development order (but see regulations 60 to 64 below);

(b) by virtue of the adoption of a simplified planning zone scheme or of alterations to such a scheme (but see regulation 65 below);

(c) by virtue of the taking effect of an order designating an enterprise zone under Schedule 32 to the Local Government, Planning and Land Act 1980, or by virtue of the approval of a modified enterprise zone scheme (but see regulation 66 below).

(3) Planning permission deemed to be granted by virtue of—

(a) a direction under section 90(1) of the Town and Country Planning Act 1990 or section 37(1) of the Town and Country Planning (Scotland) Act 1972 in respect of development for which an authorisation has been granted under section 1 or 3 of the Pipe-lines Act 1962,

(b) a direction under section 5(1) of the Pipe-lines Act 1962,

(c) a direction under section 90(1) of the Town and Country Planning Act 1990 or section 37(1) of the Town and Country Planning (Scotland) Act 1972 in respect of development for which a consent has been given under section 36 or 37 of the Electricity Act 1989,

(d) a direction under section 90(2) of the Town and Country Planning Act 1990 or paragraph 7 of Schedule 8 to the Electricity Act 1989, or

(e) a direction under section 90(2A) of the Town and Country Planning Act 1990 (which relates to development in pursuance of an order under section 1 or 3 of the Transport and Works Act 1992),

shall be reviewed in accordance with the following provisions of this Part in conjunction with the review of the underlying authorisation, consent or order.

(4) In the case of planning permission deemed to have been granted in any other case by a direction under section 90(1) of the Town and Country Planning Act 1990 or section 37(1) of the Town and Country Planning (Scotland) Act 1972, the local planning authority shall—

(a) identify any such permission which they consider falls to be reviewed under regulations 50 and 51, and

(b) refer the matter to the government department which made the direction;

and the department shall, if it agrees that the planning permission does fall to be so reviewed, thereupon review the direction in accordance with those regulations.

(5) Save as otherwise expressly provided, regulations 50 and 51 do not apply to planning permission granted or deemed to be granted by a public general Act of Parliament.

(6) Subject to paragraphs (3) and (4), where planning permission granted by the Secretary of State falls to be reviewed under regulations 50 and 51—

(a) it shall be reviewed by the local planning authority, and

(b) the power conferred by section 97 of the Town and Country Planning Act 1990 or section 42 of the Town and Country Planning (Scotland) Act 1972 (revocation or modification of planning permission) shall be exercisable by that authority as in relation to planning permission granted on an application under Part III of that Act.

In a non-metropolitan county in England and Wales the function of reviewing any such planning permission shall be exercised by the district planning authority unless it relates to a county matter (within the meaning of Schedule 1 to the Town and Country Planning Act 1990) in which case it shall be exercised by the county planning authority.

56 Planning permission: consideration on review

(1) In reviewing any planning permission or deemed planning permission in pursuance of regulations 50 and 51, the competent authority shall, in England and Wales—

(a) consider whether any adverse effects could be overcome by planning obligations under section 106 of the Town and Country Planning Act 1990 being entered into, and

(b) if they consider that those effects could be so overcome, invite those concerned to enter into such obligations;

and so far as the adverse effects are not thus overcome the authority shall make such order under section 97 of that Act (power to revoke or modify planning permission), or under section 102 of or paragraph 1 of Schedule 9 to that Act (order requiring discontinuance of use, etc.), as may be required.

(2) In reviewing any planning permission or deemed planning permission in pursuance of regulations 50 and 51, the competent authority shall, in Scotland—

(a) consider whether any adverse effects could be overcome by an agreement under section 50 (agreements regulating development or use of land) of the Town and Country Planning (Scotland) Act 1972 being entered into, and

(b) if they consider that those effects could be so overcome, invite those concerned to enter into such an agreement;

and so far as the adverse effects are not thus overcome, the authority shall make such order under section 42 of that Act (power to revoke or modify planning permission), or under section 49 of that Act (orders requiring discontinuance of use, etc.) as may be required.

(3) Where the authority ascertain that the carrying out or, as the case may be, the continuation of the development would adversely affect the integrity of a European site, they nevertheless need not proceed under regulations 50 and 51 if and so long as they consider that there is no likelihood of the development being carried out or continued.

57 Effect of orders made on review: England and Wales

(1) An order under section 97 of the Town and Country Planning Act 1990 (power to revoke or modify planning permission) made pursuant to regulation 55 shall take effect upon service of the notices required by section 98(2) of that Act or, where there is more than one such notice and those notices are served at different times, upon the service of the last such notice to be served.

(2) Where the Secretary of State determines not to confirm such an order, the order shall cease to have effect from the time of that determination, and the permission revoked or modified by the order shall thereafter have effect as if the order had never been made, and—

- (a) any period specified in the permission for the taking of any action, being a period which had not expired prior to the date upon which the order took effect under paragraph (1) above, shall be extended by a period equal to that during which the order had effect; and

- (b) there shall be substituted for any date specified in the permission as being a date by which any action should be taken, not being a date falling prior to the date upon which the order took effect under paragraph (1) above, such date as post-dates the specified date by a period equal to that during which the order had effect.

(3) An order under section 102 of, or under paragraph 1 of Schedule 9 to, the Town and Country Planning Act 1990 (order requiring discontinuance of use, etc.) made pursuant to regulation 55 shall insofar as it requires the discontinuance of a use of land or imposes conditions upon the continuance of a use of land, take effect upon service of the notices required by section 103(3) or, where there is more than one such notice and those notices are served at different times, upon service of the last such notice to be served.

(4) Where the Secretary of State determines not to confirm any such order, the order shall cease to have effect from the time of that determination and the use which by the order was discontinued or upon whose continuance conditions were imposed—

- (a) may thereafter be continued as if the order had never been made, and

- (b) shall be treated for the purposes of the Town and Country Planning Act 1990 as if it had continued without interruption or modification throughout the period during which the order had effect.

(5) An order under section 97 of that Act (power to revoke or modify planning permission) made in pursuance of regulation 55 shall not affect so much of the development authorised by the permission as was carried out prior to the order taking effect.

(6) An order under section 102 of, or under paragraph 1 of Schedule 9 to, that Act (order requiring discontinuance of use, etc.) made in pursuance of regulation 55 shall not affect anything done prior to the site becoming a European site or, if later, the commencement of these Regulations.

. . .

59 Planning permission: supplementary provisions as to compensation

(1) Where the Secretary of State determines not to confirm—

- (a) an order under section 97 of the Town and Country Planning Act 1990 (revocation or modification of planning permission) which has taken effect under regulation 57(1), or

- (b) an order under section 42 of the Town and Country Planning (Scotland) Act 1972 (revocation or modification of planning permission) which has taken effect under regulation 58(1), any claim for compensation under section 107 of the Act of 1990 or section 153 of the Act of 1972 shall be limited to any loss or damage directly attributable to the permission being suspended or temporarily modified for the duration of the period between the order so taking effect and the Secretary of State determining not to confirm the order.

(2) Where the Secretary of State determines not to confirm—

(a) an order under section 102 of the Town and Country Planning Act 1990 (order requiring discontinuance of use, etc.) which has taken effect under regulation 57(3) above, or

(b) an order under section 49 of the Town and Country Planning (Scotland) Act 1972 (order requiring discontinuance of use, etc.) which has taken effect under regulation 58(3) above,

any claim for compensation under section 115 of the Act of 1990 or section 159 of the Act of 1972 shall be limited to any loss or damage directly attributable to any right to continue a use of the land being, by virtue of the order, suspended or subject to conditions for the duration of the period between the order so taking effect and the Secretary of State determining not to confirm the order.

(3) Where compensation is payable in respect of—

(a) an order under section 97 of the Town and Country Planning Act 1990, or

(b) any order mentioned in section 115(1) of that Act (compensation in respect of orders under s.102, etc.), or to which that section applies by virtue of section 115(5), and the order has been made pursuant to regulation 50, the question as to the amount of the compensation shall be referred, by the authority liable to pay the compensation, to and be determined by the Lands Tribunal unless and to the extent that in any particular case the Secretary of State has indicated in writing that such a reference and determination may be dispensed with.

(4) . . .

60 General development orders

(1) It shall be a condition of any planning permission granted by a general development order, whether made before or after the commencement of these Regulations, that development which—

(a) is likely to have a significant effect on a European site in Great Britain (either alone or in combination with other plans or projects), and

(b) is not directly connected with or necessary to the management of the site,

shall not be begun until the developer has received written notification of the approval of the local planning authority under regulation 62.

(2) It shall be a condition of any planning permission granted by a general development order made before the commencement of these Regulations that development which—

(a) is likely to have a significant effect on a European site in Great Britain (either alone or in combination with other plans or projects), and

(b) is not directly connected with or necessary to the management of the site, and which was begun but not completed before the commencement of these Regulations,

shall not be continued until the developer has received written notification of the approval of the local planning authority under regulation 62.

(3) Nothing in this regulation shall affect anything done before the commencement of these Regulations.

61 General development orders: opinion of appropriate nature conservation body

(1) Where it is intended to carry out development in reliance on the permission granted by a general development order, application may be made in writing to the appropriate nature conservation body for their opinion whether the development is likely to have such an effect as is mentioned in regulation 60(1)(a) or (2)(a).

The application shall give details of the development which is intended to be carried out.

(2) On receiving such an application, the appropriate nature conservation body shall consider whether the development is likely to have such an effect.

(3) Where they consider that they have sufficient information to conclude that the development will, or will not, have such an effect, they shall in writing notify the applicant and the local planning authority of their opinion.

(4) If they consider that they have insufficient information to reach either of those conclusions, they shall notify the applicant in writing indicating in what respects they consider the information insufficient; and the applicant may supply further information with a view to enabling them to reach a decision on the application.

(5) The opinion of the appropriate nature conservation body, notified in accordance with paragraph (3), that the development is not likely to have such an effect as is mentioned in regulation 60(1)(a) or (2)(a) shall be conclusive of that question for the purpose of reliance on the planning permission granted by a general development order.

62   General development orders: approval of local planning authority

(1) Where it is intended to carry out development in reliance upon the permission granted by a general development order, application may be made in writing to the local planning authority for their approval.

(2) The application shall—
   (a) give details of the development which is intended to be carried out; and
   (b) be accompanied by—
      (i) a copy of any relevant notification by the appropriate nature conservation body under regulation 61, and
      (ii) any fee required to be paid.

(3) For the purposes of their consideration of the application the local planning authority shall assume that the development is likely to have such an effect as mentioned in regulation 60(1)(a) or (2)(a).

(4) The authority shall send a copy of the application to the appropriate nature conservation body and shall take account of any representations made by them.

(5) If in their representations the appropriate nature conservation body state their opinion that the development is not likely to have such an effect as is mentioned in regulation 60(1)(a) or (2)(a), the local planning authority shall send a copy of the representations to the applicant; and the sending of that copy shall have the same effect as a notification by the appropriate nature conservation body of its opinion under regulation 61(3).

(6) In any other case the local planning authority shall, taking account of any representations made by the appropriate nature conservation body, make an appropriate assessment of the implications of the development for the European site in view of that site's conservation objectives.

In the light of the conclusions of the assessment the authority shall approve the development only after having ascertained that it will not adversely affect the integrity of the site.

63   General development orders: supplementary

(1) The local planning authority for the purposes of regulations 60 to 62 shall be the authority to whom an application for approval under regulation 62 would fall to be made if it were an application for planning permission.

(2) The fee payable in connection with an application for such approval is—
   (a) £25 in the case of applications made before 3rd January 1995, and
   (b) £30 in the case of applications made on or after that date.

(3) Approval required by regulation 60 shall be treated—
   (a) for the purposes of the provisions of the Town and Country Planning Act 1990, or the Town and Country Planning (Scotland) Act 1972 relating to appeals, as

approval required by a condition imposed on a grant of planning permission; and

(b) for the purposes of the provisions of any general development order relating to the time within which notice of a decision should be made, as approval required by a condition attached to a grant of planning permission.

64 Special development orders

(1) A special development order made after the commencement of these Regulations may not grant planning permission for development which—

(a) is likely to have a significant effect on a European site in Great Britain (either alone or in combination with other plans or projects), and

(b) is not directly connected with or necessary to the management of the site;

and any such order made before the commencement of these Regulations shall, on and after that date, cease to have effect to grant such permission, whether or not the development authorised by the permission has been begun.

(2) Nothing in this regulation shall affect anything done before the commencement of these Regulations.

65 Simplified planning zone

The adoption or approval of a simplified planning zone scheme after the commencement of these Regulations shall not have effect to grant planning permission for development which—

(a) is likely to have a significant effect on a European site in Great Britain (either alone or in combination with other plans or projects), and

(b) is not directly connected with or necessary to the management of the site;

and every simplified planning zone scheme already in force shall cease to have effect to grant such permission, whether or not the development authorised by the permission has been begun.

66 Enterprise zones

An order designating an enterprise zone, or the approval of a modified scheme, if made or given after the commencerment of these Regulations, shall not have effect to grant planning permission for development which—

(a) is likely to have a significant effect on a European site in Great Britain (either alone or in combination with other plans or projects), and

(b) is not directly connected with or necessary to the management of the site;

and where the order or approval was made or given before that date, the permission granted by virtue of the taking effect of the order or the modifications shall, from that date, cease to have effect to grant planning permission for such development, whether or not the development authorised by the permission has been begun.

67 Simplified planning zones and enterprise zones: supplementary provisions as to compensation

(1) Where in England and Wales—

(a) planning permission is withdrawn by regulation 65 or 66, and

(b) development authorised by the permission had been begun but not completed before the commencement of these Regulations, and

(c) on an application made under Part III of the Town and Country Planning Act 1990 before the end of the period of 12 months beginning with the date of commencement of these Regulations, planning permission for the development is refused or is granted subject to conditions other than those imposed by the scheme, section 107(1)(a) of that Act (compensation in respect of abortive expenditure) shall apply as if the permission granted by the scheme had been granted by the local planning authority under Part III of that Act and had been revoked or modified by an order under section 97 of that Act.

(2) ...

(3) Paragraphs (1) and (2) above do not apply in relation to planning permission for the development of operational land by statutory undertakers.

68   Construction as one with planning legislation

Regulations 54 to 67 shall be construed as one—

(a) in England and Wales, with the Town and Country Planning Act 1990; and

(b) in Scotland, with the Town and Country Planning (Scotland) Act 1972.

...

Environmental controls

83   Authorisations under Part I of the Environmental Protection Act 1990

(1) Regulations 48 and 49 (requirement to consider effect on European site) apply in relation to the granting of an authorisation under Part I of the Environmental Protection Act 1990 (integrated pollution control and local authority air pollution control).

(2) Where in such a case the competent authority consider that any adverse effects of the plan or project on the integrity of a European site would be avoided if the authorisation were subject to conditions, they may grant an authorisation, or cause an authorisation to be granted, subject to those conditions.

(3) Regulations 50 and 51 (requirement to review existing decisions and consents, &c.) apply to any such authorisation as is mentioned in paragraph (1).

(4) Where on the review of such an authorisation the competent authority consider that any adverse effects on the integrity of a European site of the carrying out or, as the case may be, the continuation of activities authorised by it would be avoided by a variation of the authorisation, they may vary it, or cause it to be varied, accordingly.

(5) Where any question arises as to agreeing to a plan or project, or affirming an authorisation on review, under regulation 49 (considerations of overriding public interest), the competent authority shall refer the matter to the Secretary of State who shall determine the matter in accordance with that regulation and give directions to the authority accordingly.

84   Licences under Part II of the Environmental Protection Act 1990

(1) Regulations 48 and 49 (requirement to consider effect on European site) apply in relation to—

(a) the granting of a waste management licence under Part II of the Environ-mental Protection Act 1990,

(b) the passing of a resolution under section 54 of that Act (provisions as to land occupied by disposal authorities themselves), and

(c) the granting of a disposal licence under Part I of the Control of Pollution Act 1974 and the passing of a resolution under section 11 of that Act.

(2) Where in such a case the competent authority consider that any adverse effects of the plan or project on the integrity of a European site would be avoided by making any licence subject to conditions, they may grant a licence, or cause a licence to be granted, or, as the case may be, pass a resolution, subject to those conditions.

(3) Regulations 50 and 51 (requirement to review existing decisions and consents, &c.) apply to any such licence or resolution as is mentioned in paragraph (1).

(4) Where on the review of such a licence or resolution the competent authority consider that any adverse effects on the integrity of a European site of the carrying out or, as the case may be, the continuation of the activities authorised by it would be avoided by a variation of the licence or resolution, they may vary it, or cause it to be varied, accordingly.

[84A   Permits under the Pollution Prevention and Control (England and Wales) Regulations 2000

(1) Regulations 48 and 49 (requirement to consider effect on European site) apply in relation to the granting of a permit under the Pollution Prevention and Control (England and Wales) Regulations 2000.

(2) Where in such a case the competent authority consider that any adverse effects of the plan or project on the integrity of a European site would be avoided if the permit were subject to conditions, they may grant a permit, or cause a permit to be granted, subject to those conditions.

(3) Regulations 50 and 51 (requirement to review existing decisions and consents, etc.) apply to any such permit as is mentioned in paragraph (1).

(4) Where on the review of such a permit the competent authority consider that any adverse effects on the integrity of a European site of the carrying out or, as the case may be, the continuation of activities authorised by it would be avoided by a variation of the permit, they may vary it, or cause it to be varied, accordingly.

(5) Where any question arises as to agreeing to a plan or project, or affirming a permit on review, under regulation 49 (considerations of overriding public interest), the competent authority shall refer the matter to the Secretary of State who shall determine the matter in accordance with that regulation and give directions to the authority accordingly.]

85   Discharge consents under water pollution legislation

(1) Regulations 48 and 49 (requirement to consider effect on European site) apply in relation to the giving of consent under—

(a) Chapter II of Part III to the Water Resources Act 1991 (control of pollution of water resources), or

(b) Part II of the Control of Pollution Act 1974 (which makes corresponding provision for Scotland).

(2) Where in such a case the competent authority consider that any adverse effects of the plan or project on the integrity of a European site would be avoided by making any consent subject to conditions, they may give consent, or cause it to be given, subject to those conditions.

(3) Regulations 50 and 51 (requirement to review existing decisions and consents, &c.) apply to any such consent as is mentioned in paragraph (1).

(4) Where on the review of such a consent the competent authority consider that any adverse effects on the integrity of a European site of the carrying out or, as the case may be, the continuation of the activities authorised by it would be avoided by a variation of the consent, they may vary it, or cause it to be varied, accordingly.

. . .

SCHEDULE 1   PROCEDURE IN CONNECTION WITH ORDERS UNDER REGULATION 22

Coming into operation

1.—(1) An original order or a restrictive amending order takes effect on its being made.

(2) The Secretary of State shall consider every such order, and the order shall cease to have effect nine months after it is made unless he has previously given notice under paragraph 6 that he has considered it and does not propose to amend or revoke it, or has revoked it.

(3) Subject to paragraphs 3(1) and 4(4), a revoking order, or an amending order which is not restrictive, does not take effect until confirmed by the Secretary of State.

(4) An amending or revoking order requiring confirmation shall stand revoked if the Secretary of State gives notice under paragraph 6 below that it is not to be confirmed.

Publicity for orders

2.—(1) The Secretary of State shall, where an order has been made, give notice setting out the order (or describing its general effect) and stating that it has taken effect or, as the case may be, that it has been made and requires confirmation.
    (2) The notice shall—
        (a) name a place in the area in which the land to which the order relates is situated where a copy of the order may be inspected free of charge at all reasonable hours; and
        (b) specify the time (not being less than 28 days from the date of the first publication of the notice) within which, and the manner in which, representations or objections with respect to the order may be made.
    (3) The notice shall be given—
        (a) by publication in the Gazette and also at least one local newspaper circulating in the area in which the land to which the order relates is situated;
        (b) by serving a like notice—
            (i) on every owner and occupier of that land (subject to sub-paragraph (4) below); and
            (ii) on the local planning authority within whose area the land is situated.
    (4) The Secretary of State may, in any particular case, direct that it shall not be necessary to comply with sub-paragraph (3)(b)(i); but if he so directs in the case of any land, then in addition to publication the notice shall be addressed to 'The owners and any occupiers' of the land (describing it) and a copy or copies of the notice shall be affixed to some conspicuous object or objects on the land.

Unopposed orders

3.—(1) Where an order has taken effect immediately and no representations or objections are duly made in respect of it or any so made are withdrawn, the Secretary of State shall, as soon as practicable after considering the order, decide either to take no action on it or to make an order amending or revoking it.
    An amending or revoking order under this sub-paragraph takes effect immediately and does not require confirmation nor shall any representation or objection with respect to it be entertained.
    (2) Where an order requiring confirmation is made and no representations or objections are duly made in respect of it, or any so made are withdrawn, the Secretary of State may confirm the order (with or without modification).

Opposed orders

4.—(1) If any representation or objection duly made with respect to an order is not withdrawn, then, as soon as practicable in the case of an order having immediate effect and before confirming an order requiring confirmation, the Secretary of State shall either—
        (a) cause a local inquiry to be held; or
        (b) afford any person by whom a representation or objection has been duly made and not withdrawn an opportunity of being heard by a person appointed by the Secretary of State for the purpose.
    (2) On considering any representations or objections duly made and the report of any person appointed to hold the inquiry or to hear representations or objections, the Secretary of State—

(a) if the order has already taken effect, shall decide either to take no action on the order, or to make an order amending or revoking it as he thinks appropriate in the light of the report, representations or objections; and

(b) if the order requires confirmation, may confirm it (with or without modifications).

(3) The provisions of section 250(2) to (5) of the Local Government Act 1972 or section 210(4) to (8) of the Local Government (Scotland) Act 1973 (local inquiries: evidence and costs) apply in relation to an inquiry held under this paragraph:

(4) An amending or revoking order made by virtue of sub-paragraph (2) above takes effect immediately and does not require confirmation nor shall any representation or objection with respect to it be entertained.

Restriction on power to amend orders or confirm them with modifications

5.   The Secretary of State shall not by virtue of paragraphs 3(1) or 4(2) amend an order which has taken effect, or confirm any other order with modifications, so as to extend the area to which the order applies.

Notice of final decision on order

6.—(1) The Secretary of State shall as soon as practicable after making an order by virtue of paragraphs 3(1) or 4(2) give notice—

(a) setting out the order (or describing its effect) and stating that it has taken effect; and

(b) naming a place in the area in which the land to which the order relates is situated where a copy of the order may be inspected free of charge at all reasonable hours.

(2) The Secretary of State shall give notice of any of the following decisions of his as soon as practicable after making the decision—

(a) a decision under paragraph 3(1) or 4(2) to take no action on an order which has already taken effect;

(b) a decision to confirm or not to confirm an order requiring confirmation under this Schedule.

(3) A notice under this paragraph of a decision to confirm an order shall—

(a) set out the order as confirmed (or describe its general effect) and state the day on which the order took effect; and

(b) name a place in the area in which the land to which the order relates is situated where a copy of the order as confirmed may be inspected free of charge at all reasonable hours.

(4) Notice under this paragraph shall be given by publishing it in accordance with paragraph 2(3) and serving a copy of it on any person on whom a notice was required to be served under paragraph 2(3) or (4).

Proceedings for questioning validity of orders

7.—(1) This paragraph applies to any order which has taken effect and as to which the Secretary of State has given notice under paragraph 6 of a decision of his to take no action or to amend the order in accordance with paragraph 4; and in this paragraph 'the relevant notice' means that notice.

(2) If any person is aggrieved by an order to which this paragraph applies and desires to question its validity on the ground that it is not within the powers of regulation 22 or that any of the requirements of this Schedule have not been complied with in relation to it, he may within six weeks from the date of the relevant notice make an application to the court under this paragraph.

(3) On any such application the court may, if satisfied that the order is not within those powers or that the interests of the applicant have been substantially prejudiced by a failure to comply with any of those requirements—

    (a) in England and Wales, quash the order, or any provision of the order, either generally or in so far as it affects the interests of the applicant; or

    (b) in Scotland, make such declarator as seems to the court to be appropriate.

(4) Except as provided by this paragraph, the validity of an order shall not be questioned in any legal proceedings whatsoever.

(5) In this paragraph 'the court' means the High Court in relation to England and Wales and the Court of Session in relation to Scotland.

Interpretation

In this Schedule—

    'amending order' and 'revoking order' mean an order which amends or, as the case may be, revokes a previous order;

    'the Gazette' means—

    (a) if the order relates in whole or in part to land in England and Wales, the London Gazette; and

    (b) if the order relates in whole or in part to land in Scotland, the Edinburgh Gazette;

    'order' means an order under regulation 22;

    'original order' means an order other than an amending or revoking order; and

    'restrictive amending order' means an amending order which extends the area to which a previous order applies.

SCHEDULE 2   EUROPEAN PROTECTED SPECIES OF ANIMALS

Common name	*Scientific name*
Bats, Horseshoe (all species)	Rhinolophidae
Bats, Typical (all species)	Vespertilionidae
Butterfly, Large Blue	Maculinea arion
Cat, Wild	Felis silvestris
Dolphins, porpoises and whales (all species)	Cetacea
Dormouse	Muscardinus avellanarius
Lizard, Sand	Lacerta agilis
Newt, Great Crested (or Warty)	Triturus cristatus
Otter, Common	Lutra lutra
Snake, Smooth	Coronella austriaca
Sturgeon	Acipenser sturio
Toad, Natterjack	Bufo calamita
Turtles, Marine	Caretta caretta
	Chelonia mydas
	Lepidochelys kempii
	Eretmochelys imbricata
	Dermochelys coriacea

NOTE. The common name or names given in the first column of this Schedule are included by way of guidance only; in the event of any dispute or proceedings, the common name or names shall not be taken into account.

SCHEDULE 3   ANIMALS WHICH MAY NOT BE TAKEN OR KILLED IN CERTAIN WAYS

Common name	*Scientific name*
Barbel	Barbus barbus
Grayling	Thymallus thymallus
Hare, Mountain	Lepus timidus
Lamprey, River	Lampetra fluviatilis
Marten, Pine	Martes martes
Polecat	Mustela putorius (otherwise known as Putorius putorius)
Salmon, Atlantic	Salmo salar (only in fresh water)
Seal, Bearded	Erignathus barbatus
Seal, Common	Phoca vitulina
Seal, Grey	Halichoerus grypus
Seal, Harp	Phoca groenlandica (otherwise known as Pagophilus groenlandicus)
Seal, Hooded	Cystophora cristata
Seal, Ringed	Phoca hispida (otherwise known as Pusa hispida)
Shad, Allis	Alosa alosa
Shad, Twaite	Alosa fallax
Vendace	Coregonus albula
Whitefish	Coregonus lavaretus

NOTE. The common name or names given in the first column of this Schedule are included by way of guidance only; in the event of any dispute or proceedings, the common name or names shall not be taken into account.

SCHEDULE 4   EUROPEAN PROTECTED SPECIES OF PLANTS

Common name	*Scientific name*
Dock, Shore	Rumex rupestris
Fern, Killarney	Trichomanes speciosum
Gentian, Early	Gentianella anglica
Lady's-slipper	Cypripedium calceolus
Marshwort, Creeping	Apium repens
Naiad, slender	Najas flexilis
Orchid, Fen	Liparis loeselii
Plantain, Floating-leaved water	Luronium natans
Saxifrage, Yellow Marsh	Saxifraga hirculus

NOTE. The common name or names given in the first column of this Schedule are included by way of guidance only; in the event of any dispute or proceedings, the common name or names shall not be taken into account.

Town and Country Planning
(General Permitted Development) Order 1995

(SI 1995, No. 418) (as amended)

SCHEDULE 2

PART 3   CHANGES OF USE

Class A

Permitted
development

A. Development consisting of a change of the use of a building to a use falling within Class A1 (shops) of the Schedule to the Use Classes Order from a use falling within Class A3 (food and drink) of that Schedule or from a use for the sale, or display for sale, of motor vehicles.

Class B

Permitted
development

B. Development consisting of a change of the use of a building—

(a) to a use for any purpose falling within Class B1 (business) of the Schedule to the Use Classes Order from any use falling within Class B2 (general industrial) or B8 (storage and distribution) of that Schedule;

(b) to a use for any purpose falling within Class B8 (storage and distribution) of that Schedule from any use falling within Class B1 (business) or B2 (general industrial).

Development
not permitted

Development is not permitted by Class B where the change is to or from a use falling within Class B8 of that Schedule, if the change of use relates to more than 235 square metres of floor space in the building.

Class C

Permitted
development

C. Development consisting of a change of use to a use falling within Class A2 (financial and professional services) of the Schedule to the Use Classes Order from a use falling within Class A3 (food and drink) of that Schedule.

Class D

Permitted
development

D. Development consisting of a change of use of any premises with a display window at ground floor level to a use falling within Class A1 (shops) of the Schedule to the Use Classes Order from a use falling within Class A2 (financial and professional services) of that Schedule.

Class E

Permitted
development

E. Development consisting of a change of the use of a building or other land from a use permitted by planning permission granted on an application, to another use which that permission would have specifically authorised when it was granted.

Development
not permitted

E.1 Development is not permitted by Class E if—

(a) the application for planning permission referred to was made before the 5th December 1988;

(b) it would be carried out more than 10 years after the grant of planning permission; or

(c) it would result in the breach of any condition, limitation or specification contained in that planning permission in relation to the use in question.

Class F

Permitted
development

F. Development consisting of a change of the use of a building—

(a) to a mixed use for any purpose within Class A1 (shops) of the Schedule to the Use Classes Order and as a single flat, from a use for any purpose within Class A1 of that Schedule;

(b) to a mixed use for any purpose within Class A2 (financial and professional services) of the Schedule to the Use Classes Order and as a single flat, from a use for any purpose within Class A2 of that Schedule;

(c) where that building has a display window at ground floor level, to a mixed use for any purpose within Class A1 (shops) of the Schedule to the Use Classes Order and as a single flat, from a use for any purpose within Class A2 (financial and professional services) of that Schedule.

Conditions

F.1 Development permitted by Class F is subject to the following conditions—

(a) some or all of the parts of the building used for any purposes within Class A1 or Class A2, as the case may be, of the Schedule to the Use Classes Order shall be situated on a floor below the part of the building used as a single flat;

(b) where the development consists of a change of use of any building with a display window at ground floor level, the ground floor shall not be used in whole or in part as the single flat;

(c) the single flat shall not be used otherwise than as a dwelling (whether or not as a sole or main residence)—

(i) by a single person or by people living together as a family, or

(ii) by not more than six residents living together as a single household (including a household where care is provided for residents).

Interpretation of Class F

F.2 For the purposes of Class F — 'care' means personal care for people in need of such care by reason of old age, disablement, past or present dependence on alcohol or drugs or past or present mental disorder.

**Class G
Permitted development**

G. Development consisting of a change of the use of a building—

(a) to a use for any purpose within Class A1 (shops) of the Schedule to the Use Classes Order from a mixed use for any purpose within Class A1 of that Schedule and as a single flat;

(b) to a use for any purpose within Class A2 (financial and professional services) of the Schedule to the Use Classes Order from a mixed use for any purpose within Class A2 of that Schedule and as a single flat;

(c) where that building has a display window at ground floor level, to a use for any purpose within Class A1 (shops) of the Schedule to the Use Classes Order from a mixed use for any purpose within Class A2 (financial and professional services) of that Schedule and as a single flat.

Development not permitted

G.1 Development is not permitted by Class G unless the part of the building used as a single flat was immediately prior to being so used used for any purpose within Class A1 or Class A2 of the Schedule to the Use Classes Order.

Statutory Nuisance (Appeals) Regulations 1995
(SI 1995, No. 2644)

1   Citation, commencement and interpretation
(1) . . .
(2) In these Regulations—
'the 1974 Act' means the Control of Pollution Act 1974;
'the 1990 Act' means the Environmental Protection Act 1990; and
'the 1993 Act' means the Noise and Statutory Nuisance Act 1993.

2   Appeals under section 80(3) of the 1990 Act
(1) The provisions of this regulation apply in relation to an appeal brought by any person

under section 80(3) of the 1990 Act (appeals to magistrates) against an abatement notice served upon him by a local authority.

(2) The grounds on which a person served with such a notice may appeal under section 80(3) are any one or more of the following grounds that are appropriate in the circumstances of the particular case—

(a) that the abatement notice is not justified by section 80 of the 1990 Act (summary proceedings for statutory nuisances);

(b) that there has been some informality, defect or error in, or in connection with, the abatement notice, or in, or in connection with, any copy of the abatement notice served under section 80A(3) (certain notices in respect of vehicles, machinery or equipment);

(c) that the authority have refused unreasonably to accept compliance with alternative requirements, or that the requirements of the abatement notice are otherwise unreasonable in character or extent, or are unnecessary;

(d) that the time, or where more than one time is specified, any of the times, within which the requirements of the abatement notice are to be complied with is not reasonably sufficient for the purpose;

(e) where the nuisance to which the notice relates—

(i) is a nuisance falling within section 79(1)(a), (d), (e), (f) or (g) of the 1990 Act and arises on industrial, trade, or business premises, or

(ii) is a nuisance falling within section 79(1)(b) of the 1990 Act and the smoke is emitted from a chimney, or

(iii) is a nuisance falling within section 79(1)(ga) of the 1990 Act and is noise emitted from or caused by a vehicle, machinery or equipment being used for industrial, trade or business purposes,

that the best practicable means were used to prevent, or to counteract the effects of, the nuisance;

(f) that, in the case of a nuisance under section 79(1)(g) or (ga) of the 1990 Act (noise emitted from premises), the requirements imposed by the abatement notice by virtue of section 80(1)(a) of the Act are more onerous than the requirements for the time being in force, in relation to the noise to which the notice relates, of—

(i) any notice served under section 60 or 66 of the 1974 Act (control of noise on construction sites and from certain premises), or

(ii) any consent given under section 61 or 65 of the 1974 Act (consent for work on construction sites and consent for noise to exceed registered level in a noise abatement zone), or

(iii) any determination made under section 67 of the 1974 Act (noise control of new buildings);

(g) that, in the case of a nuisance under section 79(1)(ga) of the 1990 Act (noise emitted from or caused by vehicles, machinery or equipment), the requirements imposed by the abatement notice by virtue of section 80(1)(a) of the Act are more onerous than the requirements for the time being in force, in relation to the noise to which the notice relates, of any condition of a consent given under paragraph 1 of Schedule 2 to the 1993 Act (loudspeakers in streets or roads);

(h) that the abatement notice should have been served on some person instead of the appellant, being—

(i) the person responsible for the nuisance, or

(ii) the person responsible for the vehicle, machinery or equipment, or

(iii) in the case of a nuisance arising from any defect of a structural character, the owner of the premises, or

(iv) in the case where the person responsible for the nuisance cannot be found or the nuisance has not yet occurred, the owner or occupier of the premises;

    (i) that the abatement notice might lawfully have been served on some person instead of the appellant being—

        (i) in the case where the appellant is the owner of the premises, the occupier of the premises, or

        (ii) in the case where the appellant is the occupier of the premises, the owner of the premises,

    and that it would have been equitable for it to have been so served;

    (j) that the abatement notice might lawfully have been served on some person in addition to the appellant, being—

        (i) a person also responsible for the nuisance, or

        (ii) a person who is also owner of the premises, or

        (iii) a person who is also an occupier of the premises, or

        (iv) a person who is also the person responsible for the vehicle, machinery or equipment,

    and that it would have been equitable for it to have been so served.

(3) If and so far as an appeal is based on the ground of some informality, defect or error in, or in connection with, the abatement notice, or in, or in connection with, any copy of the notice served under section 80A(3), the court shall dismiss the appeal if it is satisfied that the informality, defect or error was not a material one.

(4) Where the grounds upon which an appeal is brought include a ground specified in paragraph (2)(i) or (j) above, the appellant shall serve a copy of his notice of appeal on any other person referred to, and in the case of any appeal to which these regulations apply he may serve a copy of his notice of appeal on any other person having an estate or interest in the premises, vehicle, machinery or equipment in question.

(5) On the hearing of the appeal the court may—

    (a) quash the abatement notice to which the appeal relates, or

    (b) vary the abatement notice in favour of the appellant in such manner as it thinks fit, or

    (c) dismiss the appeal; and an abatement notice that is varied under sub-paragraph (b) above shall be final and shall otherwise have effect, as so varied, as if it had been so made by the local authority.

(6) Subject to paragraph (7) below, on the hearing of an appeal the court may make such order as it thinks fit—

    (a) with respect to the person by whom any work is to be executed and the contribution to be made by any person towards the cost of the work, or

    (b) as to the proportions in which any expenses which may become recoverable by the authority under Part III of the 1990 Act are to be borne by the appellant and by any other person.

(7) In exercising its powers under paragraph (6) above the court—

    (a) shall have regard, as between an owner and an occupier, to the terms and conditions, whether contractual or statutory, of any relevant tenancy and to the nature of the works required, and

    (b) shall be satisfied before it imposes any requirement thereunder on any person other than the appellant, that that person has received a copy of the notice of appeal in pursuance of paragraph (4) above.

3 Suspension of notice

(1) Where—

    (a) an appeal is brought against an abatement notice served under section 80 or section 80A of the 1990 Act, and—

    (b) either—

      (i) compliance with the abatement notice would involve any person in expenditure on the carrying out of works before the hearing of the appeal, or

      (ii) in the case of a nuisance under section 79(1)(g) or (ga) of the 1990 Act, the noise to which the abatement notice relates is noise necessarily caused in the course of the performance of some duty imposed by law on the appellant, and

    (c) either paragraph (2) does not apply, or it does apply but the requirements of paragraph (3) have not been met,

the abatement notice shall be suspended until the appeal has been abandoned or decided by the court.

    (2) This paragraph applies where—

      (a) the nuisance to which the abatement notice relates—

        (i) is injurious to health, or

        (ii) is likely to be of a limited duration such that suspension of the notice would render it of no practical effect, or

      (b) the expenditure which would be incurred by any person in the carrying out of works in compliance with the abatement notice before any appeal has been decided would not be disproportionate to the public benefit to be expected in that period from such compliance.

    (3) Where paragraph (2) applies the abatement notice—

      (a) shall include a statement that paragraph (2) applies, and that as a consequence it shall have effect notwithstanding any appeal to a magistrates' court which has not been decided by the court, and

      (b) shall include a statement as to which of the grounds set out in paragraph (2) apply.

Environmental Licences (Suspension And Revocation) Regulations 1996
(SI 1996, No. 508)

1   . . .

2   Interpretation
In these Regulations—

    'holder' in relation to an environmental licence means the person liable to pay any charges due and payable in respect of the subsistence of that licence.

3   Notice demanding payment
The appropriate procedure, where a new Agency proposes to suspend or revoke an environmental licence under section 41(6) of the Environment Act 1995, is as follows—

    (a) before taking any action under regulation 5 below to suspend or revoke an environmental licence, the new Agency shall first serve on the holder of the environ-mental licence a notice demanding payment within twenty-eight days after the service of the notice of any charges due and payable in respect of the subsistence of the licence; and

    (b) the new Agency shall allow the period of twenty-eight days to expire before taking further action to suspend or revoke the environmental licence.

4   Contents of notice demanding payment
A notice demanding the payment of any charges which is served for the purposes of regulation 3 shall state—

    (a) that the environmental licence may be suspended or revoked if the charges are not paid within twenty-eight days after the service of the notice; and

    (b) the effect of suspension or revocation.

5 Notice of suspension or revocation

(1) Suspension or revocation of a licence under section 41(6) of the Environment Act 1995 shall be effected by the service of a notice of suspension or revocation on the holder of the environmental licence.

(2) A notice of suspension or revocation shall—

    (a) set out the reason for the suspension or revocation and the date and time at which it will take effect; and

    (b) in the case of a suspension of an environmental licence, set out the circumstances in which the suspension may be lifted.

Special Waste Regulations 1996

(SI 1996, No. 972) (as amended)

1 Citation, commencement, extent, application and interpretation

(1) These Regulations may be cited as the Special Waste Regulations 1996 and shall come into force on 1st September 1996.

    (2) . . .

    (3) . . .

(4) In these Regulations, unless the context otherwise requires—

'the 1990 Act' means the Environmental Protection Act 1990;

'the 1994 Regulations' means the Waste Management Licensing Regulations 1994;

'Agency' means

    (a) in relation to places, premises and sites in England and Wales, the Environment Agency established by section 1 of the Environment Act 1995 and

    (b) . . .

'the approved classification and labelling guide' means the document entitled 'Approved guide to the classification and labelling of substances and preparations dangerous for supply ([Fourth] edition)' approved by the Health and Safety Commission on [12th October 1999] for the purposes of the Chemicals (Hazard Information and Packaging for Supply) Regulations 1994;

'the approved supply list' means the document entitled 'Approved Supply List ([Sixth Edition])—Information approved for the classification and labelling of substances and preparations dangerous for supply' (c) approved by the Health and Safety Commission on [15th August 2000] for the purposes of the Chemicals (Hazard Information and Packaging for Supply) Regulations 1994; 'carrier', in relation to a consignment of special waste, means the person who collects that waste from the premises at which it is being held and transports it to another place;

'carrier's round' in relation to consignments of special waste, means a journey made by a carrier during which he collects more than one consignment of special waste and transports all consignments collected to the same consignee who is specified in the consignment note;

'carrier's schedule' means a schedule prepared in accordance with regulation 8;

'consignee', in relation to a consignment of special waste, means the person to whom that waste is to be transported;

'consignment note', in relation to a consignment of special waste, means a note in a form corresponding to the form set out in Schedule 1 to these Regulations, or in a form substantially to the like effect, and giving at any time the details required by these Regulations to be shown in respect of that consignment (including, where the consignment is one in a succession of consignments, any details required to be shown in respect of other consignments in the succession);

'consignor', in relation to a consignment of special waste, means the person who causes that waste to be removed from the premises at which it is being held;

'controlled waste' has the same meaning as in Part II of the 1990 Act (d);

'conveyance' includes a vehicle designed to carry goods by road or rail and a vessel designed to carry goods by water;

'harbour area' has the same meaning as in the Dangerous Substances in Harbour Areas Regulations 1987;

'the Hazardous Waste Directive' means Council Directive 91/689/EEC on hazardous waste, as amended by Council Directive 94/31/EC;

['household waste' means waste which is household waste for the purposes of Part II of the 1990 Act or which is treated as household waste for those purposes by virtue of regulation 2(1) of the Controlled Waste Regulations 1992, other than—

    (a) asbestos;

    (b) waste from a laboratory;

    (c) waste from a hospital, other than waste from a self-contained part of a hospital which is used wholly for the purposes of living accommodation.]

'premises' includes any ship;

'relevant code', in relation to a consignment note or carrier's schedule, means the code assigned in accordance with regulation 4 to the consignment of special waste to which the consignment note or carrier's schedule relates or, where the consignment is one in a carrier's round, to the consignments in that round;

'risk phrase' means the risk phrase shown under Part III of the approved supply list;

'ship' means a vessel of any type whatsoever operating in the marine environment including submersible craft, floating craft and any structure which is a fixed or floating platform;

'special waste' has the meaning given by regulation 2 of these Regulations; and

'waste management licence' has the meaning given by section 35(1) of the 1990 Act.

[2   Meaning of special waste

    (1) Any controlled waste, other than household waste,—

        (a) to which a six-digit code is assigned in the list set out in Part I of Schedule 2 to these Regulations (which reproduces the list of hazardous waste annexed to Council Decision 94/904/EC establishing a list of hazardous waste pursuant to Article 1(4) of the Hazardous Waste Directive); and

        (b) which displays any of the properties specified in Part II of that Schedule (which reproduces Annex III to the Hazardous Waste Directive),

is special waste.

    (2) Any other controlled waste, other than household waste, which—

        (a) displays the property H3A (first indent), H4, H5, H6, H7 or H8 specified in Part II of Schedule 2, to these Regulations; or

        (b) is a medicinal product, as defined in section 130 of the Medicines Act 1968 (meaning of 'medicinal product' etc.), of a description, or falling within a class, specified in an order under section 58 of that Act (medicinal products on prescription only),

is special waste.

    (3) For the purposes of paragraphs (1) and (2) waste shall be treated as displaying none of the properties H4 to H8 specified in Part II of Schedule 2 to these Regulations if it satisfies none of the criteria set out in Part III of that Schedule.

(4) Part IV of Schedule 2 to these Regulations (which contains rules for the interpretation of that Schedule) shall have effect.]

3 Certain radioactive waste to be special waste

Section 62 (special provision with respect to certain dangerous and intractable waste) of the 1990 Act shall have effect, without modification, so as to empower the Secretary of State to make provision for waste which would be controlled waste but for the fact that it is radioactive waste within the meaning of the Radioactive Substances Act 1993; and paragraphs (1) and (2) of regulation 2 shall apply to any such waste as if it were controlled waste.

4 Coding of consignments

(1) [Subject to paragraph (3),] an Agency shall assign or supply forthwith to any person, on request, for the purpose of assigning to a consignment of special waste or, where the consignment is one in a carrier's round, to the consignments in that round, a code unique to that consignment or round, as the case may be.

(2) A code assigned or supplied in accordance with paragraph (1) may consist of letters, numbers or symbols, or any combination of letters, numbers and symbols, or a bar code which enables the consignment or carrier's round, as the case may be, to be identified electronically.

[(3) The Agency need not assign or supply a code for a consignment or round until any fee required in respect of it under regulation 14(1) has been paid.]

5 Consignment notes: standard procedure

(1) Except in a case to which regulation 6, 8 or 9 applies, this regulation applies where a consignment of special waste is to be removed from the premises at which it is being held.

(2) Before the consignment is removed—
- (a) five copies of the consignment note shall be prepared, and, on each copy, Parts A and B shall be completed and the relevant code entered;
- (b) the consignor shall ensure that one of those copies (on which Parts A and B have been completed and the relevant code entered) is furnished to the Agency for the place to which the consignment is to be transported;
- (c) the carrier shall complete Part C on each of the four remaining copies; and
- (d) the consignor—
  - (i) shall complete Part D on each of those copies;
  - (ii) shall retain one copy (on which Parts A to D have been completed and the relevant code entered); and
  - (iii) shall give the three remaining copies (on which Parts A to D have been completed and the relevant code entered) to the carrier.

(3) The carrier shall ensure that the copies which he has received—
- (a) travel with the consignment; and
- (b) are given to the consignee on delivery of the consignment.

(4) Subject to regulation 10, on receiving the consignment the consignee shall—
- (a) complete Part E on the three copies of the consignment note given to him;
- (b) retain one copy;
- (c) give one copy to the carrier; and
- (d) forthwith furnish one copy to the Agency for the place to which the consignment has been transported.

(5) The carrier shall retain the copy of the consignment note given to him by the consignee.

6 Consignment notes: cases in which pre-notification is not required

(1) For the purposes of regulation 7, except in a case to which regulation 8 applies, this regulation applies—

(a) subject to paragraph (2)(a), to the removal, from the premises at which it is being held, of each of the second and any subsequent consignment of special waste in a succession of consignments of special waste,

(b) subject to paragraph (2)(b), to the removal as a consignment of special waste of a product or material for the purposes of the return by the person to whom the product or material had been supplied to the person who supplied it to him or who manufactured it,

(c) subject to paragraph (2)(c), to the removal of a consignment of special waste where the consignor and the consignee are bodies corporate belonging to the same group,

(d) to the removal from a ship in a harbour area of a consignment of special waste to a conveyance for transportation to a place outside that area, and

(e) to the removal of a consignment of special waste which consists entirely of lead acid [. . .] batteries.

(2) This regulation does not apply unless—

(a) in the case mentioned in paragraph (1)(a), in respect of each consignment—

(i) the waste is of the same description as the waste in the first of the consignments in the succession;

(ii) the consignor is the same person;

(iii) the consignee is the same person;

(iv) the premises from which the consignment is removed are the same;

(v) the place to which the consignment is transported is the same; and

(vi) the removal of the consignment takes place within one year of the removal of the first consignment in the succession;

(b) in the case mentioned in paragraph (1)(b), the person to whom the product or material was supplied is satisfied that, as supplied, the product or material fails to meet any specification which he expected it to meet;

(c) in the case mentioned in paragraph (1)(c), the removal is for the purposes of an operation within either paragraph 15 of Part III, or paragraph 13 of Part IV, of Schedule 4 to the 1994 Regulations, and the consignee either—

(i) is the holder of a waste management licence which authorises the relevant operation; or

(ii) carries on any activity to which section 33(1)(a) and (b) of the 1990 Act does not apply by virtue of regulation 16 or 17 of the 1994 Regulations.

(3) In paragraph (1)(c) 'group', in relation to a body corporate, means that body corporate, any other body corporate which is its holding company or subsidiary and any other body corporate which is a subsidiary of that holding company; and for these purposes—

'body corporate' does not include a corporation sole or a Scottish partnership, but includes a company incorporated elsewhere than in Great Britain; and

'holding company' and 'subsidiary' have the meaning given by section 736 of the Companies Act 1985.

7 Consignment notes: procedure where pre-notification is not required

Paragraph (2), with the exception of sub-paragraph (b), and paragraphs (3) to (5) of regulation 5 shall apply in cases to which regulation 6 applies as if—

(a) 'four' were substituted for 'five' in sub-paragraph (a) of paragraph (2);

[(aa) references to the relevant code in regulation 5(2)(a) were references, in relation to the case mentioned in regulation 6(1)(a), to the relevant code and the code for the first consignment in that succession;]

(b) references to the consignor were references—

(i) in relation to the case mentioned in regulation 6(1)(b), to the person to whom the product or material was supplied; and

(ii) in relation to the case mentioned in regulation 6(1)(d), to the master of the ship; and

(c) references to the consignee were references, in relation to the case mentioned in regulation 6(1)(b), to the person to whom the product or material is to be returned.

8   Consignment notes: carrier's rounds

(1) This regulation applies to a carrier's round or to a succession of such rounds by the same carrier starting and ending within a twelve month period in respect of which:

(a) every consignor is a person specified in the consignment note or in the schedule prepared in accordance with paragraph (2)(b)(iii) or whose particulars are notified in writing to the Agency not less than 72 hours before the removal of the first waste on the carrier's round;

(b) the premises from which the special waste is removed are:

(i) specified in the consignment note or in the schedule prepared in accordance with paragraph (2)(b)(iii) or notified in writing to the Agency not less than 72 hours before the removal of the first waste on the carrier's round; and

(ii) so located that the Agency for each of those premises is the same;

(c) the special waste is of a description specified in the consignment note; and

(d) in the case of a single round other than a round that satisfies the requirements of regulation 14(2)(a), the time between the collection of the first consignment and delivery to the consignee is no more than [72] hours.

(2) Before the first removal of waste, the carrier shall,

(a) on any carrier's round which is not in a succession or on the first round in such a succession, ensure that

(i) Parts A and B of the consignment note are completed and that the relevant code is entered;

(ii) [except where the special waste to be collected on the carrier's round consists entirely of lead acid [. . .] batteries,] one copy of the consignment note is furnished to the Agency for the place to which the special waste is to be transported;

(b) on every round—

(i) prepare [three] copies of the consignment note in addition to one copy for each consignor from whom waste is to be collected during the round;

(ii) complete on those copies Parts A and B, the carrier's particulars and particulars of transport in Part C, the code assigned or supplied under regulation 4 in respect of the round and, if it is a second or subsequent round, the code in respect of the first round; and

(iii) ensure that four copies of a schedule are prepared in the form set out in Part II of Schedule 1 to these Regulations, or in a form substantially to the like effect, in addition to one consignor's copy for each site from which waste is to be collected during that round.

[(2A) In a case where waste of more than one description is specified in the consignment note, either—

(a) the schedule referred to in paragraph (2)(b)(iii) shall contain a separate entry for each description of waste to be collected from each consignor showing the description of waste to which that entry relates; or

(b) each entry in the schedule shall show the different descriptions of the waste to be collected and, for each such description, the quantity of the waste to be collected.]

(3) The consignor shall, before the removal of waste from a site, complete on all the copies that part of the schedule indicated on it as for completion by him.

(4) The carrier shall ensure, before the removal of the waste, that—

(a) the part of the schedule indicated on it as for completion by him is completed on all the copies [and includes a record of the time at which it is completed]; and

(b) he has all copies of the schedule (on which the part to be completed by the consignor has been completed) except the copy to be retained by the consignor under paragraph (5).

(5) The consignor shall retain in respect of each site one copy of the consignment note and of that part of the schedule on which the parts to be completed by him and by the carrier have been completed.

[(5A) Before the removal of the last consignment of waste on the carrier's round, the carrier shall complete Part C on the three copies of the consignment note retained by him.]

(6) The carrier shall ensure that the copies of the consignment note and of the schedule which he has received—

(a) [. . .]

(b) travel with the waste to which they refer;

(c) are given to the consignee on delivery of the waste.

(7) Subject to regulation 10, on receiving the waste collected on each round, the consignee shall—

(a) complete Part E on the three copies of the consignment note given to him;

(b) retain one copy of the consignment note and one copy of the schedule;

(c) give to the carrier a copy of the consignment note and a copy of the schedule; and

(d) forthwith furnish to the Agency for the place to which the consignment has been transported one copy of the consignment note and one copy of the schedule.

(8) The carrier shall retain the copies given to him in accordance with paragraph (7)(c).

9 Consignment notes: removal of ships' waste to reception facilities

(1) This regulation applies where special waste is removed from a ship in a harbour area to—

(a) reception facilities provided within that harbour area; or

(b) by pipeline to any such facilities provided outside a harbour area.

(2) Before the waste is removed from the ship—

(a) three copies of the consignment note shall be prepared and Parts A and B shall be completed and the relevant code entered on each of those copies;

(b) the operator of the facilities shall complete Part C on each of those copies; and

(c) the master of the ship—

  (i) shall ensure that Part D is completed on each of those copies;

  (ii) shall retain one copy (on which Parts A to D have been completed); and

  (iii) shall give the two remaining copies (on which Parts A to D have been completed) to the operator of the facilities.

(3) On receiving a consignment of special waste the operator of the facilities shall—

(a) complete Part E on the copies of the consignment note which he has received;

(b) retain one copy; and

(c) forthwith furnish the other copy to the Agency for the place where the facilities are situated.

10 Consignment notes etc.: duty of consignee not accepting delivery of a consignment

(1) This regulation applies where the consignee does not accept delivery of a consignment of special waste.

(2) In a case to which this regulation applies the requirements of regulation 5(4) (including that paragraph as applied in cases to which regulation 6 applies) or 8(7), as the case may be, shall not apply to the consignee.

(3) If, in a case to which this regulation applies, copies of the consignment note have been given to the consignee he shall—

- (a) indicate on Part E of each copy that he does not accept the consignment and the reasons why he does not accept the consignment;
- (b) retain one copy;
- (c) ensure that one copy, accompanied by one copy of any carrier's schedule given to him in accordance with regulation 8, [(annotated to show which consignment is not accepted)], are furnished forthwith to the Agency for the place to which the special waste has been transported; and
- (d) ensure that the other copy is returned to the carrier forthwith.

(4) If, in a case to which this regulation applies, no copies of the consignment note have been given to the consignee he shall ensure that a written explanation of his reasons for not accepting delivery, including such details of the consignment and of the carrier as are known to him, is furnished forthwith to the Agency for the place to which the special waste has been transported.

(5) In a case to which this regulation applies—

- (a) on being informed that the consignee will not accept delivery of the consignment, the carrier shall inform the Agency and seek instructions from the consignor;
- (b) the consignor shall forthwith inform the carrier and the Agency of his intentions as regards the consignment; and
- (c) the carrier shall take all reasonable steps to ensure that the consignor's intentions are fulfilled.

(6) For the purposes of paragraph (5), the consignor may propose one of the following, namely—

- (a) the delivery of the consignment to the premises from which it had been collected;
- (b) the delivery of the consignment to the premises at which it had been produced;
- (c) the delivery of the consignment to other specified premises in respect of which there is held any waste management licence necessary to authorise the receipt of the waste.

[10A   Consignment notes: requirement for a new consignment note

(1) This regulation applies where, in accordance with regulation 10(6)(c), a consignor proposes that a consignment be delivered to other specified premises in respect of which there is held any waste management licence necessary to authorise receipt of the waste.

(2) Before the consignment is delivered to those premises—

- (a) four copies of a new consignment note shall be prepared and
  - (i) on each copy Parts A and B shall be completed and the relevant code (including the previous code) shall be entered;
  - (ii) to each copy shall be attached a copy of any relevant previous carrier's schedule, annotated to show which consignment was not accepted;
- (b) the carrier shall complete Part C on each of those copies;
- (c) the consignor, subject to paragraph (3) below—
  - (i) shall complete Part D on each of those copies;
  - (ii) shall retain one copy (on which Parts A to D have been completed and the relevant codes entered); and
  - (iii) shall give the three remaining copies (on which Parts A to D have been completed and the relevant codes entered) to the carrier.

(3) The carrier may, where he has received written instructions from the consignor to that effect, complete Part D of each of the copies of the consignment note on behalf of the

consignor, and where he does so he shall send to the consignor the consignor's copy (on which Parts A to D have been completed and the relevant codes entered).

(4) The carrier shall ensure that the three copies of the consignment note which he has received (or, if paragraph (3) applies, retained)—

    (a) travel with the consignment; and

    (b) are given to the consignee on delivery of the consignment.

(5) Subject to regulation 10, on receiving the consignment the consignee shall—

    (a) complete Part E on all copies of the consignment note given to him;

    (b) retain one copy;

    (c) give one copy to the carrier; and

    (d) forthwith furnish one copy to the Agency for the place to which the consignment has been transported.

(6) The carrier shall retain the copy of the consignment note given to him by the consignee.]

11   Consignment notes: duties of the Agencies

(1) Subject to paragraph (2), where—

    (a) an Agency ('the receiving Agency') has been furnished with a copy of a consignment note under regulation 5, 7, 8, 9 or 10 or with a copy of the explanation under regulation 10(4); and

    (b) the other Agency is the Agency for the premises from which the special waste was removed,

the receiving Agency shall, within two weeks of receipt, send to the other Agency one copy of the consignment note or explanation as the case may be.

(2) Where copies have been furnished—

    (a) under regulation 7 in a case to which regulation 6 applies by virtue of paragraph (1)(d) of that regulation, or

    (b) under regulation 9(3)(c),

paragraph (1) shall have effect as if the reference to the premises from which the special waste was removed were a reference to the harbour area in which the special waste was removed from the ship.

12   Consignment notes: provisions as to furnishing

(1) Subject to paragraphs (2), (3) and (6), a copy of a consignment note required by regulation 5 or 8 to be furnished to an Agency must be furnished not more than one month and not less than 72 hours before the removal of the consignment.

(2) Subject to paragraphs (3) and (6), a copy of a consignment note required to be furnished by regulation 8(2)(a)(ii) shall be furnished not less than 72 hours before the removal of the first consignment to which the consignment note relates.

(3) The copy of the consignment note mentioned in paragraphs (1) and (2) may be furnished to the Agency within 72 hours before the removal where—

    (a) the consignment is to be delivered to other specified premises pursuant to a proposal under regulation 10(6)(c);

    (b) the consignment cannot lawfully remain where it is for 72 hours.

(4) The requirements of paragraphs (1) and (2) shall be treated as satisfied if—

    (a) a facsimile of the copy is furnished to the Agency by telephonic, electronic or other similar means of transmission in compliance with the time limits set out in those paragraphs, and

    (b) the copy is furnished to the Agency before or, in accordance with paragraph (5) below, forthwith upon removal of the consignment.

(5) A copy of a consignment note or a written explanation of reasons for refusing to accept delivery of any special waste is furnished to an Agency in accordance with this paragraph if it, and any document required to be furnished with it, is—

(a) delivered to the Agency, or

(b) posted to the Agency by pre-paid first class post, within one day of the receipt, removal or refusal to accept delivery of the special waste in question, as the case may be.

(6) In reckoning any period of hours for the purposes of paragraphs (1), (2) and (3), the hours of any Saturday, Sunday, Good Friday, Christmas Day, bank holiday or other public holiday shall be disregarded.

13   Consignment notes: Importers and exporters

(1) Subject to paragraphs (3) and (4), regulations 5 to 12 shall apply to special waste imported into Great Britain from Northern Ireland or Gibraltar as if—

(a) any reference to the consignor were a reference to the person importing the special waste;

(b) any reference to the premises at which the special waste is being held and from which it is removed were a reference to the place where it first enters Great Britain; and

(c) the special waste is removed from that place at the time when it first enters Great Britain.

(2) Subject to paragraph (4), these Regulations shall apply to special waste exported from Great Britain to Northern Ireland or Gibraltar as if—

(a) any reference to the consignee were a reference to the person exporting the waste; and

(b) the consignment of special waste is received by that person at the place where and the time when it leaves Great Britain.

(3) Paragraph (1) does not apply in a case to which either regulation 6(1)(d) or regulation 9 applies.

(4) Nothing in regulations 5 to 12 shall apply in relation to shipments of waste to which the provisions of Council Regulation (EEC) No. 259/93 other than Title III of that Regulation, apply.

14   Fees

(1) Subject to paragraph (2), [in connection with the assignment or supply of] a code for a consignment or a carrier's round in accordance with regulation 4(1), an Agency shall require payment of a fee [prescribed for the purposes by a charging scheme under section 41 of the Environment Act 1995.]

(2) An Agency shall not require payment of a fee where the code is assigned or supplied in connection with:

(a) a second or subsequent carrier's round in a succession of [such rounds in which a single vehicle is used and in respect of which]—

(i) [. . .]

(ii) no more than one consignment is collected from any consignor during the succession;

(iii) the total weight of special waste collected in each round [in the succession] does not exceed 400 kg; and

(iv) the time between the collection of the first consignment on the first round in the succession and the delivery of the last consignment to the place to which it is to be transported is no more than one week.

(b) the removal of a single consignment of special waste for the purposes set out in regulation 6(1)(b) provided that the person to whom the product or material was supplied is satisfied that it fails to meet any specification which he expected it to meet; or

(c) the removal of special waste from a ship in a harbour area—

(i)   to a conveyance for transportation to a place outside that area;

(ii) to reception facilities provided within the same harbour area; or

(iii) by pipeline to reception facilities provided outside the harbour area.

[(3) Where an Agency assigns or supplies a code under regulation 4(1) without the fee required under this regulation having been paid to it, the person who requested the assignment or supply shall be required to pay the fee to that Agency within the period of two months beginning with the date on which the request was made.]

15   Registers

(1) At each site from which any consignment of special waste has been removed, the consignor shall keep a register containing—

(a) a copy of the consignment note; and

(b) where the consignment is one to which regulation 8 applies, a copy of that part of the carrier's schedule retained under regulation 8(5),

applicable to each consignment removed from that site.

(2) Every carrier shall keep a register containing—

(a) a copy of the consignment note; and

(b) where the consignment is one to which regulation 8 applies, a copy of the carrier's schedule,

applicable to each consignment which he has transported.

(3) At each site at which any consignment of special waste has been received, the consignee shall keep a register containing—

(a) a copy of the consignment note; and

(b) where the consignment is one to which regulation 8 applies, a copy of the carrier's schedule,

applicable to each consignment, other than a consignment to which regulation 10 applies, received at that site.

(4) A consignment note or carrier's schedule required by paragraph (1) or (2) to be kept in a register shall be retained in the register for not less than three years from the date on which the waste to which it relates was removed from the premises at which it was being held.

(5) Subject to paragraphs (6) and (7), consignment notes and carrier's schedules required by paragraph (3) to be kept by a person shall be retained until his waste management licence for the site in question is surrendered or revoked entirely, at which time he shall send the register to the Agency for the site; and that Agency shall retain the register for not less than three years after its receipt.

(6) Where, by virtue of regulation 16(1)(a) or (b) of the 1994 Regulations, section 33(1)(a), (b) and (c) of the 1990 Act does not apply to any of the activities carried on at a site at which special waste is received, paragraph (5) shall have effect as if any reference to the surrender or revocation of a person's waste management licence were a reference to the surrender or revocation of his authorisation under Part I of the 1990 Act for the site in question.

[(6A) Where, by virtue of regulation 16(1)(ba) or (bb) of the 1994 Regulations, section 33(1)(a), (b) and (c) of the 1990 Act does not apply to any of the activities carried on at a site at which special waste is received, paragraph (5) shall have effect as if any reference to the surrender or revocation of a person's waste management licence were a reference to the surrender or revocation of his permit under the Pollution Prevention and Control (England and Wales) Regulations 2000 for the site in question.]

(7) Where, in circumstances other than those mentioned in paragraph (6) [or (6A)], section 33(1)(a) and (b) of the 1990 Act does not apply to any of the activities carried on at a site at which special waste is received, each consignment note and carrier's schedule required to be kept in a register shall be kept in that register for not less than three years from the date on which the consignment of special waste to which it relates was received at the site to which it was transported.

(8) Insofar as is consistent with the foregoing provisions of this regulation, registers under this regulation may be kept in any form.

16 Site records

(1) Any person who makes a deposit of special waste in or on any land shall record the location of each such deposit, shall keep such records until his waste management licence is surrendered or revoked and shall then send the records to the Agency for the site.

(2) Such records shall comprise either—
- (a) a site plan marked with a grid, or
- (b) a site plan with overlays on which deposits are shown in relation to the contours of the site.

(3) Deposits shall be described in such records by reference to the register of consignment notes kept under regulation 15, save that where waste is disposed of—
- (a) by pipeline, or
- (b) within the curtilage of the premises at which it is produced, the deposits shall be described by reference to a record of the quantity and composition of the waste and the date of its disposal.

(4) In the case of liquid wastes discharged without containers into underground strata or disused workings the record shall comprise only a written statement of the quantity and composition of special waste so discharged and the date of its disposal.

(5) Every record made pursuant to regulation 14 of the Control of Pollution (Special Waste) Regulations 1980 shall—
- (a) be kept with the records referred to in paragraph (1) above for so long as is mentioned in that paragraph, and
- (b) shall accompany those records when they are sent to the Agency in accordance with that paragraph.

17 Restrictions on mixing special waste

(1) Subject to paragraph (2), an establishment or undertaking which carries out the disposal or recovery of special waste, or which collects or transports special waste, shall not—
- (a) mix different categories of special waste; or
- (b) mix special waste with waste which is not special waste.

(2) Paragraph (1) above shall not apply if the mixing—
- (a) is authorised by a waste management licence or under an authorisation granted under Part I of the 1990 Act [or under a permit granted under the Pollution Prevention and Control (England and Wales) Regulations 2000] or
- (b) is an activity to which, by virtue of regulation 17 of the 1994 Regulations, section 33(1)(a) and (b) of the 1990 Act does not apply.

18 Offences

(1) Subject to paragraph (2) below, it shall be an offence for a person (other than a member, officer or employee of an Agency who is acting as authorised by that Agency,) to fail to comply with any of the foregoing provisions of these Regulations insofar as that provision imposes any obligation or requirement upon him.

(2) It shall be a defence for a person charged with an offence under paragraph (1) to prove that he was not reasonably able to comply with the provision in question by reason of an emergency or grave danger and that he took all steps as were reasonably practicable in the circumstances for—
- (a) minimising any threat to the public or the environment; and
- (b) ensuring that the provision in question was complied with as soon as reasonably practicable after the event.

(3) A person who, in purported compliance with a requirement imposed by or under any of the foregoing provisions of these Regulations to furnish any information, makes a

statement which he knows to be false or misleading in a material particular, or recklessly makes any statement which is false or misleading in a material particular, commits an offence.

(4) A person who intentionally makes a false entry in any record or register required to be kept by virtue of any of the foregoing provisions of these Regulations commits an offence.

(5) Where the commission by any person of an offence under this regulation is due to the act or default of some other person, that other person may be charged with and convicted of an offence by virtue of this paragraph whether or not proceedings are taken against the first-mentioned person.

(6) Where an offence under this regulation which has been committed by a body corporate is proved to have been committed with the consent or connivance of, or to have been attributable to, any neglect on the part of a director, manager, secretary or other similar officer of the body corporate, or any person who was purporting to act in any such capacity, he, as well as the body corporate, shall be liable to be proceeded against and punished accordingly.

(7) Where the affairs of a body corporate are managed by its members, paragraph (6) shall apply in relation to the acts or defaults of a member in connection with his functions of management as if he were a director of the body corporate.

(8) Where, in Scotland, an offence under this regulation which has been committed by a partnership or an unincorporated association (other than a partnership) is proved to have been committed with the consent or connivance of, or to have been attributable to any neglect on the part of, a partner in the partnership or, as the case may be, a person concerned in the management or control of the association, he, as well as the partnership or association, shall be liable to be proceeded against and punished accordingly.

(9) A person who commits an offence under this regulation shall be liable—

    (a) on summary conviction, to a fine not exceeding level 5 on the standard scale;

    (b) on conviction on indictment, to a fine or to imprisonment for a term not exceeding two years, or to both.

19   Responsibilities of the Agencies

The Agencies shall be responsible for supervising the persons and activities subject to any provision of these Regulations.

20   Transitional provisions for certificates of technical competence

(1) This regulation applies in relation to—

    (a) waste defined as special waste under regulation 2 of these Regulations which was not so defined under regulation 2 of the Control of Pollution (Special Waste) Regulations 1980 ('waste now defined as special waste'); and

    (b) persons to be treated as technically competent for the purposes of section 74(3)(b) of the 1990 Act—

        (i) pursuant to regulation 4 of the 1994 Regulations; or

        (ii) pursuant to regulation [5(1)] of the 1994 Regulations, or to regulation 4(1) or (3) of the Waste Management Licensing (Amendment etc.) Regulations 1995.

(2) For the purposes only of operations concerning waste now defined as special waste and provided that both the conditions set out in paragraph (3) are satisfied, the persons referred to in paragraph (1)(b) shall continue to be treated as technically competent—

    (a) in the case of those referred to in paragraph (1)(b)(i), until 10th August 2000; and

    (b) in the case of those referred to in paragraph (1)(b)(ii), in accordance with the Regulations mentioned there, except that paragraph (1) of regulation 5 of the 1994 Regulations and paragraphs (1) and (4) of regulation 4 of the Waste Management Licensing (Amendment etc.) Regulations 1995 shall have effect as if for the date '10th August 1999' there were substituted the date '10th August 2000'.

(3) The conditions referred to in paragraph (2) are that:

(a) before 1st March 1997, the person applies to the Waste Management Industry Training and Advisory Board for a certificate of technical competence at Level 4 in respect of special waste; and

(b) before 1st September 1996, the person was entitled to act as the manager of a facility in respect of which there was in force a waste management licence authorising activities concerning waste now defined as special waste.

[20A   Transitional provisions and 'grandfather rights'

A person who by virtue of paragraph (2) of regulation 5 of the 1994 Regulations is treated as being technically competent for the purposes of section 74(3)(b) of the 1990 Act, shall continue to be so treated in accordance with paragraphs (2) and (4) of that regulation as if waste now defined as special waste within the meaning of regulation 20(1)(a) were not special waste.]

Regulation 2   SCHEDULE 2

                                    SPECIAL WASTE

                          PART I   HAZARDOUS WASTE LIST

Waste code (6 digits)/ Chapter Heading (2 and 4 digits)	Description
02	WASTE FROM AGRICULTURAL, HORTICULTURAL, HUNTING, FISHING AND AQUACULTURE PRIMARY PRODUCTION, FOOD PREPARATION AND PROCESSING
0201	PRIMARY PRODUCTION WASTE
020105	agrochemical wastes
03	WASTES FROM WOOD PROCESSING AND THE PRODUCTION OF PAPER, CARDBOARD, PULP, PANELS AND FURNITURE
0302	WOOD PRESERVATION WASTE
030201	non-halogenated organic wood preservatives
030202	organochlorinated wood preservatives
030203	organometallic wood preservatives
030204	inorganic wood preservatives
04	WASTES FROM THE LEATHER AND TEXTILE INDUSTRIES
0401	WASTES FROM THE LEATHER INDUSTRY
040103	degreasing wastes containing solvents without a liquid phase
0402	WASTES FROM TEXTILE INDUSTRY
040211	halogenated wastes from dressing and finishing
05	WASTES FROM PETROLEUM REFINING, NATURAL GAS PURIFICATION AND PYROLYTIC TREATMENT OF COAL
0501	OILY SLUDGES AND SOLID WASTES
050103	tank bottom sludges
050104	acid alkyl sludges
050105	oil spills

Waste code (6 digits)/ Chapter Heading (2 and 4 digits)	Description
050107	acid tars
050108	other tars
0504	SPENT FILTER CLAYS
050401	spent filter clays
0506	WASTE FROM THE PYROLYTIC TREATMENT OF COAL
050601	acid tars
050603	other tars
0507	WASTE FROM NATURAL GAS PURIFICATION
050701	sludges containing mercury
0508	WASTES FROM OIL REGENERATION
050801	spent filter clays
050802	acid tars
050803	other tars
050804	aqueous liquid waste from oil regeneration
06	WASTES FROM INORGANIC CHEMICAL PROCESSES
0601	WASTE ACIDIC SOLUTIONS
060101	sulphuric acid and sulphurous acid
060102	hydrochloric acid
060103	hydrofluoric acid
060104	phosphoric and phosphorous acid
060105	nitric acid and nitrous acid
060199	waste not otherwise specified
0602	ALKALINE SOLUTIONS
060201	calcium hydroxide
060202	soda
060203	ammonia
060299	wastes not otherwise specified
0603	WASTE SALTS AND THEIR SOLUTIONS
060311	salts and solutions containing cyanides
0604	METAL-CONTAINING WASTES
060402	metallic salts (except 0603)
060403	wastes containing arsenic
060404	wastes containing mercury
060405	wastes containing heavy metals
0607	WASTES FROM HALOGEN CHEMICAL PROCESSES
060701	wastes containing asbestos from electrolysis
060702	activated carbon from chlorine production

Waste code (6 digits)/ Chapter Heading (2 and 4 digits)	Description
0613	WASTES FROM OTHER INORGANIC CHEMICAL PROCESSES
061301	inorganic pesticides, biocides and wood preserving agents
061302	spent activated carbon (except 060702)
07	WASTES FROM ORGANIC CHEMICAL PROCESSES 0701 WASTE FROM THE MANUFACTURE, FORMULATION, SUPPLY AND USE (MFSU) OF BASIC ORGANIC CHEMICALS
070101	aqueous washing liquids and mother liquors
070103	organic halogenated solvents, washing liquids and mother liquors
070104	other organic solvents, washing liquids and mother liquors
070107	halogenated still bottoms and reaction residues
070108	other still bottoms and reaction residues
070109	halogenated filter cakes, spent absorbents
070110	other filter cakes, spent absorbents
0702	WASTE FROM THE MFSU OF PLASTICS, SYNTHETIC RUBBER AND MAN-MADE FIBRES
070201	aqueous washing liquids and mother liquors
070203	organic halogenated solvents, washing liquids and mother liquors
070204	other organic solvents, washing liquids and mother liquors
070207	halogenated still bottoms and reaction residues
070208	other still bottoms and reaction residues
070209	halogenated filter cakes, spent absorbents
070210	other filter cakes, spent absorbents
0703	WASTE FROM THE MFSU FOR ORGANIC DYES AND PIGMENTS (EXCLUDING 0611)
070301	aqueous washing liquids and mother liquors
070303	organic halogenated solvents, washing liquids and mother liquors
070304	other organic solvents, washing liquids and mother liquors
070307	halogenated still bottoms and reaction residues
070308	other still bottoms and reaction residues
070309	halogenated filter cakes, spent absorbents
070310	other filter cakes, spent absorbents
0704	WASTE FROM THE MFSU FOR ORGANIC PESTICIDES (EXCEPT 020105)
070401	aqueous washing liquids and mother liquors
070403	organic halogenated solvents, washing liquids and mother liquors
070404	other organic solvents, washing liquids and mother liquors
070407	halogenated still bottoms and reaction residues
070408	other still bottoms and reaction residues
070409	halogenated filter cakes, spent absorbents

Waste code (6 digits)/ Chapter Heading (2 and 4 digits)	Description
070410	other filter cakes, spent absorbents
0705	WASTE FROM THE MFSU OF PHARMACEUTICALS
070501	aqueous washing liquids and mother liquors
070503	organic halogenated solvents, washing liquids and mother liquors
070504	other organic solvents, washing liquids and mother liquors
070507	halogenated still bottoms and reaction residues
070508	other still bottoms and reaction residues
070509	halogenated filter cakes, spent absorbents
070510	other filter cakes, spent absorbents
0706	WASTE FROM THE MFSU OF FATS, GREASE, SOAPS, DETERGENTS, DISINFECTANTS AND COSMETICS
070601	aqueous washing liquids and mother liquors
070603	organic halogenated solvents, washing liquids and mother liquors
070604	other organic solvents, washing liquids and mother liquors
070607	halogenated still bottoms and reaction residues
070608	other still bottoms and reaction residues
070609	halogenated filter cakes, spent absorbents
070610	other filter cakes, spent absorbents
0707	WASTE FROM THE MFSU OF FINE CHEMICALS AND CHEMICAL PRODUCTS NOT OTHERWISE SPECIFIED
070701	aqueous washing liquids and mother liquors
070703	organic halogenated solvents, washing liquids and mother liquors
070704	other organic solvents, washing liquids and mother liquors
070707	halogenated still bottoms and reaction residues
070708	other still bottoms and reaction residues
070709	halogenated filter cakes, spent absorbents
070710	other filter cakes, spent absorbents
08	WASTES FROM THE MANUFACTURE, FORMULATION, SUPPLY AND USE (MFSU) OF COATINGS (PAINTS, VARNISHES AND VITREOUS ENAMELS), ADHESIVE, SEALANTS AND PRINTING INKS
0801	WASTES FROM MFSU OF PAINT AND VARNISH
080101	waste paints and varnish containing halogenated solvents
080102	waste paints and varnish free of halogenated solvents
080106	sludges from paint or varnish removal containing halogenated solvents
080107	sludges from paint or varnish removal free of halogenated solvents
0803	WASTES FROM MFSU OF PRINTING INKS
080301	waste ink containing halogenated solvents
080302	waste ink free of halogenated solvents

Waste code (6 digits)/ Chapter Heading (2 and 4 digits)	Description
080305	ink sludges containing halogenated solvents
080306	ink sludges free of halogenated solvents
0804	WASTES FROM MFSU OF ADHESIVE AND SEALANTS (INCLUDING WATER-PROOFING PRODUCTS)
080401	waste adhesives and sealants containing halogenated solvents
080402	waste adhesives and sealants free of halogenated solvents
080405	adhesives and sealants sludges containing halogenated solvents
080406	adhesives and sealants sludges free of halogenated solvents
09	WASTES FROM THE PHOTOGRAPHIC INDUSTRY
0901	WASTES FROM PHOTOGRAPHIC INDUSTRY
090101	water based developer and activator solutions
090102	water based offset plate developer solutions
090103	solvent based developer solutions
090104	fixer solutions
090105	bleach solutions and bleach fixer solutions
090106	waste containing silver from on-site treatment of photographic waste
10	INORGANIC WASTES FROM THERMAL PROCESSES
1001	WASTES FROM POWER STATION AND OTHER COMBUSTION PLANTS (EXCEPT 1900)
100104	oil fly ash
100109	sulphuric acid
1003	WASTES FROM ALUMINIUM THERMAL METALLURGY
100301	tars and other carbon-containing wastes from anode manufacture
100303	skimmings
100304	primary smelting slags/white drosses
100307	spent pot lining
100308	salt slags from secondary smelting
100309	black drosses from secondary smelting
100310	waste from treatment of salt slags and black drosses treatment
1004	WASTES FROM LEAD THERMAL METALLURGY
100401	slags (1st and 2nd smelting)
100402	dross and skimmings (1st and 2nd smelting)
100403	calcium arsenate
100404	flue gas dust
100405	other particulates and dust
100406	solid waste from gas treatment
100407	sludges from gas treatment

Waste code (6 digits)/ Chapter Heading (2 and 4 digits)	Description
1005	WASTES FROM ZINC THERMAL METALLURGY
100501	slags (1st and 2nd smelting)
100502	dross and skimmings (1st and 2nd smelting)
100503	flue gas dust
100505	solid waste from gas treatment
100506	sludges from gas treatment
1006	WASTES FROM COPPER THERMAL METALLURGY
100603	flue gas dust
100605	waste from electrolytic refining
100606	solid waste from gas treatment
100607	sludges from gas treatment
11	INORGANIC WASTE WITH METALS FROM METAL TREATMENT AND THE COATING OF METALS; NON FERROUS HYDRO-METALLURGY
1101	LIQUID WASTES AND SLUDGES FROM METAL TREATMENT AND COATING OF METALS (e.g. GALVANIC PROCESSES, ZINC COATING PROCESSES, PICKLING PROCESSES, ETCHING, PHOSPHATIZING, ALKALINE DE-GREASING)
110101	cyanidic (alkaline) wastes containing heavy metals other than chromium
110102	cyanidic (alkaline) wastes which do not contain heavy metals
110103	cyanide-free wastes containing chromium
110105	acidic pickling solutions
110106	acids not otherwise specified
110107	alkalis not otherwise specified
110108	phosphatizing sludges
1102	WASTES AND SLUDGES FROM NON-FERROUS HYDROMETALLURGICAL PROCESSES
110202	sludges from zinc hydrometallurgy (including jarosite, goethite)
1103	SLUDGES AND SOLIDS FROM TEMPERING PROCESSES
110301	wastes containing cyanide
110302	other wastes
12	WASTES FROM SHAPING AND SURFACE TREATMENT OF METALS AND PLASTICS
1201	WASTES FROM SHAPING (INCLUDING FORGING, WELDING, PRESSING, DRAWING, TURNING, CUTTING AND FILING)
120106	waste machining oils containing halogens (not emulsioned)
120107	waste machining oils free of halogens (not emulsioned)
120108	waste machining emulsions containing halogens
120109	waste machining emulsions free of halogens
120110	synthetic machining oils

Waste code (6 digits)/ Chapter Heading (2 and 4 digits)	Description
120111	machining sludges
120112	spent waxes and fats
1203	WASTES FROM WATER AND STEAM DEGREASING PROCESSES (EXCEPT 1100)
120301	aqueous washing liquids 120302 steam degreasing wastes
13	OIL WASTES (EXCEPT EDIBLE OILS, 0500 AND 1200)
1301	WASTE HYDRAULIC OILS AND BRAKE FLUIDS
130101	hydraulic oils, containing PCBs or PCTs
130102	other chlorinated hydraulic oils (not emulsions)
130103	non-chlorinated hydraulic oils (not emulsions)
130104	chlorinated emulsions
130105	non-chlorinated emulsions
130106	hydraulic oils containing only mineral oil
130107	other hydraulic oils
130108	brake fluids
1302	WASTE ENGINE, GEAR AND LUBRICATING OILS
130201	chlorinated engine, gear and lubricating oils
130202	non-chlorinated engine, gear and lubricating oils
130203	other machine, gear and lubricating oils
1303	WASTE INSULATING AND HEAT TRANSMISSION OILS AND OTHER LIQUIDS
130301	insulating or heat transmission oils and other liquids containing PCBs or PCTs
130302	other chlorinated insulating and heat transmission oils and other liquids
130303	non-chlorinated insulating and heat transmission oils and other liquids
130304	synthetic insulating and heat transmission oils and other liquids
130305	mineral insulating and heat transmission oils
1304	BILGE OILS 130401 bilge oils from inland navigation
130402	bilge oils from jetty sewers
130403	bilge oils from other navigation
1305	OIL/WATER SEPARATOR CONTENTS
130501	oil/water separator solids
130502	oil/water separator sludges
130503	interceptor sludges
130504	desalter sludges or emulsions
130505	other emulsions
1306	OIL WASTE NOT OTHERWISE SPECIFIED
130601	oil waste not otherwise specified
14	WASTES FROM ORGANIC SUBSTANCES EMPLOYED AS SOLVENTS (EXCEPT 0700 AND 0800)

Waste code (6 digits)/ Chapter Heading (2 and 4 digits)	Description
1401	WASTES FROM METAL DEGREASING AND MACHINERY MAINTENANCE
140101	chlorofluorocarbons
140102	other halogenated solvents and solvent mixes
140103	other solvents and solvent mixes
140104	aqueous solvent mixes containing halogens
140105	aqueous solvent mixes free of halogens
140106	sludges or solid wastes containing halogenated solvents
140107	sludges or solid wastes free of halogenated solvents
1402	WASTES FROM TEXTILE CLEANING AND DEGREASING OF NATURAL PRODUCTS
140201	halogenated solvents and solvent mixes
140202	solvent mixes or organic liquids free of halogenated solvents
140203	sludges or solid wastes containing halogenated solvents
140204	sludges or solid wastes containing other solvents
1403	WASTES FROM THE ELECTRONIC INDUSTRY
140301	chlorofluorocarbons
140302	other halogenated solvents
140303	solvents and solvent mixes free of halogenated solvents
140304	sludges or solid wastes containing halogenated solvents
140305	sludges or solid wastes containing other solvents
1404	WASTES FROM COOLANTS, FOAM/AEROSOL PROPELLANTS
140401	chlorofluorocarbons
140402	other halogenated solvents and solvent mixes
140403	other solvents and solvent mixes
140404	sludges or solid wastes containing halogenated solvents
140405	sludges or solid wastes containing other solvents
1405	WASTES FROM SOLVENT AND COOLANT RECOVERY (STILL BOTTOMS)
140501	chlorofluorocarbons
140502	halogenated solvents and solvent mixes
149503	other solvents and solvent mixes
140504	sludges containing halogenated solvents
140505	sludges containing other solvents
16	WASTES NOT OTHERWISE SPECIFIED IN THE CATALOGUE
1602	DISCARDED EQUIPMENT AND SHREDDER RESIDUES
160201	transformers and capacitors containing PCBs or PCTs
1604	WASTE EXPLOSIVES
160401	waste ammunition

Waste code (6 digits)/ Chapter Heading (2 and 4 digits)	Description
160402	fireworks waste
160403	other waste explosives
1606	BATTERIES AND ACCUMULATORS
160601	lead batteries
160602	Ni-Cd batteries
160603	mercury dry cells
160606	electrolyte from batteries and accumulators
1607	WASTE FROM TRANSPORT AND STORAGE TANK CLEANING (EXCEPT 0500 AND 1200)
160701	waste from marine transport tank cleaning, containing chemicals
160702	waste from marine transport tank cleaning, containing oil
160703	waste from railway and road transport tank cleaning, containing oil
160704	waste from railway and road transport tank cleaning, containing chemicals
160705	waste from storage tank cleaning, containing chemicals 160706 waste from storage tank cleaning, containing oil
17	CONSTRUCTION AND DEMOLITION WASTE (INCLUDING ROAD CONSTRUCTION)
1706	INSULATION MATERIALS
170601	insulation materials containing asbestos
18	WASTES FROM HUMAN OR ANIMAL HEALTH CARE AND/OR RELATED RESEARCH (EXCLUDING KITCHEN AND RESTAURANT WASTES WHICH DO NOT ARISE FROM IMMEDIATE HEALTH CARE)
1801	WASTE FROM NATAL CARE, DIAGNOSIS, TREATMENT OR PREVENTION OF DISEASE IN HUMANS
180103	other wastes whose collection and disposal is subject to special requirements in view of the prevention of infection
1802	WASTE FROM RESEARCH, DIAGNOSIS, TREATMENT OR PREVENTION OF DISEASE INVOLVING ANIMALS
180202	other wastes whose collection and disposal is subject to special requirements in view of the prevention of infection
180204	discarded chemicals
19	WASTES FROM WASTE TREATMENT FACILITIES, OFF-SITE WASTE WATER TREATMENT PLANTS AND THE WATER INDUSTRY
1901	WASTES FROM INCINERATION OR PYROLYSIS OF MUNICIPAL AND SIMILAR COMMERCIAL, INDUSTRIAL AND INSTITUTIONAL WASTES
190103	fly ash
190104	boiler dust
190105	filter cake from gas treatment
190106	aqueous liquid waste from gas treatment and other aqueous liquid wastes
190107	solid waste from gas treatment

Waste code (6 digits)/ Chapter Heading (2 and 4 digits)	Description
190110	spent activated carbon from flue gas treatment
1902	WASTES FROM SPECIFIC PHYSICO/CHEMICAL TREATMENTS OF INDUSTRIAL WASTES (e.g. DECHROMATATION, DECYANIDATION, NEUTRALIZATION)
190201	metal hydroxide sludges and other sludges from metal insolubilization treatment
1904	VITRIFIED WASTES AND WASTES FROM VITRIFICATION
190402	fly ash and other flue gas treatment wastes
190403	non-vitrified solid phase
1908	WASTES FROM WASTE WATER TREATMENT PLANTS NOT OTHERWISE SPECIFIED
190803	grease and oil mixture from oil/waste water separation
190806	saturated or spent ion exchange resins
190807	solutions and sludges from regeneration of ion exchangers
20	MUNICIPAL WASTES AND SIMILAR COMMERCIAL, INDUSTRIAL AND INSTITUTIONAL WASTES INCLUDING SEPARATELY COLLECTED FRACTIONS
2001	SEPARATELY COLLECTED FRACTIONS
200112	paint, inks, adhesives and resins
200113	solvents
200117	photo chemicals
200119	pesticides
200121	fluorescent tubes and other mercury containing waste

PART II   HAZARDOUS PROPERTIES

H1 'Explosive': substances and preparations which may explode under the effect of flame or which are more sensitive to shocks or friction than dinitrobenzene.

H2 'Oxidizing': substances and preparations which exhibit highly exothermic reactions when in contact with other substances, particularly flammable substances.

H3–A 'Highly flammable':
— liquid substances and preparations having a flash point below 21°C (including extremely flammable liquids), or
— substances and preparations which may become hot and finally catch fire in contact with air at ambient temperature without any application of energy, or
— solid substances and preparations which may readily catch fire after brief contact with a source of ignition and which continue to burn or to be consumed after removal of the source of ignition, or
— gaseous substances and preparations which are flammable in air at normal pressure, or
— substances and preparations which, in contact with water or damp air, evolve highly flammable gases in dangerous quantities.

H3–B   'Flammable': liquid substances and preparations having a flash point equal to or greater than 21°C and less than or equal to 55°C.

H4   'Irritant': non-corrosive substances and preparations which, through immediate, prolonged or repeated contact with the skin or mucous membrane, can cause inflammation.

H5   'Harmful': substances and preparations which, if they are inhaled or ingested or if they penetrate the skin, may involve limited health risks.

H6   'Toxic': substances and preparations (including very toxic substances and preparations) which, if they are inhaled or ingested or if they penetrate the skin, may involve serious, acute or chronic health risks and even death.

H7   'Carcinogenic': substances and preparations which, if they are inhaled or ingested or if they penetrate the skin, may induce cancer or increase its incidence.

H8   'Corrosive': substances and preparations which may destroy living tissue on contact.

H9   'Infectious': substances containing viable micro-organisms or their toxins which are known or reliably believed to cause disease in man or other living organisms.

H10   'Teratogenic': substances and preparations which, if they are inhaled or ingested or if they penetrate the skin, may induce non-hereditary congenital malformations or increase their incidence.

H11   'Mutagenic': substances and preparations which, if they are inhaled or ingested or if they penetrate the skin, may induce hereditary genetic defects or increase their incidence.

H12   Substances and preparations which release toxic or very toxic gases in contact with water, air or an acid.

H13   Substances and preparations capable by any means, after disposal, of yielding another substance, e.g. a leachate, which possesses any of the characteristics listed above.

H14   'Ecotoxic': substances and preparations which present or may present immediate or delayed risks for one or more sectors of the environment.

PART III   THRESHOLDS FOR CERTAIN HAZARDOUS PROPERTIES

In the waste:

— the total concentration of substances classified as irritant and having assigned to them any of the risk phrases R36 ('irritating to the eyes'), R37 ('irritating to the respiratory system') or R38 ('irritating to the skin') is equal to or greater than 20%;

— the total concentration of substances classified as irritant and having assigned to them the risk phrase R41 ('risk of serious damage to eyes') is equal to or greater than 10%;

— the total concentration of substances classified as harmful is equal to or greater than 25%;

— the total concentration of substances classified as very toxic is equal to or greater than 0.1%;

— the total concentration of substances classified as toxic is equal to or greater than 3%;

— the total concentration of substances classified as carcinogenic and placed by the approved classification and labelling guide in category 1 or 2 of that classification is equal to or greater than 0.1%;

— the total concentration of substances classified as corrosive and having assigned to them the risk phrase R34 ('causes burns') is equal to or greater than 5%; and

— the total concentration of substances classified as corrosive and having assigned to them the risk phrase R35 ('causes severe burns') is equal to or greater than 1%.

[PART IV   RULES FOR THE INTERPRETATION OF THIS SCHEDULE

1. Except in the case of a substance listed in the approved supply list, the test methods to be used for the purposes of deciding which (if any) of the properties mentioned in Part II of this Schedule are to be assigned to a substance are those described in Annex V to Council Directive 67/548/EEC as amended by Commission [Directives 92/69/EEC, 93/21/EEC, 96/54/EEC, 98/73/EC, 2000/32/EC, 2000/33/EC.

2. Any reference in Part III of this Schedule to a substance being classified as having a hazardous property, having assigned to it a particular risk phrase, or being placed within a particular category of a classification is a reference to that substance being so classified, having that risk phrase assigned to it or being placed in that category—

    (i)   in the case of a substance listed in the approved supply list, on the basis of Part [I] of that list;

    (ii) in the case of any other substance, on the basis of the criteria laid down in the approved classification and labelling guide.

3. Any reference in Part III of this Schedule to the total concentration of any substances being equal to or greater than a given percentage is a reference to the proportion by weight of those substances in any waste being equal to or, as the case may be, greater than that percentage.]

Control of Pollution (Applications, Appeals and Registers) Regulations 1996
(SI 1996, No. 2971) (as amended)

1   Citation, commencement and interpretation

(1) These Regulations may be cited as the Control of Pollution (Applications, Appeals and Registers) Regulations 1996 and shall come into force on 31st December 1996.

(2) In these Regulations—

'discharge consent' has the same meaning as in section 91(8) of the Water Resources Act 1991;

'register' means a register maintained by the Agency under section 190 of that Act (pollution control registers).

2   Advertisements

(1) Subject to regulation 4, an application for—

    (a) a discharge consent or the variation of a discharge consent;

    (b) a consent for the purposes of section 89(4)(a) of the Water Resources Act 1991 (consents for the deposit of solid refuse from mines or quarries on land near inland freshwaters); or

    (c) a consent for the purposes of section 90(1) or (2) of that Act (consents for the removal of deposits or for the cutting or uprooting of vegetation in or near inland freshwaters),

shall be advertised in accordance with the following provisions of this regulation and regulation 3.

(2) Notice of the application shall be published—

    (a) in one or more newspapers circulating in—

        (i)   the locality in which the activities which are the subject matter of the application are proposed to be carried on; and

        (ii) the locality in which the controlled waters which may be affected by the proposed activities are situated; and

    (b) in the London Gazette.

(3) Subject to paragraph (4) below, the notice shall—

(a) state the name of the applicant;

(b) Specify where the activities which are the subject matter of the application are proposed to be carried on;

(c) describe briefly the nature of the proposed activities;

(d) state where the register containing information about the application may be inspected, the times at which the register is open for inspection and that the register may be inspected free of charge; and

(e) explain that any person may make representations in writing to the Agency, specify when the period allowed for making representations ends and give the address of the Agency to which representations are to be sent.

(4) Nothing in paragraph (3) above shall require the disclosure of any information which is not to be included in a register by virtue of section 191A or 191B of the Water Resources Act 1991 (exclusion from registers of information affecting national security and of certain confidential information).

3   Timing of advertisements

(1) An application to which regulation 2, applies shall be advertised in accordance with paragraph (2) of that regulation within the period of 28 days beginning 14 days after the relevant date.

(2) Subject to paragraphs (3) to (5) below, the relevant date in relation to an application shall be the date on which the application is received by the Agency.

(3) In a case where the Agency has notified the applicant within 14 days of the receipt of the application that it refuses to proceed with the application until information required by section 90A(4) of, or paragraph 1(3) or (4) of Schedule 10 to, the Water Resources Act 1991 (duty to provide Agency with information) is provided, the relevant date shall be the date on which the Agency is finally provided with the information required.

(4) In a case where a matter falls to be determined under section 191A of the Water Resources Act 1991 (exclusion from registers of information affecting national security), the relevant date shall be the date on which the Secretary of State notifies the applicant of his determination.

(5) In a case where a matter falls to be determined under section 191B of the Water Resources Act 1991 (exclusion from registers of certain confidential information), the relevant date shall be—

(a) if the Agency is treated by virtue of section 191B(3) of that Act as having determined that the information in question is commercially confidential, the date on which the period of 14 days mentioned in section 191B(3) expires;

(b) if the Agency determines under section 191B(2) or (4) of that Act that the information in question is commercially confidential, the date on which the Agency notifies the applicant of its determination;

(c) if the Agency determines under section 191B(2) or (4) of that Act that the information in question is not commercially confidential—

(i) the date on which the period for appealing expires without an appeal having been made;

(ii) the date on which the Secretary of State notifies the applicant of his final determination of the appeal; or

(iii) the date on which the appeal is withdrawn.

(6) Where the relevant date for the purposes of this regulation in relation to an application is later than the date on which the application is received, a period of four months beginning with the relevant date shall be substituted for the period of four months specified in paragraph 3(2) of Schedule 10 to the Water Resources Act 1991 (failure to determine application within four months or longer period agreed with applicant).

4   Exemption from advertising requirements

The Agency may determine that an application is not required to be advertised if it appears to the Agency that it is appropriate to dispense with advertising the application because—

(a) section 191A of the Water Resources Act 1991 (exclusion from registers of information affecting national security) applies; or

(b) the Agency considers that the activities which are the subject matter of the application are unlikely to have an appreciable effect on controlled waters in the locality in which those activities are proposed to be carried on; or

(c) the application is made before 1st April 1997 and it relates to discharges of a kind which the applicant, or a predecessor of his, was authorised to make by virtue of a consent to which paragraph 21 of Schedule 23 to the Environment Act 1995 applied but notice in accordance with sub-paragraph (2)(b)(ii) of that paragraph was not given by him or his predecessor,

and, in any case where the Agency so determines, the application shall be exempt from the requirements of section 90A(1)(b) of, or, as the case may be, paragraph 1(1)(b) of Schedule 10 to, the Water Resources Act 1991 (requirement to advertise applications).

5   Consultation

(1) Subject to paragraph (3) below, the persons to be consulted under paragraph 2 of Schedule 10 to the Water Resources Act 1991 (consultation in connection with applications) in relation to an application for, or for the variation of, a discharge consent are—

(a) every local authority or water undertaker within whose area any of the proposed discharges are to be made;

(b) each of the Ministers if any of the proposed discharges are to be made into coastal waters, relevant territorial waters or waters outside the seaward limits of relevant territorial waters;

(c) the harbour authority within the meaning of section 57(1) of the Harbours Act 1964 if any of the proposed discharges are to be made into a harbour managed by the authority; and

(d) the local fisheries committee, if any of the proposed discharges are to be made into relevant territorial waters or coastal waters within the sea fisheries district of that committee.

(2) The specified period for notification of those persons under paragraph 2 of Schedule 10 to the Water Resources Act 1991 (consultation in connection with applications) is the period of 14 days beginning with the relevant date and, for this purpose, 'relevant date' has the same meaning as in regulation 3.

(3) The requirements of paragraph 2 of Schedule 10 to the Water Resources Act 1991 (consultation in connection with applications) shall not apply in relation to any of the bodies mentioned in paragraph (1)(a), (c) or (d) above—

(a) in so far as they would require the disclosure of any information which is not to be included in a register by virtue of section 191A or 191B of the Water Resources Act 1991 (exclusion from registers of information affecting national security and of certain confidential information);

(b) in relation to an application for, or for the variation of, a discharge consent which need not be advertised as a result of an exemption under regulation 4.

(4) A period of six weeks beginning with the last date on which the making of the application was advertised in pursuance of paragraph 1(1)(b) of Schedule 10 to the Water Resources Act 1991 shall be substituted for the period specified in paragraph 2(6)(b) of that Schedule (period allowed for making representations).

6   Transmitted applications

(1) The following provisions of this regulation shall apply where an application for, or for the variation of, a discharge consent is transmitted to the Secretary of State under paragraph

5(1) of Schedule 10 to the Water Resources Act 1991 (reference to the Secretary of State of certain applications for consent).

(2) Paragraph 2 of Schedule 10 to the Water Resources Act 1991 (consultation in connection with applications) shall apply subject to the modification that representations made to the Agency within the period allowed for making representations shall, instead of being considered by the Agency, be sent by the Agency to the Secretary of State and shall be considered by him along with any representations made by the Agency.

(3) Any request to be heard by the applicant or the Agency with respect to the application shall be made in writing to the Secretary of State within the period of 28 days beginning with the day on which the applicant is informed by the Agency of the transmission of his application to the Secretary of State.

7 Discharge consents without applications

The provisions of Schedule 1 to these Regulations shall apply where the Agency gives a discharge consent under paragraph 6 of Schedule 10 to the Water Resources Act 1991 (discharge consents without applications).

8 Appeals

(1) A person who wishes to appeal to the Secretary of State under section 91 or 191B(5) of the Water Resources Act 1991 (appeals in respect of consents under Chapter II of Part III and appeals in relation to information which the Agency has determined is not commercially confidential) shall give the Secretary of State notice of the appeal.

(2) The notice of appeal shall—
- (a) specify the grounds of appeal; and
- (b) indicate whether the appellant wishes the appeal to be determined on the basis of a hearing or written representations.

(3) The notice of appeal shall be accompanied by copies of any application, consent, correspondence, decision, notice or other document relevant to the appeal.

(4) At the same time as the appellant gives notice of the appeal to the Secretary of State, the appellant shall send the Agency a copy of his notice of appeal, together with a list of the documents provided to the Secretary of State under paragraph (3) above.

(5) If the appellant wishes at any time to withdraw his appeal he shall do so by notice informing the Secretary of State and shall send a copy of the notice to the Agency.

9 Time limit for bringing appeal

(1) Subject to the following provisions of this regulation, notice of appeal in accordance with regulation 8(1) shall be given—
- (a) in the case of an appeal against the revocation of a consent, before the revocation takes effect;
- (b) in the case of an appeal against an enforcement notice, before the expiry of the period of 21 days beginning with the date on which the enforcement notice is received;
- (c) in the case of an appeal against a determination under section 191B(2) or (4) of the Water Resources Act 1991 (exclusion from registers of certain confidential information) that information is not commercially confidential, before the expiry of the period of 21 days beginning with the date on which the appellant is notified of the determination; and
- (d) in any other case, before the expiry of the period of three months beginning with—
  - (i) the date on which the appellant is notified of the decision which is the subject matter of the appeal; or
  - (ii) if paragraph 3(2) of Schedule 10 to the Water Resources Act 1991 (failure to determine application within 4 months or longer period agreed with

applicant) applies, the date on which the applicable period under paragraph 3(2) expires.

(2) Subject to paragraph (3) below, the Secretary of State may allow notice of appeal to be given after the expiry of the relevant period mentioned in paragraph (1) above.

(3) Paragraph (2) above shall not apply in the case of an appeal against—

(a) a decision to revoke a discharge consent;

(b) a decision to modify the conditions of any such consent;

(c) a decision to provide that any such consent which was unconditional shall be subject to conditions;

(d) a determination under section 191B(2) or (4) of the Water Resources Act 1991 (exclusion from registers of certain confidential information) that information is not commercially confidential.

10   Action upon receipt of notice of appeal

(1) Subject to paragraph (5) below, the Agency shall, within 14 days of receipt of the copy of the notice of appeal in accordance with regulation 8(4)—

(a) in the case of an appeal against a decision—

(i) to revoke a discharge consent; or

(ii) to modify the conditions of any such consent, or to provide that any such consent which was unconditional shall be subject to conditions, unless in either case the decision was made in response to an application for a variation,

give notice of the appeal to any person who appears to the Agency likely to have a particular interest in its subject matter; and

(b) in any other case give notice of the appeal—

(i) to any person who made representations or objections to the Agency with respect to the grant or variation of the consent; and

(ii) to any person who was required to be consulted in relation to the grant or variation of the consent under paragraph 2(1) or 6(4) of Schedule 10 to the Water Resources Act 1991 pursuant to regulation 5(1) or paragraph 3(1) of Schedule 1 to these Regulations.

(2) A notice under paragraph (1) above shall—

(a) inform the person on whom it is served that an appeal to the Secretary of State has been made; and

(b) state—

(i) that any representations made to the Secretary of State in writing by the recipient of the notice will be considered by the Secretary of State if they are made within the period of 21 days beginning with the date of receipt of the notice;

(ii) that copies of the representations will be sent to the appellant and the Agency;

(iii) that copies of the representations will be placed on registers maintained under section 190 of the Water Resources Act 1991 (pollution control registers);

(iv) that any person who makes any such representations will be informed about the hearing of the appeal if there is to be a hearing held wholly or partly in public, and shall be accompanied by a copy of the notice of appeal.

(3) The Agency shall, within 14 days of sending a notice under paragraph (1) above, notify the Secretary of State of the name and address of every person who was sent such a notice in relation to the appeal and the date on which it was sent.

(4) Where an appeal is withdrawn after a notice under paragraph (1) above has been sent, the Agency shall inform every person who was sent such a notice in relation to the appeal.

(5) This regulation shall not apply in relation to an appeal under section 91(1)(h) or 191B(5) of the Water Resources Act 1991 (appeals against enforcement notices and appeals against determinations that information is not commercially confidential).

11 Written representations

(1) Where the appellant informs the Secretary of State that he wishes the appeal to be disposed of on the basis of written representations, the Agency shall submit any written representations to the Secretary of State—

    (a) in the case of an appeal against an enforcement notice, not later than 14 days after receiving a copy of the notice of appeal in accordance with regulation 8(4); and

    (b) in all other cases, not later than 28 days after receiving a copy of the notice of appeal in accordance with regulation 8(4).

(2) The appellant shall make any further representations by way of reply not later than 14 days after receiving the Agency's representations under paragraph (1) above.

(3) The Secretary of State shall send to the appellant and the Agency copies of any representations made to him in relation to the appeal under regulation 10 and shall allow them each a period of 14 days from the date of the receipt of those copies in which to make representations thereon.

(4) The Secretary of State may in any particular case—

    (a) set shorter or longer time limits than those mentioned in this regulation;

    (b) allow the parties to make representations in addition to those mentioned in paragraphs (1) to (3) above.

(5) Any representations made by a party to the appeal shall be dated with the date on which they are submitted to the Secretary of State.

(6) Where either party to the appeal submits any representations to the Secretary of State they shall at the same time send a copy to the other party.

12 Hearings

(1) The Secretary of State shall give the appellant and the Agency at least 28 days notice (unless they agree to a shorter period of notice) of the date, time and place fixed for a hearing in relation to an appeal under section 91 or 191B(5) of the Water Resources Act 1991 (appeals in respect of consents under Chapter II of Part III and appeals in relation to information which the Agency has determined is not commercially confidential).

(2) Subject to paragraph (4) and (5) below, in the case of a hearing which is to be held wholly or partly in public, the Secretary of State shall, at least 21 days before the date fixed for the hearing—

    (a) publish a copy of the notice given under paragraph (1) above in a newspaper circulating in the locality which he considers may be affected by any matter which falls to be determined in relation to the appeal; and

    (b) serve a copy of the notice given under paragraph (1) above on every person who has made representations or objections in writing to the Secretary of State under regulation 10 in relation to the appeal.

(3) The Secretary of State may vary the date fixed for the hearing and paragraphs (1) and (2) above shall apply, with necessary modifications, to the variation of the date.

(4) The Secretary of State may also vary the time or place for the holding of a hearing but shall give such notice of any such variation as appears to him to be reasonable.

(5) Paragraph (2) above shall not apply in the case of a hearing in relation to an appeal under section 191B(5) of the Water Resources Act 1991 (appeals in relation to information which the Agency has determined is not commercially confidential).

(6) The persons entitled to be heard at a hearing are—

    (a) the appellant;

    (b) the Agency; and

    (c) any person required under regulation 10(1)(b)(ii) to be notified of the appeal.

(7) Nothing in paragraph (6) above shall prevent the person appointed to conduct the hearing of the appeal from permitting any other person to be heard at the hearing and such permission shall not be unreasonably withheld.

(8) After the conclusion of a hearing, the person appointed to conduct the hearing shall, unless he was appointed under section 114(1)(a) of the Environment Act 1995 (power of Secretary of State to delegate his functions of determining appeals), make a report in writing to the Secretary of State which shall include his conclusions and his recommendations or his reasons for not making any recommendations.

13   Notification of determination

(1) The Secretary of State shall notify the appellant in writing of his determination of the appeal and shall provide him with a copy of any report mentioned in regulation 12(8).

(2) The Secretary of State shall at the same time send—

(a) a copy of the documents mentioned in paragraph (1) above to the Agency and to any persons required under regulation 10(1)(b)(ii) to be notified of the appeal; and

(b) a copy of his determination of the appeal to any other person who made representations to the Secretary of State under regulation 10 and, if a hearing was held, to any other person who made representations in relation to the appeal at the hearing.

14   Consents for discharges by the Agency

(1) Section 88 of the Water Resources Act 1991 (defence to principal offences in respect of authorised discharges) shall have effect in relation to cases in which consents for the purposes of subsection (1)(a) of that section are required by the Agency as if for subsection (2) there were substituted—

'(2) Schedule 2 to the Control of Pollution (Applications, Appeals and Registers) Regulations 1996 shall apply with respect to the making of applications by the Agency for consents under this Chapter for the purposes of subsection (1)(a) above and with respect to the giving, revocation and modification of such consents.'

(2) Schedule 2 to these Regulations (which deals with consents for discharges by the Agency) shall have effect.

15   Pollution control registers

Subject to sections 191A and 191B of the Water Resources Act 1991 and regulations 16 and 17, registers maintained by the Agency under section 190 of that Act (pollution control registers) shall contain full particulars of—

(a) notices of water quality objectives and other notices served under section 83 of that Act;

(b) applications made for consents, or for the variation of consents, under Chapter II of Part III of that Act, together with information provided in connection with such applications;

(c) consents given under that Chapter, the conditions to which the consents are subject and any variation of the consents;

(d) the date and time of each sample of water or effluent taken by the Agency for the purposes of the water pollution provisions of that Act (including details of the place where it was taken) and the result of the analysis of each sample and the steps, if any, taken in consequence by the Agency;

(e) information corresponding to that mentioned in paragraph (d) above with respect to samples of water or effluent taken by any other person, and the analysis of those samples, acquired by the Agency from that person under arrangements made by the Agency for the purposes of any of the water pollution provisions of that Act, including any steps taken by that person in consequence of the results of the analysis of any sample;

(f) prohibition notices served under section 86(1) of that Act;

(g) enforcement notices served under section 90B of that Act;

(h) revocations of discharge consents under paragraph 7 of Schedule 10 to that Act;

(i) notices of appeal under section 91 of that Act, correspondence provided to the Secretary of State under regulation 8(3), the decisions or notices which are the subject matter of the appeals, representations made under regulation 10, written notifications of the Secretary of State's determination of appeals and reports accompanying any such notification;

(j) directions given by the Secretary of State in relation to the Agency's functions under the water pollution provisions of that Act, with the exception of directions under section 191A(2) of that Act (directions in relation to information affecting national security);

(k) convictions, for offences under Part III of that Act, of persons who have the benefit of discharge consents, including the name of the offender, the date of conviction, the penalty imposed, the costs, if any, awarded against the offender and the name of the Court;

(l) returns and other information about the nature, origin, composition, temperature, volume and rate of discharges provided to the Agency in pursuance of conditions of discharge consents; and

(m) information which was entered on the registers under the Control of Pollution (Registers) Regulations 1989.

[(n) works notices under section 161A of the Act;

(o) notices of appeal under section 161C of the Act, documents provided to the Secretary of State in connection with appeals under that section, written notifications of the determinations of such appeals and any report accompanying any such written notification; and

(p) any conviction of any person for any offence under section 161D of the Act, including the name of the offender, the date of conviction, the penalty imposed, the costs, if any, awarded against the offender, and the name of the court.]

16 Entry of particulars on register, removal of certain particulars and indexing of registers

(1) Subject to sections 191A and 191B of the Water Resources Act 1991 and paragraph (2) below, where registers are by virtue of regulation 15 to contain any particulars, those particulars shall be entered on the registers—

(a) if they relate to an application or notice which is to be advertised under regulation 2(2), paragraph 1(1) of Schedule 1 or paragraph 1(2) of Schedule 2, before the beginning of the period of 28 days during which the application or notice is required to be advertised;

(b) if they relate to an enforcement notice served under section 90B of that Act, not later than 7 days after it is served;

[(ba) if they relate to a works notice under section 161A of the Act, not later than 7 days after the notice is served;

(bb) if they relate to any matters mentioned in regulation 15(o), not later than 14 days after those particulars become available to the Agency;]

(c) in all other cases, not later than 28 days after those particulars become available to the Agency.

(2) Where an application for a consent, or for the variation of a consent, is withdrawn at any time before it is determined—

(a) no further particulars relating to the application shall be entered on the registers after the application is withdrawn; and

(b) all particulars relating to the application shall be removed from the registers not less than 2 months, and not more than 3 months, after the application is withdrawn.

(3) The Agency shall keep records in each register showing the dates on which particulars are entered on that register.

(4) Each register shall be indexed in a way which facilitates access to particulars entered on it.

17   Period after which information may be removed from pollution control registers

(1) Nothing in regulation 15 shall require the Agency to keep on a register—

(a) monitoring information more than four years after that information was entered on the register; or

(b) other information which has been superseded by later information more than four years after that later information was entered on the register.

(2) In this regulation 'monitoring information' means information entered on the register by virtue of regulation 15(d), (e) or (l).

18   Revocation of existing regulations

(1) Subject to paragraph (2) below, the following regulations are hereby revoked—

(a) the Control of Pollution (Consents for Discharges etc.) (Secretary of State Functions) Regulations 1989;

(b) the Control of Pollution (Discharges by the National Rivers Authority) Regulations 1989;

(c) the Control of Pollution (Registers) Regulations 1989.

(2) Subject to paragraph (3) below, nothing in paragraph (1)(a) or (b) above shall affect—

(a) the application of the Control of Pollution (Discharges by the National Rivers Authority) Regulations 1989, and regulations 2 to 6 of the Control of Pollution (Consents for Discharges etc.) (Secretary of State Functions) Regulations 1989, in relation to any application made under paragraph 1 of Schedule 10 to the Water Resources Act 1991 (applications for discharge consents) before 31st December 1996 or any consent given under paragraph 5 of that Schedule (discharge consents granted without applications) before that date; or

(b) the application of regulations 2 and 7 of the Control of Pollution (Consents for Discharges etc.) (Secretary of State Functions) Regulations 1989 (appeals in respect of consents under Chapter II of Part III of that Act), in relation to any appeal under that section made in relation to a decision taken before 31st December 1996.

(3) Paragraph (2)(a) above shall not apply in relation to an application made under paragraph 1 of Schedule 10 to the Water Resources Act 1991 before 31st December 1996 if—

(a) the application relates to discharges of a kind which the applicant, or a predecessor of his, was authorised to make by virtue of a consent to which paragraph 21 of Schedule 23 to the Environment Act 1995 (transitional provisions in relation to discharge consents) applied; and

(b) notice in accordance with sub-paragraph (2)(b)(ii) of that paragraph was not given by him or his predecessor.

Regulation 7   SCHEDULE 1

DISCHARGE CONSENTS WITHOUT APPLICATIONS

1   Advertisements

(1) Notice of any discharge consent given by the Agency under paragraph 6 of Schedule 10 to the Water Resources Act 1991 (discharge consents without applications) shall be published—

(a) in one or more newspapers circulating in—

    (i)   the locality in which the discharges are made; and

    (ii) the locality in which the controlled waters which may be affected by the discharges are situated; and

  (b) in the London Gazette.

(2) Subject to sub-paragraph (3) below, the notice shall—

  (a) state the name of the person to whom the discharge consent was given;

  (b) specify where the discharges are made;

  (c) describe briefly the nature of the discharges;

  (d) state where the register containing information about the discharges may be inspected, the times at which the register is open for inspection and that the register may be inspected free of charge;

  (e) explain that any person may make representations in writing to the Agency, specify when the period allowed for making representations ends and give the address of the Agency to which representations are to be sent.

(3) Nothing in sub-paragraph (1) or (2) above shall require the disclosure of any information which is not to be included in a register by virtue of section 191A or 191B of the Water Resources Act 1991 (exclusion from registers of information affecting national security and of certain confidential information).

2   Timing of advertisements

(1) In the case of any discharge consent to which paragraph 1 above applies, advertisements required by sub-paragraph (1) of that paragraph shall be published within the period of 28 days beginning with the relevant date.

(2) Subject to sub-paragraphs (3) and (4), the relevant date in relation to any such discharge consent shall be the date on which it comes into force.

(3) In a case where a matter falls to be determined under section 191A of the Water Resources Act 1991 (exclusion from registers of information affecting national security), the relevant date shall be the date on which the Secretary of State notifies the applicant of his determination.

(4) In a case where a matter falls to be determined under section 191B of the Water Resources Act 1991 (exclusion from registers of certain confidential information), the relevant date shall be—

  (a) if the Agency determines under section 191B(4) of that Act that the information in question is commercially confidential, the date on which the Agency notifies the applicant of its decision;

  (b) if the Agency determines under section 191B(4) of that Act that the information in question is not commercially confidential—

    (i)   the date on which the period for appealing expires without an appeal having been made;

    (ii) the date on which the Secretary of State notifies the applicant of his final determination of the appeal; or

    (iii) the date on which the appeal is withdrawn.

3   Consultation

(1) Subject to sub-paragraph (4) below, copies of the discharge consent shall be sent, within the period of 28 days beginning with the relevant date, to—

  (a) every local authority or water undertaker within whose area any of the discharges are made;

  (b) each of the Ministers if any of the discharges are made into coastal waters, relevant territorial waters or waters outside the seaward limits of relevant territorial waters;

  (c) the harbour authority within the meaning of section 57(1) of the Harbours Act 1964 if any of the discharges are made into a harbour managed by the authority; and

(d) the local fisheries committee, if any of the discharges are made into relevant territorial waters or coastal waters within the sea fisheries district of that committee.

(2) The Agency need only consider representations or objections under paragraph 6(5) of Schedule 10 to the Water Resources Act 1991 which have not been withdrawn if they were made in writing to the Agency within the period allowed under sub-paragraph (3) below.

(3) The period allowed for making representations or objections is—

(a) in the case of a person who is required to be consulted under sub-paragraph (1) above, the period of six weeks beginning with the date on which a copy of the discharge consent is sent to him; and

(b) in the case of any other person, the period of six weeks beginning with the last date on which the making of the application was advertised under paragraph 1(1) above.

(4) Nothing in sub-paragraph (1) above shall require the disclosure in relation to any of the bodies mentioned in sub-paragraph (1)(a), (c) or (d) of any information which is not to be included in a register by virtue of section 191A or 191B of the Water Resources Act 1991 (exclusion from registers of information affecting national security and of certain confidential information).

(5) In this paragraph, 'the relevant date', in relation to a discharge consent, has the same meaning as it has in paragraph 2 above.

| Regulation 14(2) | SCHEDULE 2 |

SCHEDULE 2

DISCHARGE CONSENTS FOR THE AGENCY

1 Application for consent

(1) An application by the Agency for a consent, for the purposes of section 88(1)(a) of the Water Resources Act 1991, for any discharges shall be made to the Secretary of State in writing accompanied by such information as he may require; and shall be advertised by the Agency in accordance with subparagraphs (2) and (3) below.

(2) Notice of the application shall be published within the period of 28 days beginning with the date on which the application is received—

(a) in one or more newspapers circulating in—

(i) the locality in which the proposed discharges are to be made; and

(ii) the locality in which the controlled waters likely to be affected by the proposed discharges are situated; and

(b) in the London Gazette.

(3) The notice shall—

(a) state that the application is made by the Agency;

(b) specify where the discharges are proposed to be made;

(c) describe briefly the nature of the proposed discharges;

(d) state where the register containing information about the application may be inspected, the times at which the register is open for inspection and that the register may be inspected free of charge; and

(e) explain that any person may make representations in writing to the Secretary of State, specify when the period allowed for making representations ends and give the address of the Secretary of State to which representations are to be sent.

(4) The Secretary of State may give the Agency notice requiring it to provide him with such further information of any description specified in the notice as he may require for the purpose of determining the application.

(5) An application made in accordance with this paragraph which relates to proposed discharges at two or more places may be treated by the Secretary of State as separate applications for consents for discharges at each of those places.

2 Consultation in connection with applications

(1) The Agency shall, within the period of 28 days beginning with the date on which any application under paragraph 1 above is made, give notice of the application, together with a copy of the application, to—

    (a) every local authority or water undertaker within whose area any of the proposed discharges are to be made;

    (b) the Minister if any of the proposed discharges are to be made into coastal or relevant territorial waters, or waters outside the seaward limits of relevant territorial waters, which are in or adjacent to England;

    (c) the harbour authority within the meaning of section 57(1) of the Harbours Act 1964 if any of the proposed discharges are to be made into a harbour managed by the authority; and

    (d) the local fisheries committee, if any of the proposed discharges are to be made into relevant territorial waters or coastal waters within the sea fisheries district of that committee.

(2) Any representations made by any persons within the period allowed under sub-paragraph (3) below and not withdrawn shall be considered by the Secretary of State in determining the application.

(3) The period allowed for making representations is—

    (a) in the case of persons given notice of the application under sub-paragraph (1) above, the period of six weeks beginning with the date on which the notice was given under that sub-paragraph; and

    (b) in the case of other persons, the period of six weeks beginning with the last date on which the making of the application was advertised under paragraph 1(2) above.

3 Consideration and determination of applications

(1) On an application under paragraph 1 above the Secretary of State shall be under a duty, if the requirements of that paragraph and paragraph 2 above are complied with, to consider whether to give the consent applied for, either unconditionally or subject to conditions, or to refuse it.

(2) The conditions subject to which a consent may be given under this paragraph shall be such conditions as the Secretary of State may think fit and, in particular, may include conditions—

    (a) as to the places at which the discharges to which the consent relates may be made and as to the design and construction of any outlets for the discharges;

    (b) as to the nature, origin, composition, temperature, volume and rate of the discharges and as to the periods during which the discharges may be made;

    (c) as to the steps to be taken, in relation to the discharges or by way of subjecting any substance likely to affect the description of matter discharged to treatment or any other process, for minimising the polluting effects of the discharges on any controlled waters;

    (d) as to the provision of facilities for taking samples of the matter discharged and, in particular, as to the provision, maintenance and use of manholes, inspection chambers, observation wells and boreholes in connection with the discharges;

    (e) as to the provision, maintenance and testing of meters for measuring or recording the volume and rate of the discharges and apparatus for determining the nature, composition and temperature of the discharges;

(f) as to the keeping of records of the nature, origin, composition, temperature, volume and rate of the discharges and, in particular, of records of readings of meters and other recording apparatus provided in accordance with any other condition attached to the consent; and

(g) as to the making of returns and the giving of other information to the Secretary of State about the nature, origin, composition, temperature, volume and rate of the discharges;

and it is hereby declared that a consent may be given under this paragraph subject to different conditions in respect of different periods.

(3) Before determining an application, the Secretary of State may, and shall, if the Agency request him to do so—

(a) cause a local inquiry to be held with respect to the application; or

(b) afford the Agency an opportunity of appearing before, and being heard by, a person appointed by the Secretary of State for the purpose.

4 Revocation of consents and alteration and imposition of conditions

(1) The Secretary of State may from time to time review any consent given under paragraph 3 above and the conditions (if any) to which the consent is subject.

(2) Where the Secretary of State has reviewed a consent under this paragraph, he may by a notice served on the Agency—

(a) revoke the consent;

(b) make modifications of the conditions of the consent; or

(c) in the case of an unconditional consent, provide that it shall be subject to such conditions as may be specified in the notice.

5 Applications for variation

(1) The Agency may make an application in writing to the Secretary of State for the variation of a consent given under paragraph 3 above; and any such application shall be accompanied by such information as the Secretary of State may require.

(2) The provisions of paragraphs 1 to 3 above shall apply (with the necessary modifications) to applications under sub-paragraph (1) above, and to the variation of consents in pursuance of such applications, as they apply to applications for, and the grant of, consents.

6 Transfer of consents

(1) A consent under paragraph 3 may be transferred by the Agency to a person who proposes to carry on making the discharges in place of the Agency.

(2) A consent under paragraph 3 above which is transferred to a person under this paragraph shall have effect on and after the date of the transfer as if it had been granted to that person under paragraph 3 of Schedule 10 to the Water Resources Act 1991, subject to such modifications as the Agency may specify in writing.

(3) Where a consent under paragraph 3 above is transferred under sub-paragraph (1) above, the Agency shall give notice of that fact to the Secretary of State.

Waste Management (Miscellaneous Provisions) Regulations 1997

(SI 1997, No. 351)

1 Citation and commencement

(1) These Regulations may be cited as the Waste Management (Miscellaneous Provisions) Regulations 1997 and, except for regulation 2, shall come into force on 1st April 1997.

(2) Regulation 2 shall come into force on 14th March 1997.

2 Relevant Offences

An offence shall be a relevant offence for the purposes of section 74(3)(a) of the Environmental Protection Act 1990 (in addition to the offences prescribed by regulation 3 of the Waste Management Licensing Regulations 1994) if it is an offence under paragraph 15(1), (3), (4) or (5) of Schedule 5 to the Finance Act 1996 (landfill tax).

3 ...

Hedgerows Regulations 1997
(SI 1997, No. 1160)

1 Citation and commencement

These Regulations may be cited as the Hedgerows Regulations 1997 and shall come into force on 1st June 1997.

2 Interpretation

(1) In these Regulations—

'the 1990 Act' means the Town and Country Planning Act 1990;

'the 1995 Act' means the Environment Act 1995;

'agriculture' includes horticulture, fruit growing, seed growing, dairy farming, the breeding and keeping of livestock (including any creature kept for the production of food, wool, skins or fur, or for the purposes of its use in the farming of land), the use of land as grazing land, meadow land, osier land, market gardens and nursery grounds, and the use of land for woodlands where that use is ancillary to the farming of land for other agricultural purposes, and 'agricultural' shall be construed accordingly;

'agricultural holding' has the same meaning as in the Agricultural Holdings Act 1986;

'common land' has the same meaning as in the Commons Registration Act 1965, and references to common land include town or village green within the meaning of that Act;

'farm business tenancy' has the same meaning as in the Agricultural Tenancies Act 1995;

'gap', in relation to a hedgerow, means any opening (whether or not it is filled);

'hedgerow removal notice' means a notice under regulation 5(1)(a);

'hedgerow retention notice' means a notice referred to in regulation 5(2);

'local planning authority', except in paragraph 5(b)(ii) of Part II of Schedule 1, means—

(a) as regards land within a National Park, the National Park Authority for that Park,

(b) as regards land within the Broads, within the meaning of the Norfolk and Suffolk Broads Act 1988, the Broads Authority,

(c) as regards the Isles of Scilly, the Council of the Isles of Scilly,

(d) as regards any other land in England, the district planning authority within the meaning of the 1990 Act,

(e) as regards any other land in Wales, the county council or county borough council;

'notice' means notice in writing;

'owner'—

(a) in relation to a hedgerow growing on any land which comprises part of an agricultural holding or which is subject to a farm business tenancy, means the person who owns the freehold of the land or the tenant;

(b) in relation to a hedgerow growing on any other land, means the person who owns the freehold of the land,

and 'owns the freehold' means is entitled, otherwise than as a mortgagee not in possession, to dispose of the fee simple;

'protected land' means—

(a) land managed as a nature reserve in pursuance of section 21 (establishment of nature reserves by local authorities) of the National Parks and Access to the Countryside Act 1949,

(b) land in relation to which a notification under section 28 (areas of special scientific interest) of the Wildlife and Countryside Act 1981 is in force; 'relevant utility operator', in relation to any hedgerow, means—

(a) any person who holds a licence granted under section 6 of the Electricity Act 1989 (power to grant licences for the generation, transmission or supply of electricity) and who wishes to remove or, as the case may be, removes the hedgerow in question for the purpose of carrying out any activity authorised by that licence;

(b) any person who holds a licence granted or treated as granted under section 7 of the Gas Act 1986 (power to grant licences for the conveyance of gas through pipes) and who wishes to remove or, as the case may be, removes the hedgerow in question for the purpose of carrying out any activity authorised by that licence;

(c) any person who holds a licence granted under section 7 of the Telecommunications Act 1984 (power to licence telecommunications systems) which applies to him the telecommunications code contained in Schedule 2 to that Act and who wishes to remove or, as the case may be, removes the hedgerow in question in pursuance of a right conferred by the telecommunications code and in accordance with the provisions of his licence;

(d) a sewerage undertaker or a water undertaker which wishes to remove or, as the case may be, removes the hedgerow in question for the purpose of carrying out its functions, within the meaning of the Water Industry Act 1991.

(2) In these Regulations a reference to a numbered regulation or Schedule is to the regulation in, or Schedule to, these Regulations which is so numbered and a reference in a regulation or Schedule to a numbered paragraph, or in a paragraph to a numbered sub-paragraph, is to a paragraph or sub-paragraph of that regulation, Schedule or paragraph.

(3) Part I of Schedule 1 shall have effect for the purposes of interpretation of that Schedule, and Schedules 2 and 3 shall have effect for the purposes of that Part.

3   Application of Regulations

(1) Subject to paragraph (3), these Regulations apply to any hedgerow growing in, or adjacent to, any common land, protected land, or land used for agriculture, forestry or the breeding or keeping of horses, ponies or donkeys, if—

(a) it has a continuous length of, or exceeding, 20 metres; or

(b) it has a continuous length of less than 20 metres and, at each end, meets (whether by intersection or junction) another hedgerow.

(2) Subject to paragraph (3), a hedgerow is also one to which these Regulations apply if it is a stretch of hedgerow forming part of a hedgerow such as is described in paragraph (1).

(3) These Regulations do not apply to any hedgerow within the curtilage of, or marking a boundary of the curtilage of, a dwelling-house.

(4) A hedgerow which meets (whether by intersection or junction) another hedgerow is to be treated as ending at the point of intersection or junction.

(5) For the purposes of ascertaining the length of any hedgerow—

(a) any gap resulting from a contravention of these Regulations; and

(b) any gap not exceeding 20 metres, shall be treated as part of the hedgerow.

4   Criteria for determining 'important' hedgerows

For the purposes of section 97 (hedgerows) of the Environment Act 1995 and these Regulations, a hedgerow is 'important' if it, or the hedgerow of which it is a stretch,—

(a) has existed for 30 years or more; and

(b) satisfies at least one of the criteria listed in Part II of Schedule 1.

5   Removal of hedgerows

(1) Subject to the exceptions specified in regulation 6, the removal of a hedgerow to which these Regulations apply is prohibited unless—

(a) the local planning authority in whose area the hedgerow is situated or, where it is situated in the area of more than one such authority, the local planning authority in whose area the greater part of the hedgerow is situated, have received from an owner of the hedgerow (subject to paragraph (10)) notice in the form set out in Schedule 4, or a form substantially to the same effect, of his proposal to remove the hedgerow ('hedgerow removal notice') together with the plan and evidence mentioned in the form set out in Schedule 4; and

(b) (i) the authority have given to the person who gave the hedgerow removal notice written notice stating that the hedgerow may be removed; or

    (ii) the period specified in paragraph (6) has expired without the authority having given to that person a hedgerow retention notice stating that the work may not be carried out; and

(c) the removal is carried out in accordance with the proposal specified in the hedgerow removal notice; and

(d) the hedgerow is removed within the period of two years beginning with the date of service of the hedgerow removal notice.

(2) A local planning authority which has received a hedgerow removal notice shall, consistently with paragraph (5) and within the period specified in paragraph (6), decide whether or not to give notice to that person stating that the work or, where the hedgerow removal notice refers to more than one hedgerow, so much of the work as may be specified by the authority in their notice, may not be carried out ('hedgerow retention notice').

(3) Where a hedgerow in respect of which the local planning authority has received a hedgerow removal notice is situated in a parish in England for which there is a parish council, or in a community in Wales for which there is a community council, that authority shall consult that council (or, where there is more than one such council, each of them) on the proposal to remove that hedgerow.

(4) The consultation referred to in paragraph (3) shall be completed before the period specified in paragraph (6) expires and before the giving of a notice under paragraph (1)(b)(i) or a hedgerow retention notice.

(5) A local planning authority—

(a) shall not give a hedgerow retention notice in respect of a hedgerow which is not an 'important' hedgerow;

(b) shall give such a notice, within the period specified in paragraph (6), in respect of an 'important' hedgerow unless satisfied, having regard in particular to the reasons given for its proposed removal in the hedgerow removal notice, that there are circumstances which justify the hedgerow's removal.

(6) The period referred to in paragraphs (1)(b)(ii), (2), (4) and (5)(b) is that of 42 days beginning with the date on which the hedgerow removal notice is received by the local planning authority or such longer period as may be agreed between the person who gave the notice and the authority.

(7) A hedgerow retention notice shall, except where regulation 8(4) applies, specify each criterion (of those listed in Schedule 1) which applies to the hedgerow to which the notice relates.

(8) A hedgerow retention notice may be withdrawn at any time by the local planning authority by giving written notice of the withdrawal to the person to whom the hedgerow retention notice was given.

(9) Where a hedgerow retention notice has been given stating that work relating to a hedgerow may not be carried out, and that notice has not been withdrawn, removal of the hedgerow consisting of or including any such work is prohibited.

(10) Where a hedgerow is or is to be removed by or on behalf of a relevant utility operator from land of which it is not the owner, paragraph (1)(a) shall apply as though the reference to the owner were instead a reference to the relevant utility operator.

6   Permitted work

(1) The removal of any hedgerow to which these Regulations apply is permitted if it is required—

   (a) for making a new opening in substitution for an existing opening which gives access to land, but subject to paragraph (2);

   (b) for obtaining temporary access to any land in order to give assistance in an emergency;

   (c) for obtaining access to land where another means of access is not available or is available only at disproportionate cost;

   (d) for the purposes of national defence;

   (e) for carrying out development for which planning permission has been granted or is deemed to have been granted, except development for which permission is granted by article 3 of the Town and Country Planning General Permitted Development Order 1995 in respect of development of any of the descriptions contained in Schedule 2 to that Order other than Parts 11 (development under local or private Acts or orders) and 30 (toll road facilities);

   (f) for carrying out, pursuant to, or under, the Land Drainage Act 1991, the Water Resources Act 1991 or the Environment Act 1995, work for the purpose of flood defence or land drainage;

   (g) for preventing the spread of, or ensuring the eradication of—

      (i) any plant pest, within the meaning of the Plant Health (Great Britain) Order 1993, in respect of which any action is being, or is to be, taken under Article 22 or 23 of that Order, or

      (ii) any tree pest, within the meaning of the Plant Health (Forestry) (Great Britain) Order 1993, in respect of which any action is being, or is to be, taken under Article 21 or 22 of that Order;

   (h) for the carrying out by the Secretary of State of his functions in respect of any highway for which he is the highway authority or in relation to which, by virtue of section 4(2) of the Highways Act 1980, he has the same powers under that Act as the local highway authority;

   (i) for carrying out any felling, lopping or cutting back required or permitted as a consequence of any notice given or order made under paragraph 9 of Schedule 4 to the Electricity Act 1989 (felling, lopping or cutting back to prevent obstruction of or interference with electric lines and plant or to prevent danger); or

   (j) for the proper management of the hedgerow.

(2) Where the removal of a hedgerow to which these Regulations apply is permitted by these Regulations only by paragraph (1)(a), the person removing it shall fill the existing opening by planting a hedge within 8 months of the making of the new opening.

(3) The fact that work is permitted under these Regulations does not affect any prohibition or restriction imposed by or under any other enactment or by any agreement.

7   Offences

(1) A person who intentionally or recklessly removes, or causes or permits another person to remove, a hedgerow in contravention of regulation 5(1) or (9) is guilty of an offence.

(2) A person who contravenes or fails to comply with regulation 6(2) is guilty of an offence.

(3) Hedgerows to which these Regulations apply are prescribed for the purposes of section 97(4)(d) of the 1995 Act (which relates to offences triable either way).

(4) A person guilty of an offence under paragraph (1) shall be liable—

   (a) on summary conviction, to a fine not exceeding the statutory maximum; or

   (b) on conviction on indictment, to a fine.

(5) A person guilty of an offence under paragraph (2) shall be liable on summary conviction to a fine not exceeding level 3 on the standard scale.

(6) In determining the amount of any fine to be imposed on a person convicted of an offence under paragraph (1) or (2), the court shall in particular have regard to any financial benefit which has accrued or appears likely to accrue to him in consequence of the offence.

(7) Section 331 (offences by corporations) of the 1990 Act shall apply in relation to offences under paragraph (1) or (2) committed by a body corporate as it applies in relation to offences under that Act committed by a body corporate.

8   Replacement of hedgerows

(1) Subject to regulation 15, where it appears to the local planning authority that a hedgerow has been removed in contravention of regulation 5(1) or (9), the authority may (whether or not proceedings are instituted under regulation 7), give a notice to the owner, requiring him to plant another hedgerow or, where the hedgerow has been removed by or on behalf of a relevant utility operator, give a notice to that operator requiring it to plant another hedgerow.

(2) A notice under paragraph (1) shall specify the species and position of the shrubs, or trees and shrubs, to be planted and the period within which the planting is to be carried out.

(3) Subsections (1), (2) and (6) of section 209 (execution and cost of works required by s. 207 notice) of the 1990 Act shall apply, with the necessary modifications, to shrubs and trees whose planting is required by a notice under paragraph (1) as if they were trees whose planting was required by a notice under subsection (1) of section 207 (enforcement of duties as to replacement of trees) of that Act.

(4) A hedgerow planted in compliance with a notice under paragraph (1) or by virtue of paragraph (3) shall be treated—

(a) for the purposes of these Regulations;

(b) for the period of 30 years beginning with the date of substantial completion of the planting,

as if it were an 'important' hedgerow within the meaning of regulation 4.

9   Appeals

(1) Subject to regulation 15, a person to whom a hedgerow retention notice or a notice under regulation 8(1) is given may, by notice given within 28 days from the date on which the notice was given to him, or such longer period as the Secretary of State may allow, appeal to the Secretary of State.

(2) The notice of appeal shall state the grounds for the appeal and the appellant shall serve a copy of it on the local planning authority which gave the hedgerow retention notice or notice under regulation 8(1).

(3) In determining the appeal the Secretary of State—

(a) may allow or dismiss it, either as to the whole or as to part;

(b) shall give any directions necessary to give effect to his determination, including directions for quashing or modifying any notice,

and he shall notify the appellant and the local planning authority of his determination of the appeal.

(4) Before determining the appeal, the Secretary of State shall afford to the appellant and the local planning authority an opportunity, if they so wish, of appearing before, and being heard by, a person appointed by the Secretary of State for the purpose.

(5) The Secretary of State may cause a local inquiry to be held in connection with an appeal and subsections (2) to (5) of section 250 of the Local Government Act 1972 (local inquiries: evidence and costs) shall apply to any such inquiry.

(6) The Secretary of State shall have the same powers to appoint a person to exercise functions in connection with appeals under this regulation as he is given by section 114 of the

1995 Act in relation to his functions specified in that section; and the provisions of Schedule 20 to that Act shall apply with respect to any such appointment as it applies to appointments under that section.

(7) The Secretary of State and any person appointed by him for any purpose of this regulation shall, except where the appeal is disposed of on the basis of written representations and other documents, have the same power to make orders under section 250(5) of the Local Government Act 1972 (orders with respect to costs of the parties) in relation to proceedings on an appeal under this regulation which do not give rise to an inquiry as he has in relation to an inquiry and section 322A (orders as to costs: supplementary) of the 1990 Act shall apply to proceedings on an appeal under this regulation as if they were proceedings under that Act.

10 Records

Each local planning authority shall compile and keep available for public inspection free of charge at all reasonable hours and at a convenient place a record containing a copy of—

    (a) every hedgerow removal notice received by them;

    (b) every hedgerow retention notice issued by them;

    (c) every notice given by them under regulation 5(1)(b)(i);

    (d) every determination notified to them under regulation 9(3).

11 Injunctions

(1) Where a local planning authority consider it necessary or expedient for an actual or apprehended offence under these Regulations to be restrained by injunction, they may apply to the court for an injunction, whether or not they have exercised or are proposing to exercise any of their other powers under these Regulations.

(2) On an application under paragraph (1) the court may grant such an injunction as the court thinks appropriate for the purpose of restraining the offence.

(3) In this regulation 'the court' means the High Court or the county court.

12 Rights to enter without a warrant

(1) Any person duly authorised in writing by a local planning authority may enter any land for the purpose of—

    (a) surveying it in connection with any hedgerow removal notice received by the authority;

    (b) ascertaining whether an offence under regulation 7 has been committed;

    (c) determining whether a notice should be given under regulation 8, if there are reasonable grounds for entering for the purpose in question.

(2) Any person duly authorised in writing by the Secretary of State may enter any land for the purpose of surveying it in connection with any appeal made under regulation 9, if there are reasonable grounds for entering for that purpose.

(3) Any right to enter by virtue of paragraph (1) or (2) shall be exercised at a reasonable hour.

(4) No right to enter by virtue of paragraph (1)(a) or (2) shall be exercised in relation to land which—

    (a) adjoins that in respect of which a hedgerow removal notice has been given or an appeal made; and

    (b) is occupied by a person other than the person who gave the hedgerow removal notice or made the appeal,

unless at least 24 hours' notice of the intended entry has been given to the occupier of that adjoining land.

(5) In a case to which regulation 5(10) applies, no right to enter any land by virtue of paragraph (1)(a) or (2) shall be exercised unless at least 24 hours' notice of the intended entry has been given to the occupier of the land.

13   Right to enter under warrant

(1) If it is shown to the satisfaction of a justice of the peace on sworn information in writing—

(a) that there are reasonable grounds for entering any land for any of the purposes mentioned in regulation 12(1) or (2); and

(b) that—

(i) admission to the land has been refused, or a refusal is reasonably apprehended; or

(ii) the case is one of urgency,

the justice may issue a warrant authorising any person duly authorised in writing by a local planning authority or, as the case may be, the Secretary of State to enter the land.

(2) For the purposes of paragraph (1)(b)(i) admission to land shall be regarded as having been refused if no reply is received to a request for admission within a reasonable period.

(3) A warrant authorises entry on one occasion only and that entry must be—

(a) within one month from the date of the issue of the warrant; and

(b) at a reasonable hour, unless the case is one of urgency.

14   Rights of entry: supplementary provisions

(1) Any power conferred by virtue of regulation 12 or 13 to enter land ('a right of entry') shall be construed as including power to take samples from any hedgerow on the land and samples of the soil.

(2) A person authorised to enter land in the exercise of a right of entry—

(a) shall, if so required, produce evidence of his authority and state the purpose of his entry before so entering;

(b) may take with him such other persons as may be necessary; and

(c) on leaving the land shall, if the occupier is not then present, leave it as effectively secured against trespassers as he found it.

(3) Any person who wilfully obstructs a person acting in the exercise of a right of entry shall be guilty of an offence and liable on summary conviction to a fine not exceeding level 3 on the standard scale.

(4) If any damage is caused to land or chattels in the exercise of a right of entry, compensation may be recovered by any person suffering the damage from the authority who gave the written authority for the entry or, as the case may be, the Secretary of State.

(5) Any question of disputed compensation under this regulation shall be referred to and determined by the Lands Tribunal.

(6) In relation to the determination of any such question, the provisions of sections 2 and 4 of the Land Compensation Act 1961 shall apply subject to any necessary modifications.

15   Local planning authorities as owners of hedgerows

(1) This regulation applies where a local planning authority are the owners (whether alone or jointly with others) of a hedgerow to which these Regulations apply.

(2) Notwithstanding anything in section 101 (arrangements for the discharge of functions by local authorities) of the Local Government Act 1972, a hedgerow removal notice given in a case to which this regulation applies may not be considered—

(a) by a committee or sub-committee of the authority concerned if that committee or sub-committee is responsible (wholly or partly) for the management of the land in which is situated the hedgerow to which the notice relates; or

(b) by an officer of the authority concerned if his responsibilities include any aspect of the management of the land in which is situated the hedgerow to which the notice relates.

(3) Regulations 8 and 9 do not apply in a case to which this regulation applies.

16 Application of other provisions of the 1990 Act

(1) Subsections (1), (3) and (6) of section 318 (ecclesiastical property) of the 1990 Act shall apply—

    (a) to notices required to be served under these Regulations on an owner of land as if those notices were notices required to be served on an owner of land under a provision of the 1990 Act; and

    (b) to compensation payable under regulation 14 of these Regulations as if that compensation were compensation payable under Part IV of the 1990 Act.

(2) Subsections (1), (2) and (4) of section 329 (service of notices) of the 1990 Act shall apply to notices under these Regulations as if those notices were notices required or authorised to be given or served under that Act.

Regulations 2(3) and 4   SCHEDULE 1

ADDITIONAL CRITERIA FOR DETERMINING 'IMPORTANT' HEDGEROWS

PART I   INTERPRETATION

In this Schedule—

'building' includes structure;

'Record Office' means—

    (a) a place appointed under section 4 of the Public Records Act 1958, (place of deposit of public records),

    (b) a place at which documents are held pursuant to a transfer under section 144A(4) of the Law of Property Act 1922 or under section 36(2) of the Tithe Act 1936, including each of those provisions as applied by section 7(1) of the Local Government (Records) Act 1962, or

    (c) a place at which documents are made available for inspection by a local authority pursuant to section 1 of the Local Government (Records) Act 1962;

'relevant date' means the date on which these Regulations are made;

'Sites and Monuments Record' means a record of archaeological features and sites adopted—

    (a) by resolution of a local authority within the meaning of the Local Government Act 1972 or

    (b) in Greater London, by the Historic Buildings and Monuments Commission;

'standard tree'—

    (a) in the case of a multi-stemmed tree, means a tree which, when measured at a point 1.3 metres from natural ground level, has at least two stems whose diameters are at least 15 centimetres;

    (b) in the case of a single-stemmed tree, means a tree which, when measured at a point 1.3 metres from natural ground level, has a stem whose diameter is at least 20 centimetres;

'woodland species' means the species listed in Schedule 2; and

'woody species' means the species and sub-species listed in Schedule 3, and any hybrid, that is to say, any individual plant resulting from a cross between parents of any species or sub-species so listed, but does not include any cultivar; and

references to the documents in paragraph 6(3)(b) and (4) are to those documents as at the relevant date, without taking account of any subsequent revisions, supplements or modifications.

PART II   CRITERIA

1   Archaeology and history

The hedgerow marks the boundary, or part of the boundary, of at least one historic parish or township; and for this purpose 'historic' means existing before 1850.

2.—The hedgerow incorporates an archaeological feature which is—

    (a) included in the schedule of monuments compiled by the Secretary of State under section 1 (schedule of monuments) of the Ancient Monuments and Archaeological Areas Act 1979; or

    (b) recorded at the relevant date in a Sites and Monuments Record.

3.—The hedgerow—

    (a) is situated wholly or partly within an archaeological site included or recorded as mentioned in paragraph 2 or on land adjacent to and associated with such a site; and

    (b) is associated with any monument or feature on that site.

4.—The hedgerow—

    (a) marks the boundary of a pre-1600 AD estate or manor recorded at the relevant date in a Sites and Monuments Record or in a document held at that date at a Record Office; or

    (b) is visibly related to any building or other feature of such an estate or manor.

5.—The hedgerow—

    (a) is recorded in a document held at the relevant date at a Record Office as an integral part of a field system pre-dating the Inclosure Acts; or

    (b) is part of, or visibly related to, any building or other feature associated with such a system, and that system—

        (i)   is substantially complete; or

        (ii) is of a pattern which is recorded in a document prepared before the relevant date by a local planning authority, within the meaning of the 1990 Act, for the purposes of development control within the authority's area, as a key landscape characteristic.

6   Wildlife and landscape

    (1) The hedgerow—

    (a) contains species listed or categorised as mentioned in sub-paragraph (3); or

    (b) is referred to in a record held immediately before the relevant date by a biological record centre maintained by, or on behalf of, a local authority within the meaning of the Local Government Act 1972, and in a form recognised by the Nature Conservancy Council for England, the Countryside Council for Wales or the Joint Nature Conservation Committee, as having contained any such species—

        (i)   in the case of animals and birds, subject to sub-paragraph (2), within the period of five years immediately before the relevant date.

        (ii) in the case of plants, subject to sub-paragraph (2), within the period of ten years immediately before the relevant date;

    (2) Where more than one record referable to the period of five or, as the case may be, ten years before the relevant date is held by a particular biological record centre, and the more (or most) recent record does not satisfy the criterion specified in sub-paragraph (1)(b), the criterion is not satisfied (notwithstanding that an earlier record satisfies it).

    (3) The species referred to in sub-paragraph (1) are those—

    (a) listed in Part I (protection at all times) of Schedule 1 (birds which are protected by special penalties), Schedule 5 (animals which are protected) or Schedule 8 (plants which are protected) to the Wildlife and Countryside Act 1981;

(b) categorised as a declining breeder (category 3) in 'Red Data Birds in Britain' Batten LA, Bibby CJ, Clement P, Elliott GD and Porter RF (Eds.), published in 1990 for the Nature Conservancy Council and the Royal Society for the Protection of Birds (ISBN 0 85661 056 9); or

(c) categorised as 'endangered', 'extinct', 'rare' or 'vulnerable' in Britain in a document mentioned in sub-paragraph (4).

(4) The documents referred to in sub-paragraph (3)(c) are—

(a) of the books known as the British Red Data Books:

1. 'Vascular Plants' Perring FH and Farrell L, 2nd Edition, published in 1983 for the Royal Society for Nature Conservation (ISBN 0 902484 04 4);

2. 'Insects' Shirt DB (Ed.), published in 1987 for the Nature Conservancy Council (ISBN 0 86139 380 5); and

3. 'Invertebrates other than insects' Bratton JH (Ed.), published in 1991 for the Joint Nature Conservation Committee (ISBN 1 873701 00 4); and

(b) of the books known as the Red Data Books of Britain and Ireland: 'Stoneworts' Stewart NF and Church JM, published in 1992 for the Joint Nature Conservation Committee (ISBN 1 873701 24 1).

7.—(1) Subject to sub-paragraph (2), the hedgerow includes—

(a) at least 7 woody species;

(b) at least 6 woody species, and has associated with it at least 3 of the features specified in sub-paragraph (4);

(c) at least 6 woody species, including one of the following—

black-poplar tree (*Populus nigra ssp betulifolia*);

large-leaved lime (*Tilia platyphyllos*);

small-leaved lime (*Tilia cordata*);

wild service-tree (*Sorbus torminalis*); or

(d) at least 5 woody species, and has associated with it at least 4 of the features specified in sub-paragraph (4),

and the number of woody species in a hedgerow shall be ascertained in accordance with sub-paragraph (3).

(2) Where the hedgerow in question is situated wholly or partly in the county (as constituted on 1st April 1997) of the City of Kingston upon Hull, Cumbria, Darlington, Durham, East Riding of Yorkshire, Hartlepool, Lancashire, Middlesbrough, North East Lincolnshire, North Lincolnshire, Northumberland, North Yorkshire, Redcar and Cleveland, Stockton-on-Tees, Tyne and Wear, West Yorkshire or York, the number of woody species mentioned in paragraphs (a) to (d) of sub-paragraph (1) is to be treated as reduced by one.

(3) For the purposes of sub-paragraph (1) (and those of paragraph 8(b))—

(a) where the length of the hedgerow does not exceed 30 metres, count the number of woody species present in the hedgerow;

(b) where the length of the hedgerow exceeds 30 metres, but does not exceed 100 metres, count the number of woody species present in the central stretch of 30 metres;

(c) where the length of the hedgerow exceeds 100 metres, but does not exceed 200 metres, count the number of woody species present in the central stretch of 30 metres within each half of the hedgerow and divide the aggregate by two;

(d) where the length of the hedgerow exceeds 200 metres, count the number of woody species present in the central stretch of 30 metres within each third of the hedgerow and divide the aggregate by three.

(4) The features referred to in sub-paragraph (1)(b) and (d) (which include those referred to in paragraph 8(b)) are—

(a) a bank or wall which supports the hedgerow along at least one half of its length;

(b) gaps which in aggregate do not exceed 10% of the length of the hedgerow;

(c) where the length of the hedgerow does not exceed 50 metres, at least one standard tree;

(d) where the length of the hedgerow exceeds 50 metres but does not exceed 100 metres, at least 2 standard trees;

(e) where the length of the hedgerow exceeds 100 metres, such number of standard trees (within any part of its length) as would when averaged over its total length amount to at least one for each 50 metres;

(f) at least 3 woodland species within one metre, in any direction, of the outermost edges of the hedgerow;

(g) a ditch along at least one half of the length of the hedgerow;

(h) connections scoring 4 points or more in accordance with sub-paragraph (5);

(i) a parallel hedge within 15 metres of the hedgerow.

(5) For the purposes of sub-paragraph (4)(h) a connection with another hedgerow scores one point and a connection with a pond or a woodland in which the majority of trees are broad-leaved trees scores 2 points; and a hedgerow is connected with something not only if it meets it but also if it has a point within 10 metres of it and would meet it if the line of the hedgerow continued.

8.—The hedgerow—

(a) is adjacent to a bridleway or footpath, within the meaning of the Highways Act 1980, a road used as a public path, within the meaning of section 54 (duty to reclassify roads used as public paths) of the Wildlife and Countryside Act 1981, or a byway open to all traffic, within the meaning of Part III of the Wildlife and Countryside Act 1981, and

(b) includes at least 4 woody species, ascertained in accordance with paragraph 7(3) and at least 2 of the features specified in paragraph 7(4)(a) to (g).

Regulation 2(3) and
Schedule 1, Part I

SCHEDULE 2
WOODLAND SPECIES

Barren strawberry (*Potentilla sterilis*)
Bluebell (*Hyacinthoides non-scriptus*)
Broad buckler fern (*Dryopteris dilatata*)
Broad-leaved helleborine (*Epipactis helleborine*)
Bugle (*Ajuga reptans*)
Common cow-wheat (*Melampyrum pratense*)
Common dog violet (*Viola riviniana*)
Common polypody (*Polypodium vulgare*)
Dog's mercury (*Mercurialis perennis*)
Early dog violet (*Viola reichenbachiana*)
Early purple orchid (*Orchis mascula*)
Enchanter's nightshade (*Circaea lutetiana*)
Giant fescue (*Festuca gigantea*)
Goldilocks buttercup (*Ranunculus auricomus*)
Great bell-flower (*Campanula latifolia*)
Greater wood-rush (*Luzula sylvatica*)
Hairy brome (*Bromus ramosus*)
Hairy woodrush (*Luzula pilosa*)
Hard fern (*Blechnum spicant*)

Hard shield fern (*Polystichum aculeatum*)
Hart's tongue (*Asplenium scolopendrium*)
Heath bedstraw (*Galium saxatile*)
Herb paris (*Paris quadrifolia*)
Herb-robert (*Geranium robertianum*)
Lady fern (*Athyrium filix-femina*)
Lords-and-ladies (*Arum maculatum*)
Male fern (*Dryopteris filix-mas*)
Moschatel (*Adoxa moschatellina*)
Narrow buckler-fern (*Dryopteris carthusiana*)
Nettle-leaved bell-flower (*Campanula trachelium*)
Oxlip (*Primula elatior*)
Pignut (*Conopodium majus*)
Primrose (*Primula vulgaris*)
Ramsons (*Allium ursinum*)
Sanicle (*Sanicula europaea*)
Scaly male-fern (*Dryopteris affinis*)
Small cow-wheat (*Melampyrum sylvaticum*)
Soft shield fern (*Polystichum setiferum*)
Sweet violet (*Viola odorata*)
Toothwort (*Lathraea squamaria*)
Tormentil (*Potentilla erecta*)
Wild strawberry (*Fragaria vesca*)
Wood anemone (*Anemone nemorosa*)
Wood avens/Herb bennet (*Geum urbanum*)
Wood false-brome (*Brachypodium sylvaticum*)
Wood horsetail (*Equisetum sylvaticum*)
Wood meadow-grass (*Poa nemoralis*)
Wood melick (*Melica uniflora*)
Wood millet (*Millium effusum*)
Wood sage (*Teucrium scorodonia*)
Wood sedge (*Carex sylvatica*)
Wood sorrel (*Oxalis acetosella*)
Wood speedwell (*Veronica montana*)
Wood spurge (*Euphorbia amygdaloides*)
Woodruff (*Galium odoratum*)
Yellow archangel (*Lamiastrum galeobdolon*)
Yellow pimpernel (*Lysimachia nemorum*)

| **Regulation 2(3) and** | . | SCHEDULE 3 |
| **Schedule 1, Part I** | | WOODY SPECIES |

Alder (*Alnus glutinosa*)
Apple, crab (*Malus sylvestris*)
Ash (*Fraxinus excelsior*)
Aspen (*Populus tremula*)
Beech (*Fagus sylvatica*)
Birch, downy (*Betula pubescens*)
Birch, silver (*Betula pendula*)
Black-poplar (*Populus nigra sub-species betulifolia*)
Blackthorn (*Prunus spinosa*)

Box (*Buxus sempervirens*)
Broom (*Cytisus scoparius*)
Buckthorn (*Rhamnus cathartica*)
Buckthorn, alder (*Frangula alnus*)
Butcher's-broom (*Ruscus aculeatus*)
Cherry, bird (*Prunus padus*)
Cherry, wild (*Prunus avium*)
Cotoneaster, wild (*Cotoneaster integerrimus*)
Currant, downy (*Ribes spicatum*)
Currant, mountain (*Ribes alpinum*)
Dogwood (*Cornus sanguinea*)
Elder (*Sambucus nigra*)
Elm (*Ulmus species*)
Gooseberry (*Ribes uva-crispa*)
Gorse (*Ulex europaeus*)
Gorse, dwarf (*Ulex minor*)
Gorse, western (*Ulex gallii*)
Guelder rose (*Viburnum opulus*)
Hawthorn (*Crataegus monogyna*)
Hawthorn, midland (*Crataegus laevigata*)
Hazel (*Corylus avellana*)
Holly (*Ilex aquilfolium*)
Hornbeam (*Carpinus betulus*)
Juniper, common (*Juniperus communis*)
Lime, large-leaved (*Tilia platyphyllos*)
Lime, small-leaved (*Tilia cordata*)
Maple, field (*Acer campestre*)
Mezereon (*Daphne mezereum*)
Oak, pedunculate (*Quercus robur*)
Oak, sessile (*Quercus petraea*)
Osier (*Salix viminalis*)
Pear, Plymouth (*Pyrus cordata*)
Pear, wild (*Pyrus pyraster*)
Poplar, grey (*Populus x canescens*)
Poplar, white (*Populus alba*)
Privet, wild (*Ligustrum vulgare*)
Rose (*Rosa species*)
Rowan (*Sorbus aucuparia*)
Sea-buckthorn (*Hippophae rhamnnoides*)
Service-tree, wild (*Sorbus torminalis*)
Spindle (*Euonymus europaeus*)
Spurge-laurel (*Daphne laureola*)
Walnut (*Juglans regia*)
Wayfaring-tree (*Viburnum lantana*)
Whitebeam (*Sorbus species*)
Willow (*Salix species*)
Yew (*Taxus baccata*)

SCHEDULE 4

. . .

Air Quality Regulations 1997
(SI 1997, No. 3043)

1 ...

2 Interpretation

(1) In these Regulations, 'the 1995 Act' means the Environment Act 1995.

(2) The provisions of the Schedule to these Regulations which follow the Table in that Schedule shall have effect for the purpose of the interpretation of that Schedule.

3 Relevant period

(1) The relevant period for the purposes of section 86(3) of the 1995 Act shall, in relation to the preparation of an action plan to which that section applies, be the period of 9 months beginning with the date on which the district council preparing the action plan first consults the relevant county council in relation to the plan pursuant to paragraph 1(2)(e) of Schedule 11 to the 1995 Act.

(2) The relevant period for the purposes of the other provisions of Part IV of the 1995 Act shall be the period beginning with the date on which these Regulations come into force and ending on 31st December 2005.

4 Air quality objectives

(1) The air quality objective for each substance listed in the first column of the Table in the Schedule to these Regulations shall be to restrict, by no later than the end of the relevant period prescribed by regulation 3(2), the level at which that substance is present in the air to the level set out in the second column of that Table for that substance.

(2) The achievement or likely achievement of an air quality objective prescribed by paragraph (1) shall be determined by reference to the quality of air at locations which are situated outside of buildings or other natural or man-made structures above or below ground and where members of the public are regularly present.

Regulations 2(2) and 4   SCHEDULE

AIR QUALITY OBJECTIVES

TABLE

Substance	Air Quality Objective levels
Benzene	5 ppb or less, when expressed as a running annual mean
1, 3-Butadiene	1 ppb or less, when expressed as a running annual mean
Carbon Monoxide	10 ppm or less, when expressed as a running 8 hour mean
Lead	0.5 micrograms per cubic metre or less, when expressed as an annual mean
Nitrogen Dioxide	150 ppb or less, when expressed as an hourly mean, and 21 ppb or less, when expressed as an annual mean
PM_{10}	50 micrograms per cubic metre or less, when expressed as the 99th percentile of daily maximum running 24 hour means
Sulphur Dioxide	100 ppb or less, when expressed as the 99.9th percentile of 15 minute means

Interpretation

For the purposes of this Schedule:

1.—'ppb' means parts per 1000 million by volume.

2.—'ppm' means parts per million by volume.

3.—'PM10' means the mass fraction of particles which if inhaled would penetrate beyond the larynx. This mass fraction shall be taken to be the thoracic convention, ET,as defined in ISO 7708:1995(E) 'Air Quality — Particle size fraction definitions for health-related sampling', published by the International Organisation for Standardisation.

4.—(1) A running annual mean is a mean which is calculated on an hourly basis, yielding one running annual mean per hour. The running annual mean for a particular substance at a particular location for a particular hour is the mean of the hourly levels for that substance at that location for that hour and the preceding 8759 hours.

(2) For the purpose of the calculation of a running annual mean, the hourly level for a particular substance at a particular location is either:

 (a) the level at which that substance is recorded as being present in the air at that location during the hour on that basis of a continuous sample of air taken during that hour for at least 30 minutes; or

 (b) the mean of the levels recorded at that location on the basis of 2 or more samples of air taken during the hour for an aggregate period of at least 30 minutes.

5.—A running 8 hour mean is a mean which is calculated on an hourly basis, yielding one running 8 hour mean per hour. The running 8 hour mean for a particular substance at a particular location for a particular hour is the mean of the hourly means for that substance at that location for that hour and the preceding 7 hours.

6.—(1) An annual mean is a mean which is calculated on a yearly basis, yielding one annual mean per calendar year. The annual mean for a particular substance at a particular location for a particular calendar year is:

 (a) in the case of lead, the mean of the daily levels for that year;

 (b) in the case of nitrogen dioxide, the mean of the hourly means for that year.

(2) For the purpose of the calculation of an annual mean, the daily level for a particular substance at a particular location for a particular day is the level at which that substance is recorded as being present in the air at that location during the week in which the day occurs on the basis of a continuous sample of air taken throughout that week (each day in that week therefore being attributed with the same daily level).

(3) For the purpose of paragraph (2) 'week' means a complete week beginning on a Monday, except that it also includes any period of less than seven days from the beginning of the calendar year until the first Monday in that year or from the beginning of the last Monday in the calendar year to the end of that year.

7.—(1) A daily maximum running 24 hour mean is a mean which is calculated on a daily basis, yielding one daily maximum running 24 hour mean per day. The daily maximum running 24 hour mean for a particular substance at a particular location for a particular day is the maximum of the 24 running 24 hour means recorded for that substance at that location during that day.

(2) For the purpose of the calculation of a daily maximum running 24 hour mean—

 (a) a running 24 hour mean is a mean which is calculated on an hourly basis, yielding one running 24 hour mean per hour, and the running 24 hour mean for a particular substance at a particular location for a particular hour is the mean of the hourly means for that substance at that location for that hour and the preceding 23 hours;

 (b) 'day' means the 24 hour period commencing immediately after midnight, Greenwich mean time.

8.—(1) The nth percentile (that is to say the 99th or the 99.9th percentile) is calculated for a calendar year (yielding one result per calendar year) as follows:

Let:

(1) N equal the number of measurements for that calendar year;

(2) k equal—

$$(n \times N)/100$$

rounded to the nearest whole number (or rounded up to the nearest whole number where the fractional part of the number is 0.5); and

(3) the N measurements be listed in ascending order:

$$X_1; X_2; X_3; \ldots X_k; \ldots X_{N-1}; X_N$$

Then: the nth percentile for that calendar year is the value of the measurement listed in the kth position; that is X_k.

(2) For the purpose of the calculation of the nth percentile, the measurements for a calendar year are:

(a) in the case of the 99th percentile of daily maximum running 24 hour means, the 365 daily maximum running 24 hour means for the calendar year in question (or 366 in the case of a leap year);

(b) in the case of the 99.9th percentile of 15 minute means, the 35040 15 minute means for the calendar year in question (or 35136 in the case of a leap year).

9.—A 15 minute mean is a mean calculated every 15 minutes. The 15 minute mean for a particular substance at a particular location for a particular 15 minutes is the mean of the levels recorded, at a frequency of not less than once every 10 seconds, for that substance at that location during that 15 minutes.

10.—An hourly mean is a mean calculated every hour. The hourly mean for a particular substance at a particular location for a particular hour is the mean of the levels recorded, at a frequency of not less than once every 10 seconds, for that substance at that location during that hour.

Mines (Notice Of Abandonment) Regulations 1998
(SI 1998, No. 892)

1   Citation, commencement and interpretation

(1) These Regulations may be cited as the Mines (Notice of Abandonment) Regulations 1998 and shall come into force on 1st July 1998.

(2) In these Regulations references to sections are to sections of the Water Resources Act 1991.

2   Prescribed information

A notice given to the Agency under—

(a) section 91B(1);

(b) section 91B(4)(b); or

(c) section 91B(5);

shall contain the information prescribed in paragraph 1, 2 or 3 respectively of Schedule 1 to these Regulations.

3   Prescribed particulars

Where a person gives a notice referred to in regulation 2 he shall publish in one or more local newspapers circulating in the locality where the mine is situated the particulars prescribed in Schedule 2 to these Regulations.

Regulation 2   SCHEDULE 1

INFORMATION PRESCRIBED UNDER SECTION 91B(1), (4)(b) AND (5)

1 Information for notice of abandonment under section 91B(1)

(1) The name and address of the operator and, if different, the owner of the mine.

(2) Details of any changes to the names and addresses referred to in sub-paragraph (1) above likely to occur before the latest date for any abandonment specified in the notice.

(3) The nature and date of each proposed abandonment, specifying (if relevant) the appropriate sub-paragraph or sub-paragraphs under section 91A(1)(a).

(4) The name and address of the mine, including an Ordnance Survey National Grid Reference for its address.

(5) A description and schematic drawing showing the area, extent and depth below the surface of—

(a) the mine;

(b) where not all of the mine is to be abandoned, that part which it is proposed to abandon;

(c) any relevant seam, vein or vein system; and

(d) any shaft or outlet of the mine.

(6) The volume of water discharged to the surface from the mine, and from any part of the mine, to be abandoned, for the two years prior to the date of the notice.

(7) The latest information available to the operator on the extent and chemical composition of underground water in the worked areas of the mine.

(8) The projected volume of water discharged to the surface from the mine, and from any part of the mine, to be abandoned for the period from the date of the notice to the date of each abandonment specified in it.

(9) Proposals for the monitoring of groundwater levels and the chemical composition of water in the worked areas of the mine from the date of the notice to the date of each abandonment specified in it.

(10) Proposals to—

(a) treat, lessen or prevent the discharge of water from the mine; or

(b) treat water in the mine.

(11) The operator's opinion as to the likelihood of any of the following matters occurring as a consequence of the abandonment—

(a) the flooding of any worked areas, such areas to be shown on a plan or a schematic drawing identifying the location and extent of such workings;

(b) the migration of water to any other mine (whether or not abandoned) and the name of any such mine;

(c) the recovery levels of ground water within the mine workings being reached and the period of time within which those levels will be reached; and

(d) the discharge of water on to land or into surface water, and the location and chemical composition of any such discharge,

together with the information on which the opinion is based.

(12) The operator's opinion as to the volume of water likely to be discharged to the surface from the mine, and from any part of the mine, to be abandoned, for a period of at least two years from the date of the last abandonment specified in the notice, together with the information on which the opinion is based.

2 Information for notice following an emergency under section 91B(4)(b)

(1) The information prescribed in paragraph 1(1), (3) to (7) and (10) to (12) above, but—

(a) in paragraph 1(3) omitting the word 'proposed';

(b) in paragraph 1(5)(b) for the words 'is to be' substituting the words 'has been', and for the words 'it is proposed to abandon' substituting the words 'has been abandoned';

(c) in paragraph 1(6) and (12) after the words 'part of the mine' omitting the words 'to be'.

(2) The nature of the emergency which necessitated the abandonment under section 91B(4)(a).

3   Information for notice from official receiver or Accountant in Bankruptcy under section 91B(5)

(1) Subject to sub-paragraph (2) below the information prescribed in paragraph 1 above but where the notice is given after the abandonment—

(a) omitting paragraph 1(2), (8) and (9);

(b) in paragraph 1(3) omitting the word 'proposed';

(c) in paragraph 1(5)(b) for the words 'is to be' substituting the words 'has been', and for the words 'it is proposed to abandon' substituting the words 'has been abandoned'; and

(d) in paragraph 1(6) and (12) after the words 'part of the mine' omitting the words 'to be'.

(2) Such information as demonstrates that the operator is a person to whom section 91B(5) applies.

Regulation 3	SCHEDULE 2

PARTICULARS PRESCRIBED UNDER SECTION 91B(6)

1.—The name and address of the mine.

2.—The name and address of the operator.

3.—The nature of each abandonment or proposed abandonment, specifying (if relevant) the appropriate sub-paragraph or sub-paragraphs under section 91A(1)(a).

4.—The date or dates of each abandonment or proposed abandonment.

5.—The address at which the notice under section 91B(1), (4)(b) or (5) may be inspected.

6.—The provisions of section 91B under which the notice has been served.

Action Programme for Nitrate Vulnerable Zones (England and Wales) Regulations 1998
(SI 1998, No. 1202)

2   Interpretation

In these Regulations—

'the enforcement authority' means the Environment Agency;

'farm' includes livestock unit and has the same meaning which it has in Annex III, paragraph 2, of Council Directive 91/676/EEC concerning the protection of waters against pollution caused by nitrates from agricultural sources;

'nitrate vulnerable zone' means any area designated as a nitrate vulnerable zone in accordance with regulation 3 of the Protection of Water against Agricultural Nitrate Pollution (England and Wales) Regulations 1996.

3   Implementation of action programme

(1) The occupier of any farm all or part of which is in a nitrate vulnerable zone shall ensure that the action programme set out in the Schedule hereto is implemented in relation to any land comprised in the farm and in the nitrate vulnerable zone.

(2) For the purposes of paragraph (1) above, the occupier of a farm shall not cease to be the occupier of the whole of the farm by reason of another agricultural producer using part of the land comprised in the farm.

4 Notice to remedy contravention of regulation 3

(1) Where the enforcement authority is of the opinion that a person—

    (a) is contravening a requirement imposed on him by regulation 3; or

    (b) has contravened such a requirement in circumstances which make it likely that the contravention will continue or be repeated,

the authority may serve a notice on that person in accordance with this regulation.

(2) A notice served in accordance with this regulation shall—

    (a) require the person upon whom it is served to carry out such works or to take such precautions and other steps as the enforcement authority considers appropriate to remedy, or to prevent the continuation or repetition of, any contravention to which the notice relates;

    (b) state the period within which any such requirement is to be complied with; and

    (c) inform the person on whom it is served of the effect in relation to the notice of regulation 5 below.

(3) The period for compliance stated in the notice shall be such period as is reasonable in the circumstances and shall not in any case be less than 28 days.

(4) The enforcement authority may at any time—

    (a) withdraw the notice;

    (b) extend the period for compliance with any requirement of the notice;

    (c) with the consent of the person on whom the notice is served, modify the requirements of the notice,

and shall do so if so directed by the Secretary of State under regulation 5(4) below.

5 Appeals against notices requiring works etc.

(1) A person served with a notice under regulation 4 above may within the period of 28 days beginning with the day on which that notice is served (or within such longer period as the Secretary of State may allow) appeal to the Secretary of State against the notice.

(2) An appeal under this regulation shall be made by the appellant serving notice on the Secretary of State and the notice shall contain or be accompanied by a statement of the grounds of appeal.

(3) Before determining an appeal under this regulation the Secretary of State shall, if requested to do so by the appellant or the enforcement authority, afford them an opportunity of appearing before and being heard by a person appointed by the Secretary of State for the purpose.

(4) On determining an appeal under this regulation the Secretary of State shall have power to direct the enforcement authority to withdraw the notice under regulation 4 above, to modify any of its requirements, to extend the period for compliance with any requirement or to dismiss the appeal.

(5) The period for compliance with a notice under regulation 4 above shall, subject to any direction under paragraph (4) above, be extended by a period equal to the period beginning with the date on which notice of appeal is served and ending on the date on which the Secretary of State finally determines the appeal or, if the appeal is withdrawn, the date on which it is withdrawn.

6 Monitoring

(1) The occupier of any farm all or part of which is in a nitrate vulnerable zone shall permit the enforcement authority, its servant or agent ('the authorised person'), accompanied by such persons as appear to the authorised person to be necessary for the purpose, at all

reasonable times, where necessary in order to monitor implementation of the action programme or to assess its effectiveness in reducing water pollution caused or induced by nitrates from agricultural sources and preventing further such pollution, to—

    (a) enter upon the land;

    (b) take samples;

    (c) install and maintain equipment; or

    (d) examine all records kept in implementation of the action programme.

(2) The occupier of any farm all or part of which is in a nitrate vulnerable zone shall render all reasonable assistance to any person acting by virtue of paragraph (1) above and in particular shall—

    (a) produce for inspection such document or record as may be reasonably required by that person; and

    (b) at the reasonable request of that person, accompany him in making the inspection of any land.

(3) In this regulation, 'occupier' shall be construed in accordance with regulation 3(2).

7 Offences by directors, etc.

(1) Where a body corporate is guilty of an offence under these Regulations, and that offence is proved to have been committed with the consent or connivance of, or to be attributable to any neglect on the part of—

    (a) any director, manager, secretary or other similar officer of the body corporate, or

    (b) any person who was purporting to act in such capacity, he, as well as the body corporate, shall be guilty of the offence and be liable to be proceeded against and punished accordingly.

(2) for the purpose of paragraph (1) above, 'director', in relation to a body corporate whose affairs are managed by its members, means a member of the body corporate.

(3) Where an offence under these Regulations is committed by a Scottish partner-ship and is proved to have been committed with the consent or connivance of, or to be attributable to any neglect on the part of, a partner, he as well as the partnership shall be guilty of the offence and be liable to be proceeded against and punished accordingly.

8 Offences

(1) Any person who fails to comply with a requirement imposed on him by regulation 3 or by a notice served on him under regulation 4, shall be guilty of an offence and liable, on summary conviction, to a fine not exceeding level 5 on the standard scale or, on conviction on indictment, to a fine not exceeding the statutory maximum.

(2) Any person who fails to comply with a requirement imposed on him by regulation 6, shall be guilty of an offence and liable, on summary conviction, to a fine not exceeding level 3 on the standard scale.

9 Revocation

Regulation 5 (code of good agricultural practice) of the Protection of Water Against Agricultural Nitrate Pollution (England and Wales) Regulations 1996 is hereby revoked.

Regulation 2(1)   SCHEDULE

ACTION PROGRAMME

1.—(1) In this Schedule—

    'autumn sown crop' means—

        (a) a cover crop sown before 1st October and not removed (whether by mechanical cultivation, herbicide or grazing) before 1st December in the same year, and

        (b) a crop, not being a cover crop, sown between 1st August and 1st November in any year;

'chemical fertiliser' means nitrogen fertiliser which is manufactured by an industrial process;

'cover crop' means a crop sown primarily for the purpose of taking up nitrogen from the soil and which is not harvested;

'crop requirement' means the amount of nitrogen fertiliser which it is reasonable to apply to land in any year having regard to the foreseeable nitrogen requirement of the crop growing or to be grown on the land and the nitrogen supply to the crop from the soil and from other sources, including any previous applications of livestock and other organic manures;

'grassland' means land on which the vegetation consists predominantly of grass species;

'livestock' means any animal kept for use or profit;

'livestock manure' means waste products excreted by livestock or a mixture of litter and waste products excreted by livestock, even in processed form;

'nitrogen compound' means any nitrogen-containing substance other than gaseous molecular nitrogen;

'nitrogen fertiliser' means any substance containing a nitrogen compound utilised on land to enhance growth of vegetation;

'organic manure' means—

    (a) livestock manure, and

    (b) nitrogen fertiliser, not being livestock manure or chemical fertiliser, derived from organic matter,

and includes sewage sludge and other organic wastes;

'sandy' in relation to soil means soil where—

    (a) in the layer up to 40 cm deep, there are—

        (i) more than 50 per cent by weight of sand sized particles (that is particles more than 0.06 mm and less than 2 mm in diameter),

       (ii) less than 18 per cent by weight of clay sized particles (that is particles less than 0.02 mm in diameter), and

      (iii) less than 5 per cent by weight of organic carbon, and

    (b) in the layer 40 cm deep and up to 80 cm deep, the sum of the percentage, by weight, of silt sized particles (that is particles more than 0.02 mm in diameter and less than 0.06 mm in diameter) and double the percentage, by weight, of clay sized particles is less than or equal to 30% of the total weight of sand, silt and clay sized particles;

'shallow' in relation to soil means less than 40 cm deep; and other expressions used in Council Directive 91/676/EEC concerning the protection of waters against pollution by nitrates from agricultural sources have the same meaning as in that Directive.

(2) For the purposes of this Schedule, material is applied to land where the material is added to the land whether by spreading on the surface of the land, injecting into the land, placing below the surface of the land or mixing with the surface layers of the land, and for the purposes of paragraph 9 below includes material deposited by livestock.

(3) In relation to a farm only part of which is in a nitrate vulnerable zone, references in this Schedule to a farm shall be taken as references to that part of the farm which is in the nitrate vulnerable zone.

2.—(1) Without prejudice to the specific provisions set out in paragraphs 3–12 below, the land application of nitrogen fertiliser shall take account of local environ-mental factors.

(2) For the purpose of paragraph (1) above local environmental factors are—

    (a) soil conditions, type and slope,

    (b) climatic conditions, rainfall and irrigation,

    (c) land use and agricultural practice.

3. Nitrogen fertiliser shall not be applied to any land in excess of the crop requirement.

4.—(1) Chemical fertiliser shall not be applied to land between the dates specified in paragraph (2) below in relation to that land.

(2) The dates specified for the purposes of paragraph (1) above are—

(a) in the case of grassland, 15th September in any year and 1st February in the following year; and

(b) in the case of other land, 1st September in any year and 1st February in the following year.

(3) The prohibition in paragraph (1) above shall not apply where, taking into account the characteristics of the crop and soil, the nitrogen requirement of the crop between the dates specified in paragraph (2) above can only be met by applying fertiliser between those dates.

5. Nitrogen fertiliser shall be applied to land in as accurate and uniform a manner as is practicably possible.

6. Nitrogen fertiliser shall not be applied to steeply sloping fields.

7. Nitrogen fertiliser shall not be applied to any land if—

(a) the soil is waterlogged;

(b) the land is flooded;

(c) the soil has been frozen for 12 hours or longer in the preceding 24; or

(d) the land is covered by snow.

8. Chemical fertiliser shall not be applied to any land in a location or manner which makes it likely that the chemical fertiliser will directly enter surface water.

9.—(1) Without prejudice to paragraph 10 below, organic manure shall not be applied to land where the application would result in the total nitrogen in kilograms contained in organic manure applied in each year to land on the farm exceeding the specified amount calculated in accordance with paragraph (2) below.

(2) For the purposes of paragraph (1) above, the specified amount is the sum of—

(a) the number of hectares of grassland on the farm multiplied by 250 kg; and

(b) the number of hectares of agricultural land other than grassland on the farm multiplied by—

(i) 210 kg in relation to a year ending on or before 19th December 2002,

(ii) 170 kg in relation to other years.

10. Organic manure shall not be applied to any field where the application would result in the total nitrogen in kilograms contained in organic manure applied in any 12 month period to any field exceeding a rate of 250 kg per hectare.

11. Organic manure shall not be applied to any land less than 10 metres from surface water.

12. Organic manure in the form of slurry, poultry manure or liquid digested sewage sludge shall not be applied to any land which has a sandy or shallow soil—

(a) between 1st September and 1st November in any year where the land is in grass or is to be sown with an autumn sown crop;

(b) between 1st August and 1st November in any year in any other case.

13. The capacity of storage vessels for livestock manure shall exceed the capacity required to store livestock manure produced throughout the longest period during which land application of livestock manure is prohibited by paragraph 12 above except where it can be demonstrated that any livestock manure in excess of the storage capacity will be disposed of in a manner which will not cause harm to the environment.

14. Records shall be made sufficient to enable any person inspecting those records readily to ascertain—

(a) the area of the farm;

(b) for each field comprised in the farm—

(i) the quantity of any chemical fertiliser applied to the field, the nitrogen content of that chemical fertiliser and the date of application,

    (ii) the quantity of any organic manure applied (other than by the animals themselves) to the field and the date of application,

    (iii) whether organic manure applied to the field (other than by the animals themselves) was farm yard manure, poultry manure, slurry, sewage sludge or other organic manure,

    (iv) the type of any crop grown and the date the crop is sown;

  (c) the number of livestock kept on the farm, their species and type, and the length of time for which they were kept on the farm;

  (d) the quantity of each type of livestock manure (whether farmyard manure, slurry, poultry manure, or other livestock manure) moved off the farm, the date of that movement and the name and address of the consignee.

15. Any record made for the purposes of paragraph 14 above shall be retained for a period of 5 years after the latest event recorded therein.

Groundwater Regulations 1998
(SI 1998, No. 2746)

1 Citation, extent, commencement and interpretation

(1) These Regulations may be cited as the Groundwater Regulations.

(2) . . .

(3) In these Regulations—

'the Groundwater Directive' means Council Directive 80/68/EEC;

'the Agency'—

  (a) in relation to England and Wales, means the Environment Agency;

  (b) . . .

'authorisation' means—

  (a) an authorisation under regulation 18 or 19;

  (b) a discharge consent within the meaning of section 91(8) of the Water Resources Act 1991;

  (c) . . .; [. . .]

  (d) an authorisation under Part I of the Environmental Protection Act 1990 in relation to a process designated for central control under section 2 of that Act; 'direct discharge' means the introduction into groundwater of any substance in list I or II without percolation through the ground or subsoil;

'groundwater' means all water which is below the surface of the ground in the saturation zone and in direct contact with the ground or subsoil;

'highway drain' means a drain which a highway authority or other person is entitled to keep open by virtue of section 100 of the Highways Act 1980;

'indirect discharge' means the introduction into groundwater of any substance in list I or II after percolation through the ground or subsoil;

'pollution' means the discharge by man, directly or indirectly, of substances or energy into groundwater, the results of which are such as to endanger human health or water supplies, harm living resources and the aquatic ecosystem or interfere with other legitimate uses of water;

. . .

'substance in list I' and 'substance in list II' shall have the meaning given by paragraphs 1 and 2 of the Schedule to these Regulations (and paragraphs 3 and 4 of that Schedule shall have effect);

and other expressions used in these Regulations which are also used in the Groundwater Directive shall have the same meaning as in that Directive [and

(e) a permit under the Pollution Prevention and Control (England and Wales) Regulations 2000 in so far as it authorises the operation of a Part A installation or Part A mobile plant within the meaning of those Regulations;]

2   Exclusions from these Regulations

(1) Nothing in these Regulations shall apply in relation to—

(a) any discharge of matter containing radioactive substances;

(b) any discharge of domestic effluent from an isolated dwelling which is not connected to a sewerage system and which is situated outside any area protected for the abstraction of water for human consumption;

(c) any discharge found by the Agency to contain substances in list I or II in a quantity and concentration so small as to obviate any present or future danger of deterioration in the quality of the receiving groundwater; or

(d) any activity for which a waste management licence (within the meaning of Part II of the Environmental Protection Act 1990) is required.

(2) The Agency shall from time to time publish a summary of its findings under paragraph (1)(c) above in such manner as it considers appropriate and shall make copies of any such summary available to the public free of charge.

3   Discharge of functions

The Agency and the Secretary of State shall for the purposes of implementing the Groundwater Directive discharge their respective functions under these Regulations, . . . Part III of the Water Resources Act 1991 (control of water pollution — England and Wales) and Part I of the Environmental Protection Act 1990 (integrated pollution control) [and the Pollution Prevention and Control (England and Wales) Regulations 2000] in accordance with the following provisions of these Regulations.

4   Measures to prevent the introduction into groundwater of list I substances

(1) An authorisation shall not be granted if it would permit the direct discharge of any substance in list I.

(2) An authorisation shall not be granted in relation to—

(a) the disposal, or tipping for the purpose of disposal, of any substance in list I which might lead to an indirect discharge of that substance; or

(b) any other activity on or in the ground which might lead to an indirect discharge of any substance in list I,

unless that activity has been subjected to prior investigation.

(3) In the light of any such investigation—

(a) an authorisation shall not be granted if it would permit the indirect discharge of any substance in list I; and

(b) any authorisation granted must include conditions which require that all necessary technical precautions are observed to prevent an indirect discharge of any substance in list I.

(4) The following powers shall be exercised if it is necessary to do so for the purpose of preventing the introduction into groundwater of substances in list I—

(a) in the case of any discharge from a highway drain . . . which contains any such substance, the powers conferred by section 86(1) of the Water Resources Act 1991 . . . (prohibition of certain discharges by notice);

(b) in the case of any activity falling within paragraph (2)(b) above and not falling within sub-paragraph (a) above, the powers conferred by regulation 19.

(5) However, a discharge of any substance in list I into groundwater may be authorised after prior investigation if—

(a) the investigation reveals that the groundwater is permanently unsuitable for other uses (especially domestic or agricultural uses), presence of that substance does not impede exploitation of ground resources and conditions are imposed which require that all technical precautions are observed to prevent that substance from reaching other aquatic systems or harming other ecosystems; or

(b) the discharge is due to the re-injection into the same aquifer of water used for geothermal purposes, water pumped out of mines and quarries or water pumped out for civil engineering works.

5   Measures to limit the introduction into groundwater of list II substances to avoid pollution

(1) An authorisation shall not be granted in relation to—

(a) any direct discharge of any substance in list II;

(b) any disposal or tipping for the purpose of disposal of any substance in list II which might lead to an indirect discharge of that substance;

(c) any other activity on or in the ground which might lead to an indirect discharge of any substance in list II,

unless that activity has been subjected to prior investigation.

(2) An authorisation may only be granted if, in the light of any such investigation, it includes conditions which require that all necessary technical precautions are observed to prevent groundwater pollution by any substance in list II.

(3) The following powers shall be exercised if it is necessary to do so for the purpose of avoiding pollution of groundwater by substances in list II—

(a) in the case of any discharge from a highway drain ... which contains such substances, the powers conferred by section 86(1) of the Water Resources Act 1991 ... (prohibition of certain discharges by notice);

(b) in the case of any activity falling within paragraph (1)(c) above and not falling within sub-paragraph (a) above, the powers conferred by regulation 19.

6   Artificial recharges for the purposes of groundwater management

Artificial recharges may be authorised on a case by case basis for the purpose of groundwater management notwithstanding regulations 4 and 5, but such authorisation shall only be granted if there is no risk of polluting groundwater.

7   Examination required in prior investigation

Any prior investigation required by regulation 4 or 5 shall include examination of—

(a) the hydrogeological conditions of the area concerned;

(b) the possible purifying powers of the soil and subsoil; and

(c) the risk of pollution and alteration of the quality of the groundwater from the discharge,

and shall establish whether the discharge of substances into groundwater is a satisfactory solution from the point of view of the environment.

8   Surveillance of groundwater

An authorisation which is subject to any of the provisions of regulation 4, 5 or 6 may only be granted if the Agency has checked that the groundwater (and, in particular, its quality) will undergo the requisite surveillance.

9   Terms of authorisation of discharge of substances in list I or II

(1) This regulation applies where—

(a) a direct discharge of any substance in list I or II is authorised in accordance with regulation 4(5) or 5; or

(b) waste water disposal which inevitably causes an indirect discharge of any substance in list II is authorised in accordance with regulation 5.

(2) In a case where this regulation applies the authorisation shall specify in particular—

(a) the place where the discharge may be made;

(b) the method of discharge which may be used;

(c) the essential precautions which must be taken, paying particular attention to the nature and concentration of any substance in list I or II present in the effluent, the characteristics of the receiving environment and the proximity of water catchment areas, in particular those for drinking, thermal and mineral water;

(d) the maximum quantity of any such substance permissible in the effluent during one or more specified periods of time and the appropriate requirements as to the concentration of any such substance;

(e) the arrangements for monitoring effluents discharged into groundwater;

(f) if necessary, measures for monitoring groundwater, and in particular its quality.

10 Terms of authorisation for disposal or tipping for the purpose of disposal

(1) This regulation applies where—

(a) any disposal, or tipping for the purpose of disposal, of any matter which might lead to an indirect discharge of any substance in list I or II is authorised in accordance with regulation 4 or 5; and

(b) in the case of a disposal, it is not a disposal of waste water to which regulation 9(1)(b) applies.

(2) In a case where this regulation applies the authorisation shall specify in particular—

(a) the place where the disposal or tipping may be done;

(b) the methods of disposal or tipping which may be used;

(c) the essential precautions which must be taken, paying particular attention to the nature and concentration of any substance in list I or II present in the matter to be disposed of or tipped, the characteristics of the receiving environment and the proximity of water catchment areas, in particular those for drinking, thermal and mineral water;

(d) the maximum quantity permissible, during one or more specified periods of time, of the matter containing any such substance and, where possible, of any such substance, to be tipped or disposed of and the appropriate requirements as to the concentration of any such substance;

(e) the technical precautions to be implemented to prevent any discharge into groundwater of any substance in list I and any pollution of such water by any substance in list II,

(f) if necessary, the measures for monitoring the groundwater, and in particular its quality.

11 Period and conditions of authorisation

(1) An authorisation of—

(a) a discharge of any substance in list I or II; or

(b) any disposal, or tipping for the purpose of disposal, of any matter which might lead to an indirect discharge of any substance in list I or II,

may be granted for a limited period only, and must be reviewed at least once in every four years when it may be renewed, amended or revoked.

(2) If the applicant for any such authorisation states, or it is otherwise evident, that he will be unable to comply with the conditions of the proposed authorisation, the authorisation shall not be granted.

(3) The Agency shall monitor compliance with the conditions of any such authorisation and the effects of discharges on groundwater.

(4) If the conditions of any such authorisation are not complied with, the appropriate steps shall be taken to ensure compliance and, if necessary, the revocation of the authorisation.

12   Inventory of authorisations

The Agency shall keep an inventory of authorisations of—

    (a)   direct or indirect discharges of any substance in list I;

    (b)   direct discharges of any substance in list II; and

    (c)   artificial recharges for the purposes of groundwater management.

13   Application of measures not to lead to pollution of groundwater

The application of the measures taken pursuant to these Regulations may on no account lead, either directly or indirectly, to pollution of groundwater.

14   Application of provisions of water pollution legislation

(1) A person shall be treated as contravening section 85 of the Water Resources Act 1991 . . . (water pollution offences) if—

    (a)   he causes or knowingly permits—

        (i)   the disposal or tipping for the purposes of disposal of any substance in list I or II in circumstances which might lead to an indirect discharge of that substance into groundwater unless it is carried on under and in accordance with an authorisation granted under regulation 18; or

        (ii)   any activity to be carried on in contravention of a prohibition imposed under regulation 19 or any authorisation granted under that regulation; or

    (b)   he contravenes the conditions of any authorisation under regulation 18 or 19.

(2) Section 88(1) of the Water Resources Act 1991 . . . (defences to water pollution offences in respect of authorised discharges) shall apply in relation to an authorisation under regulation 18 or 19 as if the reference—

    (a)   in section 88(1)(a) to a consent under Chapter II of Part III of the Water Resources Act 1991;

    (b)   . . . included a reference to such an authorisation.

(3) Sections 191A and 191B of the Water Resources Act 1991 . . . (exclusion from registers of information affecting national security and certain confidential information) shall apply in relation to the particulars mentioned in regulation 22(1) as if information furnished for the purposes mentioned in paragraphs (a) to (c) of subsection (2) of section 191A . . . included information furnished to the Agency for the purposes of regulation 18 or 19.

(4) Paragraph 11 of Schedule 10 to the Water Resources Act 1991 (transfer of discharge consents) shall apply in relation to an authorisation under regulation 18—

    (a)   as if any reference to a consent included a reference to such an authorisation;

    (b)   as if references to paragraphs 3 and 6 of that Schedule were references to regulation 18; and

    (c)   as if references to carrying on or making discharges were references to carrying on the activities regulated by the authorisation.

15   Application of section 71 of the Environmental Protection Act 1990

Section 71 of the Environmental Protection Act 1990 (obtaining of information) shall apply for the purposes of these Regulations as if any reference to functions under Part II of that Act included a reference to functions under these regulations.

16   Application of sections 41, 42 and 123 of the Environment Act 1995

(1) Sections 41 and 42 of the Environment Act 1995 (charging schemes) shall apply in relation to an authorisation under regulation 18 or 19 as if any reference to an environmental licence included a reference to such an authorisation.

(2) Section 123 of the Environment Act 1995 (provisions relating to the service of documents) shall apply to the service of notices under regulation 18 or 19 as it applies to the service of documents under that Act.

. . .

18   Authorisation of disposal or tipping of substances in list I or II

(1) An application for an authorisation for the purposes of regulation 14(1)(a)(i) shall be made in writing to the Agency.

(2) If in any case the Agency considers that there are special reasons why the application should be advertised, it may by notice in writing served on the applicant require him to advertise the application in such manner as may be specified in the notice.

(3) The Agency may either—

    (a) grant an authorisation in writing subject to such conditions as it thinks fit; or

    (b) by notice in writing served on the applicant, refuse the application and the notice shall state the Agency's reasons for refusal.

(4) The Agency may, by notice in writing served on the person holding an authorisation under this regulation, at any time vary or revoke the authorisation and a notice of variation or revocation shall state the Agency's reasons.

19   Notice to prevent or control indirect discharges of substances in list I or II

(1) Subject to paragraph (2), where—

    (a) any person is carrying on, or proposing to carry on, any activity on or in the ground; and

    (b) that activity might lead to an indirect discharge of any substance in list I or pollution of groundwater as a result of an indirect discharge of any substance in list II, the Agency may serve notice in writing on that person prohibiting him from carrying on that activity or authorising him to carry on that activity subject to such conditions as are specified in the notice and which are necessary to prevent an indirect discharge of any substance in list I or pollution of groundwater as a result of an indirect discharge of any substance in list II.

(2) This regulation shall not apply to the disposal, or tipping for the purpose of disposal, of any substance in list I or II except in a case falling within regulation 23(3) during the period whilst the application in question is pending.

(3) The Agency may at any time, by notice in writing served on the person on whom a notice under paragraph (1) was served, vary or revoke that notice and a notice of variation or revocation shall state the Agency's reasons.

20   Appeals

(1) A person may appeal by notice in writing to the Secretary of State against any decision of the Agency under regulation 18 or 19—

    (a) in the case of a decision under regulation 18, within a period of three months; or

    (b) in the case of a decision under regulation 19, within a period of 21 days, beginning in either case with the date on which he was notified of the Agency's decision, or within such longer period as the Secretary of State may allow.

(2) Where—

    (a) an application has been made to the Agency in accordance with regulation 18 above; and

    (b) the Agency has not notified the applicant of its decision in relation to that application within—

        (i) a period of four months beginning with the date on which it received the application (or, if the application must be advertised, the date on which advertising is completed); or

        (ii) if the Agency and the applicant agree in writing to a longer period, that period, the applicant may for the purposes of this regulation treat this as a refusal by the Agency of the application and appeal to the Secretary of State.

(3) An appeal under this regulation shall be made by the appellant serving notice in writing on the Secretary of State and the notice shall state the appellant's grounds of appeal.

(4) Before determining an appeal under this regulation the Secretary of State shall—

    (a) take into account any written representations of the appellant and of the Agency; and

    (b) if requested to do so by the appellant or the Agency, afford them an opportunity of appearing before and being heard by a person appointed by the Secretary of State for the purpose.

(5) On determining an appeal under this regulation the Secretary of State shall have power to dismiss the appeal or to direct the Agency to take such steps in exercise of its powers under regulation 18 or 19 as the Secretary of State considers appropriate to give effect to his decision on the appeal.

21   Codes of practice

(1) The Ministers may from time to time approve for the purposes of these Regulations (or withdraw their approval of) codes of practice issued for the purpose of giving practical guidance to persons engaged in any activity falling within regulation 4(2)(b) or 5(1)(c) about the steps they should take to prevent substances in list I from entering groundwater or to avoid pollution of such water by substances in list II.

(2) In deciding whether or not it is necessary to exercise the Agency's powers under regulation 19, the Agency shall consider whether or not any guidance, which is contained in a relevant code of practice for the time being approved under paragraph (1) above, has been, or is likely to be, followed.

(3) When the Ministers exercise their powers under paragraph (1) above they shall—

    (a) notify the Agency of their approval (or withdrawal of their approval) of the relevant code of practice; and

    (b) make such arrangements as they consider appropriate for publicising their approval or, as the case may be, its withdrawal.

(4) The Agency shall make appropriate arrangements for bringing each code of practice for the time being approved under paragraph (1) above to the attention of persons engaged in the relevant activity.

(5) In this regulation 'the Ministers' means any Minister of the Crown within the meaning of the Ministers of the Crown Act 1975 acting either alone or jointly with one or more such Ministers.

22   Particulars to be included in registers

(1) Subject to regulation 14(3) and paragraph (2) below, the Agency shall, as soon as reasonably practicable, enter on registers maintained by it under section 190 of the Water Resources Act 1991 or . . . (pollution control registers) full particulars of—

    (a) any authorisation under regulation 18;

    (b) any application for such an authorisation;

    (c) any variation or revocation of such an authorisation;

    (d) any notice under regulation 19;

    (e) any variation or revocation of any such notice;

    (f) any information furnished to the Agency for the purposes of regulation 18 or 19;

    (g) any monitoring information provided in connection with any authorisation under regulation 18 or 19;

    (h) any conviction for an offence under section 85 of the Water Resources Act 1991 or . . . by virtue of regulation 14(1);

    (i) any finding of the Agency under regulation 2(1)(c), any determination of the Agency under paragraph 1(2) or 2(2) of the Schedule to these Regulations, any notification by the Secretary of State under paragraph 3(2) of that Schedule and any summary published under regulation 2(2) or paragraph 4 of that Schedule; and

    (j) any code of practice for the time being approved under regulation 21 above.

(2) Nothing in paragraph (1) above shall require the Agency to keep on a register—

    (a) monitoring information more than four years after that information was entered on the register;

    (b) other information which has been superseded by later information more than four years after that later information was entered on the register; or

    (c) information relating to an application for an authorisation under regulation 18 after the application has been withdrawn.

23 Transitional provisions

(1) This regulation applies where any application is made before 1st April 1999 to the Agency for an authorisation for the purposes of regulation 14(1)(a)(i).

(2) The application shall be dealt with in the same manner as an application made on or after 1st April 1999 but—

    (a) an appeal by virtue of regulation 20(2) shall not be made in relation to the application before 1st August 1999; and

    (b) an authorisation issued before 1st April 1999 in relation to the application shall have effect on and after that date as an authorisation under regulation 18.

(3) Where—

    (a) the application has not been finally disposed of before 1st April 1999; and

    (b) the application relates to an activity which is substantially the same as an activity carried on by the applicant or his predecessor before that date at the place to which the application relates;

the Agency shall be deemed to have given the authorisation applied for and the deemed authorisation shall continue in force until the application is finally disposed of or, if before that date a notice under regulation 19 is served on the applicant in relation to the activity in question, until the date of service of that notice.

(4) An application shall be treated as finally disposed of for the purposes of paragraph (1)(3) above on—

    (a) the date on which the application is withdrawn;

    (b) if the Agency gives or refuses its authorisation, the expiration (without an appeal being made) of the time limit for appealing against that decision; or

    (c) if an appeal is duly made against the Agency's decision, the date on which that appeal is determined or withdrawn.

Regulation 1(2)   SCHEDULE

LIST 1

1.—(1) Subject to sub-paragraph (2) below, a substance is in list I if it belongs to one of the following families or groups of substances—

    (a) organohalogen compounds and substances which may form such compounds in the aquatic environment;

    (b) organophosphorus compounds;

    (c) organotin compounds;

    (d) substances which possess carcinogenic, mutagenic or teratogenic properties in or via the aquatic environment (including substances which have those properties which would otherwise be in list II);

    (e) mercury and its compounds;

    (f) cadmium and its compounds;

    (g) mineral oils and hydrocarbons;

    (h) cyanides.

(2) A substance is not in list I if it has been determined by the Agency to be inappropriate to list I on the basis of a low risk of toxicity, persistence and bioaccumulation.

LIST II

2.—(1) A substance is in list II if it could have a harmful effect on groundwater and it belongs to one of the following families or groups of substances—

(a) the following metalloids and metals and their compounds:

Zinc	Tin
Copper	Barium
Nickel	Beryllium
Chromium	Boron
Lead	Uranium
Selenium	Vanadium
Arsenic	Cobalt
Antimony	Thallium
Molybdenum	Tellurium
Titanium	Silver.

(b) biocides and their derivatives not appearing in list I;

(c) substances which have a deleterious effect on the taste or odour of ground-water, and compounds liable to cause the formation of such substances in such water and to render it unfit for human consumption;

(d) toxic or persistent organic compounds of silicon, and substances which may cause the formation of such compounds in water, excluding those which are biologically harmless or are rapidly converted in water into harmless substances;

(e) inorganic compounds of phosphorus and elemental phosphorus;

(f) fluorides;

(g) ammonia and nitrites.

(2) A substance is also in list II if—

(a) it belongs to one of the families or groups of substances set out in paragraph 1(1) above;

(b) it has been determined by the Agency to be inappropriate to list I under paragraph 1(2); and

(c) it has been determined by the Agency to be appropriate to list II having regard to toxicity, persistence and bioaccumulation.

3.—(1) The Secretary of State may review any decision of the Agency in relation to the exercise of its powers under paragraph 1(2) or 2(2).

(2) The Secretary of State shall notify the Agency of his decision following a review under sub-paragraph (1) above and it shall b' the duty of the Agency to give effect to that decision.

4.   The Agency shall from time to time publish a summary of the effect of its determinations under this Schedule in such manner as it considers appropriate and shall make copies of any such summary available to the public free of charge.

Town and Country Planning (Environmental Impact Assessment) (England and Wales) Regulations 1999
(SI 1999, No. 293) (as amended)

PART I   GENERAL

1   Citation, commencement and application

(1) These Regulations may be cited as the Town and Country Planning (Environmental

Impact Assessment) (England and Wales) Regulations 1999 and shall come into force on 14th March 1999.

(2) Subject to paragraph (3), these Regulations shall apply throughout England and Wales.

(3) Paragraphs (2) and (5)(a) of regulation 14 shall not apply to the Isles of Scilly and, in relation to the Isles of Scilly, the reference in paragraph (6) of that regulation to paragraph (5) of that regulation shall be construed as a reference to paragraph (5)(b).

2   Interpretation

(1) In these Regulations—

'the Act' means the Town and Country Planning Act 1990 and references to sections are references to sections of that Act;

['the 1991 Act' means the Planning and Compensation Act 1991;]

['the 1995 Act' means the Environment Act 1995;]

'the consulation bodies' means—

(a) any body which the relevant planning authority is required to consult, or would, if an application for planning permission for the development in question were before them, be required to consult by virtue of article 10 (consultations before the grant of permission) of the Order or of any direction under that article; and

(b) the following bodies if not referred to in sub-paragraph (a)—

(i) any principal council for the area where the land is situated, if not the relevant planning authority;

(ii) where the land is situated in England, the Countryside Commission and the Nature Conservancy Council for England;

(iii) where the land is situated in Wales, the Countryside Council for Wales; and

(iv) the Environment Agency;

'the Directive' means Council Directive 85/337/EEC;

['EEA State' means a State party to the Agreement on the European Economic Area;]

'EIA application' means an application for planning permission for EIA development;

'EIA development' means development which is either—

(a) Schedule 1 development; or

(b) Schedule 2 development likely to have significant effects on the environment by virtue of factors such as its nature, size or location;

'environmental information' means the environmental statement, including any further information, any representations made by any body required by these Regulations to be invited to make representations, and any representations duly made by any other person about the environmental effects of the development;

'environmental statement' means a statement—

(a) that includes such of the information referred to in Part I of Schedule 4 as is reasonably required to assess the environmental effects of the development and which the applicant can, having regard in particular to current knowledge and methods of assessment, reasonably be required to compile, but

(b) that includes at least the information referred to in Part II of Schedule 4;

'exempt development' means development which comprises or forms part of a project serving national defence purposes or in respect of which the Secretary of State has made a direction under regulation 4(4);

'further information' has the meaning given in regulation 19(1);

'General Regulations' means the Town and Country Planning General Regulations 1992;

'inspector' means a person appointed by the Secretary of State pursuant to Schedule 6 to the Act to determine an appeal;

'the land' means the land on which the development would be carried out or, in relation to development already carried out, has been carried out;

'the Order' means the Town and Country Planning (General Development Procedure) Order 1995;

'principal council' has the meaning given by sub-section (1) of section 270 (general provisions as to interpretation) of the Local Government Act 1972;

'register' means a register kept pursuant to section 69 (registers of applications etc.) and 'appropriate register' means the register on which particulars of an application for planning permission for the relevant development have been placed or would fall to be placed if such an application were made;

['relevant mineral planning authority' means the body to whom it falls, fell, or would, but for a direction under paragraph—

(a) 7 of Schedule 2 to the 1991 Act;

(b) 13 of Schedule 13 to the 1995 Act; or

(c) 8 of Schedule 14 to the 1995 Act,

fall to determine the ROMP application in question;]

'relevant planning authority' means the body to whom it falls, fell, or would, but for a direction under section 77 (reference of applications to Secretary of State), fall to determine an application for planning permission for the development in question;

['ROMP application' means an application to a relevant mineral planning authority to determine the conditions to which a planning permission is to be subject under paragraph—

(a) 2(2) of Schedule 2 to the 1991 Act (registration of old mining permissions);

(b) 9(1) of Schedule 13 to the 1995 Act (review of old mineral planning permissions); or

(c) 6(1) of Schedule 14 to the 1995 Act (periodic review of mineral planning permissions);

'ROMP development' means development which has yet to be carried out and which is authorised by a planning permission in respect of which a ROMP application has been or is to be made;]

'Schedule 1 application' and 'Schedule 2 application' mean an application for planning permission for Schedule 1 development and Schedule 2 development respectively;

'Schedule 1 development' means development, other than exempt development, of a description mentioned in Schedule 1;

'Schedule 2 development' means development, other than exempt development, of a description mentioned in Column 1 of the table in Schedule 2 where—

(a) any part of that development is to be carried out in a sensitive area; or

(b) any applicable threshold or criterion in the corresponding part of Column 2 of that table is respectively exceeded or met in relation to that development;

'scoping direction' and 'scoping opinion' have the meanings given in regulation 10;

'screening direction' means a direction made by the Secretary of State as to whether development is EIA development;

'screening opinion' means a written statement of the opinion of the relevant planning authority as to whether development is EIA development;

'sensitive area' means any of the following—

(a) land notified under sub-section (1) of section 28 (areas of special scientific interest) of the Wildlife and Countryside Act 1981;

(b) land to which sub-section (3) of section 29 (nature conservation orders) of the Wildlife and Countryside Act 1981 applies;

(c) an area to which paragraph (u)(ii) in the table in article 10 of the Order applies;

(d) a National Park within the meaning of the National Parks and Access to the Countryside Act 1949;

(e) the Broads;

(f) a property appearing on the World Heritage List kept under article 11 (2) of the 1972 UNESCO Convention for the Protection of the World Cultural and Natural Heritage;

(g) a scheduled monument within the meaning of the Ancient Monuments and Archaeological Areas Act 1979;

(h) an area of outstanding natural beauty designated as such by an order made by the Countryside Commission, as respects England, or the Countryside Council for Wales, as respects Wales, under section 87 (designation of areas of outstanding natural beauty) of the National Parks and Access to the Countryside Act 1949 as confirmed by the Secretary of State;

(i) a European site within the meaning of regulation 10 of the Conservation (Natural Habitats etc.) Regulations 1994;

(2) Subject to paragraph (3), expressions used both in these Regulations and in the Act have the same meaning for the purposes of these Regulations as they have for the purposes of the Act.

(3) Expressions used both in these Regulations and in the Directive (whether or not also used in the Act) have the same meaning for the purposes of these Regulations as they have for the purposes of the Directive.

(4) In these Regulations any reference to a Council Directive is a reference to that Directive as amended at the date these Regulations were made.

(5) In these Regulations references to the Secretary of State shall not be construed as references to an inspector.

[(6) In its application to Wales, these Regulations shall have effect, with any necessary amendments, as if each reference to 'the Secretary of State' were a reference to 'the National Assembly for Wales.']

3   Prohibition on granting planning permission without consideration of environmental information

(1) This regulation applies—

(a) to every EIA application received by the authority with whom it is lodged on or after the commencement of these Regulations; and

(b) to every EIA application lodged by an authority pursuant to regulation 3 or 4 (applications for planning permission) of the General Regulations on or after that date;

and for the purposes of this paragraph, the date of receipt of an application by an authority shall be determined in accordance with paragraph (3) of article 20 (time periods for decision) of the Order.

(2) The relevant planning authority or the Secretary of State or an inspector shall not grant planning permission pursuant to an application to which this regulation applies unless they have first taken the environmental information into consideration, and they shall state in their decision that they have done so.

PART II   SCREENING

4   General provisions relating to screening

(1) Subject to paragraphs (3) and (4), the occurrence of an event mentioned in paragraph (2) shall determine for the purpose of these Regulations that development is EIA development.

(2) The events referred to in paragraph (1) are—

(a) the submission by the applicant or appellant in relation to that development of a statement referred to by the applicant or appellant as an environmental statement for the purposes of these Regulations; or

(b) the adoption by the relevant planning authority of a screening opinion to the effect that the development is EIA development.

(3) A direction of the Secretary of State shall determine for the purpose of these Regulations whether development is or is not EIA development.

(4) The Secretary of State may direct that particular proposed development is exempted from the application of these Regulations in accordance with Article 2(3) of the Directive (but without prejudice to Article 7 of the Directive) and shall send a copy of any such direction to the relevant planning authority.

(5) Where a local planning authority or the Secretary of State has to decide under these Regulations whether Schedule 2 development is EIA development the authority or Secretary of State shall take into account in making that decision such of the selection criteria set out in Schedule 3 as are relevant to the development.

(6) Where—
    (a) a local planning authority adopt a screening opinion; or
    (b) the Secretary of State makes a screening direction under these Regulations;
to the effect that development is EIA development—
    (i) that opinion or direction shall be accompanied by a written statement giving clearly and precisely the full reasons for that conclusion; and
    (ii) the authority or the Secretary of State, as the case may be, shall send a copy of the opinion or direction and a copy of the written statement required by sub-paragraph (i) to the person who proposes to carry out, or who has carried out, the development in question.

(7) The Secretary of State may make a screening direction irrespective of whether he has received a request to do so.

(8) The Secretary of State may direct that particular development of a description mentioned in Column 1 of the table in Schedule 2 is EIA development in spite of the fact that none of the conditions contained in sub-paragraphs (a) and (b) of the definition of 'Schedule 2 development' is satisfied in relation to that development.

(9) The Secretary of State shall send a copy of any screening direction to the relevant planning authority.

5   Requests for screening opinions of the local planning authority

(1) A person who is minded to carry out development may request the relevant planning authority to adopt a screening opinion.

(2) A request for a screening opinion shall be accompanied by—
    (a) a plan sufficient to identify the land;
    (b) a brief description of the nature and purpose of the development and of its possible effects on the environment; and
    (c) such other information or representations as the person making the request may wish to provide or make.

(3) An authority receiving a request for a screening opinion shall, if they consider that they have not been provided with sufficient information to adopt an opinion, notify in writing the person making the request of the points on which they require additional information.

(4) An authority shall adopt a screening opinion within three weeks beginning with the date of receipt of a request made pursuant to paragraph (1) or such longer period as may be agreed in writing with the person making the request.

(5) An authority which adopts a screening opinion pursuant to paragraph (4) shall forthwith send a copy to the person who made the request.

(6) Where an authority—
    (a) fail to adopt a screening opinion within the relevant period mentioned in paragraph (4); or

(b) adopt an opinion to the effect that the development is EIA development;

the person who requested the opinion may request the Secretary of State to make a screening direction.

(7) The person may make a request pursuant to paragraph (6) even if the authority has not received additional information which it has sought under paragraph (3).

6 Requests for screening directions of the Secretary of State

(1) A person who pursuant to regulation 5(6) requests the Secretary of State to make a screening direction shall submit with his request—

(a) a copy of this request to the relevant planning authority under regulation 5(1) and the documents which accompanied it;

(b) a copy of any notification under regulation 5(3) which he has received and of any response;

(c) a copy of any screening opinion he has received from the authority and of any accompanying statement of reasons; and

(d) any representations that he wishes to make.

(2) When a person makes a request pursuant to regulation 5(6) he shall send to the relevant planning authority a copy of that request and of any representations he makes to the Secretary of State.

(3) The Secretary of State shall, if he considers that he has not been provided with sufficient information to make a screening direction, notify in writing the person making the request pursuant to regulation 5(6) of the points on which he requires additional information, and may request the relevant planning authority to provide such information as they can on any of those points.

(4) The Secretary of State shall make a screening direction within three weeks beginning with the date of receipt of a request pursuant to regulation 5 (6) or such longer period as he may reasonably require.

(5) The Secretary of State shall send a copy of any screening direction made pursuant to paragraph (4) forthwith to the person who made the request.

PART III   PROCEDURES CONCERNING APPLICATIONS FOR PLANNING PERMISSION

7 Application made to a local planning authority without an environmental statement

(1) Where it appears to the relevant planning authority that—

(a) an application for planning permission which is before them for determination is a Schedule 1 application or Schedule 2 application; and

(b) the development in question has not been the subject of a screening opinion or screening direction; and

(c) the application is not accompanied by a statement referred to by the applicant as an environmental statement for the purposes of these Regulations,

paragraphs (3) and (4) of regulation 5 shall apply as if the receipt or lodging of the application were a request made under regulation 5(1).

(2) Where an EIA application which is before a local planning authority for determination is not accompanied by a statement referred to by the applicant as an environmental statement for the purposes of these Regulations, the authority shall notify the applicant in writing that the submission of an environmental statement is required.

(3) An authority shall notify the applicant in accordance with paragraph (2) within three weeks beginning with the date of receipt of the application or such longer period as may be agreed in writing with the applicant; but where the Secretary of State, after the expiry of that period of three weeks or of any longer period so agreed, makes a screening direction to the

effect that the development is EIA development, the authority shall so notify the applicant within seven days beginning with the date the authority received a copy of that screening direction.

(4) An applicant receiving a notification pursuant to paragraph (2) may, within three weeks beginning with the date of the notification, write to the authority stating—

    (a) that he accepts their view and is providing an environmental statement; or

    (b) unless the Secretary of State has made a screening direction in respect of the development, that he is writing to the Secretary of State to request a screening direction.

(5) If the applicant does not write to the authority in accordance with paragraph (4), the permission sought shall, unless the Secretary of State has made a screening direction to the effect that the development is not EIA development, be deemed to be refused at the end of the relevant three week period, and the deemed refusal—

    (a) shall be treated as a decision of the authority for the purposes of paragraph (4)(c) of article 25 (register of applications) of the Order; but

    (b) shall not give rise to an appeal to the Secretary of State by virtue of section 78 (right to appeal against planning decisions and failure to take such decisions).

(6) An authority which has given a notification in accordance with paragraph (2) shall, unless the Secretary of State makes a screening direction to the effect that the development is not EIA development, determine the relevant application only by refusing planning permission if the applicant does not submit an environmental statement and comply with regulation 14(5).

(7) A person who requests a screening direction pursuant to sub-paragraph (4)(b) shall send to the Secretary of State with his request copies of—

    (a) his application for planning permission;

    (b) all documents sent to the authority as part of the application; and

    (c) all correspondence between the applicant and the authority relating to the proposed development,

and paragraphs (2) to (5) of regulation 6 shall apply to a request under this regulation as they apply to a request made pursuant to regulation 5(6).

8 Application referred to the Secretary of State without an environmental statement

(1) Where it appears to the Secretary of State that an application for planning permission which has been referred to him for determination—

    (a) is a Schedule 1 application or Schedule 2 application; and

    (b) the development in question has not been the subject of a screening opinion or screening direction; and

    (c) the application is not accompanied by a statement referred to by the applicant as an environmental statement for the purposes of these Regulations,

paragraphs (3) and (4) of regulation 6 shall apply as if the referral of the application were a request made by the applicant pursuant to regulation 5(6).

(2) Where it appears to the Secretary of State that an application which has been referred to him for determination is an EIA application and is not accompanied by a statement referred to by the applicant as an environmental statement for the purposes of these Regulations, he shall notify the applicant in writing that the submission of an environmental statement is required and shall send a copy of that notification to the relevant planning authority.

(3) The Secretary of State shall notify the applicant in accordance with paragraph (2) within three weeks beginning with the date he received the application or such longer period as he may reasonably require.

(4) An applicant who receives a notification under paragraph (2) may within three weeks

beginning with the date of the notification write to the Secretary of State stating that he proposes to provide an environmental statement.

(5) If the applicant does not write in accordance with paragraph (4), the Secretary of State shall be under no duty to deal with the application; and at the end of the three week period he shall inform the applicant in writing that no further action is being taken on the application.

(6) Where the Secretary of State has given a notification under paragraph (2), he shall determine the relevant application only by refusing planning permission if the applicant does not submit an environmental statement and comply with regulation 14(5).

9   Appeal to the Secretary of State without an environmental statement

(1) Where on consideration of an appeal under section 78 (right to appeal against planning decisions and failure to take such decisions) it appears to the Secretary of State that—

- (a) the relevant application is a Schedule 1 application or Schedule 2 application; and
- (b) the development in question has not been the subject of a screening opinion or screening direction; and
- (c) the relevant application is not accompanied by a statement referred to by the appellant as an environmental statement for the purposes of these Regulations,

paragraphs (3) and (4) of regulation 6 shall apply as if the appeal were a request made by the appellant pursuant to regulation 5(6).

(2) Where an inspector is dealing with an appeal and a question arises as to whether the relevant application is an EIA application and it appears to the inspector that it may be such an application, the inspector shall refer that question to the Secretary of State and shall not determine the appeal, except by refusing planning permission, before he receives a screening direction.

(3) Paragraphs (3) and (4) of regulation 6 shall apply to a question referred under paragraph (2) as if the referral of that question were a request made by the appellant pursuant to regulation 5(6).

(4) Where it appears to the Secretary of State that the relevant application is an EIA application and is not accompanied by a statement referred to by the appellant as an environmental statement for the purposes of these Regulations, he shall notify the appellant in writing that the submission of an environmental statement is required and shall send a copy of that notification to the relevant planning authority.

(5) An appellant who receives a notification under paragraph (4) may within three weeks beginning with the date of the notification write to the Secretary of State stating that he proposes to provide an environmental statement.

(6) If the appellant does not write in accordance with paragraph (5), the Secretary of State or, where relevant, the inspector shall be under no duty to deal with the appeal; and at the end of the three week period he shall inform the appellant that no further action is being taken on the appeal.

(7) Where the Secretary of State has given a notification under paragraph (4), the Secretary of State or, where relevant, the inspector shall determine the appeal only by refusing planning permission if the appellant does not submit an environmental statement and comply with regulation 14(5).

PART IV   PREPARATION OF ENVIRONMENTAL STATEMENTS

10   Scoping opinions of the local planning authority

(1) A person who is minded to make an EIA application may ask the relevant planning authority to state in writing their opinion as to the information to be provided in the environmental statement (a 'scoping opinion').

(2) A request under paragraph (1) shall include—

(a) a plan sufficient to identify the land;

(b) a brief description of the nature and purpose of the development and of its possible effects on the environment; and

(c) such other information or representations as the person making the request may wish to provide or make.

(3) An authority receiving a request under paragraph (1) shall, if they consider that they have not been provided with sufficient information to adopt a scoping opinion, notify the person making the request of the points on which they require additional information.

(4) An authority shall not adopt a scoping opinion in response to a request under paragraph (1) until they have consulted the person who made the request and the consultation bodies, but shall, subject to paragraph (5), within five weeks beginning with the date of receipt of that request or such longer period as may be agreed in writing with the person making the request, adopt a scoping opinion and send a copy to the person who made the request.

(5) Where a person has, at the same time as making a request for a screening opinion under regulation 5(1), asked the authority for an opinion under paragraph (1) above, and the authority have adopted a screening opinion to the effect that the development is EIA development, the authority shall, within five weeks beginning with the date on which that screening opinion was adopted or such longer period as may be agreed in writing with the person making the request, adopt a scoping opinion and send a copy to the person who made the request.

(6) Before adopting a scoping opinion the authority shall take into account—

(a) the specific characteristics of the particular development;

(b) the specific characteristics of development of the type concerned; and

(c) the environmental features likely to be affected by the development.

(7) Where an authority fail to adopt a scoping opinion within the relevant period mentioned in paragraph (4) or (5), the person who requested the opinion may under regulation 11(1) ask the Secretary of State to make a direction as to the information to be provided in the environmental statement (a 'scoping direction').

(8) Paragraph (7) applies notwithstanding that the authority may not have received additional information which they have sought under paragraph (3).

(9) An authority which has adopted a scoping opinion in response to a request under paragraph (1) shall not be precluded from requiring of the person who made the request additional information in connection with any statement that may be submitted by that person as an environmental statement in connection with an application for planning permission for the same development as was referred to in the request.

11 Scoping directions of the Secretary of State

(1) A request made under this paragraph pursuant to regulation 10(7) shall include—

(a) a copy of the relevant request to the relevant planning authority under regulation 10(1);

(b) a copy of any relevant notification under regulation 10(3) and of any response;

(c) a copy of any relevant screening opinion received by the person making the request and of any accompanying statement of reasons; and

(d) any representations that the person making the request wishes to make.

(2) When a person makes a request under paragraph (1) he shall send to the relevant planning authority a copy of that request, but that copy need not include the matters mentioned in sub-paragraphs (a) to (c) of that paragraph.

(3) The Secretary of State shall notify in writing the person making the request of any points on which he considers the information provided pursuant to paragraph (1) is insufficient to enable him to make a scoping direction; and may request the relevant planning authority to provide such information as they can on any of those points.

(4) The Secretary of State shall not make a scoping direction in response to a request under paragraph (1) until he has consulted the person making the request and the consultation bodies, but shall, within five weeks beginning with the date of receipt of that request or such longer period as he may reasonably require, make a direction and send a copy to the person who made the request and to the relevant planning authority.

(5) Before making a scoping direction the Secretary of State shall take into account the matters specified in regulation 10(6).

(6) Where the Secretary of State has made a scoping direction in response to a request under paragraph (1) neither he nor the relevant planning authority shall be precluded from requiring of the person who made the request additional information in connection with any statement that may be submitted by that person as an environmental statement in connection with an application for planning permission for the same development as was referred to in the request.

12   Procedure to facilitate preparation of environmental statements

(1) Any person who intends to submit an environmental statement to the relevant planning authority or the Secretary of State under these Regulations may give notice in writing to that authority or the Secretary of State under this paragraph.

(2) A notice under paragraph (1) shall include the information necessary to identify the land and the nature and purpose of the development, and shall indicate the main environmental consequences to which the person giving the notice proposes to refer in his environmental statement.

(3) The recipient of—

   (a) such notice as is mentioned in paragraph (1); or
   (b) a written statement made pursuant to regulation 7(4)(a), or 8(4) or 9(5)

shall—

   (i)   notify the consultation bodies in writing of the name and address of the person who intends to submit an environmental statement and of the duty imposed on the consultation bodies by paragraph (4) to make information available to that person; and
   (ii) inform in writing the person who intends to submit an environmental statement of the names and addresses of the bodies so notified.

(4) Subject to paragraph (5), the relevant planning authority and any body notified in accordance with paragraph (3) shall, if requested by the person who intends to submit an environmental statement enter into consultation with that person to determine whether the [authority or] body has in its possession any information which he or they consider relevant to the preparation of the environmental statement and, if they have, the [authority or] body shall make that information available to that person.

(5) Paragraph (4) shall not require the disclosure of information which is capable of being treated as confidential, or must be so treated, under regulation 4 of the Environmental Information Regulations 1992.

(6) A reasonable charge reflecting the cost of making the relevant information available may be made by [an authority or body], which makes information available in accordance with paragraph (4).

PART V   PUBLICITY AND PROCEDURES ON SUBMISSION OF ENVIRONMENTAL STATEMENTS

13   Procedure where an environmental statement is submitted to a local planning authority

(1) When an applicant making an EIA application submits to the relevant planning authority a statement which he refers to as an environmental statement for the purposes of

these Regulations he shall provide the authority with three additional copies of the statement for transmission to the Secretary of State and, if at the same time he serves a copy of the statement on any other body, he shall—

    (a) serve with it a copy of the application and any plan submitted with the application (unless he has already served these documents on the body in question);

    (b) inform the body that representations may be made to the relevant planning authority; and

    (c) inform the authority of the name of every body whom he has so served and of the date of service.

(2) When a relevant planning authority receive in connection with an EIA application such a statement as is first mentioned in paragraph (1) the authority shall—

    (a) send to the Secretary of State, within 14 days of receipt of the statement, three copies of the statement and a copy of the relevant application and of any documents submitted with the application;

    (b) inform the applicant of the number of copies required to enable the authority to comply with sub-paragraph (c) below; and

    (c) forward to any consultation body which has not received a copy direct from the applicant a copy of the statement and inform any such consultation body that they may make representations.

(3) The applicant shall send the copies required for the purposes of paragraph (2)(c) to the relevant planning authority.

(4) The relevant planning authority shall not determine the application until the expiry of 14 days from the last date on which a copy of the statement was served in accordance with this regulation.

14   Publicity where an environmental statement is submitted after the planning application

(1) Where an application for planning permission has been made without a statement which the applicant refers to as an environmental statement for the purposes of these Regulations and the applicant proposes to submit such a statement, he shall, before submitting it, comply with paragraphs (2) to (4).

(2) The applicant shall publish in a local newspaper circulating in the locality in which the land is situated a notice stating—

    (a) his name and that he is the applicant for planning permission and the name and address of the relevant planning authority;

    (b) the date on which the application was made and, if it be the case, that it has been referred to the Secretary of State for determination or is the subject of an appeal to him;

    (c) the address or location and the nature of the proposed development;

    (d) that a copy of the application and of any plan and other documents submitted with it together with a copy of the environmental statement may be inspected by members of the public at all reasonable hours;

    (e) an address in the locality in which the land is situated at which those documents may be inspected, and the latest date on which they will be available for inspection (being a date not less than 21 days later than the date on which the notice is published);

    (f) an address (whether or not the same as that given under sub-paragraph (e)) in the locality in which the land is situated at which copies of the statement may be obtained;

    (g) that copies may be obtained there so long as stocks last;

    (h) if a charge is to be made for a copy, the amount of the charge;

(i) that any person wishing to make representations about the application should make them in writing, before the date named in accordance with sub-paragraph (e), to the relevant planning authority or (in the case of an application referred to the Secretary of State or an appeal) to the Secretary of State; and

(j) in the case of an application referred to the Secretary of State or an appeal, the address to which representations should be sent.

(3) The applicant shall, unless he has not, and was not reasonably able to acquire, such rights as would enable him to do so, post on the land a notice containing the information specified in paragraph (2), except that the date named as the latest date on which the documents will be available for inspection shall be not less than 21 days later than the date on which the notice is first posted.

(4) The notice mentioned in paragraph (3) must—

(a) be left in position for not less than seven days in the 28 days immediately preceding the date of the submission of the statement; and

(b) be affixed firmly to some object on the land and sited and displayed in such a way as to be easily visible to, and readable by, members of the public without going on to the land.

(5) The statement, when submitted, shall be accompanied by—

(a) a copy of the notice mentioned in paragraph (2) certified by or on behalf of the applicant as having been published in a named newspaper on a date specified in the certificate; and

(b) a certificate by or on behalf of the applicant which states either—

(i) that he has posted a notice on the land in compliance with this regulation and when he did so, and that the notice was left in position for not less than seven days in the 28 days immediately preceding the date of the submission of the statement, or that, without any fault or intention on his part, it was removed, obscured or defaced before seven days had elapsed and he took reasonable steps for its protection or replacement, specifying the steps taken; or

(ii) that the applicant was unable to comply with paragraphs (3) and (4) above because he did not have the necessary rights to do so; that he has taken such reasonable steps as are open to him to acquire those rights; and has been unable to do so, specifying the steps taken.

(6) Where an applicant indicates that he proposes to provide such a statement and in such circumstances as are mentioned in paragraph (1), the relevant planning authority, the Secretary of State or the inspector, as the case may be, shall (unless disposed to refuse the permission sought) suspend consideration of the application or appeal until receipt of the statement and the other documents mentioned in paragraph (5); and shall not determine it during the period of 21 days beginning with the date of receipt of the statement and the other documents so mentioned.

(7) If any person issues a certificate which purports to comply with the requirements of paragraph (5)(b) and which contains a statement which he knows to be false or misleading in a material particular, or recklessly issues a certificate which purports to comply with those requirements and which contains a statement which is false or misleading in a material particular, he shall be guilty of an offence and liable on summary conviction to a fine not exceeding level 3 on the standard scale.

(8) Where it is proposed to submit an environmental statement in connection with an appeal, this regulation applies with the substitution, except in paragraph (2)(a), of references to the appellant for references to the applicant.

15 Provision of copies of environmental statements and further information for the Secretary of State on referral or appeal

Where an applicant for planning permission has submitted to the relevant planning authority in connection with his application a statement which he refers to as an environmental statement for the purposes of these Regulations, or further information, and—

(a) the application is referred to the Secretary of State under section 77 (reference of applications to Secretary of State); or

(b) the applicant appeals under section 78 (right to appeal against planning decisions and failure to take such decisions),

the applicant shall supply the Secretary of State with three copies of the statement and, where relevant, the further information unless, in the case of a referred application, the relevant planning authority have done so when referring the application to him.

16   Procedure where an environmental statement is submitted to the Secretary of State

(1) This regulation applies where an applicant submits to the Secretary of State, in relation to an EIA application which is before the Secretary of State or an inspector for determination or is the subject of an appeal to the Secretary of State, a statement which the applicant or appellant refers to as an environmental statement for the purposes of these Regulations.

(2) The applicant or appellant shall submit four copies of the statement to the Secretary of State who shall send one copy to the relevant planning authority.

(3) If at the same time as he submits a statement to the Secretary of State the applicant or appellant serves a copy of it on any other body, he shall comply with regulations 13(1)(a) and 13(1)(b) as if the reference in regulation 13(1)(b) to the relevant planning authority were a reference to the Secretary of State, and inform the Secretary of State of the matters mentioned in regulation 13(1) (c).

(4) The Secretary of State shall comply with regulation 13(2) (except subparagraph (a) of that regulation) and the applicant or appellant with regulation 13(3) as if—

(a) references in those provisions to the relevant planning authority were references to the Secretary of State; and,

(b) in the case of an appeal, references to the applicant were references to the appellant;

and the Secretary of State or the inspector shall comply with regulation 13(4) as if it referred to him instead of to the relevant planning authority.

17   Availability of copies of environmental statements

An applicant for planning permission or an appellant who submits in connection with his application or appeal a statement which he refers to as an environmental statement for the purposes of these Regulations shall ensure that a reasonable number of copies of the statement are available at the address named in the notices published or posted pursuant to article 8 of the Order or regulation 14 as the address at which such copies may be obtained.

18   Charges for copies of environmental statements

A reasonable charge reflecting printing and distribution costs may be made to a member of the public for a copy of a statement made available in accordance with regulation 17.

19   Further information and evidence respecting environmental statements

(1) Where the relevant planning authority, the Secretary of State or an inspector is dealing with an application or appeal in relation to which the applicant or appellant has submitted a statement which he refers to as an environmental statement for the purposes of these Regulations, and is of the opinion that the statement should contain additional information in order to be an environmental statement, they or he shall notify the applicant

or appellant in writing accordingly, and the applicant or appellant shall provide that additional information; and such information provided by the applicant or appellant is referred to in these Regulations as 'further information'.

(2) Paragraphs (3) to (9) shall apply in relation to further information, except in so far as the further information is provided for the purposes of an inquiry held under the Act and the request for that information made pursuant to paragraph (1) stated that it was to be provided for such purposes.

(3) The recipient of further information pursuant to paragraph (1) shall publish in a local newspaper circulating in the locality in which the land is situated a notice stating—

> (a) the name of the applicant for planning permission or the appellant (as the case may be) and the name and address of the relevant planning authority;
>
> (b) the date on which the application was made and, if it be the case, that it has been referred to the Secretary of State for determination or is the subject of an appeal to him;
>
> (c) the address or location and the nature of the proposed development;
>
> (d) that further information is available in relation to an environmental statement which has already been provided;
>
> (e) that a copy of the further information may be inspected by members of the public at all reasonable hours;
>
> (f) an address in the locality in which the land is situated at which the further information may be inspected and the latest date on which it will be available for inspection (being a date not less than 21 days later than the date on which the notice is published);
>
> (g) an address (whether or not the same as that given pursuant to sub-paragraph (f) in the locality in which the land is situated at which copies of the further information may be obtained;
>
> (h) that copies may be obtained there so long as stocks last;
>
> (i) if a charge is to be made for a copy, the amount of the charge;
>
> (j) that any person wishing to make representations about the further information should make them in writing, before the date specified in accordance with sub-paragraph (f), to the relevant planning authority, the Secretary of State or the inspector (as the case may be); and
>
> (k) the address to which representations should be sent.

(4) The recipient of the further information shall send a copy of it to each person to whom, in accordance with these Regulations, the statement to which it relates was sent.

(5) Where the recipient of the further information is the relevant planning authority they shall send to the Secretary of State three copies of the further information.

(6) The recipient of the further information may by notice in writing require the applicant or appellant to provide such number of copies of the further information as is specified in the notice (being the number required for the purposes of paragraph (4) or (5)).

(7) Where information is requested under paragraph (1), the relevant planning authority, the Secretary of State or the inspector, as the case may be, shall suspend determination of the application or appeal, and shall not determine it before the expiry of 14 days after the date on which the further information was sent to all persons to whom the statement to which it relates was sent or the expiry of 21 days after the date that notice of it was published in a local newspaper, whichever is the later.

(8) The applicant or appellant who provides further information in accordance with paragraph (1) shall ensure that a reasonable number of copies of the information is available at the address named in the notice published pursuant to paragraph (3) as the address at which such copies may be obtained.

(9) A reasonable charge reflecting printing and distribution costs may be made to a member of the public for a copy of the further information made available in accordance with paragraph (8).

(10) The relevant planning authority or the Secretary of State or an inspector may in writing require an applicant or appellant to produce such evidence as they may reasonably call for to verify any information in his environmental statement.

PART VI   AVAILABILITY OF DIRECTIONS ETC. AND NOTIFICATION OF DECISIONS

20   Availability of opinions, directions etc. for inspection

(1) Where particulars of a planning application are placed on Part I of the register, the relevant planning authority shall take steps to secure that there is also placed on that Part a copy of any relevant—

  (a) screening opinion;
  (b) screening direction;
  (c) scoping opinion;
  (d) scoping direction;
  (e) notification given under regulation 7(2), 8(2) or 9(4);
  (f) direction under regulation 4(4);
  (g) environmental statement, including any further information;
  (h) statement of reasons accompanying any of the above.

(2) Where the relevant planning authority adopt a screening opinion or scoping opinion, or receive a request under regulation 10(1) or 11(2), a copy of a screening direction, scoping direction, or direction under regulation 4(4) before an application is made for planning permission for the development in question, the authority shall take steps to secure that a copy of the opinion, request, or direction and any accompanying statement of reasons is made available for public inspection at all reasonable hours at the place where the appropriate register (or relevant section of that register) is kept. Copies of those documents shall remain so available for a period of two years.

21   Duties to inform the public and the Secretary of State of final decisions

(1) Where an EIA application is determined by a local planning authority, the authority shall—

  (a) in writing, inform the Secretary of State of the decision;
  (b) inform the public of the decision, by publishing a notice in a newspaper circulating in the locality in which the land is situated, or by such other means as are reasonable in the circumstances; and
  (c) make available for public inspection at the place where the appropriate register (or relevant section of that register) is kept a statement containing—
    (i) the content of the decision and any conditions attached thereto;
    (ii) the main reasons and considerations on which the decision is based; and
    (iii) a description, where necessary, of the main measures to avoid, reduce and, if possible, offset the major adverse effects of the development.

(2) Where an EIA application is determined by the Secretary of State or an inspector, the Secretary of State shall—

  (a) notify the relevant planning authority of the decision; and
  (b) provide the authority with such a statement as is mentioned in sub-paragraph (1)(c).

(3) The relevant planning authority shall, as soon as reasonably practicable after receipt of a notification under sub-paragraph (2)(a), comply with sub-paragraphs (b) and (c) of paragraph (1) in relation to the decision so notified as if it were a decision of the authority.

PART VII   SPECIAL CASES

22   Development by a local planning authority

(1) Where the relevant planning authority is also (or would be) the applicant (whether alone or jointly with any other person), these Regulations shall apply to a Schedule 1 application or Schedule 2 application (or proposed application) subject to the following modifications—

(a) subject to sub-paragraph (b) of this paragraph and to paragraphs (2) and (3) below, regulations 5 and 6 shall not apply;

(b) paragraphs (2) to (7) of regulation 7 shall not apply, and paragraph 7(1) shall apply as if the reference to paragraph (3) of regulation 5 were omitted;

(c) regulations 10 and 11 shall not apply;

(d) paragraphs (1) to (3) of regulation 12 shall not apply, and regulation 12(4) shall apply to any consultation body from whom the relevant planning authority requests assistance as it applies to a body notified in accordance with regulation 12(3);

(e) save for the purposes of regulations 16(3) and (4), regulation 13 shall apply as if—

(i) for paragraph (1), there were substituted;

'(1) When a relevant planning authority making an EIA application lodge a statement which they refer to as an environmental statement for the purposes of these Regulations, they shall—

(a) serve a copy of that statement, the relevant application and any plan submitted with it on each consultation body;

(b) inform each consultation body that representations may be made to the relevant planning authority; and

(c) send to the Secretary of State within 14 days of lodging the statement three copies of the statement and a copy of the relevant application and of any documents submitted with the application.'

(ii) paragraphs (2) and (3) were omitted;

(f) regulation 16 shall apply as if paragraph (2) were omitted.

(2) An authority which is minded to make a planning application in relation to which it would be the relevant planning authority may adopt a screening opinion or request the Secretary of State in writing to make a screening direction, and paragraphs (3) and (4) of regulation 6 shall apply to such a request as they apply to a request made pursuant to regulation 5(6).

(3) A relevant planning authority which proposes to carry out development which they consider may be—

(a) development of a description specified in Schedule 2 to the Town and Country Planning (General Permitted Development) Order 1995 other than development of a description specified in article 3(12) of that Order; or

(b) development for which permission would be granted but for regulation 23(1),

may adopt a screening opinion or request the Secretary of State to make a screening direction, and paragraphs (3) and (4) of regulation 6 shall apply to such a request as they apply to a request made pursuant to regulation 5(6).

(4) A request under paragraph (2) or (3) shall be accompanied by—

(a) a plan sufficient to identify the land;

(b) a brief description of the nature and purpose of the development and of its possible effects on the environment; and

(c) such other information or representations as the authority may wish to provide or make.

(5) An authority making a request under paragraph (2) or (3) shall send to the Secretary of State any additional information he may request in writing to enable him to make a direction.

23   Restriction of grant of permission by old simplified planning zone schemes or enterprise zone orders

(1) Any:

(a) adoption or approval of a simplified planning zone scheme;

(b) order designating an enterprise zone; or

(c) approval of a modified scheme in relation to an enterprise zone,

which has effect immediately before the commencement of these Regulations to grant planning permission shall, on and after that date, cease to have effect to grant planning permission for Schedule 1 development, and cease to have effect to grant planning permission for Schedule 2 development unless either:

(i) the relevant planning authority has adopted a screening opinion; or

(ii) the Secretary of State has made a screening direction,

to the effect that the particular proposed development is not EIA development.

(2) Paragraph (1) shall not affect the completion of any development begun before the commencement of these Regulations.

24   Restriction of grant of permission by new simplified planning zone schemes or enterprise zone orders

No:

(a) adoption or approval of a simplified planning zone scheme;

(b) order designating an enterprise zone made; or

(c) modified scheme in relation to an enterprise zone approved,

after the commencement of these Regulations shall:

(i) grant planning permission for EIA development; or

(ii) grant planning permission for Schedule 2 development unless that grant is made subject to the prior adoption of a screening opinion or prior making of a screening direction that the particular proposed development is not EIA development.

25   Unauthorised development

Prohibition on the grant of planning permission for unauthorised EIA development

(1) The Secretary of State shall not grant planning permission under subsection (1) of section 177 (grant or modification of planning permission on appeals against enforcement notices) in respect of EIA development which is the subject of an enforcement notice under section 172 (issue of enforcement notice) ('unauthorised EIA development') unless he has first taken the environmental information into consideration, and he shall state in his decision that he has done so.

Screening opinions of the local planning authority

(2) Where it appears to the local planning authority by whom or on whose behalf an enforcement notice is to be issued that the matters constituting the breach of planning control comprise or include Schedule 1 development or Schedule 2 development they shall, before the enforcement notice is issued, adopt a screening opinion.

(3) Where it appears to the local planning authority by whom or on whose behalf an enforcement notice is to be issued that the matters constituting the breach of planning control comprise or include EIA development they shall serve with a copy of the enforcement notice a notice ('regulation 25 notice') which shall—

(a) include the screening opinion required by paragraph (2) and the written statement required by regulation 4(6); and

(b) require a person who gives notice of an appeal under section 174 to submit to the Secretary of State with the notice four copies of an environmental statement relating to that EIA development.

(4) The authority by whom a regulation 25 notice has been served shall send a copy of it to—

(a) the Secretary of State; and

(b) the consultation bodies.

(5) Where an authority provide the Secretary of State with a copy of a regulation 25 notice they shall also provide him with a list of the other persons to whom a copy of the notice has been or is to be sent.

Screening directions of the Secretary of State

(6) Any person on whom a regulation 25 notice is served may apply to the Secretary of State for a screening direction and the following shall apply—

(a) an application under this paragraph shall be accompanied by—

(i)   a copy of the regulation 25 notice;

(ii) a copy of the enforcement notice which accompanied it; and

(iii) such other information or representations as the applicant may wish to provide or make;

(b) the applicant shall send to the authority by whom the regulation 25 notice was served, at such time as he applies to the Secretary of State, a copy of the application under this paragraph and of any information or representations provided or made in accordance with sub-paragraph (a)(iii);

(c) if the Secretary of State considers that the information provided in accordance with sub-paragraph (a) is insufficient to enable him to make a direction, he shall notify the applicant and the authority of the matters in respect of which he requires additional information; and the information so requested shall be provided by the applicant within such reasonable period as may be specified in the notice;

(d) the Secretary of State shall send a copy of his direction to the applicant;

(e) without prejudice to sub-paragraph (d), where the Secretary of State directs that the matters which are alleged to constitute the breach of planning control do not comprise or include EIA development, he shall send a copy of the direction to every person to whom a copy of the regulation 25 notice was sent.

Provision of information

(7) The relevant planning authority and any person, other than the Secretary of State, to whom a copy of the regulation 25 notice has been sent ('the consultee') shall, if requested by the person on whom the regulation 25 notice was served, enter into consultation with that person to determine whether the consultee has in his possession any information which that person or the consultee consider relevant to the preparation of an environmental statement and, if they have, the consultee shall make any such information available to that person.

(8) The provisions of regulations 12(5) and 12(6) shall apply to information under paragraph (7) as they apply to any information falling within regulation 12(4).

Appeal to the Secretary of State without a screening opinion or screening direction

(9) Where on consideration of an appeal under section 174 it appears to the Secretary of State that the matters which are alleged to constitute the breach of planning control comprise or include Schedule 1 development or Schedule 2 development and, in either case, no screening opinion has been adopted and no screening direction has been made in respect of that development, the Secretary of State shall, before any notice is served pursuant to paragraph (12), make such a screening direction.

(10) If the Secretary of State considers that he has not been provided with sufficient information to make a screening direction he shall notify the applicant and the authority by whom the regulation 25 notice was served of the matters in respect of which he requires additional information; and the information so requested shall be provided by the applicant within such reasonable period as may be specified in the notice.

(11) If an appellant to whom notice has been given under paragraph (10) fails to comply with the requirements of that notice:

(a) the application which is deemed to have been made by virtue of the appeal made under section 174 ('the deemed application'); and

(b) the appeal in so far as it is brought under the ground mentioned in section 174(2)(a) ('the ground (a) appeal'),

shall lapse at the end of the period specified in the notice.

Appeal to the Secretary of State without an environmental statement

(12) Where the Secretary of State is considering an appeal under section 174 and the matters which are alleged to constitute the breach of planning control comprise or include unauthorised EIA development, and the documents submitted to him for the purposes of the appeal do not include a statement referred to by the appellant as an environmental statement for the purposes of these Regulations, the following procedure shall apply—

(a) the Secretary of State shall, subject to sub-paragraph (b), within the period of three weeks beginning with the day on which he receives the appeal, or such longer period as he may reasonably require, notify the appellant in writing of the requirements of sub-paragraph (c) below;

(b) notice need not be given under sub-paragraph (a) where the appellant has submitted a statement which he refers to as an environmental statement for the purposes of these Regulations to the Secretary of State for the purposes of an appeal under section 78 (right to appeal against planning decisions and failure to take such decisions) which—

(i) relates to the development to which the appeal under section 174 relates; and

(ii) is to be determined at the same time as that appeal under section 174;

and that statement, any further information, and the representations (if any) made in relation to it shall be treated as the environmental statement and representations for the purpose of paragraph (1) of this regulation;

(c) the requirements of this sub-paragraph are that the appellant shall, within the period specified in the notice or such longer period as the Secretary of State may allow, submit to the Secretary of State four copies of an environmental statement relating to the unauthorised EIA development in question;

(d) the Secretary of State shall send to the relevant planning authority a copy of any notice sent to the appellant under sub-paragraph (a);

(e) if an appellant to whom notice has been given under sub-paragraph (a) fails to comply with the requirements of sub-paragraph (c), the deemed application and the ground (a) appeal (if any) shall lapse at the end of the period specified or allowed (as the case may be);

(f) as soon as reasonably practicable after the occurence of the event mentioned in sub-paragraph (e), the Secretary of State shall notify the appellant and the local planning authority in writing that the deemed application and the ground (a) appeal (if any) have lapsed.

Procedure where an environmental statement is submitted to the Secretary of State

(13) Where the Secretary of State receives (otherwise than as mentioned in paragraph (12)(b)) in connection with an enforcement appeal a statement which the appellant refers to as an environmental statement for the purposes of these Regulations he shall—

(a) send a copy of that statement to the relevant planning authority, advise the authority that the statement will be taken into consideration in determining the deemed application and the ground (a) appeal (if any), and inform them that they may make representations; and

(b) notify the persons to whom a copy of the relevant regulation 25 notice was sent that the statement will be taken into consideration in determining the deemed application and the ground (a) appeal (if any), and inform them that they may make representations and that, if they wish to receive a copy of the statement or any part of it, they must notify the Secretary of State of their requirements within seven days of the receipt of the Secretary of State's notice; and

(c) respond to requirements notified in accordance with sub-paragraph (b) by providing a copy of the statement or of the part requested (as the case may be).

Further information and evidence respecting environmental statements

(14) Regulations 19(1) and 19(10) shall apply to statements provided in accordance with this regulation with the following modifications—

(a) where the Secretary of State notifies the appellant under regulation 19(1), the appellant shall provide the further information within such period as the Secretary of State may specify in the notice or such longer period as the Secretary of State may allow;

(b) if an appellant to whom a notice has been given under sub-paragraph (a) fails to provide the further information within the period specified or allowed (as the case may be), the deemed application and the ground (a) appeal (if any) shall lapse at the end of that period.

(15) Paragraph (13) shall apply in relation to further information received by the Secretary of State in accordance with paragraph (14) as it applies to such a statement as is referred to in that paragraph.

Publicity for environmental statements or further information

(16) Where an authority receive a copy of a statement or further information by virtue of paragraph (13)(a) they shall publish in a local newspaper circulating in the locality in which the land is situated a notice stating—

(a) the name of the appellant and that he has appealed to the Secretary of State against the enforcement notice;

(b) the address or location of the land to which the notice relates and the nature of the development;

(c) that a copy of the statement or further information may be inspected by members of the public at all reasonable hours;

(d) an address in the locality in which the land is situated at which the statement or further information may be inspected, and the latest date on which it will be available for inspection (being a date not less than 21 days later than the date on which the notice is published);

(e) that any person wishing to make representations about any matter dealt with in the statement or further information should make them in writing, no later than 14 days after the date named in accordance with sub-paragraph (d), to the Secretary of State; and

(f) the address to which any such representations should be sent.

(17) The authority shall as soon as practicable after publication of a notice in accordance with paragraph (16) send to the Secretary of State a copy of the notice certified by or on behalf of the authority as having been published in a named newspaper on a date specified in the certificate.

(18) Where the Secretary of State receives a certificate under paragraph (17) he shall not determine the deemed application or the ground (a) appeal in respect of the development to which the certificate relates until the expiry of 14 days from the date stated in the published notice as the last date on which the statement or further information was available for inspection.

Public inspection of documents

(19) The relevant planning authority shall make available for public inspection at all

reasonable hours at the place where the appropriate register (or relevant part of that register) is kept a copy of—

    (a) every regulation 25 notice given by the authority;

    (b) every notice received by the authority under paragraph (12)(d); and

    (c) every statement and all further information received by the authority under paragraph (13)(a);

and copies of those documents shall remain so available for a period of two years or until they are entered in Part II of the register in accordance with paragraph (20), whichever is the sooner.

(20) Where particulars of any planning permission granted by the Secretary of State under section 177 are entered in Part II of the register the relevant planning authority shall take steps to secure that that Part also contains a copy of any of the documents referred to in paragraph (19) as are relevant to the development for which planning permission has been granted.

(21) The provisions of regulations 21(2) and 21(3) apply to a deemed application and a grant of planning permission under section 177 as they apply to an application for and grant of planning permission under Part III of the Act.

26 Unauthorised development with significant transboundary effects

(1) Regulation 27 shall apply to unauthorised EIA development as if—

    (a) for regulation 27(1)(a) there were substituted—

        '(a) on consideration of an appeal under section 174 the Secretary of State is of the opinion that the matters which are alleged to constitute the breach of planning control comprise or include EIA development and that the development has or is likely to have significant effects on the environment in another [EEA State]; or'

    (b) in regulation 27(3)(a) the words 'a copy of the application concerned' were replaced by the words 'a description of the development concerned';

    (c) in regulation 27(3)(b) the words 'to which that application relates' were omitted; and

    (d) in regulation 27(6) the word 'application' was replaced by the word 'appeal'.

[ROMP Applications

General application of the Regulations to ROMP applications

26A—(1) These Regulations shall apply to—

    (a) a ROMP application as they apply to an application for planning permission;

    (b) ROMP development as they apply to development in respect of which an application for planning permission is, has been or is to be made;

    (c) a relevant mineral planning authority as they apply to a relevant planning authority;

    (d) a person making a ROMP application as they apply to an applicant for planning permission; and

    (e) the determination of a ROMP application as they apply to the granting of a planning permission,

subject to the modifications and additions set out below.

Modification of provisions on prohibition of granting planning permission

(2) In regulation 3(1) (prohibition on granting planning permission without consideration of environmental information)—

    (a) in paragraph (a) for the words 'these Regulations' substitute 'the Town and Country Planning (Environmental Impact Assessment) (England and Wales) (Amendment) Regulations 2000';

(b) in paragraph (b) for the words '3 or 4 (applications for planning permission)' substitute '11 (other consents)';

(c) for the words 'determined in accordance with paragraph (3) of article 20 (time periods for decision) of the Order' substitute 'the date on which a ROMP application has been made which complies with the provisions of paragraphs 2(3) to (5) and 4(1) of Schedule 2 to the 1991 Act, 9(2) of Schedule 13 to the 1995 Act, or 6(2) of Schedule 14 to the 1995 Act'.

Modification of provisions on application to local planning authority without an environmental statement

(3) In regulation 7(4) (application made to a local planning authority without an environmental statement)—

(a) for the word 'three' substitute 'six'; and

(b) after 'the notification' insert ', or within such other period as may be agreed with the authority in writing,'.

Disapplication of Regulations and modification of provisions on application referred to or appealed to the Secretary of State without an environmental statement

(4) Regulations 7(5) and (6), 8(5) and (6), 9(6) and (7), 22, and 32 shall not apply.

(5) In regulation 8(4) (application referred to the Secretary of State without an environmental statement) and 9(5) (appeal to the Secretary of State without an environmental statement)—

(a) for the word 'three' substitute 'six';

(b) after 'the notification' insert ', or within such other period as may be agreed with the Secretary of State in writing,'.

Substitution of references to section 78 right of appeal and modification of provisions on appeal to the Secretary of State

(6) In regulations 9(1) and 15(b), for the references to 'section 78 (right to appeal against planning decisions and failure to take such decisions)' substitute—

'paragraph 5(2) of Schedule 2 to the 1991 Act, paragraph 11(1) of Schedule 13 to the 1995 Act or paragraph 9(1) of Schedule 14 to the 1995 Act (right of appeal)'.

(7) In regulation 9(2) (appeal to the Secretary of State without an environmental statement) omit the words ', except by refusing planning permission,'.

Modification of provisions on preparation, publicity and procedures on submission of environmental statements

(8) In regulations 10(9) and 11(6) for the words 'an application for planning permission for' substitute 'a ROMP application which relates to another planning permission which authorises'.

(9) In regulation 13 (procedure where an environmental statement is submitted to a local planning authority) after paragraph (3) insert—

'(3A) Where an applicant submits an environmental statement to the authority in accordance with paragraph (1), the provisions of article 8 of and Schedule 3 to the Order (publicity for applications for planning permission) shall apply to a ROMP application under paragraph—

(a) 2(2) of Schedule 2 to the 1991 Act; and

(b) 6(1) of Schedule 14 to the 1995 Act,

as they apply to a planning application falling within paragraph 8 (2) of the Order except that for the references in the notice in Schedule 3 to the Order to "planning permission" there shall be substituted "determination of the conditions to which a planning permission is to be subject" and that notice shall refer to the relevant provisions of the 1991 or 1995 Act pursuant to which the application is made.'

(10) In regulation 14 (publicity where an environmental statement is submitted after the planning application)—

(a) in paragraph (2)(a) for the words 'and that he is the applicant for planning permission' substitute—

', that he has applied for determination of the conditions to which a planning permission is to be subject, the relevant provisions of the 1991 or 1995 Act pursuant to which the application is made';

(b) in paragraph (6) for the words—

(i) '(unless disposed to refuse the permission sought) suspend consideration of the application or appeal until receipt of the statement and the other documents mentioned in paragraph (5)' substitute—

'suspend consideration of the application or appeal until the date specified by the authority or the Secretary of State for submission of the environmental statement and compliance with paragraph (5)';

(ii) 'so mentioned' substitute 'mentioned in paragraph (5)'.

(11) In regulation 15 (provision of copies of environmental statements and further information for the Secretary of State on referral or appeal), in paragraph (a) for 'section 77' substitute 'paragraph 7(1) of Schedule 2 to the 1991 Act, paragraph 13(1) of Schedule 13 to the 1995 Act or paragraph 8(1) of Schedule 14 to the 1995 Act'.

(12) In regulation 17 (availability of copies of environmental statements) after the words 'the Order' insert '(as applied by regulation 13(3A) or by paragraph 9(5) of Schedule 13 to the 1995 Act),'

(13) In regulation 19 (further information and evidence respecting environmental statements)—

(a) in paragraph (3) for the words 'applicant for planning permission or the appellant (as the case may be)' substitute—

'person who has applied for or who has appealed in relation to the determination of the conditions to which the planning permission is to be subject, the relevant provisions of the 1991 or 1995 Act pursuant to which the application is made';

(b) in paragraph (7) after the words 'application or appeal' insert 'until the date specified by them or him for submission of the further information'.

Modification of provisions on application to the High Court and giving of directions

(14) For regulation 30 (application to the High Court) substitute—

'Application to the High Court

30. For the purposes of Part XII of the Act (validity of certain decisions), the reference in section 288, as applied by paragraph 9(3) of Schedule 2 to the 1991 Act, paragraph 16(4) of Schedule 13 to the 1995 Act or paragraph 9(4) of Schedule 14 to the 1995 Act, to action of the Secretary of State which is not within the powers of the Act shall be taken to extend to the determination of a ROMP application by the Secretary of State in contravention of regulation 3.'.

(15) The direction making power substituted by regulation 35(8) shall apply to ROMP development as it applies to development in respect of which a planning application is made.

Suspension of minerals development

(16) Where the authority, the Secretary of State or an inspector notifies the applicant or appellant, as the case may be, that—

(a) the submission of an environmental statement is required under regulation 7(2), 8(2) or 9(4) then such notification shall specify the period within which the environmental statement and compliance with regulation 14(5) is required; or

(b) a statement should contain additional information under regulation 19(1) then such notification shall specify the period within which that information is to be provided.

(17) Subject to paragraph (18), the planning permission to which the ROMP application relates shall not authorise any minerals development (unless the Secretary of State has made a screening direction to the effect that the ROMP development is not EIA development) if the applicant or the appellant does not—

(a) write to the authority or Secretary of State within the six week or other period agreed pursuant to regulations 7(4), 8(4) or 9(5);

(b) submit an environmental statement and comply with regulation 14(5) within the period specified by the authority or the Secretary of State in accordance with paragraph (16) or within such extended period as is agreed in writing; or

(c) provide additional information within the period specified by the authority, the Secretary of State or an inspector in accordance with paragraph (16) or within such extended period as is agreed in writing.

(18) Where paragraph (17) applies, the planning permission shall not authorise any minerals development from the end of—

(a) the relevant six week or other period agreed in writing as referred to in paragraph (17)(a);

(b) the period specified or agreed in writing as referred to in paragraphs (17)(b) and (c), ('suspension of minerals development') until the applicant has complied with all of the provisions referred to in paragraph (17) which are relevant to the application or appeal in question.

(19) Particulars of the suspension of minerals development and the date when that suspension ends must be entered in the appropriate part of the register as soon as reasonably practicable.

(20) Paragraph (17) shall not affect any minerals development carried out under the planning permission before the date of suspension of minerals development.

(21) For the purposes of paragraphs (17) to (20) 'minerals development' means development consisting of the winning and working of minerals, or involving the depositing of mineral waste.

Determination of conditions and right of appeal on non-determination

(22) Where it falls to—

(a) a mineral planning authority to determine a Schedule 1 or a Schedule 2 application, paragraph 2(6)(b) of Schedule 2 to the 1991 Act, paragraph 9(9) of Schedule 13 to the 1995 Act or paragraph 6(8) of Schedule 14 to the 1995 Act shall not have effect to treat the authority as having determined the conditions to which any relevant planning permission is to be subject unless either the mineral planning authority has adopted a screening opinion or the Secretary of State has made a screening direction to the effect that the ROMP development in question is not EIA development;

(b) a mineral planning authority or the Secretary of State to determine a Schedule 1 or a Schedule 2 application—

(i) section 69 (register of applications, etc), and any provisions of the Order made by virtue of that section, shall have effect with any necessary amendments as if references to applications for planning permission included ROMP applications under paragraph 9(1) of Schedule 13 to the 1995 Act and paragraph 6(1) of Schedule 14 to the 1995 Act; and

(ii) where the relevant mineral planning authority is not the authority required to keep the register, the relevant mineral planning authority must provide the authority required to keep it with such information and documents as that authority requires to comply with section 69 as applied by sub-paragraph (i), with regulation 20 as applied by paragraph (1), and with paragraph (19).

(23) Where it falls to the mineral planning authority or the Secretary of State to determine an EIA application which is made under paragraph 2(2) of Schedule 2 to the 1991 Act, paragraph 4(4) of that Schedule shall not apply.

(24) Where it falls to the mineral planning authority to determine an EIA application, the authority shall give written notice of their determination of the ROMP application within 16 weeks beginning with the date of receipt by the authority of the ROMP application or such extended period as may be agreed in writing between the applicant and the authority.

(25) For the purposes of paragraph (24) a ROMP application is not received by the authority until—

(a) a document referred to by the applicant as an environmental statement for the purposes of these Regulations;

(b) any documents required to accompany that statement; and

(c) any additional information which the authority has notified the applicant that the environmental statement should contain,

has been received by the authority.

(26) Where paragraph (22)(a) applies—

(a) paragraph 5(2) of Schedule 2 to the 1991 Act, paragraph 11(1) of Schedule 13 to the 1995 Act and paragraph 9(1) of Schedule 14 to the 1995 Act (right of appeal) shall have effect as if there were also a right of appeal to the Secretary of State where the mineral planning authority have not given written notice of their determination of the ROMP application in accordance with paragraph (24); and

(b) paragraph 5(5) of Schedule 2 to the 1991 Act, paragraph 11(2) of Schedule 13 to the 1995 Act and paragraph 9(2) of Schedule 14 to the 1995 Act (right of appeal) shall have effect as if they also provided for notice of appeal to be made within six months from the expiry of the 16 week or other period agreed pursuant to paragraph (24).

(27) In determining for the purposes of paragraphs—

(a) 2(6)(b) of Schedule 2 to the 1991 Act, 9(9) of Schedule 13 to the 1995 Act and 6(8) of Schedule 14 to the 1995 Act (determination of conditions); or

(b) paragraph 5(5) of Schedule 2 to the 1991 Act, paragraph 11(2) of Schedule 13 to the 1995 Act and paragraph 9(2) of Schedule 14 to the 1995 Act (right of appeal) as applied by paragraph (26)(b),

the time which has elapsed without the mineral planning authority giving the applicant written notice of their determination in a case where the authority have notified an applicant in accordance with regulation 7(2) that the submission of an environmental statement is required and the Secretary of State has given a screening direction in relation to the ROMP development in question no account shall be taken of any period before the issue of the direction.

ROMP application by a mineral planning authority

(28) Where a mineral planning authority proposes to make or makes a ROMP application to the Secretary of State under regulation 11 (other consents) of the General Regulations which is a Schedule 1 or a Schedule 2 application (or proposed application), these Regulations shall apply to that application or proposed application as they apply to a ROMP application referred to the Secretary of State under paragraph 7(1) of Schedule 2 to the 1991 Act, paragraph 13(1) of Schedule 13 to the 1995 Act or paragraph 8(1) of Schedule 14 to the 1995 Act (reference of applications to the Secretary of State) subject to the following modifications—

(a) subject to paragraph (29) below, regulations 5, 6, 7, 9, 10, 11, 13 (save for the purposes of regulations 16(3) and (4)) 15 and 21 (1) shall not apply;

(b) in regulation 4 (general provisions relating to screening)—

    (i)   in paragraph (4), omit the words 'and shall send a copy of such direction to
          the relevant planning authority';
    (ii) paragraph (9) shall be omitted;
(c) in regulation 8(2) (application referred to the Secretary of State without an
    environmental statement), omit the words 'and shall send a copy of that
    notification to the relevant planning authority';
(d) in regulation 12 (procedure to facilitate preparation of environmental
    statements)—
    (i)   in sub-paragraph (3)(b) for the words '7(4)(a), or 8(4) or 9(5)' substitute
          '8(4)';
    (ii) in paragraph (4) omit the words 'the relevant planning authority and';
(e) in regulation 14(2) (publicity where an environmental statement is submitted
    after the planning application)—
    (i)   in sub-paragraph (a) omit the words 'and the name and address of the
          relevant planning authority';
    (ii) for sub-paragraph (b) substitute—
          '(b) the date on which the application was made and that it has been made to
               the Secretary of State under regulation 11 of the General Regulations;';
(f) in regulation 16 (procedure where an environmental statement is submitted to
    the Secretary of State), in paragraph (2) omit the words 'who shall send one copy
    to the relevant planning authority';
(g) in regulation 19(3) (further information and evidence respecting environmental
    statements)—
    (i)   in sub-paragraph (a) omit the words 'and the name and address of the
          relevant planning authority';
    (ii) for sub-paragraph (b) substitute—
          '(b) the date on which the application was made and that it has been made to
               the Secretary of State under regulation 11 of the General Regulations;';
(h) regulations 20 (availability of opinions, directions etc. for inspection) and 21(2)
    (duties to inform the public and the Secretary of State of final decisions) shall
    apply as if the references to a 'relevant planning authority' were references to a
    mineral planning authority.
(29) A mineral planning authority which is minded to make a ROMP application to the
Secretary of State under regulation 11 of the General Regulations may request the Secretary of
State in writing to make a screening direction, and paragraphs (3) and (4) of regulation 6 shall
apply to such a request as they apply to a request made pursuant to regulation 5(6) except that
in paragraph (3) the words ', and may request the relevant planning authority to provide such
information as they can on any of those points' shall be omitted.
(30) A request under paragraph (29) shall be accompanied by—
    (a) a plan sufficient to identify the land;
    (b) a brief description of the nature and purpose of the ROMP development and of its
         possible effects on the environment; and
    (c) such other information as the authority may wish to provide or make.
(31) An authority making a request under paragraph (29) shall send to the Secretary of
State any additional information he may request in writing to enable him to make a direction.']

PART VIII   DEVELOPMENT WITH SIGNIFICANT
TRANSBOUNDARY EFFECTS

**27 Development in England and Wales likely to have significant effects in
another [EEA State]**
    (1) Where—

(a) it comes to the attention of the Secretary of State that development proposed to be carried out in England or Wales is the subject of an EIA application and is likely to have significant effects on the environment in another [EEA State]; or

(b) another [EEA State] likely to be significantly affected by such development so requests,

the Secretary of State shall—

(i) send to the [EEA State] as soon as possible and no later than their date of publication in The London Gazette referred to in subparagraph (ii) below, the particulars mentioned in paragraph (2) and, if he thinks fit, the information referred to in paragraph (3); and

(ii) publish the information in sub-paragraph (i) above in a notice placed in The London Gazette indicating the address where additional information is available; and

(iii) give the [EEA State] a reasonable time in which to indicate whether it wishes to participate in the procedure for which these Regulations provide.

(2) The particulars referred to in paragraph (1)(i) are—

(a) a description of the development, together with any available information on its possible significant effect on the environment in another [EEA State]; and

(b) information on the nature of the decision which may be taken.

(3) Where a [EEA State] indicates, in accordance with paragraph (1)(iii), that it wishes to participate in the procedure for which these Regulations provide, the Secretary of State shall as soon as possible send to that [EEA State] the following information—

(a) a copy of the application concerned;

(b) a copy of the environmental statement in respect of the development to which that application relates; and

(c) relevant information regarding the procedure under these Regulations,

but only to the extent that such information has not been provided to the [EEA State] earlier in accordance with paragraph (1)(i).

(4) The Secretary of State, insofar as he is concerned, shall also—

(a) arrange for the particulars and information referred to in paragraphs (2) and (3) to be made available, within a reasonable time, to the authorities referred to in Article 6(1) of the Directive and the public concerned in the territory of the [EEA State] likely to be significantly affected; and

(b) ensure that those authorities and the public concerned are given an opportunity, before planning permission for the development is granted, to forward to the Secretary of State, within a reasonable time, their opinion on the information supplied.

(5) The Secretary of State shall in accordance with Article 7(4) of the Directive—

(a) enter into consultations with the [EEA State] concerned regarding, inter alia, the potential significant effects of the development on the environment of that [EEA State] and the measures envisaged to reduce or eliminate such effects; and

(b) determine in agreement with the other [EEA State] a reasonable period of time for the duration of the consultation period.

(6) Where a [EEA State] has been consulted in accordance with paragraph (5), on the determination of the application concerned the Secretary of State shall inform the [EEA State] of the decision and shall forward to it a statement of—

(a) the content of the decision and any conditions attached thereto;

(b) the main reasons and considerations on which the decision is based; and

(c) a description, where necessary, of the main measures to avoid, reduce and, if possible, offset the major adverse effects of the development.

28 Projects in another EEA State likely to have significant transboundary effects

(1) Where the Secretary of State receives from another [EEA State] pursuant to Article 7(2) of the Directive information which that [EEA State] has gathered from the developer of a proposed project in that [EEA State] which is likely to have significant effects on the environment in England and Wales, the Secretary of State shall, in accordance with Article 7(4) of the Directive:

(a) enter into consultations with that [EEA State] regarding, inter alia, the potential significant effects of the proposed project on the environment in England and Wales and the measures envisaged to reduce or eliminate such effects; and

(b) determine in agreement with that [EEA State] a reasonable period, before development consent for the project is granted, during which members of the public in England and Wales may submit to the competent authority in that [EEA State] representations pursuant to Article 7(3)(b) of the Directive.

(2) The Secretary of State, insofar as he is concerned, shall also—

(a) arrange for the information referred to in paragraph (1) to be made available, within a reasonable time, both to the authorities in England and Wales which he considers are likely to be concerned by the project by reason of their specific environmental responsibilities, and to the public concerned in England and Wales; and

(b) ensure that those authorities and the public concerned in England and Wales are given an opportunity, before development consent for the project is granted, to forward to the competent authority in the relevant [EEA State], within a reasonable time, their opinion on the information supplied.

PART IX   MISCELLANEOUS

29 Service of notices etc.

Any notice or other document to be sent, served or given under these Regulations may be served or given in a manner specified in section 329 (service of notices).

30 Application to the High Court

For the purposes of Part XII of the Act (validity of certain decisions), the reference in section 288 to action of the Secretary of State which is not within the powers of the Act shall be taken to extend to a grant of planning permission by the Secretary of State in contravention of regulations 3 or 25(1).

31 Hazardous waste and material change of use

A change in the use of land or buildings to a use for a purpose mentioned in paragraph 9 of Schedule I involves a material change in the use of that land or those buildings for the purposes of paragraph (1) of section 55 (meaning of 'development' and 'new development').

32 Extension of the period for an authority's decision on a planning application

(1) In determining for the purposes of section 78 (right to appeal against planning decisions and failure to take such decisions) the time which has elapsed without the relevant planning authority giving notice to the applicant of their decision in a case where—

(a) the authority have notified an applicant in accordance with regulation 7(2) that the submission of an environmental statement is required; and

(b) the Secretary of State has given a screening direction in relation to the development in question,

no account shall be taken of any period before the issue of the direction.

(2) Where it falls to an authority to determine an EIA application, article 20 (time periods for decision) of the Order shall have effect as if—

    (a) for the reference in paragraph (2)(a) of that article to a period of 8 weeks there were substituted a reference to a period of 16 weeks;

    (b) after paragraph (3)(b) of that article there were inserted—

        '(ba) the environmental statement required to be submitted in respect of the application has been submitted, together with the documents required to accompany that statement; and.'

33 Extension of the power to provide in a development order for the giving of directions as respects the manner in which planning applications are dealt with

The provisions enabling the Secretary of State to give directions which may be included in a development order by virtue of section 60 (permission granted by development order) shall include provisions enabling him to direct that development which is both of a description mentioned in Column 1 of the table in Schedule 2, and of a class described in the direction is EIA development for the purposes of these Regulations.

34 Revocation of Statutory Instruments and transitional provisions

(1) The instruments in Schedule 5 are hereby revoked to the extent shown in that Schedule.

(2) Nothing in paragraph (1) shall affect the continued application of the Instruments revoked by that paragraph to any application lodged or received by an authority before the commencement of these Regulations, to any appeal in relation to such an application, or to any matter in relation to which a local planning authority has before that date issued an enforcement notice under section 172; and these Regulations shall not apply to any such application, appeal, or matter.

35 Miscellaneous and consequential amendments [. . .]

Regulation 2(1)	SCHEDULE 1

DESCRIPTIONS OF DEVELOPMENT FOR THE PURPOSES OF THE DEFINITION OF 'SCHEDULE 1 DEVELOPMENT'

Interpretation

In this Schedule—

    'airport' means an airport which complies with the definition in the 1944 Chicago Convention setting up the International Civil Aviation Organisation (Annex 14);

    'express road' means a road which complies with the definition in the European Agreement on Main International Traffic Arteries of 15 November 1975;

    'nuclear power station' and 'other nuclear reactor' do not include an installation from the site of which all nuclear fuel and other radioactive contaminated materials have been permanently removed; and development for the purpose of dismantling or decommissioning a nuclear power station or other nuclear reactor shall not be treated as development of the description mentioned in paragraph 2(b) of this Schedule.

Descriptions of development

The carrying out of development to provide any of the following—

1. Crude-oil refineries (excluding undertakings manufacturing only lubricants from crude oil) and installations for the gasification and liquefaction of 500 tonnes or more of coal or bituminous shale per day.

2.

    (a) Thermal power stations and other combustion installations with a heat output of 300 megawatts or more; and

  (b) Nuclear power stations and other nuclear reactors (except research installations for the production and conversion of fissionable and fertile materials, whose maximum power does not exceed 1 kilowatt continuous thermal load).

3.

  (a) Installations for the reprocessing of irradiated nuclear fuel. (b) Installations designed—
   (i) for the production or enrichment of nuclear fuel,
   (ii) for the processing of irradiated nuclear fuel or high-level radioactive waste,
   (iii) for the final disposal of irradiated nuclear fuel,
   (iv) solely for the final disposal of radioactive waste,
   (v) solely for the storage (planned for more than 10 years) of irradiated nuclear fuels or radioactive waste in a different site than the production site.

4.

  (a) Integrated works for the initial smelting of cast-iron and steel;
  (b) Installations for the production of non-ferrous crude metals from ore, concentrates or secondary raw materials by metallurgical, chemical or electrolytic processes.

5. Installations for the extraction of asbestos and for the processing and transformation of asbestos and products containing asbestos—

  (a) for asbestos-cement products, with an annual production of more than 20,000 tonnes of finished products;
  (b) for friction material, with an annual production of more than 50 tonnes of finished products; and
  (c) for other uses of asbestos, utilisation of more than 200 tonnes per year.

6. Integrated chemical installations, that is to say, installations for the manufacture on an industrial scale of substances using chemical conversion processes, in which several units are juxtaposed and are functionally linked to one another and which are—

  (a) for the production of basic organic chemicals;
  (b) for the production of basic inorganic chemicals;
  (c) for the production of phosphorous-, nitrogen- or potassium-based fertilisers (simple or compound fertilisers);
  (d) for the production of basic plant health products and of biocides;
  (e) for the production of basic pharmaceutical products using a chemical or biological process;
  (f) for the production of explosives.

7.

  (a) Construction of lines for long-distance railway traffic and of airports with a basic runway length of 2,100 metres or more;
  (b) Construction of motorways and express roads;
  (c) Construction of a new road of four or more lanes, or realignment and/or widening of an existing road of two lanes or less so as to provide four or more lanes, where such new road, or realigned and/or widened section of road would be 10 kilometres or more in a continuous length.

8.

  (a) Inland waterways and ports for inland-waterway traffic which permit the passage of vessels of over 1,350 tonnes;
  (b) Trading ports, piers for loading and unloading connected to land and outside ports (excluding ferry piers) which can take vessels of over 1,350 tonnes.

9. Waste disposal installations for the incineration, chemical treatment (as defined in Annex IIA to Council Directive 75/442/EEC under heading D9), or landfill of hazardous waste (that is to say, waste to which Council Directive 91/689/EEC applies).

10. Waste disposal installations for the incineration or chemical treatment (as defined in Annex IIA to Council Directive 75/442/EEC under heading D9) of non-hazardous waste with a capacity exceeding 100 tonnes per day.

11. Groundwater abstraction or artificial groundwater recharge schemes where the annual volume of water abstracted or recharged is equivalent to or exceeds 10 million cubic metres.

12.

(a) Works for the transfer of water resources, other than piped drinking water, between river basins where the transfer aims at preventing possible shortages of water and where the amount of water transferred exceeds 100 million cubic metres per year;

(b) In all other cases, works for the transfer of water resources, other than piped drinking water, between river basins where the multi-annual average flow of the basin of abstraction exceeds 2,000 million cubic metres per year and where the amount of water transferred exceeds 5% of this flow.

13. Waste water treatment plants with a capacity exceeding 150,000 population equivalent as defined in Article 2 point (6) of Council Directive 91/271/EEC.

14. Extraction of petroleum and natural gas for commercial purposes where the amount extracted exceeds 500 tonnes per day in the case of petroleum and 500,000 cubic metres per day in the case of gas.

15. Dams and other installations designed for the holding back or permanent storage of water, where a new or additional amount of water held back or stored exceeds 10 million cubic metres.

16. Pipelines for the transport of gas, oil or chemicals with a diameter of more than 800 millimetres and a length of more than 40 kilometres.

17. Installations for the intensive rearing of poultry or pigs with more than—

(a) 85,000 places for broilers or 60,000 places for hens;

(b) 3,000 places for production pigs (over 30 kg); or

(c) 900 places for sows.

18. Industrial plants for—

(a) the production of pulp from timber or similar fibrous materials;

(b) the production of paper and board with a production capacity exceeding 200 tonnes per day.

19. Quarries and open-cast mining where the surface of the site exceeds 25 hectares, or peat extraction where the surface of the site exceeds 150 hectares.

20. Installations for storage of petroleum, petrochemical or chemical products with a capacity of 200,000 tonnes or more.

Regulation 2(1)   SCHEDULE 2

DESCRIPTIONS OF DEVELOPMENT AND APPLICABLE THRESHOLDS AND CRITERIA FOR THE PURPOSES OF THE DEFINITION OF 'SCHEDULE 2 DEVELOPMENT'

1.   In the table below—

'area of the works' includes any area occupied by apparatus, equipment, machinery, materials, plant, spoil heaps or other facilities or stores required for construction or installation;

'controlled waters' has the same meaning as in the Water Resources Act 1991

'floorspace' means the floorspace in a building or buildings.

2.   The table below sets out the descriptions of development and applicable thresholds and criteria for the purpose of classifying development as Schedule 2 development.

Table

Column 1	Column 2
Description of development	**Applicable thresholds and criteria**
The carrying out of development to provide any of the following—	
1. Agriculture and aquaculture (a) Projects for the use of uncultivated land or semi-natural areas for intensive agricultural purposes;	The area of the development exceeds 0.5 hectare.
(b) Water management projects for agriculture, including irrigation and land drainage projects;	The area of the works exceeds 1 hectare.
(c) Intensive livestock installations (unless included in Schedule 1);	The area of new floorspace exceeds 500 square metres.
(d) Intensive fish farming;	The installation resulting from the development is designed to produce more than 10 tonnes of dead weight fish per year.
(e) Reclamation of land from the sea.	All development.
2. Extractive industry (a) Quarries, open-cast mining and peat extraction (unless included in Schedule 1); (b) Underground mining;	All development except the construction of buildings or other ancillary structures where the new floorspace does not exceed 1,000 square metres.
(c) Extraction of minerals by fluvial dredging;	All development.

(d) Deep drillings, in particular—
  (i) geothermal drilling;
  (ii) drilling for the storage of nuclear waste material;
  (iii) drilling for water supplies; with the exception of drillings for investigating the stability of the soil.
	(i) In relation to any type of drilling, the area of the works exceeds 1 hectare; or
	(ii) in relation to geothermal drilling and drilling for the storage of nuclear waste material, the drilling is within 100 metres of any controlled waters.

(e) Surface industrial installations for the extraction of coal, petroleum, natural gas and ores, as well as bituminous shale.	The area of the development exceeds 0.5 hectare.
3. Energy industry (a) Industrial installations for the production of electricity, steam and hot water (unless included in Schedule 1);	The area of the development exceeds 0.5 hectare.
(b) Industrial installations for carrying gas, steam and hot water;	The area of the works exceeds 1 hectare.
(c) Surface storage of natural gas; (d) Underground storage of combustible gases; (e) Surface storage of fossil fuels;	(i) The area of any new building, deposit or structure exceeds 500 square metres; or (ii) a new building, deposit or structure is to be sited within 100 metres of any controlled waters.
(f) Industrial briquetting of coal and lignite;	The area of new floorspace exceeds 1,000 square metres.
(g) Installations for the processing and storage of radioactive waste (unless included in Schedule 1);	(i) The area of new floorspace exceeds 1,000 square metres; or

Column 1	Column 2
Description of development	**Applicable thresholds and criteria**
	(ii) the installation resulting from the development will require an authorisation or the variation of an authorisation under the Radioactive Substances Act 1993.
(h) Installations for hydroelectric energy production;	The installation is designed to produce more than 0.5 megawatts.
(i) Installations for the harnessing of wind power for energy production (wind farms).	(i) The development involves the installation of more than 2 turbines: or (ii) the hub height of any turbine or height of any other structure exceeds 15 metres.

4. Production and processing of metals
(a) Installations for the production of pig iron or steel (primary or secondary fusion) including continuous casting;
(b) Installations for the processing of ferrous metals—
    (i) hot-rolling mills;
    (ii) smitheries with hammers;
    (iii) applications of protective fused metal coats.
(c) Ferrous metal foundries;
(d) Installations for the smelting, including the alloyage, of non-ferrous metals, excluding precious metals, including recovered products (refining, foundry casting, etc.);
(e) Installations for surface treatment of metals and plastic materials using an electrolytic or chemical process;
(f) Manufacture and assembly of motor vehicles and manufacture of motor-vehicle engines;
(g) Shipyards;
(h) Installations for the construction and repair of aircraft;
(i) Manufacture of railway equipment;
(j) Swaging by explosives;
(k) Installations for the roasting and sintering of metallic ores.
	The area of new floorspace exceeds 1,000 square metres.

5. Mineral industry (a) Coke ovens (dry coal distillation); (b) Installations for the manufacture of cement; (c) Installations for the production of asbestos and the manufacture of asbestos-based products (unless included in Schedule 1); (d) Installations for the manufacture of glass including glass fibre; (e) Installations for smelting mineral substances including the production of mineral fibres;	The area of new floorspace exceeds 1,000 square metres.

Column 1	Column 2
Description of development	**Applicable thresholds and criteria**
(f) Manufacture of ceramic products by burning, in particular roofing tiles, bricks, refractory bricks, tiles, stonewear or porcelain.	
6. Chemical industry (unless included in Schedule 1) (a) Treatment of intermediate products and production of chemicals; (b) Production of pesticides and pharmaceutical products, paint and varnishes, elastomers and peroxides;	The area of new floorspace exceeds 1,000 square metres.
(c) Storage facilities for petroleum, petrochemical and chemical products.	(i) The area of any new building or structure exceeds 0.05 hectare; or (ii) more than 200 tonnes of petroleum, petrochemical or chemical products is to be stored at any one time.
7. Food industry (a) Manufacture of vegetable and animal oils and fats; (b) Packing and canning of animal and vegetable products; (c) Manufacture of dairy products; (d) Brewing and malting; (e) Confectionery and syrup manufacture; (f) Installations for the slaughter of animals; (g) Industrial starch manufacturing installations; (h) Fish-meal and fish-oil factories; (i) Sugar factories.	The area of new floorspace exceeds 1,000 square metres.
8. Textile, leather, wood and paper industries (a) Industrial plants for the production of paper and board (unless included in Schedule 1); (b) Plants for the pre-treatment (operations such as washing, bleaching, mercerisation) or dyeing of fibres or textiles; (c) Plants for the tanning of hides and skins; (d) Cellulose- processing and production installations.	The area of new floorspace exceeds 1,000 square metres.
9. Rubber industry Manufacture and treatment of elastomer-based products.	The area of new floorspace exceeds 1,000 square metres.
10. Infrastructure projects (a) Industrial estate development projects; (b) Urban development projects, including the construction of shopping centres and car parks, sports stadiums, leisure centres and multiplex cinemas;	The area of the development exceeds 0.5 hectare.

Column 1	Column 2
Description of development	**Applicable thresholds and criteria**
(c) Construction of intermodal transshipment facilities and of intermodal terminals (unless included in Schedule 1);	
(d) Construction of railways (unless included in Schedule 1);	The area of the works exceeds 1 hectare.
(e) Construction of airfields (unless included in Schedule 1);	(i) The development involves an extension to a runway; or (ii) the area of the works exceeds 1 hectare
(f) Construction of roads (unless included in Schedule 1);	The area of the works exceeds 1 hectare.
(g) Construction of harbours and port installations including fishing harbours (unless included in Schedule 1);	The area of the works exceeds 1 hectare.
(h) Inland-waterway construction not included in Schedule 1, canalisation and flood-relief works; (i) Dams and other installations designed to hold water or store it on a long-term basis (unless included in Schedule 1); (j) Tramways, elevated and underground railways, suspended lines or similar lines of a particular type, used exclusively or mainly for passenger transport;	The area of the works exceeds 1 hectare.
(k) Oil and gas pipeline installations (unless included in Schedule 1); (l) Installations of long-distance aqueducts;	(i) The area of the works exceeds 1 hectare; or, (ii) in the case of a gas pipeline, the installation has a design operating pressure exceeding 7 bar gauge.
(m) Coastal work to combat erosion and maritime works capable of altering the coast through the construction, for example, of dykes, moles, jetties and other sea defence works, excluding the maintenance and reconstruction of such works;	All development.
(n) Groundwater abstraction and artificial groundwater recharge schemes not included in Schedule 1; (o) Works for the transfer of water resources between river basins not included in Schedule 1;	The area of the works exceeds 1 hectare.
(p) Motorway service areas.	The area of the development exceeds 0.5 hectare.
11. Other projects (a) Permanent racing and test tracks for motorised vehicles;	The area of the development exceeds 1 hectare.

Column 1	Column 2
Description of development	**Applicable thresholds and criteria**
(b) Installations for the disposal of waste (unless included in Schedule 1);	(i) The disposal is by incineration; or (ii) the area of the development exceeds 0.5 hectare; or (iii) the installation is to be sited within 100 metres of any controlled waters.
(c) Waste-water treatment plants (unless included in Schedule 1);	The area of the development exceeds 1,000 square metres.
(d) Sludge-deposition sites; (e) Storage of scrap iron, including scrap vehicles;	(i) The area of deposit or storage exceeds 0.5 hectare; or (ii) a deposit is to be made or scrap stored within 100 metres of any controlled waters.
(f) Test benches for engines, turbines or reactors; (g) Installations for the manufacture of artificial mineral fibres; (h) Installations for the recovery or destruction of explosive substances; (i) Knackers' yards.	The area of new floorspace exceeds 1,000 square metres.
12. Tourism and leisure (a) Ski-runs, ski-lifts and cable-cars and associated developments;	(i) The area of the works exceeds 1 hectare; or (ii) the height of any building or other structure exceeds 15 metres.
(b) Marinas;	The area of the enclosed water surface exceeds 1,000 square metres.
(c) Holiday villages and hotel complexes outside urban areas and associated developments; (d) Theme parks;	The area of the development exceeds 1 hectare.
(e) Permanent camp sites and caravan sites;	The area of the development exceeds 1 hectare.
(f) Golf courses and associated developments.	The area of the development exceeds 1 hectare.
13. (a) Any change to or extension of development of a description listed in Schedule 1 or in paragraphs 1 to 12 of Column 1 of this table, where that development is already authorised, executed or in the process of being executed, and the change or extension may have significant adverse effects on the environment;	(i) In relation to development of a description mentioned in Column 1 of this table, the thresholds and criteria in the corresponding part of Column 2 of this table applied to the change or extension (and not to the development as changed or extended). (ii) In relation to development of a description mentioned in a paragraph in Schedule 1 indicated below, the thresholds and criteria in Column 2 of the paragraph of this table indicated below applied to the change or extension (and not to the development as changed or extended):

Column 1	Column 2
Description of development	**Applicable thresholds and criteria**
	Paragraph in Schedule 1 — Paragraph of this table

Paragraph in Schedule 1	Paragraph of this table
1	6(a)
2(a)	3(a)
2(b)	3(g)
3	3(g)
4	4
5	5
6	6(a)
7(a)	10(a) (in relation to railways)
1	or 10(e) (in relation to airports)
7(b) and (c)	10(f)
8(a)	10(h)
8(b)	10(g)
9	11(b)
10	11(b)
11	10(n)
12	10(o)
13	11(c)
14	2(e)
15	10(i)
16	10(k)
17	1(c)
18	8(a)
19	2(a)
20	6(c)

Column 1	Column 2
(b) Development of a description mentioned in Schedule 1 undertaken exclusively or mainly for the development and testing of new methods or products and not used for more than two years.	All development.

Regulation 4(5)   SCHEDULE 3

SELECTION CRITERIA FOR SCREENING SCHEDULE 2 DEVELOPMENT

1 Characteristics of development

The characteristics of development must be considered having regard, in particular, to—

   (a) the size of the development;
   (b) the cumulation with other development;
   (c) the use of natural resources;
   (d) the production of waste;
   (e) pollution and nuisances;
   (f) the risk of accidents, having regard in particular to substances or technologies used.

2 Location of development

The environmental sensitivity of geographical areas likely to be affected by development must be considered, having regard, in particular, to—

(a) the existing land use;

(b) the relative abundance, quality and regenerative capacity of natural resources in the area;

(c) the absorption capacity of the natural environment, paying particular attention to the following areas—

    (i) wetlands;

    (ii) coastal zones;

    (iii) mountain and forest areas;

    (iv) nature reserves and parks;

    (v) areas classified or protected under Member States' legislation; areas designated by Member States pursuant to Council Directive 79/409/EEC on the conservation of wild birds and Council Directive 92/43/EEC on the conservation of natural habitats and of wild fauna and flora;

    (vi) areas in which the environmental quality standards laid down in Community legislation have already been exceeded;

    (vii) densely populated areas;

    (viii) landscapes of historical, cultural or archaeological significance.

3 Characteristics of the potential impact

The potential significant effects of development must be considered in relation to criteria set out under paragraphs 1 and 2 above, and having regard in particular to—

(a) the extent of the impact (geographical area and size of the affected population);

(b) the transfrontier nature of the impact;

(c) the magnitude and complexity of the impact;

(d) the probability of the impact;

(e) the duration, frequency and reversibility of the impact.

Regulation 2(1)

SCHEDULE 4

INFORMATION FOR INCLUSION IN
ENVIRONMENTAL STATEMENTS

PART I

1. Description of the development, including in particular—

(a) a description of the physical characteristics of the whole development and the land-use requirements during the construction and operational phases;

(b) a description of the main characteristics of the production processes, for instance, nature and quantity of the materials used;

(c) an estimate, by type and quantity, of expected residues and emissions (water, air and soil pollution, noise, vibration, light, heat, radiation, etc.) resulting from the operation of the proposed development.

2. An outline of the main alternatives studied by the applicant or appellant and an indication of the main reasons for his choice, taking into account the environmental effects.

3. A description of the aspects of the environment likely to be significantly affected by

the development, including, in particular, population, fauna, flora, soil, water, air, climatic factors, material assets, including the architectural and archaeological heritage, landscape and the inter-relationship between the above factors.

4.   A description of the likely significant effects of the development on the environment, which should cover the direct effects and any indirect, secondary, cumulative, short, medium and long-term, permanent and temporary, positive and negative effects of the development, resulting from:

(a) the existence of the development;

(b) the use of natural resources;

(c) the emission of pollutants, the creation of nuisances and the elimination of waste,

and the description by the applicant of the forecasting methods used to assess the effects on the environment.

5.   A description of the measures envisaged to prevent, reduce and where possible offset any significant adverse effects on the environment.

6.   A non-technical summary of the information provided under paragraphs 1 to 5 of this Part.

7.   An indication of any difficulties (technical deficiences or lack of know-how) encountered by the applicant in compiling the required information.

PART II

1.   A description of the development comprising information on the site, design and size of the development.

2.   A description of the measures envisaged in order to avoid, reduce and, if possible, remedy significant adverse effects.

3.   The data required to identify and assess the main effects which the development is likely to have on the environment.

4.   An outline of the main alternatives studied by the applicant or appellant and an indication of the main reasons for his choice, taking into account the environmental effects.

5.   A non-technical summary of the information provided under paragraphs 1 to 4 of this Part.

SCHEDULE 5

Regulation 34(1) [. . .]

Anti-Pollution Works Regulations 1999
(SI 1999, No. 1006)

1 Citation, commencement and interpretation

(1) These Regulations may be cited as the Anti-Pollution Works Regulations 1999 and shall come into force on 29th April 1999.

(2) In these Regulations 'the Act' means the Water Resources Act 1991; and for the purposes of these Regulations the parties to an appeal are the appellant, the Agency and any person who is served with a copy of a notice of an appeal in accordance with regulation 3(4)(b).

2   Content of works notices

A works notice shall—

(a) in the case of a potential pollution incident, describe the nature of the risk to controlled waters, identifying the controlled waters which may be affected and the place from which the matter in question is likely to enter those waters;

(b) in the case of an actual pollution incident, describe the nature and extent of the pollution, identifying the controlled waters affected by it;

(c) specify the works or operations required to be carried out by the person on whom the notice is served, stating his name and address;

(d) give the Agency's reasons for serving the notice on that person and for requiring those works or operations to be carried out;

(e) inform the person on whom the notice is served of his right of appeal under section 161C of the Act (including the time for appealing) and of the requirements imposed by regulation 3 in relation to its exercise;

(f) state that the Agency is entitled (unless the notice is quashed or withdrawn) to recover from the person on whom the notice is served its costs or expenses reasonably incurred in carrying out such investigations as are mentioned in section 161(1) of the Act; and

(g) set out the contents of section 161 D(1) to (4) of the Act (consequences of not complying with a works notice).

3   Appeals against works notices

(1) A person who wishes to appeal to the Secretary of State under section 161C of the Act (appeals against works notices) shall give the Secretary of State notice of the appeal.

(2) The notice of appeal shall state—

(a) the name and address of the appellant and of all persons to be served with a copy of the notice of appeal;

(b) the grounds on which the appeal is made; and

(c) whether the appellant wishes the appeal to be determined on the basis of written representations or a hearing.

(3) The notice of appeal shall be accompanied by copies of any application, consent, correspondence, decision, notice or other document relevant to the appeal.

(4) At the same time as the appellant gives notice of the appeal to the Secretary of State, the appellant shall send to—

(a) the Agency, and

(b) where a ground of appeal is that the notice might lawfully have been served on some other person, that person,

a copy of the notice of appeal, together with a list of the documents provided to the Secretary of State under paragraph (3).

(5) If the appellant wishes at any time to withdraw his appeal he shall do so by notice informing the Secretary of State and shall send a copy of the notice to the Agency and any other person on whom he is required to serve a copy of his notice of appeal.

4   Written representations

(1) Where the appellant informs the Secretary of State that he wishes the appeal to be disposed of on the basis of written representations, the Agency, and any party to the appeal other than the appellant, shall submit any written representations to the Secretary of State not later than 14 days after receiving a copy of the notice of appeal.

(2) The appellant shall submit any further representations by way of reply not later than 14 days after receiving whichever is the latest of the representations referred to in paragraph (1).

(3) The Secretary of State may in any particular case—

(a) set longer time limits than those mentioned in this regulation,

(b) allow the parties to make representations in addition to those mentioned in paragraphs (1) and (2).

(4) Any representations made by a party to the appeal shall be dated with the date on which they are submitted to the Secretary of State.

(5) A party to the appeal who submits any representations to the Secretary of State shall at the same time send a copy to every other party.

5 Hearings

(1) If a party to the appeal so requests or the Secretary of State so decides, the appeal shall be or continue in the form of a hearing (which may, if the person hearing the appeal so decides, be held, or held to any extent, in private).

(2) The Secretary of State shall give the parties to the appeal at least 28 days' notice (unless they agree to a shorter period of notice) of the date, time and place fixed for the hearing.

(3) In the case of a hearing which is to be held wholly or partly in public, the Secretary of State shall, at least 21 days before the date fixed for the hearing, publish a copy of the notice given under paragraph (2) in a newspaper circulating in each locality which he considers may be affected by any matter which falls to be determined in relation to the appeal.

(4) The Secretary of State may vary the date fixed for the hearing and paragraphs (2) and (3) shall apply to the new date as they apply to the original date.

(5) The Secretary of State may also vary the time or place fixed for the hearing but shall give such notice of any such variation as appears to him to be reasonable.

(6) Each party to the appeal is entitled to be heard at a hearing.

(7) Nothing in paragraph (6) shall prevent the person appointed to hear the appeal from permitting any other person to be heard at the hearing and such permission shall not be unreasonably withheld.

(8) After the conclusion of a hearing, the person appointed to hear the appeal shall, unless he was appointed under section 114(1)(a) of the Environment Act 1995 (power of Secretary of State to delegate his functions of determining appeals), make a report in writing to the Secretary of State which shall include his conclusions and his recommendations or his reasons for not making any recommendations.

6 Notification of determination

(1) The Secretary of State shall notify the appellant in writing of the determination of the appeal and shall provide him with a copy of any report mentioned in regulation 5(8).

(2) The Secretary of State shall at the same time send a copy of the documents mentioned in paragraph (1) to the Agency and to every other party to the appeal.

7 Compensation for grant of rights under section 161B
The Schedule to these Regulations shall have effect—

(a) for prescribing the period within which a person who grants, or joins in granting, any rights pursuant to section 161B(2) of the Act may apply for compensation for the grant of those rights;

(b) for prescribing the manner in which, and the person to whom, such an application may be made; and

(c) for prescribing the manner of determining such compensation, for determining the amount of such compensation and for making supplemental provision relating to such compensation.

. . .

Regulation 7   SCHEDULE

COMPENSATION FOR GRANT OF RIGHTS

1 Interpretation
In this Schedule—

'the grantor' means the person who grants, or joins in granting, any right pursuant to section 161 B(2) of the Act; and

'relevant interest' means an interest in land out of which a right has been granted or which is bound by a right granted.

2   Period for making an application

An application for compensation shall be made before the expiry of a period of 12 months beginning with—

    (a)   the date of the grant of the rights in respect of which compensation is claimed, or

    (b)   where there is an appeal against the notice in relation to which those rights were granted, the date on which the appeal is determined or withdrawn; whichever is the later date.

3   Manner of making an application

(1) An application for compensation shall be made in writing and delivered at or sent by pre-paid post to the last known address for correspondence of the person to whom the right was granted.

(2) The application shall contain—

    (a)   a copy of the grant of rights in respect of which the grantor is applying for compensation and of any plans attached to such grant;

    (b)   a description of the exact nature of any interest in land in respect of which compensation is applied for; and

    (c)   a statement of the amount of compensation applied for, distinguishing the amounts applied for under each of sub-paragraphs (a) to (e) of paragraph 4 and showing how the amount applied for under each sub-paragraph has been calculated.

4   Loss and damage for which compensation payable

Compensation shall be payable for loss and damage of the following descriptions—

    (a)   any depreciation in the value of any relevant interest to which the grantor is entitled which results from the grant of the right;

    (b)   loss or damage, in relation to any relevant interest to which he is entitled, which—

        (i)   is attributable to the grant of the right or the exercise of it;

        (ii)   does not consist of depreciation in the value of that interest; and

        (iii) is loss or damage for which he would have been entitled to compensation by way of compensation for disturbance, if that interest had been acquired compulsorily under the Acquisition of Land Act 1981, in pursuance of a notice to treat served on the date on which the grant of the right was made;

    (c)   damage to, or injurious affection of, any interest in land to which the grantor is entitled which is not a relevant interest and which results from the grant of the right or from the exercise of it;

    (d)   any loss or damage sustained by the grantor, other than in relation to any interest in land to which he is entitled, which is attributable to the grant of the right or the exercise of it; and

    (e)   the amount of any valuation and legal expenses reasonably incurred by the grantor in granting the right and in the preparation of the application for and the negotiation of the amount of compensation.

5   Basis on which compensation assessed

(1) The rules set out in section 5 of the Land Compensation Act 1961 (rules for assessing compensation) shall, so far as applicable and subject to any necessary modifications, have effect for the purpose of assessing any compensation under paragraph 4, as they have effect for the purpose of assessing compensation for the compulsory acquisition of an interest in land.

(2) Where the relevant interest in respect of which any compensation is to be assessed is subject to a mortgage—

(a) the compensation shall be assessed as if the interest were not subject to the mortgage;

(b) no compensation shall be payable in respect of the interest of the mortgagee (as distinct from the interest which is subject to the mortgage); and

(c) any compensation which is payable in respect of the interest which is subject to the mortgage shall be paid to the mortgagee or, if there is more than one mortgagee, to the first mortgagee and shall, in either case, be applied by him as if it were proceeds of sale.

6   Determination of disputes

(1) Any question of disputed compensation shall be referred to and determined by the Lands Tribunal.

(2) In relation to the determination of any such question of compensation the provisions of sections 2 and 4 of the Land Compensation Act 1961 (procedure on references to the Lands Tribunal and costs) shall apply as if—

(a) the reference in section 2 of the Land Compensation Act 1961 to section 1 of that Act were a reference to sub-paragraph (1); and

(b) references in section 4 of the Land Compensation Act 1961 to the acquiring authority were references to the person to whom the rights were granted.

Contaminated Land (England) Regulations 2000
(SI 2000, No. 227) (as amended)

1   Citation, commencement, extent and interpretation

(1) These Regulations may be cited as the Contaminated Land (England) Regulations 2000 and shall come into force on 1st April 2000.

(2) These Regulations extend to England only.

(3) In these Regulations, unless otherwise indicated, any reference to a numbered section is to the section of the Environmental Protection Act 1990 which bears that number.

2   Land required to be designated as a special site

(1) Contaminated land of the following descriptions is prescribed for the purposes of section 78C(8) as land required to be designated as a special site—

(a) land to which regulation 3 applies;

(b) land which is contaminated land by reason of waste acid tars in, on or under the land;

(c) land on which any of the following activities have been carried on at any time—

(i) the purification (including refining) of crude petroleum or of oil extracted from petroleum, shale or any other bituminous substance except coal; or

(ii) the manufacture or processing of explosives;

(d) land on which a prescribed process designated for central control has been or is being carried on under an authorisation where the process does not comprise solely things being done which are required by way of remediation;

[(da) land on which an activity has been or is being carried on in a Part A(1) installation or by means of Part A(1) mobile plant under a permit where the activity does not comprise solely things being done which are required by way of remediation;]

(e) land within a nuclear site;

(f) land owned or occupied by or on behalf of—

(i) the Secretary of State for Defence;

      (ii) the Defence Council;

      (iii) an international headquarters or defence organisation; or

      (iv) the service authority of a visiting force, being land used for naval, military or air force purposes;

  (g) land on which the manufacture, production or disposal of—

      (i) chemical weapons;

      (ii) any biological agent or toxin which falls within section 1(1)(a) of the Biological Weapons Act 1974 (restriction on development of biological agents and toxins); or

      (iii) any weapon, equipment or means of delivery which falls within section 1(1)(b) of that Act (restriction on development of biological weapons), has been carried on at any time;

  (h) land comprising premises which are or were designated by the Secretary of State by an order made under section 1(1) of the Atomic Weapons Establishment Act 1991 (arrangements for development etc of nuclear devices);

  (i) land to which section 30 of the Armed Forces Act 1996 (land held for the benefit of Greenwich Hospital) applies; and

  (j) land which—

      (i) is adjoining or adjacent to land of a description specified in subparagraphs (b) to (i) above; and

      (ii) is contaminated land by virtue of substances which appear to have escaped from land of such a description.

(2) For the purposes of paragraph (1)(b) above, 'waste acid tars' are tars which—

  (a) contain sulphuric acid;

  (b) were produced as a result of the refining of benzole, used lubricants or petroleum; and

  (c) are or were stored on land used as a retention basin for the disposal of such tars.

(3) In paragraph (1)(d) above, 'authorisation' and 'prescribed process' have the same meaning as in Part I of the Environmental Protection Act 1990 (integrated pollution control and air pollution control by local authorities) and the reference to designation for central control is a reference to designation under section 2(4) (which provides for processes to be designated for central or local control).

[(3A) In paragraph (1)(da) above, 'Part A(1) installation', 'Part A(1) mobile plant' and 'permit' have the same meaning as in the Pollution Prevention and Control (England and Wales) Regulations 2000.]

(4) In paragraph (1)(e) above, 'nuclear site' means—

  (a) any site in respect of which, or part of which, a nuclear site licence is for the time being in force; or

  (b) any site in respect of which, or part of which, after the revocation or surrender of a nuclear site licence, the period of responsibility of the licensee has not come to an end;

and 'nuclear site licence', 'licensee' and 'period of responsibility' have the meaning given by the Nuclear Installations Act 1965.

(5) For the purposes of paragraph (1)(f) above, land used for residential purposes or by the Navy, Army and Air Force Institutes shall be treated as land used for naval, military or air force purposes only if the land forms part of a base occupied for naval, military or air force purposes.

(6) In paragraph (1)(f) above—

'international headquarters' and 'defence organisation' mean, respectively, any international headquarters or defence organisation designated for the purposes of the International Headquarters and Defence Organisations Act 1964;

'service authority' and 'visiting force' have the same meaning as in Part I of the Visiting Forces Act 1952.

(7) In paragraph (1)(g) above, 'chemical weapon' has the same meaning as in subsection (1) of section 1 of the Chemical Weapons Act 1996 disregarding subsection (2) of that section.

3   Pollution of controlled waters

For the purposes of regulation 2(1)(a), this regulation applies to land where—

(a) controlled waters which are, or are intended to be, used for the supply of drinking water for human consumption are being affected by the land and, as a result, require a treatment process or a change in such a process to be applied to those waters before use, so as to be regarded as wholesome within the meaning of Part III of the Water Industry Act 1991 (water supply);

(b) controlled waters are being affected by the land and, as a result, those waters do not meet or are not likely to meet the criterion for classification applying to the relevant description of waters specified in regulations made under section 82 of the Water Resources Act 1991 (classification of quality of waters); or

(c) controlled waters are being affected by the land and—

(i) any of the substances by reason of which the pollution of the waters is being or is likely to be caused falls within any of the families or groups of substances listed in paragraph 1 of Schedule 1 to these Regulations; and

(ii) the waters, or any part of the waters, are contained within underground strata which comprise wholly or partly any of the formations of rocks listed in paragraph 2 of Schedule 1 to these Regulations.

4   Content of remediation notices

(1) A remediation notice shall state (in addition to the matters required by section 78E(1) and (3))—

(a) the name and address of the person on whom the notice is served;

(b) the location and extent of the contaminated land to which the notice relates (in this regulation referred to as the 'contaminated land in question'), sufficient to enable it to be identified whether by reference to a plan or otherwise;

(c) the date of any notice which was given under section 78B to the person on whom the remediation notice is served identifying the contaminated land in question as contaminated land;

(d) whether the enforcing authority considers the person on whom the notice is served is an appropriate person by reason of—

(i) having caused or knowingly permitted the substances, or any of the substances, by reason of which the contaminated land in question is contaminated land, to be in, on or under that land;

(ii) being the owner of the contaminated land in question; or

(iii) being the occupier of the contaminated land in question;

(e) particulars of the significant harm or pollution of controlled waters by reason of which the contaminated land in question is contaminated land;

(f) the substances by reason of which the contaminated land in question is contaminated land and, if any of the substances have escaped from other land, the location of that other land;

(g) the enforcing authority's reasons for its decisions as to the things by way of remediation that the appropriate person is required to do, which shall show how any guidance issued by the Secretary of State under section 78E(5) has been applied;

(h) where two or more persons are appropriate persons in relation to the contaminated land in question—

(i) that this is the case;

(ii) the name and address of each such person; and

(iii) the thing by way of remediation for which each such person bears responsibility;

(i) where two or more persons would, apart from section 78F(6), be appropriate persons in relation to any particular thing which is to be done by way of remediation, the enforcing authority's reasons for its determination as to whether any, and if so which, of them is to be treated as not being an appropriate person in relation to that thing, which shall show how any guidance issued by the Secretary of State under section 78F(6) has been applied;

(j) where the remediation notice is required by section 78E(3) to state the proportion of the cost of a thing which is to be done by way of remediation which each of the appropriate persons in relation to that thing is liable to bear, the enforcing authority's reasons for the proportion which it has determined, which shall show how any guidance issued by the Secretary of State under section 78F(7) has been applied;

(k) where known to the enforcing authority, the name and address of—

(i) the owner of the contaminated land in question; and

(ii) any person who appears to the enforcing authority to be in occupation of the whole or any part of the contaminated land in question;

(l) where known to the enforcing authority, the name and address of any person whose consent is required under section 78G(2) before any thing required by the remediation notice may be done;

(m) where the notice is to be served in reliance on section 78H(4), that it appears to the enforcing authority that the contaminated land in question is in such a condition, by reason of substances in, on or under the land, that there is imminent danger of serious harm, or serious pollution of controlled waters, being caused;

(n) that a person on whom a remediation notice is served may be guilty of an offence for failure, without reasonable excuse, to comply with any of the requirements of the notice;

(o) the penalties which may be applied on conviction for such an offence;

(p) the name and address of the enforcing authority serving the notice; and

(q) the date of the notice.

(2) A remediation notice shall explain—

(a) that a person on whom it is served has a right of appeal against the notice under section 78L;

(b) how, within what period and on what grounds an appeal may be made; and

(c) that a notice is suspended, where an appeal is duly made, until the final determination or abandonment of the appeal.

5 Service of copies of remediation notices

(1) Subject to paragraph (2) below, the enforcing authority shall, at the same time as it serves a remediation notice, send a copy of it to each of the following persons, not being a person on whom the notice is to be served—

(a) any person who was required to be consulted under section 78G(3) before service of the notice;

(b) any person who was required to be consulted under section 78H(1) before service of the notice;

(c) where the local authority is the enforcing authority, the Environment Agency; and

(d) where the Environment Agency is the enforcing authority, the local authority in whose area the contaminated land in question is situated.

(2) Where it appears to the enforcing authority that the contaminated land in question is in such a condition by reason of substances in, on or under it that there is imminent danger of serious harm, or serious pollution of controlled waters, being caused, the enforcing authority shall send any copies of the notice pursuant to paragraph (1) above as soon as practicable after service of the notice.

6 Compensation for rights of entry etc.

Schedule 2 to these Regulations shall have effect—

(a) for prescribing the period within which a person who grants, or joins in granting, any rights pursuant to section 78G(2) may apply for compensation for the grant of those rights;

(b) for prescribing the manner in which, and the person to whom, such an application may be made; and

(c) for prescribing the manner in which the amount of such compensation shall be determined and for making further provision relating to such compensation.

7 Grounds of appeal against a remediation notice

(1) The grounds of appeal against a remediation notice under section 78L(1) are any of the following—

(a) that, in determining whether any land to which the notice relates appears to be contaminated land, the local authority—

(i) failed to act in accordance with guidance issued by the Secretary of State under section 78A(2), (5) or (6); or

(ii) whether by reason of such a failure or otherwise, unreasonably identified all or any of the land to which the notice relates as contaminated land;

(b) that, in determining a requirement of the notice, the enforcing authority—

(i) failed to have regard to guidance issued by the Secretary of State under section 78E(5); or

(ii) whether by reason of such a failure or otherwise, unreasonably required the appellant to do any thing by way of remediation;

(c) that the enforcing authority unreasonably determined the appellant to be the appropriate person who is to bear responsibility for any thing required by the notice to be done by way of remediation;

(d) subject to paragraph (2) below, that the enforcing authority unreasonably failed to determine that some person in addition to the appellant is an appropriate person in relation to any thing required by the notice to be done by way of remediation;

(e) that, in respect of any thing required by the notice to be done by way of remediation, the enforcing authority failed to act in accordance with guidance issued by the Secretary of State under section 78F(6);

(f) that, where two or more persons are appropriate persons in relation to any thing required by the notice to be done by way of remediation, the enforcing authority—

(i) failed to determine the proportion of the cost stated in the notice to be the liability of the appellant in accordance with guidance issued by the Secretary of State under section 78F(7); or

(ii) whether, by reason of such a failure or otherwise, unreasonably determined the proportion of the cost that the appellant is to bear;

(g) that service of the notice contravened a provision of subsection (1) or (3) of section 78H (restrictions and prohibitions on serving remediation notices) other than in circumstances where section 78H(4) applies;

(h) that, where the notice was served in reliance on section 78H(4) without compliance with section 78H(1) or (3), the enforcing authority could not reasonably have taken the view that the contaminated land in question was in such a condition by reason of substances in, on or under the land, that there was imminent danger of serious harm, or serious pollution of controlled waters, being caused;

(i) that the enforcing authority has unreasonably failed to be satisfied, in accordance with section 78H(5)(b), that appropriate things are being, or will be, done by way of remediation without service of a notice;

(j) that any thing required by the notice to be done by way of remediation was required in contravention of a provision of section 78J (restrictions on liability relating to the pollution of controlled waters);

(k) that any thing required by the notice to be done by way of remediation was required in contravention of a provision of section 78K (liability in respect of contaminating substances which escape to other land);

(l) that the enforcing authority itself has power, in a case falling within section 78N(3)(b), to do what is appropriate by way of remediation;

(m) that the enforcing authority itself has power, in a case falling within section 78N(3)(e), to do what is appropriate by way of remediation;

(n) that the enforcing authority, in considering for the purposes of section 78N(3)(e), whether it would seek to recover all or a portion of the cost incurred by it in doing some particular thing by way of remediation—

    (i) failed to have regard to any hardship which the recovery may cause to the person from whom the cost is recoverable or to any guidance issued by the Secretary of State for the purposes of section 78P(2); or

    (ii) whether by reason of such a failure or otherwise, unreasonably determined that it would decide to seek to recover all of the cost;

(o) that, in determining a requirement of the notice, the enforcing authority failed to have regard to guidance issued by the Environment Agency under section 78V(1);

(p) that a period specified in the notice within which the appellant is required to do anything is not reasonably sufficient for the purpose;

(q) that the notice provides for a person acting in a relevant capacity to be personally liable to bear the whole or part of the cost of doing any thing by way of remediation, contrary to the provisions of section 78X(3)(a);

(r) that service of the notice contravened a provision of section 78YB (interaction of Part IIA of the Environmental Protection Act 1990 with other enactments), and

    (i) in a case where subsection (1) of that section is relied on, that it ought reasonably to have appeared to the enforcing authority that the powers of the Environment Agency under section 27 might be exercised;

    (ii) in a case where subsection (3) of section 78YB is relied on, that it ought reasonably to have appeared to the enforcing authority that the powers of a waste regulation authority or waste collection authority under section 59 might be exercised; or

(s) that there has been some informality, defect or error in, or in connection with, the notice, in respect of which there is no right of appeal under the grounds set out in sub-paragraphs (a) to (r) above.

(2) A person may only appeal on the ground specified in paragraph (1)(d) above in a case where—

(a) the enforcing authority has determined that he is an appropriate person by virtue of subsection (2) of section 78F and he claims to have found some other person who is an appropriate person by virtue of that subsection;

(b) the notice is served on him as the owner or occupier for the time being of the contaminated land in question and he claims to have found some other person who is an appropriate person by virtue of that subsection; or

(c) the notice is served on him as the owner or occupier for the time being of the contaminated land in question, and he claims that some other person is also an owner or occupier for the time being of the whole or part of that land.

(3) If and in so far as an appeal against a remediation notice is based on the ground of some informality, defect or error in, or in connection with, the notice, the appellate authority shall dismiss the appeal if it is satisfied that the informality, defect or error was not a material one.

8 Appeals to a magistrates' court

(1) An appeal under section 78L(1) to a magistrates' court against a remediation notice shall be by way of complaint for an order and, subject to section 78L(2) and (3) and regulations 7(3), 12 and 13, the Magistrates' Courts Act 1980 shall apply to the proceedings.

(2) An appellant shall, at the same time as he makes a complaint,—
(a) file a notice ('notice of appeal') and serve a copy of it on—
  (i) the enforcing authority;
  (ii) any person named in the remediation notice as an appropriate person;
  (iii) any person named in the notice of appeal as an appropriate person; and
  (iv) any person named in the remediation notice as the owner or occupier of the whole or any part of the land to which the notice relates;
(b) file a copy of the remediation notice to which the appeal relates and serve a copy of it on any person named in the notice of appeal as an appropriate person who was not so named in the remediation notice; and
(c) file a statement of the names and addresses of any persons falling within paragraph (ii), (iii) or (iv) of sub-paragraph (a) above.

(3) The notice of appeal shall state the appellant's name and address and the grounds on which the appeal is made.

(4) On an appeal under section 78L(1) to a magistrates' court—
(a) the justices' clerk or the court may give, vary or revoke directions for the conduct of proceedings, including—
  (i) the timetable for the proceedings;
  (ii) the service of documents;
  (iii) the submission of evidence; and
  (iv) the order of speeches;
(b) any person falling within paragraph (2)(a)(ii), (iii) or (iv) above shall be given notice of, and an opportunity to be heard at, the hearing of the complaint and any hearing for directions, in addition to the appellant and the enforcing authority; and
(c) the court may refuse to grant a request by the appellant to abandon his appeal against a remediation notice, where the request is made after the court has notified the appellant in accordance with regulation 12(1) of a proposed modification of that notice.

(5) Rule 15 of the Family Proceedings Courts (Matrimonial Proceedings etc.) Rules 1991 (delegation by justices' clerk) shall apply for the purposes of an appeal under section 78L(1) to a magistrates' court as it applies for the purposes of Part II of those Rules.

(6) In this regulation, 'file' means deposit with the [justices' chief executive.].

9 Appeals to the Secretary of State

(1) An appeal to the Secretary of State against a remediation notice shall be made to him by a notice ('notice of appeal') which shall state—
(a) the name and address of the appellant;
(b) the grounds on which the appeal is made; and
(c) whether the appellant wishes the appeal to be in the form of a hearing or to be disposed of on the basis of written representations.

(2) The appellant shall, at the same time as he serves a notice of appeal on the Secretary of State,—

    (a) serve a copy of it on—

        (i) the Environment Agency;

        (ii) any person named in the remediation notice as an appropriate person;

        (iii) any person named in the notice of appeal as an appropriate person; and

        (iv) any person named in the remediation notice as the owner or occupier of the whole or any part of the land to which the notice relates;

and serve on the Secretary of State a statement of the names and addresses of any persons falling within paragraph (ii), (iii) or (iv) above; and

    (b) serve a copy of the remediation notice to which the appeal relates on the Secretary of State and on any person named in the notice of appeal as an appropriate person who is not so named in the remediation notice.

(3) Subject to paragraph (5) below, if the appellant wishes to abandon an appeal, he shall do so by notifying the Secretary of State in writing and the appeal shall be treated as abandoned on the date the Secretary of State receives that notification.

(4) The Secretary of State may refuse to permit an appellant to abandon his appeal against a remediation notice where the notification by the appellant in accordance with paragraph (3) above is received by the Secretary of State at any time after the Secretary of State has notified the appellant in accordance with regulation 12(1) of a proposed modification of that notice.

(5) Where an appeal is abandoned, the Secretary of State shall give notice of the abandonment to any person on whom the appellant was required to serve a copy of the notice of appeal.

10   Hearings and local inquiries

(1) Before determining an appeal, the Secretary of State may, if he thinks fit—

    (a) cause the appeal to take or continue in the form of a hearing (which may, if the person hearing the appeal so decides, be held, or held to any extent, in private); or

    (b) cause a local inquiry to be held, and the Secretary of State shall act as mentioned in sub-paragraph (a) or (b) above if a request is made by either the appellant or the Environment Agency to be heard with respect to the appeal.

(2) The persons entitled to be heard at a hearing are—

    (a) the appellant;

    (b) the Environment Agency; and

    (c) any person (other than the Agency) on whom the appellant was required to serve a copy of the notice of appeal.

(3) Nothing in paragraph (2) above shall prevent the person appointed to conduct the hearing of the appeal from permitting any other person to be heard at the hearing and such permission shall not be unreasonably withheld.

(4) After the conclusion of a hearing, the person appointed to conduct the hearing shall, unless he has been appointed under section 114(1)(a) of the Environment Act 1995 (power of Secretary of State to delegate his functions of determining appeals) to determine the appeal, make a report in writing to the Secretary of State which shall include his conclusions and his recommendations or his reasons for not making any recommendations.

11   Notification of Secretary of State's decision on an appeal

(1) The Secretary of State shall notify the appellant in writing of his decision on an appeal and shall provide him with a copy of any report mentioned in regulation 10(4).

(2) The Secretary of State shall, at the same time as he notifies the appellant, send a copy of the documents mentioned in paragraph (1) above to the Environment Agency and

to any other person on whom the appellant was required to serve a copy of the notice of appeal.

12   Modification of a remediation notice

(1) Before modifying a remediation notice under section 78L(2)(b) in any respect which would be less favourable to the appellant or any other person on whom the notice was served, the appellate authority shall—

(a) notify the appellant and any persons on whom the appellant was required to serve a copy of the notice of appeal of the proposed modification;

(b) permit any persons so notified to make representations in relation to the proposed modification; and

(c) permit the appellant or any other person on whom the remediation notice was served to be heard if any such person so requests.

(2) Where, in accordance with paragraph (1) above, the appellant or any other person is heard, the enforcing authority shall also be entitled to be heard.

13   Appeals to the High Court

An appeal against any decision of a magistrates' court in pursuance of an appeal under section 78L(1) shall lie to the High Court at the instance of any party to the proceedings in which the decision was given (including any person who exercised his entitlement under regulation 8(4)(b) to be heard at the hearing of the complaint).

14   Suspension of a remediation notice

(1) Where an appeal is duly made against a remediation notice, the notice shall be of no effect pending the final determination or abandonment of the appeal.

(2) An appeal against a remediation notice is duly made for the purposes of this regulation if it is made within the period specified in section 78L(1) and the requirements of regulation 8(2) and (3) (in the case of an appeal to a magistrates' court) or regulation 9(1) and (2) (in the case of an appeal to the Secretary of State) have been complied with.

15   Registers

(1) Schedule 3 to these Regulations shall have effect for prescribing—

(a) for the purposes of subsection (1) of section 78R, the particulars of or relating to the matters to be contained in a register maintained under that section; and

(b) other matters in respect of which such a register shall contain prescribed particulars pursuant to section 78R(1)(l).

(2) The following descriptions of information are prescribed for the purposes of section 78R(2) as information to be contained in notifications for the purposes of section 78R(1)(h) and (j)

(a) the location and extent of the land sufficient to enable it to be identified;

(b) the name and address of the person who it is claimed has done each of the things by way of remediation;

(c) a description of any thing which it is claimed has been done by way of remediation; and

(d) the period within which it is claimed each such thing was done.

(3) The following places are prescribed for the purposes of subsection (8) of section 78R as places at which any registers or facilities for obtaining copies shall be available or afforded to the public in pursuance of paragraph (a) or (b) of that sub section—

(a) where the enforcing authority is the local authority, its principal office; and

(b) where the enforcing authority is the Environment Agency, its office for the area in which the contaminated land in question is situated.

Regulation 3(c)   SCHEDULE 1

SPECIAL SITES

1.   The following families and groups of substances are listed for the purposes of regulation 3(c)(i)—

organohalogen compounds and substances which may form such compounds in the aquatic environment;

organophosphorus compounds;

organotin compounds;

substances which possess carcinogenic, mutagenic or teratogenic properties in or via the aquatic environment;

mercury and its compounds;

cadmium and its compounds;

mineral oil and other hydrocarbons;

cyanides.

2.   The following formations of rocks are listed for the purposes of regulation 3(c)(ii)—

Pleistocene Norwich Crag;

Upper Cretaceous Chalk;

Lower Cretaceous Sandstones;

Upper Jurassic Corallian;

Middle Jurassic Limestones;

Lower Jurassic Cotteswold Sands;

Permo-Triassic Sherwood Sandstone Group;

Upper Permian Magnesian Limestone;

Lower Permian Penrith Sandstone;

Lower Permian Collyhurst Sandstone;

Lower Permian Basal Breccias, Conglomerates and Sandstones;

Lower Carboniferous Limestones.

Regulation 6   SCHEDULE 2

COMPENSATION FOR RIGHTS OF ENTRY ETC.

1   Interpretation

In this Schedule—

'the 1961 Act' means the Land Compensation Act 1961;

'grantor' means a person who has granted, or joined in the granting of, any rights pursuant to section 78G(2);

'relevant interest' means an interest in land out of which rights have been granted pursuant to section 78G(2).

2   Period for making an application

An application for compensation shall be made within the period beginning with the date of the grant of the rights in respect of which compensation is claimed and ending on whichever is the latest of the following dates—

    (a)   twelve months after the date of the grant of those rights;

    (b)   where an appeal is made against a remediation notice in respect of which the rights in question have been granted, and the notice is of no effect by virtue of regulation 14, twelve months after the date of the final determination or abandonment of the appeal; or

    (c)   six months after the date on which the rights were first exercised.

3   Manner of making an application

(1) An application shall be made in writing and delivered at or sent by pre-paid post to the last known address for correspondence of the appropriate person to whom the rights were granted.

(2) The application shall contain, or be accompanied by—

    (a) a copy of the grant of rights in respect of which the grantor is applying for compensation, and of any plans attached to that grant;

    (b) a description of the exact nature of any interest in land in respect of which compensation is applied for; and

    (c) a statement of the amount of compensation applied for, distinguishing the amounts applied for under each of sub-paragraphs (a) to (e) of paragraph 4 below, and showing how the amount applied for under each sub-paragraph has been calculated.

4   Loss and damage for which compensation payable

Subject to paragraph 5(3) and (5)(b) below, compensation is payable under section 78G for loss and damage of the following descriptions—

    (a) depreciation in the value of any relevant interest to which the grantor is entitled which results from the grant of the rights;

    (b) depreciation in the value of any other interest in land to which the grantor is entitled which results from the exercise of the rights;

    (c) loss or damage, in relation to any relevant interest to which the grantor is entitled, which—

        (i)   is attributable to the grant of the rights or the exercise of them;

        (ii) does not consist of depreciation in the value of that interest; and

        (iii) is loss or damage for which he would have been entitled to compensation by way of compensation for disturbance, if that interest had been acquired compulsorily under the Acquisition of Land Act 1981 in pursuance of a notice to treat served on the date on which the rights were granted;

    (d) damage to, or injurious affection of, any interest in land to which the grantor is entitled which is not a relevant interest, and which results from the grant of the rights or the exercise of them; and

    (e) loss in respect of work carried out by or on behalf of the grantor which is rendered abortive by the grant of the rights or the exercise of them.

5   Basis on which compensation assessed

(1) The following provisions shall have effect for the purpose of assessing the amount to be paid by way of compensation under section 78G.

(2) The rules set out in section 5 of the 1961 Act (rules for assessing compensation) shall, so far as applicable and subject to any necessary modifications, have effect for the purpose of assessing any such compensation as they have effect for the purpose of assessing compensation for the compulsory acquisition of an interest in land.

(3) No account shall be taken of any enhancement of the value of any interest in land, by reason of any building erected, work done or improvement or alteration made on any land in which the grantor is, or was at the time of erection, doing or making, directly or indirectly concerned, if the Lands Tribunal is satisfied that the erection of the building, the doing of the work, the making of the improvement or the alteration was not reasonably necessary and was undertaken with a view to obtaining compensation or increased compensation.

(4) In calculating the amount of any loss under paragraph 4(e) above, expenditure incurred in the preparation of plans or on other similar preparatory matters shall be taken into account.

(5) Where the interest in respect of which compensation is to be assessed is subject to a mortgage—

    (a) the compensation shall be assessed as if the interest were not subject to the mortgage; and

    (b) no compensation shall be payable in respect of the interest of the mortgagee (as distinct from the interest which is subject to the mortgage).

(6) Compensation under section 78G shall include an amount equal to the grantor's reasonable valuation and legal expenses.

6 Payment of compensation and determination of disputes

(1) Compensation payable under section 78G in respect of an interest which is subject to a mortgage shall be paid to the mortgagee or, if there is more than one mortgagee, to the first mortgagee and shall, in either case, be applied by him as if it were proceeds of sale.

(2) Amounts of compensation determined under this Schedule shall be payable—

    (a) where the appropriate person and the grantor or mortgagee agree that a single payment is to be made on a specified date, on that date;

    (b) where the appropriate person and the grantor or mortgagee agree that payment is to be made in instalments at different dates, on the date agreed as regards each instalment; and

    (c) in any other case, subject to any direction of the Lands Tribunal or the court, as soon as reasonably practicable after the amount of the compensation has been finally determined.

(3) Any question of the application of paragraph 5(3) above or of disputed compensation shall be referred to and determined by the Lands Tribunal.

(4) In relation to the determination of any such question, sections 2 and 4 of the 1961 Act (procedure on reference to the Lands Tribunal and costs) shall apply as if—

    (a) the reference in section 2(1) of that Act to section 1 of that Act were a reference to sub-paragraph (3) of this paragraph; and

    (b) references in section 4 of that Act to the acquiring authority were references to the appropriate person.

Regulation 15   SCHEDULE 3

REGISTERS

A register maintained by an enforcing authority under section 78R shall contain full particulars of the following matters—

1 Remediation notices

In relation to a remediation notice served by the authority—

    (a) the name and address of the person on whom the notice is served;

    (b) the location and extent of the contaminated land to which the notice relates (in this paragraph referred to as the 'contaminated land in question'), sufficient to enable it to be identified whether by reference to a plan or otherwise;

    (c) the significant harm or pollution of controlled waters by reason of which the contaminated land in question is contaminated land;

    (d) the substances by reason of which the contaminated land in question is contaminated land and, if any of the substances have escaped from other land, the location of that other land;

    (e) the current use of the contaminated land in question;

    (f) what each appropriate person is to do by way of remediation and the periods within which they are required to do each of the things; and

    (g) the date of the notice.

2 Appeals against remediation notices
Any appeal against a remediation notice served by the authority.

3 Any decision on such an appeal.

4 Remediation declarations
Any remediation declaration prepared and published by the enforcing authority under section 78H(6).

5 In relation to any such remediation declaration—
   (a) the location and extent of the contaminated land in question, sufficient to enable it to be identified whether by reference to a plan or otherwise; and
   (b) the matters referred to in sub-paragraphs (c), (d) and (e) of paragraph 1 above.

6 Remediation statements
Any remediation statement prepared and published by the responsible person under section 78H(7) or by the enforcing authority under section 78H(9).

7 In relation to any such remediation statement—
   (a) the location and extent of the contaminated land in question, sufficient to enable it to be identified whether by reference to a plan or otherwise; and
   (b) the matters referred to in sub-paragraphs (c), (d) and (e) of paragraph 1 above.

8 Appeals against charging notices
In the case of an enforcing authority, any appeal under section 78P(8) against a charging notice served by the authority.

9 Any decision on such an appeal.

10 Designation of special sites
In the case of the Environment Agency, as respects any land in relation to which it is the enforcing authority, and in the case of a local authority, as respects any land in its area,—
   (a) any notice given by a local authority under subsection (1)(b) or (5)(a) of section 78C, or by the Secretary of State under section 78D(4)(b), which, by virtue of section 78C(7) or section 78D(6) respectively, has effect as the designation of any land as a special site;
   (b) the provisions of regulation 2 or 3 by virtue of which the land is required to be designated as a special site;
   (c) any notice given by the Environment Agency under section 78Q(1)(a) of its decision to adopt a remediation notice; and
   (d) any notice given by or to the enforcing authority under section 78Q(4) terminating the designation of any land as a special site.

11 Notification of claimed remediation
Any notification given to the authority for the purposes of section 78R(1)(h) or (j).

12 Convictions for offences under section 78M
Any conviction of a person for any offence under section 78M in relation to a remediation notice served by the authority, including the name of the offender, the date of conviction, the penalty imposed and the name of the Court.

13 Guidance issued under section 78V(1)
In the case of the Environment Agency, the date of any guidance issued by it under subsection (1) of section 78V and, in the case of a local authority, the date of any guidance issued by the Agency to it under that subsection.

14 Other environmental controls
Where the authority is precluded by virtue of section 78YB(1) [or 78YB(2B)] from serving a remediation notice—

(a) the location and extent of the contaminated land in question, sufficient to enable it to be identified whether by reference to a plan or otherwise;

(b) the matters referred to in sub-paragraphs (c), (d) and (e) of paragraph 1 above; and

(c) any steps of which the authority has knowledge, carried out under section 27 [or by means of enforcement action (within the meaning of section 78YB(2C)], towards remedying any significant harm or pollution of controlled waters by reason of which the land in question is contaminated land.

15.   Where the authority is precluded by virtue of section 78YB(3) from serving a remediation notice in respect of land which is contaminated land by reason of the deposit of controlled waste or any consequences of its deposit—

(a) the location and extent of the contaminated land in question, sufficient to enable it to be identified whether by reference to a plan or otherwise;

(b) the matters referred to in sub-paragraphs (c), (d) and (e) of paragraph 1 above; and

(c) any steps of which the authority has knowledge, carried out under section 59, in relation to that waste or the consequences of its deposit, including in a case where a waste collection authority (within the meaning of section 30(3)) took those steps or required the steps to be taken, the name of that authority.

16.   Where, as a result of a consent given under Chapter II of Part III of the Water Resources Act 1991 (pollution offences), the authority is precluded by virtue of section 78YB(4) from specifying in a remediation notice any particular thing by way of remediation which it would otherwise have specified in such a notice—

(a) the consent;

(b) the location and extent of the contaminated land in question, sufficient to enable it to be identified whether by reference to a plan or otherwise; and

(c) the matters referred to in sub-paragraphs (c), (d) and (e) of paragraph 1 above.

Air Quality (England) Regulations 2000
(SI 2000, No. 928)

1   Citation, commencement and extent

(1) These Regulations may be cited as the Air Quality (England) Regulations 2000 and shall come into force on the seventh day after the day on which they are made.

(2) These Regulations extend to England only.

2   Interpretation

(1) In these Regulations, 'the 1995 Act' means the Environment Act 1995.

(2) The provisions of the Schedule to these Regulations which follow the Table in that Schedule shall have effect for the purpose of the interpretation of that Schedule.

3   Relevant periods

(1) The relevant period for the purposes of section 86(3) of the 1995 Act shall be, in relation to the preparation of an action plan to which that section applies, the period of 9 months beginning with the date on which the district council preparing the action plan first consults the relevant county council in relation to the plan pursuant to paragraph 1(2)(e) of Schedule 11 to the 1995 Act.

(2) The relevant period for the purposes of any other provision of Part IV of the 1995 Act shall be, in relation to an air quality objective, the period beginning with the date on which these Regulations come into force and ending on the date set out in the third column of the Table in the Schedule which relates to that objective.

4   Air quality objectives

(1) It is an air quality objective for each substance listed in the first column of the Table in the Schedule to these Regulations that the level at which that substance is present in the air is restricted to a level set out in the second column of that Table for that substance by no later than the date set out in the third column of that Table for that substance and level.

(2) The achievement or likely achievement of an air quality objective prescribed by paragraph (1) shall be determined by reference to the quality of air at locations—

    (a) which are situated outside of buildings or other natural or man-made structures above or below ground; and

    (b) where members of the public are regularly present.

5   Revocation

The Air Quality Regulations 1997 are hereby revoked in so far as they extend to England.

Regulations 2(2), 3(2) and 4   SCHEDULE

AIR QUALITY OBJECTIVES

Table

Substance	Air quality objective levels	Air quality objective dates
Benzene	16.25 micrograms per cubic metre or less, when expressed as a running annual mean	31st December 2003
1,3-Butadiene	2.25 micrograms per cubic metre or less, when expressed as a running annual mean	31st December 2003
Carbon monoxide	11.6 milligrams per cubic metre or less, when expressed as a running 8 hour mean	31st December 2003
Lead	0.5 micrograms per cubic metre or less, when expressed as an annual mean	31st December 2004
	0.25 micrograms per cubic metre or less, when expressed as an annual mean	31st December 2008
Nitrogen dioxide	200 micrograms per cubic metre, when expressed as an hourly mean, not to be exceeded more than 18 times a year	31st December 2005
	40 micrograms per cubic metre or less, when expressed as an annual mean	31st December 2005
PM_{10}	50 micrograms per cubic metre or less, when expressed as a 24 hour mean, not to be exceeded more than 35 times a year	31st December 2004
	40 micrograms per cubic metre or less, when expressed as an annual mean	31st December 2004
Sulphur dioxide	125 micrograms per cubic metre or less, when expressed as a 24 hour mean, not to be exceeded more than 3 times a year	31st December 2004
	350 micrograms per cubic metre or less, when expressed as an hourly mean, not to be exceeded more than 24 times a year	31st December 2004
	266 micrograms per cubic metre or less, when expressed as a 15 minute mean, not to be exceeded more than 35 times a year	31st December 2005

Interpretation

For the purposes of this Schedule:

1. 'PM$_{10}$' means particulate matter which passes through a size-selective inlet with a 50% efficiency cut-off at 10 μm aerodynamic diameter.

2.—(1) A running annual mean is a mean which is calculated on an hourly basis, yielding one running annual mean per hour. The running annual mean for a particular substance at a particular location for a particular hour is the mean of the hourly levels for that substance at that location for that hour and the preceding 8759 hours.

(2) For the purpose of the calculation of a running annual mean, the hourly level for a particular substance at a particular location is either:

(a) the level at which that substance is recorded as being present in the air at that location during the hour on the basis of a continuous sample of air taken during that hour for at least 30 minutes; or

(b) the mean of the levels recorded at that location on the basis of 2 or more samples of air taken during the hour for an aggregate period of at least 30 minutes.

3. A running 8 hour mean is a mean which is calculated on an hourly basis, yielding one running 8 hour mean per hour. The running 8 hour mean for a particular substance at a particular location for a particular hour is the mean of the hourly means for that substance at that location for that hour and the preceding 7 hours.

4.—(1) An annual mean is a mean which is calculated on a yearly basis, yielding one annual mean per calendar year. The annual mean for a particular substance at a particular location for a particular calendar year is:

(a) in the case of lead, the mean of the daily levels for that year;

(b) in the case of nitrogen dioxide, the mean of the hourly means for that year;

(c) in the case of PM10, the mean of the 24 hour means for that year.

(2) For the purpose of the calculation of the annual mean for lead, the daily level for lead at a particular location for a particular day is the level at which lead is recorded as being present in the air at that location during the week in which the day occurs on the basis of a continuous sample of air taken throughout that week (each day in that week therefore being attributed with the same daily level).

(3) For the purpose of sub-paragraph (2) 'week' means a complete week beginning on a Monday, except that it also includes any period of less than seven days from the beginning of the calendar year until the first Monday in that year or from the beginning of the last Monday in the calendar year to the end of that year.

5. An hourly mean is a mean calculated every hour. The hourly mean for a particular substance at a particular location for a particular hour is the mean of the levels recorded, at a frequency of not less than once every 10 seconds, for that substance at that location during that hour.

6. A 24 hour mean is a mean calculated every 24 hours. The 24 hour mean for a particular substance at a particular location for a particular 24 hour period is the level at which that substance is recorded as being present in the air at that location on the basis of a continuous sample of air taken throughout the period.

7. A 15 minute mean is a mean calculated every 15 minutes. The 15 minute mean for a particular substance at a particular location for a particular 15 minutes is the mean of the levels recorded, at a frequency of not less than once every 10 seconds, for that substance at that location during that 15 minutes.

8. The reference to a number of micrograms or milligrams per cubic metre of a substance is a reference to the number of micrograms or milligrams per cubic metre of that substance when measured with the volume standardised at a temperature of 293K and at a pressure of 101.3 kPa.

Pollution Prevention and Control (England and Wales) Regulations 2000

(SI 2000, No. 1973) (as amended)

PART I   GENERAL

1   Citation, commencement and extent

(1) These Regulations may be cited as the Pollution Prevention and Control (England and Wales) Regulations 2000 and shall come into force on the 1st August 2000.

(2) These Regulations extend to England and Wales only.

(3) For the purpose of paragraph (2), 'England and Wales' includes the territorial waters adjacent to England and Wales.

2   Interpretation: general

(1) In these Regulations, except in so far as the context otherwise requires—

['the 2002 Regulations' means the Landfill (England and Wales) Regulations 2002;]

'change in operation' means, in relation to an installation or mobile plant, a change in the nature or functioning or an extension of the installation or mobile plant which may have consequences for the environment; and 'substantial change in operation' means, in relation to an installation or mobile plant, a change in operation which, in the opinion of the regulator, may have significant negative effects on human beings or the environment;

'the Directive' means Council Directive 96/61/EC concerning integrated pollution prevention and control;

'emission' means—

    (i)   in relation to Part A installations, the direct or indirect release of substances, vibrations, heat or noise from individual or diffuse sources in an installation into the air, water or land;

    (ii) in relation to Part B installations, the direct release of substances or heat from individual or diffuse sources in an installation into the air;

    (iii) in relation to Part A mobile plant, the direct or indirect release of substances, vibrations, heat or noise from the mobile plant into the air, water or land;

    (iv) in relation to Part B mobile plant, the direct release of substances or heat from the mobile plant into the air;

'emission limit value' means the mass, expressed in terms of specific parameters, concentration or level of an emission, which may not be exceeded during one or more periods of time;

'enforcement notice' has the meaning given by regulation 24(1);

'general binding rules' has the meaning given by regulation 14(1);

'installation' means—

    (i)   a stationary technical unit where one or more activities listed in Part 1 of Schedule 1 are carried out; and

    (ii) any other location on the same site where any other directly associated activities are carried out which have a technical connection with the activities carried out in the stationary technical unit and which could have an effect on pollution, and, other than in Schedule 3, references to an installation include references to part of an installation;

['landfill' means a landfill to which the 2002 Regulations apply;]

'mobile plant' means plant which is designed to move or to be moved whether on roads or otherwise and which is used to carry out one or more activities listed in Part 1 of Schedule 1;

'off-site condition' has the meaning given by regulation 12(12);

operator', subject to paragraph (2), means, in relation to an installation or mobile plant, the person who has control over its operation;

'Part A installation', 'Part A(1) installation', 'Part A(2) installation' and 'Part B installation' shall be interpreted in accordance with Part 3 of Schedule 1;

'Part A mobile plant', 'Part A(1) mobile plant', 'Part A(2) mobile plant' and 'Part B mobile plant' shall be interpreted in accordance with Part 3 of Schedule 1;

'permit' means a permit granted under regulation 10;

'pollution' means emissions as a result of human activity which may be harmful to human health or the quality of the environment, cause offence to any human senses, result in damage to material property, or impair or interfere with amenities and other legitimate uses of the environment; and 'pollutant' means any substance, vibration, heat or noise released as a result of such an emission which may have such an effect;

'regulator' means, in relation to the exercise of functions under these Regulations, the authority by whom, under regulation 8, the functions are exercisable; and 'local authority regulator' means a regulator which is a local authority as defined in regulation 8(15) and (16);

'revocation notice' has the meaning given by regulation 21(1);

'specified waste management activity' means any one of the following activities—

(a) the disposal of waste in a landfill, whether or not the disposal falls within Section 5.2 of Part 1 of Schedule 1;

(b) the disposal of waste falling within Section 5.3 of that Part of that Schedule;

(c) the recovery of waste falling within paragraphs (i), (ii), (v) or (vii) of paragraph (c) of Part A(1) of Section 5.4 of that Part of that Schedule; 'substance' includes any chemical element and its compounds and any biological entity or micro-organism, with the exception of radioactive substances within the meaning of Council Directive 80/836/Euratom, genetically modified micro-organisms within the meaning of Council Directive 90/219/EEC and genetically modified organisms within the meaning of Council Directive 90/220/EEC;

'suspension notice' has the meaning given by regulation 25(1);

'variation notice' has the meaning given by regulation 17(5).

(2) For the purposes of these Regulations—

(a) where an installation or mobile plant has not been put into operation, the person who will have control over the operation of the installation or mobile plant when it is put into operation shall be treated as the operator of the installation or mobile plant;

(b) where an installation or mobile plant has ceased to be in operation, the person who holds the permit which applies to the installation or mobile plant shall be treated as the operator of the installation or mobile plant.

(3) In these Regulations—

(a) a reference to a release into water includes a release into a sewer (within the meaning of section 219(1) of the Water Industry Act 1991);

(b) a reference to a Council Directive is a reference to that Directive together with any amendment made before the date on which these Regulations are made.

(4) Part 1 of Schedule 1 shall be interpreted in accordance with the provisions as to interpretation in Part 1 and 2 of that Schedule.

(5) Parts 1 and 2 of Schedule 3 shall be interpreted in accordance with Part 3 of that Schedule.

3 Interpretation: 'best available techniques'

(1) For the purpose of these Regulations, 'best available techniques' means the most effective and advanced stage in the development of activities and their methods of operation which indicates the practical suitability of particular techniques for providing in principle the basis for emission limit values designed to prevent and, where that is not practicable, generally to reduce emissions and the impact on the environment as a whole; and for the purpose of this definition—

    (a) 'available techniques' means those techniques which have been developed on a scale which allows implementation in the relevant industrial sector, under economically and technically viable conditions, taking into consideration the cost and advantages, whether or not the techniques are used or produced inside the United Kingdom, as long as they are reasonably accessible to the operator;

    (b) 'best' means, in relation to techniques, the most effective in achieving a high general level of protection of the environment as a whole;

    (c) 'techniques' includes both the technology used and the way in which the installation is designed, built, maintained, operated and decommissioned.

(2) Schedule 2 shall have effect in relation to the determination of best available techniques.

4 Fit and proper person

(1) This regulation applies for the purpose of the discharge of any function under these Regulations which requires the regulator to determine whether a person is or is not a fit and proper person to carry out a specified waste management activity.

(2) Whether a person is or is not a fit and proper person to carry out a specified waste management activity shall be determined by reference to the fulfilment of the conditions of the permit which apply or will apply to the carrying out of that activity.

(3) Subject to paragraph (4), a person shall be treated as not being a fit and proper person if it appears to the regulator that—

    (a) he or another relevant person has been convicted of a relevant offence;

    [(b) he has not made, or will not before commencement of the specified waste management activity make, adequate financial provision (either by way of financial security or its equivalent) to ensure that—

        (i) the obligations (including after-care provisions) arising from the permit in relation to that activity are discharged; and

        (ii) any closure procedures required by the permit in relation to that activity are followed;

    (c) he and all staff engaged in carrying out that activity will not be provided with adequate professional technical development and training; or

    (d) the management of that activity will not be in the hands of a technically competent person.]

(4) The regulator may, if it considers it proper to do so in any particular case, treat a person as a fit and proper person notwithstanding that paragraph (3)(a) applies in his case.

(5) For the purposes of paragraph (3)—

    (a) 'relevant offence' means an offence prescribed under section 74(6) of the Environmental Protection Act 1990 for the purposes of section 74(3)(a) of that Act; and

    (b) the qualifications and experience required of a person for the purposes of section 74(3)(b) of that Act which are prescribed under section 74(6) of that Act shall be treated as the qualifications and experience required of a person for the purposes of paragraph (3) [. . .]

(6) In paragraph (3)(a), 'another relevant person' means, in relation to the holder or proposed holder of a permit—

    (a) any person who has been convicted of a relevant offence committed by him in the course of his employment by the holder or proposed holder of the permit or in the course of the carrying on of any business by a partnership one of the members of which was the holder or proposed holder of the permit;

    (b) a body corporate which has been convicted of a relevant offence committed when the holder or proposed holder of the permit was a director, manager, secretary or other similar officer of that body corporate; or

(c) where the holder or proposed holder of the permit is a body corporate, a person who is a director, manager, secretary or other similar officer of that body corporate and who—
  (i) has been convicted of a relevant offence; or
  (ii) was a director, manager, secretary or other similar officer of another body corporate at a time when a relevant offence for which that other body corporate has been convicted was committed.

5 Application to the Crown

(1) Subject to the provisions of this regulation, these Regulations [and the 2002 Regulations] bind the Crown.

(2) No contravention by the Crown of any provision of these Regulations [or the 2002 Regulations] shall make the Crown criminally liable under regulation 32 [below or under regulation 17 of the 2002 Regulations] and no proceedings may be taken against the Crown under regulation 33 but the High Court may, on the application of a regulator, declare unlawful any act or omission of the Crown which constitutes such a contravention.

(3) Notwithstanding anything in paragraph (2), the provisions of these Regulations [and the 2002 Regulations] shall apply to persons in the public service of the Crown as they apply to other persons.

(4) If the Secretary of State certifies that it appears to him, as respects any Crown premises and any specified powers of entry exercisable under section 108 of the Environment Act 1995 in relation to functions conferred or imposed by these Regulations [or the 2002 Regulations], that it is requisite or expedient that, in the interests of national security, the powers of entry should not be exercisable in relation to the premises, those powers shall not be exercisable in relation to those premises; and in this paragraph 'specified' means specified in the certificate and 'Crown premises' means premises held or used by or on behalf of the Crown.

(5) The following persons shall be treated as if they were the operator of the installation or mobile plant concerned for the purpose of any notice served or given or any proceedings instituted in relation to an installation or mobile plant operated or controlled by any person acting on behalf of the Royal Household, the Duchy of Lancaster or the Duke of Cornwall or other possessor of the Duchy of Cornwall—
  (a) in relation to an installation or mobile plant operated or controlled by a person acting on behalf of the Royal Household, the Keeper of the Privy Purse;
  (b) in relation to an installation or mobile plant operated or controlled by a person acting on behalf of the Duchy of Lancaster, such person as the Chancellor of the Duchy appoints in relation to that installation or mobile plant;
  (c) in relation to an installation or mobile plant operated or controlled by a person acting on behalf of the Duchy of Cornwall, such person as the Duke of Cornwall, or the possessor for the time being of the Duchy of Cornwall, appoints in relation to that installation or mobile plant.

6 Notices

(1) Any notice served or given under these Regulations [or the 2002 Regulations] by the Secretary of State or a regulator shall be in writing.

(2) Any such notice may be served on or given to a person by leaving it at his proper address or by sending it by post to him at that address.

(3) Any such notice may—
  (a) in the case of a body corporate, be served on the secretary or clerk of that body;
  (b) in the case of a partnership, be served on or given to a partner or person having the control or management of the partnership business.

(4) For the purpose of this regulation and of section 7 of the Interpretation Act 1978 (service of documents by post) in its application to this regulation, the proper address of any

person on or to whom any such notice is to be served or given shall be his last known address, except that—

    (a) in the case of a body corporate or their secretary or clerk, it shall be the address of the registered or principal office of that body;

    (b) in the case of a partnership or person having the control or management of the partnership business, it shall be the principal office of the partnership,

and for the purposes of this paragraph the principal office of a company registered outside the United Kingdom or of a partnership carrying on business outside the United Kingdom shall be their principal office within the United Kingdom.

(5) If the person to be served with or given any such notice has specified an address in the United Kingdom other than his proper address within the meaning of paragraph (4) as the one at which he or someone on his behalf will accept notices of the same description as that notice, that address shall also be treated for the purposes of this regulation and section 7 of the Interpretation Act 1978 as his proper address.

7 Applications

(1) A regulator may require any application or type of application made to it under any provision of these Regulations to be made on a form made available by the regulator.

(2) A form made available by a regulator under paragraph (1) shall specify the information required by the regulator to determine the application, which shall include any information required to be contained in the application by the provision of these Regulations under which the application is made.

(3) Where a regulator makes available a form under paragraph (1) in relation to the making of applications to it under a provision of these Regulations any application made to it under that provision shall be made on that form.

(4) Any application made under these Regulations may, with the agreement of the regulator, be sent to the regulator electronically.

(5) Where an application which is required to be accompanied by a fee, map or plan is sent electronically, the fee, map or plan may be sent to the regulator separately from the application but the application shall not be treated as having been received by the regulator until the fee, map or plan has also been received.

(6) An application made under these Regulations may be withdrawn at any time before it is determined.

8 Discharge and scope of functions

(1) This regulation determines the authority by whom the functions conferred or imposed by these Regulations on a regulator are exercisable and the purposes for which they are exercisable.

(2) Those functions, in their application to a Part A(1) installation or Part A(1) mobile plant, shall be functions of the Environment Agency and shall be exercisable for the purpose of achieving a high level of protection of the environment taken as a whole by, in particular, preventing or, where that is not practicable, reducing emissions into the air, water and land.

(3) Subject to regulation 13, those functions, in their application to a Part A(2) installation or Part A(2) mobile plant, shall be functions of the local authority in whose area the installation is (or will be) situated or the mobile plant is (or will be) operated and shall be exercisable for the purpose of achieving a high level of protection of the environment taken as a whole by, in particular, preventing or, where that is not practicable, reducing emissions into the air, water and land.

(4) Those functions, in their application to a Part B installation, shall be functions of the local authority in whose area the installation is (or will be) situated and shall be exercisable for the purpose of preventing or, where that is not practicable, reducing emissions into the air.

(5) Those functions, in their application to a Part B mobile plant, shall be functions of—

(a) where the operator of the mobile plant has his principal place of business in England and Wales, the local authority in whose area that place of business is;

(b) where the operator of the mobile plant has his principal place of business outside of England and Wales and the mobile plant is not covered by a permit, the local authority in whose area the plant is first operated or, where the plant has not been operated in England and Wales, the local authority in whose area it is intended by the operator that the plant should first be operated;

(c) where the operator has his principal place of business outside of England and Wales and the mobile plant is covered by a permit, the local authority which granted the permit,

and shall be exercisable for the purpose of preventing or, where that is not practicable, reducing emissions into the air.

(6) The Secretary of State may, as respects functions under these Regulations exercisable by a local authority specified in the direction, direct that those functions shall be exercised instead by the Environment Agency while the direction remains in force or during a period specified in the direction.

(7) A transfer of functions under paragraph (6) to the Environment Agency relating to Part B installations or Part B mobile plant does not make them exercisable by the Agency for any other purpose than that mentioned in paragraphs (4) and (5).

(8) The Secretary of State may, as respects functions under these Regulations exercisable by the Environment Agency specified in the direction, direct that those functions shall be exercised instead by a local authority while the direction remains in force or during a period specified in the direction.

(9) A direction under paragraph (6) may transfer functions exercisable by a local authority in relation to all or any description of installations or mobile plant (a 'general direction') or in relation to a specific installation or mobile plant specified in the direction (a 'specific direction') but a direction under paragraph (8) may only be a specific direction.

(10) A direction under paragraph (6) or (8) may include such saving and transitional provisions as the Secretary of State considers necessary or expedient.

(11) The Secretary of State, on giving or withdrawing a general direction under paragraph (6), shall—

(a) serve notice of it on the Environment Agency and on the local authorities affected by the direction; and

(b) cause notice of it to be published as soon as practicable in the London Gazette and in at least one newspaper circulating in the area of each authority affected by the direction,

and any such notice shall specify the date on which the direction is to take (or took) effect and (where appropriate) its duration.

(12) The Secretary of State, on giving or withdrawing a specific direction under paragraph (6) or (8), shall—

(a) serve notice on the Environment Agency, the local authority and the operator or the person appearing to the Secretary of State to be the operator of the installation or mobile plant affected; and

(b) cause notice of it to be published in the London Gazette and in at least one newspaper circulating in the authority's area,

and any such notice shall specify the date on which the direction is to take (or took) effect and (where appropriate) its duration.

(13) The requirements of sub-paragraph (b) of paragraph (11), or, as the case may be, sub-paragraph (b) of paragraph (12) shall not apply in any case where, in the opinion of the Secretary of State, the publication of the notice in accordance with that sub-paragraph would be contrary to the interests of national security.

(14) It shall be the duty of regulators to follow developments in best available techniques.

(15) In this regulation, 'local authority' means, subject to paragraph (16)—

    (a) in Greater London, a London borough council, the Common Council of the City of London, the Sub-Treasurer of the Inner Temple and the Under Treasurer of the Middle Temple;

    (b) in England outside Greater London, a district council or, in relation to an area for which there is a county council but no district council, the county council, and the Council of the Isles of Scilly;

    (c) in Wales, a county council or county borough council.

(16) Where, by an order under section 2 of the Public Health (Control of Disease) Act 1984, a port health authority has been constituted for any port health district, the port health authority shall have, as respects its district, the functions conferred or imposed by these Regulations in their application to a Part B installation; and 'local authority' and 'area' shall be construed accordingly.

PART II   PERMITS

9   Requirement for permit to operate installation and mobile plant

(1) No person shall operate an installation or mobile plant after the prescribed date for that installation or mobile plant except under and to the extent authorised by a permit granted by the regulator.

(2) In paragraph (1), the 'prescribed date' means the appropriate date set out in or determined in accordance with Schedule 3.

10   Permits: general provisions

(1) An application for a permit to operate an installation or mobile plant shall be made to the regulator in accordance with paragraphs 1 to 3 of Part I of Schedule 4 and shall be accompanied by any fee prescribed in respect of the application under section 41 of the Environment Act 1995 or regulation 22.

(2) Subject to paragraphs (3) and (4), where an application is duly made to the regulator, the regulator shall either grant the permit subject to the conditions required or authorised to be imposed by regulation 12 [below (or regulation 8 of the 2002 Regulations)] or refuse the permit.

(3) A permit shall not be granted if the regulator considers that the applicant will not be the person who will have control over the operation of the installation or mobile plant concerned after the grant of the permit or will not ensure that the installation or mobile plant is operated so as to comply with the conditions which would be included in the permit.

(4) In the case of an application for a permit that will authorise the carrying out of a specified waste management activity at an installation or by means of mobile plant, the permit shall not be granted unless—

    (a) the regulator is satisfied that the applicant is a fit and proper person to carry out that activity; and

    (b) in the case of an installation where the use of the application site for the carrying out of that activity requires planning permission granted under the Town and Country Planning Act 1990, such planning permission is in force in relation to that use of the land.

(5) For the purpose of paragraph (4)(b), a certificate under section 191 of the Town and Country Planning Act 1990 (certificate of lawful use or development) in relation to the use of the application site for the carrying out of the specified waste management activity, and an established use certificate under section 192 of that Act, as originally enacted, in relation to that use which continues to have effect for the purpose of subsection (4) of that section, shall be treated as if it were a grant of planning permission for that use.

(6) A permit may authorise the operation of—
  (a) more than one Part A installation or Part A mobile plant on the same site operated by the same operator;
  (b) more than one Part B installation on the same site operated by the same operator; or
  (c) more than one Part B mobile plant operated by the same operator, but may not otherwise authorise the operation of more than one installation or mobile plant.

(7) A permit authorising the operation of a Part A mobile plant may only authorise the operation of that plant on a site specified in the permit and only one site may be specified in each such permit (accordingly, the operation of the plant on a different site shall require a distinct permit).

(8) A permit authorising the operation of an installation or Part A mobile plant shall include a map or plan showing the site of the installation or plant covered by the permit and, in the case of an installation, the location of the installation on that site.

(9) A permit shall be transferred only in accordance with regulation 18 and shall cease to have effect only in accordance with regulation 19 or 20 (surrender) or regulation 21 (revocation) or paragraph (10) (consolidation).

(10) Where—
  (a) the conditions of a permit have been varied under regulation 17 or affected by a partial transfer, surrender or revocation under regulations 18 to 21; or
  (b) there is more than one permit applying to installations on the same site operated by the same operator or to mobile plant operated by the same operator, the regulator may replace the permit or permits, as the case may be, with a consolidated permit applying to the same installations or mobile plant and subject to the same conditions as the permit or permits being replaced.

(11) Paragraphs 4 to 8 of Part 1 of Schedule 4 shall have effect with respect to applications made under paragraph (1).

(12) Part 2 of Schedule 4 shall have effect in relation to the determination of applications for permits.

(13) Parts 1 and 2 of Schedule 4 shall have effect subject to Part 3 of that Schedule (national security).

(14) This regulation is subject to paragraphs 5 and 9 of Schedule 3 (applications for a permit to operate existing installations or mobile plant, as defined in that Schedule).

11 Conditions of permits: general principles

(1) When determining the conditions of a permit, the regulator shall take account of the general principles set out in paragraph (2) and, in the case of a permit authorising the operation of a Part A installation or Part A mobile plant, the additional general principles set out in paragraph (3).

(2) The general principles referred to in paragraph (1) are that installations and mobile plant should be operated in such a way that—
  (a) all the appropriate preventative measures are taken against pollution, in particular through application of the best available techniques; and
  (b) no significant pollution is caused.

(3) The additional general principles referred to in paragraph (1) in relation to a permit authorising the operation of a Part A installation or a Part A mobile plant are that the installation or mobile plant should be operated in such a way that—
  (a) waste production is avoided in accordance with Council Directive 75/442/ EEC on waste; and where waste is produced, it is recovered or, where that is technically and economically impossible, it is disposed of while avoiding or reducing any impact on the environment;

(b) energy is used efficiently;

(c) the necessary measures are taken to prevent accidents and limit their consequences,

and that, upon the definitive cessation of activities, the necessary measures should be taken to avoid any pollution risk and to return the site of the installation or mobile plant to a satisfactory state.

12   Conditions of permits: specific requirements

(1) Subject to paragraphs (15) and (16) and regulations 13 and 14, there shall be included in a permit—

(a) such conditions as the regulator considers appropriate to comply with paragraphs (2) to (8); and

(b) in relation to any Part A installation or Part A mobile plant authorised by the permit—

(i) such other conditions applying in relation to the Part A installation or Part A mobile plant as the regulator considers appropriate to comply with paragraph (9); and

(ii) such other conditions (if any) applying in relation to the Part A installation or Part A mobile plant, in addition to those required by sub-paragraphs (a) and (b)(i), as appear to the regulator to be appropriate, when taken with the condition implied by paragraph (10), for the purpose of ensuring a high level of protection for the environment as a whole, taking into account, in particular, the general principles set out in regulation 11;

(c) in relation to any Part B installation or Part B mobile plant authorised by the permit, such other conditions (if any) applying in relation to the Part B installation or Part B mobile plant as appear to the regulator to be appropriate, when taken with the condition implied by paragraph (10), for the purpose of preventing or, where that is not practicable, reducing emissions into the air, taking into account, in particular, the general principles set out in regulation 11(2).

(2) Subject to paragraph (8), a permit shall include emission limit values for pollutants, in particular those listed in Schedule 5, likely to be emitted from the installation or mobile plant in significant quantities, having regard to their nature and, in the case of emissions from a Part A installation or a Part A mobile plant, their potential to transfer pollution from one environmental medium to another.

(3) Where appropriate, the emission limit values required by paragraph (2) may apply to groups of pollutants rather than to individual pollutants.

(4) The emission limit values required by paragraph (2) shall normally apply at the point at which the emissions leave the installation or mobile plant, any dilution being disregarded when determining them.

(5) The effect of a waste water treatment plant may be taken into account when determining the emission limit values applying in relation to indirect releases into water from a Part A installation or Part A mobile plant provided that an equivalent level of protection of the environment as a whole is guaranteed and taking such treatment into account does not lead to higher levels of pollution.

(6) Subject to paragraph (7), the emission limit values required by paragraph (2) shall be based on the best available techniques for the description of installation or mobile plant concerned but shall take account of the technical characteristics of the particular installation or mobile plant being permitted, and, in the case of an installation or Part A mobile plant, its geographical location and the local environmental conditions.

(7) Where an environmental quality standard requires stricter emission limit values than those that would be imposed pursuant to paragraph (6), paragraph (2) shall require those stricter emission limit values; and for the purpose of this paragraph 'environmental quality

standard' means the set of requirements which must be fulfilled at a given time by a given environment or particular part thereof, as set out in Community legislation.

(8) Where appropriate, the emission limit values required by paragraph (2) may be supplemented or replaced by equivalent parameters or technical measures.

(9) A permit authorising the operation of a Part A installation or Part A mobile plant shall also include conditions—

(a) aimed at minimising long distance and transboundary pollution;

(b) ensuring, where necessary, appropriate protection of the soil and ground-water and appropriate management of waste generated by the installation or mobile plant;

(c) relating to the periods when the installation or mobile plant is not operating normally where there is a risk that the environment may be adversely affected during such periods, including, in particular, conditions relating to the start up of operations, leaks, malfunctions and momentary stoppages;

(d) setting out the steps to be taken prior to the operation of the installation or mobile plant and after the definitive cessation of operations;

(e) setting out suitable emission monitoring requirements, specifying the measurement methodology and frequency and the evaluation procedure, and ensuring that the operator supplies the regulator with the data required to check compliance with the permit;

(f) requiring the operator to supply the regulator regularly with the results of the monitoring of emissions and to inform the regulator, without delay, of any incident or accident which is causing or may cause significant pollution.

(10) Subject to paragraph (11), there is implied in every permit a condition that, in operating the installation or mobile plant, the operator shall use the best available techniques for preventing or, where that is not practicable, reducing emissions from the installation or mobile plant.

(11) The obligation implied by virtue of paragraph (10) shall not apply in relation to any aspect of the operation of the installation or mobile plant in question which is regulated by a condition imposed under any other paragraph of this regulation.

(12) A permit authorising the operation of an installation or Part A mobile plant may include a condition (an 'off-site condition') requiring an operator to carry out works or do other things in relation to land not forming part of the site of the installation or mobile plant notwithstanding that he is not entitled to carry out the works or do the things and any person whose consent would be required shall grant, or join in granting, the operator such rights in relation to that land as will enable the operator to comply with any requirements imposed on him by the permit.

(13) Schedule 6 shall have effect in relation to compensation where rights are granted pursuant to paragraph (12).

(14) A permit may, without prejudice to the generality of the previous provisions of this regulation, include conditions—

(a) imposing limits on the amount or composition of any substance produced or utilised during the operation of the installation or mobile plant in any period;

(b) which are supplemental or incidental to other conditions contained in the permit.

(15) The Secretary of State may give directions to regulators—

(a) as to the specific conditions which are, or are not, to be included in all permits, in permits of a specified description or in any particular permit;

(b) as to the objectives which are to be achieved by conditions included in such permits,

and the regulators shall include in such permits such conditions as are specified or required to comply with such directions.

(16) Guidance issued by the Secretary of State under regulation 37 may sanction reliance by a regulator on any arrangements referred to in the guidance to operate to secure a particular result as an alternative to including a condition in the permit pursuant to this regulation [or regulation 8 of the 2002 Regulations].

(17) Where a Part B mobile plant authorised by a permit is used to carry out an activity on the site of an installation which is authorised by a separate permit, then if different requirements are imposed in the permits as respect the carrying out of the activity the requirements in the permit authorising the operation of the installation shall prevail in the event of any inconsistency.

13   Conditions of permits: Environment Agency notice in relation to emissions into water

(1) In the case of a Part A installation or Part A mobile plant in relation to which a local authority regulator exercises functions under these Regulations, the Environment Agency may, at any time, give notice to the local authority regulator specifying the emission limit values or conditions (not containing emission limit values) which it considers are appropriate in relation to preventing or reducing emissions into water.

(2) Where a notice under paragraph (1) specifies emission limit values, the emission limit values required by paragraph (2) of regulation 12 in relation to emissions into water from the installation or mobile plant concerned shall be those specified in that notice or such stricter emission limit values as may be determined by the local authority regulator in accordance with paragraph (6) of that regulation or required by paragraph (7) of that regulation.

(3) Where a notice under paragraph (1) specifies conditions in relation to emissions into water from an installation or mobile plant, the permit authorising the operation of that installation or mobile plant shall include those conditions or any more onerous conditions dealing with the same matters as the local authority regulator considers to be appropriate.

14   General binding rules

(1) Subject to paragraph (2), the Secretary of State may make rules ('general binding rules') containing requirements applying to certain types of installation or mobile plant.

(2) The Secretary of State shall only make general binding rules under this regulation applying to Part A installations or Part A mobile plant if he is satisfied that the operation of such installations or mobile plant under the rules will result in the same high level of environmental protection and integrated prevention and control of pollution as would result from the operation of the installations or mobile plant under the conditions that would be included in the permits for those installations or mobile plant pursuant to regulation 12 if the rules did not apply.

(3) Where the Secretary of State makes general binding rules a regulator may, at the request of the operator, include in a permit authorising the operation of an installation or mobile plant covered by the rules a condition (a 'general binding rules condition') providing that the aspects of the operation of the installation or mobile plant covered by the requirements in the rules shall be subject to those requirements instead of to conditions included in the permit pursuant to regulation 12.

(4) Where a permit includes a general binding rules condition the requirements in the general binding rules shall be treated as if they were conditions of the permit for the purpose of regulations 23, 24 and 32(1)(b).

(5) The Secretary of State may vary general binding rules by means of a notice of variation specifying the variations and the date on which the variations are to take effect, which shall be not less than 3 months after the date on which notice of the variation is given in the London Gazette pursuant to paragraph (9)(c).

(6) The Secretary of State may revoke general binding rules by means of a notice of revocation.

(7) Where aspects of the operation of an installation or mobile plant are covered by the requirements in general binding rules which are revoked, the regulator shall vary the permit authorising the operation of the installation or mobile plant under regulation 17 to delete the general binding rules condition and to insert the conditions that will be required by regulations 11 and 12 when the requirements in the general binding rules no longer apply.

(8) Where the Secretary of State revokes general binding rules the requirements in the general binding rules shall continue to be treated under paragraph (4) as if they were conditions of a permit until the variations of the permit required by paragraph (7) take effect.

(9) Where the Secretary of State makes, varies or revokes general binding rules he shall—

(a) serve a copy of the rules, notice of variation or notice of revocation on the Environment Agency and on all local authority regulators;

(b) publish the rules, notice of variation or notice of revocation in such manner as he considers appropriate for the purpose of bringing the rules or notice to the attention of operators likely to be affected by them;

(c) give notice of the making, variation or revocation of the rules in the London Gazette.

15   Review of conditions of permits

(1) Regulators shall periodically review the conditions of permits and may do so at any time.

(2) Without prejudice to paragraph (1), a review of a permit under this regulation shall be carried out where—

(a) the pollution caused by the installation or mobile plant covered by the permit is of such significance that the existing emission limit values of the permit need to be revised or new emission limit values need to be included in the permit;

(b) substantial changes in the best available techniques make it possible to reduce emissions from the installation or mobile plant significantly without imposing excessive costs; or

(c) the operational safety of the activities carried out in the installation or mobile plant requires other techniques to be used.

16   Proposed change in the operation of an installation

(1) Subject to paragraph (4), where an operator of an installation which is permitted under these Regulations proposes to make a change in the operation of that installation he shall, at least 14 days before making the change, notify the regulator.

(2) A notification under paragraph (1) shall be in writing and shall contain a description of the proposed change in the operation of the installation.

(3) A regulator shall, by notice served on the operator, acknowledge receipt of any notification received under paragraph (1).

(4) Paragraph (1) shall not apply where the operator applies under regulation 17(2) for the variation of the conditions of his permit before making the proposed change and the application contains a description of the change.

17   Variation of conditions of permits

(1) The regulator may at any time vary the conditions of a permit and shall do so if it appears to the regulator at that time, whether as a result of a review under regulation 15, a notification under regulation 13 or 16 or otherwise, that regulations 11 and 12 [above or regulation 8 of the 2002 Regulations] require conditions to be included which are different from the subsisting conditions.

(2) An operator of an installation or mobile plant which is permitted under these Regulations may apply to the regulator for the variation of the conditions of his permit.

(3) An application under paragraph (2) shall be made in accordance with paragraph 1 of Part 1 of Schedule 7 and shall be accompanied by any fee prescribed in respect of the

application under section 41 of the Environment Act 1995 or regulation 22; and paragraphs 2 and 3 of Part 1 of Schedule 7 shall have effect with respect to such applications.

(4) Where an application is duly made to the regulator under paragraph (2), the regulator shall determine, in accordance with regulations 11 and 12 [above or regulation 8 of the 2002 Regulations], whether to vary the conditions of the permit.

(5) Where the regulator decides to vary the conditions of the permit, whether on an application under paragraph (2) or otherwise, it shall serve a notice on the operator (a 'variation notice') specifying the variations of the conditions of the permit and the date or dates on which the variations are to take effect and, unless the notice is withdrawn, the variations specified in the notice shall take effect on the date or dates so specified.

(6) A variation notice served under paragraph (5) shall, unless served for the purpose of determining an application under paragraph (2), require the operator to pay, within such period as may be specified in the notice, any fee prescribed in respect of the variation notice under section 41 of the Environment Act 1995 or regulation 22.

(7) Where the regulator decides on an application under paragraph (2) not to vary the conditions of the permit, it shall give notice of its decision to the operator.

(8) Part 2 of Schedule 7 shall have effect in relation to the determination of applications under paragraph (2) and the issuing of variation notices.

(9) Parts 1 and 2 of Schedule 7 shall have effect subject to Part 3 of that Schedule (national security).

(10) This regulation and Schedule 7 apply to the variation of any provision other than a condition which is contained in a permit as they apply to the variation of a condition.

18 Transfer of permits

(1) Where the operator of an installation or mobile plant wishes to transfer, in whole or in part, his permit to another person ('the proposed transferee') the operator and the proposed transferee shall jointly make an application to the regulator to effect the transfer.

(2) An application under paragraph (1) shall be accompanied by the permit and any fee prescribed in respect of the transfer under section 41 of the Environment Act 1995 or regulation 22 and shall contain—

    (a) the operator's and the proposed transferee's telephone number and address and, if different, any address to which correspondence relating to the application should be sent;

    (b) in the case of an application to effect the transfer of a permit or part of a permit that authorises the carrying out of a specified waste management activity, any information which the applicants wish the regulator to take into account when considering whether the transferee is a fit and proper person to carry out that activity.

(3) Where the operator wishes to retain part of his permit (a 'partial transfer'), an application under paragraph (1) shall—

    (a) identify the installation or mobile plant to which the transfer applies (the 'transferred unit'); and

    (b) where the transfer applies to the operation of an installation or Part A mobile plant, contain a map or plan identifying the part of the site used for the operation of that installation or mobile plant (the 'identified part of the site').

(4) Subject to paragraph (5), the regulator shall effect the transfer unless the regulator considers that the proposed transferee will not be the person who will have control over the operation of the installation or mobile plant covered by the transfer after the transfer is effected or will not ensure compliance with the conditions of the transferred permit.

(5) In the case of an application to effect the transfer of a permit or part of a permit which authorises the carrying out of a specified waste management activity, the regulator shall only

effect the transfer if the regulator is satisfied that the proposed transferee is a fit and proper person to carry out that activity.

(6) The regulator shall effect a transfer under this regulation by—

(a) in the case of a partial transfer—

(i) issuing a new permit to the proposed transferee which applies to the transferred unit and, where the transfer applies to the operation of an installation or Part A mobile plant, the identified part of the site covered by the transfer, and includes the conditions required by paragraph (7); and

(ii) returning the original permit to the operator, endorsed to record the transfer and varied to show the installation or mobile plant and, where the transfer applies to the operation of an installation or Part A mobile plant, the site covered by the permit after the transfer and the conditions applying after the transfer as required by paragraph (7);

(b) in the case of a transfer of the whole permit, causing the permit to be endorsed with the name and other particulars of the proposed transferee as the operator of the installation or mobile plant concerned,

and the transfer shall take effect from such date as may be agreed with the applicants and specified in the endorsement and, in the case of a partial transfer, the new permit.

(7) In the case of a partial transfer effected under this regulation, the conditions included in the new permit and original permit after the transfer shall be the same as the conditions included in the original permit immediately before the transfer in so far as they are relevant to any installation, site and mobile plant covered by the new permit or the original permit, as the case may be, but subject to such variations as, in the opinion of the regulator, are necessary to take account of the transfer.

(8) If within the period of two months beginning with the date on which the authority receives an application under paragraph (1), or within such longer period as the regulator and the applicants may agree in writing, the regulator has neither effected the transfer nor given notice to the applicants that it has rejected the application, the application shall, if the applicants notify the regulator in writing that they treat the failure as such, be deemed to have been refused at the end of that period or that longer period, as the case may be.

(9) The regulator may, by notice, require the operator or the proposed transferee to furnish such further information specified in the notice, within the period so specified, as the regulator may require for the purpose of determining an application under this regulation.

(10) Where a notice is served on an operator or proposed transferee under paragraph (9)—

(a) for the purpose of calculating the period of two months mentioned in paragraph (8), no account shall be taken of the period beginning with the date on which notice is served and ending on the date on which the information specified in the notice is furnished; and

(b) if the specified information is not furnished within the period specified, the application shall, if the regulator gives notice to the operator and proposed transferee that it treats the failure as such, be deemed to have been withdrawn at the end of that period.

19 Application to surrender a permit for a Part A installation or Part A mobile plant

(1) This regulation applies where an operator of a Part A installation or Part A mobile plant ceases or intends to cease operating the installation (in whole or in part) or the mobile plant.

(2) Where this regulation applies, the operator may—

(a) if he has ceased or intends to cease operating all of the installations and mobile plant covered by the permit, apply to the regulator to surrender the whole permit;

(b) in any other case, apply to the regulator to surrender the permit in so far as it authorises the operation of the installation or mobile plant ('the surrender unit') which he has ceased or intends to cease operating (a 'partial surrender').

(3) An application under paragraph (2) shall be accompanied by any fee prescribed in respect of the application under section 41 of the Environment Act 1995 or regulation 22, and shall contain the following information—

(a) the operator's telephone number and address and, if different, any address to which correspondence relating to the application should be sent;

(b) in the case of a partial surrender, a description of the surrender unit and a map or plan identifying the part of the site used for the operation of the surrender unit (the 'identified part of the site');

(c) a site report describing the condition of the site, or the identified part of the site, as the case may be ('the report site'), identifying, in particular, any changes in the condition of the site as described in the site report contained in the application for the permit; and

(d) a description of any steps that have been taken to avoid any pollution risk on the report site resulting from the operation of the installation or mobile plant or to return it to a satisfactory state.

(4) If the regulator is satisfied, in relation to the report site, that such steps (if any) as are appropriate to avoid any pollution risk resulting from the operation of the Part A installation or Part A mobile plant and to return the site to a satisfactory state have been taken by the operator, it shall accept the surrender and give the operator notice of its determination and the permit shall cease to have effect or, in the case of partial surrender, shall cease to have effect to the extent surrendered, on the date specified in the notice of determination.

(5) If, in the case of a partial surrender, the regulator is of the opinion that it is necessary to vary the conditions included in the permit to take account of the surrender, the regulator shall specify the necessary variations in the notice of determination given under paragraph (4) and the variations specified in the notice shall take effect on the date specified in the notice.

(6) If the regulator is not satisfied as mentioned in paragraph (4), it shall give to the operator a notice of its determination stating that the application has been refused.

(7) The regulator shall give notice of its determination of an application under this regulation within the period of three months beginning with the date on which the regulator receives the application or within such longer period as the regulator and the operator may agree in writing.

(8) If the regulator fails to give notice of its determination accepting the surrender or refusing the application within the period allowed by or under paragraph (7) the application shall, if the operator notifies the regulator in writing that he treats the failure as such, be deemed to have been refused at the end of that period.

(9) The regulator may, by notice to the operator, require him to furnish such further information specified in the notice, within the period so specified, as the regulator may require for the purpose of determining an application under this regulation.

(10) Where a notice is served on an operator under paragraph (9)—

(a) for the purpose of calculating the period of three months mentioned in paragraph (7), no account shall be taken of the period beginning with the date on which notice is served and ending on the date on which the information specified in the notice is furnished; and

(b) if the specified information is not furnished within the period specified the application shall, if the regulator gives notice to the operator that it treats the failure as such, be deemed to have been withdrawn at the end of that period.

(11) For the purpose of deciding whether a pollution risk results from the operation of a Part A installation or Part A mobile plant for the purpose of this regulation—

(a) where the operation of the installation or plant involved the carrying out of a specified waste management activity, only risks resulting from carrying out that activity after the relevant date for that activity shall be treated as resulting from the operation of the installation or mobile plant;

(b) where the operation of the installation or mobile plant involved the carrying out of other activities, only risks resulting from the carrying out of those other activities after the date on which the permit applying to the installation or mobile plant was granted shall be treated as resulting from the operation of the installation or mobile plant.

(12) The relevant date for a specified waste management activity for the purpose of paragraph (11)(a) is—

(a) where the activity was carried out on the site of the installation or mobile plant under a waste management licence which, by virtue of section 35(11A) of the Environmental Protection Act 1990, ceased to have effect in relation to the carrying out of that activity on that site on the granting of the permit applying to the installation or mobile plant, the date on which that waste management licence was granted;

(b) in any other case, the date on which the permit applying to the installation or mobile plant was granted.

(13) In paragraph (12)(a), 'waste management licence' has the same meaning as in section 35(12) of the Environmental Protection Act 1990 (and includes a disposal licence which is treated as a site licence by virtue of section 77(2) of that Act).

20 Notification of surrender of a permit for a Part B installation or Part B mobile plant

(1) This regulation applies where an operator of a Part B installation or Part B mobile plant ceases or intends to cease operating the installation (in whole or in part) or the mobile plant.

(2) Where this regulation applies, the operator may—

(a) if he has ceased or intends to cease operating all of the installations and mobile plant covered by the permit, notify the regulator of the surrender of the whole permit;

(b) in any other case, notify the regulator of the surrender of the permit in so far as it authorises the operation of the installation or mobile plant ('the surrender unit') which he has ceased or intends to cease operating (a 'partial surrender').

(3) A notification under paragraph (2) shall contain the following information—

(a) the operator's telephone number and address and, if different, any address to which correspondence relating to the notification should be sent;

(b) in the case of a partial surrender of a permit applying to Part B installations, a description of the surrender unit and a map or plan identifying the part of the site used for the operation of the surrender unit (the 'identified part of the site');

(c) in the case of a partial surrender of a permit applying to Part B mobile plant, a list of the mobile plant to which it applies;

(d) the date on which the surrender is to take effect, which shall be at least 28 days after the date on which the notice is served on the regulator.

(4) Subject to paragraph (5), where a surrender is notified under this regulation the permit shall cease to have effect on the date specified in the notification or, in the case of partial surrender, shall cease to have effect on that date to the extent surrendered.

(5) If, in the case of a partial surrender, the regulator is of the opinion that it is necessary to vary the conditions of the permit to take account of the surrender, the regulator shall—

(a) notify the operator of its opinion; and

(b) serve a variation notice under regulation 17 on the operator specifying the variations of the conditions necessitated by the surrender,

and the permit shall cease to have effect to the extent surrendered on the date on which the variations specified in the variation notice take effect if that date is after the date specified in the notification of the surrender.

21 Revocation of permits

(1) The regulator may at any time revoke a permit, in whole or in part, by serving a notice ('a revocation notice') on the operator.

(2) Without prejudice to the generality of paragraph (1), the regulator may serve a notice under this regulation in relation to a permit where—

(a) the permit authorises the carrying out of a specified waste management activity and it appears to the regulator that the operator of the installation or mobile plant concerned has ceased to be a fit and proper person to carry out that activity by reason of his having been convicted of a relevant offence within the meaning of regulation 4(5)(a) or by reason of the management of that activity having ceased to be in the hands of a technically competent person;

(b) the holder of the permit has ceased to be the operator of the installation or mobile plant covered by the permit.

(3) A revocation notice may—

(a) revoke a permit entirely;

(b) revoke a permit only in so far as it authorises the operation of some of the installations or mobile plant to which it applies;

(c) revoke a permit only in so far as it authorises the carrying out of some of the activities which may be carried out in an installation or by means of mobile plant to which it applies.

(4) A revocation notice shall specify—

(a) in the case of a revocation mentioned in sub-paragraph (b) or (c) of paragraph (3) (a 'partial revocation'), the extent to which the permit is being revoked;

(b) in all cases, the date on which the revocation shall take effect, which shall be at least 28 days after the date on which the notice is served.

(5) If, in the case of a revocation mentioned in sub-paragraph (a) or (b) of paragraph (3) applying to a Part A installation or Part A mobile plant, the regulator considers that it is appropriate to require the operator to take steps, once the installation or mobile plant is no longer in operation, to—

(a) avoid any pollution risk resulting from the operation of the installation or mobile plant on the site or, in the case of a partial revocation, that part of the site used for the operation of that installation or mobile plant, or

(b) return the site, or that part of the site, to a satisfactory state, the revocation notice shall specify that this is the case and, in so far as those steps are not already required to be taken by the conditions of the permit, the steps to be taken.

(6) Subject to paragraph (7) and regulation 27(6), a permit shall cease to have effect, or, in the case of a partial revocation, shall cease to have effect to the extent specified in the revocation notice, from the date specified in the notice.

(7) Where paragraph (5) applies the permit shall cease to have effect to authorise the operation of the Part A installation or Part A mobile plant from the date specified in the revocation notice but shall continue to have effect in so far as the permit requires steps to be taken once it is no longer in operation until the regulator issues a certificate stating that it is satisfied that all such steps have been taken.

(8) Where a permit continues to have effect as mentioned in paragraph (7), any steps specified in a revocation notice pursuant to paragraph (5) shall be treated as if they were

required to be taken by a condition of the permit and regulations 17, 23, 24, and 32(1)(b) shall apply in relation to the requirement to take such steps, and to any other conditions in the permit which require steps to be taken once the installation is no longer in operation, until the regulator issues a certificate as mentioned in paragraph (7).

(9) A regulator which has served a revocation notice may, before the date on which the revocation takes effect, withdraw the notice.

(10) Regulation 19(11) shall apply for the purpose of deciding whether a pollution risk results from the operation of a Part A installation or Part A mobile plant for the purpose of this regulation as it applies for the purpose of regulation 19.

22   Fees and charges in relation to local authority permits

(1) There shall be charged by and paid to regulators such fees and charges as may be prescribed from time to time by a scheme under paragraph (2) (whether by being specified in or made calculable under the scheme).

(2) The Secretary of State may make and from time to time revise a scheme prescribing—

(a) fees payable in respect of applications for the grant of local authority permits;

(b) fees payable in respect of, or of applications for, the variation, transfer and surrender of such permits; and

(c) charges payable in respect of the subsistence of such permits.

(3) The Secretary of State shall, on making or revising a scheme under paragraph (2), lay a copy of the scheme or of the revisions made to the scheme or, if he considers it more appropriate, the scheme as revised, before each House of Parliament.

(4) A scheme under paragraph (2) may, in particular—

(a) make different provision for different cases, including different provision in relation to different persons, circumstances or localities;

(b) allow for reduced fees or charges to be payable in respect of permits granted to the same person;

(c) provide for the times at which and the manner in which the payments required by the scheme are to be made (subject to the requirements in these Regulations as to the times at which payment is required); and

(d) make such incidental, supplementary and transitional provisions as appears to the Secretary of State to be appropriate.

(5) The Secretary of State, in framing a scheme under paragraph (2), shall, so far as practicable, secure that the fees and charges payable under the scheme are sufficient, taking one year with another, to cover the expenditure incurred by—

(a) local authority regulators in exercising their functions under these Regulations in relation to local authority permits;

(b) the Environment Agency in exercising its functions under regulation 13(1) or in preparing guidance in relation to the authorisation of installations and plants covered by local authority permits.

(6) A scheme under paragraph (2) shall provide that to the extent that sums paid to a local authority regulator under the scheme relate to the expenditure incurred by the Environment Agency mentioned in paragraph (5)(b) those sums shall be paid by the local authority regulator to the Environment Agency.

(7) If it appears to the local authority regulator that an operator has failed to pay a charge due in respect of the subsistence of a permit, it may revoke the permit under regulation 21.

(8) In this regulation, 'local authority permit' means a permit applying to installations or mobile plant in relation to which a local authority exercises functions under these Regulations.

PART III   ENFORCEMENT

23   Duty of regulator to ensure compliance with conditions

While a permit is in force it shall be the duty of the regulator to take such action under these Regulations as may be necessary for the purpose of ensuring that the conditions of the permit are complied with.

24   Enforcement notices

(1) If the regulator is of the opinion that an operator has contravened, is contravening or is likely to contravene any condition of his permit, the regulator may serve on him a notice (an 'enforcement notice').

(2) An enforcement notice shall—

(a) state that the regulator is of that opinion;

(b) specify the matters constituting the contravention or the matters making it likely that the contravention will arise, as the case may be;

(c) specify the steps that must be taken to remedy the contravention or to remedy the matters making it likely that the contravention will arise, as the case may be; and

(d) specify the period within which those steps must be taken.

(3) The steps that may be specified in an enforcement notice as steps that must be taken to remedy the contravention of any condition of a permit may include both steps that must be taken to make the operation of the installation or mobile plant comply with the conditions of the permit and steps that must be taken to remedy the effects of any pollution caused by the contravention.

(4) The regulator may withdraw an enforcement notice at any time.

25   Suspension notices

(1) If the regulator is of the opinion, as respects an installation or mobile plant authorised under these regulations, that the operation of the installation or mobile plant, or the operation of it in a particular manner, involves an imminent risk of serious pollution, it shall, unless it intends to arrange for steps to be taken under regulation 26(1) in relation to the risk, serve a notice under this regulation (a 'suspension notice') on the operator of the installation or mobile plant.

(2) Paragraph (1) applies whether or not the particular manner of operating the installation or mobile plant in question is regulated by or contravenes a condition of the permit.

(3) If the regulator is of the opinion, as respects the carrying out of specified waste management activities under a permit, that the operator carrying out the activities has ceased to be a fit and proper person in relation to those activities by reason of their management having ceased to be in the hands of a technically competent person, it may serve a suspension notice on that operator.

(4) A suspension notice shall—

(a) state the regulator's opinion, as mentioned in paragraph (1) or (3), as the case may be;

(b) in the case of a notice served under paragraph (1), specify—

(i) the imminent risk involved in the operation of the installation or mobile plant;

(ii) the steps that must be taken to remove it and the period within which they must be taken;

(c) state that the permit shall, until the notice is withdrawn, cease to have effect to authorise the operation of the installation or mobile plant or the carrying out of specified activities in the installation or by means of the mobile plant; and

(d) where the permit is to continue to have effect to authorise the carrying out of activities, state any steps, in addition to those already required to be taken by the conditions of the permit, that are to be taken in carrying out those activities.

(5) Where a suspension notice is served under this regulation the permit shall, on the service of the notice, cease to have effect as stated in the notice.

(6) The regulator may withdraw a suspension notice at any time and shall withdraw a notice when it is satisfied—

(a) in the case of a notice served under paragraph (1), that the steps required by the notice to remove the imminent risk of serious pollution have been taken;

(b) in the case of a notice served under paragraph (3), that the management of the specified waste management activities is in the hands of a technically competent person.

26   Power of regulator to prevent or remedy pollution

(1) If the regulator is of the opinion, as respects the operation of an installation or mobile plant authorised under these regulations, that the operation of the installation or mobile plant, or the operation of it in a particular manner, involves an imminent risk of serious pollution, the regulator may arrange for steps to be taken to remove that risk.

(2) Where the commission of an offence under regulation 32(1)(a), (b) or (d) causes any pollution the regulator may arrange for steps to be taken towards remedying the effects of the pollution.

(3) A regulator which intends to arrange for steps to be taken under paragraph (2) shall, at least seven days before the steps are taken, notify the operator of the steps that are to be taken.

(4) Subject to paragraph (5), where a regulator arranges for steps to be taken under this regulation it may recover the cost of taking those steps from the operator concerned.

(5) No costs shall be recoverable under paragraph (4) where the regulator arranges for steps to be taken under paragraph (1) if the operator shows that there was no imminent risk of serious pollution requiring any such steps to be taken and no other costs shall be recoverable which the operator shows to have been unnecessarily incurred by the regulator.

PART IV   APPEALS

27   Appeals to the Secretary of State

(1) Subject to paragraph (3), the following persons, namely—

(a) a person who has been refused the grant of a permit under regulation 10;

(b) a person who has been refused the variation of the conditions of a permit on an application under regulation 17(2);

(c) a person who is aggrieved by the conditions attached to his permit following an application under regulation 10 or by a variation notice following an application under regulation 17(2);

(d) a person whose application under regulation 18(1) for a regulator to effect the transfer of a permit has been refused or who is aggrieved by the conditions attached to his permit to take account of such a transfer;

(e) a person whose application under regulation 19(2) to surrender a permit has been refused, or who is aggrieved by the conditions attached to his permit to take account of the surrender,

[(f) a person whose request to initiate the closure procedure is not approved under regulation 15(3)(b) of the 2002 Regulations;

(g) a person who is aggrieved by a decision under paragraph 1(6) (b) of Schedule 4 to the 2002 Regulations]

may appeal against the decision of the regulator to the Secretary of State.

(2) Subject to paragraph (3), a person on whom a variation notice is served, other than following an application under regulation 17(2), or on whom a revocation notice, an enforcement notice [a suspension notice or a closure notice under regulation 16(1) of the 2002 Regulations] is served may appeal against the notice to the Secretary of State.

(3) Paragraphs (1) and (2) shall not apply where the decision or notice, as the case may be, implements a direction of the Secretary of State given under regulations 12(15) or 36 or paragraph (4) of this regulation or paragraph 14(6) of Schedule 4 or 6(6) of Schedule 7.

(4) On determining an appeal against a decision of a regulator under paragraph (1) the Secretary of State may—

(a) affirm the decision;
(b) where the decision was a refusal to grant a permit or to vary the conditions of a permit, direct the regulator to grant the permit or to vary the conditions of the permit, as the case may be;
(c) where the decision was as to the conditions attached to a permit, quash all or any of the conditions of the permit;
(d) where the decision was a refusal to effect the transfer or accept the surrender of a permit, direct the regulator to effect the transfer or accept the surrender, as the case may be,

and where he exercises any of the powers in paragraph (b) or (c) he may give directions as to the conditions to be attached to the permit.

(5) On the determination of an appeal under paragraph (2) the Secretary of State may either quash or affirm the notice and, if he affirms it, may do so either in its original form or with such modifications as he may in the circumstances think fit.

(6) Where an appeal is brought under paragraph (2) against a revocation notice, the revocation shall not take effect pending the final determination or the withdrawal of the appeal.

(7) Where an appeal is brought under paragraph (1)(c), (d) or (e) in relation to the conditions attached to a permit, the bringing of the appeal shall not have the effect of suspending the operation of the conditions.

(8) Where an appeal is brought under paragraph (2) against a variation notice, an enforcement notice or a suspension notice, the bringing of the appeal shall not have the effect of suspending the operation of the notice.

[(8A) Where an appeal is brought under paragraph (1)(g) in relation to a requirement to initiate the closure procedure or under paragraph (2) in relation to a closure notice, the closure procedure shall not be initiated pending the final determination or the withdrawal of the appeal.]

(9) Regulations 11 and 12 [above or regulation 8 of the 2002 Regulations] shall apply where the Secretary of State, in exercising any of the powers in sub-paragraph (b) or (c) of paragraph (4), gives directions as to the conditions to be attached to a permit as they would apply to the regulator when determining the conditions of the permit.

(10) Schedule 8 shall have effect in relation to the making and determination of appeals under this regulation.

(11) This regulation and Schedule 8 are subject to section 114 of the Environment Act 1995 (delegation of reference of appeals).

[(12) Where an appeal is brought under paragraph (1)(g) in relation to which a waste management licence within the meaning of Part II of the Environmental Protection Act 1990 ('a licence') is in force, this regulation and Schedule 8 shall apply as if:

(a) references to a permit were references to a licence;
(b) references to the operator were references to the licence holder; and
(c) references to an installation or mobile plant were references to a landfill.]

PART V INFORMATION AND PUBLICITY

28 Information

(1) For the purpose of the discharge of his functions under these Regulations [or the 2002 Regulations], the Secretary of State may, by notice served on a regulator, require the regulator to furnish such information about the discharge of its functions as a regulator as he may require.

(2) For the purposes of the discharge of their functions under these Regulations [or the 2002 Regulations], the Secretary of State or a regulator may, by notice served on any person, require that person to furnish such information as is specified in the notice, in such form and within such period following service of the notice or at such time as is so specified.

(3) For the purposes of this regulation, the discharge by the Secretary of State of an obligation of the United Kingdom under the Community Treaties or any international agreement relating to the environment shall be treated as a function of his under these Regulations and the compilation of an inventory of emissions (whether or not from installations or mobile plant) shall be treated as a function of the Environment Agency under these Regulations.

(4) The information which a person may be required to furnish by a notice served under paragraph (2) includes information on emissions which, although it is not in the possession of that person or would not otherwise come into the possession of that person, is information which it is reasonable to require that person to compile for the purpose of complying with the notice.

29 Public registers of information

(1) Subject to regulations 30 and 31 and to paragraphs 2 to 5 of Schedule 9, it shall be the duty of each regulator, as respects installations or mobile plant for which it is the regulator, to maintain a register containing the particulars described in paragraph 1 of that Schedule.

(2) Subject to paragraph (3), the register maintained by a local authority regulator shall also contain any particulars contained in any register maintained by the Environment Agency relating to the operation of an installation or Part A mobile plant in the area of the local authority regulator in relation to which the Environment Agency has functions under these Regulations.

(3) Paragraph (2) does not apply to port health authorities but each local authority regulator whose area adjoins that of a port health authority shall include in its register the information that it would have had to include under paragraph (2) in relation to the operation of installations and Part A mobile plant in the area of the port health authority if the port health authority had not been constituted.

(4) The Environment Agency shall furnish each local authority regulator with the particulars which are necessary to enable it to discharge its duty under paragraphs (2) and (3).

(5) Where information of any description is excluded from any register by virtue of regulation 31, a statement shall be entered in the register indicating the existence of information of that description.

(6) It shall be the duty of each regulator—
   (a) to secure that the registers maintained by them under this regulation are available, at all reasonable times, for inspection by the public free of charge; and
   (b) to afford to members of the public facilities for obtaining copies of entries, on payment of reasonable charges.

(7) Registers under this regulation may be kept in any form.

30 Exclusion from registers of information affecting national security

(1) No information shall be included in a register maintained under regulation 29 if and so long as, in the opinion of the Secretary of State, the inclusion in the register of that information, or information of that description, would be contrary to the interests of national security.

(2) The Secretary of State may, for the purpose of securing the exclusion from registers of information to which paragraph (1) applies, give to regulators directions—

(a) specifying information, or descriptions or information, to be excluded from their registers; or

(b) specifying descriptions of information to be referred to the Secretary of State for his determination,

and no information referred to the Secretary of State in pursuance of sub-paragraph (b) shall be included in any such register until the Secretary of State determines that it should be so included.

(3) The regulator shall notify the Secretary of State of any information it excludes from the register in pursuance of directions under paragraph (2).

(4) A person may, as respects any information which appears to him to be information to which paragraph (1) may apply, give a notice to the Secretary of State specifying the information and indicating its apparent nature; and, if he does so—

(a) he shall notify the regulator that he has done so; and

(b) no information so notified to the Secretary of State shall be included in any such register until the Secretary of State has determined that it should be so included.

31   Exclusion from registers of certain confidential information

(1) No information relating to the affairs of any individual or business shall be included in a register maintained under regulation 29, without the consent of that individual or the person for the time being carrying on that business, if and so long as the information—

(a) is, in relation to him, commercially confidential; and

(b) is not required to be included in the register in pursuance of a direction under paragraph (9),

but information is not commercially confidential for the purposes of this regulation unless it is determined under this regulation to be so by the regulator or, on appeal, by the Secretary of State.

(2) Where information is furnished to a regulator for the purpose of these Regulations the person furnishing it may apply to the regulator to have the information excluded from the register on the ground that it is commercially confidential (as regards himself or another person) and the regulator shall determine whether the information is or is not commercially confidential.

(3) Notice of determination under paragraph (2) shall be given to the applicant within the period of 28 days beginning with the date of the application or within such longer period as may be agreed with the applicant.

(4) If the regulator fails to give notice of its determination of an application under paragraph (2) within the period allowed by or under paragraph (3), the regulator shall, if the applicant notifies the regulator in writing that he treats the failure as such, be deemed to have determined at the end of that period that the information is not commercially confidential.

(5) Where it appears to a regulator that any information which has been obtained by the regulator under or by virtue of any provision of these Regulations and is required to be included in the register unless excluded under this regulation might be commercially confidential, the regulator shall (unless the information is the subject of an application under paragraph (2))—

(a) give to the person to whom or whose business it relates notice that that information is required to be included in the register unless excluded under this regulation; and

(b) give that person a reasonable opportunity—

    (i) of objecting to the inclusion of the information on the ground that it is commercially confidential; and

    (ii) of making representations to the regulator for the purpose of justifying any such objection,

and, if any representations are made, the regulator shall, having taken the representations into account, give that person notice of its determination as to whether the information is or is not commercially confidential.

    (6) Where, under paragraph (2) or (5), a regulator determines that information not commercially confidential—

    (a) the information shall not be entered in the register until the end of the period of 21 days beginning with the date on which the determination is notified to the person concerned or the determination is deemed to have been made under paragraph (4), as the case may be;

    (b) that person may, before the end of that period, appeal to the Secretary of State against the decision,

and, where an appeal is brought in respect of any information, the information shall not be entered in the register until the end of the period of seven days following the day on which the appeal is finally determined or is withdrawn.

    (7) A person who wishes to appeal to the Secretary of State under paragraph (6) shall give to the Secretary of State written notice of the appeal together with a statement of the grounds of appeal and a statement indicating whether the appellant wishes the appeal to be in the form of a hearing or to be disposed of by way of written representations and shall, at the same time, send to the regulator a copy of that notice together with those statements.

    (8) Before giving notice of his determination of an appeal under paragraph (6), the Secretary of State may afford the appellant and the regulator an opportunity of appearing before and being heard by a person appointed by him and he shall do so in any case where a request is duly made by the appellant or the regulator to be so heard.

    (9) The Secretary of State may give to the regulator directions as to specified information, or descriptions of information, which the public interest requires to be included in registers maintained under regulation 29 notwithstanding that the information may be commercially confidential.

    (10) Information excluded from a register shall be treated as ceasing to be commercially confidential for the purposes of this regulation at the expiry of the period of four years beginning with the date of the determination by virtue of which it was excluded or at the expiry of such shorter period as may be specified in the notice of that determination for the purpose of this paragraph; but the person who furnished it may apply to the regulator for the information to remain excluded from the register on the ground that it is still commercially confidential and the regulator shall determine whether or not that is the case.

    (11) Paragraphs (6) to (8) shall apply in relation to a determination under paragraph (10) as they apply in relation to a determination under paragraph (2) or(5).

    (12) Information is, for the purposes of any determination under this regulation, commercially confidential, in relation to any individual or other person, if its being contained in the register would prejudice to an unreasonable degree the commercial interests of that individual or other person.

    (13) Paragraph (6) is subject to section 114 of the Environment Act 1995.

PART VI   PROVISION AS TO OFFENCES

32   Offences

    (1) It is an offence for a person—

    (a) to contravene regulation 9(1);

(b) to fail to comply with or to contravene a condition of a permit;

(c) to fail to comply with regulation 16(1);

(d) to fail to comply with the requirements of an enforcement notice, [a suspension notice or a closure notice under regulation 16 of the 2002 Regulations;]

(e) to fail, without reasonable excuse, to comply with any requirement imposed by a notice under regulation 28(2);

(f) to make a statement which he knows to be false or misleading in a material particular, or recklessly to make a statement which is false or misleading in a material particular, where the statement is made—

    (i) in purported compliance with a requirement to furnish any information imposed by or under any provision of these Regulations [or the 2002 Regulations;]

    (ii) for the purpose of obtaining the grant of a permit to himself or any other person, or the variation, transfer or surrender of a permit;

(g) intentionally to make a false entry in any record required to be kept under the condition of a permit;

(h) with intent to deceive, to forge or use a document issued or authorised to be issued under a condition of a permit or required for any purpose under a condition of a permit or to make or have in his possession a document so closely resembling any such document as to be likely to deceive;

(i) to fail to comply with an order made by a court under regulation 35.

(2) A person guilty of an offence under sub-paragraph (a), (b), (d) or (i) of paragraph (1) shall be liable—

(a) on summary conviction, to a fine not exceeding £20,000 or to imprisonment for a term not exceeding six months or to both;

(b) on conviction on indictment, to a fine or to imprisonment for a term not exceeding five years or to both.

(3) A person guilty of an offence under sub-paragraph (c), (e) and (f) to (h) of paragraph (1) shall be liable—

(a) on summary conviction, to a fine not exceeding the statutory maximum;

(b) on conviction on indictment, to a fine or to imprisonment for a term not exceeding two years or to both.

(4) Where an offence under this regulation committed by a body corporate is proved to have been committed with the consent or connivance of, or to have been attributable to any neglect on the part of, any director, manager, secretary or other similar officer of the body corporate or a person who was purporting to act in any such capacity, he as well as the body corporate shall be guilty of that offence and shall be liable to be proceeded against and punished accordingly.

(5) Where the affairs of a body corporate are managed by its members, paragraph (4) shall apply in relation to the acts or defaults of a member in connection with his functions of management as if he were a director of the body corporate.

(6) Where the commission by any person of an offence under this regulation is due to the act or default of some other person, that other person may be charged with and convicted of the offence by virtue of this paragraph whether or not proceedings for the offence are taken against the first-mentioned person.

33 Enforcement by High Court

If the regulator is of the opinion that proceedings for an offence under regulation 32(1)(d) would afford an ineffectual remedy against a person who has failed to comply with the requirements of an enforcement notice or a suspension notice, the regulator may take proceedings in the High Court for the purpose of securing compliance with the notice.

34   Admissibility of evidence
Where—
> (a) by virtue of a condition of a permit granted by a local authority regulator an entry is required to be made in any record as to the observance of any condition of the permit; and
> (b) the entry has not been made, that fact shall be admissible as evidence that that condition has not been observed.

35   Power of court to order cause of offence to be remedied
(1) Where a person is convicted of an offence under regulation 32(1)(a), (b) or (d) in respect of any matters which appear to the court to be matters which it is in his power to remedy, the court may, in addition to or instead of imposing any punishment, order him, within such time as may be fixed by the order, to take such steps as may be specified in the order for remedying those matters.

(2) The time fixed by an order under paragraph (1) may be extended or further extended by order of the court on an application made before the end of the time as originally fixed or extended under this paragraph, as the case may be.

(3) Where a person is ordered under paragraph (1) to remedy any matters, that person shall not be liable under regulation 32 in respect of those matters in so far as they continue during the time fixed by the order or any further time allowed under paragraph (2).

PART VII   SECRETARY OF STATE'S POWERS

36   Directions to regulators
(1) The Secretary of State may give directions to regulators of a general or specific character with respect to the carrying out of any of their functions under these Regulations [or the 2002 Regulations.]

(2) Without prejudice to the generality of the power conferred by paragraph (1), a direction under that paragraph may direct regulators—
> (a) to exercise any of their powers under these Regulations [or the 2002 Regulations] or to do so in such circumstances as may be specified in the directions or in such manner as may be so specified; or
> (b) not to exercise those powers, or not to do so in such circumstances or such manner as may be specified in the directions.

(3) Where the Secretary of State receives information pursuant to Article 17(1) of the Directive in relation to the operation of an installation outside of the United Kingdom which is likely to have a significant negative effect on the environment of England or Wales, he shall, for the purpose of complying with Article 17(2) of the Directive, direct the Environment Agency to take such steps as he considers appropriate for the purpose of bringing the information to the attention of the persons in England or Wales likely to be affected by the operation of the installation and providing them with an opportunity to comment on that information.

(4) Any direction given under these Regulations shall be in writing and may be varied or revoked by a further direction.

(5) It shall be a duty of a regulator to comply with any direction which is given to it under these Regulations.

37   Guidance to regulators
(1) The Secretary of State may issue guidance to regulators with respect to the carrying out of any of their functions under these Regulations [or the 2002 Regulations.]

(2) A regulator, in carrying out any of its functions under these Regulations [or the 2002 Regulations], shall have regard to any guidance issued by the Secretary of State under this regulation.

38   Plans relating to emissions

(1) The Secretary of State may make plans for—

(a) the setting of limits on the total amount, or the total amount in any period, of emissions from all or any description of source within England and Wales; or

(b) the allocation of quotas relating to such emissions.

(2) Where the Secretary of State allocates a quota in a plan made under paragraph (1) he may also make a scheme for the trading or other transfer of the quota so allocated.

(3) In this regulation, 'emission' means the direct or indirect release of any substance from individual or diffuse sources into the air, water or land.

Regulation 2

SCHEDULE 1

ACTIVITIES, INSTALLATIONS AND MOBILE PLANT

PART 1   ACTIVITIES

CHAPTER 1—ENERGY INDUSTRIES

SECTION 1.1—COMBUSTION ACTIVITIES

Part A(1)

(a) Burning any fuel in an appliance with a rated thermal input of 50 megawatts or more.

(b) Burning any of the following fuels in an appliance with a rated thermal input of 3 megawatts or more but less than 50 megawatts unless the activity is carried out as part of a Part A(2) or B activity—

(i)   waste oil;

(ii) recovered oil;

(iii) any fuel manufactured from, or comprising, any other waste.

Interpretation of Part A(1)

1.   For the purpose of paragraph (a), where two or more appliances with an aggregate rated thermal input of 50 megawatts or more are operated on the same site by the same operator those appliances shall be treated as a single appliance with a rated thermal input of 50 megawatts or more.

2.   Nothing in this Part applies to burning fuels in an appliance installed on an offshore platform situated on, above or below those parts of the sea adjacent to England and Wales from the low water mark to the seaward baseline of the United Kingdom territorial sea.

3.   In paragraph 2, 'offshore platform' means any fixed or floating structure which—

(a) is used for the purposes of or in connection with the production of petroleum; and

(b) in the case of a floating structure, is maintained on a station during the course of production,

but does not include any structure where the principal purpose of the use of the structure is the establishment of the existence of petroleum or the appraisal of its characteristics, quality or quantity or the extent of any reservoir in which it occurs.

4.   In paragraph 3, 'petroleum' includes any mineral oil or relative hydrocarbon and natural gas existing in its natural condition in strata but does not include coal or bituminous shales or other stratified deposits from which oil can be extracted by destructive distillation.

Part A(2)

Nil.

Part B

Unless falling within paragraph (a) of Part A(1) of this Section—

(a) Burning any fuel, other than a fuel mentioned in paragraph (b) of Part A(1) of this Section, in a boiler or furnace or a gas turbine or compression ignition engine with, in the case of any of these appliances, a rated thermal input of 20 megawatts or more but less than 50 megawatts.

(b) Burning any of the following fuels in an appliance with a rated thermal input of less than 3 megawatts—
   (i) waste oil;
   (ii) recovered oil;
   (iii) a solid fuel which has been manufactured from waste by an activity involving the application of heat.

(c) Burning fuel manufactured from or including waste, other than a fuel mentioned in paragraph (b), in any appliance—
   (i) with a rated thermal input of less than 3 megawatts but at least 0.4 megawatts; or
   (ii) which is used together with other appliances which each have a rated thermal input of less than 3 megawatts, where the aggregate rated thermal input of all the appliances is at least 0.4 megawatts.

Interpretation of Part B

1. Nothing in this Part applies to any activity falling within Part A(1) or A(2) of Section 5.1.

2. In paragraph (c), 'fuel' does not include gas produced by biological degradation of waste.

Interpretation of Section 1.1

For the purpose of this Section—

'waste oil' means any mineral based lubricating or industrial oil which has become unfit for the use for which it was intended, such as used combustion engine oil, gearbox oil, mineral lubricating oil, oil for turbines and hydraulic oil;

'recovered oil' means waste oil which has been processed before being used.

SECTION 1.2 — GASIFICATION, LIQUEFACTION AND REFINING ACTIVITIES

Part A(1)

(a) Refining gas where this is likely to involve the use of 1,000 tonnes or more of gas in any period of 12 months.

(b) Reforming natural gas.

(c) Operating coke ovens.

(d) Coal or lignite gasification.

(e) Producing gas from oil or other carbonaceous material or from mixtures thereof, other than from sewage, unless the production is carried out as part of an activity which is a combustion activity (whether or not that combustion activity is described in Section 1.1).

(f) Purifying or refining any product of any of the activities falling within paragraphs (a) to (e) or converting it into a different product.

(g) Refining mineral oils.

(h) The loading, unloading or other handling of, the storage of, or the physical, chemical or thermal treatment of—
   (i) crude oil;
   (ii) stabilised crude petroleum;
   (iii) crude shale oil;
   (iv) where related to another activity described in this paragraph, any associated gas or condensate;
   (v) emulsified hydrocarbons intended for use as a fuel.

(i)   The further refining, conversion or use (otherwise than as a fuel or solvent) of the product of any activity falling within paragraphs (g) or (h) in the manufacture of a chemical.

(j)   Activities involving the pyrolysis, carbonisation, distillation, liquefaction, gasification, partial oxidation, or other heat treatment of coal (other than the drying of coal), lignite, oil, other carbonaceous material or mixtures thereof otherwise than with a view to making charcoal.

Interpretation of Part A(1)

1.   Paragraph (j) does not include the use of any substance as a fuel or its incineration as a waste or any activity for the treatment of sewage.

2.   In paragraph (j), the heat treatment of oil, other than distillation, does not include the heat treatment of waste oil or waste emulsions containing oil in order to recover the oil from aqueous emulsions.

3.   In this Part, 'carbonaceous material' includes such materials as charcoal, coke, peat, rubber and wood.

Part A(2)

(a)   Refining gas where this activity does not fall within paragraph (a) of Part A(1) of this Section.

Part B

(a)   Odorising natural gas or liquefied petroleum gas, except where that activity is related to a Part A activity.

(b)   Blending odorant for use with natural gas or liquefied petroleum gas.

(c)   The storage of petrol in stationary storage tanks at a terminal, or the loading or unloading at a terminal of petrol into or from road tankers, rail tankers or inland waterway vessels.

(d)   The unloading of petrol into stationary storage tanks at a service station, if the total quantity of petrol unloaded into such tanks at the service station in any period of 12 months is likely to be 100m ^{3}or more.

Interpretation of Part B

1.   In this Part—

'inland waterway vessel' means a vessel, other than a sea-going vessel, having a total dead weight of 15 tonnes or more;

'petrol' means any petroleum derivative (other than liquefied petroleum gas), with or without additives, having a Reid vapour pressure of 27.6 kilopascals or more which is intended for use as a fuel for motor vehicles;

'service station' means any premises where petrol is dispensed to motor vehicle fuel tanks from stationary storage tanks;

'terminal' means any premises which are used for the storage and loading of petrol into road tankers, rail tankers or inland waterway vessels.

2.   Any other expressions used in this Part which are also used in Directive 94/63/EC on the control of volatile organic compound (VOC) emissions resulting from the storage of petrol and its distribution from terminals to service stations have the same meaning as in that Directive.

CHAPTER 2 — PRODUCTION AND PROCESSING OF METALS

SECTION 2.1 — FERROUS METALS

Part A(1)

(a)   Roasting or sintering metal ore, including sulphide ore, or any mixture of iron ore with or without other materials.

   (b) Producing, melting or refining iron or steel or any ferrous alloy, including continuous casting, except where the only furnaces used are—
      (i) electric arc furnaces with a designed holding capacity of less than 7 tonnes, or
      (ii) cupola, crucible, reverbatory, rotary, induction or resistance furnaces.
   (c) Processing ferrous metals and their alloys by using hot-rolling mills with a production capacity of more than 20 tonnes of crude steel per hour.
   (d) Loading, unloading or otherwise handling or storing more than 500,000 tonnes in total in any period of 12 months of iron ore, except in the course of mining operations, or burnt pyrites.

Part A(2)
   (a) Producing pig iron or steel, including continuous casting, in a plant with a production capacity of more than 2.5 tonnes per hour unless falling within paragraph (b) of Part A(1) of this Section.
   (b) Operating hammers in a forge, the energy of which is more than 50 kilojoules per hammer, where the calorific power used is more than 20 megawatts.
   (c) Applying protective fused metal coatings with an input of more than 2 tonnes of crude steel per hour.
   (d) Casting ferrous metal at a foundry with a production capacity of more than 20 tonnes per day.

Part B
   (a) Producing pig iron or steel, including continuous casting, in a plant with a production capacity of 2.5 tonnes or less per hour, unless falling within paragraph (b) of Part A(1) of this Section.
   (b) Producing, melting or refining iron or steel or any ferrous alloy (other than producing pig iron or steel, including continuous casting) using—
      (i) one or more electric arc furnaces, none of which has a designed holding capacity of 7 tonnes or more; or
      (ii) a cupola, crucible, reverberatory, rotary, induction or resistance furnace, unless falling within paragraph (a) or (d) of Part A(2) of this Section.
   (c) Desulphurising iron, steel or any ferrous alloy.
   (d) Heating iron, steel or any ferrous alloy (whether in a furnace or other appliance) to remove grease, oil or any other non-metallic contaminant (including such operations as the removal by heat of plastic or rubber covering from scrap cable) unless—
      (i) it is carried out in one or more furnaces or other appliances the primary combustion chambers of which have in aggregate a rated thermal input of less than 0.2 megawatts;
      (ii) it does not involve the removal by heat of plastic or rubber covering from scrap cable or of any asbestos contaminant; and
      (iii) it is not related to any other activity falling within this Part of this Section.
   (e) Casting iron, steel or any ferrous alloy from deliveries of 50 tonnes or more of molten metal, unless falling within Part A(1) or Part A(2) of this Section.

Interpretation of Section 2.1
In this Section, 'ferrous alloy' means an alloy of which iron is the largest constituent, or equal to the largest constituent, by weight, whether or not that alloy also has a non-ferrous metal content greater than any percentage specified in Section 2.2.

SECTION 2.2 — NON-FERROUS METALS

Part A(1)

    (a) Unless falling within Part A(2) of this Section, producing non-ferrous metals from ore, concentrates or secondary raw materials by metallurgical, chemical or electrolytic activities.

    (b) Melting, including making alloys, of non-ferrous metals, including recovered products (refining, foundry casting etc.) where—

        (i) the plant has a melting capacity of more than 4 tonnes per day for lead or cadmium or 20 tonnes per day for all other metals; and

        (ii) any furnace, bath or other holding vessel used in the plant for the melting has a design holding capacity of 5 tonnes or more.

    (c) Refining any non-ferrous metal or alloy, other than the electrolytic refining of copper, except where the activity is related to an activity described in paragraph (a) of Part A(2), or paragraph (a), (d), or (e) of Part B, of this Section.

    (d) Producing, melting or recovering by chemicals means or by the use of heat, lead or any lead alloy, if—

        (i) the activity may result in the release into the air of lead; and

        (ii) in the case of lead alloy, the percentage by weight of lead in the alloy in molten form is more than 23 per cent if the alloy contains copper and 2 per cent in other cases.

    (e) Recovering any of the following elements if the activity may result in their release into the air: gallium; indium; palladium; tellurium; thallium.

    (f) Producing, melting or recovering (whether by chemical means or by electrolysis or by the use of heat) cadmium or mercury or any alloy containing more than 0.05 per cent by weight of either of those metals or, in aggregate, of both.

    (g) Mining zinc or tin bearing ores where the activity may result in the release into water of cadmium or any compound of cadmium in a concentration which is greater than the background concentration.

    (h) Manufacturing or repairing involving the use of beryllium or selenium or an alloy containing one or both of those metals if the activity may result in the release into the air of any of the substances listed in paragraph 12 of Part 2 to this Schedule; but an activity does not fall within this paragraph by reason of it involving an alloy that contains beryllium if that alloy in molten form contains less than 0.1 per cent by weight of beryllium and the activity falls within paragraph (a) or (d) of Part B of this Section.

    (i) Pelletising, calcining, roasting or sintering any non-ferrous metal ore or any mixture of such ore and other materials.

Interpretation of Part A(1)

In paragraph (g), 'background concentration' means any concentration of cadmium or any compound of cadmium which would be present in the release irrespective of any effect the activity may have had on the composition of the release and, without prejudice to the generality of the foregoing, includes such concentration of those substances as is present in—

    (i) water supplied to the site where the activity is carried out;

    (ii) water abstracted for use in the activity; and

    (iii) precipitation onto the site on which the activity is carried out.

Part A(2)

    (a) Melting, including making alloys, of non-ferrous metals, including recovered products (refining, foundry casting, etc.) where—

(i) the plant has a melting capacity of more than 4 tonnes per day for lead or cadmium or 20 tonnes per day for all other metals; and

(ii) no furnace, bath or other holding vessel used in the plant for the melting has a design holding capacity of 5 tonnes or more.

Part B

(a) Melting, including making alloys, of non-ferrous metals (other than tin or any alloy which in molten form contains 50 per cent or more by weight of tin), including recovered products (refining, foundry casting, etc.) in plant with a melting capacity of 4 tonnes or less per day for lead or cadmium or 20 tonnes or less per day for all other metals.

(b) The heating in a furnace or any other appliance of any non-ferrous metal or non-ferrous metal alloy for the purpose of removing grease, oil or any other non-metallic contaminant, including such operations as the removal by heat of plastic or rubber covering from scrap cable, if not related to another activity described in this Part of this Section; but an activity does not fall within this paragraph if—

  (i) it involves the use of one or more furnaces or other appliances the primary combustion chambers of which have in aggregate a net rated thermal input of less than 0.2 megawatts; and

  (ii) it does not involve the removal by heat of plastic or rubber covering from scrap cable or of any asbestos contaminant.

(c) Melting zinc or a zinc alloy in conjunction with a galvanising activity at a rate of 20 tonnes or less per day.

(d) Melting zinc, aluminium or magnesium or an alloy of one or more of these metals in conjunction with a die-casting activity at a rate of 20 tonnes or less per day.

(e) Unless falling within Part A(1) or A(2) of this Section, the separation of copper, aluminium, magnesium or zinc from mixed scrap by differential melting.

Interpretation of Part B

In this Part 'net rated thermal input' is the rate at which fuel can be burned at the maximum continuous rating of the appliance multiplied by the net calorific value of the fuel and expressed as megawatts thermal.

Interpretation of Section 2.2

1. In this Section 'non-ferrous metal alloy' means an alloy which is not a ferrous alloy, as defined in Section 2.1.

2. Nothing in paragraphs (c) to (h) of Part A(1) or in Part B of this Section shall be taken to refer to the activities of hand soldering, flow soldering or wave soldering.

SECTION 2.3 — SURFACE TREATING METALS AND PLASTIC MATERIALS PART A(1)

(a) Surface treating metals and plastic materials using an electrolytic or chemical process where the aggregated volume of the treatment vats is more than $30m^3$.

Part A(2)
Nil.

Part B

(a) Any process for the surface treatment of metal which is likely to result in the release into air of any acid-forming oxide of nitrogen and which does not fall within Part A(1) of this Section.

CHAPTER 3 — MINERAL INDUSTRIES

SECTION 3.1 — PRODUCTION OF CEMENT AND LIME

Part A(1)

[(a) Producing cement clinker or producing and grinding cement clinker.]
(b) Producing lime—
(i)   in kilns or other furnaces with a production capacity of more than 50 tonnes per day; or
(ii) where the activity is likely to involve the heating in any period of 12 months of 5,000 tonnes or more of calcium carbonate or calcium magnesium carbonate or, in aggregate, of both.

Part A(2)

[(a) Unless falling within Part A(1) of this Section, grinding cement clinker.
(b) Unless falling within Part A(1) of Section 2.1 or 2.2, grinding metallurgical slag in plant with a grinding capacity of more than 250,000 tonnes in any period of 12 months.]

Part B

(a) Storing, loading or unloading cement or cement clinker in bulk prior to further transportation in bulk.
(b) Blending cement in bulk or using cement in bulk other than at a construction site, including the bagging of cement and cement mixtures, the batching of ready-mixed concrete and the manufacture of concrete blocks and other cement products.
(c) Slaking lime for the purpose of making calcium hydroxide or calcium magnesium hydroxide.
(d) Producing lime where the activity is not likely to involve the heating in any period of 12 months of 5,000 tonnes or more of calcium carbonate or calcium magnesium carbonate or, in aggregate, of both.

SECTION 3.2 — ACTIVITIES INVOLVING ASBESTOS

Part A(1)

(a) Producing asbestos or manufacturing products based on or containing asbestos.
(b) Stripping asbestos from railway vehicles except—
(i)   in the course of the repair or maintenance of the vehicle;
(ii) in the course of recovery operations following an accident; or
(iii) where the asbestos is permanently bonded in cement or in any other material (including plastic, rubber or resin).
(c) Destroying a railway vehicle by burning if asbestos has been incorporated in, or sprayed on to, its structure.

Part A(2)

Nil.

Part B

(a) The industrial finishing of any of the following products where not related to an activity falling within Part A(1) of this Section—
asbestos cement;
asbestos cement products;
asbestos fillers;
asbestos filters;
asbestos floor coverings;

asbestos friction products;
asbestos insulating board;
asbestos jointing, packaging and reinforcement material;
asbestos packing;
asbestos paper or card;
asbestos textiles.

Interpretation of Section 3.2

1. In this Section 'asbestos' includes any of the following fibrous silicates: actinolite, amosite, anthophyllite, chrysotile, crocidolite and tremolite.

SECTION 3.3 — MANUFACTURING GLASS AND GLASS FIBRE

Part A(1)
- (a) Manufacturing glass fibre.
- (b) Manufacturing glass frit or enamel frit and its use in any activity where that activity is related to its manufacture and the aggregate quantity of such substances manufactured in any period of 12 months is likely to be 100 tonnes or more.

Part A(2)
- (a) Manufacturing glass, unless falling within Part A(1) of this Section, where the melting capacity of the plant is more than 20 tonnes per day.

Part B
Unless falling within Part A(1) or A(2) of this Section—
- (a) Manufacturing glass at any location where the person concerned has the capacity to make 5,000 tonnes or more of glass in any period of 12 months, and any activity involving the use of glass which is carried out at any such location in conjunction with its manufacture.
- (b) Manufacturing glass where the use of lead or any lead compound is involved.
- (c) Manufacturing any glass product where lead or any lead compound has been used in the manufacture of the glass except—
  - (i) making products from lead glass blanks; or
  - (ii) melting, or mixing with another substance, glass manufactured elsewhere to produce articles such as ornaments or road paint.
- (d) Polishing or etching glass or glass products in the course of any manufacturing activity if—
  - (i) hydrofluoric acid is used; or
  - (ii) hydrogen fluoride may be released into the air.
- (e) Manufacturing glass frit or enamel frit and its use in any activity where that activity is related to its manufacture.

SECTION 3.4 — PRODUCTION OF OTHER MINERAL FIBRES

Part A(1)
- (a) Unless falling within Part A(1) or A(2) of Section 3.3, melting mineral substances in plant with a melting capacity of more than 20 tonnes per day.
- (b) Unless falling within Part A(1) of Section 3.3, producing any fibre from any mineral.

Part A(2)
Nil.

Part B
Nil.

SECTION 3.5 — OTHER MINERAL ACTIVITIES

Part A(1)
Nil.

Part A(2)
    [(a) Manufacturing cellulose fibre reinforced calcium silicate board using unbleached pulp.]

Part B
    (a) Unless falling within Part A(1) or Part A(2) of any Section in this Schedule, the crushing, grinding or other size reduction, other than the cuffing of stone, or the grading, screening or heating of any designated mineral or mineral product except where the operation of the activity is unlikely to result in the release into the air of particulate matter.
    (b) Any of the following activities unless carried on at an exempt location—
        (i) crushing, grinding or otherwise breaking up coal, coke or any other coal product;
        (ii) screening, grading or mixing coal, coke or any other coal product;
        (iii) loading or unloading petroleum coke, coal, coke or any other coal product except unloading on retail sale.
    (c) The crushing, grinding or other size reduction, with machinery designed for that purpose, of bricks, tiles or concrete.
    (d) Screening the product of any activity described in paragraph (c).
    (e) Coating road stone with tar or bitumen.
    (f) Loading, unloading, or storing pulverised fuel ash in bulk prior to further transportation in bulk.
    (g) The fusion of calcined bauxite for the production of artificial corundum.

Interpretation of Part B
    1. In this Part—
'coal' includes lignite;
'designated mineral or mineral product' means—
        (i) clay, sand and any other naturally occurring mineral other than coal or lignite;
        (ii) metallurgical slag;
        (iii) boiler or furnace ash produced from the burning of coal, coke or any other coal product;
        (iv) gypsum which is a by-product of any activity; 'exempt location' means—
        (i) any premises used for the sale of petroleum coke, coal, coke or any coal product where the throughput of such substances at those premises in any period of 12 months is in aggregate likely to be less than 10,000 tonnes; or
        (ii) any premises to which petroleum coke, coal, coke or any coal product is supplied only for use there;
'retail sale' means sale to the final customer.
    2. Nothing in this Part applies to any activity carried out underground.

SECTION 3.6 — CERAMIC PRODUCTION

Part A(1)
    (a) Manufacturing ceramic products (including roofing tiles, bricks, refractory bricks, tiles, stoneware or porcelain) by firing in kilns, where—

(i) the kiln production capacity is more than 75 tonnes per day; or

(ii) the kiln capacity is more than 4m ^{3} and the setting density is more than 300 kg/m ^{3},

and a reducing atmosphere is used other than for the purposes of colouration.

Part A(2)

(a) Unless falling within Part A(1) of this Section, manufacturing ceramic products (including roofing tiles, bricks, refractory bricks, tiles, stoneware or porcelain) by firing in kilns, where—

(i) the kiln production capacity is more than 75 tonnes per day; or

(ii) the kiln capacity is more than 4m ^{3} and the setting density is more than 300 kg/m ^{3}.

Part B

(a) Unless falling within Part A(1) or A(2) of this Section, firing heavy clay goods or refractory materials (other than heavy clay goods) in a kiln.

(b) Vapour glazing earthenware or clay with salts.

Interpretation of Part B

In this Part—

'clay' includes a blend of clay with ash, sand or other materials;

'refractory material' means material (such as fireclay, silica, magnesite, chrome-magnesite, sillimanite, sintered alumina, beryllia and boron nitride) which is able to withstand high temperatures and to function as a furnace lining or in other similar high temperature applications.

CHAPTER 4 — THE CHEMICAL INDUSTRY

Interpretation of Chapter 4

In Part A(1) of the Sections of this Chapter, 'producing' means producing in a chemical plant by chemical processing for commercial purposes substances or groups of substances listed in the relevant sections.

SECTION 4.1 — ORGANIC CHEMICALS

Part A(1)

(a) Producing organic chemicals such as—

(i) hydrocarbons (linear or cyclic, saturated or unsaturated, aliphatic or aromatic);

(ii) organic compounds containing oxygen, such as alcohols, aldehydes, ketones, carboxylic acids, esters, ethers, peroxides, phenols, epoxy resins;

(iii) organic compounds containing sulphur, such as sulphides, mercaptans, sulphonic acids, sulphonates, sulphates and sulphones and sulphur heterocyclics;

(iv) organic compounds containing nitrogen, such as amines, amides, nitrous-, nitro- or azo-compounds, nitrates, nitriles, nitrogen heterocyclics, cyanates, isocyanates, di-isocyanates and di-isocyanate prepolymers;

(v) organic compounds containing phosphorus, such as substituted phosphines and phosphate esters;

(vi) organic compounds containing halogens, such as halocarbons, halogenated aromatic compounds and acid halides;

(vii) organometallic compounds, such as lead alkyls, Grignard reagents and lithium alkyls;

(viii) plastic materials, such as polymers, synthetic fibres and cellulose-based fibres;

(ix) synthetic rubbers;

        (x)   dyes and pigments;

        (xi) surface-active agents.

(b) Producing any other organic compounds not described in paragraph (a).

(c) Polymerising or co-polymerising any unsaturated hydrocarbon or vinyl chloride (other than a pre-formulated resin or pre-formulated gel coat which contains any unsaturated hydrocarbon) which is likely to involve, in any period of 12 months, the polymerisation or co-polymerisation of 50 tonnes or more of any of those materials or, in aggregate, of any combination of those materials.

(d) Any activity involving the use in any period of 12 months of one tonne or more of toluene di-isocyanate or other di-isocyanate of comparable volatility or, where partly polymerised, the use of partly polymerised di-isocyanates or prepolyrners containing one tonne or more of those monomers, if the activity may result in a release into the air which contains such a di-isocyanate monomer.

(e) The flame bonding of polyurethane foams or polyurethane elastomers.

(f) Recovering—

        (i)   carbon disulphide;

        (ii) pyridine or any substituted pyridine.

(g) Recovering or purifying acrylic acid, substituted acrylic acid or any ester of acrylic acid or of substituted acrylic acid.

Part A(2)

Nil.

Part B

(a) Unless falling within Part A(l) of this Section any activity involving in any period of 12 months—

        (i)   the use of less than 1 tonne of toluene di-isocyanate or other di-isocyanate of comparable volatility or, where partially polymerised, the use of partly polymerised di-isocyanates or prepolymers containing less than 1 tonne of those monomers; or

        (ii) the use of 5 tonnes or more of diphenyl methane di-isocyanate or other di-isocyanate of much lower volatility than toluene di-isocyanate or, where partly polymerised, the use of partly polymerised di-isocyanates or prepolymers containing 5 tonnes or more of these less volatile monomers,

      where the activity may result in a release into the air which contains such a di-isocyanate monomer.

(b) Cutting polyurethane foams or polyurethane elastomers with heated wires.

(c) Any activity for the polymerisation or co-polymerisation of any pre-formulated resin or pre-formulated gel coat which contains any unsaturated hydro-carbon, where the activity is likely to involve, in any period of 12 months, the polymerisation or co-polymerisation of 100 tonnes or more of unsaturated hydrocarbon.

Interpretation of Section 4.1

In this Section, 'pre-formulated resin or pre-formulated gel coat' means any resin or gel coat which has been formulated before being introduced into polymensation or co-polymerisation activity, whether or not the resin or gel coat contains a colour pigment, activator or catalyst.

SECTION 4.2 — INORGANIC CHEMICALS

Part A(1)

(a) Producing inorganic chemicals such as—

     (i) gases, such as ammonia, hydrogen chloride, hydrogen fluoride, hydrogen cyanide, hydrogen sulphide, oxides of carbon, sulphur compounds, oxides of nitrogen, hydrogen, oxides of sulphur, phosgene;

    (ii) acids, such as chromic acid, hydrofluoric acid, hydrochloric acid, hydrobromic acid, hydroiodic acid, phosphoric acid, nitric acid, sulphuric acid, oleum and chlorosulphonic acid;

   (iii) bases, such as ammonium hydroxide, potassium hydroxide, sodium hydroxide;

   (iv) salts, such as ammonium chloride, potassium chlorate, potassium carbonate, sodium carbonate, perborate, silver nitrate, cupric acetate, ammonium phosphomolybdate;

    (v) non-metals, metal oxides, metal carbonyls or other inorganic compounds such as calcium carbide, silicon, silicon carbide, titanium dioxide;

   (vi) halogens or interhalogen compound comprising two or more of halogens, or any compound comprising one or more of those halogens and oxygen.

(b) Unless falling within another Section of this Schedule, any manufacturing activity which uses, or which is likely to result in the release into the air or into water of, any halogens, hydrogen halides or any of the compounds mentioned in paragraph (a)(vi), other than the treatment of water by chlorine.

(c) Unless falling within another Section of this Schedule, any manufacturing activity involving the use of hydrogen cyanide or hydrogen sulphide.

(d) Unless falling within another Section of this Schedule, any manufacturing activity, other than the application of a glaze or vitreous enamel, involving the use of any of the following elements or compound of those elements or the recovery of any compound of the following elements—

antimony;
arsenic;
beryllium;
gallium;
indium;
lead;
palladium;
platinum;
selenium;
tellurium;
thallium,

where the activity may result in the release into the air of any of those elements or compounds or the release into water of any substance listed in paragraph 13 of Part 2 of this Schedule.

(e) Recovering any compound of cadmium or mercury.

(f) Unless falling within another Section of this Schedule, any manufacturing activity involving the use of mercury or cadmium or any compound of either element or which may result in the release into air of either of those elements or their compounds.

(g) Unless carried out as part of any other activity falling within this Schedule—

    (i) recovering, concentrating or distilling sulphuric acid or oleum;

   (ii) recovering nitric acid;

   (iii) purifying phosphoric acid.

(h) Any manufacturing activity (other than the manufacture of chemicals or glass or the coating, plating or surface treatment of metal) which—

    (i) involves the use of hydrogen fluoride, hydrogen chloride, hydrogen bromide or hydrogen iodide or any of their acids; and

    (ii) may result in the release of any of those compounds into the air.

(i) Unless carried out as part of any other activity falling within this Schedule, recovering ammonia.

(j) Extracting any magnesium compound from sea water.

Part A(2)

Nil.

Part B

Nil.

SECTION 4.3 — CHEMICAL FERTILISER PRODUCTION

Part A(1)

(a) Producing (including any blending which is related to their production) phosphorus, nitrogen or potassium based fertilisers (simple or compound fertilisers).

(b) Converting chemical fertilisers into granules.

Part A(2)

Nil.

Part B

Nil.

SECTION 4.4 — PLANT HEALTH PRODUCTS AND BIOCIDES

Part A(1)

(a) Producing plant health products or biocides.

(b) Formulating such products if this may result in the release into water of any substance listed in paragraph 13 of Part 2 of this Schedule in a quantity which, in any period of 12 months, is greater than the background quantity by more than the amount specified in that paragraph for that substance.

Part A(2)

Nil.

Part B

Nil.

SECTION 4.5 — PHARMACEUTICAL PRODUCTION

Part A(1)

(a) Producing pharmaceutical products using a chemical or biological process.

(b) Formulating such products if this may result in the release into water of any substance listed in paragraph 13 of Part 2 of this Schedule in a quantity which, in any period of 12 months, is greater than the background quantity by more than the amount specified in that paragraph for that substance.

Part A(2)

Nil.

Part B

Nil.

SECTION 4.6 — EXPLOSIVES PRODUCTION

Part A(1)
    (a) Producing explosives.

Part A(2)
Nil.

Part B
Nil.

SECTION 4.7 — MANUFACTURING ACTIVITIES INVOLVING CARBON DISULPHIDE OR AMMONIA

Part A(1)
    (a) Any manufacturing activity which may result in the release of carbon disulphide into the air.
    (b) Any activity for the manufacture of a chemical which involves the use of ammonia or may result in the release of ammonia into the air other than an activity in which ammonia is only used as a refrigerant.

Part A(2)
Nil.

Part B
Nil.

SECTION 4.8 — THE STORAGE OF CHEMICALS IN BULK

Part A(1)
Nil.

Part A(2)
Nil.

Part B
    (a) The storage in tanks, other than in tanks for the time being forming part of a powered vehicle, of any of the substances listed below except where the total storage capacity of the tanks installed at the location in question in which the relevant substance may be stored is less than the figure specified below in relation to that substance—

any one or more acrylates	20 tonnes (in aggregate)
acrylonitrile	20 tonnes
anhydrous ammonia	100 tonnes
anhydrous hydrogen fluoride	1 tonne
toluene di-isocyanate	20 tonnes
vinyl chloride monomer	20 tonnes
ethylene	8,000 tonnes.

CHAPTER 5 — WASTE MANAGEMENT
SECTION 5.1 — DISPOSAL OF WASTE BY INCINERATION

Part A(1)
    (a) The incineration of any waste chemical or waste plastic arising from the manufacture of a chemical or the manufacture of a plastic.

(b) The incineration, other than incidentally in the course of burning other waste, of any waste chemical being, or comprising in elemental or compound form, any of the following—

bromine;
cadmium;
chlorine;
fluorine;
iodine;
lead;
mercury;
nitrogen;
phosphorus;
sulphur;
zinc.

(c) Unless falling within Part B of this Section, the incineration of (any other) hazardous waste in an incineration plant other than of specified hazardous waste in an exempt incineration plant.
(d) The incineration of municipal waste in an incineration plant with a capacity of more than 3 tonnes per hour.
(e) The incineration of any waste, including animal remains, otherwise than as part of a Part B activity, in an incineration plant with a capacity of 1 tonne or more per hour.
(f) The cleaning for reuse of metal containers used for the transport or storage of a chemical by burning out their residual content.

Part A(2)
Nil.

Part B

(a) The incineration of specified hazardous waste in an incineration plant with a capacity of 10 tonnes or less per day and less than 1 tonne per hour, unless the plant is an exempt incineration plant.
(b) The incineration of any non hazardous waste in an incineration plant, other than an exempt incineration plant, with a capacity of less than 1 tonne per hour.
(c) The cremation of human remains.

Interpretation of Section 5.1
In this Section—

'clinical waste', in the definition of 'exempt incineration plant', means waste (other than waste consisting wholly of animal remains) which falls within sub-paragraph (a) or (b) of the definition of such waste in paragraph (2) of regulation 1 of the Controlled Waste Regulations 1992 (or would fall within one of those sub-paragraphs but for paragraph (4) of that regulation);

'exempt incineration plant' means any incineration plant on premises where there is plant designed to incinerate waste, including animal remains, at a rate of 50 kilogrammes or less per hour, not being an incineration plant employed to incinerate clinical waste, sewage sludge, sewage screenings or municipal waste; and the for purposes of this definition, the weight of waste shall be determined by reference to its weight as fed into the incineration plant;

'hazardous waste' means waste as defined in Article 1(4) of Council Directive 91/689/EEC on hazardous waste;

'incineration' includes pyrolysis;

'incineration of hazardous waste in an incineration plant' means the incineration by oxidation of hazardous wastes, with or without recovery of the combustion heat generated, including pre-treatment and thermal treatment processes, for example, plasma process, in so far as their products are subsequently incinerated, and includes the incineration of such wastes as regular or additional fuel for any industrial process;

'municipal waste' means municipal waste as defined in Council Directives 89/369/EEC and 89/429/EEC;

'specified hazardous waste' means—

(a) combustible liquid wastes, including waste oils as defined in Article 1 of Council Directive 75/43 9/EEC on the disposal of waste oil, provided that they meet the following three criteria—

(i) the mass content of polychlorinated aromatic hydrocarbons, for example, polychlorinated biphenyls or pentachlorinated phenol, amounts to concentrations not higher than those set out in the relevant Community legislation;

(ii) these wastes are not rendered hazardous by virtue of containing other constituents listed in Annex II to Council Directive 91/689/EEC on hazardous waste in quantities or in concentrations which are inconsistent with the achievement of the objectives set out in Article 4 of Council Directive 75/442/EEC on waste; and

(iii) the net calorific value amounts to 30 MJ or more per kilogramme;

(b) combustible liquid wastes which cannot cause, in the flue gas directly resulting from their combustion, emissions other than those from gas oil, as defined in Article 1(1) of Council Directive 75/716/EEC on the approximation of the laws of Member States relating to the sulphur content of certain liquid fuels or a higher concentration of emissions than those resulting from the combustion of gas oil as so defined;

(c) sewage sludges from the treatment of municipal waste waters which are not rendered hazardous by virtue of containing constituents listed in Annex II to Council Directive 91/689/EEC on hazardous waste in quantities or in concentrations which are inconsistent with the achievement of the objectives set out in Article 4 of Council Directive 75/442/EEC on waste; and

(d) infectious clinical waste, provided that such waste is not rendered hazardous as a result of the presence of constituents listed in Annex II to Council Directive 91/689/EEC on hazardous waste other than constituent C35 in that list (infectious substances).

SECTION 5.2 — DISPOSAL OF WASTE BY LANDFILL

Part A(1)

(a) The disposal of waste in a landfill receiving more than 10 tonnes of waste in any day or with a total capacity of more than 25,000 tonnes, excluding disposals in landfills taking only inert waste.

[(b) The disposal of waste in any other landfill to which the 2002 Regulations apply;]

Part A(2)

Nil.

Part B

Nil.

SECTION 5.3 — DISPOSAL OF WASTE OTHER THAN BY INCINERATION OR LANDFILL

Part A(1)

    (a) The disposal of hazardous waste (other than by incineration or landfill) in a facility with a capacity of more than 10 tonnes per day.

    (b) The disposal of waste oils (other than by incineration or landfill) in a facility with a capacity of more than 10 tonnes per day.

    (c) Disposal of non-hazardous waste in a facility with a capacity of more than 50 tonnes per day by—

        (i) biological treatment, not being treatment specified in any paragraph other than paragraph D8 of Annex IIA to Council Directive 75/442/EEC, which results in final compounds or mixtures which are discarded by means of any of the operations numbered D1 to D12 in that Annex (D8); or

        (ii) physico-chemical treatment, not being treatment specified in any paragraph other than paragraph D9 in Annex IIA to Council Directive 75/442/EEC, which results in final compounds or mixtures which are discarded by means of any of the operations numbered D1 to D12 in that Annex (for example, evaporation, drying, calcination, etc.) (D9).

Interpretation of Part A(1)

    1.   In this Part—

'disposal' in paragraph (a) means any of the operations described in Annex IIA to Council Directive 75/442/EEC on waste;

'hazardous waste' means waste as defined in Article 1(4) of Council Directive 91/689/EEC.

    2.   Paragraph (b) shall be interpreted in accordance with Article 1 of Council Directive 75/439/EEC.

    3.   Nothing in this Part applies to the treatment of waste soil by means of mobile plant.

    4.   The reference to a D paragraph number in brackets at the end of paragraphs (c)(i) and (ii) is to the number of the corresponding paragraph in Annex IIA to Council Directive 75/442/EEC on waste (disposal operations).

Part A(2)

Nil.

Part B

Nil.

SECTION 5.4 — RECOVERY OF WASTE

Part A(1)

    (a) Recovering by distillation of any oil or organic solvent.

    (b) Cleaning or regenerating carbon, charcoal or ion exchange resins by removing matter which is, or includes, any substance listed in paragraphs 12 to 14 of Part 2 of this Schedule.

    (c) Unless carried out as part of any other Part A activity, recovering hazardous waste in plant with a capacity of more than 10 tonnes per day by means of the following operations—

        (i)   the use principally as a fuel or other means to generate energy (R1);

        (ii) solvent reclamation/regeneration (R2);

        (iii) recycling/reclamation of inorganic materials other than metals and metal compounds (R5);

        (iv) regeneration of acids or bases (R6);

        (v) recovering components used for pollution abatement (R7);

(vi) recovery of components from catalysts (R8);

(vii) oil re-refining or other reuses of oil (R9).

Interpretation of Part A(1)

1. Nothing in paragraphs (a) and (b) of this Part applies to—

   (a) distilling oil for the production or cleaning of vacuum pump oil; or

   (b) an activity which is ancillary to and related to another activity, whether described in this Schedule or not, which involves the production or use of the substance which is recovered, cleaned or regenerated,

except where the activity involves distilling more than 100 tonnes per day.

2. Nothing in this Part applies to the treatment of waste soil by means of mobile plant.

3. The reference to a R paragraph number in brackets at the end of paragraphs (c)(i) to (vii) is to the number of the corresponding paragraph in Annex IIB of Council Directive 75/442/EEC on waste (recovery operations).

Part A(2)

Nil.

Part B

Nil.

SECTION 5.5 — THE PRODUCTION OF FUEL FROM WASTE

Part A(1)

(a) Making solid fuel (other than charcoal) from waste by any process involving the use of heat.

Part A(2)

Nil.

Part B

Nil.

CHAPTER 6 — OTHER ACTIVITIES
SECTION 6.1 — PAPER, PULP AND BOARD MANUFACTURING ACTIVITIES

Part A(1)

(a) Producing in industrial plant pulp from timber or other fibrous materials.

(b) Producing in industrial plant paper and board where the plant has a production capacity of more than 20 tonnes per day.

(c) Any activity associated with making paper pulp or paper, including activities connected with the recycling of paper such as de-inking, if the activity may result in the release into water of any substance listed in paragraph 13 of Part 2 of this Schedule in a quantity which, in any period of 12 months, is greater than the background quantity by more than the amount specified in that paragraph in relation to that substance.

Interpretation of Part A(1)

In paragraph (c), 'paper pulp' includes pulp made from wood, grass, straw and similar materials and references to the making of paper are to the making of any product using paper pulp.

Part A(2)

[(a) Manufacturing wood particleboard, oriented strand board, wood fibreboard, plywood, cement-bonded particleboard or any other composite wood-based board.]

Part B
Nil.

SECTION 6.2 — CARBON ACTIVITIES

Part A(1)
- (a) Producing carbon or hard-burnt coal or electro graphite by means of incineration or graphitisation.

Part A(2)
Nil.

Part B
Nil.

SECTION 6.3 — TAR AND BITUMEN ACTIVITIES

Part A(1)
- (a) The following activities—
  - (i) distilling tar or bitumen in connection with any process of manufacture; or
  - (ii) heating tar or bitumen for the manufacture of electrodes or carbon-based refractory materials,

  where the carrying out of the activity by the person concerned at the location in question is likely to involve the use in any period of 12 months of 5 tonnes or more of tar or of bitumen or, in aggregate, of both.

Part A(2)
Nil.

Part B
- (a) Any activity not falling within Part A(l) of this Section or of Section 6.2 involving—
  - (i) heating, but not distilling, tar or bitumen in connection with any manufacturing activity; or
  - (ii) oxidising bitumen by blowing air through it, at plant where no other activities described in any Section in this Schedule are carried out,

  where the carrying out of the activity is likely to involve the use in any period of 12 months of 5 tonnes or more of tar or of bitumen or, in aggregate, of both.

Interpretation of Part B
In this Part 'tar' and 'bitumen' include pitch.

SECTION 6.4 — COATING ACTIVITIES, PRINTING AND TEXTILE TREATMENTS

Part A(1)
- (a) Applying or removing a coating material containing any tributyltin compound or triphenyltin compound, if carried out at a shipyard or boatyard where vessels of a length of 25 metres or more can be built, maintained or repaired.
- (b) Pre-treating (by operations such as washing, bleaching or mercerization) or dyeing fibres or textiles in plant with a treatment capacity of more than 10 tonnes per day.
- (c) Treating textiles if the activity may result in the release into water of any substance listed in paragraph 13 of Part 2 of this Schedule in a quantity which, in any

period of 12 months, is greater than the background quantity by more than the amount specified in that paragraph in relation to that substance.

Part A(2)

(a) Unless falling within Part A(l) of this Section, surface treating substances, objects or products using organic solvents, in particular for dressing, printing, coating, degreasing, waterproofing, sizing, painting, cleaning or impregnating, in plant with a consumption capacity of more than 150 kg per hour or more than 200 tonnes per year.

Part B

(a) Unless falling within Part A(1) or A(2) of this Section or paragraph (c) of Part A(2) of Section 2.1, any process (other than for the repainting or re-spraying of or of parts of aircraft or road or railway vehicles) for applying to a substrate, or drying or curing after such application, printing ink or paint or any other coating material as, or in the course of, a manufacturing activity, where the process may result in the release into the air of particulate matter or of any volatile organic compound and is likely to involve the use in any period of 12 months of—

   (i)   20 tonnes or more of printing ink, paint or other coating material which is applied in solid form;
   (ii) 20 tonnes or more of any metal coating which is sprayed on in molten form;
   (iii) 25 tonnes or more of organic solvents in respect of any cold set web offset printing activity or any sheet fed offset litho printing activity; or
   (iv) 5 tonnes or more of organic solvents in respect of any activity not mentioned in sub-paragraph (iii).

(b) Unless falling within Part A(2) of this Section, repainting or re-spraying road vehicles or parts of them if the activity may result in the release into the air of particulate matter or of any volatile organic compound and the carrying on of the activity is likely to involve the use of 1 tonne or more of organic solvents in any period of 12 months.

(c) Repainting or re-spraying aircraft or railway vehicles or parts of them if the activity may result in the release into the air of particulate matter or of any volatile organic compound and the carrying out of the activity is likely to involve the use in any period of 12 months of—

   (i)   20 tonnes or more of any paint or other coating material which is applied in solid form;
   (ii) 20 tonnes or more of any metal coatings which are sprayed on in molten form; or
   (iii) 5 tonnes or more of organic solvents.

Interpretation of Part B

1.   In this Part—

'aircraft' includes gliders and missiles;

'coating material' means paint, printing ink, varnish, lacquer, dye, any metal oxide coating, any adhesive coating, any elastomer coating, any metal or plastic coating and any other coating material.

2.   The amount of organic solvents used in an activity shall be calculated as—

(a) the total input of organic solvents into the process, including both solvents contained in coating materials and solvents used for cleaning or other purposes; less

(b) any organic solvents that are removed from the process for re-use or for recovery for re-use.

SECTION 6.5 — THE MANUFACTURE OF DYESTUFFS, PRINTING INK
AND COATING MATERIALS

Part A(1)
Nil.

Part A(2)
Nil.

Part B

(a) Unless falling within Part A(1) or A(2) of any Section in this Schedule—

(i) manufacturing or formulating printing ink or any other coating material containing, or involving the use of, an organic solvent, where the carrying out of the activity is likely to involve the use of 100 tonnes or more of organic solvents in any period of 12 months;

(ii) manufacturing any powder for use as a coating material where there is the capacity to produce 200 tonnes or more of such powder in any period of 12 months.

Interpretation of Part B

1. In this Part, 'coating material' has the same meaning as in Section 6.4.
2. The amount of organic solvents used in an activity shall be calculated as—

(i) the total input of organic solvents into the process, including both solvents contained in coating materials and solvents for cleaning or other purposes; less

(ii) any organic solvents, not contained in coating materials, that are removed from the process for re-use or for recovery for re-use.

SECTION 6.6 — TIMBER ACTIVITIES

Part A(1)

(a) Curing, or chemically treating, as part of a manufacturing process, timber or products wholly or mainly made of wood if any substance listed in paragraph 13 of Part 2 of this Schedule is used.

Part A(2)
Nil.

Part B

(a) [Unless falling within Part A(2) of Section 6.1, manufacturing] products wholly or mainly of wood at any works if the activity involves the sawing, drilling, shaping, turning, planing, curing or chemical treatment of wood ('relevant activities') and the throughput of the works in any period of 12 months is likely to be more than—

(i) 10,000 cubic metres, in the case of works at which wood is sawed but at which wood is not subjected to any other relevant activities or is subjected only to relevant activities which are exempt activities; or

(ii) 1,000 cubic metres in any other case.

Interpretation of Part B

In this Part—

'relevant activities' other than sawing are 'exempt activities' where, if no sawing were carried out at the works, the activities carried out there would be unlikely to result in the release into the air of any substances listed in paragraph 12 of Part 2 of this Schedule in a quantity which is capable of causing significant harm;

'throughput' shall be calculated by reference to the amount of wood which is subjected to any of the relevant activities, but where, at the same works, wood is subject to two or more relevant activities, no account shall be taken of the second or any subsequent activity;

'wood' includes any product consisting wholly or mainly of wood; and

'works' includes a sawmill or any other premises on which relevant activities are carried out on wood.

SECTION 6.7 — ACTIVITIES INVOLVING RUBBER

Part A(1)
Nil.

Part A(2)
[(a) Manufacturing new tyres (but not remoulds or retreads) if this involves the use in any period of 12 months of 50,000 tonnes or more of one or more of the following—
  (i)   natural rubber;
  (ii) synthetic organic elastomers;
  (iii) other substances mixed with them.]

Part B
(a) Unless falling within Part A(1) or A(2) of any Section in this Schedule, the mixing, milling or blending of—
  (i) natural rubber; or
  (ii) synthetic organic elastomers, if carbon black is used.
(b) Any activity which converts the product of an activity falling within paragraph (a) into a finished product if related to an activity falling within that paragraph.

SECTION 6.8 — THE TREATMENT OF ANIMAL AND VEGETABLE MATTER AND FOOD INDUSTRIES

Part A(1)
(a) Tanning hides and skins at plant with a treatment capacity of more than 12 tonnes of finished products per day.
(b) Slaughtering animals at plant with a carcass production capacity of more than 50 tonnes per day.
(c) Disposing of or recycling animal carcasses or animal waste, other than by rendering, at plant with a treatment capacity exceeding 10 tonnes per day of animal carcasses or animal waste or, in aggregate, of both.
(d) Treating and processing materials intended for the production of food products from—
  (i) animal raw materials (other than milk) at plant with a finished product production capacity of more than 75 tonnes per day;
  (ii) vegetable raw materials at plant with a finished product production capacity of more than 300 tonnes per day (average value on a quarterly basis).
(e) Treating and processing milk, the quantity of milk received being more than 200 tonnes per day (average value on an annual basis).
(f) Processing, storing or drying by the application of heat of the whole or part of any dead animal or any vegetable matter (other than the treatment of effluent so as to permit its discharge into controlled waters or into a sewer unless the treatment involves the drying of any material with a view to its use as animal feedstuff) if—

    (i) the processing, storing or drying does not fall within another Section of this Schedule or Part A(2) of this Section and is not an exempt activity; and

    (ii) it may result in the release into water of any substance listed in paragraph 13 of Part 2 of this Schedule in a quantity which, in any period of 12 months, is greater than the background quantity by more than the amount specified in relation to the substance in that paragraph.

Part A(2)

(a) Disposing of or recycling animal carcasses or animal waste by rendering at plant with a treatment capacity exceeding 10 tonnes per day of animal carcasses or animal waste, or, in aggregate, of both.

Part B

(a) Processing, storing or drying by the application of heat of the whole or part of any dead animal or any vegetable matter (other than the treatment of effluent so as to permit its discharge into controlled waters or into a sewer unless the treatment involves the drying of any material with a view to its use as animal feedstuff) if—

    (i) the processing, storing or drying does not fall within another Section of this Schedule or Part A(1) or Part A(2) of this Section and is not an exempt activity; and

    (ii) the processing, storing or drying may result in the release into the air of a substance described in paragraph 12 of Part 2 of this Schedule or any offensive smell noticeable outside the premises on which the activity is carried out.

(b) Breeding maggots in any case where 5 kg or more of animal matter or of vegetable matter or, in aggregate, of both are introduced into the process in any week.

Interpretation of Section 6.8

In this Section—

'animal' includes a bird or a fish;

'exempt activity' means—

    (i) any activity carried out in a farm or agricultural holding other than the manufacture of goods for sale;

    (ii) the manufacture or preparation of food or drink for human consumption but excluding—

        (1) the extraction, distillation or purification of animal or vegetable oil or fat otherwise than as a activity incidental to the cooking of food for human consumption;

        (2) any activity involving the use of green offal or the boiling of blood except the cooking of food (other than tripe) for human consumption;

        (3) the cooking of tripe for human consumption elsewhere than on premises on which it is to be consumed;

    (iii) the fleshing, cleaning and drying of pelts of fur-bearing mammals;

    (iv) any activity carried on in connection with the operation of a knacker's yard, as defined in article 3(1) of the Animal By-Products Order 1999;

    (v) any activity for the manufacture of soap not falling within Part A(1) of [Section 4.1;]

    (vi) the storage of vegetable matter not falling within any other Section of this Schedule;

    (vii) the cleaning of shellfish shells;

    (viii) the manufacture of starch;

    (ix) the processing of animal or vegetable matter at premises for feeding a recognised pack of hounds registered under article 13 of the Animal By-Products Order 1999;

(x)   the salting of hides or skins, unless related to any other activity listed in this Schedule;

(xi)   any activity for composting animal or vegetable matter or a combination of both, except where that activity is carried on for the purposes of cultivating mushrooms;

(xii)   any activity for cleaning, and any related activity for drying or dressing, seeds, bulbs, corms or tubers;

(xiii)   the drying of grain or pulses;

(xiv)   any activity for the production of cotton yarn from raw cotton or for the conversion of cotton yarn into cloth;

'food' includes—

(i)   drink;

(ii)   articles and substances of no nutritional value which are used for human consumption; and

(iii)   articles and substances used as ingredients in the preparation of food;

'green offal' means the stomach and intestines of any animal, other than poultry or fish, and their contents.

SECTION 6.9 — INTENSIVE FARMING

Part A(1)

(a)   Rearing poultry or pigs intensively in an installation with more than:

(i)   40,000 places for poultry;

(ii)   2,000 places for production pigs (over 30 kg); or

(iii)   750 places for sows.

Part A(2)

Nil.

Part B

Nil.

PART 2   INTERPRETATION OF PART 1

1.   The following rules apply for the interpretation of Part 1 of this Schedule.

2.—(1) Subject to sub-paragraph (2), an activity shall not be taken to be a Part B activity if it cannot result in the release into the air of a substance listed in paragraph 12 or there is no likelihood that it will result in the release into the air of any such substance except in a quantity which is so trivial that it is incapable of causing pollution or its capacity to cause pollution is insignificant.

(2) Sub-paragraph (1) does not apply to an activity which may give rise to an offensive smell noticeable outside the site where the activity is carried out.

3.   An activity shall not be taken to be an activity falling within Part 1 if it is carried out in a working museum to demonstrate an industrial activity of historic interest or if it is carried out for educational purposes in a school as defined in section 4(1) of the Education Act 1996,

4.   The running on or within an aircraft, hovercraft, mechanically propelled road vehicle, railway locomotive or ship or other vessel of an engine which propels or provides electricity for it shall not be taken to be an activity falling within Part 1.

5.   The running of an engine in order to test it before it is installed or in the course of its development shall not be taken to be an activity falling within Part 1.

6.—(1) The use of a fume cupboard shall not be taken to be an activity falling within Part 1 if it is used as a fume cupboard in a laboratory for research or testing and it is not—

    (i) a fume cupboard which is an industrial and continuous production activity enclosure; or

    (ii) a fume cupboard in which substances or materials are manufactured.

(2) In sub-paragraph (1) 'fume cupboard' has the meaning given by the British Standard 'Laboratory fume cupboards' published by the British Standards Institution numbered BS7258 : Part I : 1990.

7.   An activity shall not be taken to fall within Part 1 if it is carried out as a domestic activity in connection with a private dwelling.

8.   References in Part 1 to related activities are references to separate activities being carried out by the same person on the same site.

9.—(1) This paragraph applies for the purpose of determining whether an activity carried out in a stationary technical unit falls within a description in Part A(1) or A(2) which refers to capacity, other than design holding capacity.

(2) Where a person carries out several activities falling within the same description in Part A(1) or A(2) in different parts of the same stationary technical unit or in different stationary technical units on the same site, the capacities of each part or unit, as the case may be, shall be added together and the total capacity shall be attributed to each part or unit for the purpose of determining whether the activity carried out in each part or unit falls within a description in Part A(1) or A(2).

(3) For the purpose of sub-paragraph (2), no account shall be taken of capacity when determining whether activities fall within the same description.

(4) Where an activity falls within a description in Part A(1) or A(2) by virtue of this paragraph it shall not be taken to be an activity falling within a description in Part B.

10.—(1) Where an activity falls within a description in Part A(1) and a description in Part A(2) that activity shall be regarded as falling only within that description which fits it most aptly.

(2) Where an activity falls within a description in Part A(1) and a description in Part B that activity shall be regarded as falling only within the description in Part A(1).

(3) Where an activity falls within a description in Part A(2) and a description in Part B that activity shall be regarded as falling only within the description in Part A(2).

11.   In Part 1 of this Schedule—

'background quantity' means, in relation to the release of a substance resulting from an activity, such quantity of that substance as is present in—

    (i)   water supplied to the site where the activity is carried out;

    (ii) water abstracted for use in the activity; and

    (iii) precipitation onto the site on which the activity is carried out;

'Part A activity' means an activity falling within Part A(1) or A(2) of any Section in Part 1 of this Schedule;

'Part A(1) activity' means an activity falling within Part A(1) of any Section in Part 1 of this Schedule;

'Part A(2) activity' means an activity falling within Part A(2) of any Section in Part 1 of this Schedule;

'Part B activity' means an activity falling within Part B of any Section in Part 1 of this Schedule.

12.   References to, or to the release into the air of, a substance listed in this paragraph are to any of the following substances—

oxides of sulphur and other sulphur compounds;

oxides of nitrogen and other nitrogen compounds;

oxides of carbon;

organic compounds and partial oxidation products;

metals, metalloids and their compounds;

asbestos (suspended particulate matter and fibres), glass fibres and mineral fibres;

halogens and their compounds;

phosphorus and its compounds;

particulate matter.

13.   References to, or to the release into water of, a substance listed in this paragraph or to its release in a quantity which, in any period of 12 months, is greater than the background quantity by an amount specified in this paragraph are to the following substances and amounts—

Substance	Amount greater than the background quantity (in grammes) in any period of 12 months
Mercury and its compounds	200 (expressed as metal)
Cadmium and its compounds	1,000 (expressed as metal)
All isomers of hexachlorocyclohexane	20
All isomers of DDT	5
Pentachlorophenol and its compounds	350 (expressed as PCP)
Hexachlorobenzene	5
Hexachlorobutadiene	20
Aldrin	2
Dieldrin	2
Endrin	1
Polychlorinated Biphenyls	1
Dichlorvos	0.2
1,2 — Dichloroethane 2,000	2,000
All isomers of trichlorobenzene	75
Atrazine	350*
Simazine	350*
Tributyltin compounds	4 (expressed as TBT)
Triphenyltin compounds	4 (expressed as TPT)
Trifluralin	20
Fenitrothion	2
Azinphos-methyl	2
Malathion	2
Endosulfan	0.5

* Where both Altrazine and Simazine are released, the figure for both substances in aggregate is 350 grammes.

14.—(1) References to a substance listed in this paragraph are to any of the following substances—

alkali metals and their oxides and alkaline earth metals and their oxides;

organic solvents;

azides;

halogens and their covalent compounds;

metal carbonyls;

organo-metallic compounds;

oxidising agents;

polychlorinated dibenzofuran and any congener thereof;

polychlorinated dibenzo-p-dioxin and any congener thereof;

polyhalogenated biphenyls, terphenyls and naphthalenes;

phosphorus;

pesticides.

(2) In sub-paragraph (1), 'pesticide' means any chemical substance or preparation prepared or used for destroying any pest, including those used for protecting plants or wood or other plant products from harmful organisms, regulating the growth of plants, giving protection against harmful creatures, rendering such creatures harmless, controlling organisms with harmful or unwanted effects on water systems, buildings or other structures, or on manufactured products, or protecting animals against ectoparasites.

PART 3   INTERPRETATION OF 'PART A INSTALLATION' ETC

15.   For the purpose of these Regulations, subject to paragraph 17—

'Part A installation' means a Part A(1) installation or a Part A(2) installation;

'Part A(1) installation' means an installation where a Part A(1) activity is carried out (including such an installation where a Part A(2) or Part B activity is also carried out);

'Part A(2) installation' means an installation, not being a Part A(1) installation, where a Part A(2) activity is carried out (including such an installation where a Part B activity is also carried out);

'Part B installation' means an installation where a Part B activity is carried out, not being a Part A installation.

16.   For the purpose of these Regulations—

'Part A mobile plant' means Part A(1) mobile plant or Part A(2) mobile plant;

'Part A(1) mobile plant' means mobile plant used to carry out a Part A(1) activity (including such plant which is also used to carry out a Part A(2) or Part B activity);

'Part A(2) mobile plant' means mobile plant, not being Part A(1) mobile plant, used to carry out a Part A(2) activity (including such mobile plant used to carry out a Part B activity);

'Part B mobile plant' means mobile plant used to carry out a Part B activity, not being Part A mobile plant.

17.—(1) An installation where a Part A(2) activity is carried out (and no Part A(1) activity) shall nevertheless be a Part A(1) installation if any waste activity is also carried out at the installation.

(2) In sub-paragraph (1) 'waste activity' means an activity mentioned in paragraph (a) or (b) of section 33(1) of the Environmental Protection Act 1990 (deposit, keeping, treatment and disposal of waste) other than—

    (a)   the incineration of waste falling within Part B of Section 5.1 of Part 1 of this Schedule; and

    (b)   an exempt activity, as defined in regulation 1(3) of and Schedule 3 to the Waste Management Licensing Regulations 1994.

18.   A Part B installation where an activity within Part B of Section 1.1 is carried out does not include any location where the associated storage, handling or shredding of tyres which are to be burned as part of that activity is carried out.

19.   A Part B installation where an activity falling within paragraph (e) of Part B of Section 2.2 is carried out does not include any location where the associated storage or handling of scrap which is to be heated as part of that activity is carried out, other than a location where scrap is loaded into a furnace.

20.   A Part B installation where an activity falling with paragraph (a) or (b) of Part B of Section 5.1 is carried out does not include any location where the associated storage or handling of wastes and residues which are to be incinerated as part of that activity is carried out, other than a location where the associated storage or handling of animal remains intended for burning in an incinerator used wholly or mainly for the incineration of such remains or residues from the burning of such remains in such an incinerator is carried out.

21.   A Part B installation where an activity falling within Part B of Section 6.4 is carried out

does not include any location where the associated cleaning of used storage drums prior to painting or their incidental handling in connection with such cleaning is carried out.

22. Where an installation is a Part A(1) installation, a Part A(2) installation or a Part B installation by virtue of the carrying out of an activity which is only carried out during part of a year that installation shall not cease to be such an installation during the parts of the year when that activity is not being carried out.

23. Where an installation is authorised by a permit granted under these Regulations to carry out Part A(1) activities, Part A(2) activities or Part B activities which are described in Part 1 by reference to a threshold (whether in terms of capacity or otherwise), the installation shall not cease to be a Part A(1) installation, a Part A(2) installation, or a Part B installation, as the case may be, by virtue of the installation being operated below the relevant threshold unless the permit ceases to have effect in accordance with these Regulations.

24. In this Part, 'Part A(1) activity', 'Part A(2) activity' and 'Part B activity' have the meaning given by paragraph 11 in Part 2 of this Schedule.

Regulation 3 SCHEDULE 2

BEST AVAILABLE TECHNIQUES

1. Subject to paragraph 2, in determining best available techniques special consideration shall be given to the following matters, bearing in mind the likely costs and benefits of a measure and the principles of precaution and prevention—

    (1) the use of low-waste technology;

    (2) the use of less hazardous substances;

    (3) the furthering of recovery and recycling of substances generated and used in the process and of waste, where appropriate;

    (4) comparable processes, facilities or methods of operation which have been tried with success on an industrial scale;

    (5) technological advances and changes in scientific knowledge and understanding;

    (6) the nature, effects and volume of the emissions concerned;

    (7) the commissioning dates for new or existing installations or mobile plant;

    (8) the length of time needed to introduce the best available technique;

    (9) the consumption and nature of raw materials (including water) used in the process and the energy efficiency of the process;

    (10) the need to prevent or reduce to a minimum the overall impact of the emissions on the environment and the risks to it;

    (11) the need to prevent accidents and to minimise the consequences for the environment;

    (12) the information published by the Commission pursuant to Article 16(2) of the Directive or by international organisations.

    2. Sub-paragraphs (1) to (3) and (9) to (12) shall not apply for the purposes of determining best available techniques in relation to Part B installations and Part B mobile plant.

Regulations 9 and 10(14) SCHEDULE 3

PRESCRIBED DATE AND TRANSITIONAL ARRANGEMENTS
PART 1—PART A INSTALLATIONS AND MOBILE PLANT

1. The prescribed date for a new Part A installation or new Part A mobile plant is—

    (a) where an application for a permit to operate the installation or mobile plant is duly made before 1st April 2001, the determination date for the installation or mobile plant;

    (b) where no such application is made, 1st January 2001.

2.—(1) Subject to paragraph 4, the prescribed date for an existing Part A installation or existing Part A mobile plant is—

(a) where an application for a permit to operate the installation or mobile plant is duly made within the relevant period (or before the beginning of the relevant period where allowed under paragraph 5), the determination date for the installation or mobile plant;

(b) where no such application is made, the day after the date on which the relevant period expires.

(2) For the purpose of sub-paragraph (1) the relevant period for an existing Part A installation or existing Part A mobile plant is the period specified for that description of installation or mobile plant in the following table—

Any installation where an activity falling within the following Section of Part 1 of Schedule 1 is carried out or any mobile plant used to carry out such an activity	Relevant Period
Section 1.1	
Part A(1)	1st January to 31st March 2006
Section 1.2	
Part A(1)	
Paragraph (c)	1st June to 31st August 2001
Remaining paragraphs	1st June to 31st August 2006
Part A(2)	[1st June to 31st August 2006]
Section 2.1	
Part A(1)	
Paragraph (c)	1st May to 31st July 2002
Remaining paragraphs	1st June to 31st August 2001
Part A(2)	[1st May to 31st July 2003]
Section 2.2	
Part A(1)	1st October to 31st December 2001
Part A(2)	1st May to 31st July 2003
Section 2.3	
Part A(1)	1st May to 31st July 2004
Section 3.1	
Part A(1)	1st June to 31st August 2001
[Part A(2)	1st April to 30th June 2003]
Section 3.2	
Part A(1)	1st June to 31st August 2006
Section 3.3	
Part A(1)	1st May to 31st July 2002
Part A(2)	[1st May to 31st July 2003]

Any installation where an activity falling within the following Section of Part 1 of Schedule 1 is carried out or any mobile plant used to carry out such an activity	Relevant Period
Section 3.4	
Part A(1)	1st May to 31st July 2002
[Section 3.5	
Part A(2)	1st April to 30th June 2003]
Section 3.6	
Part A(1)	1st January to 31st March 2004
Part A(2)	1st January to 31st March 2004
Section 4.1 Part A(1)	
Paragraphs (a)(i), (v), (vi), (vii), (b), (f), (g)	1st January to 31st March 2003
Paragraphs (a)(ii), (iii), (iv)	1st June to 31st August 2003
Paragraphs (a)(viii), (ix), (c), (d), (e)	1st January to 31st March 2006
Paragraphs (a)(x)-(xi)	1st June to 31st August 2006
Section 4.2 Part A(1)	
Paragraphs (a)(i), (ii), (iii), (vi), (b) to (j)	1st October to 31st December 2004
Paragraphs (a)(iv), (v)	1st June to 31st August 2005
Section 4.3	
Part A(1)	1st June to 31st August 2005
Section 4.4	
Part A(1)	1st January to 31st March 2006
Section 4.5	
Part A(1)	1st January to 31st March 2006
Section 4.6	
Part A(1)	1st January to 31st March 2006
Section 4.7	
Part A(1)	1st October to 31st December 2004
Section 5.1	
Part A(1)	1st June to 31st August 2005
[Section 5.2	
Part A(1)	The period specified in the notice served on the operator under paragraph 1(9) of Schedule 4 to the 2002 Regulations.]
Section 5.3 Part A(1)	
Paragraph (a)	1st June to 31st August 2005
Paragraph (b)	1st June to 31st August 2005
Paragraph (c)(i)	1st January to 31st March 2004

Any installation where an activity falling within the following Section of Part 1 of Schedule 1 is carried out or any mobile plant used to carry out such an activity	Relevant Period
Paragraph (c)(ii)	1st June to 31st August 2004
Section 5.4	
Part A(1)	1st January to 31st March 2005
Section 5.5	
Part A(1)	1st January to 31st March 2004
Section 6.1	
Part A(1)	1st December 2000 to 28th February 2001
[Part A(2)	1st April to 30th June 2003]
Section 6.2	
Part A(1)	1st January to 31st March 2004
Section 6.3 Part A(1)	
Paragraph (a)(i)	1st January to 31st March 2004
Paragraph (a)(ii)	1st October to 31st December 2001
Section 6.4	
Part A(1)	1st May to 31st July 2002
Part A(2)	1st May to 31st July 2003
Section 6.6	
Part A(1)	1st June to 31st August 2006
[Section 6.7	
Part A(2)	1st April to 30th June 2003]
Section 6.8	
Part A(1)	
Paragraph (a)	1st May to 31st July 2002
Paragraphs (b), (c), (d)(i)	1st June to 31st August 2004
Paragraphs (d)(ii), (e), (f)	1st January to 31st March 2005
Part A(2)	1st June to 31st August 2004
Section 6.9	
Part A(1)	1st November 2006 to 31st January 2007

(3) For the purpose of sub-paragraph (2), where an activity falls within a description in Part A(1) of more than one Section of Part 1 of Schedule 1 or within a description in Part A(2) of more than one Section of Part 1 of Schedule 1 it shall be regarded as falling only within that description which fits it most aptly.

(4) Subject to sub-paragraph (5), where more than one activity falling within Part A(1) or A(2) of any Section in Part 1 of Schedule 1 is carried out in an existing Part A installation or using an existing Part A mobile plant, the relevant period for that installation or mobile plant shall be the period beginning with the earliest date listed against one of those activities in the table in sub-paragraph (2).

(5) Where more than one activity falling within Part A(1) or A(2) of any Section in Part 1 of Schedule 1 is carried out in an existing Part A installation, the operator of the installation may apply to the regulator to determine that the relevant period for the installation shall not be the period determined by sub-paragraph (4) but the later period listed in the table in sub-paragraph (2) against the primary activity of the installation.

(6) An application under sub-paragraph (5) shall be in writing and shall—

    (a) identify the installation concerned;

    (b) list the activities falling within Part A(1) or A(2) of any Section in Part 1 of Schedule 1 which are carried out in the installation;

    (c) identify which of those activities the operator considers to be the primary activity,

and shall be submitted at least 3 months before the beginning of the period which would be the relevant period for the installation concerned under sub-paragraph (4).

(7) Where a regulator receives a duly made application under sub-paragraph (5) it shall, if it agrees with the operator that the activity identified pursuant to sub-paragraph (6)(c) is the primary activity, serve notice of this determination on the operator, and the period listed against that activity in sub-paragraph (2) shall be the relevant period for the installation.

(8) Where the regulator does not agree with the operator as mentioned in sub-paragraph (7) it shall serve notice of this determination on the operator and the relevant period for the installation shall be the period determined by sub-paragraph (4).

(9) A regulator shall serve notice of its determination of any application made under sub-paragraph (5) within 2 months of receiving the application.

(10) Where there is more than one operator of an installation, an application under sub-paragraph (5) shall be made by the operators of the installation jointly and the references in sub-paragraphs (6) to (8) to the operator shall be construed as a reference to all of the operators.

(11) For the purpose of sub-paragraphs (5) to (9) the primary activity of an installation is the activity the carrying out of which constitutes the primary purpose for operating the installation.

[(12) If—

    (a) an activity falling within Part A(1) of Section 5.2 in Part 1 of Schedule 1 is carried out in an existing Part A installation; and

    (b) an activity falling within some other Section in Part 1 of Schedule 1 is also carried out in the same installation ('a transitional landfill installation'),

the preceding provisions of this paragraph shall apply as if there were two separate existing Part A installations one consisting of the part of the installation where the activity falling within Part A(1) of Section 5.2 in Part 1 of Schedule 1 is carried out and the other consisting of the remainder of the installation.

(13) If—

    (a) the relevant period has expired for a transitional landfill installation; and

    (b) an application for a permit to operate the installation has been duly made but has not been determined at 15th June 2002, then—

      (i) the application shall be treated as an application to operate the parts of the installation other than those where the activity falling within Part A(1) of Section 5.2 in Part 1 of Schedule 1 is carried out; and

     (ii) the prescribed date for the remaining part of the installation shall be determined as if it were a separate installation.]

3. For the purpose of paragraphs 1 and 2, where separate applications are made to operate different parts of a Part A installation—

    (a) the date by which applications have been made in relation to all parts of the installation shall be treated as the date on which an application for a permit to operate the installation is made;

    (b) an application for a permit to operate the installation shall only be treated as having been duly made if each of the separate applications are duly made;

    (c) the determination date for the installation shall be, in relation to each part of the installation which is covered by a separate application, the determination date for that part of the installation.

4.—[. . .]

    (2) Where there is a substantial change in the operation of an existing Part A installation on or after 1st [April] 2001, the prescribed date for that part of the installation affected by the change shall be the date on which the change is made if earlier than the date which would be the prescribed date for the installation under paragraph 2.

5.—(1) Subject to sub-paragraph (2), an application for a permit to operate an existing Part A installation or Part A mobile plant shall not be made before the beginning of the relevant period for that installation or mobile plant without the consent of the regulator.

    (2) Where an operator of an existing Part A installation proposes to make a substantial change in the operation of the installation he may make an application before the beginning of the relevant period for a permit to operate that part of the installation that will be affected by the substantial change.

6. In this Part of this Schedule—

    'determination date' means—

    (a) for an installation, part of an installation or mobile plant in relation to which a permit is granted, the date on which it is granted, whether in pursuance of the application for the permit or, on an appeal, of a direction to grant it;

    (b) for an installation, part of an installation or mobile plant in relation to which a permit is refused and the applicant for the permit appeals against the refusal, the date of the affirmation of the refusal;

    (c) for an installation, part of an installation or mobile plant in relation to which a permit is refused and no appeal is made against the refusal, the date immediately following the last day, determined in accordance with paragraph 2 of Schedule 8, on which notice of appeal might have been given.

    ['existing' means, in relation to a Part A installation or a Part A mobile plant—

    (a) an installation or mobile plant which is put into operation before 1st April 2001; or

    (b) an installation or mobile plant which is put into operation on or after that date if—

      (i) its operation was authorised by the relevant authorisation before that date; or

     (ii) an application for such authorisation was duly made before that date;]

    'new' means, in relation to a Part A installation or a Part A mobile plant, an installation or plant which is put into operation on or after [1st April 2001] other than an existing Part A installation or Part A mobile plant;

'relevant authorisation' means, in relation to the operation of a Part A installation or Part A mobile plant—

(a) where the operation of the installation or mobile plant immediately before [1st April 2001] requires an authorisation under Part I of the Environmental Protection Act 1990, an authorisation under that Part of that Act;

(b) where the operation of the installation or mobile plant immediately before [1st April 2001] requires a waste management licence under Part II of the Environmental Protection Act 1990, a waste management licence under that Part of that Act;

(c) in any other case, planning permission granted under the Town and Country Planning Act 1990;

'relevant period' shall be interpreted in accordance with paragraph 2.

PART 2   PART B   INSTALLATIONS AND MOBILE PLANT

7. The prescribed date for a new Part B installation or a new Part B mobile plant is the relevant date for that installation or mobile plant.

8. The prescribed date for an existing Part B installation or existing Part B mobile plant is the determination date for that installation or mobile plant.

9.—(1) Subject to the following provisions of this paragraph, no application for a permit to operate an existing Part B installation or existing Part B mobile plant shall be made to the regulator.

(2) Where an operator of a Part B installation or a Pert B mobile plant proposes to put the installation or mobile plant into operation during the period of four months ending on the relevant date for the installation or mobile plant, he may make an application for a permit to operate that installation or mobile plant.

(3) The operator of an existing Part B installation or existing Part B mobile plant shall, unless he has made an application to operate the installation or mobile plant under sub-paragraph (2), be deemed to have made an application for a permit to operate that installation or mobile plant on the relevant date for that installation or mobile plant.

(4) Where sub-paragraph (3) applies in relation to an existing Part B installation and different parts of the installation are operated by different operators, each operator shall be deemed to have been made an application to operate that part of the installation which he operates.

(5) Schedule 4 shall not apply to a deemed application under sub-paragraph (3).

(6) The regulator shall give notice of its determination of a deemed application under sub-paragraph (3) to the applicant within the period of 12 months beginning with the date on which the application is deemed to have been made and if the regulator fails to give notice of its determination within that period the application shall, if the applicant notifies the authority in writing that he treats the failure as such, be deemed to have been refused at the end of that period.

(7) Where sub-paragraph (3) applies the regulator shall, within 2 months of the date on which the application is deemed to have been made, notify the operator of the installation or mobile plant of the deemed application and of the requirements of sub-paragraph (6).

(8) Where separate applications are deemed to have been made under sub-paragraph (4) to operate different parts of a Part B installation the prescribed date for the installation shall be, in relation to each part of the installation covered by a separate application, the determination date for that part of the installation.

10.—(1) For the purpose of this Part of this Schedule the relevant date for a Part B installation or a Part B mobile plant is the date specified for that description of installation or mobile plant in the following table—

Any installation where an activity falling within Part B of the following Sections of Part 1 of Schedule 1 is carried out or any mobile plant used to carry out such an activity	Relevant Date
Section 1.1	1st April 2003
Section 1.2	1st April 2005
Section 2.1	1st April 2004
Section 2.2	1st April 2004
Section 2.3	1st April 2004
Section 3.1	1st April 2003
Section 3.2	1st April 2003
Section 3.3	1st April 2005
Section 3.5	1st April 2003
Section 3.6	1st April 2003
Section 4.1	1st April 2005
Section 4.8	1st April 2005
Section 5.1	1st April 2003
Section 6.3	1st April 2005
Section 6.4	1st April 2004
Section 6.5	1st April 2004
Section 6.6	1st April 2003
Section 6.7	1st April 2004
Section 6.8	1st April 2005

(2) For the purpose of sub-paragraph (1), where an activity falls within a description in Part B of more than one Section of Part 1 of Schedule 1 it shall be regarded as falling only within that description which fits it most aptly.

(3) Where more than one activity falling within Part B of any Section in Part 1 of Schedule 1 is carried out in an existing Part B installation or using an existing Part B mobile plant, and the activities have different relevant dates, the relevant date for that installation or mobile plant shall be the earliest of those dates.

11.   In this Part of this Schedule—

'determination date' means—

> (a) for an installation, part of an installation or mobile plant in relation to which a permit is granted, the date on which it is granted, whether in pursuance of the application for the permit or, on an appeal, of a direction to grant it;
>
> (b) for an installation, part of an installation or mobile plant in relation to which a permit is refused and the applicant for the permit appeals against the refusal, the date of the affirmation of the refusal;
>
> (c) for an installation, part of an installation or mobile plant in relation to which a permit is refused and no appeal is made against the refusal, the date immediately following the last day, determined in accordance with paragraph 2 of Schedule 8, on which notice of appeal might have been given.

'existing' means, in relation to a Part B installation or Part B mobile plant, an installation or mobile plant which is put into operation before the relevant date for that installation or mobile plant;

'new' means, in relation to a Part B installation or Part B mobile plant, an installation or mobile plant which is put into operation on or after the relevant date for that installation or mobile plant;

'relevant date' shall be interpreted in accordance with paragraph 10.

<table>
<tr><td>**Regulation 12(2)**</td><td>SCHEDULE 5</td></tr>
</table>

POLLUTANTS

Indicative list of the main polluting substances to be taken into account if they are relevant for fixing emission limit values

AIR

1. Sulphur dioxide and other sulphur compounds.
2. Oxides of nitrogen and other nitrogen compounds.
3. Carbon monoxide.
4. Volatile organic compounds.
5. Metals and their compounds.
6. Dust.
7. Asbestos (suspended particulates, fibres).
8. Chlorine and its compounds.
9. Fluorine and its compounds.
10. Arsenic and its compounds.
11. Cyanides.
12. Substances and preparations which have been proved to possess carcinogenic or mutagenic properties or properties which may affect reproduction via the air.
13. Polychlorinated dibenzodioxins and polychlorinated dibenzofurans.

WATER

1. Organohalogen compounds and substances which may form such compounds in the aquatic environment.
2. Organophosphorus compounds.
3. Organotin compounds.
4. Substances and preparations which have been proved to possess carcinogenic or mutagenic properties or properties which may affect reproduction in or via the aquatic environment.
5. Persistent hydrocarbons and persistent and bioaccumulable organic toxic substances.
6. Cyanides.
7. Metals and their compounds.
8. Arsenic and its compounds.
9. Biocides and plant health products.
10. Materials in suspension.
11. Substances which contribute to eutrophication (in particular, nitrates and phosphates).
12. Substances which have an unfavourable influence on the oxygen balance (and can be measured using parameters such as BOD, COD, etc.).

<table>
<tr><td>**Regulation 29**</td><td>SCHEDULE 9</td></tr>
</table>

REGISTERS

1. A register maintained by a regulator under regulation 29 shall contain—
    (a) all particulars of any application made to the regulator for a permit;

(b) all particulars of any notice to the applicant by the regulator under paragraph 4 of Schedule 4 and paragraph 3 of Schedule 7 and of any information furnished in response to such a notice;

(c) all particulars of any advertisement published pursuant to paragraph 5 of Schedule 4 or paragraph 4(8) of Schedule 7 and of any representations made by any person in response to such an advertisement, other than representations which the person who made them requested should not be placed in the register;

(d) in a case where any such representations are omitted from the register at the request of the person who made them, a statement by the regulator that representations have been made which have been the subject of such a request (but such statement shall not identify the person who made the representations in question);

(e) all particulars of any representations made by any person required to be given notice under paragraph 9 of Schedule 4 or paragraph 4(5)(c) of Schedule 7;

(f) all particulars of any permit granted by the regulator;

(g) all particulars of any notification of the regulator given under regulation 16(1);

(h) all particulars of any application made to the regulator for the variation, transfer or surrender of a permit;

(i) all particulars of any variation, transfer and surrender of any permit granted by the regulator;

(j) all particulars of any revocation of a permit granted by the regulator;

(k) all particulars of any enforcement notice or suspension notice [or closure notice under the 2002 Regulations] issued by the regulator;

(l) all particulars of any notice issued by the regulator withdrawing an enforcement notice or a suspension notice;

(m) all particulars of any notice of appeal under regulation 27 against a decision by the regulator or a notice served by the regulator and of the documents relating to the appeal mentioned in paragraph 1(2)(a), (d) and (e) of Schedule 8;

(n) all particulars of any representations made by any person in response to a notice given under paragraph 3(1) of Schedule 8, other than representations which the person who made them requested should not be placed in the register;

(o) in a case where any such representations are omitted from the register at the request of the person who made them, a statement by the regulator that representations have been made which have been the subject of such a request (but such statement shall not identify the person who made the representations in question);

(p) all particulars of any written notification of the Secretary of State's determination of such an appeal and any report accompanying any such written notification;

(q) details of any conviction of or formal caution given to any person for any offence under regulation 32(1) [above or regulation 17(1) of the 2002 Regulations] which relates to the operation of an installation or mobile plant under a permit granted by the regulator, or without such a permit in circumstances where one is required by regulation 9, including the name of the person, the date of conviction or formal caution, and, in the case of a conviction, the penalty imposed and the name of the Court;

(r) all particulars of any monitoring information relating to the operation of an installation or mobile plant under a permit granted by the regulator which has been obtained by the regulator as a result of its own monitoring or furnished to the regulator in writing by virtue of a condition of the permit or under regulation 28(2);

(s) in a case where any such monitoring information is omitted from the register by virtue of regulation 31, a statement by the regulator, based on the monitoring information from time to time obtained by or furnished to them, indicating whether or not there has been compliance with any relevant condition of the permit;

(t) all particulars of any other information furnished to the authority in compliance with a condition of the permit, a variation notice, enforcement notice or suspension notice, or regulation 28(2) [or a closure notice under the 2002 Regulations];

(u) where a permit granted by the regulator authorises the carrying out of a specified waste management activity, all particulars of any waste management licence (within the meaning of regulation 19(13)) which ceased to have effect on the granting of the permit in so far as they may be relevant for the purpose of determining under regulation 19 whether any pollution risk results from the carrying out of such an activity on the site covered by the permit;

(v) all particulars of any report published by a regulator relating to an assessment of the environmental consequences of the operation of an installation in the locality of premises where the installation is operated under a permit granted by the regulator; and

(w) all particulars of any direction (other than a direction under regulation 30(2)) given to the regulator by the Secretary of State under any provision of these Regulations.

[(x) all particulars of any site conditioning plan or notice submitted under sub-paragraph 1(3) or (5) of Schedule 4 to the 2002 Regulations;

(y) all particulars of any notice requiring a landfill to close (in whole or part) issued under paragraph 1(6) of Schedule 4 to the 2002 Regulations;

(z) all particulars of any notification or report required before definitive closure of a landfill under regulation 15(4) of the 2002 Regulations.]

2. Where an application is withdrawn by the applicant at any time before it is determined, all particulars relating to that application which are already in the register shall be removed from the register not less than two months and not more than three months after the date of withdrawal of the application, and no further particulars relating to that application shall be entered in the register.

3. Where, following the amendment of Schedule 1, these Regulations cease to apply to a description of installation or mobile plant, all particulars relating to installations or mobile plant of that description shall be removed from the register not less than two months and not more than three months after the date on which the amendment comes into force.

4. Nothing in paragraph 1 shall require a regulator to keep in a register maintained by it—

(a) monitoring information relating to a particular installation or a mobile plant four years after that information was entered in the register; or

(b) information relating to a particular installation or mobile plant which has been superseded by later information relating to that installation or mobile plant four years after that later information was entered in the register,

but this paragraph shall not apply to any aggregated monitoring data relating to overall emissions of any substance or class of substance from installations or mobile plant generally or from any class of installations or mobile plant.

5. Any details of a formal caution included in a register pursuant to paragraph 1(q) shall be removed from the register after five years have elapsed since the date on which the caution was given.

The Air Quality Limit Values Regulations 2001
(SI 2001, No. 2315)

1 Citation, commencement and extent

(1) These Regulations may be cited as the Air Quality Limit Values Regulations 2001 and shall come into force on 19th July 2001.

(2) With the exception of regulation 10 which shall apply to the whole of the United Kingdom, these Regulations shall apply to England only.

2 Definitions

In these Regulations—

'agglomeration' means a zone with a population concentration in excess of 250,000 inhabitants, or, where the population concentration is 250,000 inhabitants or less, a population density per km² for which the Secretary of State considers that the need for ambient air to be assessed or managed is justified;

'alert threshold' has the meaning given by regulation 8(2);

'ambient air' means outdoor air in the troposphere, excluding work places;

'assessment' means any method used to measure, calculate, predict or estimate the level of a relevant pollutant in the ambient air;

'fixed measurements' means measurements taken at fixed sites either continuously or by random sampling, the number of measurements being sufficiently large to enable the levels observed to be determined;

'level' means the concentration of a relevant pollutant in ambient air;

'limit value' has the meaning given in regulation 3(1);

'lower assessment threshold' has the meaning given in regulation 5(5);

'natural events' means volcanic eruptions, seismic activities, geothermal activities, wild-land fires, high-wind events or the atmospheric resuspension or transport of natural particles from dry regions;

'oxides of nitrogen' means the sum of nitric oxide and nitrogen dioxide added as parts per billion and expressed as nitrogen dioxide in microgrammes per cubic metre;

'$PM_{2.5}$' means particulate matter which passes through a size-selective inlet with a 50% efficiency cut-off at 2.5 μm aerodynamic diameter;

'PM_{10}' means particulate matter which passes through a size-selective inlet with a 50% efficiency cut-off at 10 μm aerodynamic diameter;

'relevant pollutants' means sulphur dioxide, nitrogen dioxide and oxides of nitrogen, particulate matter and lead;

'upper assessment threshold' has the meaning given in regulation 5(5); and

'zone' means a part of the territory of England shown on a map published by the Secretary of State on 19th January 2001, deposited at the offices of the Department for Environment, Food and Rural Affairs, Ashdown House, 123 Victoria Street, London SW1E 6DE and displayed on the Department's website at http://www.environment.detr.gov.uk.

3 Duty to ensure that ambient air quality is improved

(1) The Secretary of State shall take the measures necessary to ensure that throughout England in each zone concentrations of relevant pollutants in ambient air, as assessed in accordance with regulations 4 to 7, do not exceed the limit values set out in Schedule 1 from the dates specified in that Schedule.

(2) The measures taken shall—

    (a) take into account an integrated approach to the protection of air, water and soil;

    (b) not contravene Community legislation on the protection of safety and health of workers at work; and

    (c) have no significant negative effects on the environment in the other Member States.

4   Assessment of ambient air quality

The Secretary of State shall ensure that ambient air quality is assessed in each zone in relation to each of the relevant pollutants in accordance with regulations 5 to 7.

5   Classification of zones

(1) The Secretary of State shall classify each zone in relation to each of the relevant pollutants according to whether ambient air quality in that zone for that pollutant is required to be assessed by—

    (a)   measurements;

    (b)   a combination of measurements and modelling techniques; or

    (c)   by the sole use of modelling or objective estimation techniques.

(2) Measurements must be used to assess ambient air quality in relation to a relevant pollutant in a zone if—

    (a)   the zone is an agglomeration;

    (b)   the levels of that pollutant in the zone are between the relevant limit values and upper assessment thresholds; or

    (c)   the levels of that pollutant in the zone exceed the limit values for that pollutant.

(3) A combination of measurements and modelling techniques may be used to assess ambient air quality in any zone in relation to a relevant pollutant where the levels of that pollutant over a representative period are below the relevant upper assessment thresholds.

(4) Where the levels of a relevant pollutant in any zone over a representative period are below the relevant lower assessment thresholds, the sole use of modelling or objective estimation techniques for assessing levels of that pollutant is permissible unless—

    (a)   the zone is an agglomeration; and

    (b)   the pollutant being assessed is sulphur dioxide or nitrogen dioxide.

(5) The upper and lower assessment thresholds for the relevant pollutants shall be determined in accordance with Schedule 2.

(6) Where a zone is classified in relation to a pollutant under paragraph (1) (a), modelling techniques may be used for supplementing the measurements taken in order to provide an adequate level of information on ambient air quality in relation to a relevant pollutant in a zone.

(7) The Secretary of State may also designate a zone classified under this regulation in relation to a relevant pollutant as follows.

(8) Where the relevant pollutant is sulphur dioxide, the zone may be designated under this paragraph if the limit values are exceeded in the zone owing to concentrations of sulphur dioxide in ambient air due to natural sources.

(9) Where the relevant pollutant is PM_{10}, the zone may be designated—

    (a)   under this sub-paragraph if due to natural events concentrations of PM_{10} in the ambient air are significantly in excess of normal background levels from natural sources;

    (b)   under this sub-paragraph if due to the resuspension of particulates following the winter sanding of roads concentrations of PM_{10} in the ambient air are significantly in excess of normal background levels from natural sources.

6   Review of classifications

(1) The Secretary of State shall review the classification of each zone under regulation 5 at least once in every five years in accordance with Part II of Schedule 2.

(2) The Secretary of State shall also review the classification of any zone under regulation 5 in the event of significant changes in activities affecting ambient concentrations in that zone of any of the relevant pollutants.

(3) In this paragraph, 'classification' includes any designation under regulation 5(7) to (9).

7   Method of assessment of ambient air quality

(1) The Secretary of State shall ensure that ambient air quality is assessed in each zone by following the appropriate method for each relevant pollutant in accordance with its current classification.

(2) Where a zone is classified under regulation 5(1)(a) or (b) in relation to a relevant pollutant—

    (a) measurements of that pollutant must be taken at fixed sites either continuously or by random sampling; and

    (b) the number of measurements must be sufficiently large to enable the levels of that pollutant to be properly determined.

(3) Schedule 3 shall have effect for the purposes of determining the location of sampling points for the relevant pollutants.

(4) For each zone classified under regulation 5(1)(a) in relation to a relevant pollutant, the Secretary of State shall ensure that the minimum number of fixed sampling points determined in accordance with Schedule 4 is used for sampling the concentrations of that pollutant in that zone.

(5) For each zone classified under regulation 5(1)(b) in relation to a relevant pollutant, the Secretary of State shall ensure that the number of fixed sampling points used for sampling that pollutant in that zone, and the spatial resolution of other techniques, shall be sufficient for the concentrations of that pollutant to be established in accordance with Part I of Schedule 3 and Part I of Schedule 5.

(6) Reference methods for—

    (a) the analysis of sulphur dioxide, nitrogen dioxide and oxides of nitrogen;

    (b) the sampling and analysis of lead; and

    (c) the sampling and measurement of PM_{10},

are set out in Schedule 6 and these methods must be used unless other methods are used which the Secretary of State considers can be demonstrated to give equivalent results.

(7) The Secretary of State shall ensure that—

    (a) measuring stations to supply representative data on concentrations of $PM_{2.5}$ are installed and operated using methods for the sampling and measurement of $PM_{2.5}$ that she considers suitable; and

    (b) sampling points for $PM_{2.5}$ are, where possible, co-located with sampling points for PM_{10}.

(8) For zones which are classified under regulation 5(1)(b) or (c), the Secretary of State shall ensure that the information set out in Part II of Schedule 5 is compiled.

(9) For sulphur dioxide, nitrogen dioxide and oxides of nitrogen measurements of volume must be standardised at a temperature of 293°K and a pressure of 101,3 kPa.

8   Action plans

(1) The Secretary of State shall draw up action plans indicating the measures to be taken in the short term where there is any risk of the limit values for any of the relevant pollutants, or the alert thresholds for sulphur dioxide or nitrogen dioxide, being exceeded, in order to reduce that risk and to limit the duration of such an occurence.

(2) The alert threshold for sulphur dioxide is set out in paragraph 1.2 of Part I of Schedule 1 and the alert threshold for nitrogen dioxide is set out in paragraph 2.2 of Part II of Schedule 1.

9   Action to be taken where limit values are exceeded

(1) The Secretary of State shall draw up a list of zones in which the levels of one or more of the relevant pollutants are higher than—

    (a) in a case where there is no margin of tolerance shown in Schedule 1 in relation to a limit value, the limit value;

(b) in any other case, the limit value plus the margin of tolerance shown in Schedule 1.

(2) The Secretary of State shall draw up a list of zones in which the levels of one or more of the relevant pollutants are between the limit value and the limit value plus any margin of tolerance.

(3) Subject to paragraphs (6), (8) and (9), the Secretary of State shall draw up for each zone listed under paragraph (1) a plan or programme for attaining the limit values for the pollutants in question within the time limits specified in Schedule 1 and shall ensure that the plan or programme is implemented.

(4) The plan or programme shall at least include the information listed in Schedule 7.

(5) Where in any zone the level of more that one pollutant is higher than the limit values, an integrated plan covering all the pollutants in question shall be prepared.

(6) For any zone designated under regulation 5(8), the Secretary of State may provide that plans or programmes shall only be required under this regulation where the limit values are exceeded owing to man-made emissions.

(7) Plans or programmes for PM_{10} which are prepared in accordance with this regulation shall also have the aim of reducing concentrations of $PM_{2.5}$.

(8) For any zone designated under regulation 5(9)(a), the Secretary of State may provide that plans or programmes shall only be required where the limit values are exceeded owing to causes other than natural events.

(9) For any zone designated under regulation 5(9)(b), the Secretary of State may provide that plans or programmes shall only be required where the limit values are exceeded owing to PM_{10} levels other than those caused by winter road sanding.

10   Consultations with other Member States of the European Union

(1) For the purpose of this regulation, a transboundary pollution issue arises when in any part of the United Kingdom the level of a relevant pollutant exceeds, or is likely to exceed, the limit value plus the margin of tolerance or, as the case may be, the alert threshold following significant pollution in another Member State of the European Union.

(2) It shall be the duty of the relevant administration to notify the Secretary of State of any transboundary pollution issue affecting Wales, Scotland or Northern Ireland.

(3) The Secretary of State shall consult any other Member State directly concerned with a pollution issue with a view to finding a solution to that issue—

(a) when she considers that a transboundary pollution issue has arisen affecting England;

(b) on receiving a notification under paragraph (2); or

(c) on being notified by any other Member State that the limit value or alert threshold for any relevant pollutant may be exceeded in that Member State as a result of pollution originating in any part of the United Kingdom.

(4) In any case which appears to her to affect Wales, Scotland or Northern Ireland respectively, the Secretary of State shall—

(a) inform the relevant administration of any notification made under paragraph (3)(c); and

(b) consult the relevant administration about any action which she proposes to take.

(5) The Commission may be present at any consultations conducted under paragraph (3).

(6) In this regulation, 'relevant administration' means—

(a) the National Assembly for Wales for matters affecting Wales;

(b) Scottish Ministers for matters affecting Scotland; and

(c) Northern Ireland Ministers for matters affecting Northern Ireland.

11   Extension of power to give directions relating to air quality

(1) For the purposes of the implementation of any obligations of the United Kingdom

under Council Directive 96/62/EC on ambient air quality assessment and management and Council Directive 99/30/EC relating to limit values for sulphur dioxide, nitrogen dioxide and oxides of nitrogen, particulate matter and lead in ambient air—

    (a) the Secretary of State shall have the same power to give directions to local authorities in Greater London and the Mayor of London; and

    (b) the Mayor of London shall have the same power to give directions to local authorities in Greater London,

as the Secretary of State has under section 85(5) of the Environment Act 1995 in relation to local authorities in England outside Greater London.

(2) The provisions of subsections (6), (6A) and (7) of section 85 of the Environment Act 1995 shall apply to directions given under this regulation as they apply to directions given under that section, and in the case of subsection (7) as if the Mayor of London were a local authority.

12   Zones where the levels are lower than the limit value

(1) The Secretary of State shall draw up a list of zones in which the levels of the relevant pollutants are below the limit values.

(2) The Secretary of State shall ensure that the levels of the relevant pollutants in these zones are maintained below the limit values and shall endeavour to preserve the best ambient air quality compatible with sustainable development.

13   Public information

(1) The Secretary of State shall ensure that up-to-date information on ambient concentrations of each of the relevant pollutants is routinely made available to the public.

(2) Information on ambient concentrations of sulphur dioxide, nitrogen dioxide and particulate matter shall be updated—

    (a) in the case of hourly values for sulphur dioxide and nitrogen dioxide, where practicable on an hourly basis;

    (b) in all other cases, as a minimum on a daily basis.

(3) Information on ambient concentrations of lead shall be updated on a three-monthly basis.

(4) Information made available under paragraph (1) shall include—

    (a) an indication of the extent to which limit values and alert thresholds for relevant pollutants have been exceeded over the averaging periods specified in Schedule 1; and

    (b) a short assessment of those exceedances and their effects on health.

(5) When an alert threshold is exceeded, the Secretary of State shall ensure that the necessary steps are taken to inform the public, and the information made available shall as a minimum include the information specified in paragraphs 1.3 of Part I and 2.3 of Part II of Schedule 1.

(6) Information to be made available to the public under this regulation shall include the map mentioned in the definition of 'zone' in regulation 2 and action plans, plans and programmes prepared under regulations 8 and 9 respectively.

(7) For the purposes of this regulation, the public includes, but is not limited to, health care bodies and organisations having an interest in ambient air quality and representing the interests of sensitive populations, consumers and the environment.

(8) Information made available under this regulation shall be clear, comprehensible and accessible.

14   Revocations of Air Quality Standards Regulations 1989 and transitional provisions

(1) The Air Quality Standards Regulations 1989, insofar as they apply to England, are hereby revoked as follows.

(2) Regulation 2(1) (limit values for sulphur dioxide and suspended particulates) and regulation 4(1) (limit value for lead in air) shall be revoked with effect from 1st January 2005.

(3) Regulations 3 (measurement of sulphur dioxide and suspended particulates), 5 (measurement of lead in air) and 7 (measurement of nitrogen dioxide in the atmosphere) shall be revoked.

(4) Regulation 6 (limit value for nitrogen dioxide in the atmosphere) shall be revoked with effect from 1st January 2010.

(5) From 19th July 2001 until 1st January 2005, if the methods prescribed by these regulations for the assessment of suspended particulate matter are used for the purpose of demonstrating compliance with [a] Annex IV. Directive 80/779/EEC of 15th July 1980 on air quality limit values and guide values for suspended particulates the data so collected shall be multiplied by a factor of 1.2.

Regulations 3(1), 8(2), 9(1)　　**SCHEDULE 1**
and (3), 13(4) and (5)

LIMIT VALUES, MARGINS OF TOLERANCE ETC.

PART I　SULPHUR DIOXIDE

1.1　Limit values for sulphur dioxide

	Averaging period	Limit value	Margin of tolerance [11]	Date by which limit value is to be met
1. Hourly limit value for the protection of human health	1 hour	$350\,\mu g/m^3$, not to be exceeded more than 24 times a calendar year	$120\,\mu g/m^3$ on 19th July 2001, reducing on 1st January of each following year by equal annual amounts to reach $0\,\mu g/m^3$ by 1st January 2005	1st January 2005
2. Daily limit value for the protection of human health	24 hours	$125\,\mu g/m^3$, not to be exceeded more than 3 times a calendar year	None	1st January 2005
3. Limit value for the protection of ecosystems	Calendar year and winter (1st October to 31st March)	$20\,\mu g/m^3$	None	19th July 2001

1.2   Alert threshold for sulphur dioxide

$500 \, \mu g/m^3$ measured over three consecutive hours at locations representative of air quality over at least $100 \, km^2$ or an entire zone, whichever is the smaller.

1.3   Minimum details to be made available to the public when the alert threshold for sulphur dioxide is exceeded

Details to be made available to the public should include at least:

— the date, hour and place of the occurrence and the reasons for the occurrence, where known;
— any forecasts of:
— changes in concentration (improvement, stabilisation, or deterioration), together with the reasons for those changes,
— the geographical area concerned,
— the duration of the occurrence;
— the type of population potentially sensitive to the occurrence;
— the precautions to be taken by the sensitive population concerned.

PART II   NITROGEN DIOXIDE (NO_2) AND OXIDES OF NITROGEN (NO_x)

2.1   Limit values for nitrogen dioxide and oxides of nitrogen

	Averaging period	Limit value	Margin of tolerance	Date by which limit value is to be met
1. Hourly limit value for the protection of human health	1 hour	$200 \, \mu g/m^3$ NO_2, not to be exceeded more than 18 times a calendar year	$90 \, \mu g/m^3$ on 19th July 2001, reducing on 1st January of each following year by equal annual amounts to reach $0 \, \mu g/m^3$ by 1st January 2010	1st January 2010
2. Annual limit value for the protection of human health	Calendar year	$40 \, \mu g/m^3$ NO_2	$18 \, \mu g/m^3$ on 19th July 2001, reducing on 1st January of each following year by equal annual amounts to reach $0 \, \mu g/m^3$ by 1st January 2010	1st January 2010
3. Annual limit value for the protection of vegetation	Calendar year	$30 \, \mu g/m^3$ NO_x	None	19th July 2001

2.2   Alert threshold for nitrogen dioxide

$400 \,\mu g/m^3$ measured over three consecutive hours at locations representative of air quality over at least $100 \,km^2$ or an entire zone or agglomeration, whichever is the smaller.

2.3   Minimum details to be made available to the public when the alert threshold for nitrogen dioxide is exceeded

Details to be made available to the public should include at least:

— the date, hour and place of the occurrence and the reasons for the occurrence, where known;
— any forecasts of:
— changes in concentration (improvement, stabilisation, or deterioration), together with the reasons for those changes,
— the geographical area concerned,
— the duration of the occurrence;
— the type of population potentially sensitive to the occurrence;
— the precautions to be taken by the sensitive population concerned.

PART III   PARTICULATE MATTER (PM_{10})

	Averaging period	Limit value	Margin of tolerance	Date by which limit value is to be met
1. 24-hour limit value for the protection of human health	24 hours	$50 \,\mu g/m^3$ PM_{10}, not to be exceeded more than 35 times a calendar year	$20 \,\mu g/m^3$ on 19th July 2001, reducing on 1st January of each following year by equal annual amounts to reach $0 \,\mu g/m^3$ by 1st January 2005	1st January 2005
2. Annual limit value for the protection of human health	Calendar year	$40 \,\mu g/m^3$ PM_{10}	$6.4 \,\mu g/m^3$ on 19th July 2001, reducing on 1st January of each following year by equal annual amounts to reach $0 \,\mu g/m^3$ by 1st January 2005	1st January 2005

PART IV   LEAD

	Averaging period	Limit value	Margin of tolerance	Date by which limit value is to be met
Annual limit value for the protection of human health	Calendar year	$0.5 \,\mu g/m^3$	$0.4 \,\mu g/m^3$ on 19th July 2001, reducing on 1st January of each following year by equal annual amounts to reach $0 \,\mu g/m^3$ by 1st January 2005	1st January 2005

Regulations 5(5) and 6(1) SCHEDULE 2

UPPER AND LOWER ASSESSMENT THRESHOLDS AND EXCEEDANCES

PART I UPPER AND LOWER ASSESSMENT THRESHOLDS

The following upper and lower assessment thresholds will apply:

(a) SULPHUR DIOXIDE

	Health protection	*Ecosystem protection*
Upper assessment threshold	60% of 24-hour limit value (75 μg/m^3), not to be exceeded more than 3 times in any calendar year	60% of winter limit value (12 μg/m^3)
Lower assessment threshold	40% of 24-hour limit value (50 μg/m^3), not to be exceeded more than 3 times in any calendar year	40% of winter limit value (8 μg/m^3)

(b) NITROGEN DIOXIDE AND OXIDES OF NITROGEN

	Hourly limit value for the protection of human health (NO_2)	*Annual limit value for the protection of human health (NO_2)*	*Annual limit value for the protection of vegetation (NO_x)*
Upper assessment value	70% of limit value (140 μg/m^3), not to be exceeded more than 18 times in any calendar year	80% of limit value (32 μg/m^3)	80% of limit value (24 μg/m^3)
Lower assessment value	50% of limit value (100 μg/m^3), not to be exceeded more than 18 times in any calendar year	65% of limit value (26 μg/m^3)	65% of limit value (19.5 μg/m^3)

(c) PARTICULATE MATTER

	24-hour average	*Annual average*
Upper assessment threshold	60% of limit value (30 μg/m^3), not to be exceeded more than seven times in any calendar year	70% of limit value (14 μg/m^3)
Lower assessment threshold	40% of limit value (20 μg/m^3), not to be exceeded more than seven times in any calendar year	50% of limit value (10 μg/m^3)

(d) LEAD

	Annual average
Upper assessment threshold	70% of limit value (0.35 μg/m³)
Lower assessment threshold	50% of limit value (0.25 μg/m³)

PART II   DETERMINATION OF EXCEEDANCES OF UPPER AND LOWER ASSESSMENT THRESHOLDS

Exceedances of upper and lower assessment thresholds must be determined on the basis of concentrations during the previous five years where sufficient data are available. An assessment threshold will be deemed to have been exceeded if during those five years the total number of exceedances of the numerical concentration of the threshold is more than three times the number of exceedances allowed each year.

Where fewer than five years' data are available, measurement campaigns of short duration during the period of the year and at locations likely to be typical of the highest pollution levels may be combined with results obtained from emission inventories and modelling to determine exceedances of the upper and lower assessment thresholds.

Regulations 7(3) and 7(5)   SCHEDULE 3

LOCATION OF SAMPLING POINTS FOR THE MEASUREMENT OF SULPHUR DIOXIDE, NITROGEN DIOXIDE AND OXIDES OF NITROGEN, PARTICULATE MATTER AND LEAD IN AMBIENT AIR

The following considerations will apply to fixed measurement.

PART I   MACROSCALE SITING

(a) Protection of human health

Sampling points directed at the protection of human health should be sited:

(i) to provide data on the areas within zones where the highest concentrations occur to which the population is likely to be directly or indirectly exposed for a period which is significant in relation to the averaging period of the limit value(s);

(ii) to provide data on levels in other areas within the zones which are representative of the exposure of the general population.

Sampling points should in general be sited to avoid measuring very small micro-environments in their immediate vicinity. As a guideline, a sampling point should be sited to be representative of air quality in a surrounding area of no less than 200 m2 at traffic-orientated sites and of several square kilometres at urban-background sites.

Sampling points should also, where possible, be representative of similar locations not in their immediate vicinity.

Account should be taken of the need to locate sampling points on islands, where that is necessary for the protection of human health.

(b) Protection of ecosystems and vegetation

Sampling points targeted at the protection of ecosystems or vegetation should be sited more than 20 km from agglomerations or more than 5 km from other built-up areas, industrial installations or motorways. As a guideline, a sampling point should be sited to be representative of air quality in a surrounding area of at least 1000 km². A sampling point may be sited at a lesser distance or to be representative of air quality in a less extended area, taking account of geographical conditions.

Account should be taken of the need to assess air quality on islands.

PART II   MICROSCALE SITING

The following guidelines should be met as far as practicable:

— the flow around the inlet sampling probe should be unrestricted without any obstructions affecting the airflow in the vicinity of the sampler (normally some metres away from buildings, balconies, trees and other obstacles and at least 0.5 m from the nearest building in the case of sampling points representing air quality at the building line);

— in general, the inlet sampling point should be between 1.5 m (the breathing zone) and 4 m above the ground. Higher positions (up to 8 m) may be necessary in some circumstances. Higher siting may also be appropriate if the station is representative of a large area;

— the inlet probe should not be positioned in the immediate vicinity of sources in order to avoid the direct intake of emissions unmixed with ambient air;

— the sampler's exhaust outlet should be positioned so that recirculation of exhaust air to the sampler inlet is avoided;

— location of traffic-orientated samplers;

— for all pollutants, such sampling points should be at least 25 m from the edge of major junctions and at least 4 m from the centre of the nearest traffic lane,

— for nitrogen dioxide, inlets should be no more than 5 m from the kerbside,

— for particulate matter and lead, inlets should be sited so as to be representative of air quality near to the building line.

The following factors may also be taken into account:

— interfering sources;

— security;

— access;

— availability of electrical power and telephone communications;

— visibility of the site in relation to its surroundings;

— safety of public and operators;

— the desirability of co-locating sampling points for different pollutants;

— planning requirements.

PART III   DOCUMENTATION AND REVIEW OF SITE SELECTION

The site-selection procedures should be fully documented at the classification stage by such means as compass-point photographs of the surrounding area and a detailed map. Sites should be reviewed at regular intervals with repeated documentation to ensure that selection criteria remain valid over time.

Regulation 7(4) SCHEDULE 4

CRITERIA FOR DETERMINING MINIMUM NUMBERS OF
SAMPLING POINTS FOR FIXED MEASUREMENT OF
CONCENTRATIONS OF RELEVANT POLLUTANTS IN
AMBIENT AIR

PART I   MINIMUM NUMBER OF SAMPLING POINTS FOR FIXED MEASUREMENT TO
ASSESS COMPLIANCE WITH LIMIT VALUES FOR THE PROTECTION OF HUMAN
HEALTH AND ALERT THRESHOLDS IN ZONES WHERE FIXED MEASUREMENT IS THE
SOLE SOURCE OF INFORMATION

(a) Diffuse sources

Population of zone (thousands)	If concentrations exceed the upper assessment threshold	If maximum concentrations are between the upper and lower assessment thresholds	For SO_2 and NO_2 in agglomerations where maximum concentrations are below the lower assessment thresholds
0–250	1	1	not applicable
250–499	2	1	1
500–749	2	1	1
750–999	3	1	1
1,000–1,499	4	2	1
1,500–1,999	5	2	1
2,000–2,749	6	3	2
2,750–3,749	7	3	2
3,750–4,749	8	4	2
4,750–5,999	9	4	2
>6,000	10	5	3
	For NO_2 and particulate matter to include at least one urban-background station and one traffic-orientated station		

(b) Point sources

For the assessment of pollution in the vicinity of point sources, the number of sampling points for fixed measurement should be calculated taking into account emission densities, the likely distribution patterns of ambient-air pollution and the potential exposure of the population.

PART II   MINIMUM NUMBER OF SAMPLING POINTS FOR FIXED
MEASUREMENTS TO ASSESS COMPLIANCE WITH LIMIT VALUES
FOR THE PROTECTION OF ECOSYSTEMS OR VEGETATION IN ZONES
OTHER THAN AGGLOMERATIONS

If maximum concentrations exceed the upper assessment threshold	If maximum concentrations are between the upper and lower assessment thresholds
1 station every 20,000 km²	1 station every 40,000 km²

In island zones the number of sampling points for fixed measurement should be calculated taking into account the likely distribution patterns of ambient-air pollution and the potential exposure of ecosystems or vegetation.

Regulation 7(5) and (8)   SCHEDULE 5

DATA-QUALITY OBJECTIVES AND COMPILATION OF RESULTS
OF AIR-QUALITY ASSESSMENT

PART I   DATA-QUALITY OBJECTIVES

The following data-quality objectives for the required accuracy of assessment methods, of minimum time coverage and of data capture of measurement are laid down to guide quality-assurance programmes.

	Suphur dioxide, nitrogen dioxide and oxides of nitrogen	*Particulate matter and lead*
Continuous measurement		
Accuracy	15%	25%
Minimum data capture	90%	90%
Indicative measurement		
Accuracy	25%	50%
Minimum data capture	90%	90%
Minimum time coverage	14% (One measurement a week at random, evenly distributed over the year, or eight weeks evenly distributed over the year.)	14% (One measurement a week at random, evenly distributed over the year, or eight weeks evenly distributed over the year.)
Modelling		
Accuracy:		
Hourly averages	50%–60%	
Daily averages	50%	50%
Annual averages	30%	50%
Objective estimation		
Accuracy:	75%	100%

The accuracy of the measurement is defined as laid down in the 'Guide to the Expression of Uncertainty of Measurements' (ISO 1993) or in ISO 5725–1 'Accuracy (trueness and precision) of measurement methods and results' (ISO 1994). The percentages in the table are given for individual measurements averaged, over the period considered, by the limit value, for a 95% confidence interval (bias + two times the standard deviation). The accuracy for continuous measurements should be interpreted as being applicable in the region of the appropriate limit value.

The accuracy for modelling and objective estimation is defined as the maximum deviation of the measured and calculated concentration levels, over the period considered by the limit value, without taking account the timing of the events.

The requirements for minimum data capture and time coverage do not include losses of data due to the regular calibration or the normal maintenance of the instrumentation.

The Secretary of State may allow for random measurements to be made instead of continuous measurements for particulate matter and lead by methods for which accuracy within the 95% confidence interval with respect to continuous monitoring has been demonstrated to be within 10%. Random sampling must be spread evenly over the year.

PART II   RESULTS OF AIR QUALITY ASSESSMENT

The following information should be compiled for zones within which sources other than measurement are employed to supplement information from measurement or as the sole means of air quality assessment:
- a description of assessment activities carried out;
- the specific methods used, with references to descriptions of the method;
- the sources of data and information;
- a description of results, including accuracies and, in particular, the extent of any area or, if relevant, the length of road within the zone over which concentrations exceed limit value(s) or, as may be, limit value(s) plus applicable margin(s) of tolerance and of any area within which concentrations exceed the upper assessment threshold or the lower assessment threshold;
- for limit values the object of which is the protection of human health, the population potentially exposed to concentrations in excess of the limit value.

Where possible maps shall be compiled showing concentration distributions within each zone.

Regulation 7(6)   SCHEDULE 6

REFERENCE METHODS FOR ASSESSMENT OF CONCENTRATIONS OF SULPHUR DIOXIDE, NITROGEN DIOXIDE AND OXIDES OF NITROGEN, PARTICULATE MATTER (PM_{10} AND $PM_{2.5}$) AND LEAD

PART I   REFERENCE METHOD FOR THE ANALYSIS OF SULPHUR DIOXIDE

ISO/FDIS 10498 (Standard in draft) Ambient air—determination of sulphur dioxide—ultraviolet fluorescence method.

PART II   REFERENCE METHOD FOR THE ANALYSIS OF NITROGEN DIOXIDE
AND OXIDES OF NITROGEN

ISO 7996: 1985 Ambient air—determination of the mass concentrations of nitrogen oxides—chemiluminescence method.

PART IIIA   REFERENCE METHOD FOR THE SAMPLING OF LEAD

The reference method for the sampling of lead will be that described in the Annex to Directive 82/884/EEC until such time as the limit value in Schedule 1 to these Regulations is to be met, when the reference method will be that for PM_{10} specified in Part IV of this Schedule.

PART IIIB   REFERENCE METHOD FOR THE ANALYSIS OF LEAD

ISO 9855: 1993 Ambient air—determination of the particulate lead content of aerosols collected in filters. Atomic absorption spectroscopy method.

PART IV   REFERENCE METHOD FOR THE SAMPLING AND MEASUREMENT OF PM_{10}

The reference method for the sampling and measurement of PM_{10} will be that described in EN 12341 'Air Quality—Field Test Procedure to Demonstrate Reference Equivalence of Sampling Methods for the PM_{10} fraction of particulate matter' [18]. The measurement principle is based on the collection on a filter of the PM_{10} fraction of ambient particulate matter and the gravimetric mass determination.

Regulation 9(4)   SCHEDULE 7

INFORMATION TO BE INCLUDED IN THE PLAN OR PROGRAMME FOR IMPROVEMENT OF AIR QUALITY

1. *Localisation of excess pollution*
    — region
    — city (map)
    — measuring station (map, geographical coordinates).
2. *General information*
    — type of zone (city, industrial or rural area)
    — estimate of the polluted area (km^2) and of the population exposed to the pollution
    — useful climatic data
    — relevant data on topography
    — sufficient information on the type of targets requiring protection in the zone.
3. *Responsible authorities*
        Names and addresses of persons responsible for the development and implementation of improvement plans.
4. *Nature and assessment of pollution*
    — concentrations observed over previous years (before the implementation of the improvement measures)
    — concentrations measured since the beginning of the project
    — techniques used for the assessment.
5. *Origin of pollution*
    — list of the main emission sources responsible for pollution (map)
    — total quantity of emissions from these sources (tonnes/year)
    — information on pollution imported from other regions.
6. *Analysis of the situation*
    — details of those factors responsible for the excess (transport, including cross-border transport, formation)
    — details of possible measures for improvement of air quality.
7. *Details of those measures or projects for improvement which existed prior to 21st November 1996*
    — local, regional, national, international measures
    — observed effects of these measures.
8. *Details of those measures or projects adopted with a view to reducing pollution following 21st November 1996*
    — listing and description of all the measures set out in the project

— timetable for implementation

— estimate of the improvement of air quality planned and of the expected time required to attain these objectives.

9.   *Details of the measures or projects planned or being researched for the long term.*

10.   *List of the publications, documents, work etc used to supplement information requested in this Schedule.*

The Control of Pollution (Oil Storage) (England) Regulations 2001
(SI 2001, No. 2954)

1   Citation, commencement, extent and interpretation

(1) These Regulations, which may be cited as the Control of Pollution (Oil Storage) (England) Regulations 2001, shall come into force on 1st March 2002 and extend to England only.

(2) In these Regulations—

'container' means a fixed tank, a drum or a mobile bowser or (even if not connected to fixed pipework) an intermediate bulk container;

'drum' means an oil drum or similar container used for storing oil;

'fixed tank' includes an intermediate bulk container which is connected to fixed pipework;

'oil' means any kind of oil and includes petrol; and

'secondary containment system' means a drip tray, an area surrounded by a bund or any other system for preventing oil which is no longer in its container from escaping from the place where it is stored.

2   Application of Regulations

(1) Subject to paragraph (2), these Regulations apply to the storage of oil on any premises.

(2) These Regulations do not apply to the storage of oil—

(a) if the oil is waste oil within the meaning of regulation 1(3) of the Waste Management Licensing Regulations 1994;

(b) in any container which is situated in a building or wholly underground;

(c) in any container with a storage capacity of 200 litres or less;

(d) on any premises used—

(i)   wholly or mainly as a private dwelling if the storage capacity of the container in which it is stored is 3500 litres or less;

(ii)   for refining oil; or

(iii) for the onward distribution of oil to other places; or

(e) on any farm if the oil is for use in connection with agriculture within the meaning of the Agriculture Act 1947.

3   Requirements for storage of oil—general

(1) Oil shall be stored in a container which is of sufficient strength and structural integrity to ensure that it is unlikely to burst or leak in its ordinary use.

(2) The container must be situated within a secondary containment system which satisfies the following requirements—

(a) subject to paragraph (5), it must have a capacity of not less than 110% of the container's storage capacity or, if there is more than one container within the system, of not less than 110% of the largest container's storage capacity or 25% of their aggregate storage capacity, whichever is the greater;

(b) it must be positioned, or other steps must be taken, so as to minimise any risk of damage by impact so far as is reasonably practicable;

(c) its base and walls must be impermeable to water and oil;

(d) its base and walls must not be penetrated by any valve, pipe or other opening which is used for draining the system; and

(e) if any fill pipe, or draw off pipe, penetrates its base or any of its walls, the junction of the pipe with the base or walls must be adequately sealed to prevent oil escaping from the system.

(3) Any valve, filter, sight gauge, vent pipe or other equipment ancillary to the container (other than a fill pipe or draw off pipe or, if the oil has a flashpoint of less than 32°C, a pump) must be situated within the secondary containment system.

(4) Where a fill pipe is not within the secondary containment system, a drip tray must be used to catch any oil spilled when the container is being filled with oil.

(5) Where any drum is used for the storage of oil in conjunction with a drip tray as the secondary containment system, it is sufficient if the tray has a capacity of not less than 25% of—

(a) the drum's storage capacity; or

(b) if there is more than one drum used at the same time with the tray, the aggregate storage capacity of the drums.

4 Fixed tanks

(1) Any fixed tank used for storing oil shall satisfy the following requirements.

(2) Any sight gauge must be properly supported and fitted with a valve which must be closed automatically when not in use.

(3) Any fill pipe, draw off pipe or overflow pipe must be positioned, or other steps must be taken, so as to minimise any risk of damage by impact so far as is reasonably practicable and—

(a) if above ground, must be properly supported;

(b) if underground—

(i) must have no mechanical joints, except at a place which is accessible for inspection by removing a hatch or cover;

(ii) must be adequately protected from physical damage;

(iii) must have adequate facilities for detecting any leaks;

(iv) if fitted with a leakage detection device which is used continuously to monitor for leaks, the detection device must be maintained in working order and tested at appropriate intervals to ensure that it works properly; and

(v) if not fitted with such a device, must be tested for leaks before it is first used and further tests for leaks must be performed, in the case of pipes which have mechanical joints, at least once in every 5 years and, in other cases, at least once in every 10 years; and

(c) if made of materials which are liable to corrosion, must be adequately protected against corrosion.

(4) The tank must be fitted with an automatic overfill prevention device if the filling operation is controlled from a place where it is not reasonably practicable to observe the tank and any vent pipe.

(5) Any screw fitting or other fixed coupling which is fitted and is in good condition must be used when the tank is being filled with oil.

(6) Where oil from the tank is delivered through a flexible pipe which is permanently attached to the container—

(a) the pipe must be fitted with a tap or valve at the delivery end which closes automatically when not in use;

(b) the tap or valve must not be capable of being fixed in the open position unless the pipe is fitted with an automatic shut off device;

(c) the pipe must be enclosed in a secure cabinet which is locked shut when not in use and is equipped with a drip tray or the pipe must—

(i) have a lockable valve where it leaves the container which is locked shut when not in use; and

(ii) be kept within the secondary containment system when not in use.

(7) Any pump must be—

(a) fitted with a non-return valve in its feed line;

(b) positioned, or other steps must be taken, so as to minimise any risk of damage by impact so far as is reasonably practicable; and

(c) protected from unauthorised use.

(8) Any permanent vent pipe, tap or valve through which oil can be discharged from the tank to the open must satisfy the following requirements—

(a) it must be situated within the secondary containment system;

(b) it must be arranged so as to discharge the oil vertically downwards and be contained within the system; and

(c) in the case of a tap or valve, it must be fitted with a lock and locked shut when not in use.

5   Mobile bowsers

(1) Any mobile bowser used for storing oil shall satisfy the following requirements.

(2) Any tap or valve permanently fixed to the unit through which oil can be discharged to the open must be fitted with a lock and locked shut when not in use.

(3) Where oil is delivered through a flexible pipe which is permanently attached to the unit—

(a) the pipe must be fitted with a manually operated pump or with a valve at the delivery end which closes automatically when not in use;

(b) the pump or valve must be provided with a lock and locked shut when not in use;

(c) the pipe must be fitted with a lockable valve at the end where it leaves the container and must be locked shut when not in use.

6   Transitional provisions

(1) Subject to paragraphs (2) and (3) below, the preceding provisions of these Regulations shall not apply until 1st September 2005 to the storage of oil in any container if the container was used for that purpose on any premises before 1st September 2001.

(2) Subject to paragraph (3), if the container or, if there is more than one container within the secondary containment system, any of them is situated less than—

(a) 10 metres away from any inland freshwaters or coastal waters; or

(b) 50 metres away from a well or borehole,

the preceding provisions of these Regulations shall apply from 1st September 2003.

(3) If a notice under regulation 7 is not complied with in relation to any container by the date specified in the notice, the preceding provisions of these Regulations shall apply from whichever is the latest of the following—

(a) the date specified in the notice;

(b) if the period for compliance is extended under regulation 7(4), the expiry of the extension;

(c) if there is an appeal against the notice, the date on which the appeal is determined or withdrawn.

7   Notices to minimise pollution risks in transitional cases

(1) In a case where—

(a) regulation 6(1) or (2) applies; and

(b) the Agency considers that there is a significant risk of pollution of controlled waters from the entry of the oil in question into those waters if steps are not immediately taken to minimise that risk,

the Agency may serve notice on the person having custody or control of that oil requiring him to carry out such works, take such precautions or such other steps as, in the opinion of the Agency, are appropriate for minimising that risk having regard to the requirements of regulations 3 to 5.

(2) The notice shall—

(a) specify or describe the works, precautions or other steps which the person is required to carry out or take;

(b) state the period within which any such requirement is to be complied with; and

(c) inform him of his rights under regulation 8.

(3) The period for compliance shall be such period as is reasonable in the circumstances and shall not in any case be less than 28 days.

(4) The Agency may at any time—

(a) withdraw the notice;

(b) extend the period for compliance with any requirement of the notice;

(c) with the consent of the person on whom it is served, modify the requirements of the notice,

and shall do so if so directed by the Secretary of State under regulation 8(4).

8   Right of appeal in transitional cases

(1) A person served with a notice under regulation 7 may within the period of 28 days beginning with the day on which the notice is served (or within such longer period as the Secretary of State may allow) appeal to the Secretary of State against the notice.

(2) An appeal shall be made by the appellant serving notice on the Secretary of State and the notice shall contain or be accompanied by a statement of the appellant's reasons for appealing and the matters which he wishes the Secretary of State to take into account in determining the appeal.

(3) Before determining an appeal the Secretary of State shall—

(a) take into account any written representations of the appellant or the Agency; and

(b) if requested to do so by the appellant or the Agency, afford them the opportunity of appearing before and being heard by a person appointed by the Secretary of State for the purpose.

(4) On determining an appeal the Secretary of State may direct the Agency to withdraw the notice under regulation 7, modify any of its requirements, extend the period for compliance or dismiss the appeal.

(5) The period for compliance with a notice under regulation 7 shall, subject to any direction under paragraph (4) be extended so that it expires on the date on which the Secretary of State determines the appeal or, if the appeal is withdrawn, the date on which it is withdrawn.

9   Offences

A person who has custody or control of any oil in circumstances in which there is a contravention of any provision of regulations 3 to 5 or the requirements of a notice under regulation 7 shall be guilty of an offence and shall be liable—

(a) on summary conviction to a fine not exceeding the statutory maximum; or

(b) on conviction on indictment, to a fine.

The Landfill (England and Wales) Regulations 2002
(SI 2002, No. 1559)

PART I
PRELIMINARY

1 Citation, commencement and extent

(1) These Regulations may be cited as the Landfill (England and Wales) Regulations 2002.

(2) These Regulations shall come into force on 15th June 2002 except for regulation 19(1) which shall come into force on 31st August 2002.

(3) These Regulations extend to England and Wales only.

2 Interpretation

In these Regulations, unless the context otherwise requires—

'the 2000 Regulations' means the Pollution Prevention and Control (England and Wales) Regulations 2000;

'biodegradable waste' means any waste that is capable of undergoing anaerobic or aerobic decomposition, such as food or garden waste and paper and cardboard;

'hazardous waste' has the meaning given by regulation 7(2);

'holder' means the producer of waste or the person who is in possession of it;

'inert waste' has the meaning given by regulation 7(4);

'landfill' means a landfill to which these Regulations apply (see regulations 3 and 4);

'landfill gas' means any gas generated from landfilled waste;

'landfill permit' has the meaning given by regulation 6(2);

'leachate' means any liquid percolating through deposited waste and emitted from or contained within a landfill;

'municipal waste' means waste from households as well as other waste which because of its nature or composition is similar to waste from households;

'non-hazardous waste' has the meaning given by regulation 7(3);

'operator' has the meaning given by regulation 2(1) and (2) of the 2000 Regulations;

'relevant authorisation' means, in relation to a landfill, the landfill permit or waste management licence for the time being in force in relation to the landfill;

'relevant waste acceptance criteria' means, in relation to a landfill, the waste acceptance criteria set out in Schedule 1 which apply to the class of landfill to which that landfill belongs;

'treatment' means physical, thermal, chemical or biological processes (including sorting) that change the characteristics of waste in order to reduce its volume or hazardous nature, facilitate its handling or enhance recovery;

'waste' means controlled waste within the meaning of section 75(4) of the Environmental Protection Act 1990;

'waste management licence' means a waste management licence within the meaning of Part II of the Environmental Protection Act 1990; and

other expressions used in these Regulations which are also used in Directive 99/31/EC on the landfill of waste shall have the same meaning as in that Directive.

3 Application of regulations

(1) Subject to regulation 4, these Regulations apply to landfills.

(2) Subject to paragraphs (3) and (4), for the purposes of this regulation, a landfill is a waste disposal site for the deposit of the waste onto or into land.

(3) Landfills include—

(a) subject to paragraph (4), any site which is used for more than a year for the temporary storage of waste; and

(b) any internal waste disposal site, that is to say a site where a producer of waste is carrying out its own waste disposal at the place of production.

(4) Landfills do not include—

(a) any facility where waste is unloaded in order to permit its preparation for further transport for recovery, treatment or disposal elsewhere;

(b) any site where waste is stored as a general rule for a period of less than three years prior to recovery or treatment; or

(c) any site where waste is stored for a period of less than one year prior to disposal.

4   Cases where regulations do not apply

These Regulations do not apply to—

(a) the spreading of sludges (including sewage sludges and sludges resulting from dredging operations) and similar matter on the soil for the purposes of fertilisation or improvement;

(b) the use of suitable inert waste for redevelopment, restoration and filling-in work or for construction purposes;

(c) the deposit of—

(i) non-hazardous dredging sludges along the bank or towpath of a waterway from which they have been dredged where that activity falls within the exemption from waste management licensing in paragraph 25 of Schedule 3 to the Waste Management Licensing Regulations 1994;

(ii) non-hazardous sludges in surface waters, including the bed and its sub-soil; or

(d) any landfill which finally ceased to accept waste for disposal before 16th July 2001.

5   Location

A planning permission under the Town and Country Planning Act 1990 may be granted for a landfill only if the requirements of paragraph 1(1) of Schedule 2 to these Regulations have been taken into consideration.

6   Extension of categories of landfill subject to the 2000 Regulations etc.

(1) . . .

(2) In these Regulations "landfill permit" means the permit which is required by the 2000 Regulations for the carrying out of the disposal of waste in a landfill.

(3) Regulations 11 and 12(1) to (11) and (14) of the 2000 Regulations shall not apply to landfills.

(4) Paragraph 5(b) in Part 1 of Schedule 4, and paragraph 4(8)(b) in Part 2 of Schedule 7 to the 2000 Regulations (requirement to advertise in the London Gazette), shall not apply to landfills falling within paragraph (b) of Part A(1) of Section 5.2 in Part 1 of Schedule 1 to those Regulations.

PART II
LANDFILL PERMITS

7   Classification of landfills

(1) Before granting a landfill permit, the Environment Agency shall classify the landfill—

(a) as a landfill for hazardous waste;

(b) as a landfill for non-hazardous waste; or

(c) as a landfill for inert waste,

and shall ensure that the classification is stated in the landfill permit.

(2) Hazardous waste means any waste as defined in Article 1(4) of Directive 91/689/EEC (hazardous waste).

(3) Non-hazardous waste is waste which is not hazardous waste.

(4) Waste is inert waste if—

(a) it does not undergo any significant physical, chemical or biological transformations;

(b) it does not dissolve, burn or otherwise physically or chemically react, biodegrade or adversely affect other matter with which it comes into contact in a way likely to give rise to environmental pollution or harm to human health; and

(c) its total leachability and pollutant content and the ecotoxicity of its leachate are insignificant and, in particular, do not endanger the quality of any surface water or groundwater.

8   Conditions to be included in landfill permits

(1) A landfill permit shall include conditions specifying the list of defined types, and the total quantity, of waste authorised to be deposited in the landfill.

(2) A landfill permit shall also include appropriate conditions—

(a) specifying requirements for—

(i) preparations for, and the carrying out of, landfilling operations;

(ii) monitoring and control procedures, including contingency plans;

(b) ensuring that the financial provision required by regulation 4(3)(b) of the 2000 Regulations is maintained until the permit is surrendered in accordance with those Regulations;

(c) ensuring that the landfill is operated in such a manner that the necessary measures are taken to prevent accidents and to limit their consequences; and

(d) requiring the operator to report at least annually to the Environment Agency on—

(i) the types and quantities of waste disposed of; and

(ii) the results of the monitoring programme required by regulations 14 and 15.

(3) A landfill permit shall also include—

(a) appropriate conditions for ensuring compliance with the requirements of the following provisions of these Regulations—

(i)   Schedule 2 (general requirements for all landfills);

(ii)   regulation 9 (prohibition of acceptance of certain wastes at landfills);

(iii)   regulation 10 (waste which may be accepted in the different classes of landfill);

(iv)   regulation 11 (costs of disposal of waste in landfills);

(v)   regulation 12 (waste acceptance procedures);

(vi)   regulation 13 (initial site inspections by Environment Agency);

(vii) regulation 14 (control and monitoring of operational landfill sites);

(viii) regulation 15 (closure and after-care procedures for landfills); and

(b) such other conditions as appear appropriate to the Environment Agency, including in particular conditions giving effect to—

(i) any requirement imposed by Community or national legislation; and

(ii) in the case of landfills falling within paragraph (a) of Part A (1) of Section 5.2 in Part 1 of Schedule 1 to the 2000 Regulations, the principle that energy should be used efficiently.

(4) The provisions of these Regulations mentioned in paragraph (3)(a) above shall impose obligations directly on an operator of a landfill (rather than through the conditions of a landfill permit) only to the extent specified in paragraph 3(3) to (5) of Schedule 4.

9   Prohibition of acceptance of certain wastes at landfills

(1) The operator of a landfill shall not accept any of the following types of waste at the landfill—

(a) any waste in liquid form (including waste waters but excluding sludge);

(b) waste which, in the conditions of landfill, is explosive, corrosive, oxidising, flammable or highly flammable;

    (c) hospital and other clinical wastes which arise from medical or veterinary establishments and which are infectious;

    (d) chemical substances arising from research and development or teaching activities, such as laboratory residues, which are not identified or which are new, and whose effects on man or on the environment are not known;

    (e) as from 16th July 2003, whole used tyres other than—

        (i) tyres used as engineering material;

        (ii) bicycle tyres; and

        (iii) tyres with an outside diameter above 1400 mm;

    (f) as from 16th July 2006, shredded used tyres other than—

        (i) bicycle tyres; and

        (ii) tyres with an outside diameter above 1400mm; and

    (g) any waste which does not fulfil the relevant waste acceptance criteria.

(2) The operator of a landfill shall ensure that the landfill is not used for landfilling waste which has been diluted or mixed solely to meet the relevant waste acceptance criteria.

(3) For the purposes of this regulation, waste is—

'corrosive' if it consists of substances and preparations which may destroy living tissue on contact;

'explosive' if it consists of substances and preparations which may explode under the effect of flame or which are more sensitive to shocks or friction than dinitrobenzene;

'flammable' if it consists of liquid substances and preparations having a flash point equal to or greater than 21°C and less than or equal to 55°C;

'highly flammable' if it consists of—

    (a) liquid substances and preparations having a flash point below 21°C (including extremely flammable liquids);

    (b) substances and preparations which may become hot and finally catch fire in contact with air at ambient temperature without any application of energy;

    (c) solid substances and preparations which may readily catch fire after brief contact with a source of ignition and which continue to burn or to be consumed after removal of the source of ignition;

    (d) gaseous substances and preparations which are flammable in air at normal pressure;

    (e) substances and preparations which, in contact with water or damp air, evolve highly flammable gases in dangerous quantities;

'infectious' if it consists of substances containing viable micro-organisms or their toxins which are known or reliably believed to cause disease in man or other living organisms; or

'oxidising' if it consists of substances and preparations which exhibit highly exothermic reactions when in contact with other substances, particularly flammable substances.

10 Waste which may be accepted in the different classes of landfill

(1) The operator of a landfill shall ensure that the landfill is only used for landfilling waste which is subject to prior treatment unless—

    (a) it is inert waste for which treatment is not technically feasible; or

    (b) it is waste other than inert waste and treatment would not reduce its quantity or the hazards which it poses to human health or the environment.

(2) The operator of a landfill for hazardous waste shall ensure that only waste which fulfils the waste acceptance criteria in paragraphs 1 and 2 of Schedule 1 is accepted at the landfill.

(3) The operator of a landfill for non-hazardous waste shall ensure that the landfill is only used for landfilling—

    (a) municipal waste;

(b) non-hazardous waste of any other origin which fulfils the waste acceptance criteria in paragraphs 1 and 3(1)(b) of Schedule 1; and

(c) stable, non-reactive hazardous waste (such as that which is solidified) with leaching behaviour equivalent to that of non-hazardous waste referred to in sub-paragraph (b) and which fulfils the waste acceptance criteria in paragraphs 1 and 3(1)(a) of Schedule 1.

(4) Where hazardous waste of the type described in paragraph (3)(c) is disposed of at a landfill for non-hazardous waste, the operator shall ensure it is not deposited in cells used or intended to be used for the disposal of biodegradable non-hazardous waste.

(5) The operator of a landfill for inert waste shall ensure that the landfill is only used for landfilling inert waste which meets the waste acceptance criteria in paragraphs 1 and 4 of Schedule 1.

11 Costs of disposal of waste in landfills

The operator of a landfill shall ensure that the charges it makes for the disposal of waste in its landfill covers all of the following—

(a) the costs of setting up and operating the landfill;

(b) the costs of the financial provision required by regulation 4(3)(b) of the 2000 Regulations; and

(c) the estimated costs for the closure and after-care of the landfill site for a period of at least 30 years from its closure.

12 Waste acceptance procedures

(1) The operator shall visually inspect the waste at the entrance to the landfill and at the point of the deposit and shall satisfy himself that it conforms to the description provided in the documentation submitted by the holder.

(2) The operator shall, in accordance with such procedures as are specified by the Environment Agency, test waste to establish whether it corresponds to the description in the accompanying documents and, if representative samples are taken for analysis, the operator shall retain the samples and results of any analysis for at least one month.

(3) The operator shall keep a register showing—

(a) the quantities of waste deposited;

(b) its characteristics;

(c) its origin;

(d) the dates of its delivery;

(e) the identity of the producer or, in the case of municipal waste, the collector; and

(f) in the case of hazardous waste, its precise location on the site.

(4) The information required to be kept under paragraph (3) shall be made available to the Environment Agency on request.

(5) The operator on accepting each delivery of waste shall provide a written receipt to the person delivering it.

(6) Where waste is not accepted at a landfill, the operator shall inform the Environment Agency of that fact as soon as reasonably possible.

13 Initial site inspections by Environment Agency

The operator of a landfill shall not commence disposal operations before the Environment Agency has inspected the site in order to ensure that it complies with the relevant conditions of the landfill permit.

14 Control and monitoring of operational landfill sites

(1) The following requirements shall apply to landfill sites from the start of the operational phase until definitive closure.

(2) The operator shall carry out the control and monitoring procedures set out in Schedule 3.

(3) Where the procedures required by paragraph (2) reveal any significant adverse environmental effects, the operator shall notify the Environment Agency as soon as reasonably possible.

(4) When it receives a notification of significant adverse environmental effects in accordance with paragraph (3), the Environment Agency shall determine the nature and timing of corrective measures that are necessary and shall require the operator to carry them out.

(5) The operator shall report at intervals specified by the Environment Agency, on the basis of aggregated data, the results of monitoring and on such other matters which the Environment Agency requires to demonstrate compliance with the conditions of the landfill permit or to increase its knowledge of the behaviour of waste in landfill.

(6) The operator shall ensure that quality control of—

(a) analytical operations of control and monitoring procedures; and

(b) analyses of representative samples taken in accordance with regulation 12(2),

is carried out by competent laboratories.

15   Closure and after-care procedures for landfills

(1) The following closure and after-care procedures shall apply to all landfill sites.

(2) The procedures may relate to the closure of the whole of the landfill or part of it.

(3) The closure procedure shall begin—

(a) when the conditions specified in the landfill permit are satisfied;

(b) when the Environment Agency approves the initiation of the closure procedure following a request from the operator; or

(c) by a reasoned decision of the Environment Agency which shall be set out in a closure notice served on the operator in accordance with regulation 16.

(4) A landfill shall not be definitively closed until—

(a) such reports as may be required by the Environment Agency have been submitted to it by the operator; and

(b) the Environment Agency—

(i) has assessed all the reports submitted by the operator;

(ii) has carried out a final on-site inspection; and

(iii) has notified the operator by notice in writing served on the operator that it approves the closure.

(5) Following definitive closure of a landfill, after-care procedures shall ensure that—

(a) the operator remains responsible for the maintenance, monitoring and control for such period as the Environment Agency determines is reasonable, taking into account the time during which the landfill could present hazards;

(b) the operator notifies the Environment Agency of any significant adverse environmental effects revealed by the control procedures and takes the remedial steps required or approved by the Agency; and

(c) the operator is responsible for monitoring and analysing landfill gas and leachate from the landfill and the groundwater regime in its vicinity in accordance with Schedule 3 for as long as the Environment Agency considers that the landfill is likely to cause a hazard to the environment.

(6) Notwithstanding regulations 19 and 21 of the 2000 Regulations (requirements on surrender or revocation of permits), the Environment Agency shall not accept any complete or partial surrender of the landfill permit, or revoke it in whole or part, for as long as the Environment Agency considers that the landfill (or the relevant part of it) is likely to cause a hazard to the environment.

(7) The operator shall not be relieved from liability under the conditions of the landfill permit by reason of the Environment Agency's approval of closure under paragraph (4)(b)(iii).

16   Closure Notices

(1) Where the Environment Agency has taken a reasoned decision under regulation 15(3)(c), it shall serve a closure notice under this regulation ("a closure notice") on the operator of the landfill.

(2) A closure notice shall—

(a) state the Environment Agency's reasons for requiring initiation of the closure procedure;

(b) specify the steps the operator is required to take to initiate the procedure; and

(c) the period within which they must be taken.

(3) The Environment Agency may withdraw a closure notice at any time.

PART III
MISCELLANEOUS

17   Offences

(1) It shall be an offence for a landfill operator to contravene—

(a) regulation 9 or 12 in each case as applied by paragraph 3(3)(a) of Schedule 4;

(b) regulation 10(1) or (2) in both cases as applied by paragraph 3(3)(b) of Schedule 4; or

(c) paragraph 3(5) of Schedule 4.

(2) A person who is guilty of an offence under paragraph (1) shall be liable—

(a) on summary conviction, to a fine not exceeding £20,000 or to imprisonment for a term not exceeding six months or to both; and

(b) on conviction on indictment, to a fine or to imprisonment for a term not exceeding five years or to both.

(3) Where an offence under this regulation committed by a body corporate is proved to have been committed with the consent or connivance of, or to have been attributable to any neglect on the part of, any director, manager, secretary of other similar officer of the body corporate or a person who was purporting to act in any such capacity, he as well as the body corporate shall be guilty of that offence and shall be liable to be proceeded against and punished accordingly.

(4) Where the affairs of a body corporate are managed by its members, paragraph (3) shall apply in relation to the acts or defaults of a member in connection with his functions of management as if he were a director of the body corporate.

(5) Where the commission by any person of an offence under this regulation is due to the act or default of some other person, that other person may be charged with and convicted of the offence by virtue of this paragraph whether or not proceedings for the offence are taken against the first-mentioned person.

18   Transitional provisions

Schedule 4 (which contains transitional provisions) shall have effect.

Regulations 2 and 10   SCHEDULE 1

WASTE ACCEPTANCE CRITERIA

1   Criteria for acceptance of waste which apply to all kinds of landfill

(1) The following criteria shall apply to the acceptance of waste at any landfill.

(2) Waste may only be accepted at a landfill where its acceptance would not—

(a) result in unacceptable emissions to groundwater, surface water or the surrounding environment;

(b) jeopardise environment protection systems (such as liners, leachate and gas collection and treatment systems) at the landfill;

(c) put at risk waste stabilisation processes (such as degradation or wash out) within the landfill; or

(d) endanger human health.

2   Additional criteria for acceptance of waste at landfills for hazardous waste

Waste may only be accepted at a landfill for hazardous waste if—

(a) it is listed on the Hazardous Waste List of the European Waste Catalogue or has similar characteristics to those so listed; and

(b) its total content or leachability—

(i) does not present a short term occupational risk or an environmental risk; and

(ii) would not prevent the stabilisation of the landfill within its projected lifetime taking account of its after care period following closure.

3   Additional criteria for acceptance of waste at landfills for non-hazardous waste

(1) Waste may only be accepted at a landfill for non-hazardous waste if—

(a) it is listed on the Hazardous Waste List of the European Waste Catalogue or has similar characteristics to those so listed (and its deposit at the landfill otherwise meets the requirements of regulation 10(3)(c) and (4)); or

(b) it is any other waste listed on the European Waste Catalogue or has similar characteristics to those so listed.

4   Additional criteria for acceptance of waste at landfills for inert waste

Waste may only be accepted at a landfill for inert waste if it is listed in the following Table or it otherwise falls within the definition of inert waste in regulation 7(4)—

Waste acceptable at landfills for inert waste

European Waste Catalogue Code	Description	Exclusions
10 11 03	Waste glass based fibrous materials	
15 01 07	Glass packaging	
17 01 01	Concrete	
17 01 02	Bricks	
17 01 03	Tiles and ceramics	
17 02 02	Glass	
17 05 04	Soil and stones	Excluding topsoil, peat
20 01 02	Glass	
20 02 02	Soil and stones	Excluding topsoil, peat

Regulations 5 and 8(3)(a)(i)   SCHEDULE 2

GENERAL REQUIREMENTS FOR LANDFILLS

1.—(1) The location of a landfill must take into consideration requirements relating to—

(a) the distances from the boundary of the site to residential and recreational areas, waterways, water bodies and other agricultural or urban sites;

(b) the existence of groundwater, coastal water or nature protection zones in the area;

(c) the geological or hydrogeological conditions in the area;

(d) the risk of flooding, subsidence, landslides or avalanches on the site; and

(e) the protection of the natural or cultural heritage in the area.

(2) A landfill permit may be issued for the landfill only if—

(a) the characteristics of the site with respect to the requirements in sub-paragraph (1); or

(b) the corrective measures to be taken,

indicate that the landfill does not pose a serious environmental risk.

(3) In this paragraph 'nature protection zone' means a site of special scientific interest within the meaning of section 52 of the Wildlife and Countryside Act 1981 or a European site within the meaning of regulation 10(1) of the Conservation (Natural Habitats, &c.) Regulations 1994.

2.—(1) Subject to the following provisions of this paragraph, appropriate arrangements shall be made with regard to the characteristics of the landfill and prevailing meteorological conditions in order to—

(a) control rainwater entering the landfill body;

(b) prevent surface water or groundwater from entering into landfilled waste;

(c) collect contaminated water and leachate and treat it to the appropriate standard so that it can be discharged.

(2) Arrangements need not be made in accordance with sub-paragraph (1)(c) if the Agency decides that the landfill poses no potential hazard to the environment in view of its location and the kinds of waste to be accepted at the landfill.

(3) This paragraph shall not apply to inert landfills.

3.—(1) The landfill must be situated and designed so as to—

(a) provide the conditions for prevention of pollution of the soil, groundwater or surface water; and

(b) ensure efficient collection of leachate as and when required by paragraph 2.

(2) Soil, groundwater and surface water is to be protected by the use of a geological barrier combined with—

(a) a bottom liner during the operational phase of the landfill; and

(b) a top liner following closure and during the after-care phase.

(3) The geological barrier shall comply with the requirements of sub-paragraph (4) and shall also provide sufficient attenuation capacity to prevent a potential risk to soil and groundwater.

(4) The landfill base and sides shall consist of a mineral layer which provides protection of soil, groundwater and surface water at least equivalent to that resulting from the following permeability and thickness requirements—

(a) in a landfill for hazardous waste: $k \Lleftarrow 1.0 \times 10^{-9}$ metre/second: thickness ≥ 5 metres;

(b) in a landfill for non-hazardous waste: $k \Lleftarrow 1.0 \times 10^{-9}$ metre/second: thickness ≥ 1 metres;

(c) in a landfill for inert waste: $k \Lleftarrow 1.0 \times 10^{-7}$ metre/second: thickness ≥ 1 metres.

(5) Where the geological barrier does not meet the requirements of subparagraph (4) naturally, it may be completed artificially and reinforced by other means providing equivalent protection; but in any such case a geological barrier established by artificial means must be at least 0.5 metres thick.

(6) A leachate collection and sealing system to ensure that leachate accumulation at the base of the landfill is kept to a minimum must also be provided in any hazardous or non-hazardous landfill in accordance with the following table—

Leachate collection and bottom sealing

Landfill category	Non-hazardous	Hazardous
Artifical sealing liner	Required	Required
Drainage layer ≥ 0.5 metres	Required	Required

(7) Where the potential hazards to the environment indicate that the prevention of leachate formation is necessary, surface sealing may be prescribed taking account of the following guidelines—

Landfill category	Non-hazardous	Hazardous
Gas drainage layer	Required	Not required
Artificial sealing liner	Not required	Required
Impermeable mineral layer	Required	Required
Drainage layer < 0.5 metres	Required	Required
Top soil cover < 1 metre	Required	Required

(8) The requirements of sub-paragraphs (3) to (7) may be reduced to an appropriate extent if on the basis of an assessment of environmental risks, having regard in particular to Directive 80/68/EEC—

    (a) it has been decided in accordance with paragraph 2 that the collection and treatment of leachate is not necessary; or

    (b) it is established that the landfill poses no potential hazard to soil, groundwater or surface water.

4.—(1) Appropriate measures must be taken in order to control the accumulation and migration of landfill gas.

(2) Landfill gas must be collected from all landfills receiving biodegradable waste and the landfill gas must be treated and, to the extent possible, used.

(3) The collection, treatment and use of landfill gas under sub-paragraph (2) must be carried on in a manner which minimises damage to or deterioration of the environment and risk to human health.

(4) Landfill gas which cannot be used to produce energy must be flared.

5.—(1) Measures must be taken to minimise the nuisances arising from the landfill in relation to—

    (a) emissions of odours and dust;

    (b) wind-blown materials;

    (c) noise and traffic;

    (d) birds, vermin and insects;

    (e) the formation of aerosols; and

    (f) fires.

(2) The landfill must be equipped so that dirt originating from the site is not dispersed onto public roads and the surrounding land.

6.—(1) The placement of waste must ensure stability of all the waste on the site and associated structures and in particular must avoid slippages.

(2) Where an artificial barrier is used, the geological substratum must be sufficiently stable, taking into account the morphology of the landfill, to prevent settlement that may cause damage to the barrier.

7.—(1) The landfill must be secured to prevent free access to the site.

(2) The gates of the landfill must be locked outside operating hours.

(3) The system of control and access to each facility must provide systems to detect and discourage illegal dumping in the facility.

Regulations 14(2) and 15(5)(c)   SCHEDULE 3

MINIMUM MONITORING PROCEDURES FOR LANDFILLS

1. This Schedule sets out minimum procedures for monitoring to be carried out to check—

(a) that waste has been accepted for disposal only if it fulfils the relevant waste acceptance criteria;

(b) that the processes within the landfill proceed as desired;

(c) that environmental protections systems are functioning fully as intended; and

(d) that the conditions of the landfill permit are fulfilled.

2.—(1) Samples of leachate or surface water (if present) must be collected at representative points.

(2) Sampling and measuring of the volume and composition of any leachate must be performed separately at each point at which leachate is discharged from the site.

(3) Monitoring of surface water (if present) shall take place at at least two points, one upstream from the landfill and one downstream.

(4) Gas monitoring must be carried out for each section of the landfill and representative samples must be collected and analysed in accordance with Table 1.

TABLE 1

	Operational phase	After-care phase[1]
Leachate volume[2]	Monthly[1,3]	Every six months
Leachate composition[2,4]	Quarterly[1]	Every six months
Volume and composition of surface water[5]	Quarterly[1]	Every six months
Potential gas emissions and atmospheric pressure[6] (CH_4, CO_2, O_2, H_2S, H_2 etc)	Monthly[1,7]	Every six months[8]

Notes to Table 1

[1] Longer intervals may be allowed if the evaluation of data indicates that they would be equally effective. For leachates, the conductivity must always be measured at least once a year.

[2] These do not apply where leachate collection is not required under paragraph 2(1)(c) of Schedule 2.

[3] The frequency of sampling may be adapted on the basis of the morphology of the landfill waste (in tumulus, buried, etc) (but only if the Environment Agency considers that the conditions of the landfill permit should allow for it).

[4] The parameters to be measured and substances to be analysed vary according to the composition of the waste deposited. They must be specified in the conditions of the landfill permit and reflect the leaching characteristics of the wastes.

[5] On the basis of the characteristics of the landfill site, the Environment Agency may determine that these measurements are not required.

[6] These measurements are related mainly to the content of the organic material in the waste.

[7] CH_4, CO_2, O_2 regularly, other gases as required, according to the composition of the waste deposited, with a view to reflecting its leaching properties.

[8] Efficiency of the gas extraction system must be checked regularly.

(5) A representative sample of leachate and water shall be taken for monitoring purposes in accordance with Table 1.

3.—(1) The sampling measurements taken must be sufficient to provide information on groundwater likely to be affected by the discharge from the landfill, with at least one measuring point in the groundwater inflow region and two in the outflow region.

(2) The number of measurements referred to sub-paragraph (1) may be increased on the basis of a specific hydrogeological survey or the need for an early identification of accidental leachate release in the groundwater.

(3) Sampling must be carried out in at least three locations before filling operations in order to establish reference values for future sampling.

4.—(1) The monitoring of groundwater shall be carried out in accordance with Table 2.

(2) The parameters to be analysed in the samples taken must be derived from the expected composition of the leachate and the groundwater quality in the area.

(3) In selecting the parameters for analysis, the mobility in the groundwater zone must be taken into account.

(4) Parameters may include indicator parameters in order to ensure an early recognition of change in water quality (the recommended parameters are pH, TOC, phenols, heavy metals, fluoride, As, oil/hydrocarbons).

TABLE 2

	Operational phase	*After-care phase*
Level of groundwater	Every six months[1]	Every six months[1]
Groundwater	Site-specific	Site-specific
composition	frequency[2,3]	frequency[2,3]

Notes to Table 2
[1] If there are fluctuating groundwater levels, the frequency must be increased.
[2] The frequency must be based on the possibility for remedial action between two samplings if a trigger level is reached, i.e. the frequency must be determined on the basis of knowledge and the evaluation of the velocity of groundwater flow.
[3] When a trigger level is reached (see paragraph 5), verification is necessary by repeating the sampling. When the level has been confirmed, a contingency plan set out in the landfill permit conditions must be followed.

5.—(1) Significant adverse environmental effects, as referred to in regulations 14(3) and 15(5)(b), should be considered to have occurred in the case of groundwater when an analysis of a groundwater sample shows a significant change in water quality.

(2) The level at which the effects referred to in sub-paragraph (1) are considered to have occurred ('the trigger level') must be determined taking account of the specific hydrogeological formations in the location of the landfill and groundwater quality.

(3) The trigger level must be set out in the conditions of the landfill permit whenever possible.

(4) The observations must be evaluated by means of control charts with established control rules and levels for each downgradient well.

(5) The control levels must be determined from local variations in groundwater quality.

6.—The topography of the site and settling behaviour of the landfill body shall be monitored in accordance with Table 3.

TABLE 3

	Operational phase	After-care phase
Structure and composition of landfill body[1]	Yearly	
Settling behaviour of the level of the landfill body	Yearly	Yearly reading

Note to Table 3

[1] Data for the status plan of the relevant landfill: surface occupied by waste, volume and composition of waste, methods of depositing, time and duration of depositing, calculation of the remaining capacity still available at the landfill.

Regulations 17(1) and 18   SCHEDULE 4

TRANSITIONAL PROVISIONS

1   Existing landfills: transitional provisions

(1) Subject to paragraph 2(1), this paragraph shall apply to a landfill if—

   (a) it is already in operation on 15th June 2002; or

   (b) it has not been brought into operation by that date but the relevant authorisation for its operation was granted before that date.

(2) A landfill to which this paragraph applies which falls within paragraph (b) of Part A(1) of Section 5.2 in Part 1 of Schedule 1 to the 2000 Regulations shall be treated as an existing installation for the purposes of Part 1 of Schedule 3 to those Regulations.

(3) If the operator proposes to continue to accept waste after 16th July 2002, the operator shall prepare a conditioning plan for the landfill site and submit it to the Environment Agency by that date.

(4) The conditioning plan required by sub-paragraph (3) must—

   (a) be prepared on a form provided for that purpose by the Environment Agency; and

   (b) contain details of any corrective measures which the operator considers will be needed in order to comply with the relevant requirements of these Regulations.

(5) If the operator does not propose to continue to accept waste after 16th July 2002, the operator shall notify the Environment Agency in writing by that date.

(6) Subject to sub-paragraph (7), where—

   (a) the operator notifies the Environment Agency that he does not propose to accept waste for disposal after 16th July 2002;

   (b) the Environment Agency decides, following the submission by the operator of a conditioning plan, that there is no reasonable prospect of the landfill or part of it meeting the relevant requirements of these Regulations (such decision, and the reasons for it, to be set out in a notice served on the operator); or

   (c) the operator fails to submit a conditioning plan as required by subparagraphs (3) and (4) or to notify the Agency as required by subparagraph (5),

the Environment Agency shall ensure that closure of the landfill site (in whole or in part) takes place as soon as possible in accordance with regulation 15.

(7) Where the operator proposes to continue to accept waste but fails to submit a conditioning plan in accordance with sub-paragraphs (3) and (4), the relevant authorisation shall cease to have effect so as to authorise the disposal of waste at the landfill, and the Environment Agency shall proceed with the closure of the site under sub-paragraph (6), unless and until a conditioning plan which complies with sub-paragraph (4) is submitted and the Agency has agreed to consider it.

(8) In any case falling within sub-paragraph (6)—
- (a) regulation 15 shall apply as if—
    - (i) references to a landfill permit were references to a relevant authorisation;
    - (ii) where the relevant authorisation is a waste management licence, references to the operator were references to the licence holder; and
    - (iii) in paragraph (6) after 'revocation of permits)' there were inserted 'and sections 38, 39 and 42 of the Environmental Protection Act 1990 (revocation, suspension and surrender of waste management licences)'; and
- (b) the Environment Agency shall, if necessary, by notice in writing served on the operator or, in the case of a waste management licence, the licence holder, vary the conditions of the relevant authorisation so that—
    - (i) waste is no longer accepted for disposal on the whole or the relevant part of the landfill site from such date as is specified in the notice; and
    - (ii) the closure and after-care procedures will operate in accordance with regulation 15.

(9) In any case where the whole of a landfill site is not subject to closure under sub-paragraph (6), the Environment Agency shall by notice served on the operator specify the period (which shall not be less than six months) within which an application must be made (accompanied by a copy of the conditioning plan)—
- (a) where no landfill permit is in force, for a landfill permit under regulation 10 of the 2000 Regulations; or
- (b) where a landfill permit is in force, for a variation of the permit under regulation 17(2) of the 2000 Regulations,

so that waste may continue to be accepted for disposal at the landfill.

(10) In any case falling within sub-paragraph (9)(b), if an application is not duly made within the period specified in the notice served on the operator under that provision, the landfill permit shall cease to authorise the disposal of waste at the landfill until the application is duly made.

(11) Where the Environment Agency decides to grant or vary a landfill permit pursuant to an application made in accordance with sub-paragraph (9), the Agency shall specify the date or dates on which the permit conditions authorised or required by these Regulations shall take effect.

(12) The Environment Agency shall exercise its powers under subparagraphs (9) and (11)—
- (a) on the basis of an assessment of environmental risks; and
- (b) with a view to achieving full compliance with the relevant requirements of these Regulations—
    - (i) as soon as possible; and
    - (ii) by 31st March 2007 at the latest.

(13) In this Schedule 'the relevant requirements of these Regulations' do not include the requirements of paragraph 1 of Schedule 2.

2.—(1) Paragraph 1 does not apply to a landfill if—
- (a) a landfill permit for its operation was granted on or after 16th July 2001 and before 15th June 2002;
- (b) it falls within paragraph (b) of Part A(1) of Section 5.2 in Part 1 of Schedule 1 to the 2000 Regulations and a waste management licence for its operation was granted on or after 16th July 2001 and before 15th June 2002; or
- (c) the prescribed date determined in accordance with Schedule 3 to the 2000 Regulations for the installation at which the landfill activity is carried out is before 15th June 2002 and an application for a landfill permit was duly made (but not determined) before 15th June 2002.

(2) In any case falling within sub-paragraph (1)(b), the waste management licence shall have effect on or after 15th June 2002 as if it were a landfill permit.

(3) In any case falling within sub-paragraph (1) the Environment Agency shall exercise its power to vary the relevant authorisation (or determine the outstanding application) so that the relevant requirements of these Regulations are complied with as soon as possible in relation to the landfill in question.

(4) In any case falling within sub-paragraph (1)(c), where an application for a waste management licence is also outstanding on 15th June 2002, there shall be no obligation on the Agency to determine the application for a waste management licence.

3.—(1) The Environment Agency shall by notice in writing served on the operator no later than 16th July 2002, classify any landfill which appears to the Agency to require classification as a landfill for hazardous waste.

(2) If a landfill classified under sub-paragraph (1) as a landfill for hazardous waste ceases to accept hazardous waste in accordance with the conditioning plan required under paragraph 1(3), the Environment Agency may at any time before 16th July 2004 by notice in writing served on the operator revoke the classification made under sub-paragraph (1).

(3) The following provisions of these Regulations shall impose obligations directly on the operator of any landfill which is for the time being classified under sub-paragraph (1) as a landfill for hazardous waste pending determination of an application made pursuant to paragraph 1(9)—

    (a) on or after 16th July 2002—
        (i) regulation 9 (prohibition of acceptance of certain wastes); and
        (ii) regulation 12 (waste acceptance procedures);
    (b) on or after 16th July 2004, regulation 10(1) and (2) (waste acceptance requirements).

(4) For the purposes of applying regulation 9(1)(g) under sub-paragraph (3)(a)(i) in relation to the period beginning on 16th July 2002 and ending on 15th July 2004, only the criteria in paragraph 1 of Schedule 1 are to be treated as relevant waste acceptance criteria.

(5) The operator of a landfill which is not classified as a landfill for hazardous waste shall only accept hazardous waste at that landfill on or after 16th July 2002 in the circumstances specified in regulation 10(3)(c) and (4).

4.—(1) This paragraph shall apply to any landfill if—

    (a) it falls within paragraph (b) of Part A(1) of Section 5.2 in Part 1 of Schedule 1 to the 2000 Regulations; and
    (b) it has not been brought into operation by 15th June 2002 but an application for a waste management licence was duly made before that date.

(2) Paragraph 1 of Part 1 of Schedule 3 to the 2000 Regulations shall apply as if in sub-paragraphs (a) and (b) '15th June 2002' were substituted for '1st January 2001'.

(3) Anything duly done by or in relation to the application for a waste management licence shall be treated as if it had been duly done in relation to an application for a landfill permit.

(4) The Environment Agency may give the applicant notice requiring him—

    (a) to provide such further information of any description specified in the notice; or
    (b) to take such further steps as it may require for the purpose of determining the application.

INDEX